GW00391154

BRIDGEND
TO
BANGKOK
(and everywhere in-between)

Extraordinary stories of an ordinary man

1

CONTENTS

*Please note: Throughout the book the following letters refer to my eldest five children:

K   -   Eldest son
R   -   Eldest daughter
G   -   Middle Son
A   -   Middle daughter (Twin 1)
Rh   -   Youngest son (Twin 2)

Youngest daughter is referred to by her real name, Amy.

Dedicated to:

My wonderful family & friends

All those people who shared the experiences

and

To all those about to read about them

Enjoy

&

Thanks to:

To family, friends and strangers who made these stories
possible.
For those who have helped in troubled times
(Particular mentions to: Warren Evans, Katie Williams, Alun
Morton, Rauf & Audra, the staff at Glanmors (cake shop in
Caerphilly), and the doctor at the Heath Hospital in Cardiff for
that intimate moment we shared - see chapter 5)
For all those who provided some of the 'not so happy'
memories
For those who have put up with me (and my stories) over the
years

And a special thanks to:
Rhian Wagstaff who proof read and edited the final draft

Prologue

Back in late 2008, following a major family upheaval, I decided to write a story of my life. It was an attempt to show how child abuse had indirectly affected me and the lives of my children. In a sense, the book was a form of self-therapy, as I tried to come to terms with the decision by my first wife to move to Middlesbrough, taking our nine year old twins with her, whilst leaving their older siblings with me in Wales. This decision created a huge split in the family that could have caused irreparable damage to relationships (i.e. parent/child, siblings, grandparents/grandchildren etc), had they not been built on solid foundations. Additionally, this also played a part in the breakdown of my second marriage as I became totally engrossed in fighting for custody of the twins, and to this day I believe I was damned if I did and damned if I didn't – a real no-win situation for all parties involved. The earlier book started out as an autobiographical account of my life, and reliving those early and happy beginnings in Bridgend in the early sixties could have been considered as a means of enjoying happy childhood memories, and to blank out the bad times experienced as an adult. Additionally, I was hoping it could be used as a tool to understand the reasons behind the events that had brought the children and I to this critical crossroads in all our lives.

In the early part of 2009 tragedy struck, my laptop had developed a fault that required a professional opinion on whether it could be repaired or not. I took it to a local computer repair shop, where I was told by a computer engineer that he would need to delete everything and *"was there anything I needed to save"*. You can guess what's coming next: *"No"* I replied. I had completely forgotten about the approximate 110 pages (over 30,000 words) of the book that was stored on the computer. As a result, the entire book was lost – disaster! I thought about restarting the book several times over the next few years but realised that I would never be able to replicate the feelings or sentiments of the original book as, emotionally, my mindset, was totally different to where it was in 2008. Therefore, I have decided to adopt a different approach this time round and have chosen to opt for a series of short stories under various subject headings. The end result is a lighter hearted book with a more reflective approach

4

to the more sensitive issues we experience in life such as; love, death, family, success, failure etc.

As you read this, I hope you raise a wry smile at some of the funnier stories, but also reflect on your own experiences, as you draw on some of the more sensitive issues. For example, the very sensitive issue of child abuse is something I touch upon, but indirectly. I have never been abused and neither have my children, but we have collectively experienced living with someone who was abused as a child. As a result, we have witnessed how destructive child abuse can still be years after the events took place. I would find it very gratifying if anything I state in this book proves to be helpful to anyone out there, albeit someone who has been abused or someone who lives with someone who has been abused. Additionally, that could be deemed as a positive outcome to a negative event. Child abuse hit the headlines in recent years with high profile revelations concerning celebrities such as Jimmy Saville, Rolf Harris, Stuart Hall and Max Clifford. Sadly, these revelations highlighted how victims were, in many cases, incorrectly perceived or accused of being liars. I learnt, from living with a victim that, whilst their abuser is alive they still feel threatened, hence many abusers are dead (i.e. Jimmy Saville) before their crimes are reported. I couldn't even begin to explain how victims are affected by these abhorrent crimes and it would be naïve of me to even try. However, during my own counselling sessions in the past, I was told that it takes years of specialist counselling for people to come to terms (if they ever do) with the effects associated with child abuse. I can only attempt to explain the effects I witnessed and the destruction it caused within our family unit. It can be considered that these may be familiar to some, similarly, they will be alien to others – each case has to be considered in its own terms and there would be different levels/extents of sexual abuse. Whatever the extent of the abuse it must always be remembered that, to each individual victim, the sexual abuse they have suffered will be more important than that experienced by any other victim. Therefore, those of us who are lucky enough not to have experienced being sexually abused need to be sympathetic and understanding and offer support to those who have (something, I admit, I didn't always achieve). We should never criticize or blame victims as it is NOT THEIR FAULT, as some people believe. The blame lies

totally with the abuser and that is a very important fact to remember.

Other important emotional issues are covered such as love, grief and humour. In relating stories from my early childhood, memories of family members that are long gone, friends throughout my life, sporting achievements (or not), good times, bad times etc, the one constant has been humour and long may it continue. Humour often helps us recover from the devastation at the passing of a much-loved family member or close friend, a lost love and it featured prominently during my time as a Sapper in the Royal Engineers. The ability to laugh at ourselves and others is important and British humour is second to none in this respect – humour is the one thing that can cross any political, religious or ethnic divide. I hope that as you read this book you will laugh, cry and generally enjoy the experiences I share, and even draw some comfort that may mirror your own life experiences. My life is ordinary and mirrors millions of others, but if this book helps anyone, even in just a small way, it will be a legacy I will be proud to have created.

Life has been a rollercoaster from the early years in Bridgend, through the Army years, lengthy rugby and football careers, two divorces, six children, life at Nuaire and recent trips to Thailand, where I have experienced a whole new culture and seen amazing historical sites etc. Hence, the name of the book *'Bridgend to Bangkok (and everywhere in between)'*. I have no doubt that there will be good times as well as bad times ahead. For now though, life is pretty good: I have finally found a steady, fun and loving relationship, I am surrounded by a loving family and great friends (as I have been all my life). I have a great job at a great company and, after qualifying to teach English to foreign learners, I am studying for a degree with the Open University. I have often been asked the question *'If I could change the past would I do anything differently?'* – Possibly, but I have accepted the fact that, regardless of whether they are positive or negative, all my actions and experiences have made me the person I am today. Whilst I apologise unreservedly to anyone I may have hurt in the past, I am happy with the person I have become and accept that I can't change the past, I can only change the future. As a result, I may not be perfect, but I think I'm a better person than the

petulant, selfish youngster I was in my teens and early twenties. My motto has been '*Enjoy life and cherish every moment, good or bad*' and I have certainly tried to follow that, in addition to using reflection to shape my future and hopefully make me a better person, but that is for others to judge!.

I hope you enjoy sharing my experiences as much as I have enjoyed writing about them – it certainly brought a smile to my face and I hope it also makes you smile and reflect on your own experiences. Brace yourself and read on, if you were a part of my life, there is every possibility you may feature in this book in some capacity. Get a brew on, grab a couple of 24 hour ration packs, pull up a sandbag and swing the light, as this might be a long few days with plenty of ups and downs..........!

Regards

Huw Thomas

October 2016

Chapter 1 – Early Years

As the name suggests the 'Early Years' feature events from those carefree days when my only worries were whether I had a football and in making sure I was home before it got dark! I was born on 17 March 1963 in Bridgend, an old market town nestled roughly halfway between Cardiff and Swansea, and about five miles from the rugged Glamorgan coastline. Despite the divorce of my parents when I was five years old (following a year living in Soham, Cambridgeshire), I spent a generally happy childhood in Bridgend up until I left school at sixteen to join the Army, and feel my upbringing was extremely privileged during those early years. I have since realised that my maternal and paternal grandparents played important roles in guiding me through those early days and provided me with a stable, loving and secure environment in which I could develop (you will be introduced to these and other family members throughout the book).

Bridgend and the surrounding areas provided me with many memories (good and bad), such as; my schooldays in both Trelales (Laleston) Primary and Bryntirion Comprehensive Schools; friends; sport; trips to the seaside, mainly Ogmore-by-Sea and Porthcawl (commonly known locally as 'Hi Butt' Bay); watching games at Bridgend R.F.C. with Kevin Freeland and John and Lloyd Williams; working on Paul Troakes' Dad's farm with Paul and Dai Lewis; cycle rides to various places i.e. the Vale of Glamorgan, Ogmore castle, Ogmore-by-Sea, Southerndown beach, Merthyr Mawr sand dunes (with our toboggans); playing badminton, squash and table tennis at the new sports centre with Tim Harries; cinema trips to the Embassy and County Cinemas and shopping in the town; hours spent down Newbridge Fields, playing football, putting (golf), mob (a form of hide and seek), climbing trees etc; my first kiss and occasional shopping trips to Cardiff or Swansea. Unfortunately, during these times I was also introduced to divorce, traffic accidents, illness and inevitably, something none of us can escape, death and all the pain and heartbreak it brings! However, these early experiences were not just confined to Bridgend. Following my parent's divorce, I didn't see my father for around three years as he made the decision to stay away, due to his continual arguments with my mother and grandmother. During this period my mother moved out into her own flat, but I stayed with my grandparents which I thought was normal at the time, but looking back, I realise now that sub-consciously I had again felt a sense of abandonment. Compounded by the fact that it would also be around three years before I started seeing my father again when I was around nine years old, but he soon remarried and moved to London with my step-mother. It felt as if my father had abandoned me for a second time! The move to London was followed a year or so later by a move to the sleepy, beautiful county of Norfolk and eventually they moved back to Wales (via Bristol) when I was sixteen years old. Therefore, I also have many treasured memories from these places such as; my first 'puppy' love; the hot summer of 1976 in Brancaster and other parts of NW Norfolk; watching my Dad play football for Docking; a school trip to Europe with Soham College (my mother's cousin (Beth) and her husband (Bernard) were teachers at this school); the long drives from Bridgend to Ely, Cambridgeshire to stay with Bernard, Beth and my cousins, Nicholas and Margaret (and back again); trips to football matches with my Father to Ninian Park, Highbury, Carrow Road, Ashton Gate and the Vetch; holidays with family and so forth. My head is filled with great childhood memories and I always remember those times fondly. Additionally, these childhood memories have been an immense source of comfort when I have encountered difficult periods as an adult, and I can look back, smile and think "yes, I was lucky to have experienced the joyous things I did as a child...they far outweigh any sad times". Some of the memories above will feature in this and other chapters and I hope you will enjoy the amusing stories, as I now have decades after they happened, and I hope you can embrace the sadness in other stories, with a simplistic "aw bless" and perhaps reflect on your own, similar experiences...so we begin.

■ ■

Frogs

This story is very important to me and is a great place to start this book as it involves one of the only memories I have of my mother, father and I doing something together before their divorce. I was only five years old at the time and we were living in Soham in Cambrideshire. There was nothing special about this particular day, we were a normal family enjoying an innocuous walk from our flat at one end of the town centre (via the town pond), to the house of my mother's cousin, Beth, her husband Bernard and Beth's mother, my Great Auntie Mary, at Staples Lane on the other side of Soham. The story involves a bucket of frogs.........and me!

The mists of time may have clouded some minor details, such as the weather, but the important details of that day, forty eight years ago, are etched in my memory.

My father, mother and I set off from our quaint, little one-bedroomed flat, a flat that adjoined the rear of a prominent Georgian house called 'The Grange', situated in Hall Street, a 5 minute walk from Soham town centre. It was normally a short walk of about 10-15 minutes to Bernard and Beth's house in Staples lane, but my father (who was strangely carrying a bucket!) suggested we took the longer route, so we could feed the ducks on the old village pond. I was clutching a large bag of stale bread as I trotted happily alongside my father, but we were soon trailing twenty to thirty metres behind my mother. Mainly, due to a mix of my mother possessing the walking pace of a member of the Light Infantry and my puzzlement causing me to continually stop and ask my father about the 'bucket'! All my father kept saying was: "It's a surprise, but you'll find out soon enough Huw!"

When we arrived at the pond, my mother and I started feeding the ducks the bread I had been carrying. My father, however started to walk around the pond, bucket in one hand clearly searching for something, his head slowly moving left and right as he scanned the ground around him! Occasionally, I would see him bend down, pick up something off the floor and carefully place it in the bucket. The intrigue got the better of me and I ran around the other side of the pond to join him. By my father's side, I looked in the bucket to see a dark green, moving mass,
"Urgh, what's that?" I shouted.
"Frogs", my father replied.
I had never seen a frog before and wasn't impressed and vehemently told my father, as any five-year-old would:
"Don't like frogs, they are yucky" and ran back to my mother on the other side of the pond and continued to feed the ducks.

When the bread had all gone my mother shouted to my father that we were ready to go. He waved to acknowledge he'd heard her and headed towards us, still carrying the bloody bucket that was now half full with frogs. When he joined us my mother asked tentatively:

"What have you got there?"

"Yucky frogs" I whispered disgustingly, under my breath.

"Frogs, I'm going to show them to Huw when we get to Bernard and Beth's...On the way home later, I can put them back in the pond" replied my father. With a shrug of her shoulders my mother said, "OK, lets go", and on we walked to Staples Lane.

A short time later we arrived at Bernard and Beth's house, as my father was carrying a bucket of frogs, we walked down the side of the house to the kitchen door that faced the garden at the back of the house. Whilst my father and I (and the dreaded bucket of frogs) stayed on a small concreted area at the back of the house my mother, knocked on the door, opened it and shouted "Beth...Bernard..." There was a muffled "in here" before my mother entered the kitchen and shut the door behind her. My father squatted down next to the bucket, which he had already placed on the floor, and called me over. He reached into the bucket and gently picked up a frog, beckoned me closer and spoke softly:

"This is a frog Huw and it won't hurt you".

I looked inquisitively at the vulnerable frog sitting in the palm of my father's hand, it was green and speckled with brown markings that glistened in the spring sunshine. I could also see its weblike feet twitching with agitation as its bulbous eyes flickered open and shut, nervously consuming the detail of its new surroundings. I began to see the frog in a new light as the fear subsided and I excitedly nodded my head when my father asked me if I would like to hold it. I held my hands out together in front of my chest and my father told me to keep still as he placed the frog on the palms of my hands. Wow! I was holding a frog, I held my breath, too scared to breathe in case I frightened it. The back door then opened, my mother appeared and asked my father to come into the house as Bernard wanted to ask him something. My father took the frog out of my hand and carefully placed it back in the bucket. He told me not to touch anything and that he wouldn't be long, he then disappeared into the house shutting the door behind him.

I was now alone with the frogs – an inquisitive unsupervised five-year-old and a bucket of frogs! What could possibly go wrong?

To this day, I can remember standing over the bucket and looking at the frogs and then glancing at the back door, looking at the frogs again and then glancing at the back door – this inane repetition seemed to last for an eternity before I thought to myself (as any five year old would), "I wonder if frogs bounce?". I reached into the bucket, glanced at the back door one more time, and picked up a frog, immediately feeling the mists of mischievous intent wash over me! I raised the hand (that held the frog) high above my head, holding it there momentarily, before lowering my hand quicker than a cricket fast bowler and released the frog...SPLAT!! The frog hit the concrete with such force that it splattered into an array of various colours. I quietly chuckled to myself like Damien from 'The Omen' and shouted, "again, again...!" I reached for another frog - the carnage had begun, SPLATT, SPLATT, SPLATT, SPLATT, until only one frog remained in the bucket. I picked the last frog out of the bucket and raised my arm high above my head. However, my unbridled joy soon turned to horror. As I speedily lowered my arm and released the last frog, my father opened the back door, stood in the doorway and witnessed the last moments of the last frog as it hit the concrete, with the now recognisable SPLAT!:
"HUW, WHAT HAVE YOU DONE? OH MY GOD, YOU'VE KILLED...", shouted my father as he attempted to process the devastation before him, in what became known as 'The Amphibian Massacre of Staples Lane, 1968'. My father, who loved animals, was hopping (excuse the pun) amongst the dead frogs that covered the back yard. At the same time, he was shouting at me incoherently, as I stood there, guilty as charged, with my head hung in shame and sobbing uncontrollably. To complete my shame, my mother, Beth, Bernard and Auntie Mary had joined us outside and they were also horrified at the massacre of the frogs – I was now surrounded by disapproving faces!

My father told me he was taking me straight home, continually berating me as we walked:
"I can't believe..."
"You killed them..."

"Such a naughty…"
"Why did you…"
"That was so cruel…"
"What were you…" etc etc.

I was sobbing gently, chin tucked into my chest not daring to look at my father, all the way home. When we arrived at our flat, I was sent straight to bed with no tea and remorsefully sobbed and sniffed myself to sleep.

The Welsh Grinch (The Boy who ruined Christmas)

Christmas has always been a magical time of year and for various reasons there have been many memorable ones over the years. Following the separation/divorce of my parents, my mother and I were now living back in Bridgend with my grandparents, Nana and Grampa Henson, at 43 Parcau Avenue. Whilst I initially enjoyed Christmas 1968, it was memorable for all the wrong reasons, as my Mother and Grandparents were robbed of the perfect Christmas…by a five-year-old!

As it started to get dark on Christmas Eve, I was reminded by my mother and grandparents that I would have to go to bed, and to sleep, early. I was told, as I'm sure were other children, that Father Christmas wouldn't leave any presents for children who tried to stay awake and catch a glimpse of the 'Bearded Wonder in the red suit'. This was enough of a threat for me to beg to go to bed early, as I didn't want a Christmas Day with no presents. With bedtime fast approaching I became extremely excited and this excitement increased tenfold when Grampa Henson suggested we leave a drink and something to eat for Father Christmas, in the hallway. Grampa disappeared into the kitchen, reappearing almost immediately, with a plate and a small glass which he carefully placed on the ornate, glass topped table that normally sat in the hallway. Nana Henson asked me to go the kitchen with her and whispered:
"Do you think Father Christmas would like a mince pie Huw"
"Yes Nana" I replied, jumping around the kitchen excitedly.
Nana opened a tin where the mince pies were kept and said:
"Pick one out for Father Christmas Huw and go and see Grampa"

13

I looked in the tin and lifted out the biggest one I could find and happily skipped into the hallway where Grampa was waiting:

"What have you got there Huw"

"Mince Pie for Father Christmas" I replied, placing it carefully on the plate and then stepping back, still looking at the mince pie and feeling really pleased with myself.

"Mmmmm, What drink do you think Father Christmas would like Huw?

"MILK, MILK, MILK…" I screamed.

Grampa laughed loudly and shouted to Nana:

"Can you bring some milk Margaret? Huw said Father Christmas drinks milk"

My nana returned to the hallway with a jug of milk and I helped her fill the glass for Father Christmas with creamy, full fat milk. My mother smiled and suggested it was time for bed. I kissed Nana and Grampa goodnight and ran up the stairs as fast as my little legs would carry me and jumped into bed. My mother chuckled, as she eventually walked into the bedroom a minute or two behind me to find me tucked into bed with my eyes firmly shut. She kissed me goodnight, gently reminded me that no sleep would mean no presents, turned the light off, leaving the door slightly open (6 inches ajar – to let in the light from the landing as I was petrified of the dark) and returned to my grandparents downstairs.

I lay there staring at the ceiling for what seemed like an eternity, but on reflection, was probably no longer than 5 or 10 minutes. My eyes soon became heavy and I drifted off to sleep with a head full of wonderment at what Christmas Day would bring!

When I woke it was difficult to contain my excitement, but as young as I was, I knew I had to be quiet in case it was too early. "Hang on!" I thought. "Where was my stocking? Perhaps Father Christmas had left it downstairs". I got up quietly and peeped around the door, all was quiet. I had no idea of the time, why would I, I was only five years old! I crept across the landing and reached my first objective – the top of the stairs. So far, so good, no-one had stirred. Like a mini Ninja, I tiptoed down the stairs, pausing on every step and listening, before proceeding to the next step. When I finally reached the bottom I sensed something was wrong, as I was sure I could hear muffled voices! But where were they coming from? As I was standing at the bottom of the stairs I peered around the corner of the bannister, in the direction of the kitchen, my heart pounding in my chest! I tried to hold my breath as I saw the slither of light coming from beneath the door of the living room, at the back of the house, and realised that the muffled voices I had heard on the stairs were coming from the television. My five-year-old mind became confused, it was 1968 and there were no television programmes on in the morning!! Panic overwhelmed me, it now dawned on me that it wasn't Christmas Day, it was still CHRISTMAS EVE! I must have slept for just a couple of hours and my initial reaction was to get back to bed quickly before I was caught. However, I was still only five years old and rationality, as I had proved with the frogs, was not a normal thought process for a child. It was then that the impish misbehavior kicked in as I thought:

"I wonder if Father Christmas has already been when I was sleeping. I know, I'll have a quick look in the front room and then I'll go to bed." The front or 'best' room was where the Christmas tree was sited in all its glory.

I slowly pushed the door open and peered into the half-lit room, the curtains were open and the tree glistened and shimmered from the street lights. Beneath and around the tree I could see an array of presents in various shapes and sizes. My heart was beating faster and my excitement was reaching new levels as I picked up the nearest present, gave it a little shake and then in a frenzy, ripped all the paper off it – pink furry slippers and they were too big - strange! I tossed them aside and reached for another present – Wow! A selection box: "Yum, yum" I thought. I moved from present to present until I had opened them all and was soon surrounded by toys, some weird presents (wallet, big pyjamas, a glass clown and more) and a sea of wrapping paper. I sat there for a moment and thought, "What have I done?", before smiling to myself, and grabbed the selection box, action man and Star Trek annual to return to my bedroom. I closed the door leaving the 'ruin of Christmas' behind me and crept back up the stairs, not noticing the untouched milk and mince pie, and back to the safety of my room (or so I thought)!

When I reached my bedroom I jumped into bed and tucked the action man up beside me, opened the chocolate buttons I had picked from the selection box and started looking at the Star Trek annual. At that moment, life was pretty good for this little five-year-old! I was so engrossed with the Star Trek annual and enjoying the milky way (I had already demolished the chocolate buttons) that I didn't hear Nana coming up the stairs. She opened the door to my bedroom and screamed:
"OH MY GOD HUW!...WHAT HAVE YOU DONE?...STAY RIGHT THERE"
I swear my nana must have made it to the bottom of the stairs in, no more than, two steps – I had never seen her move so quick (before or since)! She burst into the front room, turned the light on, screamed again and shouted:
"STANLEY...TRINA...COME AND SEE WHAT HUW HAS DONE!"
I heard voices downstairs (my name was mentioned a few times) as I took another bite of the milky-way and turned over to the next page in the Star Trek annual. Life was still good at this point, but I sensed this was about to change when I heard footsteps on the stairs. Nana reappeared in the room, but this time my mother had joined her and I received a dual lecture (wasted on a five year old) on how I had ruined Christmas for everybody – the action man, Star Trek annual and selection box (with exception of the remaining piece of the milky way I'd hidden under the bedclothes) were confiscated. I received a joint glare from My nana and mother before they turned off the light and went back downstairs. Feeling slightly sorry for myself, I ate the last piece of the milky-way and wondered when I would see the action man and Star Trek annual again! Life was so simple as a five-year-old!

Daffodil

March 1st 1969...to us Welsh people March 1st is commonly known as St David's Day. A day when the boys would go to school dressed as knights from a bygone age, and girls would be dressed in the Welsh national costume and both wearing either a leek or a daffodil (national emblems). There would be a mini Eisteddfod of singing and poems and it would be a half day finish. My St David's Day celebration that year would be cut short by a daffodil...!

16

Nana Henson finished pinning a daffodil on my jumper and armed with my wooden sword and shield that Grampa Henson had made, I was ready for school. When I arrived at school I noticed that all the other boys in my class had all eaten the yellow flower from their daffodil. Understandably, I didn't want to feel left out so I ate mine too. Everything appeared fine at first as I charged around the playground with my friends, playing nothing in particular! These demented, diagonal dashes saw us weave in and out of the older children, who tried to ignore our inane and pointless running, as they stood in small groups chatting. They only reacted to give the occasional five-year-old a clip around the head when they got too close...or even worse, accidentally bumped into them! Ding-a-ling-a-ling, ding-a-ling-a-ling, ding-a-ling-a-ling, ding-a-ling-a-ling went the school bell, and we all sprinted from wherever we were in the school yard...all attempting to be the first in the class line-up. After a great deal of pushing and shoving (mainly by the boys) we had lined up in a semi-orderly queue ready to be taken to class by our teacher, Mrs Morgan, who was still furiously ringing the school bell...attempting to round-up the stragglers!

As we entered the classroom, and without warning, I covered the centre of the classroom (the area we used for story time) in a multi-coloured yawn of epic proportions, splashing classmates as they attempted to run for cover from the relentless projectile vomiting. The horrific and chaotic scene was amplified by screams from the girls and shouts of "oh my God" from Mrs Morgan. I was quickly ushered to the toilets, across the corridor, as the screams receded to low moans of disgust! After ten minutes or so, I was sat on a chair in the corridor, covered in my own vomit and awaiting the imminent arrival of my mother. I was feeling very sorry for myself and vowing I would never eat a daffodil again!

Later that day my mother explained the difference between a leek and a daffodil (well, I was only five years old and I didn't know that daffodils were poisonous – nor did I realise my friends were wearing leeks...not daffodils) and strange as it may seem, I never did eat a daffodil again! Nan Henson completed the rehabilitation and healing process by making sure it was a leek she pinned on my jumper on the St David's Days that followed.

Adrian

When I was about eight years old one of my best friends in school was Adrian Lowe. For many years I have credited Adrian as the person who taught me how to tie my shoelaces. I am not sure if this is true or whether I used this simplistic action as a means to remember Adrian, but I can say that I still use the 'two loops' (bunny ears) method I learnt during those days in Trelales (Laleston) Primary School. This story tells of the tragic events (as I remember them) that unfolded on one fateful summer evening in 1971...

I don't have any recollection of the date but I know it was summertime, due to the light evenings. It would have been a fairly ordinary day of going to school and playing with friends. I couldn't tell you how I got to school, what we learnt that day, who played with who in the playground or what was on the menu in the school dining hall. All I knew was that I had been invited to Adrian Lowe's house to have tea, something I know I would have been excited about throughout that day.

Once school had finished, we went to Adrian's house which was only a two minute walk and probably played for a short while before having tea – another detail I couldn't describe from that day is what Adrian's mother gave us to eat! After we had finished tea, Adrian asked his Mother if we could go to our school's playing field to play football.

As children, we spent many hours on this field which was separated from school by a public footpath. Adjacent to the second of two entrances to the school buildings there was a gated entrance to the large school playing field. The top part of the field was fairly non-descript and properties from Laleston village backed on to the topmost section and a third of the way down the sloping field, in a fairly central position, was a sandpit that was used as a long jump pit whenever we had inter house sports days or competitions against other schools. The other side of the sandpit was the first set of rugby posts that marked the beginning of the school rugby field which took up the remainder of the field including the bottom set of posts. The whole area was fenced off and was considered a safe place for the children of the village to play. As you looked down the left-hand side of the field, on the other side of the fence there was a hedgerow that ran the entire length of the field. On the right-hand side was the footpath, nestled between the fences of the field and the school. This footpath carried on past the school grounds onto and through the middle of two fields (separated by a hedgerow and stile) to a gate, stile and another hedgerow that led onto the side of the A48. At the time, the A48 was a major road that linked both Cardiff and Swansea (a busy road even in 1971 as at that time the M4, from London, stopped at Newport)!

Adrian's Mother reluctantly gave us permission to go to the school playing field, but with strict instructions to be careful crossing the roads and to be back before it got dark. Adrian gathered up his football and we set off, laughing and larking about as we walked down the street in direction of the school. Within a few minutes we were on the playing field and decided to head for the rugby posts (that we would use as goalposts) at the bottom of the field. It's from this point that the unfortunate chain of events would unfold that led to an unnecessary tragedy of unspeakable proportions – a tragedy which has been etched in my memory for approximately forty-five years!

Adrian and I had happily been playing football for about twenty minutes, taking it in turns to be the goalkeeper until the other had scored three goals. We were no different to the boys of today, as we also pretended to be our favourite players, providing a continual running commentary, as we dribbled around imaginary defenders before shooting. If we scored, we copied the elaborate goal celebrations of players we had seen on BBCs 'Match of the Day' or ITVs 'The Big Match'. Our joy and fun was shortlived when an older boy of about twelve or thirteen years old approached us (to this day I have no idea who it was) and snatched Adrian's football. We made every attempt to get the ball back but the boy was bigger and stronger than us and he foiled all our efforts before running off with Adrian's ball. He was laughing loudly as he ran towards the bottom right hand corner of the field and threw the ball over the fence. In almost one movement, he climbed over the fence, retrieved the ball, and ran off down the path that meandered through the field immediately behind the rugby pitch, and as the ground dropped away he quickly disappeared from view.

I told Adrian not to worry about the ball, your Mother will understand when we tell her what happened. I said, "Come on, lets go", and turned to walk away. Adrian, however, started running in the same direction as the older boy and shouted, "I want my ball back Huw". Adrian was almost over the fence before I had reacted, and by the time I reached it, he was already fifteen to twenty metres down the same path the older boy had run down minutes before. I eventually made it over the fence and set-off down the path, but Adrian was now a good thirty metres in front of me. As I approached the centre of the field I could see that Adrian was starting to climb over the stile that would take him into field next to the A48. As I ran towards the stile I glanced to my right and noticed the older boy, still holding Adrian's ball, hiding in some bushes on the edge of a small copse. I immediately shouted:
"ADRIAN", but here was no response from Adrian, I paused as I climbed over the stile and again shouted;
"ADRIAN" quickly followed by, "ADRIAN, STOP!" I could now hear the sound of the traffic from the A48 and presumed that it was now drowning out my shouts, and why Adrian was ignoring my repeated pleas to stop. I landed on the other side of the stile and again sprinted after Adrian, repeatedly shouting his name, but the noise of the traffic and the shortness of breath, from the chase, reduced the effect of my continued pleas. In the distance, I could see Adrian fast approaching the stile and gate that separated the field from the edge of the A48. I was still shouting his name as he climbed over the stile, but the roar of the traffic was now deafening. A few seconds later, I approached the same stile and could see Adrian standing on the edge of the grass verge. He was craning his head to the right, in an attempt to see around the bend in the road, to determine if it was safe to cross. As I put my foot on the stile and pulled myself up, I shouted one last time;
"ADRIAN, NO…!"
Sadly, he didn't hear me and, as if in slow motion, I watched him step out into the road. There was a sickening 'thud' as a car came from nowhere and hit Adrian, leaving him motionless in the gutter, his left arm draped helplessly across the grass – as if it was one last futile attempt to cling to safety.

As I stepped down off the stile on to the grass verge, I glanced to my left to see that the car, a white Ford Anglia, had stopped about fifty metres up the road. As shock began to envelop me, I took a couple of tentative steps closer to Adrian and attempted to recognise my best friend, but I couldn't see any of the familiar features of his face. In their place, was a featureless, crimson mess that, as an eight-year-old, I found difficult to comprehend. I took a step back and froze, the enormity of the situation began to hit home and I glanced to my left and saw that the Ford Anglia was reversing. It stopped about ten to fifteen metres away and the last thing I remember was noticing that the wing mirror, on the passenger side, was missing and also seeing the driver get out of the car and walk towards me…the rest is blank!

I look back on that evening and still don't know how I got home and I don't remember discussing it with my mother, grandparents or teachers. I cannot be sure, but I presume that, as a coping mechanism, I shut out the events that followed the accident. The next thing I do remember is the news, being announced to the class, that Adrian had died in a tragic accident. This announcement must have been the following day, but it was much later that I learnt that he had been pronounced dead, in the ambulance, on the way to the hospital. I can't ever remember discussing it with school friends at the time or later and don't know if they ever realised that I was with Adrian on that fateful evening. It's possible that I am still carrying the burden of guilt that I couldn't save him, but I have never forgotten him or our friendship - The boy who taught me to tie my shoelaces!

London – 1973

My father and stepmother, Shirley, moved to London when I was nine years old. My father found a job as a caretaker at a Jewish old peoples home, Heinrich Stahl House, on Bishops Avenue, East Finchley. It was during the Easter holidays that I travelled to London, with my Nan Thomas, to stay with my father and Shirley for a memorable week, visiting some of the great landmarks in London, such as; Westminster Abbey, the Houses of Parliament, Tower of London (including the crown jewels), St Paul's Cathedral, Regents Park Zoo, Natural History Museum. Abiding memories of that week however,

21

*involved a pigeon in Oxford Street and a set of steps leading to
the Embankment…!!*

The Pigeon and the Glasses

After visiting one of the many museums in London, my father,
Shirley, Nan Thomas and I were walking past Marble Arch in
the direction of Oxford Street. The wider pavements of Oxford
Street struggled to contain the teeming hordes of tourists of
varying ages and nationalities, mixing with Londoners in a
hub of seemingly meaningless activity. The weather was
inclement with an uninviting grey sky overhead that was
providing persistent April showers, but thankfully, as we
walked down Oxford Street there was a welcome break in the
incessant rainfall. As we passed Selfridges, and another of the
umpteenth street stalls that littered the London streets and sold
the normal array of souvenirs, my nan turned to me to ask me
a question (I have no idea what the question was, and as you
will soon see, the nature of the question is irrelevant!). I turned
to face her and respond to the question when 'IT' happened! A
pigeon flying above released its 'load' with an unerring
accuracy that resulted in a direct hit on the inside of my Nan's
glasses, completely covering one lens in pigeon shit! For a
split second I stared in disbelief at the sight before me, and my
nan stared back at me (through the other unaffected lens!),
before we both began laughing hysterically, each doubled over
as I repeatedly pointed at her glasses and the splattered shit
over the left side of her face - What a shot!

My father and Shirley, who had been walking slightly in front
of us when the pigeon struck, turned towards us and told us to
be quiet. The space around us grew bigger, as our behaviour
was greeted with a mixture of nervousness and contempt by
other pedestrians. The more my father and Shirley told us to
"Be quiet" and "ssshhh", the more we laughed, and we
struggled on as tears streamed down our faces and our
stomach's ached with continued laughter. Eventually, we
gained our composure and carried on down Oxford Street,
occasionally receiving glances of disgust from my father and
Shirley, as my nan frantically cleaned her glasses (and her
face!). Soon all the traces of the pigeon's 'dirty deed' had been
removed from my nan's face and glasses, but how we
laughed! Over the years, my nan and I remembered and re-told

that story many times and each time we laughed, as we had on the day my nan received the direct hit from the 'Dive bombing Pigeon of Oxford Street'…!

St Paul's Cathedral, the photograph and the steps!

My father, Shirley, Nan and I emerged from St Paul's Cathedral. I was clutching my new Kodak instamatic camera (a Birthday present from my father and Shirley), and immediately ran down the steps and across the paved area in front of the main entrance. I was eager to take a photograph of the impressive building that had represented Britain's defiance to Germany during 'The Blitz' (I had recently seen the iconic photograph that showed London ablaze around St Paul's Cathedral during the Second World War!). I found a suitable place where I could capture the essence of this impressive and important landmark or from the perspective of a ten year old with a cheap camera, 'I could fit the entire cathedral into the little window!' I took the photograph and with an accomplished grin, I ran back to my father, Shirley and nan, who were waiting patiently at the foot of the steps that lead up to the main entrance of St Paul's.

My father suggested that we walk the short distance, along the embankment, to the Tower of London. We walked around the right-hand side of St Paul's and then crossed the road onto Peter's Hill (a wide paved area that headed straight down to the Embankment (where the Millennium Bridge is now located). I said to my father, "Can I run on ahead to take another photo of St Pauls" (with your back to the River Thames there is a fantastic view of the side profile of St Paul's Cathedral framed between and rising above the buildings on either side of Peter's Hill). My father nodded, allowing me to run ahead and I was soon about a hundred metres in front of my father, Shirley and nan. I turned to face St Paul's and brought the camera to my eye, "damn", I thought, "I can't get it all in" and started to walk backwards. In the distance, I could see my father, Shirley and nan waving at me, so I waved back! I continued to walk back slowly and noticed my father, Shirley and Nan were still waving (my nan was waving with both hands) and I, again waved back. As their waving continued and appeared to become more frantic, I thought, "that's strange, why are they waving all the time?" It was with sudden realisation that I understood the waving wasn't just a friendly gesture but a warning, as the next backwards step I took was into thin air! I had unknowingly reached (and obviously not seen) the steps that led down to the embankment. As I fell back, my legs immediately flipped into a vertical position as I disappeared into the abyss behind me – still clutching my new camera! I landed on my back, with a 'thud' on the wide steps with the sound of hurried footsteps and shouts of "Huw" getting nearer and nearer. I realised quickly that I was unhurt (and the camera was still in one piece) and started to giggle uncontrollably. I looked up to see my father, Shirley and nan staring down at me, open mouthed, but they too, were soon laughing when they realised I was fine. Again, similar to the incident in Oxford Street, we were getting some strange looks from disapproving people in the immediate vicinity. I was still laughing when I finally stood up, and my nan, who was struggling to contain herself, described what she had seen when I fell back, legs flipped as I disappeared from their view!

I finally took the photo of St Paul's from the second step, and with a wry smile skipped down the steps to re-join my father, Shirley and nan. As we walked along the embankment, we sporadically broke out into fits of laughter at my calamitous disappearing act down the steps of Peter's Hill!

Fring Hall and its Ghost!

Next stop for my Father and Shirley was Norfolk where they were employed by a Mr Brun (a Dane who had come to Britain on a pushbike with only £15 in his pocket and ended up becoming the second biggest landowner in Norfolk behind the Queen) who owned Fring Hall and most of the village. My father was employed as the Butler/Chaffeur/General Handyman and my stepmother as the Maid/Cook/Cleaner. The jobs came with a free flat, located high on the second floor/attic and accessed via a 'servants' stairwell, next to the main kitchen. It was here, for Easter in 1974, that I went with my grandparents (Nan and Grampa Thomas) to stay for a short holiday with my Father and Shirley. It soon became obvious we were not the only ones in the house…!

Grampa Thomas, Shirley and my father finished putting their coats on and said their farewells, leaving Nan Thomas and me alone in the flat. They were going for a few drinks at a pub called 'The Hare', which was located in the next village of Docking, as Fring didn't have a pub; in fact, it didn't have a shop – the only thing of note was a Victorian post box! My nan and I were all smiles as they left, but as they disappeared down the stairs we looked at each other nervously, as we remembered the eerie events of the previous evening…!

During the stay, I was sharing a bedroom with my grandparents; sleeping on a camp bed in the corner of the room. In the darkness of the previous night, the sound of Grampa's snoring (occasionally interrupted by the haunting sound of an owl hooting somewhere in the distance) was all that could be heard. Suddenly, the temperature in the room dropped dramatically, and there was a sense that someone or something else was also in the room. I lay there too scared to breath with my eyes tightly shut, too afraid to open them and unable to move. Within an instant, the temperature rose back to normal as dramatically as it had dropped. The silence was again broken by my Grandfather's snoring and my Nan asking, "Huw, you ok! Did you feel that?"
"Yes" I replied.
Nothing more was said and my eyes remained firmly shut as I lay there willing myself to sleep!

Back in the present, my Nan and I went into the kitchen where the cure to all evils was kept… tea!
"Do you want a cup of tea Huw?"
"Yes please Nan and can I have a biscuit please?
She chuckled quietly, "Of course you can", our nervousness now forgotten.

At this point, it is important to attempt to describe the layout of the flat. When you reached the top of the stairwell, you were on a landing area where the kitchen, bathroom and two bedrooms were located. The living room, however, was detached from the other rooms, situated approximately 20 metres down a corridor that separated the two bedrooms. The corridor continued past the living room for about another seven or eight meters before turning right and then immediately left, up a couple of steps to a door that gave access to the attic above the main house. The attic was large and with exception of a table tennis table and full size snooker table, it was no different to the attic of a small house, where memories of the family were packed away in dusty boxes of various sizes and strewn around the musty, badly lit attic.

The kettle whistled its announcement of readiness and my Nan, tea towel in hand, poured the hot water into two cups that each contained a solitary tea bag. The milk and sugar soon followed and with our tea ready, I grabbed a biscuit and followed my Nan to the sanctuary of the living room. At night, the corridor to the living room seemed longer than usual and we were almost jogging to get there quicker. Nan went in first, turned on the light and television, I followed and shut the door behind me, giving it a second tug to ensure it was firmly closed. We settled down to watch TV, happy in the knowledge that we were safely secure in the living room...or so we thought!

It must have been about an hour later when my Nan whispered;
"What was that?"
She immediately stood up, moved quickly to the television and turned the volume right down. It was then I could hear it...distant footsteps and the faint squeak of an unoiled door opening or closing.
"What is it Nan?" I whispered with a tell-tale fear in my voice.
We could hear the footsteps coming slowly down the corridor towards us and my Nan and I moved to the window on the wall opposite the door to the corridor. We stood either side of the window gently grasping at the curtain as if searching for some sort of comfort. Then the footsteps stopped outside the door to the living room, my Nan and I glanced at each other and then back at the door, an inevitable realisation that...this is it! As if in slow motion, we watched the round brass door handle turning and we held our breaths, our fate determined by whatever was on the other side of the door! It seemed like an eternity before the door opened and suddenly, without warning, a cheery, happy face peered around the door;
"Good evening Mrs Thomas, are you and your Grandson well? Just thought I'd look in on you both as I knew you were on your own".

It was Charles Brun, the eldest son of the house owner. We were both speechless and just nodded and smiled inanely, as we continued to hold onto the curtains, overcome with a mixture of fear and relief!

"Well goodnight then!" Charles said, perplexed at the scene before him; two strange, common Welsh people hanging on to the curtains, grinning and staring into space like long term patients in a mental asylum. We both mumbled something incoherently that could have been 'goodnight' as Charles closed the door. The curtains continued being a source of comfort as Charles' footsteps faded away into the distance. The only noise that could then be heard was our laboured breathing, and our old friend the owl revealed his presence with a solitary hoot!

My Nan looked at me and we both started laughing, and as we finally let go of the curtains she gave me a wink and said; "Kitchen!"

"Yeah, I think we need another cup of tea Nan".

We made a hasty retreat to the kitchen where we drank more tea and waited for Grampa, Shirley and my Father to return from the pub. As we waited, we relived the events, laughing as we retold the story again and again - "What must Charles have thought seeing us....?", "we were holding onto the curtains...", "I was petrified...", etc. When the others came home they found Nan and I laughing and laughing with tears streaming down our faces. What a night!

Thunder storm in the Alps

The Summer of 1974, before I started at Bryntirion Comprehensive School, I was fortunate to be invited on a holiday with Bernard, Beth, Nicholas and Margaret and Soham College. The trip saw us visit seven European countries in two weeks and it was an amazing experience of crossing the English Channel on Hovercraft and seeing the Rhine Falls, the Black Forest in Bavaria, Basle Zoo etc, but the night we came into Austria under cover of darkness was pretty special!

The two buses had left Remich on the Luxembourg/West German border early that morning and we were en-route for Bludenz in Austria. We had travelled through Germany, enjoying the incredible, serene beauty of the Black Forest and also briefly stopping at the equally impressive Rhine Falls. It was raining and dark when we finally reached the West German/Austrian border and after passport checks, that held us up for about 30 minutes, we finally drove into Austria. It was almost midnight when we approached Bludenz, and unlike most of the other children, who were sleeping, I was peering into the dark, through the rain lashed windows, attempting to make out the shapes of buildings we passed (I always struggled to sleep when I was travelling). The rain became heavier and had developed into a powerful electrical storm. It was this terrifying force of nature that provided me with the abiding memory from this holiday, and those images have stayed with me to this day! Every flash of lightning and pronged bolt created a very special moment as, for a split second, the Alps around Bludenz were lit up in all their glory. A silhouette of wonderment that left you gasping in astonishment and those brief images removed the fear element that is often associated with thunder and lightning! Every storm I have witnessed since, takes me back to that night, and the wondrous sights I saw through the distortions of the rain covered windows on that bus!

‘The Talk!’

The ‘birds and the bees’ is an uncomfortable and often embarrassing situation none of the participants want to be part of, something we have all experienced. My memory of the inevitable part of everyone’s life, passed me by without me even realizing it had happened. It would be years later when I looked back on ‘that’ evening that I realised I had totally misunderstood the deep meaning of that momentous occasion…wasted on a naïve (as I was then), eleven year old!

I was in the bathroom humming Mud’s ‘Lonely this Christmas’ whilst I applied the finishing touches for my big date with Jayne Pascoe. I was eleven years old and excited at the prospect of heading to the cinema on my first ever date…ever! I reached for the new bottle of Aramis aftershave my Mother had bought me for Christmas, unscrewed the top and lifted the bottle to my nose…mmm, that smells good! This was my first time wearing aftershave. My confidence grew as I poured a small quantity into the palm of my right hand, put the bottle on the windowsill, rubbed my hands together and applied the Aramis to my face...aaarrrrgh! I discovered, long before Macaulay Culkin, that aftershave bloody stings. Through watery eyes and with a slight dent in my confidence, I managed to replace the top on the bottle of Aramis and put it back in the bathroom cabinet. A quick dab of the eyes with a towel and a final look in the mirror and I was ready. I unlocked the bathroom door, stepped into the hall, turned to the left to a see a welcoming committee standing in the kitchen – my Mother, Grampa and Nan Henson all silently waiting for me!

Apprehensively, I stepped into the kitchen and quietly asked if everything was ok, thinking had I done something wrong...again! My grandparents looked on nervously as my Mother cleared her throat and said "No, everything's fine Huw. Just wanted a quick chat before you went out!"
"What about Mum?"
"Well, you are taking a girl out for the first time and I want to make sure you behave yourself and don't do anything you shouldn't do!"
Nan Henson started looking for something in the fridge and my Grandfather started to take great interest in the ceiling, as I stood there with absolutely no idea of *what* my Mother was talking about! I was eleven years old and going out with a girl to the cinema, what did my Mother honestly think I was going to do?
"What do you mean Mum?"
"Well...just don't do anything you...shouldn't do!"
"Like what?" I asked, my face a picture of complete puzzlement.
"Just behave yourself...use your manners and...well...you...you know...treat her with respect!"
My Nan still hadn't found what she was looking for in the fridge and Grampa was now on a chair carrying out a thorough investigation of the ceiling...strange! What was wrong with everyone? Very confusing for an eleven-year-old just trying to leave the house to take a girl to the cinema!
"What do you mean?"
"Just be a good boy Huw...I don't want...I mean...don't let me hear...if this girl's parents knock the door saying...well...you know what I mean!!"

I was now totally confused, but…in this confusion I just replied; "OK Mum".

I could see my Nan nodding her approval as she still searched for the mysterious item that must have been well hidden in our fridge! At this point, Grampa brought a semblance of common sense to the room when he turned to my Mother and said, "I think it's time to let Huw go now Trina"

My Mother sighed and nodded in agreement.

"Off you go Huw…have a great time and…BE GOOD!"

"OK Mum. Bye then, see you all later"

I ran for the door, opened it and in a mixture of confusion and relief, I stepped out into the dark and set off for Jayne's house!

I skipped down Longfellow Drive, again singing Lonely this Christmas, before I slowed to a steady walk and can remember thinking to myself; "What was my Mother talking about? Did she think I was going to show Jayne how impressive my stone throwing was or how high I could pee up a wall or even steal sweets from the kiosk and sneak us both into the cinema without paying!" I quickly forgot about it all and was soon at Jayne's house and with a feeling of nervousness and excitement, I plucked up the courage and knocked the door!

We went to the cinema and as far as I can remember I behaved myself, but there was no second date and it would be a couple of years before I had my first girlfriend. It's only now when I look back at that evening that I realised my Mother had made a feeble attempt at telling me about the 'birds and the bees'! I laugh now when I think back to those first years of comprehensive in the early/mid 70s, when we were much more naïve and immature than children are today. Innocence was a precious commodity we enjoyed for longer, and thankfully, there were no other attempts by my Mother or Grandparents to provide me with a sex education!

Swan Lake

When I was growing up, my grandparents (Nan and Grampa Thomas) had a picture of the ballet, Swan Lake, above the fireplace in the living room of their flat, 8a Derllwyn Close, Tondu. As small children, my cousins and I would all ask, "who are they in the picture?" We would always be told, "that's me and Nanny when we young" or "that's me and

Grampa before we got married" – None of us ever doubted what we were told, why would we, we were small children! The performance of Swan Lake I witnessed at Christmas in 1975 was breathtaking and something I'll never forget...ever!

Christmas dinner was finished... and as Nan Thomas and my Auntie Glenys washed the last of the mountain of dishes that Christmas always produced; Grampa, Uncle Ivor, my cousins Michelle and Nicola, and I escaped to the comfort of the living room. Grampa sat in his 'special' chair and instantly fell into a deep sleep...judging by the snoring that was coming from his corner of the room! Michelle, humming to herself, had taken up position on the rug in front of the roaring coal fire, a fire that was throwing heat into every corner of the room, and she was happily colouring in one of her new colouring books. Uncle Ivor, with Nicola on his lap, was sat in the armchair directly in front of Michelle and the fire place, and I was in the chair next to the window enjoying the last remnants of the Christmas Top of the Pops, Queen were singing their classic, *Bohemian Rhapsody,* deservedly the Christmas Number One in 1975. Nanny and Auntie Glenys soon joined us and made themselves comfortable on the settee next to Grampa (who was still snoring), just in time for the start of the Queen's Christmas message (a tradition enjoyed by most families). Billy Smarts Christmas Circus followed the Queen's message...this brought an abrupt end to Michelle's colouring, as she joined Nanny and her Mother on the settee. She nestled in between them, and helped herself to a chocolate from the Quality Street tin, strategically placed on the trolley behind the door, far enough away from the heat of the fire to ensure they didn't melt!

The afternoon film that Christmas Day was *The Wizard of Oz*, a timeless musical, starring Judy Garland as Dorothy – a family classic! Everyone was quiet until the Munchkins started singing "Ding dong, the wicked witch is dead...", Grampa opened his eyes and mumbled "Judy bloody Garland...again...for God's sake...this is on every bloody Christmas". He stood up, still mumbling profanities about; "Bloody Munchkins...bloody tin man...oh my God...here comes that cowardly bloody Lion...That's all I bloody need..." and left the room, his grumblings still heard from other parts of the flat! Nan Thomas sighed, rolled her eyes and confirmed what we now already knew; "Father...Grampa...hates the Wizard of Oz...silly old sod!" She rocked her head back and laughed loudly. A few minutes later he was back in the room, with a frown on his face obviously looking for something!

"Anyone seen my glasses...put them down somewhere now I...I'll give you bloody yellow brick road...ah, found them".

With impeccable timing, the Straw Man started singing "If I only had a brain...".

This prompted a sharp reply from Grampa, "Aye and If only I had a bloody shotgun..."

My Nan glared at him, "Language Eddie...there's children in the room!"

Grampa left the room again still mumbling "Green witch, hah!...flying monkeys...stupid bloody film...no wonder kids today are bloody messed up..."

Nan stood up, sighed again and cheerfully said, "Tea anyone?" We all shouted, "Yes please.." and carried on watching the Wizard of Oz, a film bursting with colour and of course...cheesy songs! We all loved it...well, everyone except Grampa!

The film was drawing to a close, as the Straw Man, Tin Man, Dorothy (holding Toto, her little dog) and the Lion were skipping down the yellow brick road towards the Emerald City, singing, "We're off to see the Wizard, the wonderful...!" The door to the living-room burst open...We were about to have the shock of our lives!

Nan came in first, prancing around the living room, similar to the dancers in the Swan Lake picture above the fire. She threw her arms out and her head back, attempting little jumps and pirouettes...laughing as she glided...no, bounced around the room wearing just a blouse and a pair of tights...gone was her skirt. What a sight! My Nan was no ballet dancer, at four foot ten and on the rather large side, she was more akin to the build of a rugby tighthead prop! My Auntie Glenys was whooping, screaming and laughing, all at the same time, as she rocked back and forth with tears rolling down her cheeks. On the other hand, Uncle Ivor, Michelle, Nicola and I, were initially in a state of shock as we were unsure as to what we were witnessing! A few seconds later, it was complete carnage as Grampa, also wearing just a shirt and a pair of my Nan's tights had now appeared and was now providing us with another poor impression of a ballet dancer – seeing my Grandfather, a sixty eight year old former coal miner and soldier, pirouetting around the living-room in a collarless shirt and a pair of my Nan's tights was too much and I burst out laughing, as did Uncle Ivor and the girls. They danced…we laughed, they danced some more…we laughed and laughed until our stomachs hurt and we could take no more! *The Wizard of Oz* was forgotten, no-one cared about Dorothy 'clicking' her red shoes so she could get back to Kansas! Nan and Grampa left the room as they had entered…arms out, heads back…the classic ballet pose, with mini kicks and half-hearted pirouettes. Absolutely priceless and a wonderful moment – God, how we needed that cup of tea my Nan had originally left the room to make!

First 'Puppy' Love – SR4HT

They say you never forget your first 'puppy' love and for me that has been no different. When my Father lived in Norfolk, when I was a teenager, I had a close-knit group of friends who lived in Brancaster, Brancaster Staithe and Burnham Deepdale, and one of those friends, Mark Richardson, had a sister – Samantha. It was with Sam, during the long, hot summer of 1976, that I experienced those feelings of being in love for the first time!

I had only been back in Norfolk a few days and my friends were all talking about a girl called Samantha, but it would be a week before I discovered why Sam was so popular! On the day I first met Sam I had been playing football with Mark Hammond and brothers Stephen and David Sutherland on Brancaster playing field. The field was where Brancaster village team played football and was just off the main NW Norfolk coast road that ran between Hunstanton and Wells-next-to-Sea. It was accessed via a small carpark, nestled behind the 71 Club (Brancaster Village Hall). A high and impenetrable hawthorn hedge (with exception of a small access point in the opposite left-hand corner, off Cross Lane) created the boundary of the field on the remaining three sides. We were having a kickabout at the Brancaster Staithe end of the field near the swings, but after about twenty minutes or so we had to stop for a drink. The heat of the sun made it difficult to play football and we sought refuge in the shade that was provided by the large hawthorn hedge. We sat with our backs to the football field, with exception of David, who was now on the nearest swing rocking gently back and forth. Suddenly, David pointed to the opposite corner of the playing field and shouted, "Here they come…Mark and Sam". We all turned round in unison to see Mark and Sam walking towards us. As they got closer, I realised why everyone was talking about her…she was beautiful! She was slim with shiny dark brown hair cut into a bob, big brown eyes and a smile that outshone the sunshine…wow! As Stephen introduced them to me, I was mesmerised by Sam's smile and almost totally ignored her brother Mark. Thankfully, I snapped out of it quickly before anyone noticed…or so I thought!

Later that day, long after Mark and Sam had gone home, it was time for the rest of us to call it a day. We said our goodbyes and see you tomorrows, and Stephen, David and Mark (Hammond) mounted their bikes and left for Burnham Deepdale and Brancaster Staithe respectively. Almost immediately Stephen called out, "Huw…wait!" I stopped and turned to see Stephen cycling back towards me, "Yes Stephen…what's the matter!"
He gave me a knowing look, "I saw the way you looked at Sam earlier"
I laughed nervously, "Was it that obvious…I…I thought I had gotten away with that!" I looked down at the ground, as I knew that I probably wasn't the only one that was attracted to Sam.
"I think she likes you too Huw" Stephen whispered.
My heart skipped a beat at the possibility that Sam liked me too. "Did…did she say anything…?"
"Trust me Huw…I know!"
"How…how can you tell Stephen?...Did she say anything?...How can you be so…sure?". My mind was racing with excitement as I fired question after question at Stephen. When it came to girls I wasn't very confident as, up to that point, I had never had a proper girlfriend.
"I'm not saying she didn't say anything Huw" Stephen grinned, gave me a wink, turned round and cycled back to the entrance to the playing field, where David and Mark were waiting for him.
"Stephen…!" I shouted.

34

He didn't turn around, he just waved and shouted back, "See you tomorrow Huw".

I stood there for a moment, unable to move and I watched them cycle off into the distance, over the brow of the hill and then they were gone. I raised my head to the sky as a warm feeling flooded through me and with a wry smile, I whispered to myself, "I can't believe it...Sam likes me!" Then a rush of the familiar self-doubt enveloped me as I thought, "Does she really like me...no, surely I can't be that lucky. Hang on!...Why shouldn't she...oh..I don't know!" The five to ten minute walk back home was filled with hope and despair, confidence and then self-doubt as I pondered the question of whether Sam liked me or not. I went to bed that night and all my thoughts were dominated by Sam, I drifted off to sleep thinking of those bewitching brown eyes and that beautiful smile...!

That summer of '76 was magical, as day after day and week after week the sun shone and the temperatures remained high, the entire summer that year didn't see a single rain drop. The fantastic weather allowed us to spend many long, fun-filled days at Brancaster Beach. A beautiful, and sometimes, dangerous place that was separated from the village by marshes and accessed either by Beach Road or on foot via the elevated footpath that ran parallel to the road. The footpath was the only way to and from the beach during high tides when the road became submerged under two to three feet of salt water! On the left as you approached the beach was the prominent feature of the Victorian clubhouse of Royal West Norfolk Golf Club. On the right, in front of the first tee of the golf course was a large car park. The golf course itself ran parallel with the beach but was separated by sand dunes 10-15m high and approximately 20m in depth. The access to the beach was via a walkway that passed the beach kiosk (selling cold and hot food/drinks, ice creams, buckets & spades, beach balls etc) and on through a small gap between the clubhouse on the left and the sand dunes on the right. The beach opened up, on the other side of the narrowing, and stretched for miles to the left and right and looked like any other beach when the tide was in. When the tide was out the scene changed dramatically, providing the hidden danger element to Brancaster Beach. The tide swept round to the left revealing a shallow river type feature and a large sandbank that included

35

an old wreck, rumoured to have been filled with concrete and used as target practice during World War II. The wreck was a good half mile walk from the beach and holidaymakers, unaware of the tidal conditions, would sometimes find themselves stranded on the sandbank, as the tide swept around behind them resulting in us witnessing the occasional air sea rescue operation! This sweeping area of natural beauty and danger became our second home during that long, hot summer. A carefree summer that provided memories of playing football and tennis, of bike rides and picnics, of swimming and carnival celebrations and above all else…experiencing the sweet innocence of a teenage love with Samantha Richardson.

By the end of that long, hot summer we became inseparable, but it would be a week after I had first met Sam that I would finally pluck up the courage to ask her if she would be my girlfriend. I waited for the right opportunity and this came during another inevitable day on Brancaster Beach. The others had gone looking for crabs amongst the mudflats, at the water's edge, about fifty metres in front of the golf clubhouse, leaving Sam and I alone together looking after everyone's clothes, drinks and food.

After a few minutes and with some degree of trepidation I said, "Sam?"

She turned to face me and raised her hand to her face to shield her eyes from the glare of the sun, "Yes Huw".

"Can…can…I ask you a…question?" I looked downwards too scared to look her in the eyes and nervously started to make swirling patterns in the sand with the index finger of my right hand.

"Of course you can Huw" and smiled.

I swallowed hard and glanced up for a moment catching a glimpse of that beautiful smile.

"I…I was wondering…if…if you would like to be my…girlfriend. It's ok…if you say…..?" Before, I had a chance to finish my sentence, without hesitation she happily said, "Yes Huw…I was…hoping you would ask me" and she flashed that beguiling smile, blushed and coyly started to twirl her hair with her fingers.

"Thank you Sam…that's…! My sentence and the beautiful moment was cut short as a football landed in front of me, kicking sand up into my face.

"Sorry Huw" Shouted David and he burst out laughing! The others were back...which made me think that they had left Sam and I on our own...on purpose!

Another day at the beach drew to a close and again it was time for us all to head off home. We left the beach, but Sam and I were walking a little way behind the others and as we reached the footpath, that led back to the village, my hand brushed against Sam's hand. She didn't move her hand away and as our fingertips touched, momentarily, for a second time, I gently clasped my hand around her petite fingers. I looked at her, smiled and gave her hand a reassuring squeeze, she gave me her usual, inimitable smile and returned the gesture. Nothing was said and no words were necessary, as we both enjoyed that first intimate moment with a feeling of mutual satisfaction – a demonstration of raw innocence! We walked on in silence, both enjoying the cool summer breeze that wrestled its way over the marshes to wash over us and then disappear into the night. After saying goodbye to the others, I walked Sam (with her brother, Mark, in tow) back to the driveway of her house on Cross Lane, we stood there for a moment and then reluctantly let go of each other's hand. Sam skipped to the door of the house, turned, smiled broadly and blew me a kiss, she followed Mark into the house, closed the door behind her, and she was gone...for now!

Carnival week in Brancaster was always a special time and that year it became extra special, because it would be the first time I would experience love's first kiss! The week started on a Saturday with a beach bar-b-cue, followed by a childrens sports day on the Sunday. Through the week there were various events, such as; pet/animal, fashion, vegetable/fruit, most beautiful baby and cake shows that would, inevitably, involve everyone in the village, regardless of age! Friday was the under 16s disco, adults disco on the Saturday and then it finished with the carnival parade on the Sunday. It was eight days of pure celebration and the carnival floats were awash with colour and various themes, decorated in the patriotic colours of red, white and blue to reflect their pride of being British.

As teenagers, our 'gang' were looking forward to the U'16s disco, a chance to impress each other with our dance moves and garish 70s garb! The talk that week centred around our musical tastes (diverse tastes from punk rock to rock and roll and a bit of disco music – well it was the 70s), clothes, the girls that the boys fancied and the boys that the girls fancied, "you like...!", "I'm going to dance with...!", "are you going to kiss...?" Normal teenage conversation prior to any disco or party! Friday arrived and it was a fantastic night, and the small hall of the 71 Club coped admirably with 30-40 kids aged between 11-16 years old. Rock and roll was still a crowd favourite amongst Norfolk children, despite the fact that the music came from an era before any of them were born. The DJ belted out song after song (from our requests) of artists, such as; Elvis, Buddy Holly, Little Richard, Bill Haley, Everley Brothers, Bay City Rollers, Slade, Sweet, Showaddywaddy, ABBA, and we all jived to the rock and roll songs in our own distinctive style, some more manic than others...Stephen! As the disco drew to a close, the mood changed as everyone prepared for the fast approaching disco ritual of the slow dances or smooches (as we called them then), 2-3 songs that created an opportunity for love to blossom! The scene was set, boys on one side of the hall, girls on the other. The DJ's announcement came that "it was time to slow things down...!", the disco lights dimmed and the unique sound of the Bee Gees singing *How Deep is your Love* was initially drowned out by the rush of platform shoes and stilettos across the dance floor as eager teenagers raced to find true love (before someone beat them to it)!

Sam and I were amongst the participants of this primal, robotic ritual; step...shuffle, step...shuffle, step...shuffle, a slow-motioned, entwined pirouette of togetherness. As the song faded to its conclusion, Sam briefly lifted her head, looked up at me and smiled before nestling back into my shoulder, as the second slow song, Leo Sayer's *When I Need You*, began playing. I moved my right hand to the nape of her neck and with a gentle stroking action I became totally immersed in feelings I was struggling to understand! We were still dancing when the song ended and the lights in the hall were switched on, signifying the abrupt end to the disco for another year! We laughed and hand in hand, ran out into the night!

When we reached the fence that faced the playing field, we stopped to catch our breath and we sat side by side and giggled quietly to ourselves. The night was still and the stars offered the only protection against the darkness and as I looked at Sam, she flashed that now familiar smile. In an instant, I placed my hand gently into the small of her back and turned to face her. Sam also turned and placed her hand on my arm, and we tenderly leant towards each other for love's first kiss! Just before our lips touched, we both experienced a natural phenomenon, as our eyes closed in expectant anticipation of this sensitive moment. Our lips met and we stayed there for a moment, each relishing the softness of the other's lips, until we both heard her brother, Mark shouting, "Sam…where are you?" We released each other from that first kiss and she shouted, "Over here Mark". He quickly joined us and was soon followed by the others…including Stephen holding his brother, David, in a familiar headlock! Mark and Sam quickly left, but not before she had gently squeezed my hand and smiled again…I watched her walk away, totally oblivious to everything else around me!

As the summer drew to a close, I wanted to seal my love for Sam by carving our initials somewhere significant (a typical teenage sign of love and affection). We chose a tree in a small wooded area adjacent to her house, one with an easily accessible large horizontal branch that was about four feet above the ground – perfect! We both clambered up and found a comfortable position where I could safely carve our initials, and within twenty minutes it was finished – SR4HT. Satisfied, we both looked at each other and I reached out to take Sam's hand, and lost myself in those beautiful brown eyes. Sam reciprocated those feelings with a broad grin as she reached out for my other hand, and we sat there in silence, holding each other's hands on the bough of that old tree!

A few days later, summer was over, I was sitting on a National Express coach In Kings Lynn waving goodbye to my Father and Shirley. As the bus pulled out of the station, I immediately thought of Sam and looked out of the window back, to what I thought was the direction of Brancaster…and Sam, and silently mouthed…*I love you*! As the coach left Kings Lynn behind, I leant against the window and gazed out to into the passing countryside and started silently singing to myself the lyrics of 'When I Need You?'.

That unforgettable summer in Norfolk was almost forty years ago, and I have never forgotten that circle of friends...especially Sam! Whenever, I hear Leo Sayer's *When I Need You*, I think of that Summer in 1976 and Sam, and of course, those eyes and that beautiful smile. Seven or eight years after carving our initials on the bough of that old tree, I returned to find that they were still there. However, the tree has now long gone and I never did see Sam again. I have no photographs of her, she only exists as the image I vaguely describe above, but there is no sadness in remembering that 'first 'puppy' love'. I don't think, 'what if?' or 'what might have been?', I just remember the innocence of a stolen kiss, the holding of hands and of loving glances in moments of silence. They all helped to create perfect, unsullied and beautiful memories. Wherever you are Sam...Thank you!

Paris 1978

In the autumn of 1978, my mother took me to Paris for a long weekend. This is significant on two levels: Firstly, it was one of the few times I remember spending quality time with my mother and secondly, the sightseeing in Paris is a rare treat, parts of which are breathtaking. As a fifteen-year-old, it was also something I could appreciate and the memories of that trip to Paris still remain...and it was the first time I had flown!

I was entering the unknown as the plane taxied towards the runway and there were numerous thoughts and scenarios running through my head – "What if the plane doesn't take off...?", "Wow! That stewardess is pretty...", "I hope the Captain knows what he's doing...!" Is there food on this plane...I'm starving?" We paused momentarily at the top of the runway, ready for take-off...this is it! We started to move off...slowly at first, then the thrusters were hit and we hurtled down the runway at speeds I'd never imagined were possible. My knuckles were white as I gripped the armrests, I closed my eyes and all I could think was, "shit...shit...shit...shit...shit...shit...please take off...please take off...yes...yes...yes...we are in the air, thank God for that!". I opened my eyes as relief swept over me and looked at

40

my mother. Judging by the look on her face, she had just experienced the same doubt and emotions that I had just lived through…we were on the way to Paris!

Just over an hour later we were descending (a little bit too quickly for my liking) into Charles de Gaulle airport. As we hit the runway, I was thinking to myself; "Brakes…BRAKES…Oh my God…**BRAKES**!", thankfully, the landing was fairly smooth and after taxiing to our allocated gate and finally stopping, we were able to leave the plane. It was a welcome relief to be on the ground again and soon we had passed through immigration and were now in the terminal itself, on an escalator passing over other escalators with other escalators passing over us, all coming from different directions in a large circular space – wow! I had not seen anything like that before (or since in fact) and compared to Cardiff Airport it was huge with a much larger volume of passengers! We soon left the airport and it wasn't long before we were on a coach heading out of Charles de Gaulle Airport and racing towards Paris.

About an hour later we were sitting in the foyer of a quaint hotel in the Montmartre area of northern Paris, not much to look at from the outside, but inside it was chic and extremely clean. The décor was stylish and the paintings that adorned the corridors and rooms were suitable reminders that we were in Montmartre, a bohemian and arguably inspirational area that, over the years, had been home to many famous artists, such as; Vincent Van Gogh, Henri Matisse, Henri de Toulouse-Lautrec, to name but a few! My Mother suggested that we take our luggage to our rooms and then venture out into the Parisian streets and find somewhere to have some lunch – good plan I thought and nodded in agreement. Twenty to thirty minutes later, my Mother and I were sat in a typical French Café, both eating a simplistic meal of sausage (similar to a frankfurter) and French fries. The Café faced the two sets of stone steps that led to Sacre Coeur, a Cathedral that is located at the top Montmartre Hill, and our destination once we had finished our meal.

We eventually arrived at the terrace in front of the entrance to Sacre Coeur with aching legs (and lungs), after combating the steps that led from the Parisian streets below. The view of

Paris was breathtaking and other famous landmarks could be seen in the distance, such as; Notre Dame, L'arc de Triomphe, Eiffel Tower and The Louvre. Sacre Coeur itself is an impressive building that towers above the Paris skyline due to its dominating position in Montmartre. It is made from Chateau-Landon Stone that bleaches with age, giving it its unique white appearance making it a spectacular image, exemplified by the large central dome and identical smaller domes on each corner. The bell tower to the left of the main building completes the impressive external images of this Parisian landmark. The interior was as equally breathtaking, as you stepped inside and embraced the beauty of the murals painted on the ceilings, the stained-glass windows and a multitude of pillars that provided a comparable impression of Roman grandeur. It was a suitable place to have begun our sightseeing in Paris.

Before we returned to the hotel my Mother wanted to show me something! We left Sacre Coeur and made the short walk to Place du Tertre, and my Mother looked at me and excitedly said, "I think you'll like this Huw!" I mumbled something along the lines of "y-y-yes Mum!", as I was still blown away by the whole Sacre Coeur experience. As we entered Place Du Tertre, I was astounded at the number of artists there were in the centre of this beautiful small square, dotted with the occasional tree and lined on all sides by a mix of cafes and shops, all beautifully painted in bright colours of red, greens and blues. The cafes all offered the typical array of exterior seating, and the small tables were littered with couples of various ages, all enjoying the contradiction of the hustle bustle and tranquility on offer in the Place du Tertre. It really was a wonderful experience wandering amongst the various artists and becoming lost in their paintings, along with so many other visitors. A truly magical place where we could have spent hours just walking around observing the artists at work, but my Mother, who suffered with rheumatoid arthritis, was becoming tired so we headed back to the hotel.

The following morning, after a continental breakfast of croissants and coffee and a short walk to the metro at Abbesses, we were soon heading towards central Paris on a packed underground train. It was difficult to contain my excitement at the prospect of visiting the iconic Eiffel tower,

L'arc du triomphe and Notre Dame, famous landmarks I had only seen in photographs, on television or from a distance the previous day. After changing at Concorde, we soon arrived at Ecole Militaire metro and attempted to make our way through the ever changing crowds, associated with underground systems the world over and back up into the autumn sunshine. Finally, outside and after walking no more than 150m we turned to the right onto Champ de Mars and there it was...the Eiffel Tower! Nothing could have prepared me for that first sighting, I had no idea it was so...huge! The Eiffel Tower is located at the far end of Champ de Mars, a green area with an array of paths and fountains and beautifully kept gardens and lawns, complete with a backdrop of the River Seine. As we got closer, the size and feat of engineering was overwhelming as we became dwarfed by this iconic and magnificent landmark. The obligatory tourist photos were taken before I left my Mother in the café at the tower's base, and started the climb up the stairway that, after a couple of stops to catch my breath, took me up to the second level. I took a few moments on each of the four sides to appreciate the amazing views over Paris, but chose not to take the elevator to the top of the tower - time was ticking by and there were other places we wanted to see. Understandably, the descent was much quicker and it wasn't long before I was sat in front of my Mother patiently waiting for her to finish her coffee! I was eager to move on to our next destination...Notre Dame!

The short journey to Notre Dame was a contradiction, in respect of time, as we had to change twice on the metro at La Motte Piquet-Grenelle and Odeon stations, to the final destination of Cite. It was still only mid-morning when we left Cite metro for another short walk to the square that faced Notre Dame...and another jaw dropping moment! A beautiful and stunning gothic structure that has stood proudly and defiantly, for centuries, on the Ile de la Cite. As you looked up at the two dominant square towers and allowed your imagination the freedom to explore, the Hunchback of Notre Dame came to life, and could be seen momentarily staring down at the expectant crowd below, before disappearing into the morning haze. When you entered the famous old cathedral, you were immediately drawn to the astonishing beauty of the altar, arguably simplistic compared to altars in other Cathedrals – it was the surroundings that made it special! The area immediately behind the altar was semi-circular in shape and adorned with three tiers of stained glass windows. These and the stained glass windows on either side, bathed the altar and its statues with natural light giving it a heavenly, serene feel, which could be considered unique! A truly beautiful cathedral, and the oldest in Paris.

Leaving Notre Dame behind us, we walked back to the metro, at Cite, for our next short trip of two stops (with one change – we were getting very proficient on the metro) to Louvre-Rivoli to visit the Louvre. On arriving at the Louvre, it was quickly evident that the crowds were significantly higher than we expected and my mother glanced at her watch and suggested we find something to eat. Hunger was 'kicking in', after our busy morning, and I eagerly smiled in agreement. We decided to take the metro (again) from Louvre-Rivoli to George V station. Emerging from the depths, we were now stood on, probably, the most famous street in Paris – the Champs Elysees. This wide and emaculate, tree-lined avenue led straight up to the imposing monumental arch of L'arc de Triomphe, another of the symbolic and well-known architectural features of Paris. The Champs Elysees housed many designer shops, restaurants, cafes and cinemas and we quickly found a typical French café to have lunch. Snails...no! Frogs legs...no! French food was a strange concept to two people from Bridgend, so it was sausage and chips again for us! I noticed that the cinema, next to the café, was showing *Grease* - a musical set in 1950s America, and catchy songs from the film had been flooding the charts all over the world! I excitedly tugged at my Mother's sleeve, "look Mum" and pointed at the cinema, "Grease...can we go and see it". It was then I realised that my Mother had given me money a few weeks earlier to watch *Grease* when it came to the Embassy Cinema in Bridgend. However, the money wasn't for the cinema...I had gone into Bridgend with friends from the school football team drinking in the pubs. Damn! I thought, as my Mother looked at me in puzzlement and said, "I thought you'd already seen it Huw!". I had to think quick...and lie! "Yeah Mum, it was brilliant, but you'd love it...the music...the clothes...the dancing...it's your era Mum. Come on, let's watch it...I don't mind seeing it again!". Thankfully, she said yes, and twenty minutes later we were in the cinema waiting for the film to start. It was a brilliant film, but it was surreal watching it for the first time (sorry Mum!), with French subtitles, in a cinema on the Champs- Elysees, in Paris...very surreal! It was early evening when we stepped back onto the street and the light was fading on that beautiful autumn day. We walked towards the L'arc de Triomphe, now beautifully illuminated, as darkness descended on another Parisian evening, and it wasn't long before we were back on the metro heading for Blanche and our next destination...the Moulin Rouge!

We could see the Moulin Rouge when we emerged from the metro at Blanche...it was lit up like a fairground...the most prominent features being the illuminated windmill and the large, red neon lighting advertising the seedy venue...M-O-U-L-I-N R-O-U-G-E! We walked over to the billboards to look at photos of the show and to find out the cost of the tickets. As we looked at the various photos of the shows there were a few that caught the attention of both of us...but for different reasons! My Mother, composed herself, cleared her throat and declared "We'll have to leave it Huw...I can't justify paying those prices for a cabaret show!".
I sighed and dejectedly said, "But...Mum...!".
"No, come on...we'll find somewhere to eat and have an early night...it's been a long day and I'm pretty tired!"
I took one last glance at the photographs of the beautiful dancers and then ran to rejoin my Mother. We never spoke about the Moulin Rouge again or the real reason for not buying tickets! No words were necessary! We both knew that the real reason we left so abruptly was because of the photographs of topless dancers in all their finery. I guess my Mother would have been too embarrassed to watch that sort of cabaret show with her fifteen year old son, who, surprise, surprise, was really quite keen on viewing the multitude of scantily clad, topless (with the exception of perhaps glitter), feathered, sultry female dancers of the Moulin Rouge...oo, la la!

The following morning at breakfast my Mother told me that we would be unable to go to the Palace of Versailles as it was too far outside of Paris, but she had a surprise in mind that she believed I would like! This was our last morning in Paris, and after packing our cases, we left for our old friend...the metro! I was filled with a mixture of disappointment that we couldn't go to the Palace of Versailles, and intrigue as to where we were going, but any questions I fired at my Mother were all dismissed with a wave of her hand, a smile and a "wait and see!" We changed at Saint Lazerre, and as we pulled out of Invalides, a couple of stops later, my Mother announced, "Our stop next!" I looked at the map on the opposite side of the carriage and could see that Varenne was the next stop, but that gave me no clues as to where we were going! As we left the metro, to our right, I could see a large domed, churchlike building called Les Invalides or Dome de Invalides, an apparently well-known monument on the Parisian landscape. We entered the pristine grounds in front of the building and I soon realised its importance when I saw a sign! The sign identified that this impressive building housed the tomb of the famous and enigmatic Napoleon Bonaparte, a scourge to Britain and many other parts of Europe, until his defeat at Waterloo in 1815.

The interior of Les Invalides was another breathtaking experience due to the extensive use of marble. The terracotta coloured tomb was located in a circular sunken area (formerly the crypt) with a beautifully patterned floor and surrounded by reliefs depicting different parts of Napoleon's reign. The openings (in the form of windows) in between the reliefs offered an ideal viewing point, from the outer walkway, where visitors could pay their respects to this former hero of France. Directly above the tomb is the dome of the former church, beautifully painted and well lit from the surrounding windows. The ground floor area offered another excellent viewing point of the tomb from above and this symbolic area is completed with a large crucifix and ornate decor of astounding beauty. A truly beautiful resting place befitting the role Napoleon Bonaparte played in French history and a fitting place to finish our weekend in Paris.

Later, as we travelled back to Charles de Gaulles Airport, I took a final look at the iconic landmarks of Paris we had visited, and reflected on the topless dancers of the Moulin Rouge...that I had nearly seen...sacre bleu and damn!

A couple of hours later we were sat on the plane, seatbelts on, waiting for the take-off and imminent return to Cardiff. We taxied to the end of the runway, stopped momentarily, and then set off down the runway, picking up speed rapidly…! It was at this point I shut my eyes, started silently praying to a God I hope existed, followed by silently mouthing, shit…shit…shit…!

Bryntirion Comprehensive School

My childhood memories wouldn't be complete if I didn't mention the school where I spent my final five years in Bridgend. Nothing of any real note happened to me during my time there…I didn't become a shining light in the academic world, my rugby career here was very unremarkable, I wasn't particularly popular with the girls and I didn't act, play a musical instrument or stand-out as a singer. It was just a period where I drifted from year to year until it became time to leave at sixteen. The only plus side was that I enjoyed friendships with many people across the various ranges of different characters found in any school. However, despite the fact I left school with literally no qualifications (unless you can count a handful of failed O Levels and a CSE Grade 4 in French…which there is a perfectly valid reason…I knew I was joining the army and had known I was joining the army since I was fifteen and a half, back in November 1978), my time at Bryntirion is a relatively happy one. Yes, it was the Seventies and teachers were far stricter, but I was never a troublemaker…I never had the cane and I can only remember one occasion when I had detention. It was, and as far as I am aware, still is a good school and my experience of my time there is a positive one. I was never bullied or mistreated by any teachers and my academic failings were not down to any dark reason, but down to my choices and immaturity and I have always spoke highly of the school (apart from the heating system) and the majority of its teachers. The reflections of my time at Bryntirion is the last entry that has made it into this book and that is due to a recent group started on facebook called 'Bryntirion Comp Catch Up.' There have been many threads over the past few weeks that have sparked the memory and made me decide to add this last short story into this book, as I reflect on some of those memories I have of a great school…

I swear I can hear my grandmother's voice, a distant "Huw, Huw…" that seemed to get louder as I clung to the comfort of my pillow, "HUW, HUW...GET UP...it's your first day at Bryntirion and you don't want to be late". "OK Nan", I said stretching, yawning and sitting up all at the same time. Finally, I was up on my feet and heading to the bathroom, I locked the door behind me and looked in the mirror at my unruly hair and groaned...every morning was a bad hair day with the styles (I use the term loosely) of the Seventies. Twenty minutes later I was sat in the living room eating my breakfast...mmm trifle (my gran let me eat what I wanted so don't judge me). My gran asked me how I was feeling and whether I was nervous...I grumbled under my breath "no, I'm fine Nan", but I wasn't, I was shitting myself. It was soon time to go and my gran wished me luck and waved me off and I was soon trudging up Longfellow Drive in my new shoes (which were killing me), my uniform which included flared trousers, white shirt, school tie, grey jumper (knitted by my nan and itchy as hell), blazer with school badge (made to measure from a gentleman's outfitters in Bridgend town centre...and I only ever wore it on that first day) and a new leather satchel. I was aware of older children looking at me, staring at the new kid with his new clothes, heading to the BIG school...I was scared as fuck! It wasn't helped by the rumours we'd heard that first formers were dragged into the toilets and had their heads flushed in the toilet bowls.

I don't remember much about the first day, but I can confirm that it was fairly uneventful and I don't know of anyone who had the their heads flushed in the toilets...it was just a day of familiarizing ourselves with our new surroundings and starting to forge new friendships and to intertwine those friendships with ones we already made from our time in Trelales. I cannot remember all of the teachers from my time at Bryntirion, but during the remaining months of 1974, Mr Owen (Maths), Mr Phillips (History), Miss Thomas (English) and Mr Hodgeson (PE) were already making an impression, the latter with his undying passion for rugby and dismissive attitude to those who didn't share that passion. They were all very different characters, but they would all leave their mark, and with the luxury of hindsight, and the fact I mention them here reveals the level of respect I had for each one of them...and fear, in respect of Mr Hodgeson.

In my first year I was introduced to a new sport...cross country running, as it turned out, it appeared I was pretty good at it. Mr Craig, one of the PE teachers, was looking for people to run in a cross country race against Ynasawdre Comprehensive, a no-nonsense comprehensive with a bad reputation, located a few miles north of Bridgend between Sarn and Brynmenyn that served the surrounding area of Aberkenfig, Tondu, Bettws (a notorious area, high on a hill overlooking Brynmenyn and Coytrahen), Sarn, Pen-y-Fai and Brynmenyn. There were about thirty participants that were eagerly waiting to start the race on the playing fields at Ynasawdre. Once we had been shown the route and told there would be marshalls located at various points to direct us around the course, we were itching to get started and we were soon on our way, following a sharp blast of a whistle by an Ynasawdre teacher. I quickly made my way to the front and was soon on my own running through a trail of thick mud of a path that traversed its way through the bracken and gorse and through streams on the common ground adjacent to the playing fields at Ynasawdre. After around twenty minutes I was back on the road and heading back towards the school, a quick glance behind me revealed that I was on my own and that no-one was near me. I had enjoyed myself running through the mud and water and had forgotten it was a race, but as I turned into the school grounds and onto one of the rugby pitches, I began to see other runners now running on the pavement on the other side of the fence. As I approached the finish line (underneath the rugby posts), I could hear Mr Craig, shouting "GO ON HUW...YOU'VE EASILY GOT THIS...ANOTHER 25 YARDS...WELL DONE". I crossed the finish line and looked behind my and the person in second was only just approaching the bottom end of the rugby field...I had won by over 100m. I was so pleased, but not as excited as Mr Craig who was jumping up and down screaming "YES HUW, YES, YES, YES". He soon regained his composure, slapped me on the back and told me to encourage the others as they approached the finish line. A couple of weeks later, I was entered in the county trials which resulted in me being selected for Glamorgan...the highlight of my time at Bryntirion was around the corner as I represented Glamorgan U13s at the Welsh Cross Country Championships at Newtown. I didn't win or even finish in the top ten, but it was definitely the highlight of my success at Bryntirion...at twelve

I had peaked too early, I didn't know it at the time, but it was a downward incline as I spent the rest of my time at Bryntirion wallowing in mediocrity.

Form 1 came and went, as did Form 2…my exam results were ok, with exception of the sciences…they were absolute pants and by the age of thirteen it was plainly obvious that the small lad from Longfellow Drive was not going to be a scientist or a doctor. Another downside was that I had only had one girlfriend in two years, and even that was only one date at the cinema (what went wrong Jayne?), no Valentine's cards and no slow dances at the Christmas disco. I did try to learn a musical instrument (only because I fancied Helen Davies from the year below) and that didn't pan out too well…my dog chewed the mouthpiece, destroying it completely, so I snuck it back in to the music room and have never touched a musical instrument since. As I headed into Form 3, this was a critical year, as our exam performances would determine whether we would be in 'o' level or CSE classes in Forms 4 and 5. There was another challenge in front of me in Form 3, I didn't want to play rugby anymore, I wanted to concentrate on football and I didn't think I'd be missed as I was only a bit part player in the second team, which meant I and other second team members were largely ignored by Mr Hodgeson…or so we thought. To give up rugby in school meant I had to have a letter off my mother detailing that she didn't want me to play rugby again…there was only one problem with this, I had to hand the letter to Mr Hodgeson or 'Clodge' as he was affectionately known. The first part was easy, I asked my mother and she only asked why I wanted to give up rugby and when I told her it was so I could concentrate on football she wrote the letter then and there…I found an envelope, put the letter inside and put it in to my school bag. The following day at the beginning of first break I made my way to Mr Hodgeson's office…I stood outside and tried to compose myself before plucking up the courage to knock. I eventually knocked and a booming "YES, WHO IS IT?..." greeted me like a punch in the stomach, I swallowed hard and shouted back "HUW THOMAS SIR, FORM 3R". Almost immediately, Mr Hodgeson was stood in the doorway "what can I do for you Huw?" I swallowed hard again and pulled the envelope out of my pocket and said "I…I…I've got a l…l…letter off my mother for you". He looked at me and held his hand out...I passed him the letter and waited as he first looked at me and opened the letter, removed my mother's letter, unfolded it and started to read it...a few seconds later, he looked up and his expression had changed. He looked angry, really angry and started to read the letter out loud, slowly and emphasizing certain words, when he had finished he leant in to me, screwing the letter up at the same time, and when his face was no more than a few inches from mine he whispered "I hope you never touch another rugby ball in your life...NOW GET OUT OF MY SIGHT". I didn't need a second invitation, I turned, ran back up the corridor, headed out of the reception area and ran out outside. When I got to the back of the toilet building I leant against the wall and let out a huge sigh of relief...I was still alive, Mr Hodgeson had read the letter off my mum and I was still alive. The rest of Form 3 passed uneventfully and my choices for Forms 4 and 5 had been made...I can't remember if we knew at the end of Form 3 which classes we would be in the following year or whether we had to wait until the start of Form 4.

Form 4 started full of promise, I was in seven 'o' level classes (maths, English language, English Literature, History, French, Art and Technical Drawing) and one CSE class (general science...no surprise there). It was a pretty uneventful school year, academically I was doing ok, but still couldn't sing, play a musical instrument or act. The only event of any real note happened outside of school when a couple of third formers mitching off school found a dead body...it was big news at the time in Bridgend, but even bigger news in Bryntirion Comprehensive as those that found the body needed counselling and the man arrested for the murder was the father of a boy in my year, Ron Chapman. Form 4 ended and after a summer of camping, bike rides and lazy days at Ogmore-by-Sea and Southerndown it was back to school for the final year.

By the time form 5 started I had already made up my mind that I wanted to join the army, despite the term starting well, by the time half-term began it looked increasingly likely that I would be leaving Bridgend in the summer of 1979 to join the army...I had passed tests and medicals at the army careers office in Cardiff and had been given a date when I would travel to the selection office at Blackdown Barracks for final tests and hopefully selection. In early November 1978, I returned from Blackdown Barracks having been accepted into the Royal Engineers and would be heading off to the Junior Leaders Regiment Royal Engineers based at Old Park Barracks in Dover...this was when my school work began to suffer. I naively believed that school was now unimportant and that I didn't need qualifications...I had a job to go to, such was my immaturity at the time. Within weeks I had dropped out of technical drawing and moved from 'o' level French to CSE and became disinterested in the other subjects. Whilst I completed homework and continued to attend school, I only done enough in lessons to keep me out of trouble with the teachers. I attended youth club most nights and when I sat my exams I didn't revise. I simply stuttered through those last weeks of school and it was with a sense of relief that I finally left school when my final exam finished. I went back to collect my results which turned out to be a total waste of time...but I can still see the disappointment in Mr John Owen's face when he told me I had failed my maths 'o' level exam by 4 marks, just 4 marks. It didn't bother me at the time, I went home and gathered all my school books together and my school tie and burnt everything in the back garden. There was no going back to sixth form, where most of my friends would be going. A month after they returned to school to start sixth form, I left Bridgend to travel to Dover and to start my army career. As I stepped onto that train at Bridgend railway station on 18th October 1979, I didn't realise at the time, but I would never live in Bridgend again...it was the end of a great life growing up in this wonderful old market town and the start of the next exciting chapter in my life.

Bryntirion Pupils I remember from those halcyon days in the Seventies are listed below, in no particular order:

Tim Harries	David Lewis	Julian Jones
Paul Evans	Alan Evans	Paul Troakes
Denise Salway	Andrea Parry	Karen Hubber
Gareth Lewis	Fiona McAllister	Susan Poole
John Williams	Lloyd Williams	Paul Jenkins
Michael Phillips	Helen Davies	Caroline Williams
Tim Rees	Susan Jones	Della Howells
Helen Fitzgerald	Miranda Morton	David Hayman
Paul Goodman	Robert Groome	Nigel Evans
Monica Long	David Burroughs	Katheyn Biddle

Claire Williams	Mike Hopkins	Peter Thomas
Brian Thomas	David De Ivy	Chris Lewis
Alison Copus	Jackie Oliver	Ben Thomas
Richard Lock	Alison Rule	Miranda Morton
Anne Thomas	Gillian Dory	Diane Campbell
Jayne Pascoe	Elaine Williams	John Morris
Mario Burke	Michael Vosper	Nicola Hold
Kevin Freeland	Suzanne Heathcote	

And many, many more who's names and faces have sadly faded from my memory.

Chapter 2 – The Army (Part 1 - Training)

I cannot tell you how old I was when I first decided that I wanted to be soldier, but what I do know is that I cannot remember a time when I didn't want to be a soldier. A childhood spent watching all the great war movies from the 1950s provided me with that yearning of wanting to be a hero, an Audie Murphy or John Wayne type of character who 'saves the day'! Looking back, those films certainly glorified war, as the atrocities and horrors of actual war were never shown, and many lads like me would come to realise that what you saw on a film was nothing compared to the real thing! However, following a series of visits to the Army Careers Office in Cardiff, and a day at the Selection Centre at Blackdown Barracks near Camberley in November 1978...I was fifteen years old and my dream of becoming a soldier would soon be a reality. Did I know what I was doing? No... absolutely not. I had no fucking idea, not a clue! Those 1950s Hollywood films were my research and had falsely filled me with romantic notions about life in the army. That November day in 1978 is still etched in my memory...a series of tests, films of various Corps (i.e. Infantry, Guards, Royal Artillery, Royal Engineers etc), trades (i.e. Bricklayers, chefs, vehicle mechanics, combat engineers, drivers, storemen etc), the sport and the social life, followed by interviews with a Selection Officer. If my memory serves me correctly, we were allowed six choices and I can still remember my first three choices (I have no idea what the other three were!). My first choice was the Parachute Regiment (no surprise there given the films I'd been watching!), but the Selection Officer looked at me (I was probably about 5' 6" and about nine stone, and hardly Para material) and immediately said, "No, that's not for you, you are not well built enough". My second choice faired no better..."Royal Armoured Corps...hmm...no, no, no, absolute waste of your intelligence". I was beginning to think my dream was slipping away as this well-spoken officer seemed to be ridiculing my choices! "Now then...Royal Engineers...hmm...! The pause seemed endless, and he leant back in his chair, looked up at the ceiling as he gently tapped his pencil on the edge of the desk in front of him. I was waiting for the inevitable excuse as to why this was also a bad choice when he leant forward, looked me in the eye and said, "Perfect...this is the Corps for you...the Royal

Engineers...absolutely" He stamped the document signifying his seal of approval, checked another document before finally filling out a form. Within minutes he handed me a slip of paper that told me I would be joining the Junior Leaders Regiment Royal Engineers at Old Park Barracks in Dover and the enlistment date was 18 October 1979...only 11 months away! The selection process was complete and I left the camp on a military bus to Farnborough North train station.

After a short train journey I was at Reading station and had a few minutes to spare before the train back to Bridgend arrived. I used the opportunity to ring my Nan Henson to tell her the good news that I would be joining the Royal Engineers. She was so pleased for me, but told me that she had something to tell me but it could wait until I got home...the pips went and she was gone. I was intrigued, what did she want to tell me! The train had now arrived at Reading, and I jumped on and headed back to South Wales...I was still wondering what my Nan wanted to tell me when I jumped off the train at Bridgend and headed home.

Later that day, when I arrived home, Nan Henson told me about my Great Grandfather Leyshon, who had been a Sapper (blacksmith) in World War 1, and who thankfully survived. She also told me about my Grampa Henson, who I knew had served in the RAF during World War II, but had apparently been transferred into the Royal Engineers sometime after D-Day (when the allies had gained air supremacy over the Germans many of the RAF ground crew were transferred into the army). I was extremely proud that I may be, unwittingly, carrying on an unplanned family tradition.

The next eleven months went by so quickly and after I had taken my Oath of Allegiance in Cardiff, I was soon waving farewell to my mother at Bridgend railway station and travelling to Dover to begin the next chapter of my life. I met other lads on the train that were also heading to Dover, lads such as; Taff Evans (never did know his Christian name), Ian (Taff) Pritchard and a, once met never forgotten, Lyndon (Taff) Davies from Merthyr Tydfil who, I swear, never stopped talking from Cardiff to London Paddington, through the underground and all the way to Dover. He told us he was going to be in the Regimental teams for every sport created by man (I remember he was a good boxer, but he did meet his match in a boxing competition against the Junior Guards Depot when he had a nose hemorrhage...I have never seen so much blood before or since!). To this day I have never met someone with so much self-confidence – by all accounts, he still hasn't stopped talking today – legend! There'll be more of Ian (Taff) Pritchard later...much more! This was it, all my dreams of being a soldier were about to be fulfilled and I was about to meet other lads from all over Britain, as I embarked on this new adventure. I was nervous, but excited at the same time, but God, was I in for a shock!! Nothing could have prepared me for what I was about to face and experience...nothing!!! However, this part of my life provided me with great memories of spending time with people that became lifelong friends. They are happy memories that often make me smile and even laugh out loud on occasions, but those episodes that make me laugh seemed like hell at the time.

Looking back, I can see that in the beginning we were a group of strangers that would have only considered self-preservation as an option during those first days and weeks at Dover. But, after the highs and lows of spending twelve months together where we were broken down and then re-built as a troop of men who would individually sacrifice their own lives to protect a fellow troop member – an amazing and unique transformation that you don't get in any other walk of life. It can't be denied that the methods the instructors used in that process were barbaric and often sadistic, but we soon learnt the meaning of teamwork and came to live by the phrase, 'a team is only as strong as its weakest member'. Therefore, we worked together helping each other through our own weaknesses to ensure no-one was left to struggle – we faced each triumph and each failure as a team! However, it wasn't that simple as we found with two members of the troop (I'll refer to as Spr 'C' and Spr Jock 'P') who couldn't fit-in, but for different reasons and they decided to leave the army and return to their families and civilian life, as did a few others. Those of us that remained experienced a multitude of emotions, but ultimately, we made it to our Passing-Out Parade at the end of the twelve months. We left behind the hours of endless cleaning, bullshit, marching (everywhere), discipline, education, physical training, abuse (mental and physical), fieldcraft training, basic combat engineer training (bridging and watermanship at Weymouth and building an assault course in Ramsgate), sport and not forgetting Fanny Morgan (the WRVS (Womens Royal Voluntary Service) representative at Old Park Barracks who had been helping Junior Leaders for many years) and much more. It may not sound like much fun, but looking back over the mists of time they were fantastic times and if I could be sixteen years old once more...I would do it all again. Thank you J.L.R.R.E. and thank you Dover (and Farnborough). Here are some of the stories from those early days in the army.

■ ■

First Impressions

The Junior Leaders Regiment Royal Engineers was based at Old Park Barracks in Dover. The camp was situated on a hill at the back of the town, and from its elevated position you could look down over Dover to the port and into the English Channel beyond. The town is described as the gateway into the garden of England. This historic place, with its prominent Norman castle c/w underground bunkers cut into the chalky ground beneath the castle that were used during World War II and the Cold War, famous white cliffs (made by famous by Vera Lynn in her wartime song) was to be my home for the next eighteen months (should have been twelve months but more of that later!).

We stepped off the train and onto the platform at Dover Priory...we had arrived in the town that would be our home for the next twelve months. A little disorientated, we joined others that were making their way towards the 'way out' sign, it seemed like the most sensible option! However, we heard much later that one lad decided, right there on the platform, the army wasn't for him and ran back over the foot bridge to catch the train back to London and to his home town! It must have been what he saw in the foyer that made him make that snap decision...! To greet us in the foyer of the station was a fierce looking character of medium build, smartly dressed in, what I now know as, No2 dress uniform c/w boots with an insane shine, that you could have used as mirrors, and a patent black peaked and navy blue hat with red piping, Royal Engineers cap badge and a slashed peak (the normal peak is

57

cut and the majority of it is then pushed up into the cap, leaving a smaller more vertical peak, that forces the wearer to push their head back in a menacing manner). As we soon discovered, to complete this intimidating vision was a strong Scottish accent (ideal for shouting at recruits as we found out later) as he said;

"Good afternoon gentlemen...please step outside where you will find a bus waiting to take you to Old Park Barracks and your new home for the next year".

Sure enough, as we stepped outside we could see a white army bus in the top right hand side of the car park. As we walked towards the bus the main topic of conversation was everyone (including me) hoping that the 'Jock Sergeant' we had just met, wouldn't be their instructor when we arrived at Old Park Barracks. We boarded the bus and waited whilst our new Jock 'friend' rounded up the stragglers! Within a few minutes, and with everyone on board, we were on our way, and a nervous hush enveloped the bus, well I say a hush, there was ONE voice that could still be heard... the Merthyr lilt of Lyndon Davies...where did he get his verbal stamina? As the bus trundled through Dover, we all gazed out of the windows, taking in our new surroundings, possibly contemplating our decisions on joining the army and thinking of our family, friends and home towns...all of which now seemed so far away! My initial thoughts about Dover were in no way positive as we passed boarded-up shops, unkempt streets of narrow terraced houses that created a general feeling of a town that was suffering from a small degree of neglect – We didn't realise at the time, but it would be two months before we would see the centre of Dover again! As a result, my initial feelings about Dover soon faded, and it was a welcome sight when I saw it again in late December!

Within about fifteen minutes we were driven through the main gates of Old Park Barracks and what struck me first was the sheer size of the camp and some of its buildings. I thought...this is it! A mixed feeling of nervous excitement and trepidation swept over me as I realised that I was now stepping into the unknown...the bungalow in Bridgend, where I had lived with Nan and Grampa Henson, now seemed like a distant memory! I can't remember much about the first day at Old Park Barracks as the mists of time have clouded the details. I can only presume that we were sent to the squadrons and troops we had been assigned to and settled into our new surroundings. One thing we found out soon after we arrived was which squadron and troop we were being sent to and who would be our instructors (in most case the instructors or permanent staff were normally sergeants). Our instructors were Sgt Kerr, Sgt Osbourne and Sgt Scholey. This was not an ideal start, as Sgt Scholey just happened to be the ferocious looking character that had greeted everyone at the station…just my luck to be landed with the Sergeant that everyone was hoping wouldn't be their sergeant…oh bugger! That first night was spent getting to know the lads that were in your troop and in particular the ones with whom you shared a room; the lads in my room were; Wils (Marc Wilson) a mixed race lad from Cockermouth in Cumbria, Rocker (Tim Smith) from Cleethorpes, Tiny Strachan (Tiny was 6ft 8 in tall, hence the ironic name of 'Tiny') from Weymouth, Turner from Blackpool and lastly, Simmons. Unfortunately, Turner and Simmons didn't last long and they were back home with their families within a few weeks. It was certainly disconcerting listening to the big lad Simmons crying himself to sleep and shouting for his mother every night…I guess you have to remember we were only sixteen years old and for some it must have been emotionally overwhelming!!

Despite marching to the block where 54 and 82 Squadrons and the junior ranks mess (canteen) were housed, none of us were aware of the significance of the many other buildings in the camp. However, this was soon rectified the following day when, as a troop, we were introduced to our troop commander, Lt Gilmour. We paraded in three ranks in the quadrangle of our three-storey block which was a sort of 'C' shape, built-up on three sides with an open end on the fourth side. It was the first parade after lunch and therefore it must have been about 1.30pm, Lt Gilmour welcomed us to 66 Squadron and J.L.R.R.E. and briefly told us what the next 12 months would entail. When he had finished his briefing, he suggested that this would be a good time for us to be shown around the camp. He offered to take us around the camp and show as the relevant buildings and areas of interest that we would become familiar with in the weeks and months that followed. I can remember thinking at the time…'what a gentleman'. But, it wouldn't be long (about two minutes to be precise) before I began thinking…'What a twat!'

Lt Gilmour gave us the command to stand to attention…most of us didn't have a clue what we were doing and just followed the few that had obviously been army cadets, He then followed this up with;
"TURN TO THE LEFT…LEFT TURN"
We turned…not as one and not all in the same direction, but at different times and with a few managing to turn the wrong way…this inept display was greeted with a mumbled response from Sgt Scholey;
"What a usless fucking pile of shite" in his distinct Scottish drawl.
"BY THE FRONT…QUICK MARCH" shouted Lt Gilmour.
We marched (well ambled) out of the quadrangle, living up to the 'pile of shite' statement from Sgt Scholey, and round the side of the building onto a long, straight path that led to the rest of the camp…which we could see in the distance! It should be pointed out at this point that we had still not been issued with our army equipment and we were still dressed in an array of civilian clothes such as, flared jeans, platform shoes (well, it was still the 70s), Wrangler/Levi jackets etc, not suitable gear for what was about to happen!! It was then we heard Lt Gilmour's command;
"BREAK INTO DOUBLE TIME…DOUBLE TIME"
What is double time, I thought!
"START RUNNING GENTLEMEN"
This was, without question, the point that I knew that I was now in the army, as we started to run around the camp with Lt Gilmour's public school voice ringing in our ears…!
"THE BUILDING TO MY RIGHT IS THE NAAFI"
I thought to myself, 'what the hell is a NAAFI?'
"OVER THERE IS THE BARBER'S SHOP, NAAFI SHOP AND JUNIOR RANKS BAR"
There's that word again…NAAFI. What is it?
"THIS IS THE GYMNASIUM, SWIMMING POOL AND SQUASH COURTS, . AND THAT BUILDING OVER THERE IS THE RHQ…REGIMENTAL HEADQUARTERS"
'That looks like a church', I said to myself!
"THE REGIMENTAL CHURCH", confirmed Lt Gilmour.

'My God! Somebody has dropped out...we've only ran about 600m' (I found out later it was a lad called Jock 'P' – more of JP later!).

"WANKER...GET BACK TO THE QUANDRANGLE AND WAIT THERE...MOVE"

'Fucking hell' I thought, as we wheeled (turned) down a block very similar to 66 Squadron block.

"54 SQUADRON...JUNIOR RANKS MESS...82 SQUADRON...REGIMENTAL SPORTS FIELDS...ASSAULT COURSE, AND THE 30M FIRING RANGE"

On we ran, and some of the bigger lads were now red-faced and beginning to blow a bit!!

"CINEMA OVER THERE ON THE LEFT"

Cinema...they've got a cinema, didn't expect that!

"MAIN GATE UP AHEAD...YOU WON'T BE GOING THROUGH THAT FOR A WHILE GENTLEMEN"

Lt Gilmour laughed at his attempt at humour and then pointed to the building on the left;

"THAT'S THE MEDICAL CENTRE...AND THE BUILDING ON THE RIGHT HAND SIDE OF THE MAIN GATE IS THE SERGEANTS MESS"

In the distance I could see our block again, nearly there...wrong!!

"GUARDROOM" Lt Gilmour shouted, as we wheeled left and ran around behind it towards, what looked like a car park!

"STORES, AND THERE'S A SMALL REGIMENTAL BANK AT THE REAR OF THE BUILDING"

We approached the car park!

"THIS IS THE MAIN SQUARE, THE REGIMENTAL SERGEANT MAJOR'S SACRED GROUND" Lt Gilmour's head rolled back as he chuckled loudly.

"DON'T LET THE RSM CATCH YOU ON HERE...EVER!"

We ran round the edge of the square to the opposite corner.

"THAT'S THE REGIMENTAL ATHLETICS TRACK, AND THAT BUILDING IS MY HOME...THE OFFICERS MESS"

We turned and ran back in the direction of the guardroom, back to what I can now describe as the main road around Old Park Barracks!

"THAT BUILDING ON THE RIGHT (opposite the Guardroom) IS THE ARMOURY"

We ran past the NAAFI again...note to self. Find out what NAAFI means – it's bugging the shit out of me!!

"THIS PART OF 66 SQUADRON'S BLOCK IS THE EDUCATION WING"
Approximately five minutes later we were back in the quadrangle of 66 Squadron, stood at ease, all blowing hard and listening to Lt Gilmour.
"GENTLEMEN...I HOPE YOU ENJOYED YOUR TOUR OF OLD PARK BARRACKS. AS THE WEEKS AND MONTHS ROLL BY YOU WILL BECOME MORE FAMILIAR WITH WHAT YOU HAVE SEEN TODAY...ANY QUESTIONS...NO! OK. THE NEXT TIME WE MEET GENTLEMAN WILL BE MONDAY MORNING...ENJOY YOUR WEEKEND. SGT KERR...THEY ARE ALL YOURS!

That was how we first saw Old Park Barracks and despite the unusual manner in which we saw it, it was impressive – Beautifully laid out with neatly mown grassy areas, shrubs, trees and dotted around at various points military vehicles (one of which we would get to know quite well) from a bygone age sited on concrete platforms completed the visual appearance of the camp. The run around the camp was a taste of what lay ahead for us in the very near future...it was going to get worse...a great deal worse!!! But as enlightening as the 'tour' was I still hadn't found out what NAAFI meant!!

Bullshit!

For those of you who don't know, 'Bullshit' rules the British Army as we found out at Dover. The endless parades, room inspections, kit inspections, rules and regulations, marching, dress codes etc kept us all on the continual merry-go-round of 'Bullshit'. If ever you want a visual of army 'bullshit' search 'Bad Lads Army' on You Tube and sit back in shock, but I guarantee you'll be crying with laughter...provided you have a twisted sense of humour! I stayed on this endless ride for over ten years, but those early days at Dover were the most intense! We lived, breathed and ate 'bullshit', but the indomitable squaddie spirit and the twisted sense of humour I mention above normally saved the day, as we took it all in our stride (most of the time!) and always ended up laughing...eventually (sometimes years later)! I thought it would be fun to share some of this 'bullshit' we experienced with you all. Those of you who know...know!

Room   inspections…Cleaning…Kit
inspections…Parades…Cleaning…Ironing…More
cleaning…Washing/drying   clothes…Even   more
cleaning…Parade   for   breakfast…Guess   what!   More
cleaning…Parade   for   work…Bed   blocks…Parade   for
lunch…Not more cleaning!...Parade for afternoon works
detail…Kit   layouts…Shaving   (every   day)…Cleaning
(again!)…Haircuts…Bulling boots (excessive shine)…More
parades…Cleaning, cleaning and I've got an idea, let's clean
something else! Yes, 'Bullshit' at Dover was intense,
continuous and relentless. Years later, when I was serving
with 24 Field Squadron RE, I remember being on guard at one
of the transit camps on Salisbury Plain. In the guard box at the
main gate there were many notable examples of squaddie
humour in the form of graffiti. There was one that I still
remember to this day, it read;
'Join the British Army and see the world. Become a Sapper
and clean the bastard!'
Looking back on those days at Old Park Barracks that
seemingly meaningless statement is a fitting tribute to those
days at Old Park Barracks when 'bullshit' was all around us
on a daily basis!

For the first two months of our time at Dover we trained by
day and cleaned by night. I may be wrong, but I have a vague
memory that our civilian clothes were locked in our suitcases
and then they, in turn, were locked in a room so we couldn't
access them! As a result, every evening after our evening meal
we would change into our army issue PE kit (red v-necked t-
shirt, navy blue PE shorts, army socks and black plimsoles) for
a fun packed five to six hours of cleaning (anything and
everything). Everything in our troop lines (rooms, corridors,
ablutions, toilets and washing/drying rooms) were designed to
maximize the full meaning of 'bullshit' – wooden floors, light
fittings, shelves, windows, tiles, toilets, baths, showers, taps,
brass fittings, painted floors, lockers/top boxes, pipework. We
polished, mopped, brushed, scrubbed and dusted it all again,
again and again! Did we ever pass a room inspection in those
first two months? Probably not, if you thought they wouldn't
find something wrong, they moved the goalposts resulting in
us failing time and time again as we endured anything up to
three room inspections every night! These inspections could

be purely a room inspection or they could include a locker inspection or additionally, a locker inspection and a 'kit layout' inspection. A kit layout inspection was where certain parts of you kit (i.e. mess tins, knife fork and spoon, mug, webbing and tin hat etc) would have to be laid out on you bed in pre-designated layout. An integral part of these inspections would be the 'bed block' which consisted of four blankets, two sheets and two pillows (c/w pillow cases). As the name suggests, it is a 'block' that is made up as follows; blanket, sheet, blanket, sheet, blanket – all folded to approx. width of 30ins and built into the block in that order. The fourth blanket is then folded in such a way that it can be wrapped around the 'block' in a picture-frame style arrangement. The pillows are then placed on top (to the same width) to complete the required military style bed block. This is all then placed on top of the bedspread at the head of the bed. There must be no sag in the middle as everything must be perfectly horizontal…this is where the use of cardboard was imperative. The final piece in this majestic form of 'squaddie' art was the bedspread. This had to be as tight as a drum, so tight that a coin could be bounced on it! This meant lying under your bed and pulling the unseen waste of the bedspread as tight as you possibly could!

The room inspections were torturous affairs and never got any easier throughout our entire army careers, but at Dover they were considerably more brutal. Our room was always the last to be inspected, and we would stand nervously at ease by our beds listening to the abuse, sounds of the contents of lockers being emptied or kit layouts crashing to the floor as beds were upturned and the shouts of 'YES SERGEANT' or 'NO SERGEANT' coming from your mates down the corridor. Then it would be your turn!
"ROOM…ROOM TENSHUN"
The collective stamping of the right foot would echo around the room. Sgt Scholey, for example, would go from bed space to bed space inspecting everything meticulously. You would silently pray that he wouldn't stop and pick something up, as that would normally bring a torrent of abuse and destruction, such as;
"WHAT THE FUCK IS THIS? (picking up you the fork off your bed and thrusting it close to your eyes to show you a particle of food the size of a spider's testacle, and barely

visible to the naked eye)...ARE YOU HUNGRY?...WERE YOU SAVING THIS FOR LATER?...YOU DISGUSTING LITTLE RUNT...WHAT ARE YOU?"

"A DISGUSTING LITTLE RUNT SERGEANT"

"CLEANLINESS IS NEXT TO WHAT THOMAS?"

"GODLINESS SERGEANT"

Then the inevitable would happen...they would target the 'BED BLOCK', regardless of how good it was in appearance, even if it looked perfect...it was the stick used to beat us!!

"THIS IS A FUCKING DISGRACE...WERE YOU PISSED WHEN YOU MADE THIS?"

"NO SERGEANT"

"YOU MUST HAVE MADE IT IN YOUR SLEEP THEN!"

"NO SERGEANT"

"YOU ARE A FUCKING WANKER THOMAS, WHAT ARE YOU?"

"I'M A FUCKING WANKER SERGEANT"

"OPEN THE WINDOW"

You'd open the nearest window and stand to attention again as Sgt Scholey would pick up your 'bed block' and walk to the window...pause and look you straight in the eye, and in an exaggerated soft and caring voice would say;

"Say goodbye to your bed block Thomas...it's going away for a little while...blow it a little kiss (I blew my bed block a kiss) there's a good lad ...wave (I waved) aw, that's so sweet!"

Then 'WOOSH' your bed block would be thrown through the window and into the darkness to land on the inevitable wet grass below (well, it was winter time!). This meant that we would have to wash and dry the blankets, sheets and pillows ready for the next night. Oh, how we laughed...Not!!

Parades were another means of creating an atmosphere of fear and uncertainty in our day to day lives. There were parades for everything; Breakfast, works parade (a.m.), lunch, works parade (p.m.), dinner, church, sports & hobbies etc. The morning works parade was by far the worst, purely because it also doubled as a kit inspection – the chances of public humiliation during these inspections was extremely high! To avoid being ripped apart, the beret had to be 'fluff' free, face clean shaven, good military haircut (typically a short back and sides or a crew cut), clothes ironed to perfection (military perfection!) and boots highly polished – there was no room for error, it had to be perfect or you entered the gates of hell, where you would be raped verbally and left feeling embarrassed and humiliated. When it came to ironing, starch was our new best friend! But, when it came to ironing, the one pet hate that would drive the permanent staff into a frenzy was seeing a 'tram line' – they expected razor sharp creases in your trouser, shirts etc, not evidence of two creases where there should only be one. A typical reaction would have been;

"HOW MANY CREASES SHOULD I SEE THERE THOMAS" enquired Sgt Kerr whilst pointing at my right leg.

"ONE SERGEANT"

"WHY THEN CAN I SEE FUCKING TWO"

"I DON'T KNOW SERGEANT"

"I DON'T KNOW SERGEANT" Repeated Sgt Kerr mockingly!

"IS IT BECAUSE I'M A WANKER" I suggested

"YES THOMAS, YOU ARE A FIRST CLASS WANKER!"

"YES SERGEANT"

"YOUR TROUSERS LOOK LIKE CLAPHAM JUNCTION…GET DOWN AND GIVE ME TWENTY"

I immediately dropped to the floor and started my press-up punishment as Sgt Kerr moved onto the next potential victim.

"NOT ANOTHER ONE…FOR FUCK SAKE!"

We suffered during those first two months, but following our return from leave in January 1980 the intensity and the number of parades lessened slightly as our collective performance improved. This highlighted the fact that we were beginning to work together as a team (the army way), as we started to support each other through any difficulties – the process had begun!

There are two huge issues in the army that are a complete 'no, no'. Firstly, all soldiers have to maintain a high level of cleanliness…personal hygiene and keeping your equipment clean are very important, especially in the field (military operations). Secondly, you do not thieve off your mates. Unfortunately, we had one member of the troop that was a grot (affectionate name for someone with low hygiene standards) and a thief…for the purposes of this book, I have kept his surname from general readers, but those who were there at the time know full well who I am referring to…J/Spr 'C'. We already knew he was a minger or a grot, but there was a certain amount of tolerance from the lads in his room, provided his low standards didn't affect them or the rest of the troop. But when one of the lads, Taff Bromley, was bedded down (ill) and confined to the room, he asked J/Spr 'C' if he would go to the bank and cash a cheque for £5 (it was a lot of money in 1979). J/Spr 'C' happily said yes, went to the bank, cashed the cheque and gave the £5 to Taff Bromley. However, when Taff Bromley was checking his bank statement a couple of weeks later he found out that the same cheque he'd given J/Spr 'C' was showing up on his statement as a debit of £15. He challenged J/Spr who eventually admitted that he'd changed the cheque to £15, pocketed the tenner and gave the £5 to Taff Bromley thinking he's get away with it...this was the straw that broke the camel's back and not long after, the word was passed around the troop that J/Spr 'C' was going to get a 'Regimental Bath'...a punishment normally reserved for 'grots'. On the night in question, the plans were in place, the bath was two thirds filled with cold water, bleach and a few other unsavoury items (those that know...know). J/Spr 'C' was pounced upon, at the agreed time, and stripped down to his manky y-fronts and carried to the bathroom. He was roughly thrown into the prepared bath and people took it in turns to scrub him down with a bass broom. It was all over in a few minutes leaving J/Spr 'C' with no illusions that being a thief and a grot were unacceptable. If my memory serves me correct he spent time in 'nick' (one of the cell's in the guardroom) before being dishonourably discharged...the troop had lost its weakest member. Not one of us felt guilty about the 'Regimental Bath' given to J/Spr 'C', considering his deceit and theft, he was lucky he got off as lightly as he did...the troop and permanent staff were glad to see the back of him, he was no loss to 'The Corps'.

Marching/drill

If there is something that everyone knows it's that soldiers love marching! This might be a slight exaggeration and is not strictly accurate, 'love' and 'marching' and even 'like' and 'marching' shouldn't really be used with each other unless the word 'don't' is included. There was an inane amount of marching and drill which became more enjoyable (not!!) when SLRs (self-loading rifles) were brought into the equation. When you next witness soldiers marching in the street, remember...an incredible amount of training went into the polished performance you are watching. When marching and drill is of a high standard it is an amazing sight to behold. However, there is a great deal of shouting and pain involved before a proficient level is reached. I want to take you back to the beginning when 'incompetence' would have better described our efforts!!!

When I joined the army I had no idea how to march, and not a clue about the intricacies of the various drills required to reach an acceptable level of competency. However, I wasn't the only one, there were many others who were being introduced to drill/marching for the first time. Therefore, it was no surprise that during that first week we were continually referred to as 'a shower of shit' and other affectionate nicknames, but despite our initial ineptitude there was hope! Luckily for us and others that went before and those that followed, the army had broken the art of marching into movements/drills that could be easily learnt. This was achieved via the assistance of individual and collective shouting of; ONE – TWO – THREE – ONE, a cry that could be continually heard throughout the camp whenever a new intake started at Old Park Barracks! The first of these that were learnt were the static drills, such as; 'standing at ease', 'standing to attention', 'turning to the left', 'turning to the right' and 'about turn (turning to face the opposite direction)', followed by 'halting', 'marking time' (marching on the spot), 'saluting' and the now recognisable 'breaking into double time'. The marching element was slightly easier (keeping in step and ensuring our arms were swung shoulder high) and was mastered quickly, however, there were still continuous shouts of 'swing your arms shoulder high' from the permanent staff. Sgt Osbourne, for example, did take this a step further with his favourite saying of;
"SWING YOUR ARMS SHOULDER HIGH OR I'LL RIP THEM OFF AND SMASH YOU OVER THE HEAD WITH THE SOGGY ENDS…NOW SWING THEM ARMS".
If we were marching anywhere near the gymnasium, NAAFI and our squadron quadrangle and made a mistake or were generally slovenly, we would have to sprint around the 'duck' (the DUKW was an amphibious military vehicle used in World War II) which sat on a concrete plinth roughly halfway between RHQ and 66 squadron block. Needless to say, we ran round the 'duck' many times!!

As mentioned above we learnt via the ONE – TWO – THREE – ONE method. For example, when standing to attention on parade, before marching off we may need to turn to the right, left or about turn, depending on which direction we were headed. Therefore, the 'ONE' would be shouted during the initial turn to face whichever direction was given in the command, the 'TWO – THREE' would be shouted to then bring the leg up (right leg if turning left and left leg if turning right or about turn) so that the thigh was horizontal with the ground, and then the final 'ONE' was shouted when the leg was driven into the ground (similar to a stamping movement). Once the static moves had been mastered, we moved onto 'saluting' and 'turning' when marching, and even the 'slow march' for more sombre occasions, such as funerals. It was only when the above had been reached and maintained to a high standard that the 'ONE – TWO – THREE – ONE' method was dropped, it was then that the final stage began – 'rifle drill'! This followed the same pattern as the drills discussed above; Firstly, static drills and then marching drills, all with our trusty SLR!

The rifle drill probably started in the second half of our training at Dover. Besides being a compulsory part of becoming a soldier, it also prepared us for our 'Passing-out Parade' at the end of our twelve months at Old Park Barracks. This drill was far harder than normal drill and mistakes were easier to make and harder to hide, and the punishment...intolerable! The drill practice on the main square had to be free of mistakes and the only way the army knew how to eradicate unwanted mistakes was via sporadic sadism...and they had an old classic ready and waiting! We would start every rifle drill practice with a full troop, but by the end there would be at least five or six running around the perimeter of the square with their SLRs held high above their heads – your heart would be pounding in your chest, sweat dripping down your face as you attempted to keep the 9.56lbs above your head...a feat none of us could successfully achieve! We all knew that as soon as any of us made a mistake we would hear immortal words, such as; "OFF YOU GO", "JOIN YOUR FRIENDS THOMAS" or "OH DEAR, HOW SAD...BYE THEN!" etc. Few escaped this torturous punishment, and believe me, it was painful and one of the worst punishments I ever experienced!! However, the army again achieved its goal, via almost illegal means, as we approached the day of our 'Passing-out Parade'. On the day of this momentous parade there was a sense of relief and pride when we halted in front of the guardroom, our time at Dover complete following a successful 'Passing-out Parade' in front of our families and friends...we were no longer Junior Sappers, we were now SAPPERS – To this day I still consider that day as one of the proudest moments of my life!

EMT (Early Morning Training)

There is no denying that fitness plays an integral part in a soldier's life. But not everyone enjoys running, and there are those who physically cannot run for a variety of reasons, such as; being overweight, asthma or other disability. There are those that may argue that to be a successful runner a person will have to train hard, be disciplined and also possess the correct footwear! However, whilst the hierarchy in the army believed in training hard and discipline, the small fact about having the correct footwear was lost on the regime that was in charge when I joined J.L.R.R.E. at Dover. We didn't have the right footwear...we weren't even close to having the right footwear...we possessed the old army faithful of a pair of DMS (directly moulded sole) boots. Oh the joy!!!

EMT was every Tuesday and Thursday, parading at 7am for the normal three to five mile run around one of the many routes in or outside of the camp. The dress code was normally red PT shirt or squadron sweatshirt, lightweight trousers, puttees and DMS boots – no running shoes or shorts!! Invariably, in a troop of thirty to thirty five soldiers there were varying degrees of fitness, thankfully, as a former cross country runner I was one of the quicker and fitter ones.

The majority of the troop increased their fitness levels as the months rolled by, and some of those who initially struggled made pleasing personal progress. However, not everyone showed signs of improvement, we had one member of the troop who continued to struggle week after week...Jock 'P'! The permanent staff had tried everything to help Jock improve, but there was an intriguing dilemma that developed...at first it could be argued that Jock 'P' may have

70

been struggling due to him being slightly overweight, but as time went on it was felt that he could have just been one those people who just couldn't run or it may have been that he was just lazy? Wils (Marc Wilson) and I found ourselves nominated as the ones to try and help Jock 'P' improve his running ability. Initially, if he started dropping back during a run, Wils and I stayed with him, offering encouragement in an attempt to drive him on and develop his progression. When this failed, they tried putting him in the front row of the troop so he was setting the pace, with Wils and I on either side of him again using encouragement, coaxing skills and even physically attempting to drag him along with us, by hooking our arms around his to keep him upright...as he continually pretended to collapse! This went on for a few months until there came a point that the permanent staff lost patience with him and his antics, and allowed him to drop out of runs and walk back to the squadron, so as not to effect the morale of the troop. It's possible that they sensed Jock 'P' was becoming isolated from other members of the troop and that it would only be a matter of time before he applied for a PVR (Pre Voluntary Release – an option open to all Junior Soldiers in the first six months!).

One morning, about four to five months in, this process was accelerated as we lined up for another EMT run. Jock 'P' was in his normal position...at the front and in the middle rank (by this time, the help he had received from Wils and I had now been withdrawn!). We set off that morning at a leisurely pace, not knowing the drama that would soon unfold! We were soon turning onto the main road around the camp and heading for the block that housed 54 Squadron, 82 Squadron and the Junior Ranks Mess Hall. As we headed toward the bottom part of the block (facing the sports fields/assault course) Jock 'P' began his normal premature 'cries of failure', such as; "I CANNEE DO IT!" and "MA CHEST IS HURRTING...I CANNEE GO ON!". Then, as we approached the centre point of the rear side of the block (probably only 600-800m from our start point) he unexpectedly collapsed (in a similar exaggerated fashion to a striker diving in the penalty box during a football match). The first two to three rows of people managed to jump over him, but it was then we came to realise that the permanent staff had obviously reached the point that they knew Jock 'P' was basically lazy, as Sgt Kerr gave a command that was eagerly obeyed by the remainder of the troop, myself included;

"DON'T RUN AROUND HIM…RUN OVER HIM!!!"

Without hesitation, the remainder of the troop either stamped on Jock 'P' or gave him a well-aimed intentional kick, borne out of frustration at what he had put us through and his distinct lack of 'fight' when the going got tough. Months of frustration, it appeared, had taken its toll on the permanent staff and all Jock 'P's peers in 4 troop. As we continued on our run, the cries and groans from Jock 'P' faded to the point that the only thing we could hear was the rhythmic drumlike beat of our boots on the tarmac. The only other noise that could be heard was labored breathing from one or two members, who did have the fight to work through their own individual pain barriers.

The events of that morning were the final straw for Jock 'P', and he must have realised that he could no longer endure this personal struggle with his own inability to run, regardless of whether he just couldn't run or was just lazy! Within a week he was on his way home, his brief army career was over. As harsh as it may sound, I believe that collectively the right decision was made that morning, whilst I am not proud of what we did it was ultimately in the best interests for 4 troop and also for Jock P.

Ghosts of Soldiers

There were many stories of ghostly sightings at Old Park Barracks, but unfortunately, they were in the 66 Squadron (formerly 'C' Squadron) block…where my troop was billeted. There were stories that had been handed down from intake to intake that included; Ghosts of soldiers who had died from their wounds following their evacuation from Dunkirk during World War II or the soldier who had hung himself, approximately ten years previous to our arrival in 1979, in the toilets off the education corridor on the first floor (the window of which was directly across from the windows of our room). Despite the many stories, the one that I found most disturbing was the one told one morning by Tim Smith (aka Rocker)…who just happened to be one my room mates!!

One morning, during those first two months, we (Wils, Tiny Strachan, Turner and me) woke up to find Rocker (Tim Smith) sat on his bed, bathed in sweat, possessing a look of unbounded fear and devoid of his normal smile and complexion. Rocker was no 'mummy's boy', he was a tough lad from Cleethorpes, but whatever had happened to him during the night must have been petrifying...and been very real!

We all listened intently when he told us the story of how, sometime after lights out (the block would have been in complete darkness with exception of the duty office on the ground floor), he dreamt that he was woken by a tap, tap, tap coming down the corridor. He explained that he didn't really think anything of it as he thought it was Cpl Meredith (one of the permanent staff) who, when carrying out reveille (wake-up call), used to walk around the lines with a broom handle tapping it on the floor as he walked. We said nothing, but all nodded furiously in agreement. Rocker continued and said that the 'tapping' stopped outside the door to our room...then the door opened slowly and Rocker told us that in the darkness all he could see was a shadowy figure peering around the partly opened door. He asked who it was...but there was no reply! Rocker attempted to wake the rest of us up, as he whispered; "Wils...Wils...Tiny...Taff...Taff...Turner" We may have stirred, but none of us woke up. During these few moments, the shadowy figure continued to peer into the room, but as Rocker jumped out of bed the door closed and the figure was gone. Rocker's voice lowered to a hushed whisper and we all leant in as he told us, "that was when I woke up from the dream and felt instantly relieved that it was just a dream...BUT!" he shouted. "When I woke up I heard tap, tap, tap...COMING DOWN THE CORRIDOR!" We all jumped back and let out a collective "FUCKING HELL...What happened next!". We all sat open-mouthed as Rocker continued to tell the story of how the reality mirrored the dream in every detail, right up to the point that the door closed and he jumped out of bed! It was about 2m from his bed to the door and he made the short distance in an instant, he stepped into the corridor and glanced to his right, where a 10m long corridor ended with a set of fire doors that led onto the stairwell...nothing! He pushed open another set of fire doors directly opposite our doorway and looked down another 10-

15m corridor to another set of fire doors that led to second stairwell…again, nothing! He swallowed hard and said "Whatever was stood at the door…just disappeared! We were all dumbfounded and it took a few seconds for us to take it all in then Wils said, "Fucking rubbish Rocker" and we all laughed nervously and never talked about the strange visitor again!!

To us it was just another story that would be added to the long list of unexplained sightings and passed down to new intakes. However, to Rocker it was very real and I swear he never left the room again after lights out, keeping a plastic bottle in his locker…in case of emergencies!!!

First Exercise

To most people the word 'exercise' defines a means of maintaining or increasing fitness levels. To a soldier the word 'Exercise' not only carries the same meaning, but also a word that signifies the wearing of combat gear i.e. camouflage clothing, tin helmet, webbing (pack, pouches, water bottle etc) and personal weapon (SLR) and leaving the comforts of camp, to sleep in bivouac or trench out in the ulu (Malay for jungle) and a common word used by all soldiers to signify 'a wilderness' where most exercises took place (i.e. Salisbury Plain, Warcop, Sennybridge etc). It could be described as an adult version of what young boys called 'war', pretend fighting in pretend scenarios. The only difference was with the number involved (sometimes in the thousands), and there were umpires to ensure fair play was observed by all! These 'Exercises' were normally designed to mimic what may happen in the event of the Cold War developing into World War III, and therefore preparing us soldiers for any eventuality that may develop. However, this 'First Exercise' was part of our basic training and designed for us to put into practice what we had learnt in fieldcraft lessons and weapons training on the camp and also lessons in the classroom. Was it fun? Yes, I believe it was, but surreal and an eye opener…certainly not enjoyed by all, which was probably due to the fact that it was mid-December. Thankfully, it was only for one night…this time!!!

We were transported by 4 tonner (army lorry) to a wooded area, approximately 6-8 miles from Old Park Barracks, and if I remember correctly it was mid-afternoon on a Saturday in mid-December 1979. It was the week before our 'Passing-in Parade' and our first leave since we had joined the army. On arrival, our first task was to set up a section (10-12 men) harbour area, which entailed setting our bivouacs (simple cover from rain) in defensive positions and compiling a rota to guard the area. There were four events that stand out in my memory during that first exercise; The attack on 3 troop, the guard rota through the night, the church parade on the Sunday morning and the forced march/yomp back to camp after the church parade!

It had been dark for a couple of hours when Sgt Osbourne entered the harbour area (following the standard 'challenge' from the sentry of; "Halt...who goes there. Friend or foe" etc) and gathered four or five of us together for a briefing. His voice was low, almost a whisper, and we all strained to hear as he explained that we were going to go on a recce (reconnaissance) to determine how strong the defences were of 3 troop's (the other new intake troop in 66 squadron) harbour area. We listened intently, all 'cammed up' (combat suit, tin hat c/w foliage and camouflage cream applied to our faces) as Sgt Osbourne briefed the plan for the patrol. He quickly looked at his watch and stated that we would be setting off at 21.00 hrs zulu (Greenwich mean time). I glanced at my watch, as Sgt Osbourne disappeared into the darkness, and I could see that it was only 19.23hrs – "Christ" I thought, "That's another one and a half hours away!" I sat there for what seemed like an eternity, but when I looked at my watch again it was still only 19.38hrs, and thought to myself, "This is going to be a long...long night". It seemed like hours before we heard the sentry say;

"Halt...Who goes there...Friend or Foe"

"Friend" whispered Sgt Osbourne

"Juliet" said the sentry, offering the first part of the password

"Quebec" whispered Sgt Osbourne, providing the second half of the password

The sentry called him through, and Sgt Osbourne whispered "well done Junior Sapper Martin" as he entered our harbour area – it was now 20.55hrs zulu!

Sgt Osborne led us out of the harbour in a line, one behind the other and with 3-4m spacing between us. This was it, the chance to put the fieldcraft skills we had learnt to the test!

Not a word was said, every command was given via hand signals; We knew when to stop, when to move on, when to crouch down and when to get up etc from the new skills we had been taught. Even walking now involved measured, critical movements to ensure there was no or minimal noise – each foot would be placed down gently with the outside edge leading to feel the way, before placing the sole of the foot flat to the floor. The sensation of being a real soldier felt good, the nervous energy was creating an adrenalin rush as we silently moved through the undergrowth, similar to a jaguar in the Amazon, toward our goal! After 20-25 minutes Sgt Osbourne finally stopped, indicating we were no more than 10m from 3 troop's harbour area. We lay down silently and pointed our SLRs menacingly towards the 'enemy' and slowed our breathing down to match the silence around us. This silence was soon shattered when a para flare lit up the whole area, and our position was compromised. All hell broke loose as 3 troop opened up on our position, and Sgt Osbourne gave us an order;
"FIRE AT WILL...FIRE AT WILL"
We needed no further invitation to the party and returned fire as the para flare ended its short life and the darkness returned, the sound and smell of gunfire filled the night air and lazer like visions, made by tracer rounds, gave psychedelic flashes of false illumination to this hell-like scene! After a few minutes we withdrew into the darkness behind us and the gunfire became more sporadic until one by one they stopped and silence returned to the woodland. We were soon back in our harbour area and the warmth of our maggots (sleeping bags), to wait for our turn 'on stag' (guard duty), with the adrenalin of what we had experienced still surging through our bodies!

It was cold that night, but despite the low temperature I eventually drifted off to sleep. What seemed like moments later I was woken up suddenly with a faraway whisper of;
"Taff...Taff...it's your turn on stag...Taff...get up you fucking Welsh wanker!"
"OK...OK...OK...Keep you fucking hair on Jock" I whispered.

I got into position and watched Jock Martin wave at me with two fingers (if you know what I mean!) before disappearing into his maggot. I turned and looked to my front as my eyes adjusted to the blackness that faced me, this was not good! I was sixteen years old and still had a slight aversion (well, more than slight!) to the dark. As I regained my focus I started to see things that weren't there, as trees and bushes began to look like people or animals. If that wasn't bad enough the wind and rain were creating strange noises in the darkness, compounding the fear levels as my heart pounded in my chest. I thought; "This is fucking scary shit". In the silence of the woodland the noises appeared amplified and my imagination was fighting with my fear at the twisted images I thought I was seeing. Gone was the bravado I felt earlier when out on patrol with Sgt Osbourne, it had been replaced with the same fear I felt as a child when told for the first time about 'Dickie Dark!'

"Fuck this for a game of soldiers!", I said to myself, and after only ten minutes (my time on stag should have been an hour) I was waking up my successor, whispering "It's your turn Tiny…Tiny…get up…you're on stag"

"Uhh…ok Taff…I'll be there in 2", groaned Tiny Strachan, half asleep.

"Ok..Tiny…I'll hang on until you're ready"

Tiny got out of his maggot and yawning continuously he dragged his 6ft 8in frame across to the sentry point!

"Get some kip Taff" whispered Tiny.

"OK Butt" I said, ridden with guilt at waking him up 45-50 minutes too early!

It was just after 1am when I crawled to my bivouac and climbed into my maggot, instantly falling asleep in the knowledge that it would be light by the time my turn came round again! I thought I was dreaming when I heard;

"Taff…Taff…Taff…for fuck sake…Taff"

I opened my eyes and in the darkness I could just make out the features of Jock Martin!

"Jock…is that you…what's going on…it's still dark!!" I said in puzzlement.

"It's your turn again…on stag…cumon Taff…get up"

This wasn't the time or place to argue so I got my shit together and took over from Jock as sentry! I looked at my watch…it was 2.22am! I inwardly chuckled as I realised that everyone else must have been shit-scared and done exactly the same as me, and only spent 5-10 mins on stag before waking up the next person! It was a long night as the 'fear factor' controlled the night and your turn would come around every one to one and a half hours. So much for big rough and tumble soldiers – we were all scared of the dark! Not the most auspicious start for us all! Thankfully, we all saw daylight again, and after eating the breakfast part of our 24 hour ration pack we were ready for our church parade!

I didn't realise at the time, but I was about to experience a significant event in my life! I had always believed in God, Jesus Christ, Heaven and the stories, I had been told/taught from the Bible as I grew up. But that was about to change! The exercise wasn't over, and following the church parade we would be marching back to camp in full kit including our new best friend, our SLR. The Sunday Service that morning was held in a field on the edge of the woodland and was in sharp contrast to the horrors of the night! The prayers and hymns were led by the Regimental Chaplain who started proceedings with an obligatory welcome followed by a prayer! Picture the scene; An army chaplain, half a dozen or so permanent staff and sixty to seventy junior soldiers in full combat gear, cammed up and with SLRs slung over our shoulders. Yes, it was a surreal scene standing there praying and singing hymns whilst dressed ready for combat with our SLRs! I do remember thinking at the time, as I looked around me, that this seemed extremely hypocritical, and for the first time I was aware that I was beginning to question the validity of religion and whether ANY God actually existed! I thought; How could it be that soldiers are fighting in the name of God or Jesus when one of the Ten Commandments is; 'Thou Shalt not kill'? This was one of the many questions I began to ask myself, and yes, that church parade in a non-descript field on the outskirts of Dover in December 1979 became a catalyst for a continued questioning of religion!

Once the church parade was over, we were given thirty minutes to prepare our equipment for the forced march back to Old Park Barracks. The time was spent ensuring our equipment was packed correctly and the weight distributed evenly throughout the various packs and pouches of our 37 pattern webbing. Additionally, we made sure our SLRs were clean so we could hand them straight back in to the armoury on our return to camp. When the time arrived, we lined up behind each other in single file ready for the march back to Old Park Barracks. Whilst we were waiting for the off, Lt Gilmour took the stretcher out of the safety vehicle (landrover), and shouted;

"P (Jock P...P (Jock P)), WHERE ARE YOU?"

A muffled voice came from the front of the line "Down the front Sir". Lt Gilmour jogged to the front and passed the stretcher to Jock P;

"Carry that P (Jock P)"

"I'M NOT FUCKING CARRYING THAT SIR" and he threw it on the floor.

"YES YOU FUCKING WILL P (Jock P)...NOW...PICK IT UP"

"NO SIR...IT'S TOO...! Before Jock P had a chance to finish his sentence, Lt Gilmour picked up the stretcher and threw it at him. Jock tried to step out of the way, but the stretcher caught him on the ankle and he fell on the floor writhing in agony and screaming "YA BASTARD SIR...YOU'VE BROKE MA FUCKING ANKLE". The rest of us tried not to laugh as Lt Gilmour tutted and said;

"P(Jock P)...YOU ARE A FUCKING WASTE OF SPACE...KNOCK AND GALLIMORE HELP THAT PIECE OF CRAP OFF THE FLOOR, OFF MY MARCH AND GET HIM TO THE SAFETY VEHICLE...WANKER!...HIGGINS, PICK UP THE STRETCHER AND PUT THAT IN THE SAFETY VEHICLE TOO... RIGHT...THE REST OF YOU...LET'S GO...BY THE FRONT QUICK MARCH!

We were off, our first forced march, as we began to tab back to camp at a steady pace!

We made good time on the march and the entire troop made it back to camp in approximately 1 hour and 20 minutes...and without any further casualties! We found out later that Jock P hadn't broken his ankle...he had some heavy bruising to both his ankle and his pride! Later that evening, I looked back on the events of the weekend and chuckled to myself...we never did discuss our sentry duties during the exercise, where each and every one of us was clearly scared of the dark!!!

Pay Parade

During the first few months at Old Park Barracks we had, I think, weekly or fortnightly 'pay parades' where part of our pay was paid over the table. This would involve marching into a room, signing for and receiving our money, from our troop commander, Lt Gilmour. Normally, this event passed without incident, but this efficient, machinelike parade suffered a hilarious moment which wouldn't have been out of place in comedy classics, such as Dads Army or It Ain't Half Hot Mum...it was pure comedy gold!!

We were lined up in the corridor outside the training room on the ground floor of 66 squadron block all ready for pay parade. Sgt Kerr came out of the training room and immediately shouted;

"QUIETEN DOWN GENTLEMEN...TROOP...TROOP TENSHUN"

We came to attention...badly! The timing was appalling and was compounded by the echo in the corridor, sounding similar to a machine gun being fired in a cave! Sgt Kerr wasted no time whatsoever letting us know how he felt!

"GENTLEMEN...NOT GOOD ENOUGH...LET'S TRY AGAIN...THIS TIME, GET IT RIGHT...STAND AT EASE"

We stood at ease...thankfully as one, but there was no time to bask in glory or enjoy a session of collective back-slapping as Sgt Kerr immediately barked out the next order;

"TROOP...TROOP TENSHUN"

This time we got it right as Sgt Kerr confirmed;

"BETTER GENTLEMEN...Thomas, Wilson...into the training room...NOW!"

Wils and I marched into the training room where Lt Gilmour was sat behind the trestle table with everything set up in front of him; Money (in an open cashbox), register (for us to sign for our money) and pens. Wils and I halted in front of the table, turned to face Lt Gilmour and saluted. Without looking up, Lt Gilmour responded;

"Good afternoon gentlemen...positions please"

We both immediately turned to face opposite directions and marched around either side of the table to enable us to flank Lt Gilmour on both sides, and act as witnesses to the impending pay parade.

Sgt Kerr was stood in the corridor in front of the doorway to the training room and called the first soldier;

"JUNIOR SAPPER BELL"

Bell responded, "SERGEANT"

Bell turned and marched into the room, halting in front of Lt Gilmour and saluted. Lt Gilmour counted out the money and Bell signed the register, took his money, saluted again, made an about turn and marched out of the room. This was the protocol we had to follow to receive 'part' of our pay. The remainder of our money was paid into a post office account which we received prior to going on our first leave at Christmas. Each soldier was called out by Sgt Kerr, and in alphabetical order;

"JUNIOR SAPPER BRAY..."

"JUNIOR SAPPER BROMLEY..."

"JUNIOR SAPPER CLAPCOTT..."

"JUNIOR SAPPER CLARK..."

"JUNIOR SAPPER COOKE..."

Etc

Everything was running like a well-oiled machine! However, one soldier, and I think it was Mackintosh (I may be wrong as the mists of time have clouded my memory!) brought this smooth, machine-like process to an abrubt halt!

"JUNIOR SAPPER MACKINTOSH" yelled Sgt Kerr.

"SERGEANT" replied Mac.

Into the room marched Mackintosh, up to the table and halted, but as he brought his right leg up he was too close to the table and the force from his knee hitting the underside of the table was too much! Mac managed to lift the table and turned it on its side, which resulted in the money, cashbox, register and pens being strewn all over the training room floor. Lt Gilmour was sitting there open-mouthed in total disbelief, Sgt Kerr had entered the room to see what the commotion was and Wils and myself were struggling not to laugh! Lt Gilmour quickly regained his composure and looked at Sgt Kerr and calmly said;

"Take Mackintosh back outside Sgt Kerr"

"RIGHT MACKINTOSH...YOU FUCKING WANKER...ABOUT TURN...QUICK MARCH...LEFT, RIGHT, LEFT, RIGHT", yelled Sgt Kerr.

Lt Gilmour glanced over his shoulders and said:

"Thomas, Wilson...pick up the money, pens and cashbox"

Wils and I jumped into action as Lt Gilmour lifted the table back into an upright position and placed the register back in its rightful place. Within a few minutes all the money had been accounted for and it was business as usual as the pay parade continued with Sgt Kerr re-calling Mac and whispered;
"Don't fuck it up this time...JUNIOR SAPPER MACKINTOSH..." (He got it right second time round!)
"JUNIOR SAPPER MACLARNON..."
"JUNIOR SAPPER McGREGOR..."
"JUNIOR SAPPER MARTIN..."
"JUNIOR SAPPER MARSHALL..."
Etc
Thankfully, the pay parade continued without any further incident!

It's funny looking back and the memory of that day still makes me smile. The moment Mac's knee hit the table was like watching something in slow motion – you could see it all happening in front of you, but you could do nothing about it! It was the only incident of any note that happened during those pay parades, but what a moment...straight out of a 'Carry on' movie!

Gas, gas, gas!

Another part of our programme was the NBC (Nuclear, Biological and Chemical) training. The classroom element of this training revealed the dangers that soldiers were now exposed to in modern warfare. It was scary shit, which normally would result in death if you didn't treat each threat seriously and follow the golden rules associated with our personal protection or NBC equipment...respirator, NBC suit (known as a 'Noddy' suit), gloves, boots, decontamination pads and atropine injectors. The classroom training was bad enough, but we also had to endure a session in the gas chamber...something I hated throughout my army career. It was disconcerting learning about what to do in the event of a nuclear explosion, a gas attack of nerve, blood or choking agents of chemical warfare or the horrors of biological warfare with the indiscriminate spread of diseases such as Anthrax. Additionally, I can still remember the taste of the CS gas as it hit the back of your throat. This is the day we experienced CS gas (or tear gas) for the first time.

None of us were looking forward to our visit to the gas chamber, we'd heard the horror stories from the senior troops that had already completed this part of their training, it was something we were all dreading. After NAAFI break we paraded in the squadron quadrangle, there wasn't the usual buzz of excitement that normally resonated around the troop on this particular parade, there was a hushed silence of nervous expectancy at our impending visit to the gas chamber…the practical element of our training was imminent and we were all fearfully entering the unknown.

We were soon marching, as a troop, to the gas chamber, located in an old gatehouse on the 'back hill' into the camp, a house that formerly marked the old entrance to Old Park Manor House. A house that once stood close to where the regimental church was now sited and the reason the camp was called Old Park Barracks. Within five minutes we were halted in front of the old gatehouse and the moment of doom was almost upon us. I believe it was Sgt Kerr that took this training, but I can't be sure, whoever it was, split us into four or five groups of between six and eight soliders…unfortunately, as always it was alphabetical and meant I was in the last group with longer to wait and longer to think of what was about to happen. Sgt Kerr explained what would happen in the gas chamber… "You will walk around the room to help dissipate the gas around the space and then, in turn, you will remove your respirator and state your name, rank and army number and then leave the gas chamber…easy as that gentlemen." And he smiled. "It sounded too good to be true…there must be a catch" I thought.

The first group entered the gas chamber and around five minutes later the door burst open and the first member of the group, Sapper Bell, staggered out with his respirator in his hand, the door immediately shutting behind him. Belly was coughing and spluttering and his eyes were screwed up tight as he screamed "AAARRGH…FUCKING TWAT" and fumbled to try and get his water bottle out of its pouch, when he succeeded he blindly unscrewed the cap and was soon pouring water into his eyes…one by one the remainder of the group staggered out of the gas chamber much the same as Belly…the rest of us looked on in silence knowing our turn was soon coming. Sgt Kerr called the next group into the chamber and the process was repeated…and then the third, fourth and finally it was our turn. We entered the gas chamber, a sealed room with no means of escape other than the way we had entered, and the empty room was filled with a cloud of gas and visibility was limited. Sgt Kerr signaled for us to start walking clockwise around the room and a minute or so later anti-clockwise. He then motioned for us to stop and then selected the first victim, I mean soldier…Rocker (Tim Smith) was soon removing his respirator and stating his name, rank and army number, as Sgt Kerr had earlier instructed…as the last digit of Rocker's army number left his lips he started coughing and squinting, and Sgt Kerr opened the door and pushed Rocker outside. One by one, those of us in the last group experienced the same ordeal that everyone else had endured. I was the last but one to be selected and had already become aware the the skin around my face, where the seal of the respirator rested and perspiration had formed, was starting to sting. I took a gulp of air and removed my respirator and started to say my name and rank, however, halfway through my army number the stinging in my eyes became instantly unbearable. As the gas dragged its acidic fingers across the back of my throat it caused me to splutter my way through the last couple of digits, I then heard the door open and felt Sgt Kerr immediately grabbed me, dragged me toward the door and pushed me outside, all in an instant. My throat, mouth, eyes, nose and ears were all stinging, and like Belly and the others, I was soon pouring water in my eyes and over my face to ease the intense stinging sensation, it was horrendous and took a good ten minutes to fully recover…it was easy to see why CS gas was used to quell riots as it is so debilitating.

It was a difficult but important part of our training and it certainly drove home the relevance of our personal NBC equipment…yes it was uncomfortable and restrictive, but used correctly, should we ever go to war and face a chemical attack, it was a sobering thought that it could potentially save our lives.

Quick Change Parade

I have mentioned those moments which were like living hell at the time, but when you look back, are absolutely hilarious.

There was one such moment that certainly wasn't funny at the time, but did drive home the reality that you could never beat the army system...ever! The quicker that was realised, the easier it was to deal with whatever was thrown your way, individually or, in this case, collectively! Most of you reading this would not have any idea what a 'quick change parade' is, but those who remember their days as a new recruit certainly would remember, and with a wry smile. As this story develops, I trust you will have some sympathy for the treatment we suffered, but at the same time end up wiping the tears of laughter from your eyes as the story reaches its climatic conclusion and highlights this perfect punishment!!!

It was just before 7pm and we were all lined up in the Hobbies corridor (the ground floor corridor that linked 66 squadron with the Education Wing and where many of the hobbies; such as; Photography, war games etc were held), dressed in works dress (beret, shirt KF, Heavy duty sweater, lightweight trousers, puttees and DMS boots) nervously waiting for Sgt Kerr. I can't remember why we were parading, but nevertheless we were certainly being punished for something and something bad? Within a few minutes we could see the double doors at the far end (opposite the NAAFI – p.s. By this time I knew what it meant 'Navy Army Air Force Institute) of the corridor open and the familiar figure of Sgt Kerr striding down the corridor towards us. When he got halfway down the corridor, he started shouting;
"RIGHT GENTLEMAN...I AM PISSED OFF HAVING TO COME HERE TONIGHT AND...YOU ARE ALL GOING TO SEE HOW PISSED OFF I AM...SO LETS BEGIN...TROOP TENSHUN...STAND AT EASE...TENSHUN...STAND AT EASE...GET A GRIP YOU FUCKERS...TENSHUN"
Sgt Kerr was now stood in front us and explained;
"I AM GOING TO INSPECT YOU ALL AND...BY GOD...IF IT'S NOT GOOD ENOUGH...YOU WILL SUFFER!"
We were like a troop of statues, too scared to move a muscle or even breath as Sgt Kerr slowly and silently moved down the line. He said nothing until he got to the end;
"MOVE ONE STEP FORWARD...MOVE"
In unison, we took the one step forward and halted as one. Sgt Kerr again slowly and silently continued his inspection of the

rear of the troop. When he had finished, he walked to roughly the middle part of the troop and let us have it;

"NOT GOOD ENOUGH GENTLEMEN...YOU ARE A SHOWER OF SHIT...YOU HAVE 5 MINUTES TO GET BACK TO YOUR ROOMS AND GET BACK DOWN HERE DRESSED IN COMBAT KIT...NOW GET AWAY...GET AWAY...GET AWAY!"

We needed no further invitation to go and sprinted up to our rooms on the second floor – a stampede of desperate and scared junior sappers on a mission, God help anyone who got in our way. Once in our rooms it was off with the works dress and on with our combat kit, there was no time to hang the clothes up that we had taken off and they were left on the floor where we had dropped them. It was now time for another stampede as we ran back to the hobbies corridor on the ground floor to parade again...in combat kit! As we lined up in front of Sgt Kerr I glanced at my watch...it was 8.05pm.

The parade followed the same format as the first, and when Sgt Kerr had finished inspecting us...guess what? Yes, we had again failed miserably as Sgt Kerr hissed;

"WHAT A PILE OF SHIT YOU REALLY ARE GENTLEMEN...YOU NEED MORE PRACTICE...YOU HAVE FIVE MINUTES TO GET BACK DOWN HERE IN BARRACK DRESS...NOW MOVE...GET AWAY...MOVE!"

The deafening noise from the stampede of our boots again filled the night air, and we started to undo our combat jackets as a torrent of camouflage made its way to the top floor. Back in our rooms it was off with the old (the combat kit joined the works dress on the floor) and on with the new; Shirts 'ceasefire' and trousers 'hands-up'(the daily order of dress for clerks) as they were affectionately known. It was now 9.12pm as I joined the others in the mass exodus from our rooms for the now familiar route down the stairwell to the hobbies corridor!

A familiar routine ensued and in roughly another hour we again back in our rooms dispensing with barrack dress and donning the latest order of dress, PE kit; Red PE t-shirt, blue shorts, army socks and black plimsoles. As we sprinted back down the stairs I noticed that it was now 10.22pm. Almost an hour later we were back in the stairwell sprinting to our rooms

with the latest dress code ringing in our ears, a strange and rather unfamiliar dress code as we were told to return to the hobbies corridor in 5 minutes dressed in 'mess tin order'. Those of you reading this who are ex-army will recognise this sadistic little number, but those of you who have no military experience may even be wondering, what is a mess tin? When I served, the army issue mess tins were supplied as a pair, they were slightly different rectangular type bowls each with a fold-in handle and the smaller mess tin fitted into the larger mess tin. Therefore, 'mess tin order' was made-up of the two mess tins, a boot lace and our tin helmets – you can use your imagination on how this was used as an official 'uniform'. If you are struggling to use your imagination or you are just too embarrassed, I can tell you that the mess tins were used in a loose attempt at hiding one's dignity, the boot lace is then used as belt looping through the handles of the mess tins to keep them where they should be kept (please note that this was inevitably an unsuccessful exercise!). It is not easy trying to run in 'mess tin order' as the 'slapping' of the tins in our nether regions as we ran down the stairs was extremely noisy, painful...and a tad embarrassing! It was 11.13pm when we reached the hobbies corridor and lined up in front of Sgt Kerr to be inspected AGAIN, complete with bruised egos, thighs and...!!!! When Sgt Kerr finished this inspection it was gone midnight and he stood in front of us all, sighed and said;
"GENTLEMEN...I HOPE YOU HAVE ENJOYED YOUR EVENING AND LEARNT A VALUABLE LESSON. I SUGGEST YOU TRY AND HAVE A GOOD NIGHT'S SLEEP AS YOU HAVE ANOTHER BIG DAY TOMORROW. I'LL SEE YOU ALL IN THE MORNING...GOODNIGHT GENTLEMEN...TROOP FALL OUT"
As we left the corridor at one end, we could hear Sgt Kerr whistling as he disappeared through the double doors at the opposite end of the corridor...we would soon find out why!!

We were all laughing and joking as we headed back up the stairwell to our rooms...dressed as 'modern' Spartan warriors in our, less than practical 'mess tin order'! We had survived another 'beasting' (harsh military treatment to instill discipline)...or so we thought! But when we walked back into our room it dawned on us immediately that we had been well and truly conned...the punishment was not over! It was complete carnage…there would have been less of a mess if someone had lobbed a hand grenade into the room and shut the door – there wasn't an inch of visible floor space as our various types of uniforms were strewn all over the floor and beds. Such was the urgency to get ready for each parade, we hadn't noticed the mess we were creating. We spent the next two hours sifting through the clothes attempting to establish which clothes belonged to who (not an easy thing to do when it came down to socks, puttees and PE kit)! When we had gathered all our own clothes and equipment we had to fold the clothes and put them back in our lockers in their rightful place (according to the locker layouts we had on the inside of the locker doors). Whenever I think of this story I have an image of Sgt Kerr walking back to his married quarter with a huge grin on his face, in the knowledge that he could go straight to bed whilst we would have to make sure the room was spotless ready for the inspections the following day…I hope he did, as that was an absolute classic punishment!

Thetford, Bellerby Camp (Yorkshire Dales), Weymouth and Margate

Our training wasn't all completed at Dover, the training programme also took us to various parts of the UK to undergo specialist training that would assist us in developing our skills as soldiers. We practiced additional fieldcraft/orienteering type skills at Thetford, bridging and watermanship at Weymouth, more fieldcraft (including survival exercise) in the training areas of the Yorkshire Dales and put into practice basic construction and combat engineering skills at Margate. They were challenging, but also enjoyable, memorable and sometimes…controversial!!

Thetford

A training area in Norfolk where we practiced more fieldcraft drills, attempted a confidence course (an assault course in the treetops – 20-30ft above the ground and without safety nets!), orienteering and possibly the most difficult assault course I ever experienced. One of the stand out memories of that week was how cold it was in Thetford, and this was driven home by Nissen huts we slept in that had no central heating – the buildings that housed 15-20 soldiers were heated by a single coal burning stove in the centre of the room. With the meagre coal rations we were given they were not enough to take the permanent chill from the rooms...it was freezing! The story below involves the NAAFI chairs and an amusing scene on the assault course!!

The nights were bitterly cold in Thetford, and with nothing but a small central stove (and restricted fuel) in our antiquated nissen hut accommodation...this was not going to be a pleasurable experience! As the nights were freezing, getting out of our army sleeping bags in the morning was not an experience filled with happiness either, you could cut shapes in our breath it was so icy! The pain didn't end there, we had to endure the arctic like conditions every morning when we left our nissen huts to go to the ablution block to shower and shave! Oh how we suffered the first night, but thankfully the remainder of the stay would be made bearable as we used our initiative! However, our resourcefulness, which was something we were actively encouraged to use, included theft...which unfortunately was something that couldn't and wouldn't be tolerated!

The transit camp we were staying in had a small NAAFI with a soft drinks bar that sold teas, coffees, cans of drink (i.e. coke, Fanta etc), crisps, chocolates and sweets and also housed a T.V. room...it also possessed hundreds of fold-up wooden chairs! The second night at the camp we thought it would be a good idea to 'purloin' two or three chairs! We discovered that the chairs made an ideal fuel substitute for our stove and the following morning our hut wasn't as cold as it had been on the previous morning. The word got around the other three nissen huts, and for the remainder of our time at Thetford both us and 3 troop enjoyed warmer nissen huts than the ice boxes we slept on on the first night! We thought that our ruse had worked and that our resourcefulness (well, theft!) had gone unnoticed. However, we failed to factor in the fact that the army accounts for everything, even down to a single paperclip! We thought that we had got away with whisking away a few chairs from the NAAFI at Thetford, and we might well have done...But the extent of our crime came to light shortly after our return to Dover! When the bill arrived in the 66 squadron office for sixty seven chairs and our 'initiative' (or crime) had been rumbled and...we were in the shit again!

The other event from Thetford that is etched in my memory concerns an assault course, a 6 ft wall and...Tiny Strachan. The assault course in Thetford was fairly non-descript and was located in a wooded area, but the difficulty level had been increased due to the 12-18 inches of mud that was evident throughout the whole course from start to finish. Sgt Scholey set us off in pairs at 10 second intervals, and as normal this followed the 'alphabetical' format meaning Wils and I were the last to set off. The first few obstacles were dealt with fairly easily, but we knew the 6ft wall was going to be tricky due to the mud! When we approached the 6ft wall we were greeted with a comical scene...Tiny Strachan was struggling to get over the wall! The comical image in front of us was of Tiny, who was 6ft 8in, leaning with both elbows on top of the wall and his legs were flailing about like a demented duck entering the water for the very first time, he was just hanging there, but achieving nothing with the flurry of activity going on below his waist! Wils and I looked at each other and for a split second looked back at the pathetic scene in front of us...I couldn't understand how somebody so tall could actually fail to get over a 6ft wall. It was bizarre! Without further hesitation Wils and I ran up to the wall and grabbed a leg each and threw Tiny over the wall. We quickly followed him, but as we landed on our feet on the other side we quickly realised that Tiny had landed on his face. He was covered in the shittiest mud you could imagine, and resembling 'Swamp Thing' from DC Comics he struggled to get to his feet! Wils and I looked at each other, laughed, looked back at Tiny and shouted;
"SEE YOU AT THE FINISH LINE TINY!"
We were still laughing when we finished, and when Tiny trotted over the finished line a few minutes later, Sgt Scholey asked him;
"WHAT THE HELL HAPPENED TO YOU STRACHAN?"
Tiny explained that we'd hastily helped him over the 6ft wall, but he'd landed face first on the other side. Wils and I looked at each other again, before smiling at Tiny and Sgt Scholey, and then shrugged our shoulders innocently...as if butter wouldn't melt...!!!

Bellerby Camp (Yorkshire Dales)

An isolated camp in the middle of the Yorkshire Dales and about two miles from the market town of Leyburn. The camp conditions were better than those at Thetford, but we did experience a survival exercise and a route march that didn't end well!

We experienced a strange phenomenon in the Yorkshire Dales during our visit to Bellerby Camp and Catterick Training Area, one that I never came close to repeating during the remainder of my army career. During a forced march through the beautiful Yorkshire Dales we thought we had been lucky with the weather, but despite the blue skies, the heat was so intense it resulted in us losing 2-3 lads from heat exhaustion. The problem came about when we were tabbing up a particularly steep hill, and with no protection from any trees (the wooded areas in and around Bolton Abbey and along the river Wharfe had provided us with much needed protection from the sun) we were at the mercy of the elements as we headed towards the pre-designated harbour area where we would spend the night! A mixture of the heat, the gradient and the distance already covered became too much resulting in the lads collapsing, and as a precaution they were taken straight to hospital. The rest of us soldiered on and eventually managed to complete the march as we reached the harbour area, a small copse high in a field and surrounded by the typical stone walls that are inherent to the landscape of the Dales.

We were resting after the march and waiting for our evening meal to arrive from Bellerby Camp, when the blue skies we had enjoyed all day were replaced by darkening clouds. By the time the meal had arrived and been dished out, the threat of rain was imminent as the former sun-kissed lush green fields that had surrounded us were replaced with a menacing sense of forboding! We could no longer see the valley below as dark clouds were nudging and bullying the peaks around us and the driving rain began to considerably reduce our visibility. The other notable change was the temperature, it had dropped almost instantly and dropped further when the rain descended on our position. We attempted to find some sort of futile protection amongst the weather beaten trees, but had to rely on our ponchos to keep us and our food dry...but for how long?

After a short while I remember I was sitting against a tree, shivering and unsuccessfully trying to keep dry when I heard a voice;

"Who's that under there?" I looked up to see Sgt Osbourne standing over me.

"Is that you Thomas" Sgt Osbourne asked sounding concerned.

I nodded and mumbled, "Yes Sergeant!"

Within ten minutes we were all sitting in the back of 4 tonners heading back to Bellerby camp...the exercise had been cancelled. Back at camp we were ordered to immediately head to the showers, change our clothing and report to the cookhouse in 30 minutes for a briefing. At the briefing the permanent staff gave us an update on the lads that had been taken to hospital...telling us they were comfortable and likely to be back with us by close of play the following day. They also explained to us that they had to bring us off the mountain as, due to the sudden change in temperature, it was too dangerous to leave us out overnight as they firmly believed that it was possible that the temperature change would result in several, if not more, cases of exposure resulting in pointless casualties...or possibly even worse! Lt Gilmour, Sgts Kerr, Osbourne and Scholey all agreed that they had never witnessed such a dramatic change in weather conditions and cancelling the exercise was the only sensible option. This highlighted to us all the dangers of mountainous areas, such as; Catterick, Sennybridge, and Warcop etc and how unforgiving they could be. I look back in admiration on the decision the permanent staff took that night and believe that, without a doubt, lives were saved by their quick thinking!

Weymouth

You can't claim to be a Sapper if you haven't stayed at Wyke Regis or Chickerell camps to enjoy the wonders of bridging and Watermanship (making rafts from planks, oil drums and rope). Despite our age we also enjoyed the nightlife in Weymouth...provided we avoided the attentions of the 'Navy Shore Patrol' as we darted in and out of the shadows of the narrow streets and alleyways in and around Weymouth town centre!!

Our training at Weymouth was a total contrast to the training we had endured at Thetford and Catterick. This had nothing to do with fieldcraft skills and running around pretending to be a part of the infantry...this was an introduction into the wonderful world of bridging! At Wyke Regis training camp the first part of our training involved making rafts from oil drums, planks of wood and rope. It sounds like fun and it was, but there was a serious side to this exercise, as it offered us the chance to work as a team and practice some of the knots we had learnt back at Dover. We were split into sections and it was a straight race to build a raft, paddle across from Wyke Regis training camp to Chesil Beach and back again, hoping the raft we made wouldn't sink or even worse...fall apart! Whilst this was fun, the main reason we were in Weymouth was for the bridging and we spent a couple of days building MGBs (Medium Girder Bridges) which can be best described as a full size adult version of meccano. As one of the smaller members of the troop, it could be considered that I was one of the lucky ones as I was part of the 'centre of bridge' party that was responsible for inserting pins to secure the top and bottom panels etc and also responsible for the sway bracing. Once the main structure of the bridge had spanned the gap, the whole troop laid the ramp units and the decking. It was impressive to see the finished bridge and certainly an achievement to be part of a team that had built it!

The sense of achievement was dwarfed by how I felt when we built a 'Bailey Bridge' later that week. The town I had grown up in, Bridgend, had several Bailey Bridges that crossed the River Ogmore in and either side of the town, a tell-tale sign of the importance of the Royal Engineers in Bridgend. Additionally, it was an iconic bridge that helped the Allies advance towards victory against Germany during World War II. The bridge we built was small (only 6 bays) in comparison, but the sense of achievement was huge. It was much more difficult to build, as the transoms were eight men lifts and the panels were six men lifts, compared to the four man lifts of the top and bottom panels of the MGB. When our small bridge was complete I, for one, was overjoyed...but tired! I also knew that our bridge didn't come close to some of the bridges built by Sappers in World War II, bridges built under enemy fire and much, much longer than ours! For example, a Bailey Bridge built to replace a bridge over the Sangro River in Italy and the Chindwin River in Burma were 1126ft and 1154ft respectively. Many Bailey Bridges are still standing today all over the world. Therefore, it is not surprising that General Eisenhower felt that the Bailey Bridge was one of three of the most influential engineering feats of World War II...Radar and Heavy Bombers being the other two. To this day, I am immensely proud that our troop became part of history when we built that small bridge in Wyke Regis back in 1980!

Ramsgate

We spent a thoroughly enjoyable week at Margate, despite living in tents in the middle of a field and enjoying the culinary delights of a field kitchen. It was a rewarding week that gave me (and I think others in the troop) a great deal of satisfaction, as we renewed an assault course for the CCF (Combined Cadet Force) at a local private school!

Our week in Ramsgate was another proud moment during our time at Old Park Barracks. It was the one and only time during my army career that I was involved in a MACC (Military Aid to the Civil Community) project. It was a construction task with a strict time limit: When we started on the Monday morning we knew that we had to be finished by Friday afternoon...so no pressure! Luckily, the weather was on our side that week and the work was almost a small distraction, as we enjoyed a week of sunshine, camping (military style), and the ice creams, promenades, beaches and fairgrounds of Ramsgate & Margate. The current assault course at the school was very old and the area it was in was overgrown rendering it totally unusable. Therefore, the first day was spent clearing the area of all the brambles, weeds, long grass etc, and the rotten wood and rusting metal from the original obstacles. It proved to be a very successful day as the whole area was completely cleared, giving us a blank canvas to start construction for the new assault course!

The next few days were spent creating the various obstacles that would make uo the assault course, and hopefully be a great addition to the CCF (Combined Cadet Force) unit at the school. We all worked hard creating each obstacle and we were assigned either as individuals (for example; I had the responsibility of cutting steps into a small mound) or as part of a team – we had become proficient working as a team, as by this time we had been together for approximately eight months. Hence, during that week I cannot remember the permanent staff having to shout or dish out any discipline/punishment to us, we had a job to do and we just got on with it! In the evenings we were free to explore Ramsgate…provided we weren't on guard detail! By close of play on the Thursday the bulk of the task had been completed, and there were just a few minor jobs to complete on the Friday and a general tidy up of the site. By late morning on the Friday we were ready to hand the site over to the school, Sgts Kerr and Scholey were happy with how the week had transpired and rewarded us with a crate of beer. But before we could drink the beer we tested out the assault course with an informal timed competition…I can't be sure but I believe I came joint second (I don't remember who won). The beer tasted sweet after a successful week; The week was over and the job was done, and collectively lauded by the permanent staff we headed back to Dover.

Leadership Training

As Junior Leaders, part of our training programme was 'Leadership Training'. This involved two weeks away at an adventure training type camp. We were sent to Halton Training Camp on the banks of the River Lune, nr Lancaster. Over the next fortnight we enjoyed rock climbing, abseiling, canoeing, a two day accompanied walk (with a member of the permanent staff) in the Lake District (climbing Scaffell Pike), and a three day unaccompanied walk in the Yorkshire Dales (climbing the three peaks of Whernside, Ingleborough and Pen-y-ghent). It was a great couple of weeks, but in addition to climbing Scaffell Pike, an incident one night near Halton Training Camp is etched in my memory and is a perfect example of how far we had come as a troop!!

Our time at Halton Camp was coming to an end, and there had certainly been some highlights; The thrill of abseiling down a rock face for the first time, experiencing the difficulties of rock climbing under the tutelage of Captain Morgan, the disappointment of reaching the top of Scafell Pike to find the visibility was zero, the 'wow' factor when stepping out of the cloud/mist and being greeted with the beautiful and

95

outstanding views of the Lake District and West Water, canoeing on the River Lune and the Carnforth Canal and not to mention, during the limited free time we had, the delights of Morcambe during the Scottish equivalent of 'Miners Fortnight' (Morcambe had been taken over by Scots and there were drunk Jocks everywhere...men and women)! It had been enjoyable, but also tiring and as a result we were having a restful day before the final task of our leadership training...a three day unaccompanied walk that involved conquering the Three Peaks in the Yorkshire Dales.

It was a pleasant summer's evening, and as it was only about 6.30pm I decided to go for a stroll down by the River Lune. I headed down to the riverside at the bottom of the camp and stood there for a moment watching the sun glisten on the surface of the water as the evening breeze kissed the water creating shivering ripples of excitement. I turned and started to head for the footpath that meandered parallel to the river through a small wood...a serene scene of natural beauty that you sometimes only see on postcards! Humming nothing in particular I headed toward the Carnforth canal. Ten minutes later I was stood beneath the aquaduct of the Carnforth canal and took the shortest route to the top, a path through the undergrowth that took you up the 70-80m steep banking to the canal above. Roughly about half way I stumbled into a clearing where ten to twelve lads of a similar age to me were laughing and joking amongst themselves. They soon stopped and stared at me menacingly...nothing was said by anyone! Then, and without warning, the lad that was directly in front of me pulled out a Bowie type hunting knife...I immediately turned and ran, not daring to look back over my shoulder. I ran...ran...ran and within minutes I was back in the safety of the camp and running up the hill to our billet. I burst through the door and tried to get my breath;
"What is it Taff" asked Rab Peacock
Blowing hard I tried to tell the lads in my room what had just happened;
"I...group of lads...knife...ran like hell...!"
"Taff...slow down...you're not making any sense!"
"I was walking up to the canal"
"hmm...hmm. Ok" said Rab
"I came into a clearing where there was a group of 10-12 lads"
"OK...carry on" said Paddy O'Malley

"...one of the lads pulled out a big hunting knife on me"

"HE DID WHAT" shouted Rab, jumping off his bed

"He pulled a knife on me" I repeated

"FUCKER...I'LL FUCKING KILL HIM...THE WEE SCROTE" yelled Rab in temper and started pulling on his boots;

"No-one pulls out a knife and threatens my mate...no-one. Little fucker!" mumbled Rab. Then without hesitation he was through the door and shouted;

"COME ON...LET'S GO...LET'S TEACH THESE FUCKERS A LESSON!"

Paddy O'Malley, me and a couple of the other lads were running through the camp a little way behind Rab who was about 10m in front of us. When Rab got to the bottom of the banking, that led up to the canal, he sensibly waited for us to catch up! He then sprinted up the path with the rest of us right behind him...within seconds we entered the clearing and the lads panicked and scattered...but not before Rab caught one and laid him out with just one punch! I saw the lad who had pulled the knife out on me earlier and another lad head towards the canal;

"THAT'S THE ONE" I shouted and pointed at the two attempting to flee.

We ran after them both as they scrambled up the path towards the canal. Once at the top, they didn't get far...with our military training we were fitter and quicker. Rab caught the boy with the knife, took the knife (it was in its sheath) off him and passed it to me...I threw it into the canal in disgust as Rab sent the lad home with a bloody nose, and possibly black eyes (when he got up the next morning!). The other lad was caught by Paddy, who lifted him off the floor with one hand and sneered;

"I hope you can swim!" and with that he threw him into the canal. 'SPLOOSH', he hit the water with a huge splash, before swimming to the opposite bank, dragging himself out of the water and running away as fast as his legs would carry him! We turned and walked away and headed back down the path that led down the steep slope to the River Lune. Pleased with the way we had dealt with the 'problem', not in a too heavy handed way, but enough to make them think twice about pulling a knife on anyone in the future, it was then that Paddy started singing, and we all joined in;

97

"WE ARE, WE ARE, WE ARE, WE ARE THE ROYAL
ENGINEERS
WE CAN, WE CAN, WE CAN, WE CAN DEMOLISH
FORTY BEERS
DRINK RUM, DRINK RUM, DRINK RUM, DRINK RUM
AND COME ALONG WITH US
COS WE DON'T GIVE A FUCK FOR ANYONE ELSE
WHO DON'T GIVE A FUCK FOR US"
We all started laughing as we walked back to the
camp...Brothers in Arms!

We were soon back in our billet in Halton Camp, and telling
the others what had happened...re-living and sharing in detail
the events from the evenings shenanigans. I now realise that
the camaraderie we shared was highlighted during the events
that evening. The permanent staff (Sgt Kerr, Sgt Scholey and
Sgt Osbourne) had done a remarkable job at Dover and the
togetherness that they had created in our troop was a credit to
their abilities as Training NCOs (non-commissioned officers).

Jock Martin's Birthday

*Ben (Jock) Martin was a good mate at Dover, a Glaswegian
and fanatic Rangers fan and protestant who was a drummer in
an Orange Band (Protestant organisations that lauded the
achievements of William IV of Orange at the Battle of the
Boyne), back home in Glasgow. Our shared love for football
resulted in us having many kickabouts on the football pitches
at Old Park Barracks. It made sense that on his seventeenth
Birthday we went out to celebrate. We had a good night in
Folkestone, but this was brought to an abrupt end the minute
we walked back into our room at the end of the
night...bastards!!*

Jock Martin and I were travelling back by train from a night
out in Folkestone, and we were talking about what a great
night we'd had on what was his seventeenth Birthday. We had
been to the cinema (I have no idea what film we saw) and had
met two local girls. After the cinema we were walking around
Folkestone getting to know the girls (if you know what I
mean!). We found ourselves in a park/garden next to the Road
of Remembrance, and Jock Martin and the girl he was with
left me and the girl I was with in a secluded part of the

98

gardens…or so we thought! I was in the process of losing my virginity, when a couple walked past and the 'tutt tutt' from the women was slightly offputting, but undeterred I carried on regardless…nothing was going to stop me achieve the end goal! Within 5-10 minutes it was all over, I had lost my virginity…but it wasn't romantic or an emotional, tender and wonderful experience shared with the love of my life! It was an act of desperate fumbling in a dark corner of a shitty town by two teenagers who had only just met and were caught up in a shared experience of rubbish sex that was over too quickly to enjoy! No lying on a deserted beach gazing at the stars, as the cool evening breeze washed over our naked bodies…it was bend down, pull your jeans up and smile politely before grabbing her hand and saying;

"Cumon…love…let's catch up with Jock and your mate…Jock and I have got a train to catch!"

That was how I lost my virginity in a town called Folkestone, but I remembered that momentous night for all the wrong reasons!! The train pulled into Dover Priory and in typical bravado style we jumped off before it had come to a standstill, ran down the platform and out of the station and started the long walk back to camp. 25-30 minutes later we began the precarious walk leading up to the 'back hill' into camp. As we approached the dark lane that led up to Old Park Barracks we nervously looked about to make sure our great night wasn't spoilt by 'squaddie bashers' (civilian lads who didn't like us Junior Leaders being in their town…sometimes hiding in the undergrowth and then cowardly attacking soldiers taking this shortcut back into Old Park Barracks). Thankfully, it was all clear and within 5 minutes we were walking past the 'old gatehouse' for the old manor house that once stood on the site of the barracks, which was now used for our CS gas training (part of our NBC (Nuclear, Biological and Chemical) training…absolutely hideous part of our training I can still remember the taste the gas as it hit the back of my throat). Jock looked at me and smiled, and asked the question he'd obviously been dying to ask since we boarded the train at Folkestone;

"What was she like Taff…nudge nudge, wink wink!" sniggered Jock and punched me in the arm playfully.

"Fuck off Jock..you wanker" and I laughed, "I'm not telling you…you'll go and tell everyone!"

"I wouldnee do that Taff?" And he grinned at me inanely.

"Yes you would…you Jock twat!"

Within a few minutes we were walking past the NAAFI heading for the hobbies corridor that led to 66 Squadron block;

"You gonna see her again Taff?"

"Nah…what's the point, another month and we'll be gone from yuh"

"True…was she a good shag then Taff?" Jock's head rocked back as he laughed uncontrollably and started shouting;

"TAFF'S NOT A VIRGIN…TAFF'S NOT A VIRGIN…TAFF'S NOT A VIRGIN..!"

"SHUT UP JOCK" and I laughed. Then we stopped walking, looked at each other and both burst out laughing.

We were now at the duty NCOs bunk and we both signed back into the squadron before heading up the stairwell with Jock still trying to wind me up;

"Did you…you know…did you…say…I LOVE YOU…when you…you know…when you…", he put his arm around me and whispered in my ear in a mocking posh accent;

"When you…EJACULATED…!"

"For fuck sake Jock, give it a rest…it happened…it wasn't special…it just…happened!"

As we went through the double doors at the top of the stairwell and into the corridor outside our room Jock asked;

"So…what was her name?"

"I dunno!"

"You dinna know…!", we stopped outside the room, looked at each other and burst out laughing;

"Fair play Taff…that's classic…absolutely classic!"

Jock pushed the door open and we both stepped into the darkness…!

Instantaneously, the lights came on…and I swear the whole troop was in the room!

"HAPPY BIRTHDAY JOCK…DID YOU THINK WE'D FORGET" they shouted in unison…and they grabbed Jock. Within seconds he was stripped to his pants and being carried out of the room high above their heads. I laughed…but not for long as Jock shouted;

"TAFF LOST HIS VIRGINITY TONIGHT WITH SOME TART IN FOLKESTONE!"

Before I had a chance to call Jock 'a bastard', I was set upon, stripped to my pants and joined Jock in the corridor. We were now both held above the heads of our mates in 4 troop…like a pair of sacrificial offerings in some sordid pagan ceremony…made all the more surreal as all the lads were singing, what had become, our troop song…'Tom Hark' by The Piranhas!

We reached the quadrangle where we were each tied to a chair, side by side, and I looked at Jock and said;
"You really are a Jock twat" and we both cracked up laughing as the windows opened on the three floors on all three sides of the quadrangle. The squadron was watching, laughing and shouting obscenities…and to add insult to injury the hosepipes were turned on and we were drenched from all three sides with cold…freezing cold water! The hosing down lasted a good few minutes before they were switched off and we sat there shivering…I looked at Jock and said;
"Have you enjoyed your Birthday?"
"Aye…was shagging that girl worth it?"
"Too right!"
We burst out laughing (again)…and we were still laughing when the lads came to untie us!

My memory of losing my virginity was not of the act itself, but more to do with the drenching Jock and I got that same night. I didn't know her name and I couldn't tell you what she looked like after all these years. What I can remember is Jock and I being tied to those chairs in our pants and thinking…What a great way to finish off a great night!!!

Passing-out Parade

This marked the end of our training at Dover, or so I thought, but more of that later! This was a chance for families to see how far we had come as a group in the past twelve months – a very proud day for us all and the end of a chapter. Sadly, it also meant that I would never see many of the other lads of 4 troop, 66 Squadron again, lads with whom I had shared many happy and tough times, and little did we know at the time, that an unbroken bond of shared experiences had been created!!

It was mid October 1980 and our last day at Dover was here, our Passing-out Parade was the final part of our transition from being a Junior Sapper to Becoming a Sapper. Following the parade in front of our families, we would leave Dover and move on to 1&3 Training Regiments RE near Farnborough to complete the B3 & B2 (trade qualification) part of our combat engineer training. Our entire intake (two troops from each of the three squadrons of 54, 66 and 82) from October 1979 was lined up, in their relevant troops, in an area adjacent to the main square, all eager to impress our watching families. We could all see that the family seating area was quickly filling up with proud parents, grandparents, girlfriends, brothers, sisters, uncles, aunties, cousins and friends: All eagerly waiting for a glimpse of their loved ones in the imminent parade. Despite my parents being divorced, they were both present; My father was there with my step-mother and my Uncle Ivor (my father's brother), and my mother was there with my Nan Henson. As we waited to march onto the square you could sense the nervous anticipation as we all wanted to make our watching families proud and were silently hoping and praying that nothing would go wrong!!

The order was given and we marched onto the square and onto our markers, the training had paid off as each troop was marching in unison to all the commands being received...like a well-oiled machine. It wasn't just our families we wanted to make proud, we also didn't want to let our permanent staff down either as they had invested so much time and patience in getting us to this point! Thankfully, there were no mishaps; No-one out of step, no dropped rifles and no soldier fainted! Everything was crisp and what was expected of us was delivered in typical military fashion...with the added pomp and ceremony of the inclusion of the Regimental band! The presiding officer stood on the raised dias to take the salute, and as each troop marched past the order was given by each Junior Sergeant of each troop to;
"EYES LEFT" our heads snapped to the left and we could see families craning their heads in an attempt to recognized loved ones. It was an immensely proud moment for everyone present and as we marched off the square and around to the armoury, there was a mixed sense of relief and pride. The families had also made their way over to the area in front of the armoury, and with expectant anticipation were waiting for us to be 'fallen out'! Eventually, it was our turn to hand in our SLRs to the armoury for the last time at Dover; Sgt Scholey stood there

and we could sense that the end was near, he took a deep breath and gave the order;

"4 TROOP…4 TROOP SHUN" We came to attention, as one.

"4 TROOP…FALL OUT"

We 'fell out' and proceeded to find our families in the throng of people…after a quick scan of the excited faces I found those of my family and waved. There was an abundance of hugging, congratulations, 'oh my God, you looked smart!', and of course…tears!

Whilst I was stood talking to my family Sgt Scholey came over, introduced himself, apologised and asked if he could speak with me for a moment. We walked away from my family and Sgt Scholey said;

"Don't worry young Thomas…WO2 Simpson would like a word with you!"

WO2 Simpson was the football officer and was in charge of the regimental football team. We found WO2 Simpson after a few minutes and he looked pleased to see us;

"Ah Sapper Thomas, just the man…I have a proposition for you…as we both know you have been a valued member of the regimental football team, and as you know, we have already qualified for the second round of the Army Youth Cup."

"Yes Sir"

"I've spoken with the CO (Commanding Officer) and I've had permission to approach you, Hutchinson, Maver, Bray, Plant, Tickle and Morris and ask if you would all be willing to return to Dover after your leave…to help the regiment win the Army Youth Cup…I've already spoken to Sappers Plant & Tickle and they have said yes…What do you think?...Would you like to stay and help us?..."

I was seventeen years old and I loved sport! I was now being asked to return to J.L.R.R.E. to play football…hell yeah, paid for playing sport…it was a 'no brainer'!

"Yes Sir…I'd love to come back and try and help the regiment win the Army Cup"

"Excellent Sapper Thomas…Sgt Scholey will fill you in on all the details and arrange travel warrants etc…see you when you come back from your leave".

"OK Sir" I said as he walked away mumbling about having to find Hutchison, Bray etc…!

My time as a Junior Leader was complete, but I did return to Dover to play football! Little did I know at the time but it would be six months before I eventually left Dover but more of that in Chapter 7. With mixed emotions it was 'farewells' to the rest of 4 troop...some of whom I would sadly never see again! I left Dover that day with my family... who were now even prouder due to my being asked to return to play football!

Back to Dover

I returned to Dover with six other lads; Geordie Hutchinson, Ron Maver, Charlie Bray, Mark Plant, Adrian Tickle and Colin Morris – we had been offered an opportunity too good to miss. The seven of us had been an integral part of the regimental football team and we had been asked if we would return to Dover to try and help J.L.R.R.E. win the Army Youth Cup. However, what do you do with seven lads who had finished their training but didn't have the qualifications or experience to be an instructor? The answer was...not a lot!!

After a week's leave I was back in Dover with the other lads from the football team; Geordie Hutchinson, Ron Maver, Charlie Bray, Adrian Tickle, Mark Plant and Colin Morris. The regiment had no idea what to do with us, as far as I was aware we were in a pretty unique position...we had finished our training as Junior Leaders, but we couldn't be instructors! Therefore, apart from playing football, we didn't do a great deal of work. The only job of note that I can remember us doing was painting a boat that was on one of the many concrete stands that were dotted around the camp. We enjoyed long days of playing pool in the NAAFI, spells of Egyptian PT (sleeping), generally relaxing and of course...football training. This was far removed from the intense twelve months of parades, beastings, bullshit and strict training programmes. There was now absolutely no structure to our day...it was a great life!

One of the only things of note that happened during this period was obviously the football, but that will be covered in Chapter 7, happened far away from the camp and it was not necessarily associated with the anything military, other than I was returning to camp when it happened. I was returning from a week's leave and found, on my arrival at London's Victoria

104

Station that I had missed the last train to Dover, and I had no choice other than to wait for the 'mail' train that departed at 4.30am. I was still only seventeen years old, fairly naïve, and as I was soon to find out, vulnerable and an obvious target for those involved in the seedier side of London! By the time I had arrived at Victoria Station the shops, cafes and bars were starting to close and there were very few travelers around the station. But there was initially an army of people cleaning the station, preparing it for another busy day! There was also a smattering of homeless people scavenging in the bins that hadn't been emptied and those who were simply trying to find a safe place to sleep, late night revelers waiting for taxis, policemen hoping for incident free shifts and as I would discover…predators and chancers!

It was almost midnight, and after wandering around the station for twenty minutes or so the station was becoming more and more deserted! For my own safety, I decided to set myself up in the well-lit large paved area in front of the platforms, and with the large entrance to the station directly 20-30 metres behind me…I felt a little more at ease when I noticed a couple of policemen patrolling the area! I sat on my sturdy army suitcase and began to read…every 10-15 minutes I would put the book down…to give my eyes a rest, and also to glance around the station to check everything was ok! A little later, around 1am, I became aware that someone was watching me and sure enough, in my peripheral vision, I could see a man nervously pacing up and down, about 10-15 metres behind me over my left shoulder. I tried to ignore him and carried on reading…then I sensed he was edging closer…a few minutes later he must have plucked up the courage to approach me and I heard him clear his throat;
"Hhemmm!...Hello, I was…wondering…if you'd like to…come back to my flat…and I'll give you £5…for your trouble!"
Without looking up I gave him a short but polite reply, afraid to antagonise him;
"No thank you..I'm ok where I am" and I carried on reading my book.
I thought that would be the end of it, but within ten minutes I could again sense a presence behind me…the same man approached me again;

105

"Excuse me, sorry to bother you again…but if I gave you £10 would that be ok…would you then come back to my flat…it's cold here…you can…you can keep warm in my flat and perhaps…have a warm drink. Then you can come back and catch your train…what do you say?…"

Again, without looking up, I gave him my answer;

"No…I'm quite happy here, thank you!"

A couple of minutes later I glanced up from my book and the area around me was again deserted…with exception of a pigeon strutting around in a vain search for his final treat of the day!

"Great!" I thought "He's gone" and carried on reading. What I hadn't bargained for was how persistent this 'stalker' or 'pervert' was, and 15-20 minutes later he was back with his latest offer! This time he seemed more direct and more agitated;

"Right…I'll tell you what I'm going to do…I'm going to give you £15 AND…pay for your taxi back to the station to catch your train…How…!" Before he could continue I firmly said;

"No...if you don't stop bothering me…I'm going to call them over!" and pointed to two policemen that had just come into view about 40-50m away, to my right!

"OK…Thank you and goodnight" and he walked away! To where I don't know and I didn't have a clue what he looked like as the fear factor had ensured I kept my head down and didn't engage him! That was that and the rest of the night passed quietly, and there was a huge sense of relief when I boarded the mail train to Dover a few hours later.

When I returned to camp I told the lads what had happened and there was a general consensus that I should have gone his flat, beat him up and stole all his money! Not a good idea considering this happened around the time that the notorious Denis Nilsen was murdering men in his flat in Muswell Hill, London (he murdered at least 12 men between 1978 and 1983). I believe I made the right decision that night…however, when I have retold this story over the years I have always jokingly said; "I was playing hard to get…and was holding out for £20!"

My eighteenth Birthday (and aftermath!)

My eighteenth Birthday was spent at Dover, a night on the town with a few of the lads I played rugby with at J.L.R.R.E. The night went pretty well...or so we thought, we were so wrong, and for the first time in my army career I was over my head and in the dark brown and smelly...!!

It was my eighteenth Birthday and a few of us from the regimental rugby team went into Dover to celebrate. If you hadn't already guessed, I was the only one who was legally old enough to drink as the others were still junior leaders...as a result, we tried to keep a low profile! Unfortunately, one of the lads, Harman (my half back partner in the rugby team), hadn't quite grasped this concept and I had already had to warn him in the first pub and told him to keep it down. We were now in the second pub and were only on our third pint of the evening when Harman started playing up again! I called him over and whispered;
"For fuck sake Harman, keep it down...you carry on like this and you'll get us kicked out of the pub...this is your last chance or you'll have to go back to camp"
"OK Taff" he said sheepishly.
Ten minutes later Harman was at it again!
"Harman...Harman..." I hissed. I got up and give him a clip and again whispered;
"I fucking told you to keep it down...get back to fucking camp...get your fucking head down and get some kip...we've got rugby training tomorrow afternoon"
"OK. Sorry Taff" and he got up and headed out the door with his tail between his legs. The rest of us went on to have a good night and didn't give Harman another thought...and we were all worse for wear by the time we got back to camp later that night!

Sometime in the middle of the night I was woken up abruptly by the duty sergeant;
"THOMAS...GET UP...YOU ARE IN THE SHIT THOMAS...GET YOUR ARSE TO THE GUARDROOM...NOW...MOVE YOUR ARSE...YOU'VE GOT FIVE MINUTES!"
I thought to myself "what the fuck is going on?" I got dressed, and still pissed, half sprinted and half staggered to the

guardroom where the duty sergeant was waiting for me…there is nothing like a good old fashioned bollocking to sober you up! The duty sergeant asked me about Harman and when was the last time I saw him! I explained that I last saw him when I told him to leave the pub and go back to camp!

"What time was that?"

"About 8.15 to 8.30pm sergeant"

"Do you know what happened to Harman"

"No sergeant"

"That's probably because you sent him back to camp…ON HIS OWN…HALF-PISSED…He decided to come back via where Thomas?

"The back hill sergeant"

"Yes Thomas…the back hill…What do you fucking think happened Thomas?"

I began to know where this was heading and was dreading what the duty sergeant was going to tell me…guilt started to wash over me and I became numb. What had I done?

"I don't know sergeant"

"SQUADDIE   BASHERS…that's   what   happened Thomas…SQUADDIE BASHERS…your stupid fucking drinking night has resulted in Junior Sapper Harman being kicked to fuck and hospitalised…I hope your fucking proud of yourself Thomas"

I swallowed hard as the reality of what I'd done hit home!

"Harman is lying in a hospital bed with broken ribs, a broken arm, detached retina and extensive heavy bruising to various parts of his body…he'll be in hospital for some time"

Guilt overwhelmed me and a whole host of thoughts went through my mind; I shouldn't have sent him back to camp on his own…Why didn't I put him in a taxi?...I should have looked after him and kept him with us etc. I felt totally to blame for Harman's injuries and wish I could have turned the clock back. The sound of the duty sergeant's voice brought me back to the reality of this horrendous situation;

"THOMAS…THOMAS…ARE   YOU   FUCKING LISTENING…GET OUT OF MY SIGHT THOMAS…FALL OUT…AND DON'T THINK THIS WILL BE THE LAST YOU HEAR ABOUT THIS!"

I slowly walked back to my room stunned by the news about Harman. I was now completely sober, and with this shocking news bouncing around in my head…with a handful of 'what ifs' it was quite a while before I drifted off into an uneasy sleep!

'BANG, BANG, BANG...' Who the hell is knocking my door! I got up, threw a towel around me and unlocked the door. There was a Junior Sapper at my door, who asked;
"Are you Sapper Thomas?"
"Yes" I answered, intrigued but fearful, given the events of last night!
"The RSM (Regimental Sergeant Major – affectionately known as 'God' in all regiments!) wants to see you straight away"
"Oh shit" I thought...this is going to be painful!
"OK thanks" and I closed the door in a feeble attempt at shutting the door on the world...and the heap of shit I was now in!
The RSM was Geordie Howe, who was an absolute nutcase...he was also the rugby officer! I couldn't even think of a future at this point...in anything! Geordie Howe had the capability to make my life a great deal more miserable than the definition of misery! After getting ready in double quick time I embarked on the short walk to the RHQ, and thinking to myself...walking through the gates of hell is going to be easier than this! I knew that nothing could prepare me for what was about to happen, I stood outside the RSM's office and hesitated and took a deep breath before knocking on the door;
"WHO IS IT?" Shouted the RSM angrily
"SAPPER THOMAS SIR"
"GET IN MY FUCKING OFFICE...NOW!"
I marched into his office and halted in front of his desk...nothing could have prepared me for the next few minutes...nothing! The RSM stood up, pushed his chair back forcefully...THUD! He came around the desk like a striking cobra and for a moment I thought he was going to hit me! He pushed his face within an inch of mine shouting incoherent obscenities, spit spraying everywhere (Geordie Howe had a habit, when shouting, of speaking out of the one side of his mouth...this became more pronounced the angrier he became) and there was 'Harman this' and 'rugby that' and 'Thomas you...', well I was everything derogatory you could imagine...and more! After a few minutes I can honestly say that my morale had now sunk to subterranean levels...in army terms, the RSM had just 'tore me a new arsehole' and made

the bollocking by the duty sergeant seem more like a pleasant chat between old friends. The RSM finished up by shouting;
"GET OUT OF MY OFFICE…GET AWAY…GET OUT OF MY SIGHT…MOVE…MOVE…!"
I didn't need a second invite to get out of his office…out of the building and if I possibly could've, I think I would have got out of the country aswell! I made an about turn and marched out his office and out of the building. I made the short walk back to my room and with a heavy heart and ridden with guilt I sat on my bed with my head in my hands. Almost immediately there was a knock on the door, 'BANG, BANG, BANG! I stood up, walked to the door and opened it, it was the same Junior Sapper from earlier;
"Yes" I said dejectedly
"The RSM wants to see you again"
'Jesus.H Christ' I thought 'can this day get any worse?'
"OK" and I stepped out of the room and locked the door behind me.
I made the short walk back to the RHQ, and I swear that with each step my legs became heavier and heavier. A couple of minutes later I was again standing outside the RSM's office…I looked at the ceiling as if I was seeking protection from a divine body! I took a deep breath and knocked the RSM's door;
"WHO IS IT?" snorted the RSM.
"SAPPER THOMAS SIR"
"GET IN MY OFFICE"
I marched in and again halted in front of his desk and was shaking uncontrollably such was the fear level! Geordie looked at me, sat back in his chair…and nothing would have prepared me for what came next, he said camly;
"Right Sapper Thomas…you've had your bollocking…" and he leant forward, "LET'S TALK FUCKING RUGBY…SIT DOWN"
I sat down and we discussed the Army final and what we were going to do now that Harman was unavailable…surreal! The more I think about Geordie Howe, he was a great man with an undescribable passion which I don't believe I've encountered since. He was also an animal and I remember a story he once told us. He was playing rugby and went into a ruck, as he arrived at the ruck and bent over to bind onto an opposing player brought his head up quickly and hit Geordie in the mouth…he told us he carried on playing, but the other player

110

had to go to hospital to get Geordie's front teeth removed from the top of his head! This explains why Geordie was such a good RSM – a mixture of passion and being an out and out animal!

1 & 3 Training Regiments RE

When I finally left Dover, I was posted to 1 & 3 Training Regiments RE at Gibraltar Barracks, Minley Manor nr Farnborough. This is where we continued our combat engineer training where, on the completion of the course, we would qualify as Class 2 Combat Engineers. During this time there were only two things that stand out; A triangular friendship and an explosives mad instructor!!

The Three Musketeers

During this time at 1 & 3 Training Regiments I became friendly with two lads, Steve Fenton (we played football at Dover) and Eric Gothard. We became inseparable during that time at Gibraltar Barracks and were the unofficial troop jokers – as we attempted to keep morale high! Little did I know at the time that Eric would introduce me to someone who would have a profound effect on my life!

"Fenton, Thomas, Gothard...this is your doing!" shouted Sgt Coulson, as he looked around the bridging hard at our entire troop doing the 'dying ant' dance (lying on your back and waving your arms and legs in the air) despite his shouts to stop! One out of the three of us would shout "DYING ANTS" at the most inopportune moments, resulting in the entire troop adopting the desired position until either me, Steve or Eric jumped up which signified the end of the dance. We had adopted the dance from a manic childrens TV programme from the 1970s and early 1980s called TISWAS, a show that made both Chris Tarrant and Lenny Henry famous! It was our attempt at a bit of light relief amidst the bullshit and beastings, a way of keeping morale high in the troop, and it worked...the permanent staff also understood what we were doing and most of the time they turned a blind eye!

Eric (Gothard) had talked Steve and me into entering a road race called the 'Barnsley 6', and also convinced the regiment that it would be good PR if the three of us entered as a team representing the Royal Engineers. This resulted in the regiment paying the entrance fee and providing running shorts and vests. The weekend of the race arrived, but I was on guard on the Friday night so we arranged that we would meet up on the Saturday evening in Barnsley. We agreed to meet at the parent's house of Eric's girlfriend, Linda (I had already met Linda and her family a couple of weeks previous when I visited Barnsley with Eric). Eric and Steve travelled up on the Friday after our training had finished, Eric travelling to Barnsley and Steve to his home town of Hull.

My guard finished at 7am and after quickly getting changed I set off on my Suzuki TS125X motor bike. An hour or so later, and as I was approaching the start of the A1 that would take me north to Barnsley, I had a minor accident! As I was driving over a roundabout…I had banked over too much and the bike went from under me resulting in me and the bike sliding to the side of the road. Thankfully, I was lucky, apart from a small cut and graze (where my hand had made contact with the floor) to the palm of my left hand, the bike and I were ok. I picked the bike up, brushed the grit from my left hand, put my glove back on properly and carried on with my journey! It was around 4pm when I arrived in Barnsley, and within ten minutes I was sat in Jean and Roy's (Linda's parents) kitchen drinking coffee with Eric, Linda and Steve...after washing my hands and applying TCP to the small cut and graze on my left hand!

Eric and Linda babysat Linda's younger brother Andrew that evening, and Steve and I took this as an opportunity to have a few pints and games of pool, and headed for the Vine Tavern on Pitt Street (a real 'spit and sawdust' pub that had minimal seating but served great beer), and wasn't far from Linda's parent's house on Princess Street (a typical terraced street that wouldn't have looked out of place in a Hovis advert!). After a couple of hours we thought we'd take a look at what was on offer in the centre of Barnsley. We left the Vine Tavern and made the short walk down a small hill into Peel Square and within a few minutes we were on a road called Cheapside where we saw a local policeman. Neither of us had experienced a night out in Barnsley and thought it would be a good idea to ask the policeman if he could recommend somewhere. We approached him and politely explained that we were visiting friends and had never enjoyed a night out in Barnsley and could he recommend a pub with...wait for it!...women, music and good beer (in that order!)! The policeman pointed to a pub located on a corner towards the top of the street, and on the left had side and said;

"Up theear...thy'll ave a great neet in theear!"

Steve and I thanked him and walked towards the noise of music, but as we got closer we sensed something wasn't quite right...judging by what we saw and heard it must have been a theme night, and the theme that night must have been 'heavy rock'...there was way too much hair, black leather and crap music for my liking...and looking at Steve's face, he felt the same. We looked back in the direction of the policeman who was laughing so hard we could hear him above the rock music coming from the pub he'd recommended! Steve and I looked at each other, laughed and said, in unison;

"What a wanker...Vine!" and we walked back the way we came, past the policeman, who was still laughing, and back to the Vine Tavern for another pint and a couple more games of pool. The night was soon over and Linda's dad Roy dropped Eric, Steve and I at the home Eric shared with his auntie and uncle in Worsborough. After a long and eventful day it was straight to bed as tomorrow was the Barnsley 6!

I woke up the following morning and something was wrong...my left arm was throbbing! I looked at my arm and I could see that the veins in my left forearm appeared to be red and inflamed...I had no idea what it was, and despite the pain I carried on as normal! However, an hour or so later, at the changing facility for the Barnsley 6, the throbbing in my arm was becoming unbearable and I could see that the red and inflamed veins were much worse and had now crept past my elbow and further up my arm. Steve called one of the St John's Ambulance representatives over, who took a look and advised me get my arm checked out at the hospital...by this time, I was dressed and ready for the race as the start time was a little under 30 minutes away! Linda and Roy took me to Barnsley and District General Hospital where a doctor greeted me on my arrival (the hospital had provided a doctor in A&E to deal specifically with any injuries from the race) and looked at my arm, he looked back at me and said;

"I can see you appear to be dressed and ready to run the Barnsley 6!"

"Yes doctor...I'm part of a three man team...is there any chance you could give me a couple of painkillers...the race is due to start in 17 minutes..."

"Well...the answer to that is...no!...if you run the race...you would probably collapse and...die!!!!"

"Pardon...die!" I said, shocked!

"In layman's terms...you have blood poisoning...any exertion would have pumped the poison around your system much quicker...when that poison reached your heart...it would be inevitable that you would have collapsed and eventually died...sorry to be so blunt!" the doctor explained.

"Wow...that's scary" I thought, as the doctor then went on to say;

"We'll have to keep you in for a minimum of 24 hours to administer a course of tetanus injections...if you wait here I'll arrange for a nurse to come and take your details!"

"OK...Thanks doctor..." I was in shock and was still coming to terms with what the doctor had said and that I could have possibly...died!

Steve and Eric ran the race, but shortly after they had to leave Barnsley and head back to camp...leaving me in the hospital facing injections in the cheeks of my arse (alternately) every six hours! Linda came into see me that evening and brought some goodies; Fruit, mint crisp (similar to a caramel shortcake) and a Yorkshire favourite...parkin (gingerbread type cake made with oatmeal and black treacle). Linda, her parents Jean and Roy and brother Andrew were a lovely, friendly family...nothing was too much trouble for them and they looked after me and made sure, when I was discharged on the Monday afternoon, that I got a train to take me back to camp. Before I left the hospital I had to clear something up that was puzzling me...when the nurse came to say I could go I asked her if I could have a quick word. She agreed that it would be ok;

"Can I ask why during my time on the ward whenever I was spoken to by the doctors, other nurses and other staff...you have all called me by surname. Yet, everyone else has been called by the Christian names...is it because I don't come from Barnsley?"

Her reply was not what I expected;

"What do you mean Mr Huw?"

There were no need for words…it was time to go!

When we left the ward Linda and I burst out laughing and we were still laughing when we got in the car with Roy, who asked Linda;

"What's so funny?"

Linda explained what had happened on the ward and Roy also saw the funny side, and had to compose himself before setting off for Doncaster so I could catch my train! My bike was left at Jean and Roy's and when I returned to pick it up a few weeks later Jean, Roy, Linda and Andrew were on holidays in Bridlington. Thankfully, a neighbour let me into the back yard of Jean and Roy's house to get my bike, and by chance it would be over a year before I saw them all again…but more about that in chapter 8…much more!!!

Sergeant Coulson

Our troop sergeant was called 'Sgt Coulson' and I soon came to the conclusion that he loved explosives. Firstly, due to the glaze in his eyes during 'booby trap' training and an incident during an exercise in the Hawley Training area, adjacent to the camp…I bet it was a while before he made Staff Sergeant!!

Thinking of two incidents during our time at Gibraltar Barracks, it has to be considered that our troop sergeant, Sgt Coulson, had issues…his love for explosives and all things that go 'BANG' was worrying! The first incident was fairly mild, but when you add the second incident into the mix Sgt Coulson may have needed 'help'!!!

Part of our combat engineer training included the need to understand explosives and how to slow the advance of enemies via 'route denial'. In addition to laying minefields, this involved blowing up bridges and roads and also using booby traps of all kinds to slow an enemies' progress. We had to learn how to 'ringmain' bridges for the maximum effect and understand the dangers associated with plastic explosives, detonators, det cord, sensors (pressure and pressure release) when creating booby traps! The 'booby trap' part of our training was carried out in an old derelict house, probably an old gatehouse for Minley Manor, and looking back, Sgt Coulson probably spent the whole morning preparing for this

115

particular part of our training. There were three or four rooms that were used, and after being split into groups of three or four, we would enter an allocated room with the intention of 'clearing' the room of booby traps and make it safe! Each group would be told how many booby traps were in the room before entering, but despite finding one or two, those of us waiting outside would hear the inevitable 'BANG', followed by Sgt Coulson shouting one of many phrases, such as;

"YOU'RE ALL DEAD...NEXT"

"OH DEAR, HOW SAD!...JOIN YOUR FRIENDS...NEXT GROUP...ROOM 3"

"BYE THEN...NEXT GROUP IN ROOM 2"

"YOU'RE DEAD...YOU'RE DEAD AND YES...YOU'RE DEAD TOO...NEXT LOSERS...I MEAN GROUP INTO ROOM 1...OFF YOU GO!" etc

This image of madness was compounded by the vacant look in his eyes and the inane grin! It's probably safe to say that this was definitely his favourite task as an instructor!

The second incident was during our final exercise shortly before the end of our training. We were in a harbour area close to Hawley lake when suddenly, and without warning there was a gas attack. The call was given;

"GAS, GAS, GAS!" and you could hear metal objects being banged together to complete the warning! Our respirators went on first, followed by our NBC (nuclear, biological and chemical) suits, gloves and boots – lastly, a frantic application of ultimate protection via the use of decontamination pads. The CS gas was not delivered conventionally, Sgt Coulson had 'rigged up' some kind of mortar system and was firing them into our harbour area, however, he went slightly overboard and miscalculated the amount used, creating a thick cloud that brought visibility down to a couple of metres. But there was another element that Sgt Coulson miscalculated...the weather conditions!! The strong south easterly breeze soon moved this hazardous cloud of CS away from our harbour area. Unfortunately, the breeze pushed the gas cloud into a nearby housing estate... resulting in the evacuation of residents, and pupils from a local primary school! Sgt Coulson was now, what is commonly known as, 'in the shit!' We never knew what happened to him with regards to his punishment, but an incident of that magnitude would have certainly impacted on his promotion chances. Additionally, like me (when I was at

Dover)...he was probably 'torn a new arsehole' by the RSM...which would have taken much longer than mine to heal!!!

ROLL OF HONOUR – 4 TROOP, 66 SQUADRON (Oct 18th 1979)

Lt Gilmour

Sgt Kerr   Sgt Osbourne
Sgt Scholey

J/Spr 'Belly' Bell	J/Spr 'Charlie' Bray
J/Spr 'Taff' Bromley	J/Spr 'Rick' Clapcott
J/Spr 'Nobby' Clarke	J/Spr ' ? ' Cooke
J/Spr ' ? ' 'C'	J/Spr 'Steve' Dare
J/Spr 'Taff' Davies	J/Spr 'Ken' Doherty
J/Spr 'Cliff' Estelle	J/Spr 'Taff' Evans
J/Spr ' ? ' Gallantree	J/Spr 'Mick' Gauntlet
J/Spr 'Clive' Gittins	J/Spr 'Jock' Higgins
J/Spr ' Nigel' Hissey	J/Spr ' Billy' Hunt
J/Spr 'Dave' Jansens	J/Spr ' ? ' Jenkins
J/Spr 'Peter' Jones	J/Spr 'Robert' Knock
J/Spr 'Pete' Lander	J/Spr 'Nick' Lye
J/Spr 'Mac' Macintosh	J/Spr 'Skin' Maclarnon
J/Spr 'Scottie' Marshall	J/Spr 'Jock'Martin
J/Spr 'Jock' McGregor	J/Spr 'Paddy' O'Malley
J/Spr 'Rab' Peacock	J/Spr 'Jock' P
J/Spr 'Paul' Raynor	J/Spr 'Taff' Roberts
J/Spr ' ? ' Simmons	J/Spr 'Rocker' Smith
J/Spr 'Tiny' Strachan	J/Spr 'Taff' Thomas (me)
J/Spr ' ? ' Turner	J/Spr 'Wils' Wilson

Please note: I have used the ranks we were given when we first joined as I cannot remember exactly who was promoted and when!

Chapter 3 – 24 Field Squadron RE

After a brief spell at 34 Field Squadron RE, who were part of 39 Engineer Regiment RE, based at Waterbeach in Cambridgeshire, I was posted to 24 Field Squadron RE because of rugby, and little did I know it at the time, but 'rugby' would govern my whole army career and ultimately be responsible for me leaving the forces nine years later. I had been looking forward to a 3-5 year posting in Cambridge as the area held special memories (as seen in Chapter one, I had lived in Soham as a child, had family living in Ely and as a result, had also started playing rugby for Ely rugby club). I was enjoying life, playing rugby for Ely U19s, I also played for Cambridgeshire U19s and was chosen to play in the Eastern Counties final trial (due to the posting to 24 Field Squadron I missed the chance to attend). I also played rugby for the Corps (Royal Engineers), the Army U19s and Combined Services U19s, and this resulted in me being told that I would not be going to Belize in January 1982 with 34 Field Squadron. Instead, I was placed on general duties and was sent to work in the officers mess. One of the roles of this new position was serving behind the bar in the mess, and it was during one of the lunchtime shifts that I received the devastating news that I was to be posted to Chatham, I can still remember the conversation to this day;

"Could I please have a tomato juice Sapper Thomas"

"Yes Sir" and I proceeded to open the Britvic bottle of tomato juice and pour it into a glass for my OC.

"Here you go Sir" The OC took the glass and turned away from the bar, but almost immediately turned around and asked;

"Do you have any Worcestershire sauce Sapper Thomas"

"Yes. Sorry Sir" and passed the bottle of Lea and Perrins Worcestershire sauce from behind the bar. The OC took the bottle shook a few drops into his tomato juice and again turned away from the bar. He instantly turned back to me and said;

"Oh, by the way...I forgot to tell you...you are posted on Monday"

"Pardon Sir" I said in astonishment

"Yes. You are posted on Monday to 24 Field Squadron. I was supposed to ask you a few days ago and get back to REMRO (Royal Engineers Manning and Records Office), but...it

slipped my damn mind. So...I knew you'd want to go because of rugby and told them that you'd love to go...so that's it...good luck Sapper Thomas"
So my time in Waterbeach came to an abrubt end and during the signing of my 'clearance' form (whenever a soldier left a regiment/squadron a clearance form had to be completed – signatures required from various departments etc within in the associated camp) I was asked several times;
"24 Field Squadron!...God, what have you done wrong?...You know it's nicknamed 24 Penal Squadron...it's where they send all the troublemakers!!"

I was still only eighteen years old when I arrived in Chattenden in November 1981 and I was twenty three years old when I left in May 1986. Looking back, they were arguably the best years of my life...young, free and single (most of the time)!!! However, I arrived with a high degree of reluctance, which was compounded during those first few months, as the amount of rugby I played isolated me from other troop members who became irritated and frustrated at having to cover for me during my enforced absences. The one occasion that started this resentment was when I was due to be on guard the night before the 1981 Sappers (Royal Engineers) v Gunners (Royal Artillery) game. Thirty minutes before the guard was due to parade, the Duty NCO received a call stating under no circumstances was I to be on guard as I had been selected to play in the game, and that someone else in my troop would have to fill-in for me...this did not endear me to fellow troop members at the time! This worsened as the months went by as I was spending more and more time on the rugby field and on average, I was only working one and a half days a week. It resulted in me becoming more and more isolated, and as a result, I withdrew into myself and it was only rugby that kept me going! Thankfully, one of the troop lance corporals, Iain George (who was also the captain of the squadron rugby team), highlighted matters to our troop commander and I was provided with some options that would hopefully alleviate my situation; I could transfer to another field troop (there were three field troops in a squadron and their main responsibilities were combat engineering and construction tasks) or transfer to HQ troop and become a driver, storeman or clerk! I chose the latter and became a

119

Clerk RE…unfortunately, this meant giving up on my chosen trade of becoming a painter and decorator!!

Following the transfer to HQ troop I began to enjoy life again and even developed friendships with members of one troop, now that their frustrations had been removed. The remainder of my time at 24 Field Squadron was incredible, despite there being many ups and downs, I met some amazing people during this period…some of whom are still friends and some who are sadly no longer with us! The high points outweigh the low ones, especially on the sporting front (with exception of boxing), but I was also promoted to lance corporal during this period, visited some amazing places in the UK and further afield (i.e. Falkland Islands, Denmark, Germany and even Senegal…for an hour whilst they refueled the plane!) and made friendships that have transcended both distance and time. My time at 24 Field Squadron was so memorable that I could have written a book purely on those experiences, but I have chosen to be selective and have tried to cover the entire period with an equilibrium befitting the events discussed. I served under four OCs (Officer Commanding) and three SSMs (Squadron Sergeant Major) and there were contrasting memories that were created as a result…some good and some not so good, but that's life!!! Additionally, throughout the entire period there were some memorable experiences that won't be covered in the stories of this chapter, such as;

Spr Coupland who had a massive drink problem and just happened to be one of my room-mates when I first arrived at Chattenden (he eventually sold all his army clothes/equipment and ended up in the drying out clinic in Woolwich);
Coming back from a weekend of rugby and seeing Christine Christmas (one of the WRACs) crying her eyes out and running naked down three troop's corridor;
Major Newns giving his farewell address to the squadron and then seeing his car (Mercedes) completely stripped (doors, wheels, bonnet, boot etc) and driven into his view on a flatbed – priceless!;
Enjoying the army obsession of 'hurry up and wait' (the art of rushing somewhere and then waiting around for hours!),
Corridor parties,
Volleyball on Salisbury Plain!,
Spr Holman refusing to soldier (all over in minutes!),

*Rab Keil's ability to start fights when he was drunk and could
barely stand…and then getting battered,*
Carl Allen's failure to pay the taxi driver in Denmark,
*Our QM, Capt Bobby Lampard, who was the elder brother of
Frank Lampard Snr and uncle to Frank Lampard;*
Trips to the Admiral Beatty in Gravesend;
The Pram Race winners at the Chattenden open day in 1983;
*The 4 tonner incident in Chatham High Street when the
wagon, driven by Spr Lyons, had picked up the married guys
from Brompton, clipped an Opel Manta on Chatham High
Street sending it crashing through an India restaurant
window. At the same time the 4 tonner tipped onto its side and
slid 30-50m down the road, with the lads bouncing around in
the back (thankfully, no-one was injured),*
*Passport hiccups (we initially couldn't get passports for two
soldiers…it was found that they weren't British citizens!),*
*LCpl Jeremy Batchelor's ability to piss everywhere…except
the toilet!;*
*On the pull with 'Taff' Pritchard – sometimes we were lucky,
other times we…well you know!;*
Lcpl Paul Weatherhill naming his new born son…Zeus!;
*The SSM driving a landrover on the M20 and the front leftside
wheel fell off and rolled down a slip road, thankfully without
hitting anything!;*
*Laith Palmer and his permanent, heavy and outswinging limp
(following a car accident) who insisted on going on squadron
parades when he was exempt;*
*Being banned for life from a Chinese restaurant (The Jade
Garden) in Chatham because Ron Quick was sampling
food…from other peoples' tables;*
*Log runs, BFTs (Battle Fitness Test) and CFTs (Combat
Fitness Test) around Lodge Hill;*
Fridays and Saturdays in the Two Sawyers/Cannon;
*Spr 'Taff' Humphrey's famous chat-up line – "You're a big
girl…do weights do you" – classic!;*
Spr 'Jake' Maiden's famous knicker collection;
*Sid falling off a railway bridge in Gravesend onto the railway
tracks 30ft below, resulting in his discharge being put back
months (you have to be medically fit before the army will
discharge you);*
Farouk Patel's dislike of curry;

Nick Tranmer and I attempting to walk Hadrian's Wall and the rain was that bad we had to pack in after 24 hrs (we never got to see any of the wall) and many, many more.

The memories below are how I remember them, but over thirty years have gone by and the finer details may be cloudy, so I apologise in advance if there are any small inaccuracies in the stories!

Chattenden and 24 Field Squadron RE hold special memories, and therefore it saddened me, on a returning to Chatham in 2014 for a 24 Field Squadron RE reunion, to find that the old camp was no longer there (with exception of the old guardroom and a streetlight by the old squadron office), it is all fenced off and overgrown waiting for a housing estate to be built!). Thankfully, demolishing Chattenden cannot erase the memories I, and others like me, created whilst being based there…or the wonderful memories I have of the people I served with in that little corner of Kent!!!

■■

OC's Orders!

Sappers Mark Methven and Kenny Emerson were both on 'three month warning orders' for various misdemeanors…any further minor indiscretion would mean being discharged from the army! They went out in style…allegedly they took a girl back to Kenny's room after 'the stomp' for a 'bit of fun' (basically a threesome)! When the 'fun' had ended they kicked her out of the room and sent her on her way! Unfortunately, she didn't ring a taxi and go quietly home…she was pissed off that they had kicked her out of Kenny's room with not as much as a 'thank you'! She must have felt used, and in an act of revenge, she went straight to the guardroom and claimed that she had been raped!! The civilian police became involved and because of the girl's reputation (of sleeping with different soldiers almost every Thursday), she had no option other than to drop the charges she had fabricated. However, the damage was done, and this didn't help Sappers Methven and Emerson…they were charged with the lesser military charge of 'taking a member of the opposite sex into the single soldiers accommodation'…a taboo in military terms. This story provides details of what happened when Spr Methven went on

122

'OC's Orders' to face the charges described above…and I was the escort!!!

"THOMAS" shouted the sergeant major.
"YES SIR" as I ran to his office and stood to attention in the doorway.
"ESCORT…FIVE MINUTES"
"YES SIR"
I waited nervously for the five minutes to pass and then returned to the corridor where the sergeant major was speaking to Spr Methven. I approached the sergeant major, and behind him Mark Methven smiled and winked at me!
"SIR"
Without looking at me he gestured with his hand and said;
"Stand there Spr Thomas…stand at ease" and then proceeded to brief us both …it was my first time on 'escort' duty and the sergeant major knew this and attempted to put me at ease! The short briefing was quickly finished and we were set for the off! The sergeant major quickly eyed us up and down and then took a deep breath…then it began!
"ORDERS…ORDERS SHUN" thankfully, Spr Methven and I, mainly through fear, came to attention simultaneously.
"TURN TO THE LEFT…LEFT TURN"
Again, we turned to the left in one mirrored movement.
"BY THE FRONT…QUICK MARCH…LEFT, RIGHT, LEFT, RIGHT, LEFT, RIGHT, LEFT…MARK TIME…HALT…TURN TO THE RIGHT…RIGHT TURN!"
Within seconds, due to the double quick time commands, we were standing in front of the OC, who was sat behind his desk reading the 252 charge report in front of him. The OC picked up the charge report, looked at Spr Methven, and read out the details on it;
"Are you 24****** (army number) Spr M.Methven…"
During this I remained perfectly still, but my mind wandered, and my eyes scanned the paintings on the walls in the room. Then suddenly…I snapped back into reality as I heard the OC say;
"Do you have anything to say Spr Methven?" and he looked directly at Mark awaiting his response! There was a slight pause before Mark answered;
"Yes Sir"

123

"Go on Spr Methven" The OC, sergeant major and I certainly could not have forseen what came next as Mark sighed heavily and said;

"I wish I was a goldfish!"

"I beg your pardon Spr Methven!!" said the OC in shock and looking astounded at what Mark had said…as if he couldn't believe a Sapper would have the audacity to be so brazen, and Mark must have felt he had the upper hand and repeated the statement with an additional add-on;

"I wish I was a goldfish…life would be so uncomplicated as a goldfish"

I glanced at the OC who for a split second was obviously thrown by what he had just heard, but then looked at the sergeant major and shouted;

"WHAT THE…SERGEANT MAJOR GET HIM OUT OF MY OFFICE!!!"

The sergeant major glared at Methven, I swallowed hard… but Mark took it all in his stride as the sergeant major screamed;

"ORDERS…ORDERS SHUN…TURN TO THE RIGHT…RIGHT TURN…BY THE FRONT QUICK MARCH…LEFT, RIGHT, LEFT, RIGHT, LEFT, RIGHT, LEFT…MARK TIME…HALT!"

The sergeant major leant into Mark and within a couple of inches of his ear, shouted;

"WHAT THE FUCK DO YOU THINK YOU ARE PLAYING AT METHVEN…THINK YOUR FUNNY DO YOU? YOU WON'T BE LAUGHING WHEN I STICK THIS UP YOUR ARSE!" and he brought his pace stick up into Mark's vision. This wasn't the way I envisaged how 'orders' would be and had no idea what was going on…I just remained perfectly still and stared straight ahead hoping this nightmare would end!!!

Within minutes we were back in front of the OC, and this time Mark behaved and accepted the OC's award…which was to be sent in front of the CO (commanding officer of 12 RSME Regiment – the OC did not have the power to discharge Spr Methven, this had to be done by the CO). Inevitably, both Mark Methven and Kenny Emerson went in front of the CO, and were both dishonorably discharged!

Looking back, immediately after my first experience of being 'escort' I was sat in the squadron office like a shell-shocked budgie!! It wasn't my last outing as an 'escort', but it always remained the most bizarre!! In my opinion, Mark knew his army career was over and chose to go out in style! He was a brave man to throw two fingers up at such a historic and disciplined military tradition, and I bet he's 'dined out' on that story over the years…the day he laughed in the face of adversity!!!

Taxi for Thomas

It was March 1982 and I was in the Queen Elizabeth Military Hospital at Woolwich (QEMH Woolwich) following a bad case of glandular fever. I had returned from two weeks sick leave, and the first question I needed to ask the doctor (a military doctor who possessed the rank of major) at his ward round the following day (Monday) was 'when would I be discharged?'…the final of the South East Minor Units rugby final against 9 Para Squadron RE was scheduled for Wednesday afternoon in Aldershot! The following day I asked the doctor the question;

"When will I be discharged Sir" The doctor was writing on my notes and without looking up he answered nonchalantly;
"Oh…tomorrow…I'd imagine Spr Thomas!"
"That's great Sir…I'm playing rugby on Wednesday" The doctor stopped writing, dropped the pen on the paper and looked up. He didn't look pleased;
"YOU WILL NOT BE PLAYING RUGBY ON WEDNESDAY SPR THOMAS" and he glared at me, popped my notes back on their rightful place at the end of the bed and moved on to the next patient!
The following day, before I had a chance to say anything, the doctor said;
"I have spoken with your squadron and have told them that you will not be available to play on Wednesday…and that's the end of it Spr Thomas!"
I was devastated, but determined to make it for the final and spent the rest of that day/night thinking, 'what can I do?'
Early the following morning I rang the MT (motor transport) back at 24 and spoke to Cpl 'Bud' Flannigan and told him I'd been discharged and I needed transport to pick me up from QEMH Woolwich and take me to Aldershot for the game! I made sure my rugby kit and other equipment was all packed…and waited!!!

It was approaching midday when Cpl 'Bud' Flannigan appeared on the ward and immediately said;

"You ready Taff?"

"I'll just go and ask the doctor again" and left Bud stood by my hospital bed looking slightly bemused!

I wandered over to the nurses station in the main corridor where the doctor was talking to one of the staff nurses. I hung around waiting for them to finish their conversation and then said;

"Excuse me Sir…can I be discharged now…" before I had a chance to finish the doctor shouted;

"SAPPER THOMAS…I HAVE TOLD YOU THAT YOU ARE NOT PLAYING RUGBY…GO BACK TO YOUR WARD BAY IMMEDIATELY AND STAY THERE"

I wandered back to where Bud was standing, and he was still a bewildered about what was going on! Bud saw me coming and said;

"Well…"

"He won't discharge me"

"What…you rang up this morning and told me you'd been discharged" he whispered

"I know…but I am going to this game…this is what we'll do…before you turn into the ward, there's a TV room…if you wait in there. I'll go out through the door there…" I pointed towards a door that led into an internal garden that couldn't be accessed from the outside, but there was a door from the TV room that opened out into the same garden!!

"…and I'll step into the garden and make my over to the TV room…you can open the door…and then we can head out of the hospital and head off to Aldershot…easy!!!"

Bud looked at me and thought about it for a second and said;

"OK…but you better not get me in the shit for this!" he whispered. I gave him my rugby bag and he headed out of the ward toward the TV room. I waited for the right opportunity and was soon knocking on the door of the TV room. Bud opened the door and within seconds we were sprinting down one of the main hospital corridors, turned right at the end of the corridor, past the hospital shop and toward the main entrance. Such was the urgency to get out of the hospital, Bud was having no problems keeping up with me and his side-stepping skills were equal to mine as we dodged patients, staff and visitors in our bid for freedom! We reached the main

126

entrance and without looking back we ran to the waiting landrover, I threw my sports bag in first and then followed it diving in to the back head first as Bud jumped into the front passenger side and shouted at the driver, Spr Roger Dewar; "GO...GO...GO...DEWAR...GET US THE FUCK OUT OF HERE!"
Roger panicked, he had no idea as to what was happening and stalled the landrover!
"For fuck sake Dewar...get a fucking grip!"
Roger started the landrover again, and we were off, and as we pulled away from the hospital he asked inquisitively;
"What's going on Bud?" and Bud tutted, pointed to me and said;
"The stupid Welsh fucker in the back has gone AWOL (absent without leave) from the hospital...just to play rugby"
"CHEERS BUD...CHEERS ROGER...THAT WAS A GOOD LAUGH" I shouted from the back in an attempt at drowning out the noise of the engine, and Bud replied;
"Fuck off Taff!" and he started laughing to himself and mumbled;
"Crazy Welsh wanker!!"

We pulled into the military stadium just before 2pm...we had made it! Thanking Bud and Roger, I then sprinted across the car park, into the clubhouse, bursting into the changing room as Iain George was delivering his pre-match 'words of wisdom' in an attempt to fire everyone up...not that they needed firing up against 9 Para Squadron RE. The changing room fell quiet as they wondered where I'd come from, all believing I was stuck in hospital!! It was Tiny Bott, SSM and one of the squadron second rows, who spoke first;
"What are you fucking doing here Thommo?...we were told you wouldn't be discharged!"
"I'm AWOL Sir!" Tiny paused momentarily, smiled knowingly and then said;
"I didn't hear that Thommo...now get your kit on..."
Looking around the changing room Tiny saw Les King and shouted;
"...KING GET THAT SHIRT OFF AND GIVE IT TO THOMMO"
Les King reluctantly gave me the shirt and I knew at that moment...he hated me for robbing him of the chance of playing in the final! I got changed and when the pre-match

'talk' and warm-up had finished we made our way to one of the pitches on Queen's Avenue (opposite the stadium) where the game would be played. As we jogged to the pitch, Tiny winked at me and said;

"We'll sort this mess out after the game...now let's go and beat these fucking para engineers!"

We won a close, hard fought match against 9 Para Squadron RE, 21 – 14, and the most enjoyable part was that the victory was in front of their entire squadron (they had made the short journey of about 600m from their camp to the rugby pitch). After we got changed Tiny and I sat in the corner of the bar to work out what we could say to the hospital;

"Right Thommo...this is what we'll do...you go straight back to Woolwich and tell them ...that...you went back to Chatham but..."

Tiny paused for a moment before banging the table with his fist and continuing;

"...but after a couple hours it was realised that you didn't have any discharge papers and...you've been sent back to Woolwich..."

He sat back momentarily and then leant forward, smiled and continued:

"Let's hope that if they decide to charge you that they ask us to deal with it...now off you go!"

There was no celebratory drink with the team, it was straight back to Woolwich with Tiny's story...seemed foolproof to me!!!

It was around 6.30pm when I sheepishly entered the ward back at QEMH Woolwich and found the duty staff nurse. I began to relay the story that Tiny had told me to use, but before I could finish, one of the nurses came out of the side room nearest the nurses station and shouted;

"HI TAFF...DID YOU WIN...DID YOU WIN!!"

Damn I was rumbled...the story unraveled and potentially, I was in the shit again! A short time later, in possession of my signed discharge papers, I left the ward with my tail firmly between my legs. I made my way back to the landrover waiting outside and Bud, Roger and I headed back to Chattenden!!!

It was about six or seven weeks later, and I was sat at my desk in the squadron office, when without warning I heard the now familiar shout of;

"THOMAS…MY OFFICE NOW!!" I was out my chair like shit off a stick and stood to attention outside the sergeant major's office in seconds;

"SIR"

The sergeant major, Tiny Bott, was an intimidating character, a 6ft 5in Yorkshireman with a deep, booming Yorkshire accent. He was stood behind his desk and holding two 252 charge reports in his hand, he looked at me and held the charge reports up so I could see them properly and said;

"Do you know what these are Thomas" I had forgotten all about going AWOL from hospital and said;

"NO SIR"

"This one I could forget…" and he waved one of the charge reports in his left hand;

"…going AWOL from the hospital" the penny now dropped, and I now realised what this was all about, but what was the second charge report for…I would soon find out as Tiny continued;

"But this one…DISOBEYING A DIRECT ORDER!!" He looked at me disapprovingly and my heart sank and the reality of the situation hit home. There was an eerie silence that descended on the room as he looked at me and then looked at the charge reports three or four times, and then with a broad smile, he screwed them up and threw them over his shoulder into the bin and said;

"Aahh fuck it…you did it for the good of the squadron…dismissed" I could hear his booming laughter as I sat back down at my desk relieved that my little ordeal was over!!!!

Falklands 1982-83

Following the Falklands conflict that ended in June 1982, there was a requirement for a re-construction program which meant there would be a major Royal Engineers presence required in the Falkland Islands. Therefore, it was no surprise that our squadron would eventually have to go, and the inevitable happened when I was on my 'clerks course' at Blackdown Barracks in Surrey…we would be leaving for a six month tour in early/mid November 1982. On hearing the news

129

there were many thoughts running through my head, such as;
What about my rugby? (I had received a letter from London
Welsh inviting me to join), what if the Argies re-invade?
(There had been rumours!!), what would the weather be like?
How are we getting there? What will our accommodation be
like? There were many, many more questions rattling around
in my head, but those questions would soon be answered! It
would be an eventful six months, and I am proud to have
served my country in the Falkland Islands, even it was only in
a small capacity!!

The OC had finished his briefing to us all about our tour to the
Falkland Islands and finished by saying;
"GENTLEMEN…THE QM WOULD LIKE A FEW
WORDS! He stepped aside and the QM (Quartermaster), Capt
Jim Benson, stood in front of us, cleared his throat, grinned
and addressed the squadron;
"RIGHT YOU'VE HAD THE BAD NEWS…NOW I'M
GOING TO GIVE YOU THE GOOD NEWS…WHEN WE
ARE IN THE FALKLANDS, WE WILL GET THE
CHANCE FOR A SPOT…OF…R&R, REST &
RECUPERATION! I HAVE CHECKED OUT POSSIBLE
LOCATIONS AND AM PLEASED TO ANNOUNCE THAT
WE HAVE FOUND THE PERFECT PLACE FOR YOU
ALL. SOMETIME DURING THE MIDDLE OF THE TOUR,
ROUND ABOUT MID JANUARY, WE WILL ALL BE
FLOWN TO ACAPULCO!!…PACK YOUR SWIMMING
TRUNKS, SUN CREAM AND SPEEDOS, IT'LL BE
GREAT…ACAPULCO
GENTLEMEN…ACA…FUCKING..PULCO…YES!!
This got a mixed reaction, there were those (myself included)
who were thrilled and positively 'bouncing' with excitement at
the thought of visiting such an iconic place, made famous by
the Elvis Presley film 'Fun in Acapulco'. However, there were
those (the 'old sweats') who didn't believe the QM…but
didn't say anything and lastly, those who had never heard of
Acapulco, never mind know where it was located!!!

A few weeks later and the night before our flight to Ascension
Island (an island in the middle of the Atlantic and just south of
the equator), we were in a large transit hall at RAF Lyneham
making those last frantic calls to loved ones before we went
'off the radar'…letters (including forces airmail – a blue fold

130

out envelope that could be written on and sent f.o.c) would be the only communication available for the next six months!!! Twenty four hours later we were on the Cunard Countess (our luxury transport to the Falklands), following a twelve hour flight (with no in-flight entertainment system…our only entertainment was looking at the peachy bum of the air hostess as she walked down the aisle of the plane! There was an hour stopover in Dakar, Senegal to refuel the plane (as we were in uniform we had to stand on the side of the runway in the midday heat), and once we landed at Ascension we were taken by helicopter to the Cunard Countess…our six month tour had begun!!

The sea voyage to Port Stanley took ten days and during that time there wasn't a great deal to do! There were a couple of token PE sessions and a couple of lectures, but most of the time we were left to our own devices. However, we were treated to some miniscule sights of nature, such as; the voracious trigger fish (eating the rubbish thrown overboard when we were moored at Ascension), two sea turtles, a whale, but the most amazing sight was the sight of an albatross gliding on the breeze in the wake of the ship…an impressive sight of, what looked like a seagull on steroids with an impressive wingspan!! One thing that did change, the further south we went, was the weather! Initially, we had been sunbathing and using the pool on deck during the first couple of days, but when we hit the 'Roaring Forties' (where the North and South Atlantic meet) and beyond it was 'batten down the hatches' and the journey was much rougher and there were certainly some 'butt-clenching' moments!! It was a welcome relief when we eventually arrived at the Falkland Islands…initially!!!

On arrival, accommodation was the first priority, and as it could still be considered as 'early days' following the conflict, there wasn't a great deal of accommodation on land, in and around Port Stanley, to house the influx of soldiers landing on the islands to deal with post-conflict requirements. However, there were ships that had been requisitioned as accommodation that were moored in the inner harbour, including the RFA Sir Tristram (the ship that was with the RFA Sir Galahad when it was bombed and consequently sunk during the conflict). It was one of these ships, the Rangatira,

131

that, along with about 20-30 members of the squadron, would be home…for the first week! I was only on the Rangatira for a short period as my bed space was the top bunk of a triple bunk system with about 12-18 inches between me and a hot-water pipe…it was like sleeping in a sauna. I quickly swapped this 'sweat box' for a room at the back of the garage, which was part of the bungalow on Davis Street where the squadron office was situated, I was lucky that I had running water…I had to 'run' and fetch it every morning!! The OC, SSM, 2ic and Chief Clerk were also housed in the bungalow on Davis Street…the remainder of the squadron were all bedded down in the town hall in Port Stanley, a large imposing building sitting on the edge of the inner harbour. Such is 'squaddie' humour the previous occupants, 50 Field Squadron RE, had left us a lovely message written on the wall which read;

"Jingle Bells, jingle bells 50's gone away
How much fun it is to have Christmas in the UK"

The main task of the squadron was re-building roads, and this involved blasting the rock at a quarry near Port Stanley airport, running these larger rocks through 'rock crushers' and then transporting the 'hardcore' by sea and land to the various sites in the Falklands (the sea route was necessary as the threat of mines was still very real!). This work was carried out by a mix of two, three and Support troops and drivers from HQ troop (a squadron is made up of 5 troops…HQ, support, 1, 2 & 3 troops). However, one troop were constructing the foundations for rub shelters/hangars for the RAF at Port Stanley airport. I was seconded to one troop for a short period and thoroughly enjoyed the nightly visits to the RAF medical centre to have all the cement dust removed from my eyes. However, one night I thought my eyes were fine so I didn't visit the medical centre. I regretted that decision, as I woke up in the morning thinking I was blind, the fine particles of cement dust had 'set' in my eyes and they were firmly shut…it was back to the medical centre to have my eyes 'opened'!!

The first couple of months saw everyone working long hours, and as clerks our long days were extended when someone in the squadron thought it would be a good idea to write to 'The Sun, Daily Mirror and Daily Star' asking for pen-pals…this quadrupled the amount of mail we received as public feeling towards servicemen and women was still running high back home!! The mail came in via a Hercules (the only large plane that could land on Port Stanley's short runway) and was a welcome sight when it could be seen coming into land in the daily flights from Ascension. Very occasionally, due to bad weather, those daily flights would be cancelled, resulting in a general 'downer' amongst the troops!! The additional mail caused by the request for pen-pals resulted in us taking a lot longer to sort the mail, but it was worth it...everyone in the squadron was now writing to 30+ pen-pals each, in addition to family and friends, and these letters were a lifeline and kept morale high during long periods of inactivity!! The hard work was rewarded at Christmas as we enjoyed two days off, and the celebration started on Christmas Eve with a squadron disco upstairs in the town hall. There was a distinct lack of local girls...well none to be precise, so the disco consisted of music, lots of beer, approximately one hundred and eighty men and a...rubber doll!!! The rubber doll was for dancing only and there was a strict rota system deployed to ensure everyone had the pleasure of dancing with this ideal woman (she didn't speak and demanded nothing!!), but as the evening drew to a close our 'latex friend' became a football, as a room full of drunken squaddies thought this would be more fun...great night!! My memory of Christmas Day is sketchy to say the least, I vaguely remember that my Christmas dinner consisted of a slice of turkey and a mince pie (I had missed Christmas dinner as I had the hangover from hell and as I was asleep in my garage they forgot about me when they went round on Christmas morning with 'gunfire': A traditional free tot of rum when soldiers served away from home). Whilst I ate my slice of turkey I put my mince pie down and someone pinched it...bastards! The only other memory I have of Christmas day 1982 is wandering around the RFA Sir Tristram with a bottle of Asbach (German brandy) in my hand, singing '*Wild Thing*' by The Troggs!!

During our tour there was a visit by Margaret Thatcher (the then British Prime Minister), a celebration of the 150th anniversary of the Falkland Islands being British, but there was one event I remember that was heartbreaking...the families of the 258 British servicemen who lost their lives in the Falklands conflict, came to visit Port Stanley. The haunting image of fathers, mothers, wives, children,

133

girlfriends etc, some of whom must have still been struggling to come to terms with their grief, are images that I would never wish to witness again! They bore resemblance to zombies as they wandered round the streets of Port Stanley probably thinking; "Did my loved one really die for THIS!" No offence to the Falkland Islanders, but those families must have seen no redeeming qualities in the islands that could have eased their suffering…to outsiders it seems like an unforgiving place…sad…very, very sad!!

As we approached the middle of our tour, the coastel (floating hotel) finally arrived and was moored overlooking Whalebone Cove, nestled in an inlet roughly halfway between Port Stanley and the airport. This accommodation was luxury compared to what we had been used to; three man rooms, fully equipped ablutions c/w hot water, a large mess hall (canteen) serving three hot meals a day and a large portakabin located within 100m that served as a bar…where the prices were VERY low; Beer/lager (30p a can), shorts (10p a tot), cigarettes (30p for a pack of 20) and cans of coke and Fanta (10p)…but no glasses! There was also a video player normally running, showing a film or a selection of porn, and as people walked to and from the bar you'd hear the familiar shout of; "SIT DOWN YOU CUNT!!" An affectionate term used between soldiers. We had some great nights in that bar; watching films (and porn), chatting, playing cards and 'singing games', and it provided a welcome relief from the long hours we worked throughout the tour!!

The latter part of the tour saw a turning point in the general mood of everyone in the squadron, people became more agitated and quick-tempered and this was highlighted one evening in a squadron get together in the squadron mess tent at Port Stanley airport! I'm not sure what happened, but Spr Roger Dewar (yes, the same Roger Dewar that drove the landrover when I went AWOL from QEMH Woolwich to play rugby) was hit by several different people that night… this included both the QM, Capt Jim Benson and our troop staff sergeant, SSgt Lonnen! After this party (well, squaddies getting drunk in a big tent!), Jack Sutton and I decided to walk back to the coastel (floating hotel), and as the 4 tonner drove past taking the lads back all I could hear coming from the back was;

"THWACK…OOH!"
"UMPH…UH!"
"KATHUD…NG!
"BOOPH…AAH!
It was Roger getting ANOTHER beating!!
In the early hours of the morning I remember going to the
toilet and could hear a noise coming from one of the cubicles,
I walked over and tentatively pushed the door open and there
was Roger…receiving another beating off the squadron welder
(his name escapes me but he was normally a quiet, easy going
lad), and he looked up and said;
"Hiya Taff"
"Everything OK Butt" I replied
"Yeah" as he hit Roger one more time and then left him
groaning and sitting next to the toilet, with his arm around the
toilet bowl and his head resting on the seat and looking
decidedly battered and bruised!! Judging by the events I had
witnessed, Roger had obviously pissed off a lot of people, but
to this day I had no idea why!!

The time came to leave the Falklands and it was our turn to
request songs on the local radio station dedicated to those
squadrons who were only half way through their tours, songs
such as; 'Sailing' by Rod Stewart, 'Tie a Yellow Ribbon' by
Dawn and 'I'm leaving on a jet plane' by Peter, Paul and
Mary. There was no regret that we were leaving…just pure
joy!! I stood on the deck of the RFA Sir Geraint, looked
towards Port Stanley and remembered some of the things from
the tour, such as; The minefield we laid in the Argentinian
minefield (I generated the required NATO minefield
map/form), the rugby and football we played (there was a
minefield behind the rugby pitch and the football pitch near
Government House used camouglage nets as goal nets!), The
squadron newsletter we published – Penguin News, the
'haulamatic incident' when the Port Ops officer decided to
load eight haulamatics on to the mexeflote (motorized floating
raft) instead of the maximum six , but the extra weight was too
much and the mexeflote tilted and the haulamatics (and
drivers) slid into the sea…thankfully, no-one was injured!, the
F.I.B.S. (Falkland Island Broadcasting Station) radio station
which was so unprofessional…but nevertheless a source of
great hilarity, the locals or 'Bennys' as we called them, named
after a TV character called 'Benny' (a backward but jovial

135

character with a wooly hat!) from a program called 'Crossroads', my friendship with a Gurkha called Agam Bahardur Limbu, the bible thumping and teetotal CO of 37 Engineer Regiment RE, Col Ivers, who I witnessed awarding an unfair punishment to a soldier (who had hit another soldier once in self-defence), his punishment was to be fined a month's wages and banned from drinking for the remainder of his tour (3 months) and finally, my 24 hours R&R on a water tanker moored in the outer harbour where I just drank myself into oblivion! If you hadn't already guessed, there was no R&R to Acapulco…the QM, Capt Jim Benson had basically lied!!!

The journey back to Ascension was horrendous…the flat bottomed RFA literally bounced back! This resulted in most of the squadron coming down with sea sickness (I was one of the few lucky ones who was OK), and with it being so hot below deck everyone used the mattress covers as sleeping bags resulting in the rooms resembling morgues. One funny story in all this misery happened one morning at breakfast, during the rougher part of the journey! I was heading toward a table with my tray (similar to those compartmental metal trays you see in prisons) of cooked breakfast, cereal and coffee…we hit a wave and 'SPLOOPH' the contents of my entire tray landed on another soldier's head! The entire mess hall erupted into fits of laughter, well, all except one person…LCpl Craig Booker who was still picking beans, egg, tinned tomatoes, cornflakes and milk out of his hair!!!

We arrived at Ascension Island, and the following morning we were airlifted by helicopter to a waiting plane that took us back to Brize Norton. The in-flight entertainment was again looking at the arse of the air hostess, but there was more perverted intent on the return journey as we hadn't seen a proper women for six months. Additionally, as we flew into Brize Norton there were shouts of;
"LOOK…A CAR!" (We didn't see any cars in the Falklands…only landrovers!)
"…TREES TAFF!" (nor trees, apart from a couple of windswept trees in Port Stanley)
"…A HOUSE…I CAN SEE A HOUSE…WITH A TILED ROOF!" (Houses in the Falkland Islands were mainly built with corrugated sheets of galvanized iron or steel).

136

If you've ever seen pictures of the Falkland Islands you might understand our excitement at seeing such basic everyday objects! Once through customs we boarded two buses and headed back to Chattenden, but as we came through London the pubs were emptying…there were women everywhere! I often wonder what they thought as our two buses drove past, with steamed-up windows, soldiers banging the glass and shouting obscenities (and lewd suggestions) out of the windows to the confused onlookers outside!! We arrived back at Chattenden just after midnight, and following the clearing of some essential laundry, and a shower, it was off to catch the mail train to London to enjoy a well-deserved four week leave!!

Water Bowser

Sitting in the 'dustbowl' that is Salisbury Plain is not a fun place to be…I was relieved, when I was delegated and ordered to go with Spr Maxwell to fill the squadron water bowser! It would be great to get off Salisbury Plain for an hour or so and this was a nice cushy number…how difficult would it be to go and fill the water bowser. As it turned out, this 'cushy number' turned into the stuff of nightmares!!!

I looked at my watch as we passed the unimpressive site of Stonehenge…it was 16.15hrs, and we'd only been away from the harbour area about fifteen minutes. I looked at the driver, Max, and he said;
"I've got an idea Taff…to save some time we could use the tank washdown point at Larkhill…to fill the water bowser" he said enthusiastically.
"OK Max…sounds good…do you…do you know how to get there?"
"Yeah…it's not far from the A303…and…it's closer than Tidworth" Max sounded pleased with himself as he drove along the Amesbury by-pass. We took the left turn at the roundabout, signposted Larkhill, and within ten minutes we were parked up! Max turned the engine off and immediately jumped out of the 4 tonner and then shut the cab door, but within seconds he re-opened the cab door and stood there looking perplexed,
"What is it Max?" I asked inquisitively.
"…Taff…the water…"

137

"Spit it out Max…what's wrong?"

"…the water…the water bowser…it's missing!"

"WHAT?...FUCK OFF MAX…STOP PISSING ABOUT" and I jumped out of the cab and walked down the side of the 4 tonner. I stopped dead in my tracks…there was a huge, empty space where the water bowser should have been!! Max and I stood there staring at each other, and then stared at the space where the water bowser should've been. Max then said;

"Told you Taff…it's not there!"

"I CAN FUCKING SEE THAT MAX…HOW THE…WHAT DO YOU…I CAN'T BELIEVE THIS IS HAPPENING…"

"NOR ME!" Max interrupted, as we both stood there in complete shock and disbelief.

"RIGHT…WE'LL HAVE TO RETRACE OUR STEPS…CUMON MAX!"

We walked back to the cab down our respective sides of the 4 tonner, climbed back in and sat there in silence for a moment as we both tried to comprehend what was happening!!

We set off and went back the way we had come scanning the area left and right as we went, and when we reached the roundabout that dissected the Amesbury bypass we turned right onto the A303 and headed towards Stonehenge! Within a couple of hundred yards Max shouted;

"THERE IT IS!"

I looked across and there it was, in a ditch at a right angle and only partially visible! We drove to the next roundabout, a few miles past Stonehenge, turned back on ourselves and were soon parked up alongside the water bowser. We jumped out of the 4 tonner and stood there scratching our heads wondering how it detached itself from the 4 tonner, and also wondering how we were going to get the damn thing out of the bloody ditch!!

As if by a stroke of luck, two 4 tonners drove past and they must have recognised our cap badges because, as it turned out, they were from 22 Engineer Regiment RE, and they turned around at the next roundabout, and a few minutes later they were parked up behind us to help their fellow Sappers! Luckily, one of their vehicles was fitted with a winch and the water bowser was soon sitting behind our 4 tonner ready to be re-hitched! We thanked our fellow 'Sappers' and they were gone. We checked over the water bowser and apart from a couple of small dents and a smashed tail light it was OK. Once we had hitched the bowser back to the 4 tonner we were soon on our way again, but this time we decided to head straight for Jellalabad Barracks, Tidworth…where we were originally told to go by the SSM, Tiny Bott!!

We spent twenty minutes driving up and down Park Road and Bulford Road, but we couldn't find Jellalabad Barracks and decided to try our luck by pulling into the nearest camp. Unfortunately, the camp we chose housed 1 RTR (Royal Tank Regiment), who we knew were part of the 'enemy' on the exercise…we were hedging our bets with this one!! We pulled up to the main gate and we were stopped by a soldier with a distinct Scottish accent and I thought "we'll be ok here as Max was also a Jock!" Max wound down the window and asked;
"Any chance of filling our water bowser laddie?"
"What's your unit?" He growled.
"24 Field Squadron RE…attached to 22 Engineer Regiment"
He reached inside the guard hut and pulled out a clipboard, and he scanned down the list in front of him before frowning and saying;
"Nay fucking chance…ma list says ur the enemy…you'll get nay fucking water here…na fuck off away ya wee shites!!"
We reversed back out as the guard laughed and flicked V's at us with his two fingers!
It was back to the drawing board, and returned to the search for Jelllalabad Barracks…after another fifteen to twenty minutes we were parked on the main square of Jellalabad Barracks, waiting for two members of the guard to bring the standpipe and hose from the guardroom!!

One of the guard was manning the standpipe, the other was sitting on the water bowser manning the hose! They were happy that everything was connected correctly, and nodded to each other in confirmation before the lad sitting on the bowser shouted;
"WATER ON"
"WATER ON" shouted his mate at the standpipe, but almost immediately…disaster!! The hose came away from the standpipe and water was spewing all over the square. In panic the lad on the bowser shouted;
"WATER OFF…WATER OFF!"

As the other guard was turning the water off…their nightmare intensified as the Regimental Sergeant Major appeared from nowhere and ranted;
"WHAT THE FUCK IS HAPPENING TO MY SQUARE YOU PAIR OF FUCKING IDIOTS…LOOK AT IT…LOOK AT IT!!"
His pride and joy was awash with water, and he continued red-faced with his military meltdown!
"I WILL PUT YOU TWO ON GUARD FOR THE REST OF YOUR NATURAL LIVES IF YOU DON'T…GET A GRIP!"
"YES SIR!" They replied in unison and the RSM disappeared as quickly as he'd appeared! The two soldiers made sure that everything ran smoothly the second time by ensuring they run the water at a reduced flow so that the pressure was less intense. The last thing they wanted to do was experience, for a second time, the wrath of the RSM, and after ten to fifteen minutes the lad on the bowser shouted;
"WATER OFF" His mate turned the water off, and as the last drops trickled from the hose, the hose was removed from the bowser, the main cover was closed and the young private jumped off onto the square. A few minutes later we were driving off the square with a full water bowser and heading to their MT section to refuel the 4 tonner. Whilst Max re-fuelled the 4 tonner I sat in the cab and looked at my watch, it was twenty past eight…we'd now been away from our harbour area for over four hours! I could see a pattern developing as we drifted into the real possibility of being 'in the shit!' for this lengthy absence…this would be compounded by events over the next couple of hours!!

The wagon was now re-fuelled and we left Jellalabad Barracks and I thought; "Great, we should be back by nine…I'll be able to get 3-4 hours sleep before my turn on stag (guard) at 1am. It was then that Max suggested;
"Why don't you get your head down Taff…I'll get us back to the squadron.
"You sure Max" I replied tentatively
"Aye…nay problem!"
"OK Butt" It had been a long day and as the headlights of other vehicles flashed past, in the dusk of that summer's evening, I found it hypnotic and within a few minutes I had drifted off into a deep sleep! The next thing I remember is hearing Max calling me;

"Taff…Taff…wake up…I'm lost!!" I stirred, rubbed my eyes, yawned and said;

"Uh…what you say?"

"I'm lost" Max repeated.

We pulled over and as Max stopped the 4 tonner I looked at my watch, it was 9.45pm! I grabbed the map and a torch, jumped out of the cab and said to Max;

"Wait here…I can see lights up ahead…I'll take a walk down there…" I pointed down the road in the direction of what looked like a small village.

"…I'll try and work out where we are…and find a way back to the harbour area"

"OK Taff" Max replied and yawned…we'd now been away from camp for nearly six hours!

I started walking in the direction of the lights and within a few minutes I was standing in front of one of those typical British village signs; 'You are now entering the picturesque village of…FENITON…! and underneath the words that shocked me to the core '…in the county of Devon'. I thought; "What had Max done? He must have got lost and then trundled down the A303 and just kept going onto the A30. How could someone by so stupid". Devon was a big county, so I followed the A30 on the map until I recognised the border of Devon/Somerset, and then looked more intently at the villages to the left and right of the A30! After a few minutes, I found Feniton on the map…it was roughly halfway between Honiton and Exeter, and I couldn't believe that Max had carried on driving for OVER 70 MILES!!! I was fuming and ran back to the 4 tonner and as I opened the cab door I could see Max was sleeping…but not for long!

"MAX…" I shouted "…WAKE UP" Max yawned and said;

"Taff…is that you"

"YES IT'S ME…" I shouted "…YOU STUPID JOCK TWAT…WE ARE ALMOST IN EXETER…WHAT DO YOU THINK YOU WERE DOING…YOU CARRIED ON DRIVING FOR 70 FUCKING MILES…WHY?...YOU SHOULD HAVE WOKEN ME UP FOR FUCK SAKE…YOU DO KNOW THAT TINY IS GOING TO RIP OUR HEADS OFF WHEN…OR IF…WE EVER GET BACK!!!"

"Sorry Taff…I didn't want to wake you because you are on guard at 1!"

"fuck me…we may not even get back in time now for me to go on stag! Cumon, let's turn this thing around and head back" "OK Taff…sorry!"

I got us back to the harbour area and needless to say, guess who was waiting for us…yes, Tiny!!
"Where the fuck have you two been…you've been gone for eight hours…eight fucking hours…this better be good gentlemen…explain" He said in a low voice as thankfully we were under exercise conditions!
We attempted to tell the SSM, Tiny Bott, about our struggle to find Jellalabad Barracks, the 1 RTR rebuttal, the disaster with the standpipe and finally getting lost and ending up near Exeter…we daren't mention the fact that the water bowser detached from the 4 tonner on the A303 or the 'world of shit' we were in would have become far worse!! Tiny looked at us both with a mixture of disgust and disbelief and with a huge sigh said;
"Wankers…dismissed…get out of my sight!"
I found my sleeping bag, and as I climbed into it I looked at my watch…it was ten minutes to midnight. "Shit…" I thought "…I'm on guard in an hour…what a shit day…cushy number my arse!!!

Denmark 1984 (Ex Bolt Gannet)

Exercise Bold Gannet was a huge NATO exercise in Denmark that involved thousands of troops from the UK. Our squadron was involved and part of 22 Engineer Regiment RE, but our role was to provide engineer support to the 16th/5th Lancers. My memories of Denmark are; Rain, rain and more rain (it was like Lincolnshire with a different language!) and pig farms everywhere, expensive (twenty eight kroner for half a litre of beer - £2 in 1984!!!), Danish pastries (mmmmmm!) and a very sexually liberated country (the hardcore porn magazines were not on the top shelf out of reach of children, but on the counter where you were served!!!). It isn't a place I would rush to visit again, but nevertheless there were plenty of discussion points surrounding our visit!

Following a ferry trip from Harwich to Esbjerg and a two hour drive in convoy, we arrived at a tented field in Randers, a town toward the north eastern part of Jutland in Denmark…it was

142

raining! I don't remember a great deal about our time in Randers, but I do remember we played football against a Danish army side…and lost!, I also remember meeting a pretty Danish girl during a night out in Randers town…we did write to each other for a short while when I returned to Chattenden, but it didn't last!, there was the continuous rain and a mini three day exercise close to Randers…I was part of a three man team manning the radio in the farmyard of a small farm (2 hours on duty and 4 hours off and we slept in a hay barn – luxury!), the OC and 2IC were staying in the same farm with the Danish family – surreal! The rest of the squadron were situated in a wooded area a short distance away…they had to sleep on the back of 4 tonners or in the back of landrovers as it was too dangerous to sleep in bivouacs or scrape holes due to the threat from wild boars!! After a week or so, we left Randers and Jutland and re-located to the large island of Sjaelland (where Copenhagen is situated) and found ourselves in another, much larger farm, between the villages of Tybjerg and Tybjerglille and close to the large town of Naestved . The farm had a large barn, large enough to house the entire squadron en masse and keep us dry…it was still raining!!! It was in this area that the main exercise (Ex Bold Gannet) was held, involving approximately 25,000 soldiers from NATO, including ourselves! It was during this carefully planned, strategic and important 'Cold War' exercise that I would be officially told…you are dead!!

Our squadron was strategically 'dug in' (sited in trenches in a defensive position) toward the back of a ploughed field, which sloped down, in front of us, to a small valley…giving us an excellent vantage point with an excellent arc of fire!! Early on the first evening, a message came down the line that the 2IC wanted to see me…and to bring my weapon, tin hat, respirator and webbing (pouches, water bottle etc). I gathered my equipment and made my way to the command post where the 2IC was waiting with Cpl 'Geordie' Robinson;
"LCpl Thomas I have a job for you…as you know we are supporting the 16th/5th Lancers…we have a problem…the distance between our position and theirs is too great and we are unable to maintain radio contact…it's imperative that this is rectified…I want you to go with Cpl Robinson and set-up a REBRO...a re-broadcast or communication link between us

and them with the radio traffic coming through you and Cpl
Robinson. OK LCpl Thomas…" I nodded and said;
"Yes Sir" The 2IC looked at Geordie Robinson;
"…Best get off then Cpl Robinson…good luck…" he nodded
and looked at me;
"…LCpl Thomas!" Geordie Robinson and I saluted, and
shouted "YES SIR" before saluting and making a hasty exit to
a waiting short-wheelbase land rover, parked on a track behind
the command post!!

Such was the nature of the task, we drove into the night
without an exact destination…this part of the task was left in
our hands and the parameters of the battle!! For the next three
or four hours we tried to keep a low profile, and where
possible we tried to stay off the main roads…preferring to use
minor roads, country lanes and the occasional track!! At one
point, during the evening, we inadvertently crossed the FEBA
(forward edge of battle area) and found ourselves 'behind
enemy lines', and almost stumbled upon an enemy convoy.
The joint skills of my map reading, Geordie's driving and the
fact we were a single vehicle meant we crossed back over the
FEBA and into a relatively safe area. In all honesty, we
struggled to find a suitable place to successfully create the
required communication link between the 16th/5th Lancers and
our squadron! However, at around 23.30hrs zulu, we luckily
stumbled across an area that served our purpose. We had
driven down a lane and after a two to three hundred metres
there was a farmhouse on the right hand side, opposite the
farm there was a track running from the lane at a right angle
that rose gradually and ran alongside a thick hedgerow.
Geordie reversed the land rover about forty to fifty metres up
the track just below the brow of the hill/slope, and I set-up the
mast in the field opposite the farmhouse. Once the mast had
been erected, we sat in the front of the land rover and took it in
turns to man the radio. The night was still, and even the rain
relented slightly until it eventually stopped in the early
hours…possibly the first time it had stopped since we had
landed at Esbjerg two weeks earlier!!!
At 04.45hrs zulu our job was complete and the REBRO was
no longer required as the 16th/5th Lancers had changed location
and could now contact our command post directly…what we
didn't realise though is that during the night the FEBA had

moved, and we were now again behind enemy lines! Unaware of the potential danger I said;

"I'll start taking the mast down Geordie"

"OK Taff…take your SMG (sub-machine gun) just in case…you just never know…" and he laughed "…as much use as it'll be!!"

"You're right Geordie" I laughed and started walking toward the mast. The first glimpses of dawn were beginning to reveal themselves, when I heard a strange rumbling noise which I initially thought was thunder! Suddenly, and without warning, three APCs (armoured personnel carriers) trundled into view down the lane and I froze and dropped to the floor. There was a soldier manning a fixed machine gun on the tail vehicle and when he spotted me he opened up…tracer rounds lit up the morning creating a hell-like scene in the half darkness and dawn mists!! As I returned fire, and in the heat of battle, I noticed that the farmer (still in his pyjamas and with ruffled hair), from the farmhouse opposite, had opened his door to see what was going on!! He quickly surveyed the scene before quickly shutting the door…he must have thought World War III had started in front of his house!! By this time, the APCs were sitting on the edge of a wooded hill about two hundred metres from me, and the farmhouse, at the end of the lane. The firing (and tracer bullets) ended and it was all over in minutes, it was then I could see one of the soldiers walking towards me across the field. He was shouting something, but I couldn't hear him properly as my ears were still ringing from the gunfire. It was only when he was about twenty metres away that I realised what he was saying, which was;

"YOU ARE DEAD…I HAVE KILLED YOU" In a strong accented voice which I presumed was Danish. As he got closer, he lowered his voice;

"You are dead…my firepower is best"

"Nah, sorry Butt…I had you in my sights…took you out no problem" I said tongue in cheek, knowing my SMG couldn't hit a barn door at 10m!

"NO…YOU DEAD!" he argued and then frowned.

"No way Butt…do you know who I am…I'm the best shot in my living room…if anyone's dead it's you…no more Danish bacon for you Butt"

"I KILLED YOU…You could not kill me with that" and he pointed at my SMG.

145

I was just about to answer when, out of the corner of my eye, I could see another uniformed figure with a clipboard walking towards us. He turned out to be a marshal and cleared up the situation immediately, much to the happiness of the 'Danish hippy' (they all had long hair!) when he pointed at me and said;

"You and your Cpl over there are DEAD..."

Before he had a chance to say any more I smiled and said;

"Are we prisoners of war now?"

"...No...you are dead...you may now go back to your squadron" and he turned and walked away! The Danish soldier gave me a knowing smile and also walked away. I, on the other hand, stood there defiantly and stuck two fingers up to them both!!

With the mast packed away, we drove down the track onto the lane and headed back to the squadron's position. After a couple of miles we saw a bakery, a solitary building in the middle of the countryside, and we stopped to see what they were selling. We walked into the shop and the smells were heavenly...it was the first time I'd seen 'Danish pastries'. I have a particular love for 'cake', but these were something else, and Geordie and I bought two each (a difficult task given the amount of choice). As it was still early in the morning the pastries were still warm...we hurriedly walked back to the land rover and each took a pastry out of the bag, and for a few seconds just looked at these magnificent items, salivating and licking our lips in anticipation. The first bite was unbelieveable and the noises we were making, to someone passing by, could have suggested we were doing more than eating Danish pastries!!! The cakes eaten it was back to reality and we set off for the trenches!!

Once the exercise had finished we had a 24hr pass, some of the lads made the short trip to Copenhagen, but the remainder of us stayed in the town of Naestved and basically got pissed! I remember entering a night club in the evening and it was similar to arriving on the set of the Al Pacino film 'Cruising', it was just wall to wall soldiers...hardly a woman in sight!! It was the only time I have ever left a nightclub when it was light outside, three of us found a taxi and I remembered the farm was between Tybjerg and Tybjerglille, which was thankfully enough information to get us back to the squadron…our time in Denmark had come to an end!!!

Tiny Bott

Tiny was the SSM (squadron sergeant major) between early 1982 to early 1984. He was an imposing figure; A 6ft 5in yorkshireman, who stamped his authority and discipline on us all! The majority of people didn't like him and considered him a bully and I think to some degree that may be true, but he was always fair with me and I would rather have had a SSM who was a complete 'bastard' all of the time, than a SSM that was two faced!! We all knew Tiny's boundaries and provided you didn't step outside those boundaries then you'd be ok! I can inwardly smile when I think about him and always knew I was in the shit if I heard a deep, booming shout of "THOMAS…MY OFFICE NOW" coming down the corridor…thankfully it didn't happen too often!!

I first met Tiny Bott when we played rugby together in the 1981 Sapper v Gunner game, I was a young Sapper of eighteen and Tiny was a SSgt in his mid-thirties. As a naïve eighteen year old his sheer size was intimidating and I quickly found this giant of a man was a tough, belligerent and uncompromising player! A short time later, in early 1982, he became the SSM (squadron sergeant major) of 24 Field Squadron RE and those qualities mentioned above were at the forefront of his leadership style…what you saw was what you got with Tiny, there was no hidden agenda! I appreciate and accept that opinion about Tiny's character and his time at 24 is split, there are those who would say Tiny had similar attributes to those I have described above. However, there are those who would describe Tiny as an egotistical bully…it's safe to say that there was a very thin line between the both!! Whatever the opinion, it can be argued that those who served under Tiny Bott, when he was the SSM of 24 Field Squadron RE, cannot deny that he was a 'huge' character and will always be remembered. I cannot and won't speak for others and it would be unfair for me to do so, these are only my thoughts and how I remember Tiny and accept that there are many who will not agree with me!! I believe that he was certainly the strongest SSM I served under during my ten year army career. In hindsight, the SSM of a squadron is not there to make friends...he is there to maintain discipline!

During Tiny's tenure at 24 there were a lot of 'strong' characters and there was still the hangover of the squadron having a 'bad lads' image! Therefore, there was a real need for the SSM to instill and maintain discipline and no-one could argue that this was something that Tiny excelled at! Tiny not only used the advantage of 'natural intimidation' through his 6ft 5in large frame and his deep, booming Yorkshire accent, but also through his God-like ability to be omnipresent...he didn't miss a trick and his 'extra duties' book was always brimming with names of those he had caught out (including mine) with misdemeanors such as; needing a haircut, being sub-standard on parade, driving offences, drunken behaviour and so forth. He didn't suffer fools or 'repeat offenders' and this is probably how the 'bully' tag was created...I will concede that he was, shall we say, overly enthusiastic at times in this area!! Tiny introduced parades that were generally disliked, such as; Newcomers reporting to SSM and sick parade. The former meant that anyone new to the squadron had to report to his office in full no2 dress (peaked hat, tie, no2 dress uniform and 'bulled boots'), and anyone below standard in terms of turnout immediately felt the 'wrath of Tiny' and had no doubts about where they were and what was expected of them, as Harry Harrison found out...but more of him later in the chapter! The latter, the sick parade, provided Tiny with the chance to check if soldiers were genuinely ill or were just attempting to 'swing the lead' (shirking work)! Therefore, before reporting to the medical centre, a soldier would have to report to the SSM c/w the large pack from their webbing filled with pre-designated items, such as; wash bag, towel etc. I am convinced this 'ordeal' stopped a lot of lads reporting sick for trivial illnesses!!

Tiny, it can be argued, did what he had to do to maintain discipline whilst he was at 24; If the squadron found itself in a stressful environment, such as in the latter weeks of our time in the Falklands, following the 'Dewar incident', he took control! Had it not been for Tiny's 'grip' on the squadron, that incident could have been the catalyst for further violence, and I can think of no further incidents during the remainder of our tour, such was Tiny's control over the squadron. Another example of Tiny's discipline came to the fore when someone smashed one of the mirrors that were located near the exits of both stairwells in the single soldier's accommodation block. We used the mirrors to check ourselves before going on parade and they were Tiny's pride and joy! When no-one would own up to the crime Tiny put an eighteen man guard in each stairwell which meant that, with approximately 100-120 soldiers in the accommodation, your turn would come round every 3-4 days. Despite that fact that the culprit never owned up (probably out of sheer fear!), it highlighted the extent of Tiny's disciplinary methods.

People may argue that as I played rugby with Tiny in the squadron team he was more lenient with me, and the screwing up of the charge reports following my going AWOL from the hospital to play rugby for the squadron could confirm that he was lenient…but I believe he saw that I was prepared to make a sacrifice for the squadron with total disregard for my own disciplinary record! Additionally, I suffered his wrath the same as anyone else, he had no favourites…he treated everyone the same! We all knew the boundaries and depending which side of the line you were on, you either stayed out of trouble or didn't…it was as simple as that! If you crossed the line…you paid the price (as I did many times), resulting in reluctant participation in many extra duties (i.e. unpaid Saturday nights in the sergeants mess serving food or drinks or washing the dishes during their many functions) or extra parades. Yes, morale may have improved when he left, but the squadron was nowhere near as disciplined as it was under Tiny!

As a rugby player he represented the Corps and the Army, and at the age of seventeen he represented Yorkshire. However, one thing he had never won was an Army Cup winners medal. Shortly before he left 24, and in his final season as a rugby player, there was one last chance, and as a team we really wanted to win the Army Minor Units Cup for him. Cruelly, we lost 4-0 to a freak try in a hard fought semi-final…we genuinely felt sorry for Tiny that day and it was the first time he showed any kind of vulnerability, and he cut a forlorn figure as he walked off the pitch that day as he knew his final chance of winning an Army Cup had gone!! I, for one, after looking back over time, have a new found respect

for Tiny Bott, and my maturity now tells me that he was a
great man and a great sergeant major…sadly, he's no longer
with us, and as I sit here thirty plus years after the events
described above, I can hear his booming laughter and those
immortal words…"THOMAS…MY OFFICE NOW!".

Christmas 1984

*Christmas at Chattenden was always special and a few days
before we went on leave there was always a Christmas carol
service in the NAAFI followed by Christmas dinner in the
junior ranks dining hall (Cpls and below). The dinner was
always a rowdy affair as the sergeants, staff sergeants,
warrant officers and officers used to serve the food to us
junior ranks. Christmas 1984 was no different…but with
added extras!!*

In keeping with normal tradition at Chattenden, we had
gathered in the NAAFI and had already enjoyed the Christmas
Carol Service…the pints were now beginning to flow on what
would be a memorable day!! One of the lads, Cpl 'Keith'
Isham, decided this would be a good time for singing, his now
familiar party piece, the Elvis classic "*Are you lonesome
tonight*" to a poor unsuspecting girl! When one of the WRACs
(Womens Royal Army Corps) became isolated from her
friends, Keith seized his opportunity and pounced, with the
speed of a striking cobra…before the girl knew what was
happening, Keith was down on one knee, holding her hand and
singing;
"*ARE YOU LONESOME TONIGHT, DO YOU MISS ME
TONIGHT…*"
The rest of us saw this is our cue and we surrounded Keith and
the girl, and rocking gently from side to side in unison, started
to hum the tune as a backing for Keith…the girl was now
boxed in and any thoughts of escaping this sweet, but
embarrassing, situation were now futile! The girl, her head in
her hands, accepted her fate and Keith continued to sing and
we continued to hum and rock gently from side to side right up
to the latter part of the song, where we all joined in with Keith,
with added 'gusto' for the big finale;
"*…IS YOUR HEART FILLED WITH PAIN, SHALL I COME
BACK AGAIN? TELL ME DEAR, ARE YOU LONESOME
TONIGHT?*"

The girl was a given a collective cheer, and red faced and giggling she quickly returned to the relative safety of her friends!!

Twenty minutes or so later we were walking the short distance of about twenty metres to the junior ranks dining hall to enjoy our Christmas dinner…the only day of the year we didn't have to spend 10-15 minutes queueing up for our food! It was on this day that all the SNCOs (i.e. Senior non-commissioned officers; Sgts, SSgts, WO2s and WO1s) and officers served our food…and more importantly, our BEER/LAGER! We were lucky at Chattenden, the standard of food was excellent and the chefs ('egg ops' or 'slop jockeys' as they were affectionately known) didn't let us down and the Christmas dinner was awesome, made all the sweeter by the fact that we were nervously served by our superiors (who were praying that it wouldn't descend into a food fight, as it did the following year)…and it was a day when any lewd comments would normally go unpunished, provided they weren't derogatory or of a personal nature! Once the Christmas pudding and cans of lager or beer had been finished it was time to head for our squadron bar on the other side of the camp!

As we walked out of the junior ranks dining hall one of the lads from 24 shouted;
"Over there…quick…squadron conga!" He pointed in the direction of the road in front of the WRAC block, as he gesticulated to other members of the squadron as they came out of the dining hall. Intrigued, we walked around the side of the building and there, on the road, were some of the lads forming the squadron conga…we ran over and joined the back of the fast forming 'conga line'! Within a few minutes the line included most of the squadron, including some of the SNCOs and officers. It must have been an impressive sight watching approximately one hundred and fifty people snaking their way through Chattenden Barracks to their ultimate destination…the squadron bar! It was great fun being part of that conga and as we made our way through the camp we continually sang: "LETS ALL DO THE CONGA…NA NA NA NA…NA NA NA NA…!" With plenty of encouragement from members of 12 RSME Regiment RE and 49 EOD Regiment RE who witnessed this unique spectacle!!

151

There was plenty more beer drank in the squadron bar, and through one eye of a drunken haze, I believe there was even a rendition of 'Sunshine Mountain', courtesy of Ish (Cpl 'Keith' Isham) and Batch (LCpl 'Jeremy' Batchelor);
"WE'RE CLIMBING UP SUNSHINE MOUNTAIN"
(climbing actions)
"WHERE THE NORTH WIND BLOWS..." (blowing noises with hands around mouth).
This eventually resulted in everyone in the bar standing on chairs belting out this classic Cub Scouts song!! The evening finished with a few of us, including Sgt Steve 'Woosh' Taylor, ending up in the Admiral Beatty, a pub in Gravesend...dressed in togas!! All was fine until the DJ played 'Nelly the Elephant' by the Toy Dolls...carnage!! Five drunken Sappers in togas created a human elephant (bent double, linking hands through our legs whilst the man at the front use his free hand as a trunk), and during the chorus charged around the pub spilling drinks and knocking people flying...very inconsiderate, but great fucking fun!!

Squadron Bar

The best kept secret in Chattenden Barracks was the 24 Field Squadron bar, open for NAAFI breaks and every Friday for 'happy hour' or to be more accurate 'happy hours' We had some pretty good times in that bar and it was one place that highlighted the unity of the squadron. In my time at 24 it had been held in three different locations such was the need to keep it secret...similar to those hidden bars during 'prohibition' in the USA!!

At the end of my first week in 24 Field Squadron RE I was taken to the squadron bar, which was hidden away in an empty bay of the MT (motor transport) building. The image that first greeted me as I walked through the door is too gross, even for this book of honest revelations, and needless to say, what I witnessed that day, scarred me for life...thankfully I never saw a repeat performance! The incident involved a certain Cpl 'Geordie' Craddock and those who knew him will understand the significance of keeping that secret amongst those that were there that day! The bar was strictly prohibited and was therefore never spoken about outside of squadron circles, but our squadron bar was a huge part of the togetherness shared by members of 24. The location was changed twice during my time at the squadron, ending up in a large room (probably a former storeroom) between the entrance off the square, that took you toward the squadron training room and offices, and the troop G10 stores that faced the square…it is here that my main memories were forged!

When the squadron bar was moved it also became a 'NAAFI break' area when Cpl 'Dave' Clement's wife and her friend, who I think was LCpl 'Jock' Anderson's wife, were given permission to sell cheese rolls, ham rolls, teas, coffees and a small selection of chocolates (i.e. Mars, Kit-kats etc). The room was fairly basic at first with just a few tables and chairs and a makeshift bar, but it enabled squadron members more actual break time instead of wasting time walking across to the other side of the camp. In addition to NAAFI breaks, the bar was normally only open on a Friday for 'Happy Hour', but sometimes, if we played rugby at Chattenden, it would open on a Wednesday. There was a small selection of alcoholic beverages available, well actually only two, lager and bitter…no cider and no shorts!! As the beer was so cheap (around half the price of beer in the pubs in and around Chatham) it was a great place to start the weekend, and then move on to 'The George' in Chattenden, and if there was enough of us, taxi's would be booked to take us to the 'Two Sawyers' or 'The Cannon' in Brompton…a stone's throw away from Brompton Barracks and nestled between Chatham and Gillingham! On particularly rowdy nights (when the glass boot came out) we would stay in the squadron bar, and barely be able to make it back to our rooms…let alone our beds!

As the months rolled by improvements were made to the bar, such as; The walls became decorated with plaques and various memorabilia (including the sign from the peace camp at RAF Molesworth, following the squadron's involvement in fencing off the camp which was going to be the second cruise missile base in the uk!), the ceiling was decorated with camouflage nets and a great addition was the table football which provided hours of fun…and misery, as no-one could beat Ish and Cpl 'Norman' Ryan, the undisputed 24 table football champions, until Norman's posting in 1985. There was a huge drinking culture in the army in the 1980s as we took the 'work hard, play hard' ideal to another level, and this could be clearly seen at 24. But saying that, in all the time I was in that squadron bar I can never remember there being any trouble…we just unwound with drinking games, rugby songs and happily getting completely pissed!! It was a great little secret we kept from the rest of the regiment, and I'm not afraid to admit that, if I wasn't duty clerk or away for the weekend, I would be the first through the door at 4'o'clock on a Friday afternoon, ready for another evening of debauchery and drunken fun. We had great times, great memories and even greater hangovers as a result of that bar, and it was exactly what it said on the tin, 24's squadron bar, no members of 12 RSME or 49 EOD would be brought in…it was 24's Narnia, our wardrobe into another world!!

The 24 Field Squadron Court Jester

There was always a squadron parade on a Monday morning (weather permitting) during my time at 24, a parade that was executed properly! However, one particular morning the parade ended in chaos following a magical interruption of comical proportions that included 'conduct unbecoming of a British army officer…!'

We had marched onto our markers and were now stood to attention facing the sergeant major (SSM), WO2 Hitchin. The five troops of the squadron were all on parade, and our troop, HQ troop, was directly in front of the SSM, a small gap then it was one troop, then two troop, three troop and lastly Support troop. We were all waiting patiently for the next order! Right on cue, the SSM shouted;
"SQUADRON…SQUADRON, STAND AT EASE"
The whole squadron, like a single clap of thunder, stood at ease.
"SQUADRON…SQUADRON, TENSHUN"
Again, the precision of carrying out the command was exemplary. The SSM turned to his left and marched to the OC, Major Newns, who was now waiting on the edge of the square. The SSM halted in front of the OC, saluted and shouted;
"24 SQUADRON IS READY FOR INSPECTION, SIR"
The OC returned the salute and marched to the position in front of the squadron where the SSM had stood a few minutes

154

earlier, he halted and immediately gave the command;

"SQUADRON…SQUADRON, STAND AT EASE"

As we stood at ease I could see movement on the roof of the three storey accommodation block facing us and directly behind the OC. Someone was throwing some sort of homemade banner of army sheets off the roof with writing on them which were at least 2ft tall. Within seconds I, and others on parade, could see what it read;

'HAPPY BIRTHDAY JIM BENSON'

This was the point that the squadron parade began to disintegrate into chaos! Firstly, there were a few sniggers, and a frown appeared on the face of the OC, who still hadn't seen the banner! It was then the figure on the roof started dancing, and we realised it was the QM, Captain Jim Benson…dressed as a court jester!! The sniggers gave way to fully blown chaotic laughter which raised an angry glare from the OC, who was still oblivious to what was going on behind him on the roof. Capt Benson danced like a demented fool and as the dancing became more manic the laughter spread like wildfire through the squadron, and despite some people maintaining some form of discipline, the SSM looked up to where people were pointing and could now see the QM dancing on the roof! The SSM immediately marched across to the OC and whispered in his ear, prompting the OC to turn around to witness the banner and the QM in all his glory! The scene on the roof was too much for the OC, and he doubled up with laughter but managed to shout to the SSM;

"GET THEM OFF THE SQUARE SERGEANT MAJOR…DISMISS THEM NOW"

The SSM managed to keep his composure and shouted;

"SQUADRON…FALL OUT…GET OFF THE SQUARE…GET AWAY GENTLEMEN…QUICK NOW!

We scuttled off the square like rats leaving a sinking ship, but throughout the clearing of the square that morning, Jim Benson carried on dancing on the roof obviously pleased with the carnage he had created below him in destroying the age old tradition of a disciplined squadron parade…it was Jim's Birthday and he certainly made it a day that no-one who was there that day would forget!!!

Remembrance Sunday 1984

Always a sombre affair, but something that everyone wanted to be involved in as a means of remembering those that had paid the ultimate sacrifice! The one Remembrance Sunday I particularly remember was a fairly simple affair and held on the square at Chattenden. But it was the nature of the proceedings that have remained with me to this day!!!

It was a cold, crisp morning in early November 1984, but despite the cold penetrating the skin of our face and hands the tingling pain was quickly forgotten when the order was given and we marched onto the square...I was honoured to be representing the squadron as part of a 'troop' of about thirty members of 24 taking part in the Remembrance parade that morning. As I sit here over 30 years later, I can now only remember one thing about that parade, as the majority of it has been dominated by the images of Lt Col Fawcus, CO of 12 RSME Regiment RE. He stood in front of us, and in the silence pulled out a small, battered book with pages yellowed by the passages of time...but a book that would have a profound effect on all of those present that morning!!

Lt Col Fawcus, who was standing in front of members of 12 RSME Regiment RE, 24 Field Squadron RE, 49 EOD Regiment RE and local dignitaries, looked up, paused for a moment, opened the book, took a deep breath and started to read. An eerie hush descended, as the gentle breeze relented and the birds heeded the unheard request for silence, it was as if the whole world was listening to the words spoken so eloquently by Lt Col Fawcus. Harrowing words that epitomized a war that should never be forgotten and a war that provided the reason we stood on that square in Chattenden, embraced in a solemn autumnal shroud. The words defined the haunting memories of a shared history that echoed across the decades to a new generation filled with hope. Each word uttered by Lt Col Fawcus wrestled with my soul, silently screaming to be heard and understood.

Lt Col Fawcus paused momentarily and looked to the sky, as if seeking the strength to continue. We waited patiently, hanging on the pause...hoping, praying for a continuation of the inspiration that each line delivered.

156

The hushed silence was deafening as Lt Col Fawcus continued to read from the delicate book in his hand and the silence of the morning roared its approval at the choice of poem for such a momentus occasion.

It was difficult not to be moved by the words we were hearing and they resonated in the silence that enveloped us, which gave them a deeper meaning. Finally, Lt Col Fawcus, took a breath, paused and closed the book and explained,
"That poem is called '*Anthem of the Doomed Youth*' and was written by a Lt Wilfred Owen. A soldier who served with the 5th Battalion of the Manchester Regiment…and one of the famous war poets that emerged from the…from the horrors of trench warfare in the First World War…sadly Lt Owen never returned home…he was sadly killed just a week before the armistice was signed…Before we proceed with this parade…I am going to read another of Owen's poems…the well-known '*Dulce et Decorum Est*'…ladies and gentlemen…pay particular attention to the poignant words that would still be relevant in the conflicts of today!!"

Lt Col Fawcus re-opened the fragile little book, flicked the yellow pages to the desired page, took another deep breath and began. I listened intently to the powerful words that Lt Col Fawcus read in his clear, unhurried tone, words that took you back to another time, another place!

Each line of the poem clawed gently at my emotions as they attempted to find solace in my heart and mind… far away from the horrors of war! Profoundly, listening to these haunting words provided me, for the first time, with the horrific sense of reality at the devastation of war.

Lt Col Fawcus changed the tone in his voice, speaking lower, slightly slower but more pronounced as the poem headed for its compelling conclusion. As the final words of the poem left the lips of Lt Col Fawcus the silence was thunderous as Lt Col Fawcus closed the little book and for a few moments, left us contemplating the helplessness and futility resounding from the words we had just heard. He cleared his throat and repeated the final words of the poem, additionally, providing the profound English translation of those last seven Latin words…"It is sweet and honorable to die for one's country!!"

"My God!..." I thought, "…that is the ultimate definition of patriotism…wow!".

The sixth sense of nature had played its dignified part, and as if nature knew, I heard a bird sing and once again felt the soft, icy breeze on my face! I stood there on that unforgettable parade and felt a renewed and increased sense of pride at being a soldier, but even though I never knew Wilfred Owen, I also felt a sense of loss and thought about the sacrifices made by Owen and his generation…At the going down of the sun and in the morning, WE WILL REMEMBER THEM!!!

Cadets Sponsored Walk

We had a cadet squadron, based at Bethnal Green in the East End of London, that was affiliated to 24 Field Squadron and I had already been on exercise with them in Easter 1984 with Iain George. This was a slightly different occasion, as the cadets were involved in a sponsored walk from Folkestone to Chattenden over one of the bank holiday weekends in May 1985. The idea was that Rab Keill and myself would, at various points, create a combat engineer type task for them to complete…but it didn't quite pan out in the way it was originally agreed!!

It was approximately 7.30pm on the Friday evening and Rab Keill and I had arrived safely at the cadet hut in Bethnal Green! We had been briefed by the cadet officer in charge of the programme for the weekend, and as our role was fairly leisurely involving the setting-up of 'stands' (engineer tasks) at pre-designated points along the route, we decided that we would head into the centre of Bethnal Green and have a few beers! There wasn't a great deal of choice in Bethnal Green and after failing to get into a couple of the 'yuppy' pubs in the area, we found an Irish bar…entering this bar probably wasn't the best decision we'd ever made!!! It was a real 'spit and sawdust' pub and when we walked in the four or five elderly men sat on bar stools stopped talking and just stared as we ordered our drinks! When we sat down the men carried on their conversation in strange Irish/cockney accents and

judging by the conversation they may well have been IRA sympathisers…I whispered to Rab;
"We may have to be careful in here!" Rab nodded confirming he knew what I meant.
With that one of the men shouted across;
"WHERE YOU FROM THEN?"
"He's Welsh and I'm Scottish" said Rab. That was good enough for them and they called us over, went through a series of introductions and for the rest of the night we drank, laughed and sang with them! When I say for the rest of the night, it was literally the rest of the night, last orders had come and gone, the doors had been locked, and when we left there at 5am we could barely speak and barely walk…what a night! We made our way back to the cadet hut, crawled into our sleeping bags and went straight to sleep!

It was around 6.30am when we were woken up and told that we would be leaving in 30 minutes…we were still pissed!! We managed to get washed, changed and a black coffee inside us, but the world still didn't look a good place through squinty, bloodshot eyes…worse still, Rab had to drive the landrover! It was time for the off, and in convoy we left Bethnal Green and headed for Folkestone! We hadn't gone far when things got a whole lot worse…on a dual carriageway leaving London, Rab had momentarily fallen asleep and drifted to the left and for a split second was heading up a grass embankment. Thankfully, he woke up and managed to right the steering and we thought we'd gotten away with Rab's minor indiscretion…but the convoy was stopped by a police car who had witnessed Rab's 'hiccup' and when we had all come to a standstill, two policemen came walking down the line of vehicles, stopped by our landrover and tapped on Rab's window. I pretended to be asleep as Rab pulled the landrover window to one side and slurred;
"Yes…Officer…how…how may I help you?"
"Everything OK soldier…where you heading?"
"Yes Officer…everything is…is tip top…and I think…Folkestone…Yes, Folkestone" slurred Rab, draped over the steering wheel.
To this day I believe that the policemen knew that Rab was drunk, but as it was early in the morning and we were in convoy, they let us off with some advice;
"Drive carefully soldier and…stay in the convoy"

159

"Yes officer…thank you!" Rab made a weak attempt at a salute and slid the window shut! An hour later we arrived at our destination, thankfully in one piece, but both Rab and I were beginning to suffer with the hangovers from hell! "It'll be ok" I thought, once the cadets and their two instructors have set-off, we can grab another hours kip…that's not quite how it panned out though!!

After a couple of minutes I decided to 'stretch my legs' and get some fresh air, in an attempt to shift the self-inflicted headache, and got out of the land rover. Almost immediately, the young officer in charge of the cadets walked over and said;"You can walk with the cadets on the first leg of the walk today…OK, LCpl…"
"Thomas" I said
"Yes…LCpl Thomas…sorry!" I nodded and thought "Lazy twat!"
So with a raging hangover, I was put in charge of about fifteen 12-15 year old cadets from the East End of London…what could possibly go wrong? Actually, as it turned out, apart from some teasing and good humoured banter between the cadets, the day went pretty well (once my hangover had disappeared!), and by early evening we had reached a clearing in a small wooded area, just off Pilgrims Way and near to the small village of Charing, which would be our home for the night. Rab was waiting for us, and like me, he looked and felt a lot better than when I had last seen him that morning! Ten minutes later the young cadet officer arrived, checked on the welfare of the cadets and when assured everything was OK, announced he was doing a 'chip shop run', took orders from everyone and left. He returned about an hour or so later, and once everyone had eaten it was time to bed down for the night, as we had another long day scheduled for the following day! The cadets were sleeping in the back of the 4 tonners, whilst Rab and I had settled down, for an uncomfortable night, in the front of the landrover! We must have been sleeping as I remember being woken by, what can only be described as, a blood curdling scream, similar to those you heard in horror films…it really sounded like a woman was being attacked! I think Rab thought the same as me, as he said;
"Taff…what the fuck was that?"
"Dunno Rab…but it didn't sound good!" I replied

160

As we had just woken up, we were a bit disoriented at first, but the second scream, amplified by the silence of the night, brought us crashing into reality, and we looked at each other and at the same time said;

"Cadets!"

We nervously jumped out of the land rover as we still didn't know what we were dealing with…why had the cadet screamed? What was happening? We ran over to where the two 4 tonners were parked as we could see that torches had now been switched on, which in the darkness, looked similar to a light show at a rock concert as distorted shadows danced in the semi darkness. We heard sobbing coming from the back on one of the 4 tonners followed by a third scream, now more pronounced as we were so close. We could see that it was one of the younger and smaller lads, and he wasn't responding to the reassurance he was receiving from some of the older lads. He was inconsolable and was continually calling for his parents to come and take him home…I looked at my watch, it was 11.35pm. The cadet officer had managed to contact his parents and just over an hour later the lad was calm and sitting in the car and was heading for home…his weekend on the sponsored walk was over!! Now that everything had calmed down again, Rab and I headed back to the land rover to try and get some sleep…thankfully, the rest of the night passed without any further incident!!

The following day (Sunday) was uneventful, with exception of the 'stand' Rab and I had set up for them, and after a day's walking (with the cadet officer) the cadets reached the area, woods at the top of Bluebell Hill (a hill that separates Rochester on one side from Maidstone on the other), where they would spend the night in bivouacs! Once everyone had eaten it was another early night ready for the final day and the last leg of the walk.

The following morning, we set off on the final leg of the cadets sponsored walk. It was a beautiful Bank Holiday Monday and Kent was bathed in sunshine, and the ridge that Pilgrims Way ran along provided us with glorious views across Maidstone and the adjoining Kent countryside. By late morning, we had reached a view that overlooked the River Medway and the town of Snodland, it was here that we veered to the right and the path ran parallel with the Medway, under the bridge that carried the M2 before we dropped down towards Rochester. We could now see the impressive sights of Rochester Castle and Rochester Cathedral which became more impressive the closer they got. We stopped for a few minutes in front of the castle for a drink before crossing over Rochester Bridge into Strood, walked along Station Road, and headed along the A228 toward Wainscott.

It was about 3pm when we reached Wainscott Camp and the cadets were strung out over a distance of about 20-30 metres, and looked like a bedraggled group of refugees as the afternoon heat and the distance they had already covered had obviously taken its toll! But now the end was in sight, there was just the hill up to Chattenden Barracks to contend with. I stopped the lads who were at the front and waited for the remainder to catch up, and then gave them a few minutes to adjust their dress and tighten their belts and ensured their headgear was worn correctly and then shouted;
"SQUAD...SQUAD SHUN...BY THE FRONT...QUICK MARCH"
They wearily followed my commands and we set off up the hill to Chattenden. As we approached the Ponderosa (the training area where the plant operatives carried out their training), I shouted;
"BREAK INTO DOUBLE TIME...DOUBLE TIME"
And we ran up the hill, into Chattenden Barracks and onto the square in front of 24 squadron accommodation block, and once I fell them out, they collapsed in crumpled heaps gasping for breath...their sponsored walk was complete! Within twenty minutes they were all sat in the back of a 4 tonner and heading back to the concrete jungle of Bethnal Green. The walk was an incredible feat for those young lads and I hope they were proud of themselves and what they had achieved!

The Stomp, Smartie Party and squaddie drinking dens in the Medway Towns

The Stomp was the disco at Chattenden Barracks on a Thursday night and the Smartie Party was the disco on a Wednesday night at Brompton Barracks...and as members of 24 we were regulars at both! The Royal Engineers HQ was based at Brompton Barracks and the camp also doubled as the place where all the artisan trade training courses were carried out. Whilst on the other side of the Medway, in

162

*Chattenden Barracks, there were ' section commanders',
'field sergeants' and 'search' (Lodge Hill Training Area
included a dummy village for NI training) courses, and 49
EOD Squadron RE (bomb disposal) and our squadron were
also based there. Therefore, it was highly likely that, as a
Sapper, you would eventually spend time in Chatham at some
point and attend one or both of the above venues. Attendance
was compulsory to sample the cheap beer and enjoy the finer
side of life from a choice of many delightful local...well, I'll
leave you to fill in the gap!!! There were also a number of
other drinking dens we frequented, such as; The Two Sawyers,
The Cannon, The George, The Command House, The Blue
Grotto, The Angel etc!*

We all loved 'the stomp' on a Thursday night at Chattenden, it
was a venue that had it all...music, booze, girls and fighting
(mainly over girls)!! Most Thursdays we'd be there and
depending what mood we were in we'd either be there looking
for a girl or just getting pissed...or a combination of both!
Most of the time we'd just head there straight from our rooms
after the three SSSs (shit, shower and shave), in our best
clobber (well nearly) and bathed in Brut, Denim or Old Spice.
However, occasionally we'd go to 'The George' first, a pub
just up the road in Chattenden village. 'The George' was a
great little boozer, but was mainly used as a 'stopping off'
pub, somewhere we'd go, have a few games of pool before
going on to 'the stomp' or heading down to Strood or
Chatham for a night out. However, I do remember some crazy
nights in there with Norman Ryan and Jim 'Panic Drinker'
Brown. The latter, Jim, had a strange drinking habit; He would
continually look at the clock, and to him it appeared that it was
always that moment just before 'last orders' was called and he
would be sinking pint after pint as if each one was his last pint
of the evening. This inevitably caused problems as Norman
and I were in rounds with him resulting in us getting into some
right states...I never learnt and believed them every time when
they knocked on my door and said;
"You coming out for a quiet drink Taff" I'd seek reassurance
and ask;
"Are you sure this is going to be a quiet one?"
"Yeah Taff...positive...we are up early in the morning for
PT" or something similar!

I'd believe it every time and every time we'd fall out of the pub at quarter past eleven after ten or eleven pints…unable to walk, unable to talk and unable to visually focus…Thanks boys!!!

I swear we could have had fun in a car park in those days of limited responsibilities, any excuse and we would have a party…even corridor parties! But 'the stomp' was the fun place to be (well, most of the time!) and luckily the army provided a bus service to collect the local girls and bring them into camp on a Thursday night. We also had a detachment of army girls (WRACs), drivers from 17 Squadron, and they were great girls with a great sense of fun…and some were up for anything! The images I have of 'the stomp' were fairly typical of many places during the 80s; The dance floor would be full of girls dancing around their handbags, sporting the latest fashion, hairdos and dance moves, whilst us men would be stood in groups either on the edge of the dance floor eying up potential 'liaisons' for later in the evening or away from the dance floor merrily getting smashed! Men would normally only be seen on the dance floor on two occasions; Firstly, when the slow dances made their ritual entry at the end of the evening or when 'Shout' by Lulu was played! 'Shout' had undergone a mini revival in the early 80s due to the famous scene from 'National Lampoons Animal House' when the whole frat house manically danced to it! However, it was the 'slow songs' that provided the comical primal behaviour at 'the stomp'; As the time approached the inevitable 'slow song' section there would be a large build-up of men around the edge of the dance floor, sometimes three or four men deep, all vying for a prime position to make their move. Carnage would ensue when the DJ announced;
"It's time to slow things down a bit now folks!"
You could feel the tension in the room, and as the first notes came through the speakers there was a mass scramble as we tried to get to our desired target…I mean girl! I remember once during one of these chaotic scene's that another soldier beat me to the girl that I'd had my eye on for over an hour. "Wanker" I thought, and turned to leave the dance floor when another girl grabbed hold of me and said;
"Quick…dance with me!" I didn't need to be asked twice and we were soon playing tonsil tennis, and within an hour we

were in her bed at her house in Gillingham sharing a tender moment...ok then having sex...thank you Tracy!!

Despite the fun times, fights would often break out, normally over a girl, but God help anyone who tried hitting someone from 24 - we were the dominant squadron at 'the stomp' and an attack on a 24 squadron member would result in the culprit being dealt with swiftly! One night I remember, following a rugby semi-final we'd played against Depot Para, we'd had a good drink in our Squadron bar before the majority of us went to 'the stomp', but Batch, Mick Stupple, Greg Gregory and Ronnie Barker went back to Batch's room and polished off a litre bottle of whiskey and a pile of cans. When they got to 'the stomp' an hour or so later they were itching for a fight; Greg was a Manc and was always fighting and Batch and Mick Stupple were big...very big Cornishmen! At some point in the evening there was a free for all with Batch, Mick and Greg right at the heart of it. The NAAFI staff had called the guardroom and the eight man guard were sent up to the NAAFI to break up the fight! However, when they burst through the door and saw that Greg, Mick and Batch were involved, they turned round and went straight back to the guardroom. We heard later that one of the guard was heard to say on his way out;
"Did you see who was fighting in there?...Batch, Mick Stupple and Greg...no way was I getting stuck in to them"
Yes 'the stomp' was legendary and having spent four and half years at Chattenden I had some great times there. I know for a fact that many a soldier met their future wives in there: Both Mick and Batch met WRAC girls at 'the stomp' and both are still happily married to those same girls over thirty years later!!

The 'Smartie Party' was the equivalent, but probably larger counterpart of 'the stomp' and was held at Brompton Barracks on Wednesday nights. Whereas Chattenden was more isolated, Brompton was nestled between Chatham and Gillingham and was much more accessible to the 'local' girls! The pattern here was pretty much the same as 'the stomp', but the only real difference was that the fights here were sometimes far worse. On one occasion, I was at the 'Smartie Party' with Knocker (Robert Knock) and Shaggy (O'Shaughnessy), and we stood near the DJ and his equipment when a fight broke out (over a girl…again!), directly opposite us on the other side of the dance floor. We watched it escalate and eventually it travelled around the room as people were pushed into others, and missed punches connected with the wrong people – the whole place soon resembled the type of mass brawls depicted in saloon bars of old western movies!! Shaggy, who by this time was pissed, mumbled something about 'hating the DJ', and when the fighting became closer to us he seized his opportunity and lunged at the DJ, but he hilariously missed, lost his footing and went crashing through the disco equipment sending speakers and lights crashing everywhere. Knocker and I stood there laughing in these surreal surroundings before picking him up off the floor, side-stepping our way through the fighting and making our way back to Chattenden. Another time, a group of us; Mick Stupple, Iki Bolton, Batch, me, Ronnie Barker and a few others were stood toward the back of the room and opposite the bar. Mick had gone to the bar and on his way back accidentally bumped into someone (about my size, 5ft 8 and 10 and a half stone), spilling a small amount of beer out of his pint. As big as Mick was (6ft 3in and 18stone with arms bigger than my thighs!) he was somewhat of a gentle giant (with exception of the incident detailed above at 'the stomp'), but because of his size was always targeted. Mick offered to buy a fresh pint for the lad, who seemed to be more content with continually prodding Mick in the chest. It wasn't long before Mick's arm lifted and we could see him clenching his fist at the same time then, 'BANG' one punch, and the lad was a crumpled heap at Mick's feet. Within seconds there was a second lad prodding Mick in the chest, this time Mick was in no mood for any nonsense, and lifted him off his feet with one hand and head-butted him, and then dropping him on the floor next to his mate!! Mick was then surrounded by four or five more! At this point we started walking over and us Mick was walking toward the exit with these boys, Iki called him;

"NEED A HAND MICK?"

"Nah…I be back in a minute" in his Cornish accent.

A few minutes later Mick was walking back into the 'Smartie Party'…on his own! We asked him what had happened and he smiled and said;

"I told'm…one at a time…orr altogetherrr…I not bothered…and they all started mumbling, turned and walked away"

166

Crazy place and crazy times!!

Prior to going to the 'Smartie Party' we would often go to either 'the Cannon' or the 'Two Sawyers', pubs that were different in so many ways! 'The Cannon' was a quaint little pub that we would frequent on a fairly regular basis, it was close to the Brompton married quarters and the US (United Services) Chatham rugby ground where the Royal Engineers rugby team also played, and therefore popular with us rugby players. I have some great memories of 'The Cannon' such as; Entertaining Gurkha's from 69 Gurkha Independent Field Squadron RE by blowing up condoms on my head…they thought it was hilarious or the time I was sat in the lounge one Saturday night after rugby with Greg and positive that I recognised the barmaid but couldn't think where I had seen her before…then the penny dropped and I told Greg that I'd seen her in a porn magazine (Escort) that I had in my room. When Greg got the next round in, he asked her and she confirmed that yes, it was her – class!...I can officially say we met a porn star that day!! 'The Cannon' is still a good little pub and I was last there in March 2014 when I attended a 24 Squadron reunion. Just around the corner from 'The Cannon' was the 'Two Sawyers' the 'fun pub of Brompton' as it was described above the door. The sort of place that you wiped your feet on the way out, but this is another place stacked with memories, such as; Standing at the bar with Taff Best and Taff Humphrey, all three of us with our trousers around our ankles…it was twenty minutes or so before the bar staff realised!; Helping Rab Keil repeatedly as he received beating after beating…he would get so pissed that he would start fights, but because he was so drunk he could never defend himself when they retaliated!!; Another indication to the standards of the place, I was stopped by a girl (who turned out be a 'pads wife' – wife of a serving solider) on my way out of the pub at 10.55pm, and by 11.05pm we were having sex in the RE stables around the corner – classy!! (my mate 'Millie' Milner was also there with another girl); a girl called Jackie continually showing me her new tattoos (including ones on her breasts), lovely girl who had three children by three different soldiers and just before I left Chatham got pregnant again, by my mate Speedy Rice…the baby was conceived on the toilet cistern in the US Chatham rugby club – again classy!; The 'Two Sawyers' was also where the best chat-up line ever was used by Taff Humphrey with, I quote, "You're a big girl…do weights do you?" and many, many more that can't be mentioned in this book. It was the type of place you would stick to the carpet (I use the term 'carpet' loosely!) and there was always the aromatic stench of cigarettes…stale beer…cheap perfume…and SWEAT!! It was also the place where I successfully restrained myself from hitting a girl who had punched me in the face…twice, and I remember Scott 'Skin'Carr and the rest of the boys trying to wind me up, and they didn't believe me when I said that I genuinely didn't know who she was! I didn't initially recognise her, but when I dragged her outside (after she tried to punch me for a third time), I detected a slight North Walian accent and remembered that she was a girl that I had 'stood up' a year earlier…and she now looked completely different (when I had previously met her she was slightly chubby, with long wavy hair tied up in some typical 80s arrangement and a North Walian accent. A year later, she was slim, short hair and her accent was similar to a Chatham accent) I had only met her once, walked her home enjoyed a few kisses and here she was a year later blaming me for the overdose she had taken, resulting in her losing the twins she was carrying (not mine and I didn't even know she was pregnant!). Not the actions of a normal person and I believe I may have had a lucky escape from that psychopath!! Yes, the 'Two Sawyers' is a pub with many dark memories and dark secrets for many, many soldiers and many, many 'local' girls!!

There were a lot of other pubs that we drank in across the Medway towns; The Monarch (Gillingham), The Chatham Arms (Chatham), The Army and Navy or 'Dive Bar' (Chatham), The Command House (Chatham), The Golden Lion or 'the Beast' (Brompton), The Angel (Strood), The Three Gardeners (Strood), The Blue Grotto (Chatham) and many, many more. If I was to pick the worse pub in the Medway towns (or anywhere for that matter!) it would have to be the 'Blue Grotto' in the Pentagon Shopping Centre in Chatham. It was one room (and toilets) with no windows, walls that had been shaped like the inside of a cave with fish tanks set in them (with no fish in them!), a pool table and the cheapest sets of chairs and tables (similar to what you would see in school classrooms!). We spent many a Saturday afternoon in there…didn't we Jake Maiden!!! To match some of the classy pubs there was a variety of classy women, such as; The Horse, Sharon, Jackie, Sonny (her daughter and grand-daughter!), Black-eyed Sue, Aiesha (who slept with three different lads from 24 in the space of a few days, got pregnant and didn't know who the father was!) and not forgetting...the Sex Dwarf! It could be considered that Chatham was the poor man's version of the Richard Gere/Debra Winger film '*An Officer and a Gentleman*', as some local girls tried to marry soldiers to escape their lives in the Medway Towns!!!

Plon 1985

This was an interesting trip, a triangular sharing of engineering equipment and skills between a German army engineer squadron, a Danish army engineer squadron and our fine squadron of stand-out characters!! Plon was a beautiful town in North West Germany, and surrounded by a collection of both lakes and forests...intermingling to create a stunning setting! Amongst this idyllic scenery was also; a pair of plastic gays, a Danish fuck up, a strange union meeting (allegedly – according to 'army rumour control') and not forgetting...a 'sunshine mountain'!!! However, there was an auspicious start...with a fight and a bad case of sickness and diarrhea!!

It didn't start well...there'd been a fight on the ferry on the way to Hamburg, between a member of 24 Squadron and a couple of guys from the East End of London who were on a stag 'do'. Prior to leaving Chatham, the OC had briefed the squadron, and we had been warned that anybody caught fighting on the ferry, and bringing the British Army into disrepute, would be severely dealt with!! Who was it? I hear you ask. Who was the drunken thug that dragged the name of the squadron, the Corps and the British Army through the mud? No...wrong, it wasn't me! It was our OC, Major Newns...the very man who had warned everybody about fighting on the ferry, but in his defence he did like a good drink!! Another slight mishap happened to one of the lads (Ronnie Barker) who I shared a room with on the ferry. When we woke up after a hefty drinking session the night before, Ron, who was sleeping in the bunk above me shouted down to me;
"Ere Taff...Can you smell sick?"
I got out of bed and the sight that greeted me was horrendous!

169

"Oh my fucking God Ron…what have you done?...you better get in the shower…you've been sick…and I think you've pissed and shit the bed aswell…it's all matted in your hair!" Ron got straight out of bed looking like 'The creature from the Black Lagoon', tried to ruffle the sheets in such a way that you couldn't see the mess he'd made and then jumped straight in the shower whilst I sprayed deodorant around the room to try and mask the foul smell! When he'd finished, we could hear the room cleaners down the corridor, so he got dressed and we got all our equipment together and left sharpish – to this day I don't know what the reaction was of the cleaners, but I dread to think, given the mess Ron had made in that bed. I had never seen anything like that before and I haven't seen anything like it since! The other funnier memory I have of the trip to Hamburg, is the tannoy announcement we heard just before we left the ferry after it had docked. We were in the middle of a troop briefing when we heard;
BING BONG followed by;
"COULD A SAPPER P.NESS PLEASE REPORT TO RECEPTION…A SAPPER P.NESS PLEASE REPORT TO RECEPTION…THANK YOU"
Needless to say that there was a general outburst of laughter, and we all knew that the message could only have been requested by a member of 24, but we never did find out who the culprit was of that hilarious prank.

A few hours after leaving the ferry, we were approaching Plon, a small German town surrounded by forests and lakes, and it was a stunningly beautiful place about 20-25 miles south east of Kiel. We were staying in a German army camp about half a mile away from the town, and were taking part in a triangular exercise involving our squadron, a German engineer squadron and a Danish engineer squadron. However, there was almost a diplomatic incident on the first night when one of the locals asked one of the lads (quite a few of us had ventured out into the town on the first night), Why were we in Plon?…and was told, incorrectly of course, but such is the British Army sense of humour, that we were there to install a new cruise missile base (public feeling was globally running high at the time against nuclear weapons, with 'peace' camps at Greenham Common and Molesworth and popular organisations, such as CND – Campaign for Nuclear Disarmament)!! The following day, angry locals marched on the burgermeister's office demanding answers…the soldier responsible for this, like the 'Sapper P.Ness' incident, was also never found!! Our trip to Plon provided me with some priceless memories such as; Iki Bolton trying to climb into bed with Jim Stead after we had convinced Jim (a young, naïve 17 year old) that Iki and me were gay, Iki's playful behaviour that night, resulted in Jim screaming and shouting for his mother!!; We played football against the Germans…and we won with a team that included; Ronnie Barker, Mark 'Garth' Hamley, Gerry Hoolachan, Me, Geordie Kelf, Russ Carter, Norman Ryan, Kevin Burroughs, Pay Sergeant, Mark 'Iki' Bolton, Jamie Richards and managed by the legendary SSgt 'Steve' Gillies (however, we did lose against the Danes…again!)!

Also, part of the military training programme involved us being split into groups of about 15-20 soldiers and visiting various different 'stands' around the camp/training area, where the Germans and Danes would show us their different engineer skills and equipment, and in return, we had 'stands' that we would show them. The one 'stand' that sticks out in my memory involved the Danes showing us the clever use of 'fascine', in layman's terms; what looks like a bundle of drain pipes which is tied to the front of a vehicle to aid the crossing of an obstacle (ditch, stream etc). A Danish officer called us over to where an APC (armoured personnel carrier) was parked in front of a ditch with a bundle of 'drainpipes' on the front. "Strange!" I thought "What's all this about?". We stood there listening to this Danish officer explain how the 'fascine' worked. He described how the vehicle would drive up to the ditch at high speed, break suddenly, tilting the APC up at a suitable angle, dropping the 'fascine' into the gap, the driver would immediately engage the forward gear and drive over the ditch. All this was explained in good English and complimented with appropriate use of hand movements…Impressive! Sounded pretty straightforward…simple but effective! The officer spoke to the APC commander in Danish and a few moments later the APC reversed back to a distance of about 100m and the officer turned to us and gestured for us to move back to a safe distance, and explained that his men were about to provide us with a demonstration. We all stood there in expectant anticipation as the driver of the APC revved the engine. The signal was given and the APC moved off, slowly at first, but was soon motoring toward the ditch, with perfect timing, just before the ditch, the driver slammed on the brakes resulting in the APC stopping immediately, tilting to an almost vertical position, releasing the 'fascine' into the ditch. Instantaneously, the APC dropped to the floor, the driver engaged the forward gear and lunged forward…"THUD!" Disaster!!! There wasn't enough fascine on the bundle and the APC had slammed into the opposite bank of the ditch and stopped dead!! The Danish officer completely lost it, and had a 'meltdown' right there in front of us, throwing his beret on the floor and berating the APC commander and driver in Danish. We compounded their misery as, with our typical British squaddie sense of humour, clapped sarcastically at the failed demonstration…laughing hysterically didn't help either!!!

Later that week everyone was preparing for the scheduled 'field exercise', but news was filtering through that the exercise was going to be postponed until the Monday…British army 'rumour control' had all the answers as to why this had happened!!!Rumour had it that the Danes had had a 'union meeting' (yes, their army possessed a Union!) because they had been told that they weren't getting 'double time' for working on the weekend, and because the issue could not be resolved, they refused to go out on exercise. Whether this was true or not is debatable, but given that the Danish army were mainly concripts and their haircuts were similar to those sported by Benny and Bjorn from the Swedish pop group, ABBA, it is more feasible to believe that the rumour was true, than to dismiss it out of hand!! Whatever the reason, the exercise was postponed until the Monday! I don't remember much about the exercise other than the hailstorm that hit our harbour area (which happened to be in a huge tin barn). When the hailstones came, I had just finished a radio stag and was trying to get some sleep, however, these were no ordinary hailstones…they were just a little smaller than the size of a golf ball, and when they hit the roof of the barn the noise was understandably deafening! As with most hail storms, it only lasted 10-15 minutes, but by far, the worse hail storm I had ever experienced, and judging by some of the small dents in the cabs of the 4 tonners and one or two broken windows, highlighted the dangers of hailstones. Thankfully, as far as I am aware there were no reports of any casualties, and I was relieved I was under cover (with exception of the noise!)…the

172

thought of being beaten unconscious by hailstones wasn't and still isn't on my 'bucket list'!!

Toward the end of our time in Plon, it may have even been the last night, a bar-b-cue had been arranged for the three squadrons. The location was a short walk away from the accommodation block we were staying in, in an area where logs had been arranged as seating with other, larger logs used as tables, flanked with the forest on one side and a lake on the other. It was a breathtaking image, made all the more spectacular by the impending sunset causing an ever-changing kaleidoscope of colours...added into this beautiful scenery was a mix of approximately six hundred German, Danish and British soldiers. However, for the first hour, hour and a half there appeared to be three separate parties, as each squadron had isolated themselves from the others, with exception of some of the officers of each squadron who had mixed in a few small groups around the central part of the bar-b-cue. How do you get soldiers to mix from three different countries? Difficult, when there was a language barrier, and what appeared to be some sort of historical hatred evident between the Danes and the Germans!! What they didn't know is that British soldiers don't give a fuck about history or politics...a party is a party and EVERYONE should be enjoying themselves. Thankfully, unbeknownst to our 'continental friends' we had a secret weapon...Keith 'Ish' Isham and Jeremy 'Batch' Batchelor!!! They had obviously seen enough and were about to roll out the greatest ever version of '*Sunshine Mountain*' ever seen...the Danes and Germans had no idea what was about to hit them!!! Initially, Ish and Batch stood on the logs and started proceedings with members of our squadron;
"WE'RE CLIMBING UP SUNSHINE MOUNTAIN"
(climbing action)
"WHERE THE NORTH WIND BLOWS..." (cupping hands around mouth and making blowing actions).
Singing through to the last part;
"YOU AND I...YOU AND I" (pointing to two people who were not singing and then to themselves).
Then there was four people standing on the logs, then eight, then sixteen, then thirty two! At this point, Ish and Batch branched out and started to involve the Danes and the Germans...I can't remember whether it was Ish or Batch, but

173

one of them picked up one German soldier, slung him over their shoulder and then placed him on a log! However, the German soldier in question was an officer, who happened to be the area commander of that part of Germany...nevertheless, he embraced the situation enthusiastically and happily, and joined in the singing and associated actions – priceless, and a stroke of genius, as it set the tone for the rest of the German soldiers!! It wasn't long before everyone was on a log attempting to sing the song and carry out the actions that matched the words! It didn't matter that it wasn't perfect, and people didn't know the words, or even worse...speak English, it was about unity, attempting to bring everyone together regardless of rank or nationality. It must have been a sight to behold, approximately six hundred soldiers, from three different countries united in one goal...singing 'Sunshine Mountain'. It worked a treat and when the singing had finished, we all started mixing in groups, enjoying the food...and the beer! As the night came to a close there were Germans with the arms around Danes and us, and vice versa, singing, eating, drinking, wearing each other's combat jackets and generally having a great night...the British Army again successfully united countries using the power of song...with a helping hand from BEER!!!

Our time in Plon was over, but we experienced one more highlight that was a gift the British Army loved to inflict on its troops! We arrived at Hamburg probably about six to seven hours before the ferry was due to depart...they didn't like cutting things fine! Therefore, we all enjoyed the aged old wonderful experience of 'hurry up and wait'...in this instance, 'HURRY UP' and get to Hamburg so we could 'WAIT' around for hours and hours...brilliant forward planning, AGAIN!!!

Mick & Karen's Wedding, Padstow 1985

I've been to quite a few weddings over the years, but this wedding in Padstow was by far the best! From the time we left Chatham to the time we returned it was a fantastic weekend...for many reasons!! But it was an honour to attend and celebrate the joining in matrimony of two dear friends...Mick and Karen Stupple! It was also an honour to

174

return to Padstow in 2015 for their 30th Wedding Anniversary…and it was nice to meet a couple of old friends!!

At around 5pm on the Friday night, we (Andy 'Scouse' Murray, Johnno Johnson, Ben Cartwright, Me and three or four WRACs that were colleagues of Karen) left Chattenden in the squadron mini bus, driven by Johnny Witchell. We had a long journey in front of us to Padstow in Cornwall, with a stopover in Southampton to pick up a couple of lads, and as a result, the first stop had to be at Safeway in Strood… to ensure we were well stocked-up with beer, fags, crisps and pies/pasties. We knew it would be a long trip, but a trip made easier by the cans of beer that were loaded on in Strood, and the first cans were 'cracked open' before we had left the car park…followed inevitably by lewd singing!! It was about seven hours later when we crossed the county line between Devon and Cornwall, and this momentous event was greeted with a collective drunken cheer!! For the next 45 minutes I drifted in and out of a drunken sleep, and then suddenly and without warning, a second cheer erupted as we passed the sign welcoming us to Padstow…I tried to look at my watch through a drunken haze and I think it was about 1am when we pulled up outside Mick's mother's house. A short time later we had been taken to our accommodation; The girls were in the Old Ship Hotel, and we were in a holiday flat in the centre of the town. We hadn't really seen any of Padstow as it was bathed in darkness…and our vision had been impaired by alcohol (with exception of Johnny Witchell of course)!!

I got up later that morning, surprisingly fresh considering how drunk I'd been and I'd only had a few hours sleep! The flat was located on the top two floors of a three storey building and after a quick shower and shave I went downstairs to where the living room and kitchen were located. I found Johnny in the kitchen and he said;
"Morning Taff…are yee wanting some Coffee?" I nodded and replied.
"Aye…please Jock"
We sat there in silence, smoked a couple of cigarettes, and drank our coffees. When we finished I said to Jock;
"I'll wake the others and then do you fancy taking a walk around outside…get our bearings…explore a bit…"
"Aye…why not" Jock replied.

Within minutes, everyone was awake and Jock and I headed down the stairs to the main door, opened it and stepped out into the streets of Padstow. It looked very different in the light of day and despite it being a grey, damp November morning, you could immediately sense the beauty of this small Cornish fishing town. There were narrow, winding streets flanked with individual styles of terraced cottages painted in an array of various pastel colours. These images and the quintessential harbour, a short walk from the flat, were the images seen on postcards found all over Cornwall, and typical of this glorious part of Britain. I thought to myself "what a beautiful setting for a wedding…". John and I then shattered this picturesque image by showing our true, immature squaddie colours, as we shouted in unison at the top of our voices;
"OOO ARR…OOO ARR!!!"
We burst into laughter, but realised that our attempt at humour hadn't been appreciated by the locals, and we retreated to the safety of the flat!!!

Back in the flat, and after another couple of cigarettes and another cup of coffee, we started getting ready. There was no particular rush, but with five people and one bathroom we had to maintain a level of military discipline to ensure we were all ready roughly around the same time. It seemed to work, and with exception of waiting for Ben to put his boots on, we were all ready for the day's big event!! Once Ben had put his boots on we made our way down the stairs and within a few minutes were stood at the bar in the Old Ship Hotel ordering our first pint of the day. Mick and his cousin Peter, the best man, soon joined us, and whilst Mick appeared relaxed I think his cousin, Peter, was feeling the pressure as he sank his pint fairly quickly and ordered another…and I don't think that first pint was his first of the day!! Mick pulled Johnny and me to one side and asked us a question;
"Jock…Taff…could you do ee a favorrr!!
"Yeah…yeah…anything Mick!" We replied in unison.
"I want ee both to be usherrrs at the church"
"Yeah…yeah…of course…" I said
"Nae problem Mick" said Johnny
We turned to walk back to the bar and I grabbed Mick's arm and said;
"Hang on Mick…what the hell does an usher do then!"

176

"You stand at the church entrance handing out the orderrr of serrvice!"

"Oh Ok...Ok" and laughed.

Our drinks were soon finished and now that the girls (Karen's WRAC friends) had joined us, we were ready for the short walk to the church. We left the Old Ship Hotel, followed Mick and Peter and walked lesuirely through the narrow streets of Padstow, passed the London Inn and the Golden Lion, and onto Church Lane where we could now see the Church for the first time. The Church overlooked the town and therefore, once we'd passed the Golden Lion, there was a gentle gradient to overcome. But within five minutes we were approaching the gate at the edge of the churchyard, and with plenty of time to spare, we stopped for a cigarette. Mick was still fairly relaxed, and in hindsight it's easy to see why...when you are sure you have met that special person you want to spend the rest of your life with, why would you be nervous!! The church of St Petroc sits above the old part of Padstow, keeping its Godly eye on the residents below, and is a beautiful fifteenth century church, sitting in a well-kept churchyard with various types of both deciduous and evergreen trees, neatly cut grass and purveyor of beautiful memories and dark secrets! Cigarettes finished, we entered the churchyard and walked past the weathered headstones, now set at various angles and varying states of disrepair, new and old, each telling their own stories of love and tragedy, where couples now lay side by side with infant children, and the love and loss were intertwined into an eternity of togetherness. If you take an alternative view of a churchyard you'll realise you are surrounded by stories of love from across time; With this in mind, what better place to celebrate the unity of two people as they set out on their own journey of love, than a church surrounded by a centuries old churchyard who's now permanent residents had celebrated their own weddings in the same church many years before!!!

Mick was now safely positioned in the church and Johnny and I, standing either side of the entrance, were taking our 'usher' roles seriously. We were welcoming the guests as they arrived, directed them to the relevant side of the church, and providing them with the 'order of ceremony'. The time of Karen's arrival was fast approaching, and the last stragglers were now finally seated...our usher duties complete, Johnny and I took our seats in the church! People were talking in hushed

177

whispers and Mick turned around a couple of times and nervously glanced in the direction of the door in search of Karen. A couple of minutes went by and then the organist was given the signal, played a quick collective note to blow the dust out of the pipes and then immediately started to play Wagner's 'Bridal Chorus'. The door opened, in walked Karen on the arm of her step-father, and she looked absolutely stunning in a traditional long white wedding dress and a full shimmering veil, which couldn't hide her beaming smile and gushing happiness…another quick glance from Mick, and he met Karen's smile with a wide grin of his own! This beautiful image was completed by the older bridesmaids, adorned in peach coloured dresses, and the younger bridesmaids in angelic white dresses, all with matching bouquets. It was a beautiful ceremony, despite the best man having to run out halfway through to relieve himself…those nervous pints in the Old Ship Hotel had certainly taken their toll!!! As Mick and Karen signed the wedding register, Johnny, Scouse, Ben, Johnno, me and one of the other lads, slipped out of the church…we had decided, that morning, that we would provide a 'Guard of Honour' for the happy couple. We set ourselves in position outside the main entrance of the church, three on either side of the path facing each other and waited patiently. When we heard the familiar chime of the church bells, that signified the wedded couple were about to leave the church, we stood to attention to honour our very good friends, just as Mick and Karen were stepping through the porch. Friends, whose romantic relationship we had watched develop, far away in Chattenden…it was obvious to everyone present, we were witnessing a special moment, and it was an absolute honour to be part of their special day!!!

The ceremony was over and it was now time for the reception, and we headed back down Church Lane toward the town, and the Old Ship Hotel where the reception would be held. However, with exception of Scouse Murray, we decided to change out of our No2 dress uniforms and into our best 'civvies' before heading to the reception. Within twenty minutes we were at the bar ordering our first drinks of the evening and looking forward to an evening of beer, food, dance and…! With drinks in hand, Johnny, Scouse, Johnno and I were stood in front of the bar, Ben had disappeared…we found out later that he had eaten his carnation, for some

178

strange reason, and was projectile vomiting in the toilet!! We watched Karen and Mick making the obligatory 'thank you' tour round the room;

"Thank you for coming…"

"It's great you could make it…"

"Thank you both so much…"   etc

They were soon stood with us and there were hugs, shaking of hands and congratulations…I think I even hugged Johnny at one point, as we told each other what wonderful ushers we had been!! Johnny then pulled a chair over for the obligatory 'garter' photo, but when Karen, without a care in the world, hitched her wedding dress up and put her foot up on the chair, it was an opportunity that was too good to miss! I placed my hand on Karen's knee and looked innocently into the distance, Scouse laughed and covered his eyes with his right hand, whilst Johnny, Mick and Johnno stared intently at the garter…without warning 'FLASH' the moment was photographed and consigned to history!!

The wedding reception turned out to be a fantastic night, and Johnny, Scouse and I were also getting on well with members of Mick's family…some might say too well! Scouse was enjoying the company of Mick's sister, Lenora, whilst Johnny and I were enjoying the company of Mick's cousins, Judy and Karen respectively. Karen was a pretty girl with blonde hair and blue eyes (not my usual type) but with a great sense of fun…and adventure, as I later found out when I took her back to our flat!! Like all good days, they eventually come to an end, and when Karen (not Mick's new wife…his cousin!) left the flat that night, the curtain came down on an excellent day, celebrating the union of two wonderful people…the new Mr and Mrs Stupple!!!

After we'd said our goodbyes on the Sunday, it was time to head back to Chattenden. It is fair to say that as I sit here now, almost thirty two years later, I can honestly say that until recently, I remembered that weekend for all the wrong reasons. Yes, it was a fun weekend of beer, dancing, laughter and…! But the real reason we were there was to celebrate the union of two wonderful people…Mick and Karen! I now look at things differently and with a more mature mind and yes, those memories above are part of me, and should not be dismissed as they have helped shape the person I am today.

But, I look at the 'garter' photo today and I see I group of close friends, and I am immensely proud and honoured that despite not seeing each other for many years we are still friends today, and with the exception of Johnno, we were back together in Padstow in 2015 to celebrate Mick and Karen's 30th wedding anniversary, I even got to meet Mick's family again, Lenora, Judy…even Karen, who delighted in telling almost everyone;
"I shagged im at the wedding!"
I also got to meet Karen and Mick's children, Herbie and Gemma, and their beautiful granddaughters. I am proud to have been at the wedding, as I believe we all witnessed, what, I now consider, to be the beginning of the greatest love story I have ever seen. A story that continues to this day, and I feel privileged and honoured to consider Mick and Karen as very special friends. Little did we know the journey they would embark on when we were in 24, back in the eighties, when Mick used to grin and tell us;
"I'm going skiing tonight!!"
Those who know…know!!!

Brindle, Kirby, Craddock, Gregory, Harrison and others

The memories I made during my time in Chatham were made greater by those I served with! Some of these, for various reasons (not always pleasant), deserve a mention! Our own memories can be selective depending on what we want to remember and events/people we choose to forget! But we can also remember trivial things and all of us who served at 24 Field Squadron RE will have memories of persons or events we may have either been directly involved with or may have just heard from others…even a shared memory could be remembered differently by different people. There are so many that it would be difficult to pick out and detail individuals but who could forget;

1. Tommy Brindle bringing an adder into the squadron bar in a brown paper bag and then taking the snake on a night out.
2. Joe Kirby's great boxing knockout at Maidstone of a guy almost twice his size (I guess they didn't know Joe was a junior amateur boxer with 47 victories out

of 48 bouts, his only loss was the Midlands ABA final where he lost to Errol Christie on points).

3. Greg Gregory's one fight too many resulting in him getting posted prematurely.

4. Harry Harrison's numerous traffic accidents and being left dressed only in his No2 dress trousers during a parade, as the rest of his kit had been thrown round the square by Tiny Bott.

5. Dave Gorrill pushing the cook's head in the beans after he'd hit Dave's hand with a ladle.

6. 'Jack' Sutton sat on my parent's settee with love bites all over his neck after a girl showed him the highlights of Maesteg…behind the rugby club;

7. The Chief Clerk, SSgt Pat Walsh's ability to run for ever.

8. Going back to Bargoed with Taff Pritch where he introduced me to his old school friend, Melinda Griffiths…let's just say that nearly getting caught in a compromising position with Melinda by her huge rugby playing brother was a close shave. But being told later by Pritch that he was watching the 'goings-on' from the dining room courtesy of a small gap in the sliding doors was hilarious.

9. Karl Tebb shitting on the straps of his NBC (nuclear, biological and chemical) suit.

10. Drinking beer, piss and other fowl substances from the glass boot in the Squadron bar and playing 'pass the yuk' (chewing food and passing it to each other mouth to mouth…mmm).

11. Norman Ryan's ability to order a banquet of a meal from Chinese takeaway in Strood when drunk and then fall asleep after two mouthfuls leaving the rest of us, who had only bought chips, to finish off his meal…thanks Norman.

12. The two WRAC girls who I overheard talking in the NAAFI that were working their way through the alphabet by means of sexual conquests…they were trying to think of someone with a surname beginning with 'R' so I guess they were doing well.

13. Training all weekend putting up fencing in preparation for the task ahead at RAF Molesworth (we didn't know the reasons why or the whereabouts at the time).

14. Weymouth Bridging Camp 1985.
15. Skin (Scott Carr) and I taking two girls back to his room one Saturday night (the night before the Squadron photograph in 1985) and having hours of fun…if you know what I mean).
16. The cook, on duty over Easter, who fell out of a second storey window and was found by the guard (they heard moaning coming from the long grass) hours later with two broken legs;
17. Laith Palmer's horrendous limp and his insistence to participate in squadron parades and as a Catholic exercising his right to attend church when we were away on exercise.

There are many, many more and it would be impossible to go through them all. My physical time at 24 Field Squadron RE came to an end in May 1986, but mentally I never left and the memories of the times and the people are fond ones (mostly)! Please see a 'roll of honour' below of people I remember, I apologise if you are not on the list but after over 30 years there are bound to be casualties that have faded or disappeared from the memory:

24 FIELD SQUADRON RE – 'ROLL OF HONOUR'

Maj Newns	Maj Owen
Maj Wyatt	
Capt 'Jim' Benson	Capt Brand
Capt 'Bobby' Lampard	Capt Sheldon
Lt 'Simon' Cannons	Lt 'Dave' Hudson
Lt 'Chris' Garner	Lt 'Jeremy' Robson
WO2 'Tiny' Bott	WO2 Fuller
WO2 Hitchin	
SSgt 'Steve' Gillies	SSgt Lonnen
SSgt 'Ken' Carr	SSgt 'John' Peers
SSgt 'Pat' Walsh	
Sgt Buckley	Sgt 'Steve Woosh' Taylor

Cpl 'Jeff' Baldock
Cpl 'Al' Bowman
Cpl 'Eddie' Carroll
Cpl 'Nick' Deppe
Cpl 'Hamish' Fotheringhame
Cpl 'Keith' Isham
Cpl 'Taff' Leadon
Cpl 'Dave' Mansell
Cpl 'Dai' Morgan
Cpl 'Norman' Ryan
Cpl 'Phill' Tillyer
Cpl 'Z' Zalewski

Cpl 'Dickie' Bird
Cpl 'David' Bruce
Cpl 'Dave' Clement
Cpl 'Bud' Flannagan
Cpl 'Bob' Hussey
Cpl Jones
Cpl 'Taff' Lewis
Cpl 'Barry' Milton
Cpl 'Stan' Roberts
Cpl 'Martin' Sealy
Cpl 'Tim' Westlake

LCpl 'Carl' Allan
LCpl 'Jeremy' Batchelor
LCpl 'Iki' Bolton
LCpl 'Jim' Brown
LCpl 'Scott Skin' Carr
LCpl 'Andy' Cockle
LCpl 'Taff' Davies
LCpl 'Pat' Fegan
LCpl 'Jon' Harvey
LCpl 'Gerry' Hoolachan
LCpl 'Rab' Keill
LCpl 'Roger' Lee
LCpl 'Scouse' Murray
LCpl 'Laith' Palmer
LCpl 'Sooty' Seteram
LCpl 'Mick' Stupple
LCpl 'Paul' Weatherhill

LCpl 'Jock' Anderson
LCpl 'Taff' Best
LCpl 'Craig' Booker
LCpl 'Eck' Callaghan
LCpl 'Vince' Clarke
LCpl 'Geordie' Craddock
LCpl 'Dixie' Duricki
LCpl 'Iain' George
LCpl 'Dave' Hodson
LCpl 'Jamie' James
LCpl 'Bill' Lakey
LCpl 'Cliff' Morris
LCpl 'Charlie' Nash
LCpl 'Ron' Quick
LCpl 'George' Strachan
LCpl 'John' Taylor
LCpl 'Mick' Williams

Spr 'Dave' Angel
Spr 'Dinger' Bell
Spr Brew
Spr 'Kevin' Brookes
Spr 'Richie' Bulliemore
Spr 'Russ' Carter
Spr 'Cinders' Cindery
Spr 'Shaun' Coupland
Spr 'Gavin' Denton
Spr 'Rick' Dyke
Spr 'Kenny' Emmerson
Spr 'David' Forbes

Spr 'Ronnie' Barker
Spr 'Mick' Bourne
Spr 'Tommy' Brindle
Spr 'Rob' Brown
Spr 'Kev' Burroughs
Spr 'Ben' Cartwright
Spr 'Clem' Clements
Spr 'Dai' Davies
Spr 'Roger' Dewar
Spr 'Bob' Ellis
Spr 'Taff' Evans
Spr 'Dave' Gibson

Spr 'Greg' Gregory
Spr 'Harry' Harrison
Spr 'Jock' Higgins
Spr 'Taff' Holman
Spr 'Phil' Humphrey
Spr 'Paul' Jenkins
Spr 'Gaz' Kearney
Spr 'Paul' Kerridge
Spr 'Joe' Kirby
Spr 'Tony' Long
Spr 'Jake' Maiden
Spr 'Jock' McPake
Spr 'Jaggy' Mcvey
Spr 'Max' Maxwell
Spr 'Millie' Milner
Spr Shaggy O'Shaughnessy
Spr 'Mark' Parker
Spr 'Farouk' Patel
Spr 'Taff' Pritchard
Spr 'Jamie' Richards
Spr 'Geordie' Rogerson
Spr 'Andy' Smith
Spr 'Jack' Sutton
Spr 'Karl' Tebb
Spr 'Nick' Tranmer
Spr 'Womble' Wellen
Spr 'Wayne' Winfield

Spr 'Garth' Hamley
Spr 'Taff' Hayward
Spr 'Andy' Hill
Spr 'Treasure' Hudson
Spr 'Billy' Hunt
Spr 'Johnno' Johnson
Spr 'Geordie' Kelf
Spr 'Les' King
Spr 'Robert' Knock
Spr 'Stevie' Lyons
Spr 'Jock' Martin
Spr 'Jock' McGregor
Spr 'Mark' Methven
Spr 'Simon' Millerick
Spr 'Pat' O'Brien
Spr 'Colin' Page
Spr 'Andy' Parkin
Spr 'Nick' Pettit
Spr 'Charlie' Rainey
Spr 'Stu' Ridgeway
Spr 'Sam' Shaw
Spr 'Jim' Stead
Spr 'Phil' Swindells
Spr 'Chris' Thomas
Spr 'Simon' Walland
Spr 'Des' Westwood
Spr 'Johnny' Witchell

Chapter 4 – MWF (Military Works Force) & Nottingham

Prior to leaving 24 Field Squadron I had been told I would be posted to 26 Engineer Regiment RE at Iserlohn in Germany. However, a week later, and without reason, this was changed to HQ MWF (Military Works Force), based at Barton Stacey, nr Andover. HQ MWF, despite having a similar strength (numbers of persons in unit) it was a totally different type of unit to 24 Field Squadron RE, and consisted of a full colonel, two lieutenant colonels (half colonels), twenty to thirty majors and captains, twenty or so WO1s and WO2s, forty or fifty Staff Sergeants and Sergeants and the remainder were Cpls and below (draughtsmen, well drillers, drivers, clerks and storemen). The majority of those that were Sgts and above were 'Clerk of Works' responsible for compiling reports detailing the materials, costs and manpower required to carry out a construction task either in the UK or globally, tasks that would be carried out by a contingent of Royal Engineers. I didn't enjoy my time in this unit, and this is reflected by the fact that I can remember very few names from my time there. My main memories are from outside of the unit, as when HQ MWF was moved to Nottingham in July 1986 (approximately two months after I joined them) I joined a local rugby club and this became the main source of my socialising over the next five years. As seen in the previous chapter, I visited various places with 24 Field Squadron, HQ MWF, by comparison didn't go anywhere as a unit and therefore my role was similar to a '9 to 5' job with the occasional weekend duty. The next seven years in Nottingham/Long Eaton (Derbyshire) were a roller-coaster of emotions, with many highs and many lows and some of these stories will be covered in other chapters!!!

The move to HQ MWF provided me with a new challenge and I threw myself into this challenge wholeheartedly, but my efforts to 'impress' my new chief clerk were wasted as I experienced a ridiculous scenario – I was called in to the chief clerk's office expecting a 'pat on the back' but was left speechless when I found out the real reason he wanted to speak to me; I had been working longer hours to put my own stamp on my new job role and sometimes missed meals in the canteen, instead eating either in the unit club or across the road in a Little Chef! I was told that mealtimes were a parade and as I wasn't eating in the canteen I was missing a parade, if I continued with this behaviour I would find myself on OC's orders. For the remainder of my time in the army I started and finished my working day at the allocated time and attended all meals!!! This was the first of many factors that would ultimately result in me deciding to leave the army. The second factor followed the fifty percent tear I received to my cruciate ligament in my left knee, as opposed to allowing army surgeons to operate on it I was awaiting an operation at Derby Royal Infirmary, under, allegedly, one of the top knee surgeons in the country, a Mr Cargill. This, and my 'rushed' marriage resulted, in me signing a document where I refused a promotion to corporal, and the posting to 22 Engineer Regiment RE, based in Tidworth. The marriage in August 1988 and my new wife becoming pregnant, roughly coincided with a period where the IRA (Irish Republican Army) had started a campaign of terror against married soliders based in Germany...this was the final straw and I signed-off in March 1989, and my daughter, 'R', arrived in the July, I left the army in March 1990, and soon found out how difficult civilian life was, compared to the 'protected' life within the forces. The timing wasn't particular good as a recession hit in the early 1990s making it difficult to find suitable employment with a living wage. If financial hardship wasn't enough, 1991 was a difficult year emotionally, as we lost my father's only sibling, my Uncle Ivor, in the February and my mother passed away in the August. In between these two losses, we welcomed another child, a son, 'G', in the April, but there were question marks over his heart as a heart murmur was detected. As it turned out, this was a misdiagnosis, and it would take two years to finally obtain a correct diagnosis and the news was devastating...he had a coarctation of the aorta and needed urgent corrective surgery. Thankfully, he had the operation and at the time of writing leads a full life, working full time, playing football and enjoying a busy social life!!!

Despite the friendships I made in the East Midlands I knew that, due to the recession, and what had happened with our son and the premature death, at 46 years old, of my mother, we had to return to Wales to be near our families. The decision was made final and we returned to Wales in October 1993...my eight year stay in Nottingham/Long Eaton was over!!

LCpl 'R', the ruler and an unexpected warning!

It was a new posting and I didn't know anyone and nobody knew me…there was nobody I'd met that I'd encountered during my previous six to seven years in the army, and it was a lonely place at first! I wanted to make an impression and threw myself wholeheartedly into the job at hand, but I didn't meet my predecessor and therefore I had no handover and had no idea what kind of person he was!!! I didn't realise that my predecessor was what could be described as a 'typical clerk'…in the army they were called REMFs (rear echelon motherfuckers) and were similar to what people would refer to as 'nerds' during their school days. Not every clerk was like that, and as you saw in the previous chapter I certainly couldn't be considered a 'nerd'. During those first couple of months at HQ MWF the orderly corporal was a lad called, shall we say, LCpl 'R'…I got to know the sort of person he was during that very first week at Barton Stacey!!!!

I was sat at my desk settling into my new role at HQ MWF, and shared my new office area with a LCpl 'Jock' Ross, a balding, slightly overweight, but jovial character with a heavy Glaswegian accent. It was still early days and I was trying to keep my head down and make an impression with my new superiors…who didn't know anything about my strengths or weaknesses! My desk faced the opposite wall where Jock Ross was sat and to my right was a bank of four or five four drawer filing cabinets that separated my desk from the open corridor. On the other side of the corridor there were offices where various officers beavered away quietly, and popping their heads out now and again to ask for a file…I was still trying to work out what everyone was doing in this strange unit! The open corridor led to another space, similar to the one where Jock and I were sat, which housed the Chief Clerk.

It was early afternoon of another unremarkable day, and if I was honest, I was struggling with the boredom of this unit and the people in it…it was far removed from the hustle and bustle of 24 Field Squadron and the good mates I'd left behind at Chattenden! I sat there for a moment, stared into space and wished I was back amongst my former 24 mates as opposed to being surrounded by these morgue like surroundings…but little did I know that the boredom was about to abruptly end!!

I was quickly dragged back into reality by the arrival of the Orderly Corporal, LCpl 'R', who I'd briefly met when I first arrived that Monday. Initially, he totally ignored me and cheerfully asked Jock Ross;

"How's the newbee getting on Jock?" referring to me!

"Yeah...he's...settling in fine" Jock replied sheepishly, keeping his head down.

R then, without saying a word, walked over to my desk and picked up my ruler, smiled at me, and instantaneously hit me across the knuckles of my left hand with the thin edge of the ruler...he laughed hysterically and called me a "Taff wanker!".

I jumped out of my seat, walked around the edge of the desk and grabbed his shirt, just above his sternum, and as his inane smile disappeared I rammed him into the filing cabinets...I leant in and whispered in his ear;

"You pull another stunt like that and I'll ram that ruler so far up your arse...you'll need an operation to have it removed..."

I pulled my head away from his ear and looked him straight in the face and said;

"...now fuck off!" and pushed him into the corridor. He scuttled away back to his office, on the other side of the building, with his tail firmly between his legs just as the Chief Clerk peered around the wall from his office;

"What was that noise LCpl Thomas?" he enquired.

"Oh...nothing Chief...LCpl 'R' tripped and fell into the filing cabinets!" I declared innocently...winking at Jock Ross.

"OK LCpl Thomas...uh...carry on" and he disappeared back into his hideaway and his own little world!!

I sat back in my chair and whispered to Jock;

"What the fuck was 'R' playing at...what is his problem?...did he think I was just going to let him get away with that...the fat Brummie twat!"

Jock smiled and said;

"Thanks Taff, it's about time someone put him in his place...he's a bully, and the lad you took over from...well, he made his life hell...I...I don't think we'll see much of him from now on!"

I got the feeling that my predecessor was not the only one that LCpl 'R' bullied, but Jock was right...LCpl 'R' kept a low profile after that and I certainly never had any further problems with him...coward!!!

Stuart's stag and the mysterious beauty!

During my short time at Barton Stacey, my cousin Stuart got married and before every wedding there's the customary 'stag', and Stuart's wedding was no different. It was a fairly quiet affair…there was no trip to Magaluf, no funny costumes and no stripping the up and coming groom and strapping him to a lamp post! It was just four men (Stuart, his two mates and me) on a mini pub crawl in Kingswood, Bristol which finished in a nite club. The most memorable event of the night involved a beautiful girl…don't they always!

Stuart, his two bus driver mates (who were older and both married), and I, were in the raised bar area that overlooked the dance floor. We were sat on bar stools at a rail with a narrow shelf (enough room for our pints) surveying the scene before us, pointing out the pretty girls to each other…and the not so pretty ones! Typical male chauvinistic behaviour, but harmless fun nevertheless…then suddenly, and without warning, we were all stood there, mouths wide open staring at a girl who had just entered the nite club. She had stopped two or three yards into the room and was stood about ten yards away…directly in front of where we were sat! She stood there for a moment, looking around, before walking across the dance floor to the opposite side of the room…for a few minutes the four of us were mesmerized by the vision of unbridled beauty, and in unison our eyes followed her every movement! She had striking features: High cheekbones, perfect teeth and big eyes (we couldn't tell the colour from where we were sat), all enhanced by a subtle application of make-up. She had blonde hair cut into a smart eighties style bob that covered her left eye, resulting in her flicking her head seductively from time to time to show the fullness of her beautiful face. She had a model-like figure that was accentuated by a sleeveless, tight-fitting black dress, stockings and red patent leather high heeled stilettos…wow! The trance-like state that we were all in was soon broken by one of Stuart's friends saying;
"Go on Huw…ask her to dance…I'll buy you a pint if you ask her to dance!"
"Damn right I will…wait until the next song comes on!!" I said, smiled sarcastically, and with that I stood up and gave them all a wink;

189

"Watch this space!!"

I was soon making my way through the throng of people on the dance floor, gyrating away to the familiar tones of Wham's 'Club Tropicana' in their garish eighties garb, and was soon standing in front of the girl we'd seen enter the room a few minutes earlier. I tried to act casual as I waited for 'Club Tropicana' to finish, but I was captivated by the girl's beauty and could now see that those beautiful eyes were a deep brown and I thought:
"She's way out of my league!" However, I swallowed hard and asked her the question;
"Would you like a dance?"
"Yeah, sure…why not", she smiled, flicked the hair out of her left eye, turned and walked onto the dance floor, I followed and gave a knowing smile to Stuart and his mates as the mysterious girl and I found a space big enough for us both! She turned and faced me, smiled that beautiful warm smile again and we started dancing to the music of Soft Cell's 'Tainted Love'…a perfect choice! Amidst the heat of the dance floor, the flashing disco lights and the dry ice, the girl leant in to speak and it was soon obvious why the girl was on her own;
"I'm surprised you asked me to dance!"
"Why?" I said intrigued.
"Well…men…men…are normally so…so scared of me cos I'm so beautiful…it's not easy for men to approach a girl so pretty…they don't know what to say!"
I nodded and smiled politely, as she continued;
"It's not easy getting a boyfriend…they all think that I'm too good for them…and friends…I don't have any friends cos other girls are jealous of how pretty I am…"
I thought to myself, "Its maybe because you love yourself too much!!!"
"…it's hard being so pretty…do you think I'm beautiful?"
"Yeah" and smiled again, quickly becoming disinterested.
"Sometimes I wish I was just a 'plain Jane'…it's hard being so stunningly pretty…"
She continued to talk but it was all about her and it got to the point where I could see her lips moving but I'd stopped listening and was praying for the song to end so I could get back to my pint! Disaster…it was the 12inch version of the song and I sighed and rolled my eyes as Marc Almond

continued singing the second part "Where Did Our Love Go?" I thought, "This girl loves herself…there's no room for anyone else in a relationship with her!" By now I was just looking around the room willing the song to end and I'd lost all interest in this vain, self-obsessed girl. A sense of relief swept over me as Marc Almond sang the last lines of the song, knowing I could get back to Stuart and his mates and leave this girl and her vanity on the dance floor. As the song ended she asked me one more question and left herself wide open; "Given that I'm so beautiful…why did you ask me to dance…weren't you scared of me?"

Grabbing the opportunity with two hands, I looked her up and down, gave my best sarcastic smile and said;

"Nah…I'll dance with anyone me!" and I immediately turned and walked away back to Stuart and his two friends!

As I reached the top of the steps, that led to the bar area, Stuart handed me my pint and said;

"What did you say to that girl…she didn't look happy when you walked away!"

I told them what the girl thought of herself and what I'd said and we all laughed and openly cursed the beautiful girl and her vanity… but with a jealous admission that we all secretly knew that girls like that were way out of our league!!!

The Toilet

The camp at Barton Stacey was old, and apparently was built as a transit camp for American soldiers during the build-up before D-Day during World War II. We were there forty two years later getting ready to leave, and once we had moved the camp would be demolished. But typical of the 'bullshit' you have already read about in Chapter one, we had to make sure everything was clean…the camp was being knocked down, but for the 'handover' it had to be CLEAN!!!

Most of the packing had been finished and the offices were becoming emptier with each passing day. Despite the camp being demolished, the inevitable cleaning program had begun and I was looking forward to leaving this antique of a camp where nothing of any note happened and excitement levels were non-existent. Additionally, I couldn't wait to leave the stench emanating from the typists office, where it was

191

believed a poisoned rat had returned to its nest to die, filling
the air with pungent and sickly aroma of death!! The time was
drawing near to us leaving for Nottingham, and Chilwell
Barracks was to be the new home for HQ MWF, but the day
before we were due to leave I was in for a special treat which
highlighted the madness that was endemic in the British
Army!

I was with Jock Ross packing the last of the files when Sgt
Webb walked into the office;
"Ah…LCpl Thomas…come with me, I have a job for you" he
said cheerfully.
"OK Sgt Webb" I replied
I followed Sgt Webb out of the office, along the corridor to the
main entrance and out of the building. I thought to myself;
"Where are we going?"
I followed Sgt Webb around the building to a door on the far
side of the building;
"Here we are" and he pulled out a bunch of keys and
attempted to find the key that would unlock the 'mystery'
door. After trying three or four keys he finally managed to
unlock the door and swung it open. I stared in a similar
disbelief at the sight before me that Howard Carter would have
done when he discovered Tutankhamun's tomb…there in front
of me was a single toilet that obviously hadn't seen the light of
day since Tutankhamun's discovery. I looked at Sgt Webb and
thought to myself;
"You want me to clean THIS…a room and a toilet that hasn't
been used in God knows how long…in a building that next
week is going to be demolished!"
"Right LCpl Thomas…we need this cleaned to military
standards…ready for handover to the MOD!" said Sgt Webb
and smiled.
I was speechless…I had nothing to say, and Sgt Webb left me
there, walked away as I looked at the toilet in disbelief, and he
disappeared back into the building! After a couple of minutes I
snapped out of the trance like state I was in and moved toward
the toilet, plucking up the courage to lift the toilet seat. After a
couple of deep breaths, I finally lifted the seat…bad
move…the blackened orange crust on the pan of the toilet
stared back at me, and was soon joined by a foul stench that
appeared to burn the hairs in my nostrils and my eyes were
soon watering!! I reeled back three or four steps and was bent

double, dry gagging, as the summer breeze struggled to bring sweeter smells from the hedgerows and surrounding fields. I thought…"This is going to be a difficult job!"

An hour or so later, I was surrounded by a multitude of cloths, scourers and three empty bottles of Jif. The toilet was now ready to be handed over…and demolished!!! I experienced some strange cleaning regimes during my time in the army, but cleaning a toilet that was going to be demolished a few days after we left Barton Stacey was by far the strangest, and a complete waste of time! We were always taught to obey the order and ask questions later…I obeyed the order, I asked questions later, but there were no answers…how could there be, it was nonsensical!!

Long Eaton R.F.C.

HQ MWF didn't have a rugby team, therefore, when we moved to Chilwell, Nottingham I had to find a rugby club so I could continue my playing career. Initially, I had made contact with Nottingham R.F.C. But I had recently bought a 'Rugby World' magazine, and when I was leafing through it I saw an advert that caught my eye…players were wanted by a club called Long Eaton R.F.C. I thought to myself "Long Eaton…I'm sure I've seen that on a road sign outside Chilwell Barracks. I looked at the telephone number, and sure enough, it was a Nottingham area dialing code. I rang the number and a man called Wayne Browne answered in a strange Australian type accent (I found out later he was a New Zealander). I told him I was new to the area, played rugby, had seen the advert in 'Rugby World' and was interested in joining the club. Wayne gave me directions to where they trained on West Park and told me to report to the captain, Danet Beckford;
"How will I know who he is?" I said
"Easy…he'll be the only black player there" Wayne said nonchanantly.
This story is about that first night at Long Eaton R.F.C.!!!

I'd borrowed a bicycle from one of the lads, John McArtney, and with a £1 in my pocket (enough for a sociable pint) I set-off for my first training session with Long Eaton R.F.C. I had no idea about any short-cuts there may be between Chilwell and West Park and had to rely on the main roads for the entire journey…I cycled past the town centre, over the canal bridge, where I could see the impressive cotton mill buildings that dominated the Long Eaton skyline, and along Derby Road passing shops, pubs, churches of different denominations, schools, terraced streets and large detached houses with well-cared for gardens. It was a quaint town, and I was suitably impressed as I approached the Wilsthorpe roundabout. This was the roundabout that I had been instructed to turn left, during my telephone conversation with Wayne Browne a couple of days earlier. I took the first left and cycled down the road on a small incline toward a large car park about three to four hundred metres away. I turned into the car park and could see the leisure centre away to my right and the park, which reminded me of Newbridge Fields back in my hometown of Bridgend. I drove into the park and immediately on my left I could see the cricket pavilion of Sawley Cricket Club and on the other side I could see twenty to thirty men, who looked like rugby players (based on their size and deameanour), and who were being led on a gentle jog around the field by…a black man who I presumed was Danet Beckford, the person I was told was the Captain of Long Eaton Rugby Club. I stopped, jumped off the bike and pushed it to where a disorderly pile of sport bags, rugby balls and tracksuits were strewn on the ground and waited for Danet and the guys to jog back around. Within minutes they were approaching and Danet shouted;

"Is your name Huw" in an accent I was now becoming used to after a couple of weeks in the area.

"Yeah…Danet?" I enquired.

"Yeah…Wayne told me you'd be coming tonight…come and join us…we're warming up"

"Ok" I shouted and ran over to join everyone. As we jogged around the field Danet introduced himself to me, and everyone else…a lot of names to remember, but I had a good feeling about joining the club, even moreso when I enquired about who the kicker was and Andy Gibb (who was the vice-captain and the scrum half) shouted;

"YOU CAN KICK…BRILLIANT!"

It was a good training session and when it finished I was invited to join them in the club, which I was told was located in an old school near the town centre! I walked with Danet, and one or two others, across West Park, a scenic and glorious expanse of land, accentuated in the dusk of the summer's evening by an array of colours from the abundance of trees and flowers, and the cotton mill that dominated the skyline toward the bottom left hand side of the park. As we walked through the park I fielded the many questions being fired at me, such as;

"How long have you played rugby?"

"What teams have you played for?

"Where are you from?" etc. They also answered questions I asked about other teams, how far we travelled etc! Knowing a lot more about each other, we eventually reached Parklands School, and the bar…time for a beer and more introductions! It was here I finally met Wayne Browne, a burly bearded Kiwi, Don Mackintosh, the Club Chairman and Derek Deacon – the latter two were both Welsh from Ebbw Vale and Kidwelly respectively! By the time Len Jones, who was from Newport, walked in 10-15 mins later I knew this was the club for me…surrounded by all these Welsh people had to be a good omen! Everyone made me feel very welcome, and the lads I would be playing with seemed like a close group of friends, as the majority had come through the colts (u19s) under the guidance of Derek Deacon. I was about to say my farewells when Ian Mackintosh (Don's son), Scottie Hutchinson, Paul Gardener and Danet announced they were going into the town for a couple of beers, and asked me if I would like to join them. I initially declined as I admitted that I had only brought enough for a pint…within a few seconds Don was thrusting a five pound note in my hand and said;

"Go on Huw…go with the boys and get to know them better" and he gave me a knowing wink.

"Cheers Don…I'll give you the money back next week if that's ok!" I replied and was soon heading into Long Eaton town for the first time with my new 'soon to be' team-mates! My first impressions of Long Eaton were positive ones, mainly due to the large concentration of pubs (including a nite club) in and around the town centre. After visiting three or four of these and enjoying a pint in each we headed back to Parklands! As I hadn't eaten anything, I was becoming a little unsteady on my feet and beginning to slur my words, and this was a problem…as it was then I remembered that I had to cycle back to Chilwell Barracks!! "Oh well!" I thought, "I'll just have one more pint and then I'll head back to camp!

Three pints later and close to midnight I staggered out of Parklands pushing the bike…I attempted to get on it, but fell off twice…and I hadn't even left the car park! Before I'd reached the top of the canal bridge, around the corner from Parklands, I'd fallen off a further three times…I slowly realised that the eight pints I'd consumed were certainly hampering my cycling skills! At one point, after further falls along Nottingham Road, Scottie pulled alongside and asked; "Everything OK Huw?"

"Yeah…yeah…yeah (hiccup)…I'll be ok…am I…I…I…going (hiccup)…the right way?" I slurred and pointed aimlessly somewhere in between the direction of Chilwell and the sky!

"Yeah…straight on to the lights…take a left, and then right at the next lights back to the Barracks…take it steady Huw!

"Thanks Scottie…I will" and then fell off the bike again!!

I got home safely, but it did take a lot longer than the cycle ride from Chilwell to West Park a few hours earlier. When I woke up the following morning I was covered in cuts, grazes and bruises…not from rugby training, but from all the falls off the bike on that return journey back to the barracks. I remember thinking at the time "What a great night…can't wait to meet the lads again, but it was the last time I cycled to Long Eaton…EVER!!!

More of Long Eaton R.F.C. in a later chapter!!!

RE 200!

In 1987 the Royal Engineers celebrated the 200th anniversary of receiving the 'Royal Warrant', and as a part of the celebration there was a two day sporting event arranged in Brompton Barracks! My fellow LCpl, Steve Roberts, and I had been playing badminton and we entered the competition and travelled to Chatham for the two day event!!!

We walked out of Chatham railway station, jumped in a taxi and ten minutes later we pulled up outside Brompton Barracks. It was almost lunchtime, so we immediately made our way to the junior ranks cookhouse. A familiar building to me, as it also housed the NAAFI where the 'Smartie Party' was held; a place where dreams were made and hearts were broken…normally, all in the same evening!! The soldiers on trade training courses hadn't broken for lunch, it appeared we were the first arrivals for the RE 200 sports events, as we were the only people, with exception of the cooks and the civvy (civilian) staff, in the cookhouse. We both made our way to the hot plates and chose our food…both settling for a simple choice of fish fingers, chips whereas I had peas with mine, Steve opted for the good old faithful…beans! Armed with our meals, the next difficult choice was 'where to sit?', faced with a huge room filled with empty chairs and tables, choosing a place to sit seemed harder than it should have been, but we settled for a table that was fairly central and sat down. We quickly realised that we didn't have a knife and fork (every solider is issued with a knife, fork, spoon and a green plastic mug when they join the army), therefore, there was no cutlery available for people to use like civilian cafaterias. I said to Steve;

"They must have plastic knives and forks for emergencies…let's go and ask the civvy staff who clean the dishes to see if they have any".

Steve and I walked across the room to a small serving hatch where I could see an elderly lady, she looked like a typical grandmother, with greying hair and gentle demeanor. As we approached the hatch she gave us a welcoming smile and asked in a strong Chatham lilt;

"Ow can I elp you boys?"

"We were wondering if you had any plastic knives and forks…and a couple of paper cups? She turned her head…we certainly weren't expecting what came next as she shouted;

"ERE JOHN…YOU GOT ANY FUCKING KNIVES AND FORKS". We heard a muffled "Yeah…how many?" coming from the back of the room and she turned to us and asked;

"Ow many of you are there then?"

"There's only us two at the moment, but there could be quite a few more coming from all over the UK and Germany…there's sporting competitions over the next couple of days to celebrate the RE 200!"

"Ow many's that then?" She asked.

"I dunno…perhaps…a couple of hundred…!" Before I had the chance to say any more she gave me a disgusted look before shouting;

"TWO FUCKING UNDRED…YOU'RE AVING A FUCKING LARFF!!" She got off her stool and walked out of sight, but we could still hear her moaning;

"Two fucking undred John…two fucking undred…no fucking warning…fucking wankers…!"

We heard a muffled "Yeah fucking out of order Irene" from John. At this point, I looked at Steve, who was red faced, bent double with his hand over his mouth in an attempt to suppress a laughing fit! The maternal matriarch image had been shattered! Within a couple of minutes she was back with two sets of plastic knives and forks and two paper cups, and passed them to me still moaning;

"Two fucking undred…un-fucking-believeable…ere you go darling…" and she gave me a wink before finishing with:

"…the rest of em can fuck right off when they come…they'll get fuck all off me…ta ta boys…better go and eat your fucking grub before it gets fucking cold!" and before I could say thanks she disappeared and began cackling and talking to herself "two fucking undred!"

I was struggling not to laugh and managed to whisper to Steve;

"Cumon Steve…let's go!" We walked back to the table and sat down, but Steve by now was red-faced with tears streaming down his face. Every time he'd attempt to talk, he'd spurt forth some gibberish, point toward the hatch before erupting into another fit of laughter! I'd warned him about Chatham women, but nothing could have prepared him for what we witnessed from the sweet old lady at Brompton Barracks…but there was more!

We never did play Badminton, as Steve was already missing his kids, and we headed back in Chatham train station to catch the next train to London. As you enter the station, ten metres in front of the entrance is the ticket barrier that leads down to the platform, and 10-15 metres to the left of the entrance was the ticket office. I said to Steve;

"I'll sort the tickets out…you wait by the barrier!"

I joined the queue at the ticket office and almost immediately there was a loud 'BANG!' as two women burst through the door of the station, one ran toward the barrier whilst the other one ran toward me! Suddenly, the girl just behind me turned and shouted to her friend;

"ADA…IF THE TRAIN FUCKING COMES, LEAVE THE FUCKING DOOR OPEN SO I CAN FUCKING JUMP ON!!"

I looked at Steve…his head had rocked back and he was laughing loudly, and I thought;

"Welcome to Chatham Steve".

A short while later we were sat on the train heading to London and Steve was still laughing about his two encounters with Chatham women!!

Paradise!!

It was Danet's stag party and a trip had been arranged to the Derby Beer Festival at the Assembly Rooms in Derby. We'd had a great time at the beer festival and were about to board the coach back to Long Eaton when Mark Davidson asked;
"Anyone up for going to Paradise Night Club?"
Never one to miss an opportunity for a chance of more drink and the possibility of meeting a new woman, shouted;
"Count me in Mark"
Therefore, whilst the others went back to Long Eaton on the coach, Mark and I caught a taxi to Paradise…where I ended up later certainly didn't live up to the exotic name of the night club!!

We'd had a great night at the Derby Beer Festival and were now all walking (and staggering) back to the bus that was waiting to take us back to Long Eaton. As we approached the bus, Mark Davidson shouted;
"ANYONE UP FOR GOING TO PARADISE?"
I turned to Chris Brookes and said;
"What's Paradise Chris?"
"It's a night club Huw" Chris replied. I thought for a moment, and then shouted;
"I'LL COME MARK…I'M OFF TOMORROW…WHAT THE HELL!"
No-one else took Mark up on his offer, and a few minutes later the two of us jumped into a taxi and Mark said;
"Paradise please driver". As we drove away I looked out of the window…this was my first time in Derby and I had no idea where we were going, but I'd taken the Friday off so I didn't really care!

I don't remember much about Paradise other than Mark and I met two girls, one was slim, pretty and smartly dressed, and I was with the other one…who was, shall we say , robust and visually challenged…in other words, I had met the resident fat, ugly bird…again!!! It could be argued that the pairs had picked themselves, as I was the less impressive male specimen out of me and Mark. Before Paradise closed, the four of us took a taxi back to the house of the girl that Mark was with, it was a small terraced house, similar to those seen in and around ITVs opening credits of 'Coronation Street'!! We stepped in off the street and the interior reflected the appearance of the owner; beautifully decorated in an array of pastel colours, chic furniture and fittings…a finish that any interior designer would have been proud of! After a quick drink the girl I was with suggested it was time we left, saying her house was only down the street. We said our farewells and walked hand in hand down the quiet, deserted street – a romantic setting completed by the stars and moonlit sky! But this romantic scene soon disappeared when she opened the door to her house; The front room that you stepped into off the street hadn't seen a paint brush in many a year, the furniture looked as if it had been dragged off a rubbish tip and the carpet…oh my God, the carpet was covered with numerous piles of dog shit, from the alsation that was now jumping up attempting to lick my face, some of the piles were a petrified creamy white colour, suggesting that they had been there for a while! Almost immediately, the smell of the dog shit filled the room…and my nostrils! This girl didn't seem at all phased or embarrassed by the mess, and after playing hopscotch through the room and through the second room (where the conditions were the same) we were stood in a sort of lean-to kitchen…sadly the décor and dog shit theme matched the other two rooms!! If I had known where I was in Derby, and didn't have my 'beer goggles' firmly fixed in place, I would have left…but those 'beer goggles' had destroyed common sense and rationality and replaced them with the animalistic urge for drunken sex, and nothing was going to stop me achieving that goal!!

At this point, I asked;
"Where's the toilet?"
"Top of the stairs…turn right, and it's straight in front of you" she replied, pointing at the stairs behind a door slightly ajar in the opposite corner of the middle room.
"Cheers" I said, and hopped across the room successfully missing the dog shit (again) and stepped into the darkness

behind the door (there was no light). I'd only taken two steps when I heard her shout;

"MIND THE ST...!!" Too late! As I took the third step...WOOSH...THUD...I dropped through the stairs in to the cupboard below, immediately stepped out casually in to the small corridor between the front and middle rooms, didn't say anything and walked/hopped back to the stairs for a second attempt at reaching the toilet! This time I made it over the two steps that were missing and finally reached the top of the stairs, turned right and the strong aromatic stench of stale urine beckoned me from the darkness! I turned the light on...urgh! The toilet was filthy (surprise, surprise!), but I was desperate and had no choice and stood there in heaven as I relived myself! When I'd finished I reached for the flush handle and pushed down...nothing...it was broken...things surely couldn't get worse...or could they?

The girl, by this time, had joined me upstairs, and holding my hand she lead me into her bedroom, where more surprises were in store! The décor matched the rest of the house and the continental quilt on the bed was stinking...it was black and didn't look as if it had been washed...EVER! Well, that didn't stop me either...the beer goggles were well and truly glued on! In true Sapper fashion the deed was done...with added extras! The shame didn't hit me until I woke in the morning...but pleased that the target had been compromised and the mission was complete!!! I was awoken by a women in the street shouting and screaming that she'd been robbed and the girl I'd been 'wrestling' with a few hours earlier was gone! Where the hell was I? What sort of place was this? The reality of the situation began to sink as I took in the surroundings with sober vision and the squalor I was in was far worse than I'd feared. I daren't go out of the house, and had to wait until she came home from work. After sitting in the house all day there was a sense of dread...and relief, when I heard keys in the front door! I think she was pleasantly surprised that I was still there, but in the light of day I was horrified by her appearance; short, unkempt greasy hair, acne around her mouth and forehead, and bigger than I'd remembered with badly fitting clothes. I knew she wasn't girlfriend material and didn't hesitate when she asked;

"Shall we go out again tonight?"

"I can't…I've arranged to go out with my friends…I'm meeting them at six thirty…is there any chance you can book a taxi" I smiled nervously.

She looked disappointed but said, "OK".

She went next door to use her neighbour's phone and booked a taxi to pick me. When the taxi arrived we said our awkward farewells and within a few minutes I was heading back to Breaston…it was 5.30pm.

After a quick bath a change of clothes and a short taxi ride into Long Eaton, I walked into the Barge Inn just after 6.30pm. Danet was already there and straight away asked me;

"What time did you get back from Derby?"

"Ten to six!"

"TEN TO SIX THIS MORNING…YOU DIRTY STOP OUT!" and he laughed.

"Ten to six…45 minutes ago". Danet's face was a picture as I told him all about my night…and day in Derby. Danet then told me what had happened to him on the bus back from Derby! The rest of the lads stripped him naked and threw him off the bus by Wilsthorpe roundabout, and he had to run naked down Parkside Avenue, across West Park, through the town centre and back to his house on Chesterfield Avenue. We were sat there laughing at each other's misfortune and were still laughing when Scottie and Geoff Charlesworth turned up a few minutes later!!!

Lucky escape!!

Jake Maiden and I were due to travel down to Chatham for a Sapper rugby match, and we normally travelled by train. But Brigadier Barr, the Chairman of the Royal Engineers R.F.C., was attending a seminar at Chilwell and offered us a lift to Chatham, in his staff car, for the game and a lift back early on the Thursday morning! We jumped at the offer, as this meant we could stay for a few beers after the game and visit the 'Smartie Party' at Brompton, as opposed to travelling back by train soon after the game had finished…brilliant!!!

After the game against the Royal Signals, which we'd won convincingly, Jake, Taff Randall and I enjoyed a few beers in the bar at the US Chatham ground in Brompton. This was followed by a beer at one of our old haunts, the 'fun pub' in

Brompton High Street, the Two Sawyers, before reaching our final destination…the Smartie Party in Brompton Barracks. We had a great night with our side-kick, Taff Randall, and it was all made possible by the fact we were being picked up by Brigadier Barr at 5am the following morning to head back to Chilwell. Normally, we'd have a couple of quick pints at the clubhouse before catching the London train from Chatham around 6pm, followed by a tube to Kings Cross/St Pancras and finally our train back to Nottingham!

Jake had left me to handover our bedding in the transit accommodation above the guardroom at Brompton Barracks, and once that was completed I joined Jake and Brigadier Barr in the staff car, parked up outside the guardroom. Jake had purposely left me the front passenger seat as the car was driven by a WRAC (Womens Royal Army Corps) driver, knowing how much I hated WRACs, following an acrimonious break-up with my WRAC girlfriend, Jenny Knight, a few months earlier. When I opened the passenger door and climbed in the driver said;
"Hello" in a strong, but gentle, scouse accent.
"Hello" I grunted and angrily stared straight ahead, as I heared Jake sniggering in the back…the twat! I thought to myself "I'll get you back for this!"
Over the next hour or so the driver attempted to make small talk, as Jake and the Brigadier snored in unison, but I continued to grunt one word replies, feeling nothing but contempt every time she started to speak! As we approached the M1 Brigadier Barr woke up and said;
"Stop at the next services please Private Fleetwood"
"Yes Sir" she replied, and ten minutes later we were pulling into Toddington Services. The staff car came to a halt and Brigadier Barr said;
"Ten minutes gentlemen…Pte Fleetwood can I get you anything?"
"No Sir, I'm fine…thank you Sir"
We got out of the car and I gave Jake a friendly clip around the head and whispered;
"Wanker!"
Jake laughed mockingly! After a quick visit to the toilet we were in the shop buying a much needed can of coke each and a newspaper. I found the newspapers and was greeted with the

same story; a fire at Kings Cross/St Pancras tube station that had killed twenty seven people. I called Jake over;
"JAKE...TAKE A LOOK AT THIS!" I held up the newspaper and the colour disappeared from his face! As I read the article aloud, we both looked at each other in horror when I read the time it had happened...19.30hrs!!
"Jake we could have got caught up in that as we normally came through there at a similar time!"
"Shit Taff...you are right!" Jake exclaimed.
The reality hit home that had we not had the lift with Brigadier Barr we could have walked straight into that fire. I purchased a copy of '*The Sun*' and we walked back to the car in silence, numbed by the realization that we had certainly had a lucky escape on the night of Wednesday 18th November 1987!!!
Soon we were back in the car and travelling up the M1 toward the East Midlands and I just stared at the headline in front of me! By the time we'd reached Nottingham, I still didn't know what Private Fleetwood looked like, but that soon changed. When we arrived at Chilwell I was told to take care of Private Fleetwood, and by the end of the day I'd warmed to this stunning scouser and had arranged to meet her at Chattenden when I was down for the next Sapper rugby match in a couple of weeks...that's a story for another book!

Dave Pickford

Dave was a quiet lad, a LCpl who appeared to have a bright future in front of him; He was eagerly waiting to start an AIPT (Assistant Instructor Physical Training) course, had a girlfriend back home, and as far as we aware, he had no money worries!! When he went out on the Saturday night with a few of the lads from HQ MWF, nobody could have foreseen what would unfold over the next twenty four hours!!

It was a Sunday morning and I'd only been on duty for about 45 mins when the phone rang;
"LCpl Thomas, Duty NCO Military Works Force speaking".
"This is Loughborough station, Leicestershire police...could you confirm that you have a LCpl D.Pickford stationed there?"
"We have a Dave Pickford here!...Is there anything I can help you with?" I asked in a tone littered with intrigue.
"We have found a body and have reason to believe that it is likely to be that of LCpl Pickford...could I please speak to

your unit Sergeant Major?" I hesitated, as I tried to comprehend what the policeman had just said.

"I'll have to send the duty driver to fetch the sergeant major...could I please take a contact number so I can call you back?" The policeman gave me the number and I said I would get the sergeant major to call them back once he had been located. I found the sergeant major's address and sent the duty driver to his house. Within ten minutes the sergeant major was stood in front of me asking;

"What's happened LCpl Thomas?" I told him about the phone call and what I'd been told...the colour drained from his face in shock, and then he asked for the number and started to dial! A couple of minutes later he put the phone down and for a moment hesitated before telling the driver to start the landrover...he had to go to Loughborough! Within a couple of minutes, I was all alone and struggling to process the information...it didn't seem real...Dave kill himself!...Nah! They must be mistaken...why! I couldn't think of a reason why he would do it? The whole situation seemed like a dream...I made a cup coffee, lit a cigarette and sat down in the chair...waited...waited...lit another cigarette and waited!! It must have been an hour and a half later when I heard the landrover pull-up in front of the building. I jumped up, knocked the ashtray, which was now half full of half-smoked cigarettes, off the table...I was clearing up the mess when the sergeant major walked into the room...he was ashen and in a zombie-like state as he attempted to tell me that he'd had to identify the body and confirmed it was Dave's!! I just stood, open mouthed listening to the sergeant major as he told me they had found Dave in his car with all the windows taped up and a pipe from the exhaust leading into passenger side window...he had committed suicide as a result of carbon monoxide poisoning!

It wasn't long before word had got round, and soon I was joined in the Duty NCO's office by my mate Rob Martin. Rob was inconsolable as he had been out with Dave the previous night and he was really struggling to come to terms with what had happened! Rob told me that a few of the lads, including Dave, had gone out for a few beers and they then decided to go to the new night club in Nottingham, 'The Black Orchid'. Dave had offered to drive as he said he didn't feel like drinking and no-one questioned it, as Rob confirmed;

"We didn't question him not wanting a drink…we were just selfishly glad we had a lift!"

After an hour or so in the club, Dave said he had a headache and would they mind if he headed back to camp.

"No-one minded Taff!" Rob sobbed. Dave cheerfully said his goodbyes and that was the last time we saw him;

"He never came back to camp did he?..." Rob said, knowing the answer! I nodded no and looked at the floor!

"…why didn't I stop him Taff…why!" Rob looked at me in the forlorn hope that I may provide the answers!

"You didn't know Rob…you didn't know he was going to do what he did…he gave you no indication…no signs…how could any of you have known!"

"But…!"

"But nothing Rob…you can't blame yourself…you had no idea!" I put a consoling arm around Rob as he sobbed uncontrollably and we both sat there remembering Dave…but neither of us understanding why he'd taken his own life!

No-one ever knew the real reasons behind Dave committing suicide…there were rumours of a suicide note, but we didn't know for sure! We did find out later that it happened around the anniversary of his younger brother's death, but we didn't know if this was the real reason for Dave's decision. His behaviour leading up to the phone call I took that Sunday morning was normal, even when he left 'The Black Orchid' that fateful evening, there were no tell-tale signs that he may have been distressed or even depressed, his demeanour was normal…there was nothing Rob and the others could have done! He'd obviously planned it all as he never went back to Chilwell after leaving 'The Black Orchid'…instead, he drove to a piece of wasteland in Loughborough, placed one end of a hose on the exhaust and the other end into the car, taped up the windows (with exception of the driver's side) and took his own life in a pre-planned suicide and no-one could have done anything to stop him!! It was a tragic event, compounded by his two brothers (both serving soldiers) arriving at the camp a few days later to collect their brother's personal belongings…after also losing their younger brother a year earlier. What an absolute tragedy!!!

Cruciate Injury

I had never received a serious injury playing sport…yes, I had suffered minor injuries, such as; bruising, cuts, grazes, groin strains and even concussion!! But I had no idea the impact that suffering a 50% tear to my cruciate ligament, whilst playing for Long Eaton in a game against Dronfield, would have on my future…there was no immediate understanding of the seriousness of the situation, but I would soon find out!!

I lay on the trolley bed in one of the many cubicles of the fracture clinic at Queen's Medical Centre, Nottingham, patiently, but nervously awaiting the arrival of a doctor…I looked down at my heavily swollen left knee, feeling very sorry for myself!! It seemed as if I had been in the cubicle for hours (in reality, it was no more than twenty minutes), before I heard voices from the other side of the curtain…then suddenly the curtain was pulled back and in stepped the doctor and said; "Huw!"
"Pete" I said shocked, recognising Pete Howard from Long Eaton rugby club.
"I heard you'd been injured…let's have a look!" and he closely examined the swelling around my knee, and attempted to move my lower leg with one hand whilst applying pressure to my knee with the other…the pain was unbearable and I winced more than once, and gripped the sides of the trolley bed. He placed my leg back on the trolley bed, stepped back and said;
"I believe it's probable that you have damaged your cruciate ligaments…but it is difficult to determine exactly what has happened from a visual examination…I'd like you to come in this weekend so I can carry out an arthroscopy…basically, put a small camera (endoscope) into your knee to determine the full extent of the damage…"
"Ok Pete" I said, not fully appreciating the seriousness of what he had said.
"I'll get the desk staff to sort out the details…I'll see you on the weekend" and with that he left the cubicle!!

The weekend of my arthroscopy turned out to be quite amusing, as the ward I was admitted to on the Friday afternoon also doubled-up as the 'emergency ward' (people involved in various types of accidents were transferred to the ward from A&E). By the Saturday evening our six person bay was full, and as you stepped into the bay the patient in the first bed on the left was the British power lifting champion who had broken his ankle when he stepped off a ladder; He was a huge man with a sense of humour to match. In the next bed was an elderly gentleman and I'm not sure what was wrong with him, then me (in the corner, by the window), opposite me was a man who had fallen off a horse; He was lying flat on the bed with his head in traction due to a suspected spinal injury. Next to him was a man who had been involved in a traffic accident, and as a result had a few broken bones including a few ribs. I can't remember who was in the last bed opposite the power lifter!! The humour element was provided by an unknown patient in the next bay who, from time to time, would let out an exaggerated series of moans followed by shouting;

"Nurse...nurse...help me...nurse..." they were pathetic attempts at trying to obtain sympathy! The problem was that every time this happened the power-lifter would make some sarcastic comment resulting in everyone in our bay breaking out in spontaneous laughter. However, the man with the broken ribs would start laughing, and then cry out in pain due to his broken ribs – making the rest of us laugh all the more! This continued throughout the night and into Sunday and I really don't think I've laughed more, and by the time I was discharged my ribs hurt more than my knee! However the one downside was that the arthroscopy confirmed that I did have a fifty percent tear in my cruciate ligament and over the next few months, the seriousness of the injury became evident and I was faced with the prospect that my rugby career was under threat; One doctor even suggested that I should think about leaving the army...I was twenty five years old and I wouldn't accept that I may not play rugby again, I stubbornly thought to myself;

"I'll decide when I retire, not a doctor!!" and I was determined to prove them wrong. But without Pete Howard it may well have been the end of my rugby career, before he left the Queen's Medical Centre for a hospital in Birmingham he spoke to a Mr Cargill at D.R.I. (Derby Royal Infirmary), a top knee surgeon (possibly the best in the country) and a former superior of Pete when he was training to be an orthopedic

surgeon. A few weeks later I was sent an appointment to see Mr Cargill, and during that appointment he asked me;
"Do you want to play rugby again?"
"Yes" I replied with a renewed sense of expectancy, and Mr Cargill explained that he would lazer the serrated edge of the tear and with extensive physiotherapy he believed I should be able to play rugby again!

After another stay in hospital and a successful operation, and six to eight weeks of extensive (Monday to Friday from 9am to 12 noon) physiotherapy, I believed I was ready to play again. I played my first game in late October for the third team and it felt good to be back on a rugby field again! On reflection, I should have missed that season and re-built the muscles around the knee to compensate for the weakness, but I managed to play rugby for another nine years until the cruciate ligament snapped totally…I was following a ball into touch in the last game of the season at Senghenydd when 'TWANG!', I hit the floor, and one of the spectators told me later that it looked as if I'd been shot by a sniper! I was thirty four years old and my twenty seven year rugby career was over!!

<u>The Wedding!!</u>

I was getting married and despite it being 'out of the blue', it seemed like the right thing to do…I believed I was in love. I had met my wife-to-be in the summer of 1984 and started a relationship that lasted about five months, and as I was in the army, the distance didn't help, resulting in me being unfaithful on a number of occasions. We met a year later and again it didn't work out, probably due to me admitting to being unfaithful during the first relationship. These should have been huge warning signs as to not entering a relationship for the third time…I was too naïve to realise that I had compounded the trust issues of somebody whowas affected by events in her childhood.. When I called in mid-May of 1988, she had a 15 month old child, 'K', and was awaiting a divorce. We arranged to meet and then quickly rushed into a disastrous marriage, getting married on 13th August 1988, but there were good things that came out of the marriage…the children!!!

The alarm went off…it was 6.30am on Saturday 13th August 1988, and I was getting married in three hours! I jumped out of bed, looked out of the window and it was raining…damn! Looking back, the weather and the fact that my dog, Cindy (a present for my thirteenth Birthday), had been put down the day before could have been considered as bad omens!! Nevertheless, at the time, I believed I was doing the right thing and couldn't wait for kick-off at 9.30am at Pontypridd Registry Office! By 7am everyone was awake and I was having breakfast with my friends from Nottingham, Andy Dyke, Mick Parr and his girlfriend Jane. At the same time my gran (Nana Henson), who was now living with my mother following a stroke in early 1983, was having her hair done by my mother's friend (a couple of days earlier she had told me she wouldn't be going to the wedding, and I believe she was disappointed that I was marrying someone who already had a child…but she didn't say as much!). I'd told her she had to be there as she had brought me up, and she was the single most important person I wanted at my wedding…thankfully, she changed her mind and was now getting ready, with help from my mother! By 8.15am everyone was ready, and by 8.30am we were on our way to Pontypridd…I thought, "this is it!" as we pulled out of Cae Bron and it wasn't lomg before Brackla and Bridgend were behind us!!

The drive to Pontypridd brought back happy memories of the many bus journeys I'd enjoyed as I child with my Nan Thomas, to visit her sister, my great auntie Beat (Beatrice), who still lived in the same house in Treforest where my gran was born. A terraced house that seemed so large to an inquisitive little boy, with its many rooms and open coal fires…I always remember it being a warm and welcoming house! Pontypridd was a town I knew well, with its bustling market, unique cafes and the open spaces of Ynysangharad Park. It was a town that my father's side of the family knew well as they'd lived in villages (Treforest, Cilfynydd and Ynysybwl) around Ponty (as it was affectionately known locally), and it seemed like the perfect place to get married! Just after 9am we had parked the cars in the large Sardis Road car park and were now taking the short walk to the Registry Office in Court House Street. Other guests were already waiting, but there was no sign of my father, Shirley and Nan (I heard later that they nearly didn't come to the wedding because I had travelled to the wedding from my mother's house!). However, just before my bride-to-be arrived, my father, Shirley, Nan Thomas, my step-brother Eric, his wife Sue and their girls (Catherine, Sarah and Sian) turned up...I was praying that everything would pass without incident, as it hadn't been easy growing up with divorced parents! Within minutes, wife-to-be arrived, driven to the Registry Office by her father, in his white Ford Sierra, suitably attired with white ribbons. She looked beautiful in a 1920s style ivory wedding dress that was stunning, a subtle veil, matched accessories and bouquet of flowers. There was a huge "AWW!" when her 15 month old son, 'K', stepped out of the car in a guards outfit!!

Once the ceremony was over we walked out onto the streets of Ponty as a married couple, and faced the inevitable deluge of confetti and rice, as the official wedding photographer (my new mother-in-law) was running around with an instamatic attempting to include everyone present in a flurry of hurried photographs! Anyone who's experienced a wedding will tell you how quick the day passes and our wedding that day was no different! Before we knew it we were at the reception venue in Llantrisant, 'The Black Prince', a legendary place in the local area that was a hotel, a venue for wedding receptions and other functions and also included a night club, and this hotel with its typical 1970s type façade was located directly across the road from the Royal Mint!

The wedding reception was fairly relaxed as the two families and friends intermingled and were chatting in small groups throughout the afternoon, but my new mother-in-law was still working that instamatic to death! The evening was more of a party atmosphere as the elder guests (and young children, including 'K') retired to their respective homes leaving a more hardcore drinking group who celebrated well into the night. The day had passed without any drama with exception of one of my new brother's-in-law, who jokingly challenged my old army mate, Jon Harvey...if only he had known who he was messing with (Jon had spent six months in a Greek prison with another Sapper, Archie Cameron, when, during an army sailing trip around Greece and the Med, they were attacked by ten or twelve local men – unfortunately, for the Greeks, Jon and Archie could handle themselves and put five or six of the Greeks in hospital) ! Eventually, the guests began to leave and

211

a good day drew to an end, and we retired to the hotel room that had been booked for us as a wedding gift! Surprise, surprise, the room had been sabotaged, and before we went to bed we had to clean-up all the confetti, balloons etc from around the room and more confetti, peanuts and crisps from the bed!!

It was a day that proved a wedding could be enjoyed without the added stress of spending thousands of pounds; The wedding car was supplied by my wife's parents, my new mother-in-law was the photographer, my mother provided the cake, I wore my army No2 dress uniform, the bridal dress cost about £80 (I think) and we paid a couple of pounds for invites from W.H.Smith! The reception food, the venue, hotel for the night and flowers were all wedding presents…the only outlay for the wedding was the 'marriage licence' and the rings!! Nevertheless, it was also a day that signaled the beginning of a very difficult period in my life, as I quickly realised that the person I'd married had been greatly affected by events in her childhood! I believe I loved her, but I was never 'in love' with her, and that proved decisive, and such was the destructive influence of what had happened to her years before, any love I may have had was quickly replaced by a great deal of resentment! In her defence, she also married a man who, due to my time in the army, struggled to show affection or emotion, and therefore, due to my own immaturity, I couldn't understand or deal with her mood swings! I was extremely naïve in thinking I could understand illness and her total mistrust of everyone around her, and the next twelve years were a continual battle…compounded by a distinct lack of money due to low wages and disastrous borrowing! But the good thing that came out of those dark days were our children…but more of that and the events surrounding our divorce in a later chapter!!!

Leaving the Army

Prior to the wedding detailed above, I had been offered promotion to Corporal with a posting (another UK posting to 22 Engineer Regiment RE based at Tidworth), but I decided to turn it down and I had to sign a form to refuse the promotion…this effectively ended my army career!! In the March of 1989 I 'signed-off' giving 12 months' notice and on

February 16th 1990, following just over ten years' service, I started my termination leave!!!

As my final day in the army approached, despite the great friendships and the memories I'd made, there were no second thoughts or regrets...at the time, I believed I was making the correct decision, not only for me, but for my family! Prior to my marriage, I only had to worry about myself, and as I had voluntarily joined the army I accepted the risks involved with being a soldier! However, when the I.R.A. (Provincial Irish Republican Army or Provos) murdered an army wife in Germany in September 1989, I knew that I had made the right decision to leave the army. The murder of Heidi Hazel made me realise that it wasn't just me I had to worry about, I was also responsible for a wife and two small children, 'K' who was now two and a half years old and two month old 'R'. My cruciate injury, my refusal of the promotion/posting and the ongoing I.R.A. attacks made the decision to leave the army much easier. Additionally, I felt that at almost twenty seven years old, I was young enough to forge another career for myself. I'd had great times in training at Dover and Farnborough, with 34 Field Squadron at Waterbeach, Cambridgeshire, and especially at 24 Field Squadron at Chattenden, and thinking of those places and the people I'd served with brought a tinge of sadness, and also a wry smile! But there were no military memories at HQ MWF, it had been like a nine to five job...with uniform! There were no six month tours, exercises in foreign lands, no parades, no 'we're in it together!', and not even much bullshit! It had been four and a half years of boredom and little or none of the camaraderie experienced in J.L.R.R.E, 1&3 Training Regiments, 34 and 24 Field Squadron! As rugby had played a major role during my army career, and especially at 24 Field Squadron, it was ironic that on my last day in the army I played for HQ MWF in a Sapper Cup game at Chilwell...against 24 Field Squadron!

We lost that final game (heavily), but it was great to see some old friends again on a day I wore my uniform and played a military game of rugby for the last time!! The following day we moved to a council house in Long Eaton...33 Bracken Close, it was a new beginning! But I still hadn't quite finished with the army though, and you'll be pleased to know that the

213

'bullshit' I'd experienced during those early days at Dover, returned to wish me a fond farewell...I had to clean the married quarter we'd been living in for the previous eighteen months from top to bottom to adhere to military style cleanliness!! After three days of relentless cleaning the married quarter was in pristine readiness for handover back to the army...I handed the keys over, and walked away from military life with a skip in my step as I faced civilian life, but also with a sense of loss at those great times I was leaving behind! I didn't know it at the time but I was in for a huge shock!!

Employment in Nottingham

After leaving the army I found out, over the next three and a half years, that civilian life was not as easy it appeared and I began to realise how protected we had been in the army...a world within a world!!! It was three years of low wages and tough times in the East Midlands as the recession of the early 1990s resulted in many businesses going into liquidation!!!

Initially, I had been lucky in finding employment in Nottingham...I had finished my resettlement leave on Friday 16th March 1990, and started my first civilian job as a telesales operative with the Nottingham Evening Post. As the role suggests I was in sales, a new experience for me, selling advertising in a large regional newspaper. If I was to describe the 'must have attribute' for this job it would be 'adaptability' as you could be laughing and joking with a customer placing an advert for, let's say, a Birthday celebration, and the next customer could be placing a death notice! I had one caller whose baby son had died in his arms shortly after being born...very difficult to cope with something like that emotionally and sometimes you would be given a quick break to gather your composure! Then there were the relentless calls from customers wanting to sell their cars, and you knew that when you heard those immortal words:
"Can I put me car in the paper Friday night me duck!" that your sales figures would plummet! The phone call I remember most though was a call I took from Tony Hately, a former professional footballer, and father of Mark Hately who played for Monaco alongside Glenn Hoddle, and was also an England international. Tony had rang to put Mark's Nottingham house

on the market…and he said I was the first to know that Mark was signing for Rangers!! I told our sports desk, but I don't think they believed me…they were kicking themselves three days later when the news was all over the back of the national papers!! After a tough year I resigned for personal reasons and for the next two or three weeks we relied solely on my wages from a cleaning job and also bar work at the Petersham pub in Long Eaton.!!

I was lucky that, due to rugby connections, I wasn't out of full time employment for much longer, as I was offered a job as a 'stationery manager' by Pat Costello (a friend at Long Eaton rugby club) at his father's company, Burton Office Equipment. The job entailed looking after the day to day running of the branch in Leicester…and came with a van!! I really enjoyed this job which involved looking after a showroom with photocopiers and faxes and providing a stationery service for companies in Leicestershire, Nottinghamshire and Lincolnshire. The wages were low, but I am convinced that the twelve months experience I gained there was instrumental in successfully applying for a job with Nuaire, where I've been for the last twenty three years. There was quite a link with Leicester rugby at Burton Office Equipment as one of our salesmen was the Leicester winger, Steve Hackney, and as a result I was always receiving calls from other Leicester players. We also employed a young Martin Johnson (the successful England Captain who famously won the world cup in 2003), for a couple of weeks when he first came back from playing in New Zealand…he was our delivery driver, and he was a humble character and a great lad! Another real funny character who joined us at Burton Office Equipment was the Leicester scrum-half, Aadel Kardooni. Unfortunately, due to the recession that was now gripping the nation, I was made redundant after twelve months and over the next sixteen months could only find temporary employment as jobs became scarcer!!

The first of those temporary jobs was with a company called Duflex in Castle Donnington. They made foam products and I was part of a maintenance team that was responsible for building a new production line, but as I was unqualified, I was given a lot of menial tasks. Nevertheless, I enjoyed the varied role and the people I worked with, but after another twelve

215

months of work I was again made redundant! I started to believe that we were now on borrowed time in the East Midlands and I felt we needed to return to Wales to be close to our families. This decision was being forced on us by the employment situation and events that will be covered in a later chapter. However, my last job in the East Midlands was another temporary job with the accounts department of British Midland Airways, who were based in Donnington House, a former stately home surrounded by fields filled with deer and close to the Donnington racetrack. I worked at this beautiful setting for three to four months, and would have loved to have stayed there, but lacked the necessary qualifications to obtain a permanent position. Therefore, the inevitable return to Wales, after fourteen years in England, drew nearer!!

Destination: Groby Road

The two years that followed the birth of our son, 'G', involved numerous visits to our local GP in Long Eaton and also visits to A&E at Queen's Medical Centre, Nottingham, attempting to determine what was medically troubling our son (there were conflicting opinions with some doctors stating 'G' had an innocent heart murmur whilst others could detect nothing and sometimes suggested he may have asthma!!). Eventually, it was a locum doctor at our local surgery in Long Eaton that decided to send 'G' for an ECG (heart scan), but reassuring us that he was sure it was just a heart murmur and just wanted to put everyone's mind at rest...this proved a critical but correct decision!!!

We looked at each other, we sensed something was wrong...the doctor and nurse were pointing at something on the monitor and speaking in hushed whispers! The doctor and nurse turned to face us, quickly glanced at each other, and then the doctor cleared his throat and said;
"Right Mr and Mrs Thomas...there's no easy way to say this...we have found that your son has a coarctation of the aorta...!"
I thought to myself momentarily, "What does that mean?" as the doctor continued;
"...in simple terms...'G' has a pinch in the main artery next to the heart...the blockage means that is heart is working harder

216

to force the blood through the narrowing…that is why we were struggling to find a pulse in the 'G's' groin…"
Devastation didn't even begin to describe how we were feeling…we were speechless, numb, as the doctor carried on; "…I know this is a lot to take in, but the coarctation can be repaired…therefore, 'G' will need an operation…I am going to make a couple of calls which will give you both a chance to digest what you've just been told…I'll try and be a quick as I can!!" He got up and walked through a door into an adjoining office and closed the door behind him! We looked at each other and then at 'G', who was sitting happily on my knee, oblivious to the seriousness of the situation and what was going on around him, and none of us knew what lay ahead! We sat there in silence, both in shock, both attempting to comprehend the devastating news…you never think something like this will happen to your child, it would always be someone else's child, a friend of a friend or to a family in a television program!! But here we were, like thousands of parents before us, attempting to accept that our 'perfect' child wasn't perfect, and actually had a life-threatening condition!! We sat there for what seemed like an eternity until the doctor returned ten to fifteen minutes later and said;
"OK…right…Mr and Mrs Thomas…I've managed to arrange for 'G' to have the required operation…1st March at Groby Road Heart Hospital in Leicester…"
If the seriousness of the situation hadn't already sunk in, it did now…I thought "today is the 1st February, to arrange an operation date that quickly meant only one thing…'G's' condition warranted an almost immediate operation", the doctor continued:
"…they'll remove the 'pinch' and re-join the two open ends of the artery…try not to worry…any operation has a danger element, but this is not open heart surgery…they'll make an incision here (the doctor pointed to 'G's' side with his pen), separate the ribs, collapse the lung…I know it's a lot to take-in, but I promise you it is a straight forward operation…", his voice faded away as I looked at 'G' and tears welled up in my eyes, and I thought…"why has this happened to our son?"

The month went by quickly and we now found ourselves in the pre-op room at Groby Road Hospital waiting for 'G' to be anaesthetised. The terrifying moment arrived, and despite 'G' only being two years old, it took three of us to hold him down

217

so he could be anaesthetised…it was heartbreaking, he had no idea nor understanding as to what was happening and I could see the fear in his eyes as he struggled. I could also see in his eyes that he could not comprehend why his parents, the two people he trusted more than anyone, were holding him down…it was a gutwrenching and heartbreaking moment…little did I know that image would continue to haunt me for many years, right up to the present. His resistance thankfully subsided quickly as he succumbed to the anaesthetic! We were advised to leave the hospital…go shopping or visit a museum, anything to keep us occupied. In their experience, it would be too stressful to wait at the hospital! I couldn't even begin to describe how it felt to walk out of a room and leave your child not knowing whether he'd be alive when we returned later that day…I knew that walking out of that room was the hardest thing I had ever done or would ever do, and I know my wife felt the same!! We decided to go to Fosse Park Retail Park, on the outskirts of Leicester, and only a ten to fifteen minute drive away from the hospital, should we need to return quickly!

We wandered around the shops at Fosse Park trying to fill the time with meaningless window shopping and our whole conversation centered on 'how' 'G' was doing!', and even walking into the shops looking at the latest clothing fashions, or electrical fads etc didn't ease the worries, doubts and hopes that were flying around our minds, and mixed emotions of elation and deep despair as we struggled to deal with the helplessness we both felt…we even tried to eat something at McDonalds, but neither of us had much of an appetite. Our thoughts were understandably dominated by 'G' and how the operation was progressing! It was a very long day, but finally, the time came when we felt it was time to return to the hospital, and twenty minutes later we were parked up in the hospital car park. We both took a deep breath, got out of the car and after closing and locking the car doors, we walked hand in hand toward the building where 'G' would be hopefully recovering!!

We nervously entered the building where 'G' would be…not knowing what to expect! Thankfully, a nurse we spoke to reassured us that 'G' was ok, that the operation had been a success and that he should be back on the ICU (intensive care unit) in twenty to thirty minutes. The nurse told us to wait in the 'family room', a room where you could make tea and coffee, read magazines or even watch TV, and a great little godsend for all the families. About fifteen minutes later, and halfway through the drinks we'd made, the same nurse popped her head around the door, smiled and said;

"Mr and Mrs Thomas…you can see 'G' now!" We didn't need to be asked twice, and putting our mugs down, immediately got up and followed the nurse to the ICU! Despite the nurse trying to prepare us for what we would see, nothing could have prepared us for what we saw when we walked into the two bed bay where 'G' was lying prostate on the farthest bed; He was laying there with both arms flailed out in a crucifix type position, still sleeping from the anaesthetic, his torso covered in iodine, and as we got closer we could see the ventilator, the chest drain and the various drips!!! It was horrific seeing him lying there so vulnerable, but a wave of relief swept over us both, and the tears rolled down our faces at seeing our son again…alive!!

The devastation we felt and the 'why us?' feelings soon disappeared, and we soon realised how lucky we were!! The baby in the bed next to 'G's' was ten days old, and talking to his (I think it was a boy) parents, we found out he had a collapsed lung, water on the brain, heart problems and other unspecified complications!! It was then we realised that whilst it is not pleasant seeing your child suffer, there were other children fighting their own battles in the hospital that were far more serious than 'G's' condition. That was confirmed later that evening when we were again in the family room enjoying, for the first time that day, a well-deserved hot drink, and a couple walked in who's baby had just passed away…it was their first child and they'd never had the chance to take their baby girl home, as she had been rushed from Leicester Royal Infirmary the day she was born, a few days earlier! We couldn't share our relief or joy with them and we knew there were no words we could say that would ease their grief, and we the four us sat there in silence, each lost in our thoughts!!

Thankfully, 'G' recovered quickly and was home a week later. Initially, he was seen regularly and his progress monitored, but the appointments became annual and then the gaps between appointments became greater. At the time of writing 'G' is twenty six years old, has a full-time job (a plumber and pipefitter), plays football, drinks, smokes and leads a full and active life. I often look at him and remember that two year old boy fighting the anaesthetic or lying there recovering on that hospital bed in Groby Road! But I also think of the baby in the next bed to 'G' in the ICU all them years ago hoping he made a full recovery, and also the parents who lost their child that day and who were denied the chance to make the memories that I have with 'G'! I hope and pray that they were able to re-build their lives and go on to have other children, whilst still remembering the little girl they lost that day back in 1993!!

Back to Wales

After fourteen years of living away from Wales…it was time to go home! The recession had killed any chance of remaining in the East Midlands, and the decision was taken to return to Wales so we could be close to our families. I thought the easiest way to find employment was to fall back on my military experience and I was lucky to find employment with Centurion Security. This enabled us to return to Wales and gave me a better chance to move into a new career in the South Wales area as we were now living locally…those first six months were difficult and there were times we questioned whether the decision to move from Long Eaton was the right one!!

I used to love driving down the M50 towards Ross-on-Wye, as I always saw it as 'the road home!' Passing Goodrich and Whitchurch on the A40, I knew that in a few minutes I'd be crossing the border into Wales and heading toward Monmouth and home! This journey would be different as I knew we were coming back to Wales to live, no weekend flying visit to see the family or a few days at Christmas…after fourteen years in England, I was going home and bringing my family with me! We were soon heading toward the last downhill stretch of the A40 before Monmouth, where the now familiar sign with its red dragon and 'Croeso i Cymru' was standing proud to inform every driver they were now entering Wales! In the darkness, I could see the sign in the distance, lit-up by the headlights of our car, and I pressed 'PLAY' on the cassette player, and after a slight pause music and words filled the car; "FAR AWAY A VOICE IS CALLING, BELLS OF MEMORY CHIME,

220

COME HOME AGAIN..."
With perfect timing, and as we passed the sign and entered
Wales the song continued;
"...WE'LL KEEP A WELCOME IN THE
HILLSIDES...WHEN YOU COME HOME AGAIN TO
WALES" As the song *"We'll keep a welcome in the hillsides"*
continued,
we were home...it was an emotional homecoming for me and
a decision that I still believe was the correct one, given the
circumstances!!!

The first five months were difficult, but security was 'money
for old rope' for an ex-soldier and the sacrifice, in the short
term, was well worth it! Despite the low hourly rates (this was
a long time before the 'minimum wage' became law), such as;
£2.10 (Barry Council Depot), £2.65 (National Folk Museum,
St Fagans) and £3.10 (L'Oreal, Pontyclun) a 'living wage'
could be earned if you were prepared to work long hours.
Thankfully, I wasn't afraid of hard work and for the next five
months 80-90 hour weeks became a standard working week
between October 1993 and March 1994...it was worth it
though to bring the family back to Wales to ensure the
children developed closer relationships with grandparents and
other family members. Initially, we lived with my wife's
parents before a failed few days renting my father's house in
Maesteg, and then finally renting a property in Clydach in the
Rhondda. It was during this period that I saw a job advertised
in the 'Wales on Sunday' for a telesales job at a company in
Caerphilly. I applied for the job and was offered an interview,
and I was delighted when, a few days after the interview, I was
offered the position. I started work at Nuaire Ltd on 24th
March 1994...where, at the time of writing, I'm still
employed.

Chapter 5 – Nuaire & Caerphilly

After six months carrying out security work at various sites in the South Wales area from L'Oreal in Pontyclun to Rexel in Llangeinor and the Folk Museum at St Fagans, I must have walked miles and miles and in the days before the 'minimum wage' I had to work about 80-90 hours a week to survive! Thankfully, I managed to find a 9to5 job at a ventilation manufacturers in Caerphilly called Nuaire and started in a tele-sales role on 24th March 1994 and met a man who became a great friend, Alan Jenkins. During my time at Nuaire I have been an estimator, a technical service administrator, team leader, major projects co-ordinator and finally a Senior Estimator. It's been a great company to work for and I have been lucky to have met some wonderful people during my time at Nuaire from within the company and outside in the wider community. My life has continued to change and despite some setbacks I can honestly say that I am content with life at the moment and looking forward to what lies ahead!

At the time of writing I have worked at Nuaire for 24 years and as a result I have lived in Caerphilly (well Abertridwr to be precise) for almost 23 years. Needless to say during this period there have been good times, there have been bad times and there have been very bad times. I will write about some of these events in this chapter whilst others will feature in Chapters 7, 8 & 9. This is a period that has seen a wedding, a wedding ceremony (Thai style), two divorces, births, deaths, mental illness, a mini health scare, holidays (some great trips to Thailand), great times with the children (and bad times), joy of grandchildren, great nights out with friends, playing and watching sport, meeting up with old army friends that I thought I would never see again (Oh, thank you Facebook) and much, much more…I think I've packed more into the last 25 years than some people manage in a lifetime!! I have been lucky to work for a great company and I have had the privilege of working with some great people, many of whom have become great friends. However, I have also met people who are not so great, but they are not worth a mention in this book…so if you have known me or knew me during my time at Nuaire and you have not been mentioned, it's either because we didn't work together closely, I've forgotten you due to age and forgetfulness or you have been excluded on purpose…take your pick, the choice is yours!!! Caerphilly (and Abertridwr) has become an area that I now consider home, the place that my children have been brought up and somewhere I have created so many memories such as; fulfilling a dream to live in a terraced house in a Welsh mining valley, experiencing the joy of having twins, Saying goodbye to two wonderful women within nine months of each other...my grandmothers, watching Barnsley F.C. live in the Premiership (well...the day they got relegated so it was a bittersweet moment!) and in two play-off finals at Wembley and the Millennium Stadium with mixed fortunes, watching Wales play rugby (live at the Millennium Stadium and also in pubs/clubs around Cardiff and Caerphilly), family holidays to Filey, Devon, Burnham-on-Sea, Magaluf, London, Cambridge, Isle of Wight and Thailand, great days out with the children to Porthcawl, the Gower, Bristol Zoo, Roath Park, Ponty Park (to play pitch and putt), Ogmore-by-Sea, Margam Park and many, many more, brilliant nights out with friends from Nuaire into Cardiff,, coaching kids football from U'8s all the way up to U'16s (there was a two year break in the middle when the twins lived in Middlesbrough), re-visiting Ely (Cambridgeshire) to stay with Bernard, Beth and cousins Nick and Margaret, Stag nights (i.e. including my own stag do, when I was dressed in a wedding dress and we went to Cardiff only to discover it was Gay Mardis Gras weekend...awkward!!!), watching my family being ripped apart (twice), great Christmases and Birthdays, great nights in Cardiff in the Ivor and the Insole with the 'Cardiff Crowd' (more on this later), meeting Jean, Roy, Linda and Andrew (the Barnsley connection) again (more on Linda in Chapter 8), saying final goodbyes to many people (i.e. great uncle Ivor, great auntie Beatrice, great auntie Ivy, my mum, Bernard, Nick, Auntie Kay, Alan Jenkins , Gareth Draper, Mike Walters and many more and also learning that old friends had also gone to the 'Sapper Bar' such as Joe Kirby, Phil Wilson, Jim Stead, Al Bowman, Tiny Bott, Kenny Moxon etc), family parties, meeting Ada almost ten years ago in Caerphilly, playing football with 'K' and 'G' and winning two leagues at the Power League 5-a-side in Cardiff, the joy of grandchildren (Alexa and Louisa), fulfilling a lifelong dream of visiting SE Asia after meeting Ada, returning to Long Eaton to play vets rugby with old friends, qualifying as a TEFL (Teaching English to Foreign Learners) and for the last four years becoming a voluntary teaching assistant at Ystrad

Mynach college which has been rewarding and interesting teaching students from Poland, Nigeria, Equador, Iraq, Bangladesh, Italy, Romania, Latvia, Lithuania, China, Hong Kong and even Thailand, returning to Chatham for a 24 Field Squadron and drinking in the Cannon and visiting the site where Chattenden Barracks once stood...sad!, returning to Padstow to see Mick and Karen Stupple, meeting old army friends at the Army v Navy rugby matches at Twickenham in 2015 and 2016, gaining my BA Open Degree after six years of studying, enjoying great parties with, what I call, the 'Thai crowd' (friends of Ada and their Welsh/English husbands) and much, much more.

It's been a great twenty five years and here's to many more as I approach the 'twilight years'. I still have so much I would like to do, but for now here are some highlights (and low points) from the last twenty five years).

■■

Nuaire

I joined Nuaire in March 1994...and at the time of writing, I am still here. A great company, with great people and I have been lucky that I have had a job where I have enjoyed getting up in the morning and going to work (well...most of the time anyway!!).

I started at Nuaire on 21st March 1994 in telesales and quickly discovered that it was a great place to work with great people. I found myself in a small sales team that included Rauf Marsh (team leader), Alan Jenkins (technical estimator), Gwyneth Jennings (order processor) and another telesales operative, Julie Jones and we looked after the Midlands. Other teams were set-up the same and looked after the remaining parts of the UK. When I started with the company the only fan I knew was the hand held fans you could typically buy in Ponty market, that ran on batteries and kept you cool in the summer – I had no idea there was a whole ventilation world out there...when I started my training it included technical training on the products, seeing how units were manufactured etc. It's ironic that my worst subject in school was physics and here I was embarking on a career that was about moving air from one place to another...basically physics. The product

224

profile and ventilation in those early days was a lot simpler…fans would be selected to suit a particular purpose, normally running at full speed, 24 hours a day for 365 days of the year in a period long before energy savings and being environmentally friendly.

In those early days Nuaire was more of a family company with approximately three hundred employees and there was an excellent relationship between the shop floor and the office staff…there was no 'us' and 'them', we sat together in the canteen, socialized together and there was generally a great rapport between the different factions within the company, even directors and senior management were known by the Christian names. I was lucky to be working with Alan Jenkins, that first twelve months, as he was willing to train me on the products and the rudiments of selecting products because I was willing to learn. Alan was a great man and in that summer of 1994 he and his wife Diane let us all stay in his beloved caravan in Porthcawl for five days…a great family holiday in a place I knew like the back of my hand being a Bridgend boy. Within 12 months, and with Alan's guidance, I moved from telesales into an estimator role, and around six months later I joined Ron Giddy (service manager) and Julie Porter (service administrator) in the service team where as a Technical Adviser, I entered a period with a steep learning curve as I became involved in fault finding, analysis of service reports, invoicing etc…I was beginning to have a much better understanding of the products and the science of air movement. Additionally, I was understanding more and more about electrical issues…more importantly I was enjoying my job. By this time, the summer of 1995, we had bought a house in Abertridwr and as I only lived up the road from Alan Jenkins, and another Nuaire employee, Gareth Draper, the three of us used to catch a taxi into work together. During this period, I was playing rugby for Senghenydd, the twins were born and I successfully passed my ONC in Building Services, justifying the faith they had shown me and the costs associated with the course that Nuaire had paid. Life was pretty good and by 1997 it got better, as I was made a Team Leader (which included a small pay rise) in the Service Department (Ron Giddy had retired by this time and Rauf Marsh was again my immediate manager). But there was trouble ahead as a recession was on the horizon.

225

In mid-1998 the recession created a situation where Nuaire had to make cutbacks and we entered a four week period that was certainly the most difficult I'd experienced in my working life. The company had to make sixty plus people redundant and as a result legislation dictated that we had to endure a four week 'consultation' period where representatives from the various departments would attend a daily meeting to determine if there could be other ways the company could make savings without having to make anyone redundant. There was also an incentive of an additional cash payment to those who took voluntary redundancy, and to those who had served ten plus years or more it was an attractive offer. But I had a young family and I decided to stick it out, and hope that in the 'dog eat dog' situation of people applying for other people's jobs that I would still have a job when the process ended. It was a horrendous time, that created suspicion and resentment, and about two weeks in I decided that I wasn't going to worry anymore about something that was out of my control. Eventually, about three weeks in it was suddenly announced that they had the necessary numbers of those wishing to take voluntary redundancy and that everyone else's jobs were safe. Personally, I was one of the fortunate ones, but it was a sad (and nervous) period where many friends such as Rauf Marsh, Julie Porter, Len Thorne and Audra Wilkes, to name but a few, left Nuaire. Life soon continued as normal and the merry-go-round of office moves and hierarchical changes were again in full swing.

I continued in my role with the Service Team ensuring our customers benefitted from our after sales service, ensuring we provided service engineers for both small and prestigious projects and maintaining a good relationship with our service providers.
As we approached mid-1999 my marriage came under enormous pressure and was starting to fall apart…a mixture of never being in love with my wife (although I hadn't admitted this to myself at the time), the long hours I was having to work to keep on top of the workload and my wife's issues were also starting to take their toll. Nuaire and friends within the company such as Alan Jenkins and Paul Harrington, provided me with the support I needed to get through a very low point in my life (please see story **End of an Era (and the**

aftermath) in this chapter). Eventually, in the latter part of 2000 the marriage was well and truly over, and I now focused on maintaining the relationships with my children, which was helped when I bought the house on High Street in Abertridwr, which was only about four hundred metres from where my children lived with their mother. I was now in my seventh year with Nuaire and friends I had were becoming more like family. There was a financial strain in running a house on one wage, paying maintenance for my children and having shared care…within those first twelve months I found myself having to take a second job with B&Q, stacking shelves between 8pm and midnight (eventually, I worked until 2am), Monday to Thursday…needs must!

By 2003 I had taken on a new role with the company and was now working with Alan Jenkins again and Stephen Hickey looking after the UK consultants and our export customers. This was another challenging role but made the more rewarding by the mix of people we had working under our manager Gary Williams. This was an interesting time and a period of extreme 'wind-ups' which culminated in me becoming the winner of the 2003 'Mug of the Year.'. In an office that included Dave Jones, Ryan Sollis, Richard Hammerton, Ed Connolly, Dan Jones, Gary Williams, Alan Jenkins, Stephen Hickey and me, there were plenty of 'wind-ups' and practical jokes, mixed with Gary Willliams singing the 'Bodyform' song from the adverts…at the top of his voice. Additionally, his continual questioning of Kostos (one of our export customer's based in Cyprus) of how was he paying his mortgage (a customer from Cyprus who always wanted quotes but never ordered anything) and teasing of Michael Klotz (a German of spurious sexual orientation who worked for our agents in Southern Ireland) were comical. We had ballot papers and a ballot box for the 'Mug of the Year' competition in 2003…and some very interesting nominations such as Dave Jones not knowing the short cut (a 5-10 minute walk) back to the office from Caerphilly town centre and walking around two miles by the only way he know…on a boiling hot day. We were about to call the local hospital when he walked through the door with a head like a redcurrant and sweating like a pig, stood in the door and said to me "you fucking twat" (I had left him in town)…or Richard Hammerton being called to reception to pick up a parcel, which he opened and found his

227

own shoes that we'd hijacked...or Ed Connolly being asked to report to Caerphilly Police Station by P.C. Roberts (me) about an alleged road rage incident...but there was no doubt about the winner, the 2-3 month wind-up, where they had me believing that one of our customer's in Hong Kong, by the name of Fanny Chau (pronounced *Chew*...yes that's right, you couldn't make this shit up), had sent in a photograph of herself...to me, and was giving me the big 'come on!" In a second e-mail Fanny told me that she was coming to see the Queen and asking to see me at the same time...all written in broken English. It was the last e-mail she sent to me when I finally realised that the joke was on me...she had sent photographs of her family and when I opened the photograph of her father...he was a sumo wrestler (which we all know is Japanese and not Chinese). Dave Jones was sat opposite me when I opened that e-mail, and when I laughed out loud he just cracked up, to the point where I thought he was going to have a clutcher. The boys had set up an e-mail account and were e-mailing from inside the office...I can still see the photograph they first sent of a pretty Chinese woman on an underground train, it wasn't even a photograph of Fanny Chau, and to this day I still don't know what she really looks like. I proudly accepted my 'Mug of the Year' award for the brilliant 'wind up' and I would like to thank Fanny Chau, without whom, none of this would have been possible. During this time I was tasked with closing down the service account with our then service provider, George S.Hall, as the working relationship between the two companies had become quite fractious...we later found out that George S.Hall were in financial trouble!

In early 2004 I left B&Q after three years and in Nuaire I was made the Major Projects Co-ordinator, which involved looking after larger, more complex projects...Liz Lewis the customer services director at the time wanted the role to provide an all-round service to our customers that our competitors couldn't offer. I carried out this role for approximately eighteen months to two years and thoroughly enjoyed working with Bev Berry and Jennet Strong before I headed back into Service and working with Alun Morton and Warren Evans again. This was a role I really enjoyed and it was a pleasure to assist customers and engineers alike in resolving on-site issues either by phone or via visiting site on the odd occasion. I also became involved in delivering the 'admin' part of the service engineer training. However, there was another crisis approaching on a personal front in 2008 when my ex-wife split the family down the middle when she took the twins to Middlesbrough, leaving the older three children here in Wales with me (please see story **The Battle with no winners!!** in this chapter). However, this affected my work, and despite Nuaire being very supportive, there were some dark forces at play within the company (people who shall remain nameless as I refuse to give them the satisfaction of revealing their names in this book) who made my life more difficult than it had already become…this was a very difficult time for me both personally and professionally. Additionally, financially, I had to get another part-time job to assist with the finances (to pay off solicitors fees) and took on a role (again stacking shelves) in the local Spar.

Eventually, I re-built my life and met Ada in 2009, we had Amy in 2010, and with more changes in Nuaire in mid-2011, an opportunity presented itself to leave a department I could no longer work in…not because of the job, but due to a heavy feeling of betrayal and mistrust toward a person working within the same department. Therefore, I became a Senior Estimator within the Commercial Department and looked forward to another new challenge, and in parallel I continued the part-time job in the Spar until 2012. There have been challenging, but enjoyable times over the past six years, and in that time I have worked with some great colleagues such as Gareth Williams; Mark Harris; James Gardiner; Ron Price; Dafydd Mearing; James Goring; Martyn Price, Martin Thomas, Thomas Hughes; Michael Mogine; Rhian Wagstaffe; James Edwards; James Pettit, Mark Nicholas; Sian Newton; Foo Wong, Lewis Williams; Jay Arnold; David McKean; Keith Georgious, Dave Jones, Ethan Greenway, Jon Matthews; James Weston; Michael Grote; Danielle Chandler, Rebecca O'Neill; Sam Phillips; Amber Edge; Kathryn Jacab; Lucy Reeves; my own daughter, 'A' and many more. I have continued to enjoy my career at Nuaire and seen the arrival of two grand-children, obtained a 2:1 in my BA Open degree at the Open University, qualified as a TEFL (Teaching English to Foreign Learners) teacher and become a voluntary teaching assistant at a local college. I consider myself to be extremely lucky to have worked for the same company for over twenty-five years and have met and worked with some fantastic people during that time, many of whom have become very good friends, and here are a few highlights of that time:

1. The many moves in the various offices due to operational changes (all for the right reasons I might add!).
2. Enjoying working relationships with external sales with some absolute legends such as Martin Draper, Stuart Smith, Chris O'Mahoney, Keith Graham, Paul Watson, Andy Warren, Paul Smith, Steve Allen, Stuart Bowers, Ken Wilson, Steve Todd, Stephen Wilkes, John Pearson, Mike Waddington, Dale Murray, Steven Macmillan and who can forget the mad Jock and avid Hibs fan, Craig Cruickshank (together we successfully turned an also ran company, FES, into Nuaire's biggest customer), and many, many more.
3. Putting the world to rights with the dinner gang of Bev Berry, Carol Horton, Jennet Strong, Sheila Tyer and Maureen Lennon.
4. Also the continuous arguments between Ed Connolly and Dennis Davey in a previous dinner gang.
5. The great nights out and 'last days'.
6. The fantastic Christmas dinners…thank you Jason, Shona, Dean and Jeanette.
7. The many site visits I went on when working in Service/After Sales…please don't send me to Glasgow again, I'm still traumatized.
8. Football matches against the shop floor and sales reps.

And many, many, more.

Abertridwr

Abertridwr lies in a small valley around two miles from Caerphilly which, in turn, is around seven miles from the centre of Cardiff. The Aber Valley consists of two villages; Abertridwr and the more infamous Senghenydd, better known for the pit explosion in 1913 that claimed the lives of 439 miners. The colleries are now long gone and nature has now claimed back an area that was once scarred by its association with coal. I have lived here for 23 years and have watched my children grow up, attending local schools and building their own bank of memories!

When I was a child I used to love visiting my Great Auntie Beatie (Beatrice) and Great Uncle Ivor, in Treforest, nr Pontypridd. I would catch the bus with my Nan Thomas in Aberkenfig and look forward to those days in Ponty…visiting Ponty Park and Taff Street and the old market in the town. But most of all I used to love going to Auntie Beatie's terraced house…I fell in love with the valleys and it was always a dream of mine to live in a terraced house. When we first moved back to Wales we moved into a rented house in the Rhondda, but six months later we were living in a rented bungalow in Beddau (between Pontypridd and Llantrisant) where we stayed for around a year before buying a house on Bryngelli Terrace in Abertridwr in the summer of 1995…my dream had come true, the boy from the market town of Bridgend had fulfilled his dream of living in a terraced house in the valleys.

I felt the sense of community as soon as we moved into the street and quickly made friends with our neighbours Vic and Anne on one side, Mrs Evans on the other and many others in the street. We were close to the infants school where 'R' and 'G' went to school and only a short walk from the Junior school which 'K' attended. However, Bryngelli was on a steep hill and our house was three-quarters up this hill, and whilst it was downhill to the shops (Spar, chip shop, newsagents), the Buffs Club and The Panteg, it was one hell of a climb back up High Street and Bryngelli to get back home. The older children ('K', 'R' and 'G'), we quickly made friends and for the first time since we'd come back to Wales in October 1993 we were finally settled in our own home. However, by the summer of 2000 we had separated and I briefly lived in a shared house in Caerphilly, but thankfully, by Christmas 2000 I had bought a house down the road from Bryngelli on High Street and I was able to have all the children for the weekend and twice in the week. Whilst she didn't appreciate me being so close, I felt it was necessary to maintain the relationships with the children…as I told her at the time; "I'm not here for you, I'm here for the children". Buying the house on High Street and fighting for the regular shared access of my children were the best decisions I have ever made. The children and I have had many happy years in that house and created some special memories, but as is life…there have also been sad times as you will see later in this chapter.

Nevertheless, at the time of writing (2020) I am still living in the same house in the Aber Valley, a valley with its rows and rows of terraced houses strewn in untidy lines up and down the valley…a living memory of the coal industry that once provided the employment for those living in these huddled streets. As the years have passed newer houses have been built in available spaces in the valley to give the Aber Valley its uniqueness. Now that the heavy industry has disappeared, the Welsh valleys once again display an element of their former beauty as they are filled with nature trails and cycle tracks, sports pitches, the rivers are full of trout and an array of different birds are once again thriving in the valleys. The Aber Valley is no different and it is a pleasure to walk or cycle in the summer around the many tracks on the former site of the Windsor Colliery. There are schools, local shops, hairdressers, takeaways, doctor's surgery, dentists, cafés, churches, a library, a YMCA (offering an array of activities for the kids) and rugby and football clubs…it suits my needs and the needs of my family. Additionally, we are only a short drive from Caerphilly and Cardiff can be reached in around twenty minutes. The M4 and the A470 are only ten minutes away so other areas are easily accessible…I'm happy in Abertridwr and it's been an excellent place to live over the past 23 years and long may it continue.

Alan Jenkins

Alan Jenkins…what can I say about this man that wouldn't have already been said! When I started work at Nuaire I was lucky enough to work in a team with Alan who, I quickly found out, was a fiercely proud family man and son of Senghenydd. Little did I know back in 1994 the journey we would take over the next twenty years…even becoming neighbours following my first divorce in 2000, our houses 'back to back' amongst the tightly packed terraced houses that litter the valley! We travelled to work together, in a taxi at first until I was able to buy a car (Alan had never learned to drive and was happily ferried around by his wife, Diane), we socialised together (those famous Wednesday nights in 'The Moat') and he was unquestionably there for me during some dark times in my life. We have laughed…laughed again and laughed some more and the image is fresh in my mind of a red faced Alan with his raspy laugh always looking as if he was on the verge of having a 'clutcher'!!

There are so many stories involving Alan, some I witnessed or was a part of and some that Alan had told me about such as returning from Scotland after one of the Scotland v Wales rugby internationals with a dead baby seal! They had found it on a beach opposite the hotel they were staying at near Edinburgh, and brought it back to the Aber valley and left it in the middle of the square in Abertridwr…imagine the puzzled look of villagers the following morning finding a dead baby seal in a village which is approximately 10 miles from the coast!! Another time, Dr Mather asked Alan what colour were his stools to which Alan replied, "teak" he told me he thought the doctor was asking what colour his breakfast stools were, "We didn't have any stools in our kitchen so I didn't want Dr Mather to think we were poor so I told her they were teak"…when Alan told Diane when he got in the car she had to explain that Dr Mather was talking about his 'shit' not breakfast stools. Inevitably this resulted in another red face, raspy laugh and potential 'clutcher'! Lastly, Alan hated cats!! Alan's chair faced the TV in the corner and behind the TV there was the back window that faced my house. One evening whilst he was watching TV a cat decided to jump on the outside window sill and stare in at Alan, much to Alan's annoyance!! Attempts to shoo the cat by Alan proved fruitless and the cat refused to budge, Alan became angrier and angrier and despite his frantic efforts…nothing!! Reaching the end of his tether he headed for the kitchen and the back door, he opened the back door (which was on the side of a single storey extension on the back of the house), grabbed a broom, stepped into the back yard and initially cornered the cat! The cat must have sensed it was in danger and attempted to make its escape, as it darted past Alan, Alan swung the broom, missed the cat completely and then he heard "C-R-A-S-H!". He looked over his shoulder at the back door where he could see the glass kitchen door was smashed and glass lay all over the floor…the head had come off the broom when Alan tried to hit the cat and went straight through the back door. I think it

233

cost £70 to replace the glass and could have only happened to Alan! There are many, many more stories!!!

Alan loved his family, his caravan in Porthcawl and simple pleasures of a quick fag (before he gave up smoking), a glass or two of strongbow and fish, chips and curry sauce. Sadly, Alan retired early due to ill health and I am ashamed to say that, despite us being neighbours, I barely saw him before he passed away in January 2017. Nevertheless, I never stopped thinking about him and would like to share with you some of my personal stories involving Alan, and as I sit here thinking of an absolute legend and a great friend I can hear his voice as clear as the mornings I picked him up for work when he would open the door, step into the car, grin and say "Morning Shag!"

I look back on my first day at Nuaire, and the first day I met Alan Jenkins, as one of those moments that shaped a large chunk of my life…and Alan was with me every step of the way…

As with any new job it was nerve-wracking entering a building where you didn't know anyone, and being subjected to those 'what have we got here?' sort of looks! However, despite the odd stare, the majority of people were very welcoming and friendly. Len Thorne, who had interviewed me, was the manager who looked after the telesales team and he introduced me to my new work colleagues…the Midlands Team – Rauf Marsh (team leader), Gwyneth Jennings (order processor), Julie Jones (my telesales colleague) and lastly a man a few inches shorter than me, smartly dressed, well-groomed and with a slight paunch (or beer belly as I later found out) who said;
"Hiya Shag…welcome to Nuaire!"
This was my first encounter with the legend that was Alan Jenkins, and he and I hit it off straight away, he helped me to immediately feel at ease in my new surroundings.

I consider myself lucky to have been put into the same team as Alan on that day in March 1994, which was the start of a great friendship with a great man, and I believe Alan is the reason I am still with Nuaire today…twenty-four years after that first meeting…

234

Soon after moving to Bryngelli Terrace in Abertridwr, around eighteen months later, Alan and another lad Gareth Draper and I, started getting a taxi to work together. In the evening we'd either get a lift back to Abertridwr with Alan's wife Diane or with Gareth's mother, Edna (who also worked at Nuaire) and his dad Pete. However, one of those trips to work in the taxi would provide us with a humerous episode – now we had a regular driver who picked us up, but on this particular morning when I heard the "B-E-E-P!" of the car horn I looked out of the window to see a dated Lada parked up outside. I shouted "GOODBYE" up the stairs…I paused, waiting for a response, but nothing, so I opened the door, stepped outside and shut the door behind me. A few seconds later I was sat in the back seat of the taxi behind the driver and said;

"Hiya Butt" to which the taxi driver replied inquisitively;

"Thomas…going to Nuaire?"

"Yes Butt…two other pick-ups though…Bridgefield Street and Upper Francis Street"

"OK" and he drove off down the hill. Two minutes later we had stopped outside Alan's house in Bridgefield Street. I jumped out of the taxi and knocked Alan's door as I thought he wouldn't recognise the car. A couple of seconds later Alan was stood in the doorway and said;

"That's not our normal taxi Shag"

"Nah…it's some fat bloke in a Lada Al".

When we were both in the taxi and taking the short drive to Upper Francis Street it soon became obvious that it wasn't a 'fat bloke' driving…it was a woman. Me and Alan looked at each other and tried not to laugh…let's just say, it was an easy mistake to make as she wasn't the most feminine of women, and she had a better moustache than Alan's mexican number. Minutes later we pulled up outside Gareth's house in Upper Francis Street…out came Gareth, opened the front passenger door, jumped in and instinctively said;

"Alright Butt…" and turning his head towards us said;

"Morning boys"

Alan and I nodded as we couldn't speak for fear of laughing and Gareth gave us a bemused look before facing the front again and saying;

"Nuaire please Butt!" Me and Alan daren't look at each other, both of us sat biting our lips as Gareth and the woman driver struck up a conversation and Gareth was none the wiser…for the entire journey. When we pulled up outside Nuaire he opened the door, got out of the taxi and shouted "CHEERS BUTT" as he closed the door.

When the three of us were walking into the building Gareth asked;

"What are you two fuckers sniggering about?"

When we told Gareth the driver was a woman he started laughing and said

"No way"

Alan and I just nodded before we both burst out laughing, and it wasn't long before Alan was caught–up in one of his famous red-faced, but 'raspy' laughs, as he kept repeating what I'd said to him outside his house;

"Oh my God…a fat bloke in a Lada…a fat bloke in a Lada…priceless…a fat bloke in a Lada…"

Alan and I often laughed and laughed about the trip to work that morning…even years later!

Over the next few years we travelled to work together and understandably we became very good friends. In 1999 following some serious personal problems, and throughout 2000, Alan was an absolute rock and was with me all the way as my marriage fell apart and finally came to an end in August of 2000. Throughout, Alan provided an 'uncomplaining' ear to my divorce problems and the usual access battle to see my children and the financial issues, as I confided in him time and time again…he couldn't have been a better friend during those dark days and Al with his wife Diane and Paul and Ceri Harrington provided a great source of comfort with a mix of piss-taking and beer. By the end of 2000, I had bought a house on High Street in Abertridwr, close to my children, but even closer to Alan as my house was just across the back lane from his. This became the start of another chapter in our friendship that brought us even closer, and provided some great, and hilarious, memories…he was becoming my surrogate older brother. I moved into the house just before Christmas and what did Alan do?...he invited me to Christmas dinner with him and his family. He knew I wasn't talking to my family and apart from my children he knew I had no-one else…he didn't have to do that, but that was Alan. I am eternally grateful for the invite he gave me that Christmas, and as my children came down at 4pm and stayed with me Christmas night and Boxing Day, it turned into the best Christmas ever.

That Christmas morning was the first time I woke up
Christmas morning without the children…it was strange and a
little sad, but I soon perked up realizing I was spending
Christmas with Alan, Diane and their family and that I would
see the children later in the day. Around 11am I took the short
walk round the corner from my house to Alan's and he
welcomed me with,
"Merry Christmas Shag…come in…just waiting for Spike and
Shuna and we'll be off down the Buffs". I walked in and
wished Di and her parents a Merry Christmas and Alan said,
"Huw do you want a quick can?"
"Aye please Al" Fair play to Al he knew what I liked to drink
and came back from the kitchen with a can of Worthington
creamflow and a glass,
"Cheers Al"
"No problem Shag"
Half way through my pint the door opened and in walked
Darren (Spike, Alan's son), Clair (Alan's daughter), Shuna
(Clair's partner) and Aylisha (Alan and Di's grand-daughter).
Merry Christmas shouted all around and Al looked at me and
said,
"Drink up Shag…we are off to the Buffs".

Ten minutes later we (Al, his father-in-law, Darren, Shuna and
me) walked into the downstairs function room in the Buffs,
and the place was heaving…with the usual suspects and
characters that I'd come to know in the valley, if not by name,
certainly by sight. An hour later we'd left the Buffs and were
stood at the bar in the Royal having a couple more pints before
heading back to Al's for Christmas dinner. There were ten of
us sat around the table in Al's living room and the normal
pulling of crackers, telling awful jokes and wearing of
colourful paper hats ensued, and the dinner…the dinner was
absolutely gorgeous. After dinner there was the Jenkins'
tradition of 'dishing out the presents'…Alan had told me that
his daughter Clair was sick of him buying cheap trainers from
Stormy Down market and was always telling Al she was
ashamed to be seen with him when he was wearing
them…"I'm going to buy a pair of tidy trainers for
Christmas…I'll get you some Nike's" she told him on more
than one occasion. Everyone was opening their presents and
there were lots of "Ahhs", "thank you's" and hugs, when
suddenly Al, who was sat in his chair that faced the television,

let out a shriek, and then his familiar raspy laugh could be heard, accompanied by the red face and wheezing,

"What's the matter Al?" asked Di. Alan couldn't speak and was just pointing down at his feet. By this point we'd all gathered around to see what the commotion was, none of us any the wiser, with Alan continually pointing down at his feet. At first none of us knew what was wrong until Alan managed to say between laughing and wheezing;

"Look…look…they are both left feet" We all looked again and could now clearly see that the expensive Nike trainers were both the same left foot…which meant that somebody somewhere was probably trying on two right footed shoes. Absolute class and could only happen to Al. An hour or so later I said my thank you's and farewells…it had been a great Christmas day with Alan and his family, and a day I've never forgotten and made all the sweeter when the kids knocked the door thirty minutes after I got in the house. It was great to see them open their presents and see the joy on their faces…it was a fantastic and special Christmas, all thanks to Al, Diane and their family.

Al and I settled into our routines, travelling to and from work, Monday to Friday and on the weekend I would have my children over and Alan and Di would make their weekly pilgrimage to their caravan in Porthcawl. At the turn of the year I started re-decorating the house, starting firstly with the bedrooms. Travelling to work one morning I jokingly said to Al that whenever I'm painting I always paint in the nude, arguing that it was easy to just jump in the shower when I'd finished. Al didn't bat an eyelid and just accepted that I was telling the truth…but I was lying through my teeth. On the way to work a couple of weeks later Al asked me how I was getting on with the decorating,

"Fine…I'm starting on the back bedroom tonight". Al didn't say anything, he just nodded. When I got home that evening I got everything ready and put on my 'painting' clothes (an old t-shirt and old jeans…already covered in dry paint from past decorating). I headed for the back bedroom and knew that I'd probably see Al, as from the bedroom window you could look down into Al's living room and see him sat in his chair, as he never shut the blinds, but not on this night…I walked in the bedroom and I looked down towards Al's house and the blinds were shut. The only time in twenty years that I have seen those

238

blinds closed…Alan must have remembered what I'd said about 'nude painting' and wasn't taking any chances. The following morning I said to Al,

"Why were you blinds closed last night?" He didn't know what to say,

"I…um…you know…it was…I can't remember…perhaps…perhaps Di…" I stopped him and said'

"Didn't you want to see me painting in the nude? And I laughed out loud.

"You bastard…I'll…" And there it was…the all familiar red face and trademark raspy laugh I knew so well. It was then it dawned on Al that I didn't and never had decorated in the nude!

Another funny episode was 'Bingate' – my bin used to mysteriously disappear after 'bin day'. After this happened a few times Al said to me,

"I know who it is…it's my bloody next door neighbour…he's always doing it…bastard!". The next bin day…it disappeared again! The weekend passed and on Monday I picked up Al as normal, and as I drove to Caerphilly Al and I were talking about the weekend when Al said,

"I know the bastard that stole your bin Huw"

"Who was it Al?"

"You'll never guess Huw"

"Was it your next door neighbour"

"No"

"Who was it then?

"It was me…I pulled your bin in off the lane by mistake" and he burst out laughing, and was still laughing and wheezing when we pulled up into Nuaire about ten minutes later. A couple of weeks later Wales were playing a World Cup Qualifier against Italy and Al asked me to come over and watch it with him,

"Don't bother walking round…come the back way…I'll leave the gate off the latch for you Shag"

"Ok Al…see you about seven-thirty"

I went in the house had a shower and something to eat and soon it was time to head to Al's. As instructed, I went the back way, stepped out into the lane, shutting my back gate behind me and walked the few metres to Alan's back gate and like he said he'd left it off the latch. But I pushed the gate and it only opened about three or four inches before it stopped…it

239

appeared to be jammed on something. I thought perhaps a
stone or a stick had got stuck underneath and put my shoulder
into and it moved a few more inches. Again, I put my shoulder
into and made enough of a gap that I could squeeze into
Alan's back garden. It was soon apparent as what the problem
was…Al had pulled two of the neighbours bins into his garden
and lined them up behind the gate. I looked down into the
house and I could see Alan's red face and his shoulders going
and I thought, "Bastard" and laughed. When I walked into
Al's house and into the living-room Al was red-faced,
laughing and wheezing and said,
"You get in OK Shag"
"You bastard Al" and were both sat there giggling like school
kids. We were still giggling when Di came in a few minutes
later and said,
"I'm not even gonna ask!" and walked into the kitchen.

Alan loved his music and during that first twelve months I
used to make compilation cassette tapes for him so he could
keep them in the car, especially for those journeys to and from
Porthcawl every weekend. One tape in particular became a
favourite of Alan's grand-daughter, Aylisha, and one song she
asked to play again, again…and again was Dean Martin's
Little Ole Wine Drinker Me, which Aylisha called 'California'.
Alan used to say that as soon as Aylisha got in the car, she'd
say,
"Put California on…put California on"
 It got to the point that Di got sick of this song as she had now
listened to it hundreds of times and jokingly cursed me for
recording it for Al. This give me an idea and I made a tape
where I started taping a song and then after about ten seconds I
would stop recording and then record the entire *Little Ole
Wine Drinker Me*, play another song and again stop recording
after about ten seconds and then record the entire *Little Ole
Wine Drinker Me* again…I repeated this for the whole tape
and told Alan what I'd done, he thought it was hilarious. Most
Wednesday's Al, me, Paul and Ceri Harrington, Ryan Sollis
and sometimes some others, would pop over the Moat House
pub after work for a couple of hours. But on the Wednesday I
gave Alan the tape we found ourselves in the pub for about an
hour longer than normal, as Di had left early to pick her
mother and bring her back to the Miners Hospital in
Caerphilly (around 200m up the road from the pub) to visit

240

Di's father who'd been admitted to hospital…Al asked Di to pick us up when they were on their way home from the hospital. It must have been about twenty past eight when Di walked through the door and found two slightly inebriated men…her husband and me and asked if we were ready. Five minutes later Alan and I were sat in the back of the car, and Alan said, after getting the 'tape' out of his jacket pocket, "Di…Huw's done another tape…here, put it on"

Alan took the tape out of its cover and passed it to Di who, in turn, put the tape into the tape player…a slight pause, and the familiar music of Abba's *Dancing Queen* could be heard, then abruptly and without warning the music stopped, and almost immediately the unmistakable voice of Dean Martin…accompanied by Alan Jenkins and Huw Thomas from the back of a Vauxhall Astra, somewhere in Caerphilly, and all singing in unison *Little Ole Wine Drinker Me*. In the front Di was nodding her head in disbelief and disaproval. She was relieved when the song finally ended and Hot Chocolate started singing *So you Win Again*, but when that again stopped about ten seconds in, Di was under no illusions as to what would happen next…Dean was back for a second rendition, again joined by Al and me as we sang at the top of our voices with no shame, and we hadn't even reached the Bowls pub in Pen-yr-Heol yet. This scenario was repeated three or four times as Di drove up the Aber Valley to drop Di's mother off at her house in the four terraces in Senghenydd. As Di drove back through Senghenydd toward Abertridwr there was still time for one more rendition, and Al and myself didn't hold back and really went for it. When Di pulled up outside their house in Bridgefield Street and turned the engine off, we were only halfway through and Al said,

"Oi…Di…turn it back on…we haven't finished singing…hic". Di turned the engine on, the music started back up and Dean, Alan and me continued to sing…Di was so embarrassed she got out of the car and went in the house, leaving me and Al in the back of the car to drunkenly finish the song. When it ended we sat there for a few minutes both wearing the same inane grin, pleased with ourselves and our performance, then laughed, shook hands and got out of the car. Alan turned the engine off and then locked the car and I started to stagger home…just before Alan went in his house he shouted,

"GREAT NIGHT…SEE YOU IN THE MORNING SHAG".

Those Wednesday nights in the Moat House were great fun, but Alan fancied doing something different and for months talked about a 'Rudry Trip' (Rudry is a village a few miles from Caerphilly). We didn't make any 'concrete' plans, but we all decided that we would go for it…it turned into a fantastic night, but not such a great Thursday morning! On the Wednesday night in question, Alan, Paul & Ceri Harrington, Ryan Sollis and I made our way, as usual, to the Moat House. We had a couple of quick drinks in the Moat House whilst we waited for Di to join us before moving on to the Goodrich pub at the bottom of Van Road in Caerphilly…it was in here that Paul Harrington made the hilarious comment that "it was so nice to be out in couples…" and looked at Al "you and Di…me and Ceri and Huw and Ryan" we all laughed…even me and Ryan (I would like to add that me and Ryan were in no way a couple…he's not my type!). From the Goodrich we went to the Maenllywd Inn where the intention was to have some food…however, as with this type of semi-planned evening, that wasn't quite how things panned out. Now the Maenllywd Inn isn't the cheapest of places to eat out and when we looked at the prices the general consensus was 'it was too expensive'…so we done what all mature adults do, we blew out all the candles in the bottom part of the restaurant and then all ran out giggling like naughty school children…yes, we were by this point becoming slightly tipsy. We headed for the Rudry Arms where Di and Ceri dropped Alan, Paul, Ryan and me before they headed off to ASDA…big mistake. There was a pool table in the back room, and with each game we played, the pints were being demolished. By the time Di and Ceri came back about an hour and a half later we were officially…drunk. Ceri and Di had a task on their hands getting us into the cars for the short trip to the Fishermans in Bedwas…where we managed to have something to eat (at more reasonable bar food prices) before finishing the evening in the White Hart in Bedwas. By the time Di dropped me off on High Street it was almost 11pm and I just about made it to the house which was all of twenty yards away, and once in the house I had an even bigger battle to get up the stairs. The following morning wasn't fun, and when I saw the state of Alan when I picked him up, I knew I wasn't the only one suffering, confirmed by Alan when he got in the car and said, "What the hell happened last night Shag?"

242

Al and I had some great times in and out of work over the next ten years, but eventually Al had to sadly retire from work with ill health. I don't want to dwell too much on the last chapter of Al's life…I would rather remember the man from the stories above than the man who's health deteriorated and who sadly passed away in 2017. He was a great friend and a great work colleague and I can honestly say that I wouldn't be half the man I am today if it wasn't for Al…he was there through the good times, but more importantly he was there for me through the bad times. My only regret is that I wasn't there for Al toward the end, but I never forgot him and I loved him like a brother, and I miss those journeys to work where we'd put the worlds to rights, our nights in the Moat House and I miss his wise words and the man he was and all he stood for. He wasn't perfect, but he was fiercely proud of his background, loved his family and would do anything for any one of them. He was an absolute legend.

"I miss you Shag!"

End of an Era (and the aftermath!)

*It's difficult to accept that a marriage is coming to an end, but that's how I was feeling at the beginning of 1998. My wife was struggling with her mental health and in part, the resultant behaviour began to affect my mental health as I tried to stay strong and positive. However, continual accusations that I was having affairs resulted in an onslaught of unreasonable questions along the same thought process and not knowing what wife was waiting for me at home (there were two extremes; I would walk through the door and the house would be immaculate, dinner on the table, children well behaved and a welcoming smile and kiss **or** she would be curled up on the settee, the house a mess and children running riot. There was nothing inbetween!!). This was beginning to take its toll on not just me, but on my wife, the children and the marriage! However, I also played a part in this developing situation as a mixture of being emotionally insensitive due to ten years in the army, a lack of understanding about mental illness, a lack of money, working too hard and…having absolutely no comprehension of what she was going through. Additionally, I had finally realised that I didn't love her and going home became harder and harder, and as a result it created*

increased stress and reduced levels of patience.
Everything...my wife...the children...work, became exhausting
and I found it increasingly difficult to function normally...to
the point that I was becoming a shadow of the happy go lucky
person you have seen in previous chapters. In hindsight, this
was the beginning of the end...almost in more ways than one
as I suffered a nervous breakdown and a few days later my
fragile mind could take no more and I was unable to process
rational thoughts!

Through my teary eyes, and lying there on the rain sodden
ground, I could see the lights of Pontypridd glistening in the
blackness of the valley below...it was a source of comfort
from the turmoil of emotional pain tearing through my mind. I
looked at the darkness above me and ignored the shouts of the
Police that were out looking for me...wishing...just wishing
that this incredible pain I felt would end..."no more" I kept
whispering to myself, hoping that the release would come
soon, that the overdose I had taken, washed down with vodka,
would bring the incredible pain to an end. I again stared at the
night sky, oblivious to the cold and the fine rain that had
started to fall, and thought about the events that had brought
me to this point...the point where I believed there was no
reason for me to carry on! The images of my children
continually swept through my sub-conscious vision
accompanied by episodes of happier times in my troubled
life...the only things that were helping me cling to this fragile
and tortured existence...
"Please, please let me go...I'm tired, so tired" I whispered, but
the breeze whispered back... "Hang-on Huw...hang on son"
I lay there with my thoughts as my only friend, and shivered
as the breeze momentarily picked up and swept over me...I
wiped the tears away with the back of my hand...tears that had
welled up in my eyes that had caused a blurring, creating a
kaleidoscope of colours from the lights in the valley below!!! I
thought of the family that were now long gone and that I
hoped to see again soon...very soon! I thought of friends from
throughout my life, their faces flashing through my mind as I
mumbled a continual stream of "goodbyes" under my breath.
But mainly, again and again, I thought of my children...and
wished I could have been stronger and a better father...and
again whispered mournful "goodbyes" to the images of their
sweet and innocent faces...and the tears continued to flow!

A noise startled me as a lone sheep, which hadn't seen me lying in the longer grass, bleated and ran off into the damp, dark and murky yonder, again leaving me battling with my dark thoughts and unrelenting demons!

Despite only being on the mountain for about two hours, it seemed as if I'd been laying in the same position for hours, but in reality, as I glanced at my watch, I realised I'd only been there, staring at the blackness above me, for about fifty minutes. The fine rain now started to get heavier, and the film of mist that had soothed my stinging eyes turned into raindrops, occasionally landing in my eyes and forcing me to squint, wince in pain and whisper unheard profanities. I soon turned my head to the side and again stared at the lights down in the valley below, following the headlights of distant cars of people heading home to their families…maybe a warm meal and a gentle, welcoming kiss from a loved one…a smile tried to creep onto my face, but it was quickly chased away by the misery and shame, as I thought of these unknown strangers going about the normal lives not aware that high up on the mountainside, laying in the cold, wet grass, was a man who saw himself as a failure and a coward, a man who wished the fading light of his wasteful life would soon be extinguished. I thought to myself, "No-one loved me, how could they? Look at me, better to go…yes…definitely. No-one would miss me…it will be better for them when I'm gone…and…and better for me. Yes…" I whispered to myself. "…Yes…" I shouted at the sky, as a feeling of resolution swept over me! Any hope I had was almost gone…gone with my dreams…carried on the wind far away from the reach of my own hands, that were now grabbing the grass at my side, scrunching it in my fists as I became overcome by anger as I thought of 'THEM' together…!!! Tears of rage welled up in my eyes as I thought about the betrayal I had heard about that day…news that my fragile mind was unable to filter, unable to comprehend and couldn't…no, wouldn't forgive!! The tears again rolled down my face as I struggled to understand why I felt so incredibly alone and emotionally drained…I could feel the last remnants of any strength I once had gripping on for dear life in one last desperate attempt to save me from myself!

The source of my salvation came from an unlikely source, and a few minutes later, and despite the ongoing battle with my demons, I was suddenly overcome by an incredible craving...I needed a cigarette, and the need was greater than I had ever felt before. The craving took hold and a new battle was developing in my mind...the need for nicotine, in the short term, was fighting my need to die. I knew I had no cigarettes...in the turmoil of my twisted mind it hadn't occurred to me to buy cigarettes before I drove up the mountain earlier that afternoon, I was now beginning to regret that decision! How could I get cigarettes? My car had been towed away by the police about an hour earlier...the need was becoming greater, swamping my, already overflowing, thoughts. I didn't know what to do...a new pain was muddling my decision making, which was now reaching an absurd level of misjudgment. I sat up and through the mist and rain I could see that I was alone on that dark, bleak mountainside. "What to do?...What to do?" I kept repeating to myself as I tapped my thighs in frustration. I stood up and started walking, continually muttering to myself...

"I'll just go to the Rose and Crown, get cigarettes, walk back up the mountain...no-one will know..."

I reached the road and with a stubbornly remembered stealth, walked towards the Rose and Crown and Eglysilan Church, and through the fine rain I could just make out the lights...a mile into the distance. Still muttering to myself and checking all around me eyes darting and focusing on any little noise I heard above the wind...

"I'll get the cigarettes...I'll be back on the mountain...10-15 minutes max...no problem..."

Only the wind heard my mutterings, the sheep occasionally bleated an occasional murmur of agreement before scappering into the darkness, and the trees gently waved as I silently walked past...still keeping my wits about me...

Still muttering, I slowed my pace, and my alertness intensified as I approached the church. I was no more than twenty metres from the pub when a figure stepped out of the shadows on the opposite side of the road. I stopped...my eyes adjusting to the image...it was a policemen and he just said...

"Huw Thomas?"

Due to my fragile mind I immediately broke down and started sobbing uncontrollably, and just nodded my head in affirmation to the question…defeated by my own insecurities. He walked towards me and guided me gently by the arm, offering reassurances that everything would be fine. He led me into the Rose and Crown and I sobbed…and sobbed…and sobbed. Only then did I become aware of the fact that I was shivering…an intense shivering of cold and frustrated anger. An ambulance soon arrived and still sobbing I was helped into the ambulance and taken away to hospital where I was immediately treated with drugs to counteract the effects of the overdose. As strange as it seemed the images of my children, the need for a cigarette and the intense cold had saved my life…despite the emotional pain searing through my body, I was alive…I would live to see another day, to fight other battles, but my damaged and fragile mind knew the road ahead was going to be long and arduous!!!

Post Note

A definite low point in my life, but something I believe I need to share as I'd like to think I turned a huge negative into a positive…sometimes we have to suffer as individuals to enable us to help others, and the 'dark' parts of my life have been sacrifices I am happy to have made as I believe it has helped me 'counsel' my own children and others whenever they have had personal problems. Thankfully, after a short spell in hospital and help from friends I made a full recovery and was able to eventually deal with the fall-out from the breakdown of a 'loveless' marriage (loveless from my perspective…it was only in hindsight that I was able to realise that I had never loved my wife and that it was wrong to stay in a marriage just for the sake of the children). Whilst I am not proud of what happened that day, I feel it is something that has shaped me as a person and I believe it happened for a reason. I'm not trying to sound blasé or arrogant, as suicide is a serious and complex issue and it is not for me to explain the 'why's' and 'wherefore's' of such a difficult subject matter. I can only attempt to understand and explain my own personal struggles, and I believe that, on reflection, I felt like many others who reach a point in their life where they think suicide is the only option. Sadly, when a person reaches those depths of despair, more often than not, the only person that can help them is themselves. I always used to think that people who commit suicide were weak or selfish, but when you reach those horrendous depths, suicide appears to be the best solution for everybody around you, then it becomes a very brave decision to try and end your life. I can only tell you that in those deep, dark moments it is not yourself you are thinking of, you are thinking of your family and friends as you believe they will be better off without you. I know I was extremely lucky that night as the outcome could have been so different…I obviously wasn't meant to die on that mountain that evening and I have used that experience to drive me forward and try and become a better person, and I believe I have done that successfully and that is why I am not ashamed at what happened…it happened, and I'm still here to tell the tale, and that's why I can't look back on it as a negative episode. The only thing that concerns me is the upset I caused the older children, but we have spoken about it many of times since it happened…it has never been a taboo subject, it has been discussed openly, as have the causes that lead to those dark events unfolding. It should never be forgotten or looked upon as a shameful episode, I feel it defines the fragility of life and how dangerous it is when events spiral out of control, a life lesson that we can, if we are lucky and with the right support, move forward and go on to live a full and fruitful life.

*Once out of hospital, I had fantastic support from people around me and eventually I was able to get my life back together, buy a house close to where my children lived and I fought for shared access…I had my children every weekend from Friday to Sunday and for two hours on a Tuesday and two hours on a Thursday, in addition to alternative Christmases and New Year's, a couple of weeks in the summer and I attended every parents evening, sports day and nativity plays. We made memories together that we still talk about today, and I believe I became a better father as a result of the divorce, and am now reaping the rewards of maintaining a strong relationship with all my children. Yes, I'm not perfect and I have made mistakes, but I think that out of something bad came a tremendous amount of good, and as a result of the strong bonds with my children we were also able to come through a particularly bad episode a few years later (see '***The Battle with no Winners'*** *below).*

Suzanne & the 'Cardiff Crowd'

*I met Suzanne Phillips-Cole on a Nuaire night out at
Walkabout in Cardiff and we hit it off pretty well on that first
night, which finished with me walking her home to Canton.
But it didn't quite work out at that time and it would be almost
a year before we started dating properly. Suzanne was a
lovely girl with a heart of gold and a great sense of fun who
lived with her daughter Olivia and parents in Canton. Her
brother Mike made up the rest of what was a very close-knit
family and it was a pleasure witnessing that closeness and
being welcomed into the fold! Another aspect of life with
Suzanne was that, in addition to her family, there was another
part of the package...what I now call the 'Cardiff Crowd', an
absolutely great bunch of friends who made an old valleys boy
feel very welcome on our 'Sunday' nights out in Cardiff and
Canton. There was Ali, Jo and Buddha (not the real one!), the
two Claires (Davies and Blakeman), Lorraine, Sharon and
many more whose names have unfortunately slipped from my
memory!! I have some fantastic memories of those manic
nights of Karaoke, pool, a shed load of beer and more often
than not...finished off with an Indian or Pizza!!*

"Huw…Huw" shouted Suzanne up the stairs. "Are you
ready?...I want to get down the Ivor to see if any of my friends
are there so I can show everyone my engagement ring"
"Coming…be there now in a minute…just put some after
shave on and I'll be down" and I chuckled to myself, as
Suzanne had no idea what I'd organized…we normally
alternated the Sunday evenings between a night out with the
Cardiff Gang and spending the evening at my house. This
week we should have been heading to my house in
Abertridwr, but Suzanne had asked if we could stay in
Cardiff…I happily agreed as that was the plan anyway,
everything was rolling along nicely and according to plan.
I heard Suzanne's muffled "OK", from somewhere
downstairs. I finished tying my laces and reached inside my
bag for my Davidoff Blue Water, opened the bottle, poured a
generous amount in my cupped hands and splashed it on to
clean shaven face…"mmm" I thought "smells good". I picked
up my wallet and fags and shouted,

"On my way". I was soon heading down the stairs toward Suzanne, who was stood by the front door, again looking at her engagement ring and beaming like a Cheshire cat. "Ready love" I said and she nodded…still smiling. We shouted our goodbyes to Suzanne's parents and hugged Olivia. A few minutes later we were walking hand in hand down Cowbridge Road toward the centre of Canton, and the Ivor Davies (Wetherspoons pub). Where I knew there would be a few surprises waiting for Suzanne.

Five minutes later we were walking through the front doors of The Ivor Davies into the usual, vibrant throng of Sunday afternoon drinkers that filled the pub. As it was fairly full, Suzanne hadn't seen our friends, that I'd arranged to be there to surprise her…one of the many surprises I'd arranged for that day, and had started earlier in the day when we had taken Olivia (her daughter) out for lunch and I had proposed and I gave her an engagement ring. Her friends had found a perfect spot towards the back of the pub and I made sure that when we were at the bar getting our first celebratory drinks Suzanne still couldn't see them. We were soon holding our first (of many) drinks and turned from the bar…I led the way, and almost immediately Suzanne caught sight of some of 'the gang' and screamed in delight, giving me a knowing glance and said,
"You planned this, didn't you?"
I laughed and just nodded in agreement, as there were hugs and congratulations all round before we settled down to an unofficial party with great company. It wasn't long before the full crowd were there, and it was fantastic for Suzanne being surrounded by her brother Mike and friends Jo, Claire Davies, Jo and Buddha, Ali, Claire Blakeman, Sharon, Lorraine and many others…you couldn't wish for better company for a special day.

After a great couple of hours in the Ivor it was time to move on to the Insole where more surprises were waiting for Suzanne. It was only a five minute walk away and we were soon walking through the door of the Insole and filling the lounge, where, not only the usual karaoke was waiting, but a buffet and an engagement cake that Suzanne, nor the others, had any idea about. We had a great night in the Insole where we were not only entertained by Ali's great singing, but also

by those songs that were 'murdered' by a few of us brave enough to have a go, including Sharon and I as we belted out our usual 'Angels' by Robbie Williams…we thought we were excellent, but it didn't matter if we weren't, we were all having a great old 'knees up'. The 'spread' (food) was a great success, as was the engagement cake…not the best thing to eat with beer or lager but everyone seemed to enjoy it. But as with all good nights, it sadly come to an end as they always do. We couldn't have spent it with a better crowd of people and this was just one of many nights that the same crowd got together in Canton…whilst the venues sometimes changed the enjoyment levels were always the same. The joy with drinking in Canton was that it never took more than 5-10 minutes to walk back to Suzanne's house…slightly tipsy…no not tipsy, slightly drunk, but extremely happy and continually giggling, we walked and staggered back to the house, sometimes taking a few steps to the side, some backwards and more importantly sometimes walking in the right direction. Finally, at the front door of the house, we played the drunken game of trying to get the key in the door…great fun, if you haven't tried it…and then eventually we were in. More giggling and shushing as the house was in darkness, and as everyone knows when you are slightly 'worse for wear', you try to be quiet, but you tend to be noiser than you would be normally. We both fell on the stairs…more giggling and shushing, before we finally made it to Suzanne's bedroom where she flopped on the bed and attempted to thank me for a wonderful evening,
"Huw…Huw…Huw….ssh, ssh, shh…" the giggling continued "…no…no…no…seriously…I mean…Huw…Huw…I wanted to (hic)…to…say…what do I want to say?…oh yeah that's it…thank you for a great…a great day (hic)…"
"That's ok Suzanne (hic)…I'm just glad, just glad…you…you…had a good time…(hiccup)." I giggled and then fell onto the bed next to Suzanne, we both giggled attempted to kiss each other…but failed, giggled again and then we both fell asleep!

Post Note

They were special times and we were surrounded by special people. We had many great nights in the pubs in and around Canton, sometimes going into Cardiff and Jumping Jacks, but mainly in Canton. I can look back on those times with Suzanne

251

and the 'Cardiff Crowd' with great affection and can appreciate them as much now as I did at the time. Genuinely nothing but happy memories from those nights out and spending time with Suzanne, Olivia and Suzanne's parents and her brother Mike...great, great people.

The Battle with no winners!!

I believe this episode is, by far, the lowest point in my life to date! It could be considered that what started as a fairly innocuous argument at a caravan park near Aberystwyth, finished with my family being completely ripped apart! The argument resulted in my ex-wife moving to Middlesbrough with the twins ('Rh' and 'A') whilst the older three ('K', 'R' and 'G') decided to remain in Wales. This decision inevitably led to a breakdown in the family units (i.e. father/son, mother/son father/daughter, mother/daughter, between siblings, grand-parents/grand-children etc), and I was left with decisions to make that resulted in me being 'damned if I did and damned if I didn't'!! As a child I had experienced my parents getting divorced, not seeing my father for 2-3 years, and shortly after I started seeing him again, he remarried and moved to London...this had a profound effect on our relationship that is still evident today. Additionally, I had experienced the negative effects of long-distance relationships, I felt that no-one realised in the family or fully appreciated how devastating distance can be on relationships. I tried to have these conversations with my ex-wife, but I don't believe she understood the potential negative implications of the proposed move. During the initial appointment with my solicitor I had a better picture of where I stood when he told me "Hmmm...on one hand, taking the twins from their father, brothers and sister, grandparents, friends, education and the area they were born and always lived and on the other hand, taking them from their mother..." and he looked me in the eye and used his hands to imitate a balancing motion and said "it's fairly even...the decision could go either way!" Despite this set-back I had to fight for what I believed was the correct thing to do and go for custody of the twins...I had to send a message to my children that I loved each and every one of them and that the right thing to do was to try and keep them together! I had no choice than to try and put my faith in a legal system that had already shown me was heavily weighted

252

in favour of mothers!!! I fought…and fought…and fought,
until I had almost lost everything as a result of an unjust
British legal system which was far worse than I feared…as
were the effects on me and my family!!

I sat in the foyer area waiting to be called into the courtroom. I had already made the decision that this was where the 'battle' would end…but on my terms, and the twenty minutes I had just spent with the CAFCASS (Children and Family Court Advisory and Support Services) Officer confirmed that my decision was correct. Everyone had been through enough, especially the twins and for once I wasn't going to be dictated to by a one-sided legal system…I was going to have my say. My solicitor couldn't make it today which meant I was representing myself…It was too good an opportunity to miss, and as I had rehearsed this moment in my head, time and time again, I knew what I was going to do once I got into the courtroom. Whilst I waited there I closed my mind to the goings on in the courthouse, and thought about the events of the last horrendous sixteen to eighteen months and the destruction caused to my family by both sides. I thought of the arguments, the fractured relationships, the lies, stopping the twins from seeing me and their sister 'R', the attempts to do everything within the bounds of the law, the broken promises, damaging letters, injustices of the CSA (Child Support Agency), unfairness of the legal system, the possible manipulation of 'A' and 'Rh', the effects on my health (physically and mentally), and the general negative affects this all had on so many people on both sides. I knew that I had to re-build the shattered relationships that were all around me…that could be re-built, that I had to accept that to carry on the fight for a fair justice for all was totally pointless. That was easier said than done as instinct was nagging away at the back of my mind to fight, fight and fight. But I knew I had to concentrate on a healing process that involved the re-building of my relationships with 'A' and 'Rh' and the relationships between all the siblings…the other relationships, I believed, would then repair naturally. As a parent it was horrendous seeing, not just the distance in miles, but also the emotional distance that had developed between 'Rh' and 'A' and their brothers and sister. As a child who had experienced the effects of not seeing my own father for 2-3 years, between the ages of five and eight years old, and him living away from Wales in

253

London, then Norfolk, followed by Bristol, when I was aged between nine and fifteen, I had experienced the damage this type of separation had on the relationship between me and my father. As a result, I foresaw the dangers that the different aspects of 'distance' can do to relationships…something my ex-wife had no comprehension of, and it was obvious to me that the judges, barristers or CAFCASS (Children and Family Court Advisory and Support Services) officers, I dealt with, had no personal experience of the damage that is inflicted on those caught up in these situations. There are no university degrees, training courses or reading of case studies that can substitute personal experience, and that was the advantage I had over both my ex-wife and the legal system, but as loud as I shouted, no-one could or would hear me. They didn't make decisions based on the facts in front of them, decisions were based on the constraints of the law and their lack of understanding of the 'personal' damage that was occurring, not just to me and all my children, but also to my ex and her husband and both of our wider familes and friends…no understanding at all. So, so frustrating and very, very painful for all concerned. I'm not a confident person, but with this situation, I knew I was right and I also knew that as long as I had a breath in my body, no-one would be able to tell me otherwise…the only thing I underestimated was the speed in which the solid foundations of all the relationships were eroded away by destructive actions and an inept legal system.

I looked at my watch as I sat there waiting to be called with all of the above continually spinning through my mind…it was twenty five past two, and I thought we could be called at any moment. There was an air of confidence running through me and I knew that this was my only chance to speak directly to a judge, not through a solicitor or a barrister, directly, and there was a nervous excitement nibbling away at my thoughts and I kept telling myself, "Huw, you have to make every second count…every second". I gritted my teeth and a steely determination enveloped me when I heard someone shouting, "Thomas versus F***** Court 2". I stood up and followed the court usher through the door into the courtroom. I was directed to my seat and my heart was racing as I made my way to seating, which happened to be directly in front of where the judge would be sitting…"perfect", I thought. I then sat down and waited, thinking to myself…"zero hour is almost here and…I'm ready, so ready."

Within a couple of minutes the judge entered the court and introduced himself, and the case he was about to hear, to all those in the room. I listened to every word, waiting for an opportunity to stand up, interrupt and say what I had to say. I didn't have to wait long for the right opportunity to present itself…the judge had been wittering on about the difficulties of the case and the sadness that the different relationships had broken down such as the one between me and 'A' and 'Rh', and the relationships between 'A' and 'Rh' and their brothers, 'K' and 'G' and sister, 'R'. The judge's comments were nothing I hadn't heard before and I knew the breakdown in relationships could have been avoided had there been a fairer legal system in place that wasn't so heavily weighted in favour of mothers. Something that I was powerless to stop…but I did try. When the judge started to state that, as 'A' and 'Rh' now lived in Middlesbrough, any future court proceedings would be transferred to that area…I seized the chance to end things right there and right now. I stood up and immediately started to address the judge directly…I was firm but polite,
"Your honour, **ALL** my children have been put through enough and this ends today…"
I paused briefly to compose myself and the judge looked at me angrily, and was about to speak when I continued,
"…the legal system has let my family down and allowed the children's mother to split the family down the middle. I will not be attending court in Middlesbrough as I have been threatened by members of my ex-wife's family…this ends now…'
Driven by anger and frustration that the British Legal system had brought us to this point, I turned and started walking out of the courtroom. The judge was obviously in shock at my audacity of hijacking his courtroom, and before he had a chance to speak I was already walking behind my ex-wife and her solicitor. As I couldn't direct my anger at the judge, I directed my pent up anger and frustration at my ex-wife and said,
"You are nothing but a disgrace as a mother and as a human being"
The judge finally found his voice and as I made my way toward the door, I heard,

255

"MR THOMAS…MR THOMAS…I HAVE NOT FINISHED…!"
Without looking back I shouted, "WELL, I HAVE"
And I walked out of the court into the waiting area outside.
The CAFCASS Officer, who had dashed out of the courtroom after me, shouted,
"MR THOMAS DON'T DO THIS, THE JUDGE HASN'T FINISHED…MR THOMAS…MR THOMAS COME BACK…PLEASE…!"
I didn't respond and I didn't look back…I calmly walked out of the building and didn't stop walking until I got back to the car, which was parked a couple of hundred metres away in the ASDA Blackwood car park.

It was a small victory in a battle where there were 'no real winners', a small victory where, in defiance, I stuck up two fingers to an establishment that had allowed this horrendous situation to happen which ultimately ripped my family apart…right down the middle!

Post Note

To many who know the journey I travelled for approximately 18 months and beyond, from the time my ex-wife announced she was moving to Middlesbrough, and the damage caused to so many people, my actions in court that day back In 2008 may seem like a hollow victory. But it was a small victory, and a very significant part in a series of events that affected so many people. My daughter 'A' and son 'Rh' sadly became estranged for around six months from myself, son 'K', daughter 'R' and other son 'G' and the stress it caused also put my job at risk. There is plenty more that could be said about the escalation of events from an argument in a caravan, to daughter 'A' and son 'Rh' returning to Wales in the middle of 2010. But even now they are extremely painful memories for everyone. Those of us who stayed in Wales, and 'A' and 'Rh' themselves are all aware that had they not returned to Wales when they did, the damage could have been irreparable. My actions in court that day may seem petulant to many people and it obviously didn't affect the decisions of the court, as the decisions had already been made. Additionally, I was lucky not to be found guilty of contempt of court, but my solicitor managed to convince the courts that my actions were borne out of frustration, stress and an acute sense of loss. But it did bring an end to all the arguments and can be considered the beginning of the healing process for everyone. Thankfully, we started having contact with the twins again and they started to stay over for holidays before finally moving back to Wales in 2010 (a little under three years after they left Wales). The relationships again became very strong between myself and the twins, and between all the children, particularly between 'R' and 'A'...who are now extremely close. Additionally, the relationships between the older children and their mother also returned to normal. However, individually, we were all affected and that unfortunately came out in other ways, but for now I don't want to dwell on those negatives. Although no longer together, my ex-wife and I will continue to support our children, to the best our abilities, in any hurdles they may encounter generally with difficulties that are thrown at them as they make their way through life. If I can turn a negative to a positive it would be that life's tough lessons have provided me with the tools to help my children, as I am sure lessons they learn will help them deal with any problems their own children encounter.

The Last Day

Throughout the year Sian Newton will remind us all how much time is left before the 'Last Day' is upon us again… "forty-nine weeks to the last day", "twenty-three weeks to the last day" and by late November she's counting down in days "27 days to the last day"!! To those who don't know, the 'Last Day' is the company's annual Christmas party which signals the beginning of the factory shutdown for the Christmas period. In my time at Nuaire it has been held in many different local locations and normally involves…food (in the form of a buffet), drink (obviously alcohol!) and a disco! It is a real high point in the Nuaire calendar, but not in a sordid way…there is very rarely any 'carrying on/shenanigans/extra-marital nonsense' with exception of one instance between two people that shall remain nameless (one year, I had agreed to give two people a lift home…as they had both decided to sit in the back I witnessed, in the rear view mirror, what can only be described as a Clinton/Lewinsky moment! It didn't end there when I pulled up in the girl's street, as a thank you she tried to kiss me…needless to say, after what I witnessed in the rear

view mirror no more than 5-10 minutes earlier I quickly pulled
away, got back in the car and drove off...at high speed!).
Additionally, the day is normally enjoyed by all, and as far as
I can remember there have been very few instances where
there has been any fighting...just a great day amongst friends
and work colleagues! Initially, in the early days when the
company was smaller it would be a few drinks and a buffet in
the staff canteen, followed by a short walk to 'The
Moathouse', a local pub across the road from where the
company is based in Caerphilly, and ending with a disco at the
49 Club. As the company has grown there have been different
venues such as the Municipal Club (or Muni as its
affectionately known locally), Bedwas Rugby Club and over
the last few years at Caerphilly Social Club (provided our
'last day' is not on a Friday as it would clash with the famous
'grab a granny' nights that the Social Club is famous for!).
We've had a 'Stars in you Eyes' competition and also X
Factor and also, what has now become an annual event,
where any newcomers to Nuaire have to get up and sing a
song of their own choice! Yes...we have had some memorable
nights, but this short story is about the 'Stars in your Eyes' we
held in, I think Christmas 1998, at the Muni (Municipal) Club
in the centre of Caerphilly!!!

We were huddled into the changing room of the Municipal
Club in Caerphilly...well, I say changing room, it was actually
the room where they kept the barrels of beer and lager. We
just managed to squeeze ourselves in...it was Christmas 1998
and it was the infamous Nuaire 'last day'. When I say 'we', I
am referring to the contestants for the Nuaire 'Stars in your
Eyes' competition...me (Dai Preslee), Dean Griffiths (Gary
Glitter...before the 'revelations', so he was still fairly
popular!), Neil Taylor (Otis Redding), Bob Duck (Elvis
Presley) and a gang of the shop floor boys (Village People).
We hadn't done anything like this before, but we were
confident we could carry it off...we got into our homemade
costumes that had been made with nowhere near the budget
that the real 'Stars in your Eyes' contestants enjoyed, no
entrance through dry ice onto an expensive set. It was wait for
your name to be shouted, walk out of the barrel store to a
drunken roar of the crowd and make your way past the bar,
through a throng of people and onto the small stage area. Who
was first I hear you ask?..."guess who?"..."yep...me". I told

258

the announcer to introduce me as Elvis Presley (all part of the plan). When the others saw what I was wearing they look mystified and Dean said,

"I thought you were Elvis!"

"No…" I said, "I'm…Dai Preslee" Again, they looked at me, all attempting to work out who Dai Preslee was! I started to explain the story and they began to understand why I was dressed in a balaclava, dai cap, white shirt, medallion (in the shape of a rugby ball), tracksuit bottoms (tucked into socks) and slippers. And when I turned around and they saw what was written on the back of the shirt 'DAI PRESLEE – KING OF THE VALLEYS' the room erupted into laughter and high fives and Dean said,

"Nice one Huw".

We agreed the order in which we would perform, and I was happy to be the first one to run the gauntlet through a baying crowd to the stage at the opposite end of the function room. I thought my mix of a Keith Isham type performance of the Elvis Presley classic, 'Are you lonesome tonight?', but with Chubby Brown's changed lyrics of the original song, would be a great pre-curser to what would follow from the other lads…a sort of shit warm-up act. I'd already agreed with the compere that he would introduce me as Elvis Presley (all part of the act). Looking around that cramped storeroom at The Village People, Gary Glitter, Otis Redding and Elvis Presley (and his two bodyguards) was fairly amusing, and a few sneaky glances into the function room told us the place was filling up nicely and there was definitely a party atmosphere building.

A few moments later there was an expectant excitement that surged through that little storeroom when there was a knock at the door, and the compere poked his head in and said,

"Ready lads…who's first?"

"ME…" I shouted "DON'T FORGET TO INTRODUCE ME AS ELVIS" and winked.

"Ok…two minutes" and he laughed when he saw what I was wearing, and I think he now understood the amusing irony of introducing me as Elvis Presley.

True to his words, no more than two minutes we heard a muffled introduction to the impending 'Stars in your Eyes' show, opened the door slightly, and then heard,

"LET'S GIVE A WARM WELCOME TO OUR FIRST ACT
THIS AFTERNOON...ALL THE WAY FROM THE
USA...IT'S ELVIS PRESLEY"

I walked out of the storeroom and made my way to the
stage...there were loud cheers, but I soon sensed the cheers
were turning to laughter...the crowd could now see what I was
wearing, it wasn't a pretty site, and the laughter seemed to get
louder when I snatched the microphone off the compere and
said,

"IT'S DAI PRESLEE...DAI PRESLEE" I turned my back to
the crowd and pointed to the back of my shirt and repeated,

"DAI PRESLEE...NOT THAT BLOODY IMPOSTER
FROM AMERICA"

I explained to the audience that, "I AM GOING TO SING
THE ORIGINAL VERSION OF 'ARE YOU LONESOME
TONIGHT?' THAT ELVIS STOLE, CHANGED THE
WORDS AND ENDED UP HAVING A BIG HIT
STATESIDE...BUT I WROTE THIS SONG ABOUT A
GIRL FROM THIS VALLEY, AND I'VE HEARD SHE'S IN
THE AUDIENCE TONIGHT"

Huge cheers as I disappeared off stage, found Karen Linder
(and a chair) and brought them onto the stage (well, dance
floor), I sat her on the chair in the middle of the dance floor
and told the crowd,

"ALL I NEED NOW IS SOME BACKING SINGERS AS
MY BACKING SINGERS ARE STRANDED IN YSTRAD
AFTER THEIR MINIBUS BROKE
DOWN...THANKFULLY SOME PEOPLE IN THE
AUDIENCE HAVE KINDLY VOLUNTEERED TO HELP
OUT...GIVE A WARM NUAIRE WELCOME TO..."

There was an instant fear in the eyes of those close to the
dance floor as I started to read out the names,

"MARK HUXTABLE"

"CERI YEO"

"ALUN MORTON"

"DAI WAUGH"

"AND...WAYNE GLOVER"

Huge roars of approval (and relief) from the crowd as the five
new members of my backing group joined me on stage. I
formed them up in a semi-circle around the chair, that Karen
was thankfully still sitting on, and explained what I wanted
them to do which was to hum the tune of 'Are you Lonesome
Tonight?' whilst swaying from side to side. They fell into their

260

new roles perfectly, and I kneeled down in front of Karen, looked into her eyes and started to sing,
"ARE YOU LONESOME TONIGHT, IS YOUR BRAZIER TOO TIGHT?
ARE YOUR KNICKERS CLUTCHING YOUR FAT HOLE?
ARE YOUR DOCTOR WHITES SNAGGING YOUR TIGHTS?..."
I noticed a confused look on Karen's face, but didn't think anything of it, and continued singing...everything was going well...the newly formed backing singers were merrily humming away and rocking from side to side, Karen was still sat on the chair and the crowd seemed to understand the irony and were finding it amusing...judging by the laughter or were they laughing at my outfit. Anyway, either way it was going down well. I was soon singing the last few lines,
"...PUT THIS BAG ON YOUR HEAD,
AND BUGGER OFF TO BED,
"IT'S NO WONDER YOU'RE LONESOME TONIGHT"
I stood up and bowed, whilst Karen didn't know what had just happened...I said to the crowd, "GIVE A BIG HAND TO THE BACKING SINGERS" and they headed back to their seats with backslaps from colleagues as I led Karen back to her seat, and to rapturous applause and laughter, I made my way back to the storeroom. Stepping inside there were more high fives all round and Dean said, "Priceless...absolutely priceless". I could relax now as it was the turn of the others to 'wow' the audience and that's exactly what they did. It was a great afternoon which I think was enjoyed by everyone...Did I win? Nah, of course I didn't, but one thing that did make me chuckle though was what Karen Linder said to me later that afternoon...
"When you sat me down on that chair I thought you were going to serenade me properly...I didn't expect you to sing something like that"
I laughed and said, "You thought I was going to sing a proper love song...wearing a balaclava, dai cap, shirt with 'Dai Presslee King of the Valleys' on the back, tracksuit bottoms (tucked into socks) and slippers...you're having a laugh!" and we both burst out laughing.

Ada

It was January 2nd 2009 and I was at the Irish Thymes in Caerphilly on a night out with Katie Williams and Craig Morgan. This turned into an unforgettable night, not just because it was the night I met my now partner, Ada, but because of a mysterious, psycho blonde and the infamous taxi getaway at the end of the night!!!

Katie, Craig and I had been in the Irish Tymes around an hour and were having a great time. Craig was getting a round in so I thought it would be a good idea to go to the toilet...I got up and started walking toward the toilet. As I got to the small area where people were dancing I was suddenly mesmerized by one of two women, who appeared to be Thai or Filipino, she had the biggest and most beautiful smile I had ever seen... "Wow..." I thought, "...she is absolutely stunning. I carried on to the toilet, and after 'breaking the seal', washed my hands, checked myself in the mirror and headed back out into the pub...there she was again, I hadn't been dreaming. I hurried back to where Katie and Craig were sitting and told them about the beautiful Asian girl I'd seen. For the next fifteen to twenty minutes all I could think of was the mysterious Asian beauty and her smile.

As the evening went on a 'psycho' blonde started bothering us, but it was mainly Craig she seemed to be interested in...she really wasn't a full ticket. She wouldn't leave us alone and we began to wonder how the hell we were going to get rid of her. It was slightly disturbing as she was telling us her boyfriend (who also seemed 'psycho' as she told us he was beating her up) had kicked her out and she had nowhere to stay...we all agreed that she was trying to latch on to us so she would have somewhere to stay...and it was poor Craig that was getting the attention. However, I couldn't get the Asian girl out of my mind and went to look for her...I found her sat down with two of her friends, who were also Asian, and I sat down next to her and attempted to talk to her, but between the loudness of the music and her English not being very good it was proving difficult to make myself understood. But I did manage to find out that the three women were all from Thailand and the one I liked was called Ada...the language barrier was proving difficult, but one of Ada's friends spoke better English and suggested I write down my phone number. After a few minutes of them searching for a pen in their handbags, I was holding a pen and scribbling my telephone number down for Ada. I asked her to "call me tomorrow", said my goodbyes and made my way back to Katie, Craig and the Psycho blonde.

It was getting late and me, Katie and Craig knew we would soon have to go…but how do we get rid of our 'problem'. When our new 'psycho' friend went to the bar a few minutes later, we agreed that when we had a chance we would try and make a dart for it. What we didn't know was that the opportunity was about to present itself…'psycho blonde' came back from the bar, put her drink on the table and drunkenly announced she was going to the toilet. This was it, this was the opportunity we needed…we waited until we had seen her close the toilet door and we were out the pub like 'shit off a stick' and jumped into a taxi, the taxi pulled off, just as the 'blonde psycho' appeared at the door of the pub, obviously looking for us. We all shot down out of sight, thankfully the lights were on green and were soon driving down Cardiff Road toward the castle. We all sat back up, heaved a sigh of relief and started laughing.
"That was close" said Katie. Craig giggled and I nodded in agreement.
We were soon leaving Caerphilly and heading back to Craig's house, but all I could think about was Ada…and her beautiful smile.

The following day, shortly after getting back from Craig's, the house phone rang and it was answered by my son, 'G' who within a couple of seconds I heard shouting down the phone, "STOP CALLING, I DON'T WANT TO BUY ANYTHING…FUCK OFF!!!" I asked inquisitively, "Who was that?"
"Just someone woman trying to sell something but I can't understand her Dad". With that the phone rang again, but this time I answered it "Hello"
"Hello…I am Ada" said a little voice in broken English.
"Hello, how are you?" I said slowly. We managed to have a short, but simple, conversation and she agreed to meet me a week later at the Tommy Cooper statue in the centre of Caerphilly at 1pm and go for lunch. I put the phone down and

couldn't stop smiling, it was just the tonic I needed after a shocking 2008. Over the next week we text each other a few times and then met up on the Sunday...I approached the Twyn car park at around five to one as I didn't want to be late, but I could see that Ada was already waiting at the statue and when I pulled up in the car, she gave me that beautiful smile that had first caught my eye in the Irish Thymes a week earlier. It was fairly low-key that first 'date' as we stayed local and went for lunch at the Cwrt Rawlin pub in Caerphilly. I wouldn't say the conversation was flowing but we managed to understand each other, she even told me that when she rang the first time somebody picked up the phone and said "not very nice words!" and I realised that the phone call that 'G' had picked up just before I spoke to Ada, was also Ada...I apologised and told her that my son thought it was someone trying to sell something. That was a close run thing and I thought I'd had a lucky roll of the dice, but also got the impression that I'd finally landed on my feet and was looking forward to where this might lead. After a lovely couple of hours I dropped her off and as I drove away and looked in the rear view mirror, I believed that my luck (or sometimes, bad choices) with women was about to change.

Over the next few months we became closer and closer and spent a lot of time together going for meals, visits to the seaside, day trips, shopping etc, and one of our favourite places to visit was Roath Park in Cardiff, with its beautiful well cared for gardens, lake, children's play area and café. Ada was a breath of fresh air and the language barrier was sometimes still there, but with Ada attending college to learn English her language skills were improving all the time. However, there were the occasional misunderstandings such as when I sent her a text and said 'I miss you xxx' and her reply of 'I not missing, I in Caerphilly' was priceless...oh how we laughed when I explained what I meant. An important factor for me was that all my children and my parents liked Ada...what was not to like, she was continually smiling, polite and wonderfully caring, and I was beginning to see how important 'family' is to Thai people. It was terribly upsetting seeing her so visibly upset when her sister, Som, passed away through cancer, a sister who had been so good to Ada when she left Ban Sam Rung for the first time and went to live with her and her family in Bangkok...Ada was on the other side of

264

the world and felt helpless and isolated that she couldn't fulfill her duty and be with her family at such a difficult time. It was heartbreaking and I really felt for her and wished I could have met Som.

Seven months into the relationship, it become clearly obvious how close we'd become when I watched Ada go through the barrier at Heathrow, she was going home to Thailand for three weeks to visit her family, I instantly missed her as she disappeared from sight and it was a lonely journey driving back to Wales. To make matters worse, contact was minimal as Ada was in a rural village where it was impossible to get a signal, making me miss her all the more. I was a happy man when three weeks later I watched her coming through the doors of 'arrivals' at Heathrow…similar to the ending of 'Love Actually' as I watched others being re-united with loved ones before being re-united with Ada. We were soon preparing for a baby when we discovered that Ada was pregnant, and Ada told me that she hoped it was a girl, as having a girl was seen as 'lucky'. We were lucky as we were blessed with a healthy baby girl On April 29th 2010 and our relationship went from strength to strength, and I strongly believed that after the previous serious relationships I had been in, that I was finally being rewarded for being the good person I believed I was, and hopefully still am. Early in 2011, we travelled to Thailand…my first trip to visit Ada's family in a beautiful country (more about the trips to Thailand in Chapter 9). I feel blessed that I met Ada as she is a beautiful person, inside and out, and she has a heart of gold that matches her beautiful smile. She is a wonderful mother and I love her with all my heart, her confidence and strong character has brushed off and me, and I credit my recent achievements to that confidence and strength she has instilled in me. To simply say 'I love her' is an injustice to Ada as a person…she is the best thing that has happened to me and I believe I am a better person and a better father as a result of sharing my life with her. But she is quick to call me a buffalo, dog or rock (in Thai) if I do or say something she thinks is stupid…'Koy hak Ada lai lai der' (I love you Ada, very, very much) from your 'Ting Tong Farang' (crazy foreigner).

James Edward's Stag do (Tenby 2012)

I have been on a few 'stag nights' (including my own), but the day we all headed to Tenby for James Edwards stag night no-one envisaged we would have such a fantastic day/night in West Wales. The Saturday morning started with us meeting early at the car park in front of the Cwrt Rawlin Tesco Express in Caerphilly, and finishing with Jag and I laughing about flowers almost incessantly the entire journey back to Caerphilly on the Sunday morning...a great time was had by all and we even got to see the teetotal James Edwards drink alcohol!!!

I was the first to arrive in the car park at the small shopping precinct of the Cwrt Rawlin estate, parked up, got out of the car and immediately walked over to the cashpoint by the Tesco Express. Others soon started to arrive, and within fifteen to twenty minutes those travelling on the minibus were seated and had cracked open the first cans. I was driving and had Martyn Price and Aled Williams as passengers...this was going to be a long day and my days of drinking from eight o'clock in the morning were long gone. I knew that pacing yourself was the key to surviving the day and as it was 'Big Cheese' weekend I wanted to get back fairly early on the Sunday to take Ada and Amy to the stalls, fair and sideshows in the castle. The minibus pulled off and I followed...we were on our way to Tenby. I chuckled to myself as I thought of the flowers that would be waiting for Martyn and Jag (James Gardiner) in their hotel room...a beautiful and romantic gesture, kindly arranged by...yes you've guessed it...me and Sian Newton!

Luckily, we had a fairly clear run and around an hour and a half later we were pulling up in the car park at Carew Karting near Tenby. I'm not sure who won the go-karting, but being a fairly conservative driver...it wasn't me. Following the go-karting, and prior to the partaking of drinking alcoholic beverages, it was decided it might be a good idea to eat something first and we all headed to a McDonalds in Pembroke...not exactly the best choice but better than having no food at all...just! As is typical of a McDonalds meal...we were all full for about 5 mins and knew that we'd have to eat something a bit more substantial between the afternoon

266

session we were about to embark on and the evening session in Tenby…or there would be drunken casualties everywhere. An hour later we were all enjoying our first pint at our accommodation for the evening, The Beach Hotel, Pendine, quickly followed by the obligatory group photo on the sea front with James dressed as one of the 'Mario Brothers' as the centerpiece. It was a fairly relaxed afternoon, playing pool and enjoying a few beers, but at the same time pacing oneself was the order of the day as an evening in Tenby was in front of us all, and by around 5ish that 'substantial' meal was calling. A few of us made our way to the chip shop that was located about 50m behind the hotel on the main road in Pendine…which also doubled as an Indian takeaway, and a rogan josh with rice and chips filled the gap and lined the stomach ready for Tenby. But first it was the 3 Ss (shit, shower and shave), the wearing of the 'glad rags' and complimentary expensive aftershave…one had to be presentable for the evening's shenanigans. At this point I have to mention Aled Williams, he worked with us in the estimating team and shall we say he was a tadge naïve…if you hadn't realised by now I like a bit of a joke, and I'd been winding Aled up all day. We were sharing bunkbeds (Aled on the top bunk and me on the bottom) in the room we were sharing with five other people. All day I'd been throwing the odd comment at Aled such as "Don't worry Aled…you'll see me naked later" or "Put your bags on the bottom bunk as we'll be sharing the top bunk tonight", it reminded me of Me, Iki Bolton and Jim Stead in Plon. I was making him nervous and it was funny as hell, his face was a picture when someone pushed the shower door open as I stepped out of the shower and he saw my lily-white arse staring at him. He went bright red and didn't know where to look I said, "Don't worry big boy, you'll see plenty more later" and I winked at him before I rocked my head back laughing hysterically…poor Aled, he was so embarrassed…and nervous.

Twenty minutes later we were all on the bus heading for Tenby…James was no longer dressed as one of the Mario Brothers, he was now dressed in a 'twister' suit (a white suit in the style of the popular game 'twister' covered in yellow, red, blue and green circles)…not exactly stylish, but certainly funny. Another thirty minutes later we were drinking our first pints in Tenby Rugby Club awaiting the arrival of brothers

Lewis and Gareth Williams (James's best man) who were
holidaying with their families in Tenby, and the 'lovers'
Martyn and Jag who had booked themselves into a hotel in
Tenby…hope they liked the flowers! It wasn't long before
everyone had arrived, but how I didn't laugh when Martyn and
Jag rolled up I don't know…Jag was full of it,
"You'll never guess what's happened at the hotel…" and he
told us the story of how they booked into the room and Martyn
was the first in the shower whilst Jag was familiarizing
himself with everything in the room. It was then he noticed the
bunch of flowers and shouted to Martyn,
"MART…THERE'S A BUNCH OF FLOWERS YUH!"
A muffled "what?" came from the bathroom
"THERE'S A BUNCH OF FLOWERS…HANG
ON…THERE'S A CARD…"
Another muffled "what?...a bunch of flowers!"
"YEAH, A BUNCH OF FLOWERS…"
"Perhaps the previous occupants had flowers but forgot to take
them with them when they left…what does the card say?"
Martyn was now out of the shower and standing in the
doorway to the bathroom drying his hair.
Jag opened the little envelope, took out the card and started to
read it,
"THANKS FOR EVERYTHING, ALL MY
LOVE…MARTYN"
Silence…Jag described to us how they both stood there
gobsmacked, and I said to Jag in a serious voice "Perhaps one
of the previous people in the room had the same name…what
a coincidence"
"NO…THIS IS THE BEST BIT…THEY WERE ORDERED
WHEN THE ROOM WAS BOOKED…CAN YOU
BELIEVE THAT"
"Perhaps Martyn fancies you Jag" and I laughed, but Jag
didn't. He had no idea and I immediately thought Sian would
love to have been here now witnessing this.

It wasn't long before a group of women turned up and
immediately took a shine to the suit James was wearing and
asking if he would lie on the floor so they could play twister.
Being the obliging person that James is he was soon lying flat
on his back…big mistake. The one girl spun the arrow and the
colour she landed on just happened to be the spot that was
covering his 'crown jewels' and she punched him straight in

the nadgers, and James let out a loud "UGHH!" and started to clutch his 'bits' whilst angrily looking at the women and shouting,

"THERE WAS NO NEED FOR THAT…WHAT DID YOU DO THAT FOR?" The rest of us thought it was hilarious and were struggling not to laugh whilst attempting to ask if he was ok. James eventually stopped rubbing his 'nadger' and it wasn't long before it was only his pride that was hurt. We stayed at the rugby club for another hour or two, and during this time I listened to Jag tell everyone (even strangers) about the flowers and innocently asking each person,

"It wasn't you that ordered them flowers...no…ok…just checking". I was continually by his side the entire time and he still had no idea it was me that had ordered the flowers…hilarious.

Next stop was the Three Mariners which was literally around the corner from the rugby club and took us no more than two minutes, but as there were so many of us we agreed to leave in small groups…we knew if we all went together it was likely they wouldn't let us in. It proved to be the right decision and after about thirty minutes the entire party were enjoying their first drinks in a pub that was complete with a small dance floor and DJ toward the rear of the pub. The first visit to the toilet, which was directly off the dance floor, was interesting as the majority of the floor was covered in about half an inch of piss, and I thought to myself "better keep an eye on this!" Jag, Aled and I positioned ourselves on the opposite side of the dance floor to the toilet, near to the bar (for obvious reasons), and therefore, far enough away from the tidal wave of piss that was building up in the excuse for a toilet. It was from this vantage point that we witnessed the only trouble we'd see that weekend…two young girls fighting on the dance floor who were soon ejected by the bouncers, but they carried on their fight outside on the paved area in front of the pub…we could see them through the windows wrestling, pulling each other's hair and slagging each other off…classy, and probably all over a boy!

It was an interesting evening in the Three Mariners, made moreso by a little game me and Jag started playing called 'spot the A-lister'. This basically involved us shouting and pointing at an unsuspecting girl/woman in the bar that, claiming they

269

were somebody famous, and despite denials from them we would tell them how much we loved them in a famous tv programme or film or even a song they had sung (we'd start singing it...badly) and the highlight came when the daughter of one of our victims looked at her mother and shouted over the music,
"MAM...YOU DIDN'T TELL ME YOU WERE FAMOUS...HOW HAVE YOU KEPT THAT A SECRET ALL THESE YEARS?"
Priceless, and just a bit of harmless fun, taken in great spirits by our victims.

Meanwhile, in the toilet, the piss was getting deeper and nearer to the door. During one visit, Jag inadvertently pissed on the feet of a guy wearing flip-flops, who had obviously been drinking all day judging by the way he was leaning against the wall via his head, in an attempt to keep his balance. He was shivering and his eyes were shut, but when the warm piss from Jag hit his feet he giggled quietly to himself and smiled...

It was getting late and after drinking pints for most of the day Jag and I fancied a change and thought we'd have a couple of the red and blue shots we could see behind the bar, one was called *sex on the beach* and the other was *blow job*. Jag was first up and soon came back with a drink each, but he told me the barmaid wouldn't serve him until he'd asked for them by their name. Within a few minutes I was stood in front of the same barmaid and told her,
"Could I have one of those please" and pointed in the direction of the shots.
"Sorry, what did you say...it's noisy in yuh"
I pointed again and said slightly louder, "One each of those please"
Pretending not to hear me she said "Pardon"
"One of those red drinks and one blue please"
"Sorry not getting that...what do you want?" and she smiled. I accepted defeat and said,
"Can I have *sex on the beach* and a *blow job*...PLEASE"
"Of course...I'll get them straight away for you" and flashed me a knowing, sarcastic smile as she passed me the drinks. I returned to Jag and said,

"You were right buddy about having to ask for the shots by name" and we both looked at the barmaid who winked and gave us both another smile…we chinked our glasses, shouted cheers, drank our shots and burst out laughing.

The piss wasn't just in the toilet now, it was starting to creep under the door, but in a beautiful and perverse way it was quite romantic the way the disco lights glistened in the reflection of the puddle of piss now developing on the dance floor…

It was fast approaching midnight and Jag still hadn't worked out who had ordered the flowers that were awaiting him and Martyn in their hotel room earlier…but suddenly and without warning, he looked at me and pointed, shouting,
"IT WAS YOU…IT WAS FUCKING YOU…"
I nodded and our heads rocked back in unison and we were crying laughing for a good few minutes as Jag kept repeating, "it was you…it was you…"

Before we left we took one look at the piss puddle…or should I say pond that had now made its way a couple of yards onto the dance floor…I might be wrong but I think there was a desperate need for both a plumber and a drains engineer to sort this out…it was way beyond the powers of a mop…

What a day we'd had and after a thirty minute bus trip and a pint back at the pub in Pendine I finally made it to bed. The following morning after a cooked breakfast I made my way to Tenby to pick up Jag and Martyn (and their flowers) from their hotel. On the return trip to Caerphilly Martyn fell asleep before we'd even got out of Tenby and every now and again, for the entire trip, me and Jag had giggling fits about the flowers…priceless and a great stag do.

"No doctor, I didn't do that…definitely not!!!"

Shortly after returning from a family holiday to Thailand in 2013 I discovered, what could have been, a potentially dangerous medical situation!! Something was wrong and I knew that I couldn't ignore the symptoms and decided I had to ring the NHS helpline for guidance…this was the start of a serious, but mildly funny, series of events that led to some intimate (and embarrassing) moments...depending on how you looked at it!!!

I stared at the blood and blood clots in the toilet bowl and at the blood on the toilet paper..."what was happening?". I stood there for a few minutes...stunned...trying to comprehend the images that faced me...I had never experienced this before and feared the worst. What else was I to think? I was over fifty, that vulnerable age when things start going wrong medically...I again looked in the toilet bowl, there was a lot of blood and I knew that wasn't natural.

"Think...think...think...what to do?" I thought, as I tried to process the information...I looked at my watch..."The doctor's are closed now" I said to myself out loud, "Right...it has to be the out of hours doctor". I took my mobile phone out of my pocket and searched for the number of my surgery and rang the number...I knew the surgery was shut and waited...and waited for the call to divert to the out of hours doctor. Within a few seconds I was talking to a woman who took all my details, apart from the symptoms...I told her, "I would rather discuss that with the doctor...it's a rather sensitive issue..." and even though I was on the phone I could feel myself blushing..."OK" she said and told me that she would get a doctor to call me back and then disconnected the call. I paced up and down the bathroom, occasionally stopping now and again to look at the 'bloody' mess staring back at me from the toilet bowl. It seemed like ages before the doctor called, but realistically it was probably only around ten minutes...when I heard the familiar tone of an incoming call I answered the phone immediately,

"Hello"

"Is that a Mr Huw Thomas"

"Yes"

"Hi Mr Thomas, I'm the emergency doctor...I...I understand you have a sensitive issue you'd wish to discuss"

"Yes"

"What seems to be the trouble"

"Well..." I was staring down into the toilet bowl, "it's a little bit...it's kind of...you know..."

"I don't know unless you tell me Mr Thomas"

"Well...it's...it's as if the world has fallen out of my backside...there's a lot of blood in the toilet bowl..."

"Has this ever happened before Mr Thomas"

272

"No...never...no way...definitely not"

"Have you been anywhere tropical recently...Africa...Caribbean..."

"Yes doctor...we came back from Thailand around three weeks ago"

"I'm sorry, but I have to ask you this...when you were in Thailand did you...". Before she had a chance to finish I thought "I know where you're going with this" and immediately interrupted her with,

"No...no...no...no...no...no...I have not been with a ladyboy...it was a family holiday" and laughed (nervously).

"Ok Mr Thomas...I have to ask to rule out any possibility of damage through..."

"I understand...but I'm straighter than straight...I don't mind visiting temples, museums and the great beaches in Thailand...but 'bum fun' is not my cup of tea"

"Ok Mr Thomas" and she laughed.

She asked a few more less probing (excuse the pun) and intimate questions, before recommending that I arrange an urgent appointment with my GP.

A couple of days later I was in the Abertridwr surgery, and after explaining the symptoms to Dr Kaushal, I was lying on my side on an examining table with my knees tucked in to my chest, waiting for him to do an investigation. I knew that this would be the first of a few intrusions into my anal passage over the next couple of weeks, and it wasn't something I was looking forward to as I wasn't, or never had been, a member of the U.G.C. (Uphill Gardening Club)...'each to their own' I always say, but it's just not for me. Following the intrusive examination Dr Kaushal didn't appear to be overly concerned, but did want me to go to Ystrad Hospital for a more thorough examination. However, this proved to be a total waste of time (as is every visit to our 'white elephant' of a hospital) as I was spoken to like a child by the hospital receptionist. Thankfully, my 'Sapper' training came to the fore as I replied with just the right amount of sarcasm,

"Oh, I am sorry...I thought the sign outside said that this was a hospital. My mistake...I'll tell you what I'll go to a real hospital tomorrow...the Heath in Cardiff is probably my best bet...thank you" and I turned to walk away but just giving me enough time to leave the receptionist speechless and looking as if she was chewing a wasp. The following day after a fairly long wait in a waiting room at the Heath (University of Wales Hospital, Cardiff), I was in a cubicle, again lying on my side with my knees tucked in to my chest, but this time the doctor was a very attractive female, with the figure of a model, and at a guess, she was only in her early/mid-twenties…awkward. She introduced herself as I explained what had happened, and then she said,

"Let's see if we can find out what's going on …" I could feel her gloved finger pushing gently into my sphincter before she continued saying, "if you could pull your knees a little bit further into your chest that would be great"

"Ok…" and thought to myself that "…there are men out there that would pay good money for this", as I sensed, like the space shuttle, she was ready for re-entry, and when she was about knuckle deep into my anus I looked over my shoulder, and looked her straight in the eye and said, "It's a shame we've had to meet like this" and smiled.

She laughed "Yes it is Mr Thomas"

I smiled again and said "Oh doctor…do please call me Huw…Mr Thomas sounds too formal for the position we currently find ourselves in…"

She laughed again and we both knew the ice was broken and that, given the circumstances, we immediately became much more relaxed in each other's company. When she had finished and I had adopted a more conventional sitting position she explained that she couldn't feel anything untoward in my back passage, but…there's always a but…she wanted me to have an endoscopy to rule everything out. Despite knowing where her finger had been I thanked her, shook her by the hand and re-joined my daughter, 'R', in the waiting room.

A couple of weeks later I was entering a procedural room at Ystrad Mynach hospital, with my arse hanging out of one of those sexy hospital gowns…a room with four middle aged women who all laughed when I stood in the doorway and said, "It's not the first time I've been naked in a room full of women…come on then girls, where do you want me?"

The one holding some sort of cable, that I presumed was the camera (thankfully the camera wasn't a Nikon that you normally associate with Japanese tourists, this was a camera on a flexible cable probably around 3-5mm in diameter), said, "Can you jump up onto the bed and pull your knees into your chest"

"Again…Ok then love…as you've asked so nicely" I jumped up and adopted the position and no more than five minutes later it was all over and I was on my way to a waiting area where I had a coffee and biscuits whilst I waited for the results.

Thankfully, my results were clear, and everything was ok…being a man in my early fifties I know that the 'finger up the bum' will become a more common procedure I have to endure as I get older and have my prostrate examined. But for now all is good…and despite the intimate moment I shared with that doctor at the Heath, I did feel a little bit used and cheap, as I never did see her again.

Facebook, 24 Field Squadron Reunion and AvN games (2015 & 2016)

There have been many negative statements about 'Facebook' such as it has led to an increase in bullying and extra-marital affairs as more and more people have become re-connected across space and time, and also the seemingly meaningless photos people post of a cup of coffee that they may be drinking highlighting they are in a well-known coffee shop chain! However, it has provided me with the opportunity to re-connect with old school and army friends I never thought I would see again. Friends that played significant roles in my life at some point or another, and without 'Facebook' it's unlikely I would ever have seen or heard from them again! Thankfully, due to 'Facebook' I attended a 24 Field Squadron reunion in March 2014 and it was an amazing experience to see so many old faces from the past and catch-up with how everyone is doing today! Additionally, it was great to see the Medway Towns again and how they had changed…and not changed in some respects! One of the notable changes was the sad fact that Chattenden Barracks is no longer there, despite the land still being owned by the MOD (Ministry of Defence) the camp has been demolished, and the only item left standing from where 24 Squadron was once sited was a lone lamp-post that stood at the foot of the steps that once led to up to the accommodation block! It was a sobering thought that life had moved on from those halcyon days in the early eighties when we hardly had a care in the world!

*Another success of 'Facebook' has to be its ability to enable
events to be well-attended and this plays a huge part in the
huge attendances at the Army v Navy rugby matches at
Twickenham in recent times...two of which I have been lucky
to have attended in 2015 and 2016 and again caught up with
so many old colleagues and fellow rugby playing team mates!
Lastly, 'Facebook' has also allowed me to stay in touch with
family members despite the distances between us and share in
the Birthdays, weddings, anniversaries etc!! Thank you
'Facebook'.*

24 Squadron Reunion – March 2015

I got out of the car and looked at the devastating sight in front
of me, I could hardly believe my eyes...it was gone...all gone.
All that remained of Chattenden Barracks was the footprint of
where the buildings once stood, and the solitary lamp post that
was next to 24 Field Squadron RE accommodation block. It
was extremely sad to see a place that held so many great
memories...demolished, overgrown and surrounded by a high
fence that included the occasional sign warning potential
intruders to 'Keep Out – Property of M.O.D.' I turned and
stared at the overgrown area of 24's former car park...now
barely unrecognisable. I closed my eyes for a moment in a
faint hope that when I re-opened them that Chattenden
Barracks would be right there in front of me, in all its glory,
but when I opened my eyes again the scene in front of me
hadn't changed...the desolation was a sober reminder that
over twenty eight years had passed since I left Chattenden in
1986. I got back in the car and headed back up Kitchener Road
toward Chattenden village, turned left and headed down
Chattenden toward the area where the married quarters
were...halfway down Chattenden Lane I could see that the
married quarters had also gone, replaced by new private
houses. I stopped the car adjacent to where the pristine sports
pitches of Chattenden Barracks were once located...I again
got out of the car and stared despondently through the fence to
where the football and rugby pitches once stood. It was a
heartbreaking sight and with a heavy heart I got back in the
car. There was one more place I wanted to see...The Old
George, the pub where I'd spent many a great night playing
pool and getting pissed with Norman Ryan and Jim 'Panic
Drinker' Brown and many others. I drove around to where the

Old George was located, the misery was now complete…the Old George was no longer a pub, but a private house. I stood there for a moment and it was as if someone had ripped out my heart, dropped it on the floor and stamped all over it. I got back in the car and headed back towards Strood and was soon driving over Rochester Bridge and familiar sites started to flash past the windows; Rochester Cathedral and Castle, The Pentagon shopping centre, Kitchener Barracks, the road that once lead down to the naval dockyard, Brompton Barracks and the United Services Chatham rugby ground. By the time I'd pulled up into the car park of the King Charles hotel I was feeling a lot better and looking forward to having a few beers in The Cannon later that evening…hopefully with a few old friends!

A couple of hours later after a shower and change of clothes I was walking past Brompton Barracks, which immediately reminded me of those numerous nights spent in the 'smartie party' (Wednesday night disco) in the N.A.A.F.I. there…crazy nights of alcohol fueled nonsense and one night stands of mutual understanding. I smiled to myself and walked on and a few minutes later I turned onto Brompton High Street, pausing slightly and thinking "Christ, this has hardly changed a bit". As I walked on I stopped again when I reached the Two Sawyers…a place packed with many memories that mainly included more drunken revelry, the roughest of the rough Chatham women, sticky carpet, the smell of stale beer, fags and sweat, watching Michael Stupple destroy some idiot who was trying to pick on him…big mistake as it was normally all over with just one punch if the idiot didn't take the hint from a patient Mick, and of Rab Keil who would always start a fight when he was too drunk to defend himself…Many a time I had to pick Rab off the floor after he lost yet another altercation…yes, great memories and I laughed as I glanced through the window. Despite it being a Friday night, it looked as if things had changed…there were just four or five lads in there playing pool. No sign of the many girls that used to be in there back in the day, however, the outside of the building hadn't changed since those days in the eighties where we'd be almost every weekend. I walked on and passed the café where we (Corps rugby players) would have a breakfast after training and prior to games on a Wednesday…couldn't believe it was still there after all these years. I continued my trip down

277

memory lane and turned the corner onto Garden Street…I
could see the familiar white building of 'The Cannon' and
thought "God, it was like stepping back in time…" as I got
closer, I again stopped "…it must be thirty years or more since
I had a drink in here" and remembered the time I blew up a
condom on my head to an audience of Gurkhas or the time I
recognised the barmaid as a girl who had bared all in 'Escort'
and confirmed by Greg who'd asked her if it was true. I
crossed the road, paused at the door and thought of those
people I would see again, people who back in the eighties
were fit young men, athletes, men with dreams who had their
whole lives in front of them, I knew the reality would be
different…a nervous excitement surged through my body, as I
took a deep breath and pushed the door open and walked into
the bar…heads turned and I immediately recognised Colin
Page, Brummie Westwood, Charlie Rainey and David Thorpe.
Colin was the first to say anything and hearing, "Taff, you
wanker" made me realise…I was home. I laughed and there
were manly hugs all round before I got to the bar to order a
beer. It was fantastic being amongst old friends again, and yes,
the young virile athletes had been replaced by balding or
greying, overweight men in their fifties with stories of life's
hardships written in the lines on their faces…but all I could
see were those faces from those halcyon days of the early
eighties. I put my beer on the bar and told Colin that I would
just pop my head into the lounge and say hello to everyone.
The first person I saw was Skin Carr who shouted,
"TAFF MY OLD MUCKER" and gave me a big bear hug.
There was Gerry Hoolachan (a fellow member of the 24 rugby
team), Mark Parker, Paul 'Millie' Milner and many others. As
I walked back into the bar I bumped into my good old mate
Mark 'Iki' Bolton, a lad I'd been in many a scrape with, who's
opening line was,
"God Taff, you are still ugly"
I laughed and replied with "Cheeky fucker, where's your hair
gone…good to see you again Buddy…" I leant in and
continued with "…remember at Plon in Germany when we
were winding up young Jim Stead by both pretending to be
gay". Iki looked my straight in the eye…deadpan, and with
serious overtones replied with, "pretended". We both laughed,
hugged, it was so good to see him after over thirty years…we
certainly had a few shared memories from back in the day. It
was a great night catching up…it was as if we'd all last seen

278

each other the day before…the years just dissolved into nothing and I thought "there's still the reunion party tomorrow night", I was so looking forward to meeting more old friends.

Most of us met again in the function room the following morning to help Skin give it the 'Sapper' touch before I took Ada and Amy out to Canterbury for the day. We had a wonderful time in Canterbury wandering around the shops in the city centre and Ada experienced her first visit to one of Britain's most famous cathedrals. She was suitably impressed with the age and amazing architecture and beautiful stain-glassed windows, each telling their own story…a truly magnificent cathedral steeped in a twisted and menacing history. After Canterbury it was back to the King Charles hotel to get ready for the official 24 Squadron Re-union.

After a shower, shave and the obligatory change of clothes I headed for the hotel bar…as I turned the last corner that faced the bar, stood there with Gerry Hoolachan was another familiar face, Jake Maiden (another fellow 24 squadron rugby player) a 'partner in many a crime' and I remembered us both being posted from 24 (12 months apart) to HQ Military Works Force in the late eighties and I had the honour of being his Best Man when he got married…I knew the affection was still there when he greeted me with,
"Thomas, you Welsh knob, what are you drinking?"
"I'll have a beer please…good to see you again Jake"
After twenty minutes or so we made our way through to the function room…and more surprises. The first surprise was seeing Iain George…Iain was still serving and was now a Lieutenant Colonel, but I remembered him as my 'protector', on and off the rugby pitch. He was a no-nonsense lance corporal when I first met him in 1981 and captain of the 24 Squadron rugby team…someone not to be messed with and someone who had looked out for me and changed my life for the better, for which I was eternally grateful…and it was great to see him again. We talked about rugby and he told me the sad news that Tiny Bott had passed away, we laughed about games we'd played in, things that happened on nights out and on away days (especially Northern Ireland and Guernsey) and even the time we trained cadets on Salisbury Plain…where Iain hilariously rigged up a thunderflash underneath a dummy mine which went off with the customery B-A-N-G!! when one

of the cadets lifted it up, sending him flying backwards with a cockney "FUCK ME...I FINK I'VE SHIT MYSELF"...me and Iain stood there laughing over thirty years later at that shared memory. Iain, Gerry, Jake and me all shared great memories of our rugby days in 24, but Jake excused himself around nine o'clock as he wasn't feeling particularly good. Despite meeting Barry Milton, Laura Richards (Garth Hamley's ex-wife), Jamie James, another old member of 24's rugby team, 'Cinders' Cindery, I spent most of the remainder of the evening talking to Gerry Hoolachan, and he provided me with one of the highlights of the weekend. Gerry began to tell me how he was woken up in the small hours, following the drunken evening in The Cannon, by loud voices coming from the room next door...judging by what was being said, or should I say shouted, it was obvious that the couple were another ex-member of 24 Field Squadron and his wife. Gerry was struggling to tell the story as every time he started to say what happened he broke out into a fit of giggles...eventually he managed to compose himself long enough to tell me what the wife of the mystery couple shouted which was,
"FOR FUCKS SAKE...YOU'VE SHIT THE BED...AGAIN!"
Gerry and I both burst out into raucous laughter, tears streaming down our faces as both repeated the word "AGAIN!". Our unknown solider had shit the bed before and was wife was still with him...this left us both in no doubt that we were at an army reunion, where an old soldier who was now in his fifties fell foul of thinking he could still hold his drink like he did in his twenties...how wrong was he. The evening ended with Colin Page giving his excellent and extremely hilarious rendition of 'Aloiette', a definite crowd pleaser and a sort of sentimental 'blast from the past'.

The following morning it was breakfast and farewells, but before Ada, Amy and I headed back to Wales we paid a visit to the excellent Royal Engineers Museum, adjacent to the King Charles Hotel. I walked around the museum and reflected not only on a fantastic weekend, but on my army career and some of the characters I'd met...good and bad. Memories, I knew, have stayed with me and it wasn't hard to realise that the weekend had been made possible by 'Facebook'...I had spent a weekend in great company with old army friends that I thought I'd never meet again, proving that used responsibly, Facebook was a wonderful way of reconnecting with people.

Army v Navy 2016

I had collected Kev Belcher from his apartment in Cardiff Bay and we were now motoring down the M4 toward London to watch the annual Army v Navy rugby match at Twickenham…my first since 1982. We had a clear run and a couple of hours later we were pulling up outside the Holiday Inn on Bath Road, opposite Heathrow Airport. Kev made a phone call and within a few minutes we were sat with Robbo and Max enjoying our first pint…it was 8.45a.m. and I thought this is going to be a long day and I need to pace myself. After a solitary pint we had been joined by Brian Parker and Geordie, and we were soon sitting on a bus heading for Hounslow. On arrival at Hounslow we thankfully headed for a busy café where we all enjoyed a full English breakfast and tea or coffee…depending on preference…at least it was a welcome break from beer (the days of drinking from 8.45a.m. in the morning were long gone, and without this sensible lull in proceedings I thought "at least I'll get to see the game…and hopefully remember it"). It was approaching 11a.m. when we all climbed on another bus and headed for the sports pitches of Kneller Hall where the Army v Navy Vets and Ladies games were being played and where…apparently, there were beer tents. I was being sensible…I wanted to enjoy the occasion, I didn't want it to be a blur, a drunken haze of vomiting and falling over…again and again and again. Max took our orders and headed to the bar, and we stood in the throng of people that had gathered there and I was enjoying the moment, taking it all in…you could see the mix of various Army, Navy, Corps, Regimental rugby shirts, people in fancy dress all around the field and there was clear evidence of people meeting people they possibly hadn't seen for many years, it was truly a wonderful sight and a great advert for, not only Services rugby, but for rugby in general – thousands of people united by common bond of serving Her Majesty the queen and by rugby. Shortly, after Max had returned with our drinks I saw someone I recognised through the crowd…I excused myself and walked toward an old friend who had been in the same troop when we both joined the army back in 1979. When

I was about ten yards away he recognised me and shouted in his still strong South Yorkshire accent,

"TAFF, YOU BALD FUCKER!"

"NOBBY, HOW YOU DOING YOU FAT TWAT" When we got close enough we embraced, and then I bent down to check he was wearing socks. Satisfied he was, I stood up, smiled and said,

"Thank fuck for that…I'm still traumatized by that weekend in Guernsey on the Corps rugby trip when we shared a room and you had no socks…we got issued our rugby kit on the first day and you wore your rugby socks all weekend…including two matches…you fucking grot"

We both laughed at the shared memory of a weekend thirty years before, which was obviously still as clear as if had happened yesterday. We posed for a couple of 'selfies' before I headed back to Kev and the boys…it was great to see Keith 'Nobby' Clark, a fellow member of 4 troop, 66 Squadron, J.L.R.R.E. and Corps team-mate. I stood there for a second wondering if I would be lucky to see any more old friends before the day was over.

A little while later, we were taking the short walk to Twickenham and to the 'Sapper Bar' beneath the South Stand (an area that ran the entire width of the stadium and could only be accessed by former Sappers or friends that possessed a special wristband). After a couple of more drinks we made our way to our seats, but as I was about to sit down I heard someone shout "TAFF", I turned around and I could see Sandy Sanderson waving at me. I left my seat and went up to have a chat with Sandy who I hadn't seen since about 1982 when we played for the Army U'19s together…I was beginning to understand why this fixture was so popular with old soldiers and sailors…it was being used as a meeting of old friends, and it was good to see Sandy again. We had a quick chat and I was just about to return to my seat when I saw Geordie Hutchison…the same Geordie Hutchinson I played football with in that J.L.R.R.E. side that won the Army Junior Cup in 1981, which incidentally was the last time I saw him…again, we had a quick chat and I returned to my seat. I thought to myself "this is brilliant…I'm so glad I came". Another bonus for me was that I wasn't feeling the slightest bit drunk and as they had shut the bar I enjoyed another respite from alcohol which, in turn, meant I was enjoying every moment of this wonderful occasion and what's more…I was also going to remember it.

The stadium was basked in sunshine and full to capacity, the teams came out, lined up and the National Anthem was sung…and I swear I had never heard 'God Save the Queen' sung so proud and loud, it was electrifying. The first half came and went and during halftime, on my way to the toilet, I bumped into Richard 'Magic' Wand, who had put on a bit…no, a lot of weight since I'd last seen him, but then again, hadn't we all, but he was still as mad as a box of frogs. Then on my way back from the toilet I bumped into a drunk Iki Bolton and his good woman, Claire, and true to form Iki insisted on kissing me…but with no tongues thankfully. The second half started and before you knew it, the final whistle was being blown…Army 29 Navy 29, but the result was secondary, it was more beer and meeting old friends that was the real reason everyone was at Twickenham…the rugby came a poor second to that feeling of seeing someone you hadn't seen for over thirty years, and I would experience that feeling a few more times before the day was out.

We were back in the Sapper Bar and it wasn't long before I saw and was talking with Nellie Nelson, Ben Calvert, Tony Wishart and Nigel Furness…all former Corps rugby players that I'd played with during my time in the army. After about half hour I told Kev and Robbo that I was going to have a wander around the Sapper Bar and see if I could find anyone else I knew. It wasn't long before I bumped into a few old members of 24 Field Squadron, Gerry Hoolachan, Jeremy Batchelor (another former rugby team-mate), Iki Bolton (again) and Nobby Clark…there were a number of selfies before Iki saw a guy dressed as a nun and to check that it was a guy he carried out the Crocodile Dundee test…before the guy (nun) knew what was happening Iki was holding his nuts, laughing and said "Just checking", thankfully the guy laughed…well he didn't have much choice as either side of Iki was Batch and Nobby…both built like brick shithouses. I said my farewells and carried on walking through the Sapper Bar, it was then I saw another old friend, Robert Knock, walking in the opposite direction…another old member of 4 troop, 66 Squadron, J.L.R.R.E., and we'd also served together in 24 Field Squadron. Ironically, it was Robert's dad that I'd given my Army U'19 rugby shirt so they could hang it up in Castle Cary Rugby Club. Robert hadn't seen me, and I turned around and started walking alongside him, after a few yards he finally noticed me and his face was a picture of surprise as he recognised me and shouted,

"OH MY FUCKING GOD TAFF…HOW YOU DOING?" in his unmistakable Somerset accent that hadn't changed since I last spoken to him on the phone, when I popped in to see his parents in South Barrow, nr Sparkford in the late nineties. Another manly embrace and I asked him,

"How are you Buddy, and how are your mum and dad?"

His mood changed and I could see the pain etched in his face, "Dad passed away a couple of years ago and mum's not to good…alzheimers Taff…mad as a hatter" and he momentarily stared, in sadness, into an imaginary space,

"Sorry to hear that Buddy…I remember your parents…lovely people…hey, is my old Army rugby shirt still hanging up on the wall in Castle Cary Rugby Club?"

He paused, and with a serious look on his face told me "The rugby club burnt down Taff…" but before I had a chance to reply, he smiled at me, leant in and whispered in my ear, "…and your fucking shirt". His head went back as he broke out in raucous laughter…in typical squaddie fashion he had turned a catastrophe into a fucking joke…priceless. He then said, "Come with me Taff" I followed him through a sea of people and the next thing I knew I was talking to Andy Smart and Simon Millerick, Simon and I used to play football together for 24 Filed Squadron. It was good to see them all again, but the reunion was brief as they were starting to close the bars and people were beginning to leave. I found Kev, Robbo, Geordie and Brian and ten minutes later we were standing at a bus stop waiting for a bus to Hounslow.

We eventually made it back to Hounslow and the general consensus was…"let's get something to eat". We settled for a large Indian restaurant which must have been popular as it was full…one thing told us that this must be a good place as the majority of the people in there were Indian…a telltale sign that the food must be good. We weren't let down…it was probably the best Indian food I'd eaten. It was approaching ten thirty by the time we got back to the hotel and it had been a long but enjoyable day. I'd managed to enjoy it, and the breaks from alcohol during the day certainly helped.

Mick and Karen's 30th Wedding Anniversary

The main part of the journey was behind us…we pulled into the car park of a guest house and the static chalet type home where my old friend Andy 'Scouse' Murray lived. I turned off the engine and got out of the car, telling Ada and Amy to stay there as I wouldn't be long…Andy must have heard the car, as he was standing in the doorway, smartly dressed in grey trousers, highly polished black shoes, white shirt, blazer and RE Corps tie, but sadly leaning on his walking stick for support. Andy, shortly after leaving the army, became a taxi driver and he had been involved in a serious accident, and during his recovery he had suffered a debilitating stroke whch left him paralysed down the one side. Made even sadder by the fact that he had once been so fit, serving in 9 Parachute Squadron RE during the Falklands Conflict and was certainly the fastest rugby player I'd ever played with. He smiled at me, and despite his condition it was great to see him again…I smiled back, we embraced and I said,
"Andy Murray…it's so good to see you again old friend…is there anything you need a hand with…a bag or suitcase?
"Yes mate…there on the table…all packed and ready to go"
I grabbed his case, stepped back outside and waited for Andy to lock the door.

We were soon eating up the ten to fifteen miles to our accommodation for the evening, a holiday park about 2 to 3 miles away from where Mick and Karen's Anniversary party was being held in Padstow. The holiday park was pretty deserted…well it was November and the holiday season had long ended…but the chalet that had kindly been organized by Mick's sister, Lenora, was perfect…two bedrooms, bathroom and an open plan kitchen/sitting-room. After Ada, Amy and I had all had quick showers and were dressed in our party clothes, we (including Andy) headed for the social club in Padstow. Ten minutes later we were parked up outside the social club and made our way into the function room. Mick saw us first, smiled and walked over, followed by Karen, and who should be in tow, none other than Mark 'Garth' Hamley (fellow, J.L.R.E.E., 24 and Corps rugby team-mate) and my old room-mate from 24 Field Squadron and driver of the minibus for the 24 rugby team and for the trip to Padstow in 1985 for Mick and Karen's wedding, Johnny Witchell. There were hugs all round...it was so good to be among old friends again, especially good friends like Mick, Karen, Andy, Garth and Johnny. I saw Lenora and went over to say hello...a little bit awkward given the history but at the least the ice was broken and then I headed back to Mick, Garth, Andy and Johnny. Karen got us all together and took photos of the four of us, and then Mick pointed to a photo album on the bar and said, "The wedding album is there if you want to take a look". It was then I realised that I'd left my glasses in the car. "Just going to get my glasses from the car...old age is a terrible thing" and laughed. I walked to the car, retrieved my glasses and headed back toward the building. To the left of the entrance was the smoking area and Lenora and another woman were both puffing on fags,

"Ere Taff, do ee remember this one" said Lenora pointing to the other woman. I looked at this woman in puzzlement and said "Nah, sorry". It was then the other woman spoke and what she said floored me...the penny dropped big time as I heard her say,

"He probably don't remember me cos I got my clothes on this time" It was Karen, Mick and Lenora's cousin...the same cousin I'd slept with at Mick and Karen's wedding thirty years before. This was the first time I'd seen her since the wedding night...how embarrassing. But that wouldn't be the end of it!

Midway through the evening I strolled outside and in the smoking area was Johnny, Lenora, Karen (Mick's wife) and Mick and Lenora's auntie, I walked over and we were all chatting and there were selfies and such like. Ten minutes later...here comes trouble...it was Karen (Mick and Lenora's cousin...from the wedding...ahem) and her opening line to her mother (Mick and Lenora's auntie) was, pointing at me, "I shagged him at Mick and Karen's wedding". Excellent, great timing and the auntie's face was a picture...her jaw dropped and she was speechless for a few seconds before she started having a pop at Karen...then as quick as she appeared and threw the cat amongst the pigeons, she disappeared back into the building. I thought it was best not to say anything to the auntie and just hope it would be forgotten as the conversation moved on to something else. Oh, but there was more, back inside the function room and around thirty minutes later I was talking to Mick and Karen's daughter, Gemma. I had just finished thanking Gemma for organizing the taxi back

286

to the holiday park when, as if by magic, Karen appeared and
without any thought for anyone looked at Gemma and
drunkenly shouted,
"I SHAGGED HIM AT YOUR PARENTS WEDDING, I
DID!" and she turned and staggered across the dance floor
leaving me and Gemma speechless, I eventually composed
myself and apologised for Karen's latest outburst, but also
embarrassingly confirming that she was in fact correct. The
remainder of the evening was really enjoyable, even the
moment when Johnny and I joined Mick and Karen, who were
the sole dancers on the dance-floor reliving their 'first' dance
experience from their wedding day thirty years before…Karen
laughing hysterically as the four of us became joined as one in
a sort of non-sexual group hug. The night was drawing to a
close and it was great seeing Amy making friends and playing
with Mick and Karen's grand-daughters, but there was still
time for one more surprise. I was again outside talking with
Lenora, Garth, Johnny and Karen (Mick's wife) when the
other Karen again appeared, thankfully there was no comment
this time as she pulled out a cigarette, put in her mouth and
after several attempts managed to light it…not a word, she just
stood there rocking gently back and forth and occasionally
shut one eye in an attempt to focus on what was around her.
She finished her cigarette and started to make her way back to
the function room, as she entered the building she dropped her
keys, she paused to get her balance and thinking of the
embarrassing "do you know who this is?" earlier in the
evening, and her outbursts thoughout the evening telling
everyone she shagged me at the wedding, I knew this was an
opportunity to good to miss…she bent down to pick up her
keys, her jacket rode-up and her arse (in jeans of course) was
on full display for everyone to see. It was then I shouted in
through the door, "OH KAREN…I RECOGNISE YOU
NOW" and laughed loudly…Karen picked up her keys and
without turning round threw up two fingers. What made it
funnier was that it was witnessed by Johnny, Garth, Lenora
and Karen…who all burst out laughing in a collective
understanding as Karen disappeared into the function room.
We were soon joined by Mick's son Herbie and Lenora's
daughter Lauren, whose opening line to me was, "My mother
told me you broke her heart". Awkward…but I responded with
a genuine honesty when I said "Yes…I was an arsehole back
then Lauren…think yourself lucky…if me and your mum had

stayed together you would have ended up being short and ugly". I think given the circumstances, it was the right answer, as she laughed and I have to say having met Lauren and her sister, Sadie, they are a credit to Lenora and her husband, as are Gemma and Herbie a credit to Mick and Karen. The night came to an end and it had been a fantastic evening, made better by the fact it was spent with great people such as Mick, Karen (Mick's wife), Lenora, Johnny Witchell, Garth Hamley and Andy 'Scouse' Murray…even Karen's (Mick's cousin) outbursts were as memorable as the time I "shagged" her on the wedding evening thirty years before.

The following morning Andy and I got a taxi from the holiday park to Padstow and collected the car, and after picking up Amy and Ada we dropped Andy back to his static bungalow, before returning to Padstow to give our thanks and say our farewells to a great couple, Mick and Karen (Mick's wife of course) and Johnny Witchell. As we headed back to Wales there were a few chuckles along the way as I thought of the events of the previous evening and considered myself blessed to have such wonderful friends.

4 Troop, 66 Squadron Re-union

On 19th October 2019 I travelled to Coventry for a re-union with some former members of the lads I joined the army with back on October 18th 1979…it was our fortieth anniversary of joining as spotty 16 year olds with 'jack the lad' attitudes, a bunch of individuals who were soon whipped into a group of fine young Sappers.

It was a fairly uneventful journey from Caerphilly, and the Premier Inn we were all staying at was easy to find. I parked the car, walked into the hotel and was immediately abused by Jock Martin who was sat with Antony Bromley, Pete Lander, Mick Gauntlett, Martin Doherty (who had come from Canada to meet us), Steve Daire and the unmistakable Sgt 'Al' Scholey. I quickly took my bags etc up to the room I was sharing with Jock Martin (the bastard had already taken the double bed and I was on the single in the corner). I returned to the others in the bar and it wasn't long before we were joined by Peter Jones and Billy Hunt, and Billy confirmed that Marc Wilson wouldn't be able to make it and that Tiny Strachan, due to illness, also wouldn't be able to make it. Another casualty was Nobby Clark, who had been dumped with the grandchildren that morning.

Our first port of call was a BT Training building and exchange, around the corner from the hotel, where Scottie Marshall was waiting for us with beers and snacks…I told Scottie I'd buy his dessert at the Indian later seeing as I'd ate his dessert back at Old Park Barracks back in 1980, resulting in him quite correctly giving me a clout. It was great catching up with everyone and reminiscing about our time at Dover and also recalling the times we enjoyed when we met-up in adult units throughout our respective careers. The evening was made complete with the arrival of Robert 'Knocker' Knock and Clive Hissey…we drank, laughed and there is nothing better than being surrounded by a bunch of former squaddies, especially ones you went through training with, as we faced things together, tough times emotionally and physically, that changed us from individuals into a tight unit…with exception of J/Spr 'C' who we all still thought was a cunt and not one of us regretted the regimental bath we gave him…especially Antony Bromley for obvious reasons. Before leaving we had in impromptu speech from Jock Martin that was spot on, quite rightly highlighting the role Sgts Al Scholey, Kerr and Osborne had in our transformation from loud mouthed youths with no direction to a troop of men that thrived on teamwork. We then had a group photo of us all with our balding or greying heads and pot bellies as a reminder of this momentus occasion. From the exchange we walked up the road to the Wetherspoons in Earlsden where the alcohol and stories continued…some of which were quite sad to listen to as personal issues were talked about, but purely reflected life and don't need to be written about in this book. They were private moments between old soldiers and old friends. The evening continued with a great Indian, photos in front of the house where The Specials met up and practiced and where two-tone was born, and finally, another pub before we headed back to the hotel and bed.

With exception of Scottie Marshall, we all met up for breakfast, watched Wales narrowly beat France, had another group photo and headed off to our respective parts of the UK.

It was a fantastic night catching up with the lads from 4 Troop and I look forward to our next re-union.

The 'Thai' crowd

Since meeting Ada I have become part of a larger 'Thai' community and we have made very good friends with people who we have something in common with! If anyone knows how to party then a Thai does...we have had some great nights, with great food, drink and music. We have watched rugby together, football, celebrated Birthdays, arrival of babies, and partied as we have said farewell to friends (who are off to live in Thailand) and much, much more! We are like a large family and the closeness reminds me of my time in the army!

This was the umpteenth time we'd been to a party at Mike and Nid's, but this one was the first proper party in their new house in Bedwas. After parking the car, I went into the house where a few people had already arrived...Nid pointed me to the 'party' room at the back of the house. I walked into the pool room where Mike, Richard and Perry were already drinking and playing pool, Mike smiled and said,
"You've still got a box of cider in the fridge from last week Buddy...better crack one open"
"OK Mike" and laughed. As I turned, I could see a familiar large cooler box behind Mike...a mixture of fear and expectation swept over me as I realised Perry had brought his 'box of pain'. In our circle of friends Perry is famous for his cocktails...this was going to be a long night!

The night started off at a nice leisurely pace (as it always did), slowly drinking my ciders, enjoying the music and playing a few games of pool. We were soon joined by Steve, Barry, Phil and their respective partners/wives, and also by Simon. We enjoyed the relative peace of the 'pool' room as the women were all talking and eating in the large kitchen/diner and we were only disturbed by the occasional appearance of the kids as they ran wildly around and under the pool table for a few minutes before disappearing to other parts of the house as their screams faded to silence. Occasionally, a couple of the women would appear, have a game of pool and disappear again to the comfort of the Thai food in the kitchen...if you don't know Thai people, then you would be amazed at their ability to continually eat, but it has to be said it is normally a healthy mix of vegetables, rice, fish and chicken (with the odd non-healthy option thrown-in). The conversation amongst us men was normally fairly high brow to begin with but normally descended into more base subjects such as rugby, army stories (Steve, like me, was an ex-soldier) and stories involving fighting or the opposite sex as the evening progressed and the alcohol flowed. An hour or so into the party I noticed Perry was hovering around the 'box of pain' and it wasn't long before the lid was off and the cocktails started to appear…shit, this was where the evening would start its descent into chaos! We were still playing pool at this point, but as the cocktails became more regular the pool cues were put away… and then the girls started to appear, the music was ramped up and the Thai songs were starting to appear as the karaoke started in earnest…the girls sure know how to party and there's nothing they love more than karaoke and dancing. As the cocktails became more regular some people were handling it better than others, eventually there were casualties, as Phil and Simon eventually disappeared…Phil to bed and Simon had gone home (after falling in the kitchen).

As it approached midnight, the party was still going strong, but thankfully the cocktails had finally stopped and people started to drift away in their ones and twos…but the girls had now returned to the kitchen to eat, and I found myself nipping in and out of the kitchen enjoying the spicy Thai sausages that Steve's partner, also called Nid, had made…really spicy, but so moreish. We had started playing pool again, and the music had returned to a more traditional mix of old classics such as AC/DC, Bee Gees, Rolling Stones, Supertramp and others…given that most of us were in our fifties. The kids were now sleeping and it wasn't long before there were only five us left in the pool room…Mike, Barry, Steve, Perry and me and we were all beginning to feel the effects of the cocktails and the copious amounts of alcohol we had drunk. Within an hour only two of us remained and Barry and I had one last game of pool before calling it a night…another successful party at the Frost Household.

We have had great nights in Bedwas, Bargoed, Caerphilly, Penclawdd, Brecon and even Cardiff and it doesn't matter whether it's a Birthday celebration, watching the six nations, the 2016 Euros, camping or even watching Thai live music the results are always the same…great company, too much alcohol, too much food, great music and a fantastic time had by all.

The Covid-19 Pandemic 2020

At the beginning of the year there were rumblings of a flu-like epidemic spreading through the streets of Wuhan in China. By late March the world was caught in the grip of a pandemic that hadn't been seen since the Spanish flu pandemic in 1918. Normal life changed as people were sent home to work or placed on furlough as only essential workplaces stayed open. Non-essential workplaces, shops (with exception of supermarkets), schools, colleges, universities, sport, bars, clubs, restaurants, takeaways etc were all closed or shutdown. There were reductions in public transport services and travel within country's borders became restricted as was travel to other countries, with borders closing and flights almost totally stopping globally…it has been a strange, sometimes scary period of something that all generations, with the exception of a handful of centarians, have never experienced before.

We sat in the office and joked about the eating of bats and that this COVID-19 nonsene would all be over in a couple of weeks. Everybody thought it was nothing more than a different type of flu to the scare-mongering that had happened when 'Bird Flu' hit the headlines back in 1997…how wrong we would be.
I was sent to work from on March 19th and it was the start of an adventure (if those are the right words) that came with a sense of 'I'll be fine…nothing will happen to me or my family'. As the first couple of weeks passed, there was a slow realization that we might be working from home for, perhaps, 2-3 months as the number of cases of those contracting COVID-19, and worst still, dying from it, steadily increased, as had happened and was still happening in other European countries, North and South America, Asia, Oceania and Africa. But the numbers of people I personally knew that had contracted the virus was only two…one person from work and my auntie June, who lived in a nursing home in Shropshire. Therefore, it was still a situation that seemed distant, far removed from my own day to day experiences. Those first

couple of months were spent being isolated from family and friends; standing at front doors once a week clapping for the NHS staff and the wonderful work they doing, sadly, sometimes making the ultimate sacrifice; working all day on the works computer in my new office - the house; going on a daily walk, as nature woke from its winter slumber and welcomed the spring and wearing a face mask as you queued at Morrisons or ASDA to do the weekly shop…but the novelty soon wore off. However, I believe, I am one of the lucky ones and have coped much better than others (probably, down to my experiences of serving in the Falkland Islands all those years ago with little or no home comforts and having no verbal contact with family and friends back in the UK, the only contact was via letters).

Summer came and went, as restrictions eased and then increased again. At the beginning of summer we were able to meet-up with family and friends again, mainly outdoors, but not forgetting the '2m apart' rule. Shaking hands and hugging also became a distant memory, but as a family, we all enjoyed one happy event, and the one highlight of the entire lockdown, with the surprise return of 'G' from Australia, following his travels in India and SE Asia. As we rolled into September, schools, colleges and universities began to open and we were briefly allowed to meet-up with friends and enjoy a few drinks, as bars and restaurants opened again, but again with social-distancing rules. I even returned to the office a couple of times to help with training staff returning from furlough. However, the new found euphoria didn't last, as we headed into October, cases again increased in the UK and we were plunged, first into a local lockdown, followed by a two week national (Wales) lockdown. We also realised that there would be no holiday to Thailand in December 2020. Therefore, we cancelled the flights and took-up the offer of accepting vouchers from Qatar Airways, valid for two years (fingers crossed we can return to Thailand within this timeframe).

It is now November and as COVID-19 infections increase, it has started to affect people we know, sometimes family members, friends or family members/friends of friends, work colleagues, neighbours or generally people locally…it now seems very real, closer to home and everyone's thoughts are about staying safe and what sort of Christmas we are going to have. It is now beginning to be accepted that it may be spring 2021 before we return to the office, but also a realization that things will probably never be the same as they once were. Society is struggling to adjust as increases in alcoholism, drug abuse, domestic violence and suicides are sadly being reported as people's mental health and well-being is affected by these unprecedented times. Thankfully, there are reports that a vaccine has been found and that in the next couple of months it will be rolled out to more vulnerable people in society…here's hoping.

Nobody knows if or when life will return to normal and we are all taking things one day and one week at a time. One thing is true no-one will forget this COVID-19 pandemic and how it has affected normal everyday life, taking away simple interactions we took for granted. Stay safe everyone, let's hope 2021 is a better year than 2020, where life has been generally put 'on hold'.

Chapter 6 – Sport (Part 1) – Boots, Balls and Bats

*I absolutely love sport and from a very young age I played
many different sports but mainly football and rugby. I was
very lucky as a child that I went to Trelales (Laleston)
Primary School nr Bridgend, a school that boasted a long
tradition of producing good rugby players…one former pupil
being the world famous Welsh rugby full-back from the
1970s…J.P.R.Williams. During my time at the school we
played football, rounders, swimming and were introduced to
competitive athletics…my speciality being the 'sack race'!
Throughout comprehensive I became involved in different
sports (whilst still playing football and rugby), I represented
Glamorgan in cross country and joined the local sports centre
in Bridgend and started playing badminton, table-tennis and
squash, and for a couple of years, travelled all over South
Wales as part of the Bridgend YMCA Athletics Team, mainly
running the 1500m. Also, when I started comprehensive school
my father and step-mother had moved to Norfolk and it was
during summer holidays here that I took up tennis!! My entire
childhood had been spent playing sport of some description
and as long as we had a ball of any shape or size we were
happy, days of playing football at Newbridge Fields in
Bridgend…26 a side and 3 hours each way with the final score
always something like 26 – 17 or 18 – 16!!! We also played
touch rugby in school break times or football with a tennis
ball, and I had a small snooker table (5ft x 2 ft 6) on which I
was taught to play snooker and billiards by my Grampa
Henson…yes, it was a great childhood of sport!!*

*I have briefly mentioned sport when I joined the army and that
I found out fairly early that if you played sport to Regimental,
Corps and even Army standard it was unlikely that you would
do much work…great news to a seventeen year old! During
my training as a Junior Leader, I returned to rugby
(accidentally), played football, cricket, and was a member of
the boxing team (I didn't actually fight) and I nearly became a
part of the Junior Leaders Gymnastic Display Team that
toured around the country…thankfully I managed to get out of
that due to the other sports I played. But it would be rugby and
football that I mainly played at Dover which led me to staying
an additional six months purely for sport…and became part of
the J.L.L.R.E. football and rugby teams that won the Army*

Junior Cups. However, despite playing football, cricket, tennis etc it was rugby that would dominate the remainder of my army career as I played in a very successful 24 Field Squadron rugby team and represented the Corps, Army U'19s & 21s and Combined Services U'19s & 21s and eventually joined Long Eaton R.F.C. when I was posted to HQ MWF in Nottingham. It was during this period that I damaged my cruciate ligaments and despite continuing to play rugby I had to retire from football…I was twenty five years old!

When I left the army I continued to play rugby at Long Eaton R.F.C. followed by two seasons at Ilkeston R.U.F.C. before returning to Wales where I enjoyed a brief spell with New Tredegar (linking up again with an old army friend…Ian (Taff) Pritchard) and a final season at Senghenydd R.F.C. In recent times I have played football, tennis, snooker and pool with my children…even playing in the same 5-a-side football team as 'K' and 'G' with Gareth ('R's partner) as we won two league cups at the Power League in Cardiff. Finally, over the past 4-5 years I have returned to Long Eaton R.F.C. and played a handful of Vets games for Long Eaton with old friends…and new! I don't know how many games of rugby I played, but it is probably in the region of 4-500 and as I was the main kicker in the majority of teams I played for, I believe my points tally was easily in excess of 1000points. Sport has given me some fantastic memories and along the way I made great friends…friends with whom I shared moments of triumph and also moments of devastation, but thankfully the former far outweighed the latter!!!

■■

Laleston – Invincibles 1973/74

In my last year in Laleston (Trelales) Primary School I was lucky enough to be a part of a very good squad of players. Under the excellent guidance of Mr Jones we managed to get to the final of the Bridgend & District Schools U'11s final following a tough semi-final replay against Pencoed, and up to this point we were undeafeated as a 15-a-side and 10-a-side team (after winning the Litchard 10-a-side competition). The rugby we played in the early-seventies wasn't the same as you see today…non-contact mini-rugby! We played the same rules as adult teams, with lineouts, scrums, rucks, mauls, tackling, conversions, drop-goals and penalties etc and the same scoring system…it was proper rugby! The team that stood between us and a perfect season was Llangewydd Primary School…we were determined to win that cup for the school and remain undefeated!!

I've returned in recent years to where it all began…the rugby pitch at Laleston Primary school, the scene of where we not only played rugby, but football, athletics and even rounders. It's strange standing on that field looking at a rugby pitch that now seems so small, but when we were eleven years old it seemed so large, and it's a place that provides so many great memories: The great games we played there, the try I scored against Bryncethin when I side-stepped my way past many of the opposition to score under the posts, the mole hills that covered the pitch, the cow pats that covered the pitch when cows broke through the bottom fence behind the rugby posts and our very own cheer leaders (Fiona McAllister, Alyson Copus, Susan Poole, Kathryn Biddle, Claire Williams, Jackie Oliver etc) who sang the songs "2-4-6-8 who do we appreciate…LALESTON!" and "2-4-6-and a quarter, who do we intend to slaughter, PENCOED" or whatever team we were playing against…fair play to the girls, they sang those songs regularly through every game we played at home.

At Laleston, in that season 1973/74, we were blessed with some great players in that team such as; Tim Harries (the Captain), Paul 'Tigger' Jenkins, Nigel Evans, Ross Bowen, Julian 'Geordie' Jones, Richard Griffiths, Kevin Freeland, David Lewis, Anthony Howells, Stephen 'Twisty' Richards, Alan & Paul Evans, Robert Groome, myself and many, many more. Back in those days I was a small right wing, and because I was small I had developed a 'sidestep' so I could avoid as much contact as possible…there would have only been one winner in a contact situation and it wouldn't have been me. Thankfully, that sidestep served me well that season and I scored quite a few tries. After a successful season, where we were currently undefeated in the 15-a-side and 10-a-side games we had played, we were on the verge of possibly becoming known as the 'invincibles' (which could be unique in Laleston Primary School history), if we won the final of the Illtyd Williams Cup against Llangewydd Primary School!

We'd been talking about the final all week, we were so excited that we were going to play the final at the Brewery Field…home to Bridgend R.F.C.…we were eleven and playing at Bridgend's ground…we had to pinch ourselves as it was difficult to believe it was real…this ground was 'Mecca' to us eleven year old rugby fanatics. Friday night it was early to bed, but sleep was difficult as the excitement was reaching levels I'd never experienced before. Eventually, I drifted off to sleep, and what seemed like only moments later I heard the faint sound of my mother's voice;

"Huw…Huw…it's time to get up…you've got a big day today!"

I opened my eyes and realised it was light outside and it was Saturday morning…the day of the final. I jumped out of bed in a panic asking what the time was, thinking it was late and I'd missed the game. My mother laughed and reassured me that it was still early and not to worry. I got ready and had breakfast and watched the clock slowly (and I mean slowly) edge towards the time when we would have to leave…in fact, time was passing by so slowly that I picked the clock up a couple of times, putting it to my ear to check it was still ticking…at the same time, also checking my mother's watch to make sure the times were the same. Eventually, it was time to leave and I was stood outside the car impatiently waiting for my mother and nana before they had even left the house…when I saw them step through the front door I shouted;

"Come on…hurry up mum…hurry up nan"

"Ok Huw…keep your hair on…we've got plenty of time"

I was so excited that I was finding it difficult to contain it, but the excitement wasn't just because of the fact we were playing on Bridgend's hallowed ground, I was excited that my mother and nan would see me play a rugby match for the first time…I didn't want to let them down.

Ten minutes later we were parked up in the car park at the Brewery Field and I shot out of the car shouting "SEE YOU LATER" as I ran to the little gate for the players, just to the left of the stand, as my mother shouted "GOOD LUCK HUW!"

I made my way to the changing rooms…the same changing rooms that were used by our idols, Welsh internationals and giants of the game. It felt good…we were eleven, but it felt that we had made the 'big time', it didn't get any better than this. Within fifteen minutes our team was now all in the changing room and starting to get ready, as Mr Jones (our rugby teacher) read the team out and handed us our shirts…No 14, right wing, I was over the moon and the butterflies in my stomach started to assemble and flutter their delicate wings. It was soon ten minutes before kick-off and we nervously sat there as Mr Jones gave us a final pep talk and Mr Baker, the headmaster, popped in to wish us luck. It was finally time…we stood up and started walking out in a single file of green and gold hoops. We ran out onto that huge Bridgend pitch to a crescendo of noise from the stands where our teachers, parents and half the school were sat…the butterflies had now subsided as I looked up into the sea of faces searching for my mother and nan, and when I finally saw them they were frantically waving as they were also trying to attract my attention, I waved and grinned like a Cheshire cat when I saw the pride etched on their faces!

The mists of time have clouded the finer details of the game, but I know we won 12-0…my abiding memories from that game were that the pitch was so big that when I got the ball on the wing there was still half the width of the pitch to run into, I also remember the grass being so long it was difficult for us eleven year olds to run, and most of all I remember the girls singing;
"2-4-6-8, who do we appreciate…LALESTON!!" again…and again…and again.
It was a great feeling climbing the steps in the main stand at the Brewery Field that day to receive the cup and our winners medals in front of a cheering crowd…I could see my mother and nan waving, tears of joy streaming down their faces, and I smiled and waved back and held up my medal to show them. Bridgend R.F.C. really looked after us that day, we had food and pop after the game and were allowed to stay in the ground as 'guests of honour' to meet the Bridgend players and watch them play that same afternoon…we felt like superstars.

The icing on the cake was that we had finished the season unbeaten and our achievements were honoured by the Community Council in Laleston who presented us with plaques at a civil reception in the village hall…I was and still am proud to have been part of the Laleston "Invincibles" of 1973/74.

Mill Utd – Double Winners 1974/75

Following the success with Laleston rugby team it would be
football that would take centre stage the following season, as I
and a few of my friends joined Mill Utd U'12s. They played on
a field at the bottom of Great Western Avenue in Pendre which
was on the other side of Bridgend to where I lived in Cefn
Glas. Again, it would be a successful season...but this time
with a round ball!!!

During my first year at comprehensive school I played football
for Mill Utd alongside Alan and Paul Evans, Julian Jones,
Richie Griffiths and others. I don't remember a great deal
about the season other than I played a different position to
where I had played for Aberkenfig U'12s the previous season,
a season that had been far from successful as we lost every
game and only scored one goal all season...in an 11-1 loss to
Brynna. And it wasn't a position where I would play for the
remainder of my footballing career...I played at left back (the
same position my father played). I have three significant
memories of that season; firstly, we won the league and cup
double in the Bridgend and District U'12s following a 1-0
away win at Garw 33 Boys Club which won the league, and a
6-0 win against Gilfach Goch in the cup final. I was beginning
to like this sport malarkey as I had now won five medals in
two seasons.

Secondly, I can remember during one game that we played at
Great Western Avenue where Geordie would score one of the
most bizarre goals I think I've ever seen on a football pitch.
Geordie, like me, played in defence and neither of us had
scored that season, but that all changed during this game when
Geordie, from within his own half, cleared the ball out of
defence...his intention to put as much leather on the ball and
send it skyward and to safety. But it didn't quite work out that
way and by putting his knee over the ball, hit it fast and hard
about six inches off the floor...it bamboozled everybody and
kept going...and going as unsighted players missed it and
eventually it seemed to be on target. He couldn't could he...he
could...it cleared the last defender and was still travelling at a
rate of knots, and the unsighted goalie was stranded, flat
footed in the middle of the goal as Geordie's clearance, come
shot, whizzed past him into the left hand side of the goal;

"GOAL"...it was a couple of seconds before the referee realised that Geordie had scored and when he blew the whistle to signify the goal, Geordie just stood there with his arms raised in the air in celebration, as we all ran over and jumped all over him...all scarcely believing what had just happened...amazing goal.

Thirdly, in the game against Garw 33 Boys Club, I was involved in a situation that would ultimately result in us winning the game. The pitch we played on was prone to flooding as on the other side of a fence of corrugated iron sheets was a stream that during the winter months tended to run all over the pitch...to counteract this phenomenon on 'normal' pitches sand is used in the worst affected areas such as the half-way line and the six-yard boxes in each goalmouth. However, this was the Welsh valleys...land of coal. There must have been a sand shortage in the Garw Valley in 1975 (I have tried googling Garw Valley sand shortage 1975 but nothing comes up!), in the absence of sand, they used the next best thing available...no, not sawdust...coal ash. Yes, you have read right...coal ash...but not any old coal ash...industrial coal ash which had large, jagged coke particles in it...as I found out to my cost halfway through the second half. In a very tight game we had managed to nick a goal, but midway through the second half their striker was through and was now one on one with our keeper, as I raced across to cover in behind. As their striker approached the goal our keeper had come out and their striker tried to place the ball under our keeper who got some contact on the ball, but despite the ball being slowed down it was still on target...me and the ball entered the six yard box at roughly the same time and I slid in...ooo...ouch...ah...ooo...ouch, and managed to clear the ball when it was about to cross the line. I managed to get a good contact on the ball and cleared it into touch on the far side, I stood up and looked down at my leg that was now a mixture of red and gray from the mixture of blood and coal ash and I looked like a burns victim...the things you do for the team when you play sport. The coach poured water on it to get rid of all the dirt and I just carried on playing. I can honestly say that the bath I had that night wasn't the most enjoyable...but at least we won the game.

301

It's bizarre the things we remember from life, trivial things but it's great to look back on them…yes, we were a great little team, but it was the one and only season we played together, but at least we won the double. As we approached our teenage years it would be girls that would become more important than sport for some…not for me though, even though I had the occasional girlfriend through school, I would be sport mad for many a more year yet!!!

Finals joy with J.L.R.R.E. (Junior Leaders Regiment Royal Engineers)

As seen in chapter 2, I was sixteen when I joined the army as a Junior Sapper. Initially, I didn't play rugby or football…I had given up rugby at thirteen in comprehensive and as a welsh boy I thought I had no chance of getting into the football team at Dover as the team would be full of much better English and Scottish boys. The first sport I played in the army was squash…it would be almost 6 months before I started playing football for the regiment, mainly off the back of having kickabouts with Jock Martin. Playing rugby again, however, was purely accidental…my troop (4 troop) were playing a game against 3 troop, both 66 Squadron, and after returning from a run I went to see how the game was getting on…with about 15 mins left of the first half and my troop losing, one of the boys said "Taff…you must know how to play rugby…go and get your boots" (this was 1980 and Wales had dominated British rugby during the 1970s so everyone thought welsh people could play rugby). Anyway, I got my boots and told the lads I used to play outside half…Billy (Simon) Hunt was playing scrum half so he threw a couple of practice passes out and we were set for the second half! I managed to score a try and a couple of conversions and eventually we won. As we walked off to the changing rooms I was stopped by an officer who turned out to be Captain Jim Wood (legend of Royal Engineers rugby) who said "Sunday…1.30pm at these changing rooms…you are playing rugby for the regiment Junior Sapper…"
"Thomas" I said in total shock and standing to attention.
"Excellent…see you Sunday Junior Sapper Thomas…1.30pm sharp…don't be late" he said in a soft Scottish accent.
"Yes Sir" I screamed.

That's how I started playing rugby again…and the rest they say is history!!!

After a close fought Army Junior Cup semi-final against the Junior Guards depot, which we won 1-0, we headed for a final against the much fancied Junior Leaders Royal Armoured Corps…they had seven players in the Army Youth team, whereas we had one, our left-back Steve Fenton. This was going to be a tough final, but at least it was going to be played in the Military Stadium in Aldershot. It was a typically grey winter's day in Aldershot on the day of the final, but thankfully it didn't rain. For those of you who don't know the Military Stadium in Aldershot it is a fine place to play both rugby and football. It is totally enclosed with a mixture of walls and fences. As you look at the stadium from the road, the building on the left hand side (behind the goal) is the clubhouse and changing rooms. As you come out of the changing rooms and look up the ground there is a concrete terrace that runs down the left hand side of the pitch and down the right hand side is the main stand and behind the goal at the top end is the garrison gymnasium. Around the football pitch is a high quality running track and the pitch itself was superbly maintained and as a result it was one of the best, if not the best surface I ever played on. It was an honour that day not just to play in that final and represent the Junior Leaders Regiment Royal Engineers, but also to play in front of the regiment…and my father and Shirley, who had made the trip that day from South Wales to Aldershot to watch me in my first army final.

The game kicked off and the first twenty minutes were difficult…The JLRAC (Junior Leaders Royal Armoured Corps) were dominating possession and stroking the ball around with ease. We were finding it difficult to get possession, and if we did, we struggled to string two passes together. Things were looking ominous and if we weren't careful this was going to be embarrassing, but the one plus during that first twenty minutes was that our back four of Steve Fenton, Charlie Bray, Mark Plant and Colin Morris were frustrating the JLRAC attack with their stout defending. They were certainly the much better side, but with an air of cockiness or arrogance that could backfire on them…that's exactly what happened. Half-way through the first half a

303

casual pass in their midfield resulted in us winning the ball, one pass and Hutch (Geordie Hutchinson) was away on the right. Ron Mavir and I raced into the box, and a perfect cross from Hutch found Ron who buried a bullet header past the JLRAC keeper…totally against the run of play we found ourselves 1-0 in front. Something happened after that goal…the JLRAC literally 'fell to pieces' and it was our turn to dominate possession, and just before half-time I managed to nick in front of a defender in the six yard box, and met an inch perfect cross from Ron for a simple tap in just inside the post…it was now 2-0. A few minutes later the whistle blew for half-time, and despite being a happy dressing room, WO2 Simpson knew it was a job only half done and managed to keep our feet firmly on the ground with his half-time talk. The second half started in the same way the first half had ended…with us dominating possession and the JLRAC were chasing shadows and already looking like a beaten team. Ten minutes later the coffin was now in place and it started to be nailed shut when I ran onto an 'over the top' ball from Charlie Bray, and as the keeper advanced I slid the ball under his despairing dive…it was now 3-0. I ran down the side of the pitch with my arm raised and fist clenched in celebration, past their fans who were still and silent, past our fans who were jumping up and cheering, and I ran to where my father and Shirley were sat…I stopped, threw my arms down by my side in a cocky 'look at me' stance as my team mates jumped all over me in celebration (my father still tells this story to my children today). If the game wasn't won then it certainly was about fifteen minutes later when Ron made it 4-0…the final nail was hammered into the JLRAC coffin. I had a chance to make it 5-0 late on and complete my hat-trick, but the JLRAC keeper flicked my goal bound header onto the bar…it didn't matter, the final whistle was blown and we were Army Youth Champions with a fine 4-0 win over the JLRAC…a team that, on paper, should have been convincing winners.

Around the same time of the latter stages of the football cup-run, I was also part of the regimental rugby team who were now starting their own assault on the Army Youth Cup. After the football final, those (Ron Mavir, Geordie Hutchinson, Adrian Tickle, Charlie Bray, Mark Plant and Colin Morris) that stayed on with me to play in that team left to go to Gibraltar Barracks to continue their combat engineer training.

I was now on my own and I didn't really do anything except play rugby…the regimental rugby team was 'marching-on' in the Army Youth Cup and we eventually made it to the final where we would play against AAC Harrogate (Army Apprentice College Harrogate, Royal Signals). The game was to be played on one of the pitches on Queens Avenue in Aldershot (opposite the Military Stadium) and my mother told me that her and my nan would travel up from South Wales to watch the game. On the day of the final, we travelled up from Dover in one of those glorious white army buses and I briefly met my mother and nan before we got changed. A little later as we ran out onto the pitch I knew this would be a game of two halves as a strong wind was blowing straight down the pitch, from left to right. I was also nervous about my new half-back partnership with Dave Nurse, as Dave was an outside-half like me and not a scrum-half, and we'd only had one training session together (as you read in Chapter 2, Harman our scrum-half had been attacked by 'squaddie bashers' on the night of my Birthday, a few days earlier, and was still recovering in hospital).

The game kicked off and despite playing with the wind we were struggling to break down the AAC Harrogate's organized defence. However, about 15 minutes in I did kick a penalty to put us 3-0 in front, but we were making heavy work of it and we knew that 3-0 would not be enough at half-time, knowing that we would be against the wind in the second half. Not even our secret weapon of the 'cannonball' move worked, a move where I would receive the ball standing still, dummy the pass to the open side and then fire a long pass to our fullback, Garth Hamley, bursting through on the blindside. Luckily though, about five minutes before half-time we had a scrum on their 22m line about six or seven metres in field from the touchline. Dave put the ball into the scrum and it was hooked back cleanly and then controlled by Tom Austin, our number eight…Dave waited and then threw a dummy out to me, picked the ball up and darted down the blindside. The AAC Harrogate's defence was slow to react, Dave had seized the initiative, chipped over their blindside winger and just as the defensive cover reached him he re-gathered the ball and was in at the corner…TRY. It was a brilliant try by Dave and totally justified our faith in picking him at scrum half. He picked the ball up and jogged back toward me, smiled and tossed the ball to me saying;

"Here you go Taff...nice easy conversion for you!"

"Cheers Dave, you tosser...you could have stepped inside and got nearer to the posts" I laughed as Dave trotted back to our own half and the others.

I made my usual mound for the ball to lift it three or four inches out of the longish grass, steadied myself, took my normal four steps back and then two to the left, bent down picked some grass and stood up, released the grass to judge the wind, made sure my breathing was right, ran forward, struck the ball and watched it sail high between the posts...I turned and jogged back to my team with us now leading 9-0. The whistle soon sounded for half-time and we were now two scores in front, and in a slightly better position to face the disadvantages posed by the wind in the second half.

The second half kicked off and we were immediately under pressure and could not get out of our own half due to a combination of the wind and the ferocious tackling by AAC Harrogate. Within the first ten minutes after relentless wave after wave of attacks our line was breached, and AAC Harrogate scored a try and kicked the conversion...the score was now 9-6. With half hour left to play we knew we'd have to dig deep if we were going to get anything out of the game...around midway through the half we managed to edge our way out of our half for the first time (and ultimately the only time in that second half) via the forwards keeping it tight and rolling off mauls. We inched deeper and deeper into their half until we were halfway between the 10m line and their 22m and about five or six metres from the touchline...PENALTY! The frustrated AAC Harrogate had collapsed the maul. Phil 'Taff' Humphrey, our captain, picked the ball up and I walked over and he asked;

"Do you think you can kick this one Taff?" I looked at the post and said;

"I reckon so Taff...we have to give it a go, it might be our only chance" Phil threw me the ball and wished me luck.

I went through the same procedure I had with the conversion in the first half, and eventually made the move towards the ball...made perfect contact with it and I knew I had given it one hell of a hoof...I stood and watched the ball sail toward the posts hoping the wind wouldn't hold it up, but thankfully it went high through the middle of the posts with plenty to spare. Half the regiment was on that touchline and they went beserk...shouts of "Well in Taff", "great kick", we were now 12-6 in front and again had a bit of breathing space. As I ran back to my team I started clapping them as that penalty was a real team effort...without the discipline and great close play of our forwards I would never have been put into a position where a successful kick was possible. That is the joy of playing a team sport, it's the combined effort of the team that wins games not an individual. With twenty minutes left to play we needed that team ethic more than anything as we knew AAC Harrogate would now throw everything they had at us...and that's exactly what they did. We tackled us a team (even me!) and we thwarted attack after attack until a couple of minutes from the end when they finally broke through and scored a try about about halfway between the posts and the touchline...the score was now 12-10 with the conversion to follow. In normal circumstances the conversion was fairly straightforward, but this was a cup final and a chance to take the game into extra time. We stood dejectedly, but completely still, behind the posts all believing we'd thrown it away and were now heading for extra time. Time stood still as the ACC Harrogate kicker, Amos, lined up the ball, stepped back, took a deep breath and ran up to ball...disaster, he completely sliced it and missed by about five metres which meant we were still winning. As I was walking to take the kick-off I heard the referee say there was only a minute left...we were almost there. I had to get this kick right to give our forwards a chance to win the ball. If I could get this right...I could use the wind, that had been our nemesis in the second half, to our advantage. I drop kicked the ball for our forwards to run on to and their job was made easier by the ball hanging in the wind allowing our Kev Hopson to pluck the ball out of the air with support from his fellow second row Andy Powney and the rest of the forwards, and they kept it tight and edged closer and closer to the touchline until the linesman put up his flag to signify the ball carrier was in touch. This brought a loud whistle from the referee that signified the end of the game...we won. We were hugging each other and those from the regiment that had made the trip up from Dover were cheering like crazy. I've played in a lot of games over the years, but that JLRRE (Junior Leaders Regiment Royal Engineers) rugby team that day epitomized everything there is about playing as a 'team', from one to fifteen it was an outstanding team effort, which was confirmed by our brilliant coaches, (Captain) Jim Wood and (WO1) Geordie Howe.

It was suggested that as I played in both the Army Youth football and rugby finals, and won, that the achievement could be unique, but nobody knows for sure. All I know is that I was blessed to play with some outstanding players in both those finals and the victories both came about as a result of us playing as a team in both games. Sadly, some of my team mates from those games I never saw again after leaving Dover, but others are still friends today. Great times.

Royal Engineers R.U.F.C., Army U'19s & 21s & Combined Services U'19s & 21s & other representative rugby

To play any sport at a higher level requires an element of skill and commitment. Additionally, an element of 'luck' is also needed…being in the right place at the right time, and in respect of team sports, playing in good teams with good players also helps! I consider myself to have had some talent as a rugby and football player, but I relied a lot on speed, a side-step (developed mainly to avoid contact with the big forwards or the 'glue-sniffing brigade' as us backs affectionately called them) and the ability to kick with either foot, and I was extremely lucky to have played in some excellent teams with many very talented players! I played in successful Royal Engineer Corps XVs team throughout my army career and also successful Army and Combined Services U'19s and U'21s rugby teams which led to trials for both Wales and England at U'19 level, however, I was not good enough for either, but still believe it an honour to have even been considered! Luck certainly played its part in turning out for Public School Wanderers once, playing for Cambridgeshire U'19s (right place at the right time!) and even playing in the England Students final trial with Rupert Moon, Tony Underwood and Steve Hackney…pure chance due to injuries they'd sustained over the weekend of the trial and them using our pitch at Long Eaton for the final trial…Jimmy Rogers and I had a fantastic letter from the England R.F.U.

308

I was seventeen when I played my first representative rugby match for the Army U'19s in a game against St Austell that should never have been played, there must have been a good four inches of water on the pitch that day. It ruined a game that finished 4-4, and a game in which our scrum-half Sandy Sanderson was convinced he would drown when he was face down in the water at the bottom of a ruck. Thankfully, the referee blew the whistle in time and a relieved Sandy got up coughing and spluttering to live another day. That was the start of a two year association with the Army U'19s that would end in us winning the inter-service championship in 1981/82 season. We had a tough fixture list playing games against the colt sides of teams such as St Austell, Plymouth Albion, London Welsh, London Scottish, London Irish, Harlequins, Bristol, Pontypool Utd, Abertillery, Boys Clubs of Wales, Leicester, Nuneaton, Orrell, Birkenhead Park and of course the Royal Navy and the Royal Air Force…all under the excellent leadership of our coach, Captain Gareth Davies and our Physio, Sgt Sid Goodall. I played with some brilliant players over those two seasons and a typical weekend of Army Colts rugby would see us travelling to the area we were playing on a Friday…meeting up in a military camp near to where our two fixtures would be that weekend. We'd normally have a couple of sociable beers on the Friday night, a training session on the Saturday morning, game Saturday afternoon, a couple of beers Saturday night (sometimes this turned into a full-on session depending on the location…as you will see later) game Sunday morning and then we'd travel back to our units. It was ideal for me as there were two of us (me and Phil 'Taff' Humphrey) who travelled from JLRRE, Dover and when I was posted to 24 Field Squadron RE, there were four of us (me, Ian 'Taff' Pritchard, Phil 'Taff' Humphrey and Andy Hill). To be selected for the Army Colts there was a 'trial' weekend and there would be sixty or so players from all over the Army, and in my experience Gareth Davies (the Head Coach) was always very fair in selecting the squads over the two years I played…the players were picked purely on their talent.

There are many stories that could be told from those two years between 1980 and 1982 such as Scouse Schears projectile vomiting in the bar at London Welsh R.F.C. after downing a jug of ale; the talented Ginge Johnson who could mimic any accent in the UK, had a repertoire of rugby and Welsh songs that no-one could match and a born joker, as Frankie Pocock bore witness when Ginge convinced him that Wales had treacle mines at Abergorki...near Abercwmfuck; Pritch's wild punch connecting with the London Irish prop just as the ruck dissipated giving the London Irish fans a birds eye view of the midemeanour; Tank Walker turning from the nicest man on the planet to an absolute animal purely by walking over the white line onto a rugby pitch; Sid Goodall's ability to know someone who ran a pub no matter where we were in the country; Beating the likes of Harlequins, London Irish, London Scottish, Plymouth Albion, Birkenhead Park, St Austell, Navy, Abertillery and R.A.F. only losing the games against Orrell (18-6), Bristol (12-10) and Boys Clubs of Wales (19-6); Me, Pritch, Andy Hill and Phil Wilson being beckoned into a nightclub on Union Street in Plymouth by three girls...we succumbed, when we should have really being going back to camp before midnight (as agreed with Gareth Davies) and the trouble we got into when they found out we came in at around three a.m. (...and no, me and Pritch didn't sleep with the sisters we met...Pritch's girl was married to a marine and my girl was engaged to a marine...time to run!!). But the three stand-out stories for me were 'The night in Treorchy', 'The Flying Pig', and the events surrounding my last game for the Army U'19s 'Army Colts v RAF Colts on 3rd April 1982'.

Firstly, we were lined up for a tough fixture against Boys Clubs of Wales on 13th February 1982 in Treorchy. On the day of the game we had travelled from the camp at Crickhowell to Treorchy, but even though there was seven or eight welsh boys in the squad...none of us came from the Rhondda and none us knew where their clubhouse was located. We drove up and down the valley three or four times and the clock was ticking, then purely by chance, we stumbled upon it and piled off the bus into the changing rooms...we had ten minutes to get changed. Once we'd changed...we were stood outside wondering where the hell the pitch was, we could not see any rugby posts anywhere. Luckily, one the Boys Clubs of Wales substitutes shouted;
"FOLLOW ME" and follow him we did down the back lane of a terraced street, over a footbridge that took us over the river, through a series of mini slag heaps...we started to hear

shouting and cheering and wondered what the noise was, then we saw the top of the rugby posts and then turned the last corner through the slag heaps and onto the pitch.

WOW!...there must have been a couple of thousand people around this pitch. We were directed to the middle of the pitch where the Boys Clubs of Wales was already lined up, we did the same, and a couple of minutes later a very smartly dressed women in her 50s with a big chain around her neck was introduced to us, shaking everyone's hand individually and stopping to have a few words with the odd player...it was the Mayoress of the Rhondda. The game had a bit of an international feel about it. But, the game was a bit of a disaster for us, with no time to prepare we were well beaten 19-6, but the day was about to get interesting. When we got into Treorchy rugby club there was the usual speeches, food, drinks...standing around the piano where Burt Greet played a number of well-known rugby songs and we all joined in with the singing. It was during this period of revelry that we found out there was going to be a disco in the function room that night...in fact, in the next hour. Negotiations were made with Gareth Davies so we could stay at the disco...an agreement was made that we could stay, provided Sid stayed with us and that we get back to Crickhowell at a reasonable time as we had a game against Abertillery in the morning 10.30a.m. kick-off...no problem...of course we'll be back at a reasonable time...honest!!! We had a fantastic night and I met a girl...Sheila Coles. At one point during the night I was talking to Sheila and had my back to the dance floor...I could see her looking over my shoulder every now and again and then she asked me;

"Are they with you?" I turned around and there was a group of about fifteen lads, all wearing the same red jumpers as me, all with their arms around each other, jumping up and down en-masse to the strains of *Jean Genie* by David Bowie...what could I say?;

"No, I've never seen them before in my life" smiled and attempted to cover up the army badge on my jumper. It was carnage when the slow dances started as the local Rhondda girls were doing the 'grabbing and dragging' onto the dance floor of the 'new meat' in the room that night. It took about an hour to get everyone on the bus, after the disco had ended...everytime it looked as if everyone was on the bus, lads would disappear off the bus and start necking (kissing) the new girls they'd met. Eventually, everyone was on the bus and we were off. We stopped once to drop a lad off in Nelson, where we convinced the fish and chip shop owner to open up and make us all sausage and chips. God knows what time we got back to Crickhowell, and by God did we have thick heads in the morning…how we got up in time for the Abertillery game was a miracle, but to beat them 34-0 was an even bigger miracle!

Secondly, in a game against Orrell on 27th February 1982 I was picked to play on the right wing. When we ran out onto the pitch that day and I saw the winger stood opposite me I remember thinking; "Get the ball out to me I'm going to run rings around this fat boy" and rubbed my hands in anticipation. But 'fat boy' got his hands on the ball before me, ran through me and though the full-back and scored under the posts…I got up and said to our full-back;
"What the fuck happened there" scratching my head.
"I dunno…beats me"
This 'fat boy freak of nature' was quicker than quick…he was like a blur. Halfway through the second half he confirmed his almost superhuman strength as he ran through our entire pack like a hybrid mix of Samson and Billy Whizz…leaving a trail of army rugby players in his wake as he scored his second try. We lost the game 18-6 that day and 'fat boy' was the definitely the difference between the two teams. In the bar after the game I asked one of the Orrell players about their mystery winger and he said;
"Come with me…I'll introduce you"
I followed him across the bar to where 'fat boy' was standing and the lad looked at me and said;
"This is the 'Flying Pig' and this is…" the lad leant in and in a whisper asked my name. I whispered "Taff";
"…and this is Taff" we shook hands and I told him that I thought he'd had an excellent game and that he was damn quick and strong. He began to tell me how this was his first season playing rugby union, and that he'd been playing rugby league at Wigan since he was about seven years old…and then said;
"Because I'm quick but also fat, the Orrell lads dubbed me 'The Flying Pig'" I have to say the nickname was apt and he was a great lad, we were stood there talking for a good half

hour before it was time for us army lads to head off back to Preston.

Lastly, my final memory was the day we beat the RAF Colts 26-10 to become the inter-service champions in 1982. I'd played full-back that day and had been fortunate to have scored eight points from two penalties and two conversions in what was a very good Army Colts side. After we had changed we got on a bus to travel to Twickenham to watch the senior game, when one of the lads jumped on the bus and held up the Sun newspaper and the headlines read *'ARGIES INVADE FALKLANDS'*. Nobody had ever heard of the Falklands and we all thought they must be off Scotland and then somebody confirmed our ignorance by saying;
"What are the Argies doing off Scotland?
We didn't really think much more about it and off we went to Twickenham unaware of the impact it would have on a few of the players from our team. During the Senior game at Twickenham it started to become apparent that something was afoot, as the tannoy announced a few times lists of names of people who should report to a designated area in the car park where transport would take them back to their units…this included four members of the Army Colts squad: Tom Austin (9 Para Squadron RE), Burt Greet (10 Field Workshops REME), Kenny 'Twenty' Williams and Ginge Johnson (1st Battalion Welsh Guards). When we returned to Aldershot early that evening we could see that the units that made up 5 Infantry Brigade, which included our four friends, were fully mobilized. This was the harsh reality of being a soldier and it certainly brought home the uncertainties we all faced. Rugby was just a game…this was the real thing and I hoped our friends would be ok!

It was a great two years with the Army Colts and winning the inter-service championship was the icing on the cake. I'd also been fortunate enough to be recognised by JLRRE a year earlier when I played in the Army v Navy Colts game, which the Army won 4-0, as apparently I was the first member of the regiment to be capped by the Army Colts for ten years…a personal achievement I still find humbling today.

In parallel with my second season with the Army Colts I was also lucky to be selected to play for the Combined Services

313

U'19s team for their Welsh Tour, where we played Cardiff and District and…my own area, Bridgend and District, a weekend of rugby that had not gone historically well for previous Combined Services teams. Additionally, I was selected to play in the game against the South of England XV in an England Area Trial. In the first game on the 'Welsh Tour' we came up against an excellent Cardiff and District side that included Mark Ring, Adrian Hadley and the current Welsh Youth captain, flanker Mike Budd. We had a glimpse of the outstanding talent of Mark Ring that day when he scored an absolutely outstanding individual try, with a combination of sidesteps and dummies that completely bamboozled our defence. But, we managed to keep him quiet for the remainder of the game, and playing outside half that day I managed to kick a drop goal and a penalty as we fought back from being 10-0 down to gain a highly respectable 10-10 draw. Mike Budd didn't legally get near me all afternoon and in frustration he tripped me from behind as we were trotting across to a breakdown…when I got up and got into position I just smiled at him to let him know his attempt to rile me hadn't worked! The following day we headed to Llanharan, near Bridgend, to play Bridgend and District, a team that included my old friend Richard Griffiths, who had already played senior rugby for Bridgend R.F.C. They had obviously heard about our result the previous day as they were already changed and warming up when we arrived. I played in my more settled position of full-back for this match, and I must have played reasonably well as I was asked if I would play for Bridgend Youth when I came home on leave or weekends and I was also seen by the Welsh selectors who offered me a Welsh Youth trial. It was a fairly even game, but late-on we had edged into a 16-10 lead and I had kicked four penalties, when suddenly Richard Griffiths broke through and only had me to beat. I remember thinking at the time, if he chips me and re-gathers the ball he was bound to win the race to the try line, as I would have to turn, and the fact that he was slightly quicker than me. Richie took the second option of trying to beat me but thankfully for me and the Combined Services U'19s team that day I managed to tackle him with probably one of the best tackles I ever made on a rugby field (many would tell you I wasn't known for my tackling skills!). The danger was snuffed out and we eventually held on to win the game 16-10…it felt good to beat my own district side.

314

Additionally, as a team we had done it! We had come to Wales and left without being beaten to two very difficult games.

The game against the South of England was classed as an England Area Trial and therefore, it was a very close game with the South of England just edging it with a score-line of 13-9. Personally, I thought I had played quite well and I also kicked three long range penalties, and when the game was over and we were walking back to the changing rooms I was soon joined by an elderly gentleman, who I thought was one of the other lad's grandfather. As we walked he said;
"You had an excellent game out there son" and smiled.
"Thank you"
"Yes…excellent kicking from the hand and also for goal…and it was great to see you joining the line and attacking from the back"
"Thanks"
"I understand you are Welsh"
"Yes I am…born in Bridgend" I said proudly.
"How come you are not playing for Wales?"
"Oh…I had a trial, but I didn't get in"
"They could have done with your kicking on Friday night when they lost to Australian Schools…are your parents Welsh?"
"Yeah…my mother is from Bridgend and my father is from just outside Ponty…Pontypridd"
"And your grandparents"
"Yeah, all Welsh" I said proudly.
We had now reached the changing rooms and he shook me by the hand and said;
"Nice talking to you Huw"
"And you…Bye" I thought for a second "How did he know my name?" But shrugged my shoulders and didn't really think any more about the elderly gent or the conversation…until I got in the bar around thirty to forty minutes later. As soon as I entered the bar I was surrounded by Peter Larter (Chief Coach and former England international second row for England), Gareth Davies (Coach and a fellow Welshman) and the coach representing the Navy, Nicholls who all proceeded to tell me that the 'elderly gent' I'd been speaking to was, in fact, the Chairman of the English Selectors and that I should have told him that "Yes, I'm Welsh, but I'd love to play for

315

England"…they also said that if I had told him that I could forget about Ebbw Vale, Abertillery and Maesteg who had already shown an interest in me, as being a Welshman born and bred in Wales, it would have been the likes of Cardiff, Swansea and Llanelli that would come knocking…there is no way they would want to see a one hundred percent Welsh person playing for England. They finished by saying that I'd probably just made the biggest mistake of my rugby playing life, but I thought I'm Welsh, I could never wear an England shirt…my family would disown me!

I was extremely proud to have represented the Corps of Royal Engineers on the rugby field from my first game against Oxford University 2nd XV in 1980, as a fresh-faced seventeen year old in a team that probably included the oldest second row partnership ever to represent the Corps…Major John Quinn and WO1 Geordie Howe, right up to my last game against the RAOC (Royal Army Ordinance Corps) in 1989. It was an honour to have been chosen to play in two Sappers v Gunners game in 1981 where we drew 13-13 and I scored two penalties and in 1987 where we lost (7-10), however it was my mistake in the second half of that game of missing a kick to touch that ultimately lost us the game…I am still haunted by the kick to this day. I was also on the bench for three others and played in many Corps games against other opposition such as the Royal Signals, RCT (Royal Corps of Transport), The REME (Royal Mechanical and Electrical Engineers), Royal Marines, Guernsey, Public School Wanderers, Cambridge University 2nd XV…and all of them more than once! However, it was the annual fixture against the Gunners that was special as it was the oldest rugby fixture in the army, having been played since 1889; games alternating between Chatham and Woolwich and the respective bands of each Corps would open proceedings at each venue and a good crowd was always guaranteed. You would also be awarded a Corps XV tie if you played in the 'Gunners' fixture and this was always worn with pride! Playing for the Corps was always a humbling experience as I played with so many great players and also played against some great players too. During this period I was also lucky enough to go on three tours to Guernsey…a pre-curser for the Gunner game which was all about 'team bonding' and getting pissed. Who can forget Terry Martin forcing us Welsh boys to throw our new mascot

316

(Welsh doll) overboard into Portsmouth harbour whilst singing the Welsh national anthem because we wouldn't agree to calling the doll 'Moby Dick', as we wanted to call it 'Myfanwy'; the kangaroo court for Russ Bedford on the ferry, as he was charged with being 'too greedy with the girls whilst being on tour'...he was found guilty of course and it was a wonderful spectacle for crew and passengers to see justice being served...who can forget Kev Bassom's Batman hat with alternating flashing lights on the ears; Jake Maiden, his foreskin and a bag of 2p coins...use your imagination!; the water pistols me, Jake and Taff Randall bought that resulted in Willie Higgins blowing up the till behind the bar when he was trying to soak Taff Randall...but missed and getting water in the electric till; me, Pritch and Grant Evans and the three women...me and Pritch got lucky and bedded two of the girls, but we left Grant Evans (a young officer) in the living room with a very big and scary girl and despite the bangs, crashes and shouts of "leave me alone" coming from Grant, we left him to his fate...we found him in the morning in the foetal position with his trousers and pants around his ankles (no sign of the 'scary' one) and he looked up at us despairingly and said "Runaway...runaway!!"; Stevie 'Woosh' Taylor spending all his beer money on the the card tables on the ferry; Jakes strip and 'Madness' dance at the Golden Monkey disco...just because there was, as Jake described him, a 'poser' on the dance floor; Double Phillips shimmying along a ledge and quietly opening the window of an officers window as the officer was 'getting it on' with a young lady...then jumping on the two of them resulting in the girl running away semi-naked screaming and the officer proclaiming "you can't do that...I'm an officer", Double Phillips just laughed and then ran out of the room; the small plane we caught one year which was tossed around the sky like nobody's business...worst flight I've ever been on; the occasional rugby match and many, many more. I have many great memories of those times playing Corps rugby and was also being selected for the 1989 tour to the United States, but unfortunately couldn't attend due to the birth of my daughter R.

I also represented the Army in the Falkland Islands in games against the Royal Navy and R.A.F. in 1983, as we won the first Inter-Services Championships played in the South Atlantic. I also represented the Army U'21s and Combined

317

Services U'21s rugby teams in 1983-84 season, culminating in being part of the Combined Services U'21s squad that played Scotland U'21s at Murrayfield. Despite us having the England winger, Rory Underwood, we were no match for a Scotland U'21s team that fielded a team that included Gary Oliver and Doug Wylie at half-backs and a centre partnership of Alan Tait and Scott Hastings all of whom gained full caps for Scotland, the latter two also playing for the British and Irish Lions, and they deservedly beat us 64-7…as much as it would have been great to actually play at Murrayfield, I think I was glad to be on the bench that day. But before the game I did get a chance to drop a couple of goals and kick a couple of place kicks between the sticks, still a great honour to be involved in that game at Murrayfield nevertheless. One of my abiding memories of playing for the Army U'21s that season was when we played Harlequins U'21s, who happened to be the club side I was playing for that same season. However, Harlequins wouldn't pick me at full-back or let me take penalties or conversions and after a couple of difficult games at outside half against Richmond and the R.A.F. I was dropped for the game against Wasps. The next being against the Army U'21s meant that I was unavailable to play for Harlequins and I knew the Army U'21s coaching staff would pick me at full-back and I was the preferred kicker. In a very close game, I kicked three penalties in a 9-7 victory at the Military Stadium in Aldershot. After the game a slightly embarrassed Chaz Bool, the Harlequins U'21s coach, admitted that he could now see that I was full-back and apologised and asked me if I was available to play against the Met Police the following week…another example of bad decision making by the petulant Huw Thomas in saying "no!", resulting in me never playing for Harlequins again! Another bizarre memory is of travelling with Phil Humphries in the back of the Bomb Disposal staff car with Major John Quinn who, when we got stuck in traffic, told the driver to put the blue lights on and give the sirens a whirl, and we sailed passed the traffic jam…class!

Another team I was lucky to represent was Cambridgeshire Colts against Essex which resulted in my being selected for the Eastern Counties final trial. Unfortunately, I was posted to Chatham before the trial and missed a good opportunity. I consider myself to have been very lucky to have played the

318

representative rugby I played in the early eighties with very good Army and Combined Services U'19s and U'21s teams and with the Royal Engineers Corps XV into the late eighties…I believe I was in the right place at the right time. I was fortunate to have created some fantastic memories, on and off the field with great players and great coaches who have also remained great friends.

24 Field Squadron RE – Rugby, football and more

I wasn't happy being posted to 24 Field Squadron as I was enjoying life at Waterbeach and playing rugby for Ely R.U.F.C. and Cambridgeshire U'19s. However, it soon became evident that something special was happening with the 24 Squadron rugby team…and I would go on to enjoy my time at Chattenden, and had the pleasure have playing with some absolutely fantastic players, many of whom still remain friends today. However, I also played other sports during my time at 24, namely; football, cricket, tennis and I flirted with boxing in what was probably the shortest boxing career in the history of the sport, but in some respects a very memorable career…for all the wrong reasons! I also played rugby for Bridgend Youth, Harlequins U'21s, US Chatham and I was invited to play for London Welsh during my time at Chattenden…the latter was scuppered due to the Falklands conflict and the six month tour I enjoyed between November 1982 and April 1983 (as written about in Chapter 3). When you mix together the experiences of Chapter 3 with my sporting experiences here…it is not hard to see why the period between November 1981 to May 1986 was such an important and enjoyable period in my life!!!

We had a very successful side during my time at 24 Field Squadron and during my time there we won the Mini-Fern Cup, Fern Cup, South East District Minor Units Cup, Army UK Minor Units Cup, Army Minor Units Cup (UK winners played the BAOR champions to determine the overall winners) and the SE District Sevens Plate Winners. It wasn't just on the field that was memorable…it was here I was introduced to the infamous rugby tradition of the 'third half'…the singing of rugby songs such as 'My sister Belinda', 'Beastiality's Best', 'Aloiette', 'Singing in the Rain', 'Old Reilly's Daughter', 'Ghostriders' 'Sloop John B' and many, many more…thank

319

you Keith 'Ish' Isham and Stevie 'Woosh' Taylor. Some of the
special memories of sport at 24 that I have are the rugby tour
to Ireland in 1982 centered around a 1ˢᵗ round cup game with
33 Indep Field Squadron in Antrim, boxing match at 36
Engineer Regiment, Maidstone in 1985, the first round of the
army cup at Shorncliffe against Infantry Junior Leaders
Battalion (IJLB) in October 1984, the Army final against the
BAOR champions in 1986 and the last rugby I played at
24...the Army Sevens in Aldershot when I played against an
army legend!!!!

Rugby was the reason I was posted to 24 Field Squadron RE,
and during my four and a half years, I would like to think I
repaid the faith they had shown in bringing me to the squadron
purely for rugby, to the detriment of my own career. I played
in teams that would end up winning the following;

The Fern (Sapper) Cup	-	1982
The South East District Minor Units Cup	-	1982,
1984, 1985 & 1986		
The South East District 7s Plate	-	1982
The Falkland Islands 7s	-	1982
The Mini-Fern Cup	-	1983
The Army Minor Units UK	-	1985 &
1986		
The Army Minor Units (UK v BAOR)	-	1985 &
1986		

We were also runners-up in the following:

The Fern (Sapper) Cup	-	1986
The Mini-Fern Cup	-	1984

And lastly we were semi-finalists in the Army 7s in 1986.

It was a successful time for 24 Field Squadron RE that I know
carried on after I got posted in May 1986. However, those
'golden' years didn't start in Chattenden, the foundations for
all that followed started far away in Antrim, Northern Ireland
in early February 1982. We flew from R.A.F. Lyneham and
the 'old sweats' (soldiers who had served in more than one

posting) in the team, who had been involved in infantry tours to Northern Ireland, enjoyed 'winding up' us younger and greener lads about the dangers with "don't do this..." and "don't do that..." and so on. By the time we approached Aldergrove airport in our Hercules I was beginning to think that this trip to Northern Ireland wasn't a good idea. When the plane had come to a stop I reluctantly joined the queue to leave the plane, but when I got to the steps of the plane I paused and looked around...nothing but darkness, so I continued down the steps. Keeping my wits about me I carefully walked across the tarmac, then suddenly and without warning I heard one of the lads shout;

"QUICK...GET DOWN!!"

I didn't need to be asked twice and dropped to the tarmac along with Taff Humphrey, Taff Pritch and Andy Hill (basically, all the youngsters). Almost immediately, the rest of the lads were laughing hysterically and pointing at the four sproggs (new soldiers) lying on the floor trying to dig themselves into the tarmac before Tiny Bott laughed and shouted;

"GET OFF THE FLOOR YOU FUCKING NUMPTIES!"

Realising we'd been had we all jumped up and followed the others, and under my breath I whispered "wankers" and laughed. It didn't get any better as we were briefed on the 'what not to do in Northern Ireland'...the main one I remember was 'under no circumstances were we to get in the black London type taxi cabs' as they were run by the I.R.A. (Irish Republican Army) as you would likely end up at the bottom of the Falls Road in Belfast with a bullet in your head. A rather sobering thought for a boy from Bridgend who had remembered 'Bloody Sunday' on the news as a ten year old. It wasn't long before we were on a bus heading for Antrim, and about an hour later we pulled up at Massereene Barracks...our home for the next week or so.

Over the next two days we carried out some light training; running through moves, kicking practice and a bit of touch rugby before we played 33 Independent Field Squadron RE on the Wednesday. The game against 33 Sqn was a one-sided affair as we won 66-0, but I now have little memory of the finer details of who scored etc. It's the off the field antics I remember more than our heroics on the field such as a visit to Portrush where we spent the afternoon in a British Legion club

321

that had bigger mortar fences around it than the police station next door, and a vault like door that led to an inner room where we spent the afternoon drinking and singing Max Boyce songs; the night Joe Kirby tried to get Sheena Easton to give him a blow job, but the problem was she was singing '9 to 5' on Top of the Pops on T.V…and that was the night we were banned from the NAAFI (we had already been banned from the Bridge Inn bar on the camp for the fighting that broke out after the match against 33 Sqn); the 33 Sqn SSM (Squadron Sergeant Major) giving is an ultimatum that "if there was any more trouble we'd find all our kit outside the front gate of the camp"; me and Andy Hill chatting to three girls in *The Steeple* pub in Antrim town centre who asked us if we wanted to go to a party. This is how the conversation went;

"Do you want to come to a fucking disco?" In their harsh Northern Irish accents.

"Where?"

"Fucking Belfast"

"How do we get there?"

"In a fucking taxi!!"

As soon as me and Andy heard the word 'taxi' we looked at each other and remembered what the man had said at the airport and in unison said;

"No, you are OK…we'll stay here"

"Suit you fucking selves" and they were gone. We then watched the news a bit worse for wear because of the drink and the newsreader said 'another soldier has been killed in Northern Ireland', I forgot that I was in a pub in Antrim in the middle of Northern Ireland and shouted at the T.V.;

"FUCKING IRISH BASTARDS!!"

The bar went quiet, Andy looked at me and drunkenly said;

"I think we'd better go…hic"

"I think you are…hic… right Andy" and we got up, left the pub and sprinted back to Massereene Barracks…and to safety. There were a couple of other games we played, but I only remember the score in one at HQ Northern Ireland at Lisburn Barracks…0-0 in what is definitely the only time I've played in a 0-0 game in rugby and it was the longest game of rugby I ever played in. The problem being that the pitch was right next to the heli-pad and every few minutes a helicopter was either landing or taking off, and every time this happened the referee would have to stop the game. It was a strange week, but the seeds had been sown and the rugby team began a success story

322

that is probably unrivalled in 24 Field Squadron's rugby history.

We went on to win, firstly the South East District Cup in a final against 9 Para Squadron RE in Aldershot, where we won the game 21-14. This memory reminds me the time I went AWOL (absent without leave) from Woolwich Hospital (see Chapter 3). I also remember Cpl Dave Clement scoring a try under the posts and then taking great delight in running straight down the touchline, where 9 Sqn supporters were stood en-masse, with his arm raised in triumph and his fist clenched shouting "WHO'S A FUCKING CRAP HAT NOW"…priceless (the paras used to call everyone who didn't wear a red beret a 'crap hat'). Meanwhile, I hurriedly took the conversion, hit the bar so hard that the ball sailed back over my head…you can't win em all. The following week we completed the double over 9 Sqn by beating them 14-6 in the Fern (Sapper) Cup in Chatham. That 1981-82 season was a good one for 24 Field Squadron RE, but there was more to follow…much, much more.

The 1982/83 was a non-event as the squadron was sent on a construction tour to the Falkland Islands and apart from a couple of friendlies before we went, a few in the Falklands and winning the 7s tournament on Boxing Day in Port Stanley the season was pretty much a write-off. The 1983/84 season was better as we won the Mini-Fern Cup (a 15-a-side tournament played in a similar way to 7s in that they were short games, I think 10 minutes each way, and there were groups and then knockout stages, all played over a day) and another South East District Minor Units win. Unfortunately, in Tiny Bott's last season of rugby before retirement we failed to provide him with the one trophy that had eluded him…an army cup winners medal, as we were beaten 4-0 in the semi-final in one of the tightest games I ever played in, as there were no kicks at goal by either side and the game was won by a cross kick that bounced back over the head of our winger Lt Jeremy Robson and straight into the arms of their winger who just fell over the line to score the only, and winning, try. The disappointment on Tiny's face when the final whistle went was painful to see and I really felt for him that day!

The 1984/85 season was a great season which saw us become runners-up in the Mini-Fern Cup, winning the South East District Minor Units Cup, The Army Minor Units UK Cup and the Army Minor Units Cup (UK v BAOR winners). But the greatest game that season wasn't any of those finals, but the 1st round of the Army Minor Units Cup against I.J.L.B. (Infantry Junior Leaders Battalion) in a rain-drenched and windy day at Shorncliffe in Folkestone…a game we should have lost, but God or somebody was on our side that day. The pitch had quite a steep gradient and mixed with the heavy rain and wind it was going to be a difficult day. We played downhill in the first half with the wind and rain both in our favour, but we struggled with the conditions and at half-time we were only 4-0 in front…it was not going to be enough. When the second half kicked off we were soon losing 9-4 and we did not look like scoring, as everything was against us, the slope; the rain; the wind, and we were playing poorly. With around five minutes left of the game we were camped in our twenty-two with the driving rain and wind in our faces and the writing was on the cards and it looked as if this would be another season where the Army Cup would elude us. Then out of the blue and totally against the run of play, a long pass by their outside half to their outside centre deep inside our twenty-two was intercepted by our Lt Jeremy Robson. He sped through the gap, and as their full-back had joined their line, there was no-one in front of him and he ran the length of the pitch to score under the posts. I kicked the conversion and we were 10-9 in front…we held out for the remaining few minutes and when the final whistle blew there was just a huge sense of shock and relief that we had won, and there were quite a few beers drank that night in celebration. On the way to the UK final we beat 19 Infantry Brigade and Signal Squadron 70-0, 10 Airborne Field Workshop REME (Royal Electrical and Mechanical Engineers) 19-0 (a team that included my old friend, Burt Greet, from our days with the Army Colts and the Irish international second row, Brian McCall), 233 Signal Squadron 18-3, and in the semi-final we beat Depot Prince of Wales Division 19-7. Revenge was ours in the final as we beat Depot Kings Division 13-6…the team that beat us 4-0 in that heartbreaking semi-final a year earlier. We went to Germany to play the BAOR (British Army of the Rhine) champions, 6 Armoured Workshop REME, and in a one sided final we beat them 27-0, and on a personal level I had the honour of winning the 'man of the match' award. We had done it…we were Army Champions. However, the Fern Cup eluded us that year as we were knocked out in the quarter final by 36 Engineer Regiment, losing 15-13 after leading 13-0, but there was a contentious decision by the referee, Mick Woollam, who controversially missed a try scored by our Phil Swindells…when Phil, who had already scored, turned and was about to run back to me to give me the ball for the conversion, he was pushed into touch by a 36 Engr Regt player…Mick gave the lineout and we lost the game.

My last season at 24 Field Squadron was another successful one as we again won the South East District Minor Units Cup, and also won the Army Minor Units UK final and the Army Minor Units (UK V BAOR winners) final. Additionally, we were the runners-up in the Fern Cup to 39 Engineer Regiment and losing semi-finalists in the Army 7s Plate competition in a game that lasted 34 minutes (twenty minutes longer due to extra-time). I don't have details of the route to the UK final of the Army Minor Units Cup, but I know we recorded the highest score in any game I've ever played in when we beat, I think, 12 Field Ambulance RAMC (Royal Army Medical Corps) 104-0 in the first round. The final itself had been postponed once due to bad weather (snow) and when we finally played Prince of Wales Division, it was rumoured they'd pulled in three or four 'ringers' from RRW (Royal Regiment of Wales) including Kev O'Hearne, the Army scrum-half. Again, the wind played its part and with around ten minutes left and playing into a strong wind we were struggling to hold on to a 10-9 lead. Bad discipline nearly cost us the game as the Prince of Wales Division piled on the pressure…resulting in us giving away three or four kickable penalties in those last ten minutes. Luckily, a combination of pressure and the weather conditions meant that Kev O'Hearne buckled under the pressure and misjudged the swirling wind in the Military Stadium and we managed to hang-on again to win the Army Minor Units UK final. We now looked forward to another game in the Military Stadium a few weeks later where we would play the BAOR champions, 16 Tank Transporter Squadron RCT (Royal Corps of Transport). On the day of the game we followed the usual routine of a light breakfast, a quick hour running through the moves (lineouts, penalties and back moves), before travelling from where we were staying at

1 & 3 Training Regiments RE at Minley, about three miles from the Military Stadium in Aldershot, where the final would be played. We arrived, had a walk around the pitch, familiarized ourselves with the weather conditions and then got changed and went through our normal individual and collective warm-up routines. When the game finally kicked off we initially had a problem…they had a huge second row and he was winning all the lineout ball (ours and theirs) and we were struggling to get any ball for our backs to utilise. About ten minutes in Sgt Stevie 'Woosh' Taylor called the 'Tetley' move at a lineout…a move that involved 'perforating' the body of a team member of the opposition similar to the perforations in a tea bag (use your imagination)! The two sets of forwards lined up for the throw-in, but our forwards had switched around in the line-out so that Woosh Taylor was lined up opposite their big second row and our flankers SSgt John Peers and Geordie Kelf were either side of Woosh. The ball was predictably thrown to their danger man in the line-out, we didn't challenge him in the air, instead we waited until he started to land on the floor, as his toes connected with the floor and with perfect timing John Peers and Geordie Kelf hit him from either side and Woosh ploughed into his back. The force of the combined tackle hit their second row, and Woosh, John and Geordie quickly rolled away as the remaining forwards stamped him into the ground, violently rucking the ball back to Dai Morgan at scrum half and I cleared 30-40m downfield for another line-out. Their second row picked himself off the floor, and brushed himself down, and I remember thinking he's just taken a shoeing and he's carrying on…fair play. We repeated the 'tetley' call at the next line-out, but this time he didn't get up and he was carried off and substituted. We never looked back and went on to win the game comfortably 32-0. I was lucky enough to score a try that day, my last try for 24 Field Squadron…I had chipped over their backs into the space between their winger and full-back who, both with their eyes on the ball, clattered into each other and the ball bounced up straight into my arms and I had a thirty metre unopposed run in to the try line. We had done the double and again received the cup, our medals and individual half-bottles of whisky from the sponsors, Whyte and Mackay and started our normal celebrations in the changing rooms and in the clubhouse at the Military Stadium. An hour or so in to the evening Jake Maiden was in the toilet having a pee when

the big second row we had despatched came into the toilet. He said to Jake;

"If I hadn't gone off you wouldn't be holding that now"

Jake finished peeing, put it away, zipped himself up and looked the guy straight in the eye and said sarcastically;

"Well you did go off and that's why I'm holding this fucking cup and not you…bye mate"

Jake waved, walked out and returned to our mad celebrations in the bar!

My last fifteen a side game was the Fern Cup final in 1986 against 39 Engineer Regiment RE. We lost a close final, but I have two memories from the game involving my old friend Phil Wilson that still make me smile. I had played many games with Phil for the Corps XV, Army Colts and Combined Services Colts teams and watched him, as open-side flanker, destroy opposing outside halfs…I knew his game, I knew exactly how he played. Midway through the first half I used that knowledge to my and my team's advantage. There was a lineout just outside out twenty two, we won the ball and I could see that Phil had adopted his normal predatory position on the periphery of the developing maul. Here it comes…Phil Swindells threw the ball out to me and out of the corner of my I could see that Phil was already out of the blocks and heading toward me. I received the ball, threw a dummy out to Keith Isham, stepped inside Phil and went through the gap…the field had opened up in front of me as their back line had stepped up with Phil expecting him to nail me. I made it deep in their twenty two before I was tackled…1-0 to Thomas, but Phil would get his revenge midway through the second half from another lineout. We again won the lineout and Phil Swindells threw the ball out to me, but the wind at our backs held it up and I caught it high above my head…at the same time my fingertips touched the ball Phil absolutely wiped me out, knocking the wind out of me as he caught me a peach in my midriff…definitely 1-1. As I lay there gasping for air, and with 39 Engineer Regiment RE winning the final, you could argue that Phil Wilson won the battle 2-1 that day.

I wore the 24 Field Squadron RE shirt for the last time at the Army 7s in Aldershot. As I've already mentioned wewere knocked out in the semi-final of the plate competition after extra-time. But it was a game during the group stage that I remember more than anything...the game against DWR (Duke of Wellington's Regiment). When I was ten years old in 1973 I had watched Bridgend play the Army, and on that night there was a young black flanker playing for the Army...a young player called Williams, who became an Army rugby legend and was affectionately known as 'Black Willy'. Here I was thirteen years later about to share a rugby pitch and play against this Army legend. I was in awe of this great Army rugby player who was now in the twilight of his career, and it was an absolute honour to play against him that day and shake his hand after the game...definitely a star struck moment and a great way to bring down the curtain on my 24 Field Squadron RE rugby career.

There are many other memories from 24 Field Squadron RE on and off the field. To start, here's a few of the 'on field' memories such as: Playing in a 'C' team in the Sapper 7s that included (Pritch with damaged ankle ligaments), Ron Quick (back problems) and me (unable to bend my left arm following a motor bike accident), and managing to beat 33 Independent Field Squadron RE...the supposed 'dark horses' of the competition; the dirty games against Kent Police, in particular when I was tackled late by their flanker who then wouldn't let me get off the floor, when I did eventually wriggle free, I jumped to my feet, grabbed the offender by the ears and proceeded to knee him in the face, luckily for me just missing as Jim Wood, the referee, grabbed me by the front of my shirt and telling me if he saw me pull a stunt like that again, he would send me off and make sure I never played rugby again; Joe Kirby's hand-off which was more of a 'grab' of an opponent's face and then dragging them along with him for a yard or two before letting go; Taff Pritch's game at scrum-half and his long awaited desire to put in 'box' kicks at every opportunity...he was our hooker; the 'Enforcer', Iain George, who I remember standing over me in the semi-final of the Fern Cup at Ripon in 1982 when I was dazed after being double tackled by two 38 Engineer Regiment RE players, and saying "who did it Taff?" I looked up at Iain, winced and said "the centres"...a few minutes later one centre was spark out and a few minutes later the second centre was spark out...thanks Iain; Tiny Bott pulling down a maul via the long hair of a college student and then telling the ref that he couldn't help it..."all that hair"; 35 Engineer Regiment RE refusing to play

328

us in the Campbell Cup (a cup played for between the UK and BAOR winners of the Fern Cup) in 1982; Al Bowman suggesting in training that we do the London marathon as a rugby team, passing the ball amongst us as we ran the course, Batch cuffed him around the head, called him a stupid fucker and said "we can't get around the field without dropping the ball, how the fuck are we going to manage for twenty-six miles"; Greg (Gregory) wanting to fight the world…on and off the field; the guile of Stan Roberts at outside half; the speed of Andy Murray; Keith Isham's tree trunk leg's that were bigger than my waist; Mick Stupple, in a game against Depot RE, punching someone in a ruck and standing there with his arm shaking from the connected punch, smiling and saying "whoever I hit isn't getting up from that one"…when the ruck broke up our other prop, Gerry Hoolachan, was lying spark out on the floor…oops!; Iki Bolton playing 7s and, as he described, getting his skull crushed by Corps winger, Sparky Watts; The No5 penalty move – Where the scrum-half turns his back to the opposition, taps the ball and as our forwards were about to run past him then kicked the ball back over his head for the forwards to run onto…did it ever work?; during the Army Cup semi-final at Lichfield the opposition hooker tackled Mick Stupple and drove him into the front of the OC's landrover, injuring Mick and forcing him to leave the field. The same hooker was spotted about ten minutes later by Garth Hamley hanging prostate out of the wrong side of a ruck (basically, on our side of the ruck) with his testacles hanging out of his shorts, Garth ran in from about fifteen metres and kicked their hooker right where it hurts…the scream was ear piercing and resounded around the pitch before he joined Mick on the sidelines, justice served; Someone shoving a ralgex stick (similar to deep heat) up Jake Maiden's arse in the changing rooms…God, Jake was quick around the field that day; Cinders (Nigel Cindery) nearly having his ear ripped off in the 1986 UK final against Prince of Wales Division and many, many more.

There were many 'off-field' memories but a lot of them have been clouded by the alcohol we drank at the time, but there are a few I remember such as sitting in the Monarch in Gillingham with Iain George and Vince Clarke trying to organise a charity game against Chatham ladies, but having to decline when the two, shall we say, 'ladies' said that we had to abide by the

rules but for them 'anything goes'...sadly, we had to decline
as we were in the middle of two cup runs and we couldn't
afford any injuries; higher than the highest mountain, deeper
than the deep blue sea...those that know, know!; the classic
rugby songs we used to sing such as "My sister Belinda",
"That was a horrible song", Beastiality's Best", "Old Riley's
Daughter", "Singing in the Rain" (c/w 'special'
actions/movements...ahem!), "Sloop John B", "Swing Low,
Sweet Chariot" "A, B, C Song" and many, many, more;
having to wear that huge, brass Maltese cross all night if you
won 'man of the match'...and the pain you'd be in when the
points prodded you in the chest...again and again and again;
Taff Best pissing on people in the showers...he'd casually
strike up a conversation with people and then start pissing on
the leg; Stevie 'Woosh' Taylor's wonderful rendition of
"Alouette"; Keith Isham's brilliant renditions of "Are you
lonesome tonight" where he would kneel down and start
singing the song to a random girl in the bar, quickly joined by
the rest of us as backing singers and to block off the escape
route of any unsuspecting female recipient...the different
reactions he got were classic; Coming back from games in
Aldershot (mainly rugby finals) and stopping at the 'Jolly
Farmers' pub just outside Reigate...we'd all pile in drunk
shouting "oo, arr...oo, arr"; Gerry Hoolachan and Woosh
Taylor running naked around the running track at the Military
Stadium, Aldershot for a now unknown misdemeanor; another
Keith Isham classic, "Ghostriders in the sky" c/w beer tray
which was used to whack people over the head during the
chorus "Yippy aye yay...(tshsh...the sound of tray on
skull)...yippy aye oh...(tshsh)...", there was always some sore
heads after that song; Karen Stupple, Val Hoolachan and
Laura Richards...our biggest fans; The night out at the
London Inn in Gutersloh after the 1985 final in Germany when
John Harvey introduced me to Fanta Korn...great night; The
half bottles of Whyte and Mckay whisky we were individually
given each time we won an Army cup as they were the
sponsors...they had always all been drunk before we even left
the bar after the game; Jonny Witchell...our long suffering
mini-bus driver and many, many more.

I also played football at 24 Sqn, and even though we weren't
as successful as the rugby team, we had some very good
players such as Gavin Denton, Mark Parker, Simon Millerick,

Dixie Duricki, Iki Bolton, Rab Keill, Tony Long and many others whose names have now escaped me over the passages of time. Nevertheless, I have a few memories that have partially remained with me to this day. Firstly, during our tour of the Falkland Islands we played a few games on the pitch that was nestled in between the military hospital in Port Stanley and Government House. It was open to the elements and the nets in each goal were camouflage nets (normally used to disguise military vehicles in the field). I can't remember much about the games other than difficulties with the wind and Dixie Duricki's goal scoring feats. Back in Chatham the following season I can remember a game against Kent Police at Chattenden…for all the wrong reasons. Just after the second half started I remember challenging the Kent Police keeper for a ball from a cross swung in from the right, he clearly caught the ball just before I had the chance to get my head on it…we were both off balance, and I hit the floor first with their keeper immediately landing on top of me, with his elbow catching me in the ribs. I was heavily winded, but when I got to my knees and then eventually to my feet and took that first breath, I screamed out in pain…I thought I'd broken my ribs from the contact, as everytime I took a breath the pain was unbearable. An ambulance (army ambulance from the camp) was called and twenty minutes later I was lying in a stretcher in the back of the ambulance heading for the medical centre at Brompton Barracks. On arrival at Brompton we were stopped at the main gate, despite me being in a great deal of discomfort in the back of the ambulance they wouldn't let us in…the reason being was that Prince Charles was visiting Brompton and we had to wait until his visit was over and he had left in the waiting helicopter, currently parked up on the main parade ground. Eventually, an hour later, I made it to the medical centre, checked over, sort of given the all clear (I hadn't broken anything, just suffered some heavy bruising)…three days later I collapsed and was rushed to Medway hospital with a suspected ruptured spleen…thankfully, after 48 hours in hospital, the tests came back clear and I was discharged, the collapse still remains a mystery to this day.

Under the guidance of SSgt (staff sergeant) Stevie Gillies, the football team played its best football in 1983-84, and it was during this period that we played a memorable game in the Army Major Units Cup against SEME Borden…the current

Army champions. On paper, they were a much stronger side than us boasting two players who went on to represent Maidstone Utd in the football league, but we gave a cracking account of ourselves and after forty-five minutes we were only losing 1-0. However, early in the second half they scored another, but we didn't buckle, we dug-in deep and started playing the better football, first to every tackle and we started to dominate possession. Twenty minutes into the second half our pressure was beginning to tell and we won a series of corners. From one of these corners I found myself wandering around the six yard box waiting for the impending cross to be swung-in...just before the cross came in I dropped off and eventually made my way, in an arc, and as the ball came into the box I found myself unmarked on the edge of the eighteen yard box – the ball was headed clear, but my gamble paid off, I kept my eye on the ball and caught the ball sweetly with my right foot and my volley through the crowded players in the box, past their unsighted keeper and high into the roof of the net...we were now 2-1 behind. Playing the better football we started to get half chances and then ten minutes from time we had a chance cleared off the line, but chasing the equaliser we left ourselves open at the back and they made it 3-1 a few minutes before the final whistle was blown. We had narrowly lost a cracking game of football to the current Army Champions, who went on to retain the trophy again that season. SSgt Stevie Gillies got us together in the changing rooms and told us how proud he was of us and that we should be proud of ourselves for the way we'd played, pushing the army champions all the way in a fairly even contest...had we scored from one of those half chances it could have been a different result.

My other great memory of SSgt Steve Gillies was when he was in charge of the 24 Sqn Boxing Team, and after he had obviously been through the records and found my boxing card, told me I was boxing in a tournament at 36 Engineer Regiment RE at Maidstone. I hadn't done any boxing training since my time at J.L.R.R.E. at Dover in 1980 (four years earlier) and even then, I had never been involved in an actual bout...sparring and shadow boxing was the extent of my boxing experience. Thinking the tournament was a few weeks away I said to Stevie Gillies;
"When is the tournament Staff?"

"Friday"

"FRIDAY…but I haven't done any training…that's…that's only two days away" I said shocked.

"Don't worry Taff…it'll be fine. First things first, we have to weigh you…"

"…Friday" I said again under my breath.

"Straight after lunch come back to my office…I'll bring my weighing scales in from home so we can weigh you and see where we are…don't eat anything!"

I went up to my room and thought "this is madness…two days to prepare for a fight"

An hour or so later I was stood in 2 troop's office on a normal bathroom scales in just a pair of shorts, Steve Gillies looking down at the dial and scratching his head before saying;

"Hmmm…we've got a bit of a problem…according to the scales you need to lose 7lb, but you have to lose that weight before Friday morning which is less than 36 hours away…right…right…" and he disappeared. A few moments later he was back with a black bin bag, tearing a hole in the bottom and smaller holes on either side;

"Put this on…and then go up to your room and put two or three layers over the top and a pair of tracksuit bottom and meet me down by the Duty NCOs bunk in about ten minutes"

I put my socks, trainers and t-shirt back on and ran up to my room to find more clothes. Ten minutes later I was stood outside the entrance to where the Duty NCO's bunk was, dressed as SSgt Stevie Gillies had ordered and waited for him to turn up. A minute or two later he trotted around the corner from the front of the office block in his trademark red tracksuit and said;

"Ready"

"Yes Staff"

"Come on then…lets go"

Off we went, onto Lochat Road and started jogging toward Lodge Hill training area. Over the next 36 hours there was more running, a session in the sauna (fully clothed c/w bin bag…I've never been in a sauna since) and even an aerobics session in the regimental gymnasium, on the Thursday morning, with the Army wives. To make matters worse, I hadn't eaten since breakfast on the Wednesday morning, and had only drank a few glasses of water…by the Friday morning I was so hungry I could have eaten a scabby dog! We went over to the official weigh-in at Invicta Park Barracks in

Maidstone, and to my surprise I had lost 10lb…damn, this meant one thing, I was definitely going to be boxing that night. I came straight out of the weigh-in and walked to the NAAFI shop and bought a couple of meat pies, crisps, a mars bar and a bottle of milkshake…they were gone in minutes, as I sat there like a rabid dog, growling at anybody who came too close to my food.

The day went by slowly, but eventually the time came for us to set off for Maidstone…those of us that were fighting, Stevie Gillies and Greg Gregory piled into the squadron minibus and we were soon on our way. On arrival at Invicta Park Barracks we made our way to the regimental gymnasium where the boxing tournament was being held…I had been here before and remembered cheering on Joe Kirby to victory in a fight that was over before the sound of the bell stopped ringing, a clubbing left then a right put pay to his opponent that night. Here I was two years later, nerves kicking in, adrenaline flowing in anticipation of my first boxing match. From the changing rooms the noise in the gym was deafening as each boxer before me took their turns in the ring…akin to gladiators entering the Colosseum in Ancient Rome. Greg was with me throughout those last nervous moments, offering advice and whipping up the aggression levels to heights I'd never experienced before;
"Taff…when the bell sounds get across that ring…get stuck into him…who's Eddie Metson…no-one, that's who…combinations…left, right…left, right, left…in trouble, hold, hold…let the referee break it up…concentrate, concentrate…jab, jab, jab, but keep that guard up…don't forget…bell…straight at him…"
We had the signal, it was time…Greg gave me a wink, ruffled my hair and said;
"Cumon Taff…do it…do it…DO IT!!"
I put my gum shield in and followed Greg out of the changing room into the cauldron as where three to four hundred soldiers were baying for blood, and the announcer announced the next bout (mine)…
"THE NEXT BOUT IS A LIGHT-WELTERWEIGHT BOUT BETWEEN, IN THE RED CORNER FROM 24 FIELD SQUADRON…LCPL THOMAS, AND IN THE BLUE CORNER FROM 9 PARA SQUADRON…LCPL METSON!!"

As I approached the ring I thought…"Eddie Metson…I'm sure I know that name", Greg then gave me one last bit of advice; "Focus Taff…fucking focus"

I could see Stevie Gillies in the red corner and climbed the steps, as the cheering and shouting reached a crescendo…like Greg in the changing rooms, he winked, held the ropes apart and I stepped into the ring and heard distant shouts of "Cumon Taff…drop the para" and "knock him out Thomo". I faced the corner whilst Steve Gillies gave me the last words of advice, and the referee came over and checked I was wearing a gum shield, checked my gloves and said;

"Box" and he lowered his eyes to my nether regions.

"Fuck…I forgot to put it in Sir" Total embarrassment ensued the announcer made everyone aware at what I'd done…or hadn't done in this case. It was made more embarrassing by the fact that I was wearing boxing gloves and couldn't put it in myself. Stevie Gillies looked at me and shook his head before placing the 'box' in my shorts to raucous cheers and laughter from the crowd…I just shrugged my shoulders. The referee called us in to the middle of the ring to read us the riot act and as soon as I saw my opponent, Eddie Metson, and quickly realised this wasn't the first time I'd seen him…I remembered him from the boxing team at J.L.R.R.E. at Dover…whereas I had never boxed before, Eddie was a good boxer with twenty or thirty fights behind him…this was going to be interesting, but this is how the British Army rolled with 'novice' boxing. Whenever a soldier was posted his 'boxing' card often mysteriously 'disappeared' and a new one would be generated and placed in the soldier's records, and 'hey presto' the soldier was a 'novice' boxer again…Joe Kirby was classed a 'novice' boxer because his boxing 'card' said he was, despite his forty plus amateur fights, losing just the one…the Midlands A.B.A. Final against Errol Christie (who later became a professional boxer). Here I was, on the verge of fighting a fellow 'novice' boxer, Eddie Metson…oh the irony! As we touched gloves…I smiled, not at Eddie…who was scowling at me, but at the irony of the situation. We went back to our corners, turned to face each other and something strange happened …despite the thunderous noise in the building, I couldn't hear anything except the referee's voice…it was as if the referee, Eddie and me were the only people in the building.

Suddenly, the bell went and I remembered what Greg had said, and sprinted...yes, sprinted across the ring, and as Eddie turned I caught him by surprise and jabbed him in the face with my left...it would be the last time during the fight that I would catch him by surprise, as his experience immediately 'kicked in'. Before I knew it, in one movement, he held me, spun me around, released me and jabbed me back with a good left...as my head snapped back I thought; "What the fuck happened there?" This became the pattern of the entire first round, I'd throw a jab...sometimes I'd connect and other times I'd miss or Eddie would parry the jab before, again, holding me, spinning me onto the ropes and jabbing me. Two minutes doesn't sound a long time but when you are continually being punched in the face by an experienced boxer, two minutes feels like an eternity. Then just before the end of the first round the tiredness and lack of strength (from not eating for two days and losing 10lb) was kicking in and I paused to take in a gulp of air, and my guard dropped...Eddie saw his chance and connected with a good punch. Down I went, my gum shield disappearing into row 3 (never did find that gum shield), and I was looking up at the referee standing above me and listening to the countdown;

"1...2...3..."

I couldn't move, my mind was saying "what just happened...who's that with the dickie bow?"

"...4...5...6..."

"Where was I...what's all that cheering about...where's it coming from?"

"...7..."

"It's nice here...I'll just lie here a bit longer"

"...8...9..."

"Who are you?"

"...10..."

I could see the man with the dickie bow waving his arms across his body and shaking his head, then I could see Stevie Gillies looking at me...what was going on? It was then I realised that I'd just been knocked out...Steve and Greg helped me to my feet and back to the corner where they brought out the smelling salts to help me come around and re-gather my thoughts. Eddie then came over, and with no hard feelings, we shook hands.

That would be my one and only fight…it may be that my boxing career is the shortest on record, as it lasted 1min 48 secs…I never even made it to the end of the first round. The funniest thing was watching it back on video that same evening…there has never been a start to a boxing match like that, before or since…as I sprinted across the ring and my jab connected with Eddie as he turned in his corner. Greg and I laughed and he said;

"You may have been shit Taff, but at least you had the guts to get in the ring!"

Long Eaton RFC (and Ilkeston R.U.F.C.)

After approximately 5-6 years of 'pressure' rugby (playing many cup games and representative rugby during my time at J.L.R.R.E. 34 and 24 Field Squadron) I enjoyed my first full season of civilian rugby at Long Eaton R.F.C. The shackles were off and personally I played with a sense of freedom and I believe that first season at Long Eaton was strangely the most enjoyable season of my entire rugby career despite winning only eight of the thirty games we played that season of 1986/87. I travelled all over the East Midlands playing rugby and enjoyed the company of great team-mates and the more senior members of the club…legends such as Jim Startin, Len Jones, Don Mackintosh, Bernard Hooper, Mike Smith, Jim Jordison and not forgetting the welsh-speaking Kidwelly born Derek Deacon. There were great times on and off the field and I had the honour of scoring the club's first ever league try in our opening league fixture when the English league system was introduced for the 1987/88 season. It was great to be part of a developing club and I have fond memories of starting our own clubhouse on West Park and the bad luck of tearing my cruciate ligaments in a home game against Dronfield. Unfortunately, due to conflict with my now ex-wife I had to leave Long Eaton and played two season with Ilkeston…despite enjoying two seasons with Ilkeston I never really wanted to leave Long Eaton R.F.C. and the friends that I had made there…but I had no choice!

My abiding memories of my time in Derbyshire are winning the player of the season at the end of my first season at Long Eaton, the Derbyshire cup game v Derby in 1987/88 season, my bogey club…Dronfield, the great Boxing Day games and

337

an event one night at training on the Gallows Field with Ilkeston R.U.F.C!!!!!

Leaving 24 Field Squadron was hard at first as I was leaving a lot of good friends and as a rugby team we had been very successful. It was time for a new challenge and in that summer of 1986 I found myself based at Chilwell in Nottingham with Military Works Force. Initially, I had made contact with Nottingham R.F.C. and was on the verge of going to a training session with them when I saw an advert for Long Eaton R.F.C. in Rugby World, and before I knew it I was training with them (see Chapter 4) and looking forward to my first proper season of civilian rugby. Long Eaton was a great little club, but when I joined they still didn't have their own clubhouse...during my first season we used Parklands Adult Education Centre, which was ideal as it was only a short walk into Town. Playing rugby at Long Eaton during that 1986-87 season I played with a freedom I'd never experienced before...the previous five or six seasons had been a continual merry go round of cup games and representative rugby where winning was all that mattered. I was turning up on a Saturday to play teams I'd never heard of, in places such as Belper, Coalville & Market Bosworth that were unknown names to a lad from South Wales. There was no pressure, at twenty-three I was one of the elder players in the team, the majority of the team (Ian Mackintosh, Scott Hutchinson, Chris Brookes, Rob Jones, Malcolm Watling, Paul Gardener, Jimmy Rogers and others) had been part of a successful Colts team a couple of years earlier and were all around twenty or twenty-one years old, therefore, the expectation wasn't too high as we were a fairly inexperienced side. Don't get me wrong, we played to win but other teams were often stronger and more experienced. But every week was an adventure and fun, and I think it showed in the rugby I played that season. I had never been a prolific try scorer in previous teams over previous seasons and tended to only score perhaps four or five tries a season, my main contribution had been as a kicker (including goal kicker) and making the odd break which put others in for tries. But this season, I probably doubled my previous try-scoring feats with some great individual tries, and my kicking from the hand, goal kicking and kick-offs appeared to have reached new levels due to this freedom I was experiencing...I was really enjoying my rugby. This was despite the fact that we only won eight and drew one of the thirty games we played. When we won the scores were fairly close in games against Rugby St Andrews (30-24), North Kesteven Old Boys (9-6) and Bingham (17-4), but when we lost, we lost heavily against some very good sides such as South Leicester (6-30), Nuneaton Old Heads (19-54), Belgrave (9-50) and Kersley (0-54). We also lost a local derby against a very good Ilkeston side 26-6, but we did do well in the Derbyshire Cup, making it to the semi-finals before losing 38-12 to Chesterfield (a game we were winning 12-10 at half-time). I played with some great players during my career, but I have to mention Danet Beckford…he was something special and I was lucky to play with him when he was in his prime. He was a left winger and our Captain during my first season and some of the tries he scored defied logic…he ran in tries from thirty to forty metres out down a tramline no wider than a metre, a burly player with electric speed and a low centre of gravity…he was difficult to stop and I was in awe of his strength and speed…great player. In addition to my new friendship with Danet, I also enjoyed new friendships I made on the field with other great players such as Andy Gibbs, Peter Podboraczynski (known affectionately as Pete Pod), Scott Hutchinson and the other young lads mentioned above which included my new partner in crime…Jimmy Rodgers. Off the field there was Don Mackintosh, Jim Startin and a great friend and 'adopted Dad' Derek Deacon…who had even driven to Norfolk Boxing Day morning to bring me back for the traditional game played against a Presidents XV. Most of my weekends would be spent with Derek, his wife Beryl (from Trimsaran) and their daughters Sarah and Sam…not forgetting 'Sian' a Great Dane who loved nibbling my moustache. Collectively, we also visited some great little pubs coming back from away games in others parts of Derbyshire, Nottinghamshire, Lincolnshire, Leicestershire etc, and when we played at home we had some fantastic nights in Long Eaton in pubs such as the 'Hole in the Wall', 'The Prince', 'The Corner Pin' and many, many more…many drunken nights which normally ended either in Platform One or in the Indian restaurant across the road. At the end of the season dinner I was shocked, but honoured, to receive the 'Player of the Year' award, something that, to this day, I am still very proud of and consider to be my greatest achievement during my rugby career.

The following season was still enjoyable but there were different and difficult challenges to overcome...a season that saw the start of the new leagues in English rugby, I was vice-captain of the 1st XV and it was a season which also resulted in a serious injury that nearly ended my rugby career. It was also the first season in which Long Eaton moved into its new clubhouse...humble beginnings of independence on West Park. Our first league game, and Long Eaton's first ever league game, was against Gainsborough and is memorable for two reasons. Firstly, I was fortunate to score Long Eaton's first ever try in the new English 'league', in a game we won 16-12, and my personal tally was twelve points (1 try, 2 conversions and 2 penalties). The other has nothing to do with the game, but with the journey to Gainsborough in Pat Costello's Vauxhall Nova...four rugby players and Pat's six month old Rottweiler, Max, what could possible go wrong? We set off from West Park and it was immediately apparent that Max didn't want to be in the 'boot' area of the car, he wanted to be in the back with me and Jimmy Rogers...we tried, and tried, and tried some more to keep Max in the boot, but after an hour me and Jimmy lost. We resigned ourselves to the fact that Max was bigger and stronger than us, and when we pulled up at Gainsborough's ground about thirty minutes later Max was lying on me and Jimmy and continually licking Jimmy in the face...probably to rub it in that he had won the battle. We only lost two games in the league that season against Belper (12-6) and a tough game against All Spartans (10-6), probably the dirtiest side I played against in twenty-seven years of rugby. After the game on West Park during the 1987-88 they were fighting amongst themselves...out and out thugs, and games against them in seasons that followed were never any different. We finished third that season which meant we just missed out on promotion to Notts, Lincs and Derbyshire Division 2. I was enjoying this second season at Long Eaton, but my season was cut short by a serious injury in a game at home to Dronfield. The first injury of the game saw another serious injury to one of their props as he dislocated his elbow and was screaming in pain and wouldn't let anyone touch him, continually screaming;
"LEAVE ME ALONE...LEAVE ME ALONE...LEAVE ME ALONE..."
We had to wait until the Ambulance turned up about twenty minutes later before he could be moved and the game could

carry on. The stoppage meant that the light started fading midway through the second half...in hindsight, the game should have probably been stopped in the first half. Ten minutes from the end of the game we had a scrum five metres from our line, Andy Gibb fed the ball into the scrum but Micky Parr hooked it so quickly that it came flying out of the back of the scrum before anyone could control it, I picked it up and was hoping to clear the ball into touch, but their openside flanker had hold of my shirt. I turned my head slightly and with one swipe of the arm I managed to successfully get free. As I turned my head to look back up the field;

"OOMPH""

The scrum had broken up and I stepped straight into the path of Dronfield's twenty-one stone hooker and it was like hitting a brick wall...my ten and a half stone frame came to a complete standstill with exception of my left leg...they could hear the tear on the touchline, about forty metres away. A noise described by someone as being similar to two strips of velcro being pulled apart...I had torn my cruciate ligaments. I tried to play on but the pain was unbearable and I had to come off...unbelievably, I played two weeks later in a 19-10 win over Keyworth and scored probably my best ever drop goal in a Long Eaton shirt. But following an operation and extensive physiotherapy it would be six months later in October 1988 before I would play first team rugby again...I was twenty five years old. I played another three seasons at Long Eaton but I was never quite the same player after that injury...I lost a half a yard of pace and whilst I was physically OK, I never mentally recovered from the injury. It was always in the back of my mind, but I successfully adapted my style of play accordingly to compensate. I still loved playing for Long Eaton, as I was surrounded by great friends and I had now become involved in the committee, firstly as players secretary (basically letting players know each week where and which team they were playing for) and then in my final season I became Club Secretary. It was during that last season as a player (and still 1st XV vice-captain) and a member of the committee that I started to have problems with my wife who was starting to suggest that I should retire...I was only twenty-eight, rugby was a huge part of my life and I wasn't ready to retire! One Sunday I was down the clubhouse for selection for the following week's games when the phone rang...it was the

341

coach of the England Students XV. They had been having trials over the weekend in Trent College (a private school in Long Eaton) and there had been a few injuries which meant they were short of a full-back and a centre. It just so happened that me (full-back) and Jimmy Rogers (centre) were at the club that morning…forty-five minutes later we found ourselves playing in the final trial of the England Students XV, both in a team with Rupert Moon (who went on to play for Llanelli and Wales) and Steve Hackney (Leicester, England 'B' and the BaaBaas). Straight from the kick-off and subsequent line-out, the opposing outside-half dummied the kick to touch and spun the ball out, the full-back joined the line…I had been covering the kick to touch and was now racing across the field to try and close down the overlap, their winger…a certain Tony Underwood (brother of England Winger Rory), only had me to beat…he showed me the inside and then stepped outside leaving me clutching at thin air. As I hit the floor and looked back Tony was now ten to fifteen metres away and racing away toward our line…TRY! I don't remember much else about the game other than I scored a try toward the end that brought the scores level at 12-12, but missed the touchline conversion. It had been a great experience, made even more special by the letter the English RFU wrote to the club thanking Jimmy and I for helping them out at short notice and that…'had we been students we would have been carefully considered for selection'. As I said above my then wife didn't like the fact I had Long Eaton R.F.C. in my life nor the friends that I had made there…she gave me an ultimatum, "Either join another rugby club or retire…or I will leave you". I had no choice…I had to leave Long Eaton R.F.C., the club where I had enjoyed playing my rugby, playing over a hundred times for the 1st XV and scoring well over seven hundred points, and where I had made fantastic friendships on and off the field. It was a very hard decision to leave Long Eaton and to this day I regret doing so…I felt that I was too young to retire at twenty eight…sad day indeed. And that's why I joined Ilkeston R.F.C.….My wife thought that I loved Long Eaton so much that I would never join another rugby club, she was wrong, as much as I loved Long Eaton Rugby Club, I loved rugby more. I didn't join Ilkeston because I wanted a new challenge, or because it was a better club…I joined for no other reason than I just wanted to play rugby…her plan had backfired.

342

I enjoyed two happy seasons at Ilkeston, but when we played Long Eaton R.F.C. in a league game…it felt strange playing against players that I'd spent five seasons with, not just playing but also on a social level. Therefore, I took no pleasure from the fact that Ilkeston won 10-0 in a very tight game. I toured Ireland with Ilkeston, but it was a bit of a let down on the rugby front as, despite taking a full strength first team, Bandon were still in a cup competition and couldn't play us and we played a game against a $2^{nd}/3^{rd}$ mixed team which we won convincingly. However, we had a great time on the social side in Bandon and Kinsale. My abiding memories of my time at Ilkeston are the day we played Derby 2nd XV in the second team cup and a night at training one summer's evening before the start of my second season. In the game against Derby, a similar incident happened that had happened in the game against Kent Police when I was at 24 Sqn…one of the Derby players tackled me late and then wouldn't let me get up. When I managed to finally wriggle free, but still lying on the floor, I swung a punch around and hit this player in the side of the head…we both started to get to our feet as players from both teams and the referee ran toward us. Luckily for me the referee got to us first and stepped between us…as we straightened up, I stopped at my height of 5ft 9in, but the Derby player kept going…and going…and going. I gulped, the player I had hit was their huge 6ft 5in South African No8…thankfully, I hit him so hard in the temple he didn't know whether it was Christmas or Easter or whether his name was Arthur or Martha. Thankfully, I got a warning (no yellow or red cards in those days). The second incident involved a young teenage couple…who were obviously very much in love with each other – we had been training on the first team pitch, but halfway through the session we split into forwards and backs. We (the backs) stayed on the first team pitch whilst the forwards went down a small banking to where the second team pitch was located. Initially, they just continued warming up and started to jog around the perimeter of the entire bottom field, when they were on the far side, where there was a lot of dead ground and long grass between the pitch and the canal, they passed a young teenage couple…who were making love in the long grass. Twenty minutes or so later the forwards re-joined us backs on the first team pitch and Ian Jones, our second row, proceeded to tell us what they had seen, finishing

343

up with one the funniest statements I'd heard about people making love which was, in a broad Ilkeston lilt;
"...she wor lying there having a whale of a time...as he wor right up t't back wheels!!"
Five minutes later, the same young teenage couple were walking up the banking, past the first team pitch and toward the *Gallows Inn* pub on the main road...we let out a huge collective cheer, and the response was brilliant...the girl was hiding, her coat hood covering her head like a criminal coming out of court, and the lad was arms raised reveling in the glory of what he had done and acting as if he'd just scored a goal in the F.A.Cup final. Brilliant!

I didn't start the 1993-94 season as we were preparing to return to Wales...I was eventually returning home after fourteen years where I would enjoy playing some more rugby before I eventually retired.

New Tredegar, Senghenydd and retirement

On returning to Wales I didn't play rugby straight away due to work commitments. I had to wait until the 1994/95 season to wear my boots again and half a season playing with an old friend, Ian 'Taff' Pritchard, at New Tredegar R.F.C. This was followed by a season at Senghenydd R.F.C. until my cruciate ligaments in my left knee snapped in the final game of the season against Taffs Well R.F.C...and as Neil Hughes said "it looked as if a sniper had shot me from Tan-y-Bryn!!

A year after moving back to Wales I found myself travelling to New Tredegar to play rugby with an old friend...Ian 'Taff' Pritchard. It was great to see Pritch again, it had been about six years since I'd last seen him. Like me, he was out of the army now and was captain of New Tredegar 1st XV, and he was waiting to start university. Following a training session I was put on the bench for the first team game against Fleurs De Lys 2nd XV, but the fifteen to twenty minutes I played that day would unfortunately be the last time I played with Pritch. This was due to two reasons, firstly, I played the next couple of games for the 2nd XV, and secondly, when Pritch joined university, UWIC (University of Wales Institute, Cardiff) stopped him playing rugby for New Tredegar R.F.C. Our brief reunion on the field was over, but we did have one more

344

memorable night out in Bargoed. After a good few beers in the New Tredegar R.F.C. clubhouse, we booked a minibus taxi to take a group of us into Bargoed, where we were dropped off at *The Plas*...as we pulled up outside *The Plas*, directly in the doorway were two lads fighting, hefty punches being thrown (and landed) by both, before the bouncers broke it up. I turned to Pritch and said;

"I see Bargoed hasn't changed then". We both laughed.

Twelve years earlier I'd been to Bargoed with Pritch when we both served together at 24 Field Squadron RE...we'd had some memorable nights in the Saturday night disco in the old Bargoed rugby club where Pritch had introduced me to his old school friend, Melinda Griffiths (see Chapter 3). But we won't mention what Pritch saw through the set of double doors that separated the living-room from the dining-room at Melinda's house...my lips are sealed!

After *The Plas* we found ourselves in *Blisters (Cleopatra's)*, Bargoed's premium, but only, nightclub...what a shithole! But at least we could drink more beer. The night took an interesting twist when we left the club, outside there was a girl crying...she was breaking her heart, I walked over and asked;

"What's the matter love?" Expecting it to be 'man' trouble, but didn't expect her to say;

"I've lost my keys...and I won't be able to get in my house" Her friend now joined us and tried to console her.

"Could you stay with your friend?"

"I wanna go home" she sobbed. Then almost immediately, she stopped crying, looked at me and said;

"Could you help me?"

"Yeah...sure" I said perplexed, wondering how I could help.

"Could you kick my front door in?" and she smiled.

"Umm...ok...do you live far from here?"

"Only round the corner...cumon" She grabbed my hand and we disappeared into a lane with her friend quickly following. I shouted to Pritch and the others where I was going and why...to be fair, they looked confused, but I said;

"HANG ON PRITCH...I WON'T BE LONG...JUST GOT TO KICK HER FRONT DOOR IN!" pointing at the girl dragging me up the lane.

Two minutes later we were stood in front of an old wooden front door on an end of terrace house.

"There you go...this one" I paused and said;

"This is definitely your house...you are not having me on"

"Yeah, yeah…don't worry, I definitely live yuh"
"So I kicked her door in…it only took one kick, the lock was broken and the door frame was splintered.
"That Ok" I said
"Thank you, oh thank you so much" She grabbed me and kissed me on the cheek. I left her waving frantically, so happy that I'd kicked her door in and that she could get in her house. I wondered if when she woke up sober in the morning she'd have a different view on things, and I wondered if she'd still feel the same about the knight in shining armour…that kicked in her door. Bizarre…but this was Bargoed, and past experiences taught me to always expect the unexpected in Bargoed. I quickly re-joined Pritch and the others who were thankfully still waiting for a taxi.

I played another half a dozen games for New Tredegar, including two consecutive weeks at probably the worst rugby pitch I had ever played on in twenty seven years of rugby…Trefil R.F.C. A pitch high above the 'heads of the valleys' road, between Tredegar and Rassau, nr Ebbw Vale, open to the elements, six to eight inches of mud and a steep slope from top to bottom. The first week I was there was with the 1st XV and we lost narrowly in the Rhymney Valley Cup, and the following week I was back with the 2nd XV and we comfortably beat their seconds. They were a great set of lads at New Tredegar, surprisingly fit for a junior civilian team and they played good rugby. But the costs associated with travelling from Beddau for training and games was getting too much and I finished the season prematurely. Additionally, I wasn't getting the same 'buzz' from playing as I once had and remembered a conversation I'd had with the RE Corps XV coach, Willie Higgins, ten years earlier when I asked him;
"When do you know when it's time to retire from rugby Willie?"
"You'll know…" he said "…you'll know"
Perhaps I was reaching that point, but I played another game at the end of the following season for Senghenydd 2nd XV in a game at Aberdare…the end was near, I was thirty-three years old, but I fancied just one more full season before finishing my rugby career. As we now lived in Abertridwr in the Aber Valley, I decided to play for Senghenydd the next season (1996-97). It was walking distance from the house and I

346

thought it would be an ideal way of getting to know more people in the valley and play rugby.

As the summer months rolled by, I was looking forward to the new season more and more and couldn't wait to start training with Senghenydd and play for the 2nd XV…I just wanted to enjoy my rugby. It was a great season and I only missed the one game…the day 'A' and 'Rh' were born. I also flirted with professionalism when I played a league game for the 1st XV against Bridgend Athletic when I got paid £10 (it would have been £15 but I'd missed one of the two training sessions that week)…I didn't let it go to my head and I didn't waste the money as I spent it all on beer that same night. Whilst playing with the seconds there was no pressure, as there were no league or cup games to worry about and even though we played to win, it didn't matter if we lost…the beer still tasted the same. The most memorable game for me was a home game against Treherbert R.F.C., a game we won 19-10, and it was memorable for two reasons. Firstly, I hit one of the sweetest drop goals I think I'd ever kicked, it sailed high between the posts and even cleared the clubhouse behind the posts…and it was in front of my children; 'K', 'R' and 'G' who were suitably impressed that their father could kick a ball so far. It wasn't the winning points of the game, but it did mean we were now two scores in front and it took the pressure off. But mainly, it was a great memory to have that my kids were proud of something I had done on a rugby field and that was better than any tries I'd scored or kicks I'd kicked previously. Secondly, on the touchline in front of the small stand there was an altercation between our winger and theirs and a couple of punches were thrown…this was a signal to our full-back, Jason Williams (who loved a good punch-up), to run twenty or thirty metres to get involved and also started throwing punches. Then something bizarre happened that I'd never seen before and that I have seen since…the handful of Treherbert supporters who were on that side of the pitch, started to drag Jason over the barrier that surrounded the pitch, punching him at the same time. All hell broke loose, and fairplay, Jason gave as good as he got, before the referee gained control and the game continued…bizarre, but funny, and in my mind, I can still see that moment when Jason was dragged over the barrier!!

347

The last game of the season saw me again playing in a 1st XV game at full-back against Taffs Well R.F.C. We got well-beaten that day as we fielded a mixed team of first and second team players against a strong Taffs Well team. About ten to fifteen minutes into the second half I was shepherding an innocuous ball into touch, but when I stopped it was my left leg that took the sudden impact from the hard ground and it suddenly crumbled under me, I hit the deck…Neil Hughes, who was standing on the banking close to where it happened, told me after the game that;

"You went down so quick I thought a sniper had shot you from Tan-y-Bryn" (council houses on the opposite side of the valley)"

Needless to say, as much as I tried to and wanted to carry on, I had to leave the pitch through injury. A trip to A&E at the Royal Gwent on the Monday confirmed that the cruciate ligaments in my left leg had finally snapped, 9 years after I tore them in 1988…that was that, my rugby career, in which I'd probably played over five hundred games and scored over a thousand points, and that had provided great memories had come to an end. A career where I was lucky to have shared rugby pitches, all over the UK, with some great rugby players, many of whom are still friends today. I believe I wasn't a bad player, however, I also believe that I was lucky that I played with great players and played for some great and highly successful teams which probably made me look better than I actually was…a very humbling experience!

I was now thirty-four years old…I hung up my boots and remembered the words of Willie Higgins;
"You'll know when it's time to retire"
It was time…or was it?

Powerleague – Cardiff

There are those that may not be familiar with the 'Powerleague' set-up; it is a series of venues that include a number of outside, floodlit and individually fenced-off 5-a-side football pitches. It would be here that I would enjoy playing competitive 5-a-side football in a team that included my sons, 'K' and 'G', and Gareth (my daughter, 'R's, partner)!!

348

In late 2009, Gareth, my daughter's ('R') boyfriend, talked about entering a 5-a-side team in the Powerleague at Whitchurch in Cardiff. The talk soon turned into reality as a few weeks later we (Gareth, 'G', 'K', Jon, Alex Langford, Paul Walsh or 'G' and me) headed to Cardiff for a 'friendly'. The finer points of 5-a-side took a bit of getting used to and that 'friendly' made us realise the importance of using 'rolling' subs every couple of minutes, using the sides of the pitch (the pitch was walled on all four sides) as a sixth man and adhering to the rules. We lost the 'friendly' but it gave us an important insight into the challenge we faced and the 'league' conditions we had to learn. The Powerleague is well run and ran pretty much like clockwork…we'd be given a time, a pitch number and a referee, and give or take a few minutes, the start times we were given were normally adhered to. As a new team, we started in the bottom division, Division Four, but that didn't mean the games were easy, as we still had to get used to the pitch, the speed of the passing etc. Thankfully, we learnt quickly and winning became a habit and we won the league…we were now promoted to Division Three. The standard in this division was similar to that in Division Four, but I noticed that as we waited for our games, we'd watch games in Divisions One and Two and they were a different level. I knew that if we got promoted again my knee wouldn't be able to keep up with the fast pace of the higher divisions nor would my knee be able to cope with the ferocity of the tackles…at forty-six, I accepted that Division Three was my limit. We did win the Division Three title and thankfully I had stayed injury free…it was time to bow out gracefully before my luck ran out. It was gratifying that even at the age I was I held my own with players twenty plus years younger than me, but playing competitive 5-a-side football with two of my sons meant the world to me and in some respects the medals we won for winning Divisions Three and Four mean more to me than other accolades I have won during my sporting career…purely as I had won them by playing in the same team as my sons. It was great sharing the anticipation before each game, playing the game itself and reliving the goals and tackles over a beer in the bar afterwards. Not many fathers and sons share moments like that in football or rugby…I feel honoured and blessed that I got to experience all those things with two of my sons, 'K' and 'G'.

Back to Long Eaton R.F.C. – Vets rugby!!!

*In recent times I have had the pleasure of returning to Long
Eaton R.F.C. and playing a handful of 'vets' games at a club
where I had so many happy memories during the late-eighties
and early-nineties. The first of these was to play in a game in
2012 that commemorated the 25th Anniversary of the opening
of the clubhouse...as I had played for the first team v
Presidents XV back in 1987 I was keen to make the trip to
Long Eaton and once again proudly wear a Long Eaton
shirt!!!!*

I pulled up into the car park at West Park Leisure Centre in
Long Eaton, and I could see Long Eaton rugby club and the
rugby pitches in the distance...it was 2012 and it felt good to
be back for a rugby match to celebrate the 25th Anniversary of
the opening of the clubhouse back in 1987. This would be my
first rugby match for fifteen years, and my first in a Long
Eaton shirt for twenty-one years...I was excited to be playing
in a team with a few former team mates and to be back at my
spiritual rugby home. Despite enjoying my rugby at Ilkeston
between September 1991 and April 1983, I'd always regretted
leaving Long Eaton R.F.C. The club was a huge part of my
life and I'd never forgotten the friends I'd made there and the
good times I'd had both on and off the field. As we walked to
the clubhouse the memories came flooding back, and the
nerves I always used to experience before games, returned for
the first time in over nineteen years. The pitches had been
moved from their previous positions close to Sawley Cricket
Club on the left hand side of West Park and were now adjacent
to the clubhouse on the right hand side of the park. I walked
through the double doors into the clubhouse and the first
person I saw was Pat Costello, who smiled and gave me a
great big hug, shouting:
"HUW THOMAS...I HEARD YOU WERE COMING TO
PLAY...GREAT TO SEE YOU AGAIN OLD FRIEND..."
and he introduced me to the colts captain, saying;
"This is the best player to have ever played for Long Eaton" I
scoffed at this exaggeration and said;
"Cumon Pat...really" Nice to hear and humbling, but given
some of the players I played with and those that had played
before me, I felt I was not worthy of that honour. Then I saw

350

Chris Brookes, we greeted each other like the old friends we were and he said;

"Right…the outside half is here". It felt as if the clock had turned back the time, as Paul Gardener, Joe Jerrett and then Darryl Webster said "Hi" and …I was home, and I couldn't wait to get on the field again, and in a Long Eaton shirt. I swore to myself that I would never play rugby for another team again, if I was to play rugby again in the future, it would only ever be in a Long Eaton shirt.

We were soon getting changed, and as the familiar smells of liniment and deep heat filled the air, and the banter levels increased in that familiar Long Eaton dialect I knew and loved, I smiled to myself and thought…"I've missed this". I was soon running out onto the field with others, and as we tossed the ball about, played touch rugby, familiarized ourselves with each other (especially with my new scrum-half , Jacko), warmed up and got a couple of practice kicks in…it was like stepping back in time. But this time I was forty-nine years old playing in a 'Vets' game against one of our old foes, 'Nottingham Moderns' to celebrate the 25th Anniversary of the opening of the clubhouse…twenty five years earlier, Chris Brookes, Paul Gardener, Pat Costello and myself had all played for the 1st XV against a President's XV to commemorate the opening of the clubhouse. It was a great game which we narrowly lost, and on a personal level I managed to play the whole game…my kicking from the hand and goal-kicking were pretty good (for an 'old timer'), but there were no telling breaks or side-stepping of the opposition, those days were long gone and whilst the mind was still willing the body certainly can't do what it used to do in my twenties…whereas I thought I was sprinting, for those watching from the side it looked more like a gentle jog or a fast walk! I enjoyed my first outing in 'Vets' rugby and was pleased to see it was played in such a great spirit. As I came off the field there were more surprises as I saw the old club chairman, Don Mackintosh, I immediately went over and gave him a big hug…it was great to see him after twenty or more years. When I got in the bar afterwards Don came over and told Ada how he remembered the first time I came to the club in 1986 and he lent me £5 to have a drink with the boys after training (see Chapter 4). I met my old partner in crime, Jimmy Rogers, and sadly an unrecognizable Mitch Grant, who was now a shadow of the bearded, burley second row I once knew, and was struggling as an Alzheimer sufferer who unfortunately didn't know who I was. After I took Ada and Amy back to the hotel I returned to the clubhouse where the hilarious Malcolm Watling had also arrived and I had a few beers with him and Chris Brookes as we remembered those days many moons ago when we all played together for the 1st XV. It was a great weekend.

I returned a few weeks later and played another game at Amber Valley with another old friend, Scott Hutchinson, who apart from a few grey hairs, hadn't changed a bit and he was still trying to mimic my welsh accent…and still failing miserably. Despite losing heavily that day it was great to play in the same team as Scott again, and also another legend from the good old days, Kev Mumby. That evening I met another Long Eaton hero in *The Hole in the Wall*, and a man I had been very much looking forward to meeting again, Danet Beckford. It was wonderful seeing him again and also Paul Yates, another winger, who had emigrated to America after my first season at Long Eaton in 1987. Meeting my fellow team mates was a dream come to true and I have travelled to Long Eaton and played another couple of times since; firstly, I went and played in Joe Jerrett's 50th Birthday game which I thought was another 'Vet's game that turned out to be a seconds/thirds mixed team and despite the speedy youngsters on the field that day, it was a fantastic game of rugby against a strong Chesterfield XV which finished in a remarkable 40-40 draw. I kicked five out of six conversions that day including a sweet conversion which my son, 'Rh', filmed and put on 'Facebook'…he was proud of me that day and that is another memory that is special to me…it takes a lot to impress 'Rh'. Secondly, I played in a triangular mini-tournament with Bingham and Nottingham Moderns, which saw me win a rugby match in a Long Eaton shirt for the first time since 1991…a long wait but well worth it in the end.

I didn't just return to Long Eaton to play rugby, I also went back in 2016 for the 'stag do' of another old friend and former 1st XV team mate, Micky Parr. We left Long Eaton on a bus and made our way to Manchester to watch Sale Sharks v Saracens and embarrassingly got dropped off at Sale's old ground…we had to re-call the bus to pick us back up and take us to the new ground that Sale Sharks share with Salford Rugby League team…a good five or six miles away. There were many of my old 1st XV team mates out that day including Scott Hutchinson, Danet Beckford, Kev Mumby, Malcolm Watling, Pat Costelow, Darren Brookes, Micky Parr and my old scrum-half, Andy Gibbs. We were joined by Don Mackintosh (still going strong in his 80s), my 24 Sqn and HQ MWF army mate, Jake Maiden (who met us at the ground). Lastly, Micky's best man, Andy Dyke was 'master of ceremony' for the day, another great friend (Mick, Andy and myself used to drink together in The Chequers in Breaston, and on a Saturday we'd often find ourselves back at Andy's house playing Trivial Pursuit…drunk!). We had a great day watching Sale Sharks play out a thrilling 36-36 draw with Saracens, before watching England beat Ireland 21-10 in the Six Nations and then heading into Manchester for a night visiting the 'real ale' pubs in the 'arty' quarter. Great night with great company!

It has been fantastic returning to Long Eaton R.F.C., playing rugby and meeting old friends again…it has and always will hold a special place in my heart. It was also an honour to have my name on the side of the 'personalised player compartment' in the 1st XV changing room as a player that played a certain amount of games over the years in a given position…there were many names in that changing room I recognised, which was a lovely gesture by the club for our past commitments. I am fifty-five years old as I write this, and I am hoping there maybe one or two games left in these old legs. There is nothing better than running onto a rugby field…it doesn't matter whether you are ten, twenty-one, thirty-four or fifty-five years old, it is a wonderful feeling and I have been lucky to experience that feeling for almost fifty years.

Other Sports

The majority of people probably have at least one sport that they enjoy playing…even if it's just darts at the local pub! However, in addition to rugby and football, I have tried playing many sports such as tennis, badminton, squash, table-tennis, hockey, basketball, fishing, golf (well pitch and putt or crazy golf!), cricket, athletics, pool, snooker, clay pigeon shooting, archery, cycling, sailing, volleyball etc…I didn't

*enjoy them all and I was certainly less than average at most,
but I had a go! There were sports that I didn't try such as
polo, water polo, horse jumping, crown green bowling, motor
racing etc, but given the chance, I probably would have. It's
easy to see that sport has played a huge part in my life and
whether playing seriously or just for fun...I was always
extremely competitive!*

As you have seen throughout this chapter, I mainly played
rugby and football competitively, and dipped my toe in the
water with boxing...well for 1 minute 48 seconds. Other
sports I played competitively include cross country
running/athletics and cricket, but on a much smaller scale. I
sort of stumbled into cross country running when our sports
teacher, Mr Craig, asked who wanted to run in a cross country
race against a team from Ynysawdre Comprehensive. I and
about fifteen others volunteered and we headed off to Sarn
(outside Bridgend) where their school was located...I won the
race by about 100m and then found myself in a trial for the
county (back in 1974 it was still Glamorgan). I didn't win the
race but I did get selected for the county team, and as a result,
represented the county in the Welsh Championships at
Newtown in Powys. I don't remember much about the race
other than I didn't finish in the top ten, but I remember more
about the journey to Newtown on the bus. The bus picked me
up at our school in Bryntirion and there were various other
pick-up points in South Wales. It was a hot day and the
temperature on the bus was uncomfortably high, this was
mixed with the continuous stop/start and travelling up and
down the hills in South Wales provided a toxic atmosphere,
especially for those prone to travel sickness. It wasn't long
before children were vomiting either on the floor or into
plastic bags...understandably the stench of the vomit created a
chain reaction and the sounds of vomiting and the stench
increased. As the bus crawled up hills the vomit would travel
toward the back of the bus, and when the bus sped down the
hills the vomit travelled down the bus and much of it on the
left hand side of the bus ended up in the stairwell where we
got on and left the bus. I remember when the bus pulled up
into the car park in Newtown and the driver opened the door, a
wave of vomit left the bus and created a puddle of sick about
1m in circumference making it difficult for us to get off the
bus...but it was great to take in a gulp of fresh air once we'd

354

left the bus – the trouble was we knew that we'd have to get back on the bus later to return home. I joined Bridgend YMCA and ran in other races, but never emulated that early success, and despite also running in 1500m races in that summer of 1975, I found it difficult to do the additional individual training required to progress in the sport. Therefore, by the time I was fourteen my once promising cross country/athletics career had ended.

I had also enjoyed playing cricket, but as a child growing up in Bridgend this was nothing more than a group of friends with a cricket bat, a tennis ball and a milk crate (for the wickets). It wasn't until I joined the army did I play cricket more competitively, briefly at Junior Leaders Regiment RE at Dover and in a limited overs competition in the summer of 1985 whilst I was at 24 Field Squadron...opening the batting with the OC, Major Newns. The only thing with cricket is that I didn't mind batting, but I found the 'fielding' part boring...so boring. I couldn't bowl...well, that's not strictly true, I was a spin bowler but without the spin, and naturally I was about as much use as an ashtray on a motorbike on the bowling front so I was always somewhere out in the field (normally safely out of the way, near the boundary), patiently waiting for the ball to come my way which, if I was lucky, might be two or three times during the opposition's innings...like I said, boring! Ideally, I would have just batted and then gone straight home afterwards. Inevitably, I never played cricket again after that summer of 1985, and it's safe to say, the likes of cricket arenas such as Lords, The Oval, Headingly or Trent Bridge didn't miss out!

As I point out in the introduction I have participated in many different sports, but mainly as hobbies or purely for enjoyment of relaxation. When I was in school, friends and I joined the leisure centre in Bridgend where we would play squash, badminton or table tennis, but never competitively in a team...it was only competitive to the point that we would all try to beat each other, but it didn't really matter whether we won or lost. Tennis was a game I enjoyed playing with friends in Brancaster Staithe during those long summers when I was a teenager or with army friends, Nick Tranmer and Steve Roberts at the tennis courts in Chattenden and Chilwell respectively. When I was fifteen, I was lucky enough to have been picked to go on weekly organized sailing trips with Bryntirion Comprehensive to the sailing club at Margam (overlooking the steel works at Port Talbot...not the best view when sailing, but great fun nevertheless). I dabbled with hockey a couple of times, but that is one sport that I consider as being way too violent, especially when you play against the girls, as we once did in school...never again. Whoever thought it was a good idea to put a hockey stick in the hands of a hormonal teenage girl must have been smoking crack-cocaine...it was carnage! I have never really played golf, but throughout my life I have always enjoyed putting, pitch and putt or just plain crazy golf...it's just great fun, and whereas other sports, as you have seen were played to win, this was purely just played for fun. One sport I enjoyed, but again purely for fun, was archery. When I was posted to 39 Engineer Regiment RE at Waterbeach one of the troop corporals, Cpl Evans, was a keen archer and I spent few Wednesday afternoons, before I was posted to Chatham, enjoying the thrill of the arrows hitting the target. Volleyball, was a game we played to while away the hours when we were on army exercise...one of the first things we'd do when we set up a harbour area on Salisbury Plain was set up the volleyball court with white tape for the line marking, the net (normally tied between two trees)...we'd then take our combat jackets off and shirts and play volleyball...it was like a poor version of the famous volleyball scene in Top Gun with Maverick and Goose, but it provided hours of fun and staved off the boredom of waiting around for hours. I've tried clay pigeon shooting, fishing, rock climbing, abseiling, canoeing and basketball a few times, but these are sports that I never fully enjoyed or never had the chance to enjoy for one reason or another. The canoeing, rock-climbing and abseiling was part of my leadership training when I was a Junior Leader at Dover, we travelled to Lancaster and partook in rock-climbing and abseiling...I wasn't scared of heights in those carefree days, but I certainly wouldn't do it now. Canoeing used muscles I never even knew existed until we canoed the Carnforth Canal...the muscle ache after was like nothing I ever experienced before or after. Another abseiling experience certainly wasn't fun as we abseiled out of a helicopter during 'helicopter training' at 24 Sqn...not for the faint-hearted! As for snooker, pool and darts (all in their many forms) they have been played since I was a kid and are just great when you play

356

for fun, which was all I ever wanted to do…I had my rugby and football…the 'pub games' were only ever played for fun or maybe for a bet of a pound or a pint…I never played in teams, as that would have removed the fun element. Lastly, who can forget swimming and cycling…I have spent hours and hours doing both of these, both great forms of exercise. We'd cycle everywhere as kids and wouldn't think twice about cycling ten to fifteen miles on trips to the many beaches in the Vale of Glamorgan as teenagers, where we would then swim in the sea playing fun games such as 'sea rugby' or 'dodge the turd'…mainly at Ogmore-by-Sea & Southerndown.

As you can see, sport has been a huge part of my life and is something I have enjoyed, and which has provided me with many great memories. Whether it has been playing in and winning a cup final in rugby, diving around a temporary volleyball court in my combat trousers and boots on Salisbury Plain, enjoying a round of crazy golf in the sunshine at Barry Island or drinking with friends and playing pool at the local pub. I loved playing sport and am glad that I have tried so many different ones, but I haven't just enjoyed playing sport, as you will see in the next chapter I also love watching sport.

Chapter 7 – Sport (Part 2) – The Fan

If I wasn't playing sport I was watching it…any sport (with exception of horse racing and motor racing)! As seen in the previous chapter…sport has been a huge part of my life and I have gained as much enjoyment from watching sport as I have had from playing it! An incredible sporting moment can be emotional such as watching Nadia Comaneci scoring a perfect ten and winning gold medals in gymnastics at the 1976 Olympics in Montreal, seeing the winning shot in tennis finals at Wimbledon or Kelly Holmes winning BOTH 800m and 1500m gold medals at the 2004 Olympics in Athens. There have been so many memorable moments in sport that provided incredible memories and when re-watched can take you back to a particular moment in your life, much the same way a song can! Whilst I enjoy most sports, especially those featured in the Olympics, it is mainly football and rugby that have dominated my viewing of sport, and I have witnessed moments in my life, both live or on television, that are iconic!

Where does this love of sport come from…well, it would have to be family! Both my father and mother enjoyed sport…my father was and still is a huge fan of football, whereas my mother enjoyed athletics and tennis. My grand-fathers and Uncle Ivor were avid football followers, but the love of rugby definitely comes from my Nana Henson…I have photos of my Nan in the fifties and early sixties travelling to both Ireland and Scotland to follow Welsh rugby…there were even photos of her in the Western Mail (a Welsh newspaper) from one trip! During my childhood I surrounded myself with friends that all loved sport…understandably, watching sport was inevitable. I have spent many an hour on the side of a football pitch, in all weathers, watching my father, my sons ('K', 'G' and 'Rh') and An play football. However, I struggled to watch teams that I played for and was not playing due to injury…that was a real struggle! Believe it or not, there are sports I don't like and watching them is like watching paint dry…I can't stand any form of motor sport (with exception of speedway) or horse-racing…BORING!!!

As you have seen in chapter 6 and as you will see in this chapter, it could be assumed that if they televised fly swatting,

358

worm racing or spider wrestling I'd probably be one of the
first ones to watch it!!!

■■

The love of football (following in father's footsteps!!)

I have loved football for as long as I can remember and my
father was a major influence in me becoming the avid football
fan I am today. Despite my parents divorcing when I was five
and not seeing my father again until I was eight or nine years
old the role my father played in my developing love of football
cannot be underestimated! When I first started seeing my
father again I can remember him taking me to watch Cardiff
City at Ninian Park...we'd catch the bus outside the police
station in Aberkenfig and travel to Cardiff on a coach filled
with football songs and chants of the time! This ended shortly
after he married my step-mother as they moved away to
London. However, over the next seven years I would stay with
them and my father took me to Highbury to watch Arsenal,
and when they moved to Norfolk, he took me to Carrow Road
to watch Norwich. When I was fifteen they moved to Bristol
and we found ourselves at Ashton Gate watching Bristol City
and prior to joining the army, they returned to Wales, where
we found ourselves at the Vetch watching Swansea City.
Therefore, as a result of my father exposing me to so much
football it was inevitable that it became so important...I was
playing football in teams, with friends in school (and out of
school) and even on my own in the garden as I attempted to
emulate my favourite players such as Kevin Keegan and Stevie
Highway (I was a huge Liverpool fan growing up) that I
watched on 'Match of the Day' or 'The Big Match'. To this
day football is the one thing my father and I can talk about for
hours!!!

From those early days catching the bus from outside
Aberkenfig Police Station to go to Ninian Park and watch
Cardiff City, the tube to Highbury to watch Arsenal, or by car
to Carrow Road and Ashton Gate to watch Norwich City and
Bristol City respectively, my father always involved me in his
love of football...it was hardly surprising that I would grow up
loving a game where twenty-two men run around a field for
ninety minutes chasing and kicking a bag of wind! Since
becoming an adult I have been to many grounds to watch the

359

beautiful game including Ninian Park, Anfield, Oakwell, White Hart Lane, Villa Park, Highbury, Carrow Road, The Vetch, Liberty Stadium and even Wembley and the Millenium Stadium and many, many more…football has been a huge part of my life and probably always will be.

I was only eight years old when my father first started taking me to Ninian Park to watch Cardiff City…I remember the crowds, the chants, and some parts of the games I watched, but most of all I remember the corned beef pasties…they were awesome! Football in that 1971/72 season was daunting to an eight year old as three-quarters of the grounds in those days were terraces full of a swaying crowd baying for the opposition to be slaughtered in some way, shape or form…and I heard my first swear words at Ninian Park along with my first football songs/chants. The first goal that I can say I still remember to this day wasn't scored by a Cardiff City player it was scored in November 1971 by Billy Hughes for Sunderland in a game that Cardiff lost 2-1. The pitch that day (as were all pitches in the 1970s) was a sea of mud, conditions not suited to flowing football and these conditions played a huge part in the winning goal…there was no danger apparent as a Cardiff City defender passed the ball back to the keeper, Bill Irwin, unfortunately, the pass back fell a long way short as the ball got stuck in the mud on the edge of the eighteen yard box, Billy Hughes came from nowhere, Bill Irwin was caught in two minds, and Billy smashed the ball into the roof of the Cardiff net. But still, for an eight year old, those pasties were the main reason I enjoyed those visits to Ninian Park with my dad…as I write this I can almost taste them.

When I was ten years old my father lived in London and when I went to visit him and Shirley I was taken to Highbury to watch Arsenal and remember watching games against the great Leeds Utd side with Bremner, Giles, Lorimer, Clarke etc, and Liverpool with Keegan, Toshack, Highway and Smith etc, but for all the wrong reasons the game I remember more than any other was the Manchester Utd game. The trouble with football around this time was the hooliganism associated with it and the Arsenal v Manchester United game in 1972/73 season was particularly bad. The away supporters were in the famous 'clock' end and we were in the opposite end and my father had lifted me up onto advertising hoardings for me to watch the game. Around five minutes to three, just before the players came out of the tunnel for the start of the game, the Manchester United supporters invaded the pitch from the 'clock' end which prompted the Arsenal fans to invade the pitch from the end where we were and for the next ten to fifteen minutes there running battles all over the pitch before the police finally regained control, making many arrests. Another vivid image during the game was a glass bottle flying over my head and landing in the crowd to my left...the next thing I saw was a fan being carried out with blood pouring from a head wound from the same bottle. Yes, the early seventies were certainly different and I am surprised I didn't just stick to watching rugby after that day, but it was too late, I had already caught the footballing bug.

My father moved to Norfolk from London and Norwich City became the next team he would take me to see before moving to Bristol when I was fifteen where I would I started watching Bristol City...but not with my dad, I now started going with my cousin Stuart and his mate Nick Theobold...during that 1978/79 season Bristol City were enjoying playing first division football (the old 'Premiership' to you youngsters reading this). In a game against Arsenal I had the pleasure of watching an absolute legend, Liam Brady...he single handedly ran the show, scored two goals and had the sweetest left foot I have ever seen, he was absolute class. There was a trip to Anfield to watch Bristol City v Liverpool, where we stood on the famous 'Kop', probably not a good idea given that my Uncle Alan (Stuart's dad) spent the entire game shouting obscenities at the Liverpool players and the ref...I swear I could feel the eyes of the whole 'Kop end' boring into the back of my skull that day in a game Bristol City lost 3-0...how we got out of the ground alive is beyond me. The game I remember most though was the day Bristol City played Bolton Wanderers in what would be, Norman Hunter's last game for Bristol City and Nick had made a banner with the words "SUPER NORM PLEASE STAY AT CITY" emblazoned across it...it was a great day and Bristol City won 4-1 and each time they scored the crowd surged forward and I swear we ended up about twenty metres further down the terracing than where we'd started from. The last thing I remember about Bristol City was the fact that 'The Wurzels' always sang before each home game...legends.

When my father returned to Wales in early 1979 we then started to watch Swansea City, who were managed by player-manager, John Toshack, who were heading for promotion to the old division two (they had already been promoted from division four the previous season). It was down to a final game of the season against Chesterfield, a game Swansea had to win and to get promotion also had to rely on results from other grounds. With twenty minutes to go it was 1-1, and this prompted John Toshack to bring himself off the bench…stroke of genius as he headed the winner. Eventually, the results from around the other grounds came in and it was confirmed, Swansea City had been promoted to division two…it was time to party.

Over the years I have watched games at Gillingham, White Hart Lane, Villa Park and the City Ground in Nottingham as my love of the game continued, but despite being a Liverpool supporter through school, my allegiances would change in 1982…because of a girl, I started supporting Barnsley F.C.

Welsh rugby in the 1970s

I was lucky to grow up in the 1970s as this was a successful period for Welsh rugby…a later BBC video would describe this wonderful period as the 'Crowning Years' due to the three Grand Slams (1971, 1976 & 1978) and six Triple Crowns (1969, 1971, 1976, 1977, 1978 & 1979). Wales were blessed with truly world class players such as Gareth Edwards, Barry John, Phil Bennett, J.P.R.Williams, J.J.Williams, Gerald Davies, Delme Thomas, Dai Morris, Terry Cobner, Allan Martin, Steve Fenwick, John Dawes and Charlie Faulkner, Bobby Windsor and Graham Price (the Pontypool front row) and many, many more. As children most welsh boys dreamt that one day they would play for Wales and I was no different, and as with the football above, we would all pretend to be our favourite players and try and copy the moves and styles of those great welsh players. In addition to watching those great Welsh teams on television as they played those 'Five Nations' games in the seventies, I was also a follower of my local team Bridgend R.F.C. I can still remember how ecstatic I was when my grand-parents bought me a season ticket. Whenever there was a home game on a Saturday or a Wednesday night I

362

*would be there with my friends Kevin Freeland and John and
Lloyd Williams…regardless of the weather we watched some
great games at the Brewery Field in the mid to late-seventies.
Their success was certainly a major influence in my playing
and watching rugby right up to the present day and
throughout my own playing career I practiced my kicking
wherever, whenever and with anything that was either a ball
or resembled a ball!!*

I grew up in the 1970s and it was a time when Wales
dominated British rugby…I would say that I religiously
watched the five nations games with my grampa Henson from
the age of eight years old…with the teams Wales fielded in
those days the expectation was extremely high. More often
than not between 1969 and 1979 Wales were victorious, but
on the odd occasion they were defeated it was a national
disaster…a nation in mourning until the next victory. As a
child it was fantastic to have so many role models from those
great Welsh sides I watched during this period, and my
personal favourites were the great Barry John, Phil Bennet and
J.P.R.Williams. It was no wonder that with those influences
that when I was ten/eleven in my last year at Trelales Primary
School in 1973/74 that we had a very successful rugby team
(as seen in Chapter 6)…we were mad about rugby and when
we weren't playing rugby, we were playing football and when
we weren't playing football, we were playing rugby…That's
how it was in the 1970s.

I watched them all; John Taylor's last minute touchline
conversion to beat Scotland in 1971; Gareth Edwards great
individual try in Cardiff in 1972, when he broke around the
blindside and realising he had no support, chipped ahead and
won the race to touch down in the corner; the famous try
Gareth Edwards scored for the BaaBaas against New Zealand
in 1973…considered still to be the greatest rugby try ever
scored; Graham Price scoring the try in France in 1975 that
gave Wales a famous victory; J.P.R.Williams scoring five of
his six tries against England and boasting the record that he
never lost in a game against England during his ten years as an
international; the speed and guile of Gerald Davies and the
kicking of Steve Fenwick…and many, many, many more great
rugby moments. After watching those great rugby games, it
would be time to re-live them in our garden…I would grab my

363

rugby ball and walk onto my own 'field of dreams' where, in my head, the crowds roared, sang and chanted my name alongside those of Edwards, John, Bennett and Williams, as I re-lived those memorable rugby matches I had just watched on T.V. and added some memorable moments of my own. I can't tell you how many times I scored the winning try against England or winning conversion against Scotland or winning drop-goal against Ireland or even a winning penalty against France. Time and time again, on that famous pitch at 30 Longfellow Drive in Bridgend I became a hero to adoring Welsh fans...I believe I was capped around 412 times for Wales during this period and never lost a game, and I scored the winning points in every game I played...and they were all played at home.

It wasn't just Wales I used to watch in the 1970s, my other great love was my hometown team...Bridgend R.F.C. I can remember coming home from school one day when I was around twelve and my nan Henson told me there was a surprise waiting for me in the living-room. Not knowing what to expect I hesitatingly walked into the living-room where a smiling grampa was sat, and pointed me towards the sideboard in the opposite corner of the room...I couldn't believe what I was seeing, my grandparents had bought me a season ticket for Bridgend R.F.C. I picked it up and opened the small greeting-card like ticket, and there was my name and membership number...I couldn't wait to go to school the following day and share the news with my friends. We (Kevin Freeland, John and Lloyd Williams and I) didn't miss a home game at the Brewery Field during that season of 1975/76, sometimes standing behind the posts at the brewery end with Kevin's dad and brother or in front of the main stand near where the players ran out of the changing rooms onto the field...sometimes we'd stand there with our autograph books trying to get the signatures of the Bridgend players, and sometimes the away players too (if we recognised them as Welsh internationals.) During the winter months Bridgend's ground was a quagmire, being close to the river, and the only blades of grass you'd see would be around the touchline, but despite the conditions we saw some cracking games there...Bridgend were a very good team in those mid to late seventies boasting a few Welsh internationals such as John Lloyd, Steve Fenwick and towards the end of his career

364

J.P.R.Williams, who had returned to his hometown club from London Welsh. Another favourite thing we did was to stand behind the posts at the bottom end of the ground (opposite the brewery end) whenever there was a penalty or conversion. There would be around half a dozen of us all vying to catch the ball from the kick and having the honour of kicking or passing the ball to one of our heroes…sometimes you were lucky, sometimes you weren't!! Yes…they were great times spent down the Brewery Field watching those players and hoping and dreaming that one day it would be us out there wearing the blue and white of Bridgend.R.F.C.

Rugby was a huge part of my life growing up in Wales and whether I watched it on T.V. or live at the Brewery Field, the excited anticipation before kick-off was always the same. We were all confident that Wales or Bridgend would win every game, but doubt would inevitably creep in during those nervous moments before every game. However, once the whistle was blown to signal the start of a game all the doubt would disappear and if…a very big if, your side did lose, it would always be blamed on some sort of injustice such as a poor decision by the ref, the weather, or that dirty number eight. It was never because your side was beaten by a better team, there was always something that would be blamed…at the end of the day, our totally biased and boss-eyed opinion was that our team was always the best and therefore, unfairly beaten. Apart from watching Wales and Bridgend during the seventies, I also enjoyed watching rugby league and remember watching the 'floodlit rugby league programme' on BBC2, and took a particular shine to Salford, mainly due to their star player, and former Welsh international rugby union player, Dai Watkins…but it was Wales and Bridgend that dominated my attention and it was certainly a great era to be growing up in Wales if you loved rugby.

My first Welsh rugby match at the National Stadium

When I was eighteen years old and part fulfilling a childhood dream of playing for my hometown club of Bridgend…well, the 'Youth' team (U'19s), I remember playing a Friday night game on 19th March 1982 (the night before Wales played Scotland in the five nations) against Scottish club Selkirk at the Brewery Field…we won a hard fought game 4 – 0…this

365

was the first time I ever played under floodlights and it wasn't the best I'd played! Following the game we were all given tickets to the Wales v Scotland game the following day...it took a while to sink in, but I was bursting with excitement when I finally realised that I would be attending my first LIVE Welsh game!!!

I arrived in Cardiff on a train that was full of Welsh rugby supporters...when I say full, I mean so full that there wasn't even room for a stray fart! When I finally managed to get out of the station there was a sea of fans, some of which were behaving as if they had already been drinking for 2-3 days...and it was only eleven in the morning! This was my first experience of a five nations 'match day' and I had no idea what to expect, I decided that I would only have a couple of pints before the game...I wanted to not only enjoy the day but also to remember the atmosphere, the game and everything that was going on around me. I made my way to St Mary Street and was welcomed by a sea of men in a mix of red and white and blue and white scarves, bobble hats and macs...it was carnage, as the 'drunk' theme was being totally adhered to by everyone. A point to note at this stage is that this crowd was not a mix of families, young men with girlfriends or gangs of young women with their heads in foam daffodils...this was a crowd of mainly men, all drinking as if it was their last day on earth. Rugby still enjoyed a mainly male fan base in the eighties and it was a site to behold, as I soaked up the atmosphere and listened to the singing by both sets of fans in a sort of unofficial 'sing-off' with Max Boyce songs from the seventies still going strong in the bars and clubs!

The time passed by quickly and I was soon heading for the National Stadium to witness a Welsh game for the first time. Once in the ground, I managed to find a small space to stand about seven or eight steps from the front...it was still a good hour before kick-off, but the stadium was starting to fill-up and the singing had started with *Cwm Rhondda* and *Calon lan* being belted out by a mass choir of around twenty thousand Welsh fans...matched by the Jock behind me who, for the last ten minutes, had repeatedly sang the first two lines of *Flower of Scotland* as he swayed and sipped whiskey from a healthy sized hip flask. I noticed that people had started to run on the playing surface which resulted in a friendly tannoy

366

announcement "COULD PEOPLE PLEASE REFRAIN FROM RUNNING ON THE PLAYING SURFACE...THANK YOU". Fair play, within a minute or two the pitch was clear. But no more than five minutes later there were again people running all over the pitch! This prompted another tannoy announcement which summed up the Welsh sense of humour perfectly when I heard "I'LL JUST REPEAT THAT LAST ANNOUNCEMENT TO MYSELF...AGAIN!!" The jock behind me was oblivious to this and continued singing the same two lines from *Flower of Scotland* again...again...and again. The ground was filling up quickly and it was soon evident why no-one was stood on the bottom step...the beer drank in the bars of Cardiff had to go somewhere and that bottom step was soon awash with urine as it was impossible to get to the toilets and men just pissed where they stood.

I heard a roar which almost immediately increased in volume as it filtered to every corner of the ground, and I could see the players making their way on to the field. Within a minute or two the crowd fell silent before *Flower of Scotland* was echoing around the ground...a song sang with passion by our friends from 'north of the border'. However, nothing prepared me for what came next when *Hen Wlad Fy Nhadau* was sung by the tens of thousands of Welshmen in the crowd...the hair on the back of my neck was standing on end and emotions I never knew existed were straining at the leash as the song reached its finale. Wow! I was so proud to be Welsh at that moment. The whistle went and the game kicked off, and the next eighty minutes were a blur as Scotland deservedly trounced Wales 34-18. When the final whistle went my new Scottish friend behind me was still swaying from side to side, still sipping whiskey from his hip flask and still singing the same two lines from Flower of Scotland....I swear I have never seen anybody so drunk and it was probably Monday before he knew the score. Despite Wales losing heavily I had enjoyed my first live Welsh game at the National Stadium. As the ground emptied and I made my way to the exit, I looked over my shoulder one last time at the pitch and noticed that the jock hadn't moved and I could still hear the faint strains of *Flower of Scotland*...I turned, laughed to myself and made my way to the train station as the crowds headed for the bars of Cardiff.

My only other abiding memory of that day was on the train journey up to Ton Pentre (I was off to see my girlfriend Sheila Coles). As the majority of the men were still in Cardiff the carriage was full of women who had been shopping, me and another man, who was sat on the opposite side of the carriage and clearly drunk, but who was thankfully sleeping and snored his way through the early part of the trip to Pontypridd. As the train left Ponty and trundled up the track towards Porth the drunk man began to stir and then suddenly, and without warning, he stood up, pulled the window down, stuck his out of the window and immediately proceeded to vomit down the side of the train. The multi-coloured yawn he produced was of mega proportions and it sprayed the windows of the remainder of the carriage in a pattern that Picasso would have been proud of. When the man finished his 'work of art' he sat back down, wiped the remnants of vomit from his mouth with his sleeve and fell straight back into a deep sleep. The grumblings from the women in the carriage made me chuckle with welshy "Bloody disgusting" and "did you see that?" and many "well I never…" and when the train stopped in Porth the majority of them left the train. When the train finally arrived in Ton Pentre I stood up and stepped off the train leaving 'sleeping beauty' with a carriage all to himself. As I walked to Sheila's house I reflected on what had been a great day watching the rugby…I couldn't wait to do it again!!

"Wales, Wales, Wales!!"

Everyone is fiercely proud of their country, its culture, its beauty and most importantly…how it performs in sporting events! I am no different…I am proud to be Welsh, proud of my culture and heritage, proud of the rugged beauty that surrounds me, but I have been, still am and always will be fiercely proud of our national teams, no matter what sport they are playing, and I am immensely proud of our sporting heroes. As mentioned above growing up in the nineteen-seventies and the 'Crowning Years' of Welsh rugby was an honour, but they ended in 1980 and despite the odd highlight we had to wait until 2005 before winning another Grand Slam and become a consistent force in World rugby again! We have always produced good football players in Wales, but we have always been three or four players short of being a great team,

368

*and despite players like Ian Rush, Mark Hughes, Gary Speed,
Kevin Ratcliffe, Ryan Giggs, Gareth Bale and Aaron Ramsey,
to name but a few, we have always struggled to qualify for
major tournaments…that changed in 2016 when we qualified
for the Euros and with the country behind them, they did quite
well! It has also been a joy to follow the individual Welsh
sportsmen and women and there have been many, in my
lifetime, that have brought pride to our small nation such as
Lynn Davies, Steve Jones, Colin Jackson, Joe Calzaghe,
Nicole Cooke, Jade Jones, Geraint Thomas (not my son, but
the cyclist and Tour De France winner), Dai Greene, Tanni
Grey-Thompson, Ian Woosnam, Non Evans and many, many
more. Yes, I'm proud to be Welsh!!!*

Despite rugby being the national sport of Wales, our small
country has produced many great sportsmen and women over
the years and I have been lucky to witness some great sporting
moments. In terms of football, throughout my lifetime the
Welsh football team have always been the 'nearly' men…we
have produced many great players, but never at the same time.
An all-time great Welsh XI team with the likes of Neville
Southall, John and Mel Charles, Kevin Ratcliffe, Terry
Yorath, Gary Speed, Ian Rush, Mark Hughes, Gareth Bale,
Ryan Giggs and Aaron Ramsey and many others would have
been a match for any side in the world. However, despite
nearly making the World Cup Finals in 1994 (we lost a crucial
qualifying game against Romania when Paul Bodin missed a
penalty) and then ten years later we missed out on the 2004
Euros after losing a two leg play-off against Russia. Wales
eventually and deservedly made it to a major finals in 2016
when they qualified for the Euros…and what a roller coaster
of emotions it turned out to be. Expectation wasn't high
amongst Welsh fans going into the tournament…everyone was
just happy that we'd qualified and put the 'ghosts of Sweden
1958' to bed. However, this team had something about them, a
togetherness we'd not seen with previous Welsh teams and
boy did they do Wales proud.

It was fantastic to watch Wales doing so well in the group
stage with amazing support at the games in France and at the
fanzone in Bute Park, Cardiff…they ended up topping the
group after victories over Slovakia (2-1) and Russia (3-0), but
losing to England (2-1). Next up was Northern Ireland in the

round of sixteen...in the battle of the British teams, Wales won a close, hard fought game 1-0. The quarter final was against the talented Belgians, a team that boasted many great players such as Kevin de Bruyne, Eden Hazard and Axel Wtisel and were the firm favourites to make it to the semi-finals...but Wales had other ideas and we had no idea what a fantastic night lay ahead at Mike and Nid's house, in what was probably the best game I have seen by a Welsh football team. After a tense first half the teams went in to the changing rooms level at 1-1...the second half started nervously as both teams probed each other's defences looking for that half chance...then on fifty-five minutes Hal Robson-Kanu received a pass in the box, swiveled and flicked the ball toward goal, taking two Belgian defenders out of the equation before sliding the ball past Courtois to put Wales 2-1 in the lead. Wales defended heroically for the thirty minutes reducing Belgium to long-range shots and as the clock ticked down they became more and more frustrated. Then in the eighty-fifth minute a precision cross from Chris Gunter was met by Sam Vokes who powered a header past Courtois...Wales were winning 3-1 and Dean Saunders and Alan Shearer in the studio, the Welsh fans in the stadium and in the fanzone in Cardiff, and all us at Mike and Nid's were going crazy...the entire Welsh nation was in dreamland. The clock ticked down and eventually the referee blew the final whistle, Wales were unbelievably in the semi-final. We went on to lose the semi-final against Portugal 2-0, but everyone was proud of a team that had displayed a togetherness and a passion I've not seen in any football team and they were deservedly received back in Wales with an open-top bus journey through Cardiff to adoring crowds...It was a special, special time for Welsh football and those players who played in Euros 2016 will long be remembered.

Wales has produced many good boxers over the years such as Tommy Farr, Freddie Welsh, 'Peerless' Jim Driscoll and Johnny Owen to name but a few, but when a boxer called Joe Calzaghe started boxing professionally in the early 1990s no-one could foresee that by the time he retired in 2008 he would finish up with an unblemished record of 46 wins from 46 fights (32 by knockout) and had been a world champion at two different weights (super-middleweight and light-heavyweight) and unifying the WBA, WBC and WBO at super-middleweight...he was a truly class act and arguably one of the best boxers Britain ever produced. It was an honour and privilege to have watched his fights on TV against the likes of Chris Eubank, Jeff Lacy, Mikkel Kessler, Bernard Hopkins and Roy Jones Jr...his showmanship and fast hands were something to behold.

My sporting viewing doesn't end with mainstream sports such as Rugby, football and boxing and I have enjoyed the performances of many other Welsh sporting stars such as Colin Jackson, a great 110m hurdler who won two world championships, four European Championships and two Commonwealth Games championships and was a truly great Welsh athlete who provided great viewing during the 1990s and early 2000s. Another great athlete was Tanni Grey Thompson who was truly inspirational as a disabled athlete and I still marvel at her achievements and was another great that I enjoyed watching during the 1990s and early 2000s. I don't enjoy watching golf, as a rule, but when there is a Welsh interest I have watched golf. This was certainly the case when the great Ian Woosnam was playing regularly and I watched many a tournament he played in. The same can be said of cycling and swimming, when Wales are involved, I'm there...glued to the T.V. cheering on my fellow Welsh compatriots and this has certainly been the case with Geraint Thomas and Nicole Cooke (cycling) and David Davies and Jazz Carling (swimming). Other sports where Wales have had success are darts and snooker and as a child growing up I was amazed at the skills of Ray Reardon and Terry Griffiths (snooker) and Leighton Rees and Alan Evan (darts). There are many, many sportsmen and women that have been produced by our small country and I've enjoyed watching their success over the years...their triumphs over adversity in their quest for that personal success that will slingshot them into the annals of Welsh sporting history.

The Mighty Reds (following Barnsley F.C. through thick and thin...mainly thin!!)

I am often asked "Barnsley...why do you support Barnsley?" – Basically, It's a long story and involves a girl. I have supported Barnsley since a cold day on 2nd October in 1982 when I first went to Oakwell. Over the years there have been

*highs and lows of both promotions and relegations, but my
support has never wavered and over those years I have seen
many a great player don the red shirt of Barnsley F.C. such as
Mick Macarthey, Ronnie Glavin, Neil Redfearn, Nicky Eaden,
Jan Aage Frortoft, Darren Barnard, David Watson, Viv
Anderson, John Stones, Craig Hignett, John Hendrie, Allan
Clarke, Chris Morgan, Norman Hunter, Ian Banks, Adie
Moses, Brian Howard, Adam Hamill and many, many more.
However, my all-time favourite is still Bruce Dyer...to me he
epitomizes what a player should possess, pace, determination
and the desire to never give-up. He played a total of 181
games for Barnsley and scored 59 goals...great player for the
club, great sportsman and an absolute legend! I have been to
Oakwell many times over the years and also watched them in
play-off finals at the old Wembley and in the Millennium
Stadium...with mixed results! Regardless of what happens in
the future I will always support Barnsley...cumon you Tykes!!!*

Supporting Barnsley came about by accident...I was staying
with Linda (see Chapter 8) and her family, but as she was a
hairdresser she worked on Saturday's. I had to do a bit of
shopping to buy a pair of shoes, trousers and a shirt and tie for
Linda's presentation night that evening (I had come to
Barnsley from a clerks course and had no 'best' clobber with
me), but I knew that would only take an hour or two...what
was I going to do for the rest of the day? Up to this point I
didn't even know that Barnsley had a football team until I read
the paper that morning and found that they were in the second
division (the championship in today's football), and were
playing at home that day against Fulham...I loved football as
you have seen above and decided to go and watch the game,
asking Jean if I could take Linda's little brother, Andrew. It
could be argued that the love for a girl led to a lifetime of love
for Barnsley F.C. from that day on 2nd October 1982.

Andrew and I made the short 10-15 minute walk to the ground
(Oakwell) and I decided that we would sit in the main stand.
Oakwell in those days was a small stadium with only one
seated stand, opposite to where we were sat and to our right,
behind the goal, were small covered terrace. To the left was an
open terrace for the away supporters. There was a good crowd
in the ground that day but I was glad that Andrew and I were
sat in the stand, in front of us to the left were three Fulham

fans, a teenager and what looked like the parents, the father was a rather large gentleman who hadn't stopped eating since we'd sat down. To the right of them were two empty seats and then a married couple in their late thirties/early forties and Barnsley fans…I thought this could get tasty if there were any contentious decisions. The game kicked off and within fifteen minutes Fulham were winning 3-0, and I began to think that this Barnsley team were shit. The scoreline prompted a few under the breath sarcastic comments from the Fulham fans in front of me and out of the corner of my eye I could see the Barnsley couple to their right were getting agitated, but just about managing to keep their cool…when out of nowhere Barnsley scored to make it 1-3, prompting the Barnsley couple to jump up pointing mockingly at the big fella in front of me…who was still eating. Then, just before half-time Barnsley had a good shout for a penalty…up jumped the Barnsley couple shouting;

"PENALTY" The referee waved play on and the Fulham man said in his London accent;

"Nah…that weren't a penalty" as he took a bite out of his mars bar…well, if he did. Up jumped the Barnsley woman, pointing and shouting and being held back by her husband;

"SHUT THY FUCKING MOUTH SOUTHERNER…WHAT DOES THY FUCKING KNOW ABOUT FOOITBALL!!!!"

Whoa…as the first swear word was leaving her lips I was covering Andrew's lug oiles (ears) to protect him from the abuse the woman was hurling across the stand. Thankfully, the half-time whistle blew and everyone could take a breather. Twenty minutes into the second half, Ian Banks scored his and Barnsley's second to make it 2-3 and straight from the kick-off, Ronnie Glavin scored a sweet half-volley to make it 3-3…what a game this was turning out to be. Fulham were shell-shocked it was now the Barnsley couple who were now mocking the Fulham fans. Five minutes later the ground erupted as Tony Cunningham climbed high above a Fulham defender and buried a sweet header in the back of the net…Barnsley were 4-3 in front and the Barnsley couple were going mental in front of me, and were now really mocking the Fulham fans who were starting to pack up to leave;

"YOU'RE NOT WINNING ANYMORE" and when they got up to leave;

"BYE SOUTHERNERS…SAFE TRIP BACK T'COCKNEY LAND…BYE"

When the final whistle was blown the ground erupted again…I just sat there for a moment wondering what I'd just witnessed…to this day that is the best live football match I've ever had the privilege of watching. Andrew and I made our way back to Princess Street, Andrew excitedly talking about the game and when we got in the house he was providing Jean and Roy with a commentary of the match, and was still going when Linda walked in from work.

I've seen Barnsley many times over the years mainly on T.V. including the night they beat Manchester Utd 3-2 in a F.A.Cup 5th round replay at Oakwell…epic night. I was lucky enough to win tickets from the *News of the World* to watch them in a Premiership game…unfortunately, it was the day they got relegated after losing 1-0 at Leicester City. The next great game I saw them play was at Wembley in 2000 when they played Ipswich in the Championship play-off Final…the winners would be going to the Premiership. What a fantastic day and I wouldn't have missed it for anything. I left Caerphilly early in the morning and caught a train to Cardiff to catch the National Express coach to London. It was a beautiful day, blue skies and glorious sunshine, and arriving in London it was great to see pockets of both Barnsley and Ipswich fans happily mixing amongst the crowds at the famous sites around London such as Covent Garden, Trafalgar Square, Oxford Street and Hyde Park etc…a fantastic relaxed mood was evident in London that day. This atmosphere continued as I stepped off the tube and headed down Wembley Way toward the stadium itself…it was awash with both sets of fans, and as I reached the top of the steps that led to the stadium, I turned and looked back down Wembley Way. It was a sea of people in intermingled colours of red and blue, and there was a real carnival atmosphere around the iconic old stadium. This was the last competitive match that was going to be played at the old Wembley and when I got inside it was easily evident as to why it was going to be re-built…this old iconic stadium, scene of many great sporting occasions such as the 1948 Olympics and England's triumph over Germany in the 1966 World Cup Final, was now looking dated and a bit 'tired'. Nevertheless, the stadium was bathed in sunshine and half the crowd was a mass of red and the other half a mass of blue. The crowds were 'whipped' into a frenzy by DJs from the respective radio stations of South Yorkshire and Suffolk…the atmosphere was electric when the teams walked out onto the hallowed turf of Wembley.

Ipswich started the better team, but it was Barnsley that took the lead, a long range effort by Craig Hignett came back off the bar, hit the back of a diving Richard Wright (Ipswich goalkeeper) before hitting the back of the net. Despite Ipswich equalizing, it was Barnsley that could have gone in at half-time 2-1 in front, but Darren Barnard missed a penalty (the first he'd missed for Barnsley)...then the half-time whistle brought a dramatic first half to an end. When the teams came out for the second half it was Ipswich that were again playing the better football, dominating possession and chances, and within twelve minutes they were leading 3-1. Barnsley did make it 3-2 from a Hignett penalty with around fifteen minutes left to play and started pressing for an equaliser...Georgie Hristov nearly provided the goal that could have taken the game to extra-time, but was foiled by a remarkable point blank save by Richard Wright. Barnsley continued to pressure Ipswich but gaps were appearing at the back and in the ninetieth minute a breakaway resulted in Ipswich scoring a fourth...ending Barnsley's dream of returning to the Premiership. It was a fantastic game, a fantastic day, and listening to other Barnsley fans, the general concensus was that Ipswich had been the better team, not just over the ninety minutes, but over the season and deserved the victory...Barnsley fans were magnanimous in defeat and we had all enjoyed a great day and felt there was always next year!

In 2006, Barnsley made it to the League One play-off final against Swansea. Myself,
My daughter, 'R' and son, 'G', had travelled to the 1st leg of the semi-final at Oakwell against Huddersfield, but Barnsley lost 1-0...thankfully, they won the 2nd leg at Huddersfield...3-1. When the tickets for the final went on general sale, I drove up to Barnsley early in the morning, arriving at Oakwell just after 9am, bought my ticket and drove back to South Wales...after popping to Princess Street for a few minutes to catch-up on some happy memories (see Chapter 8). On the day of the game it was a short trip to Cardiff, as they were still re-building Wembley Stadium and the play-offs and F.A.Cup finals were still being played at the Millenium Stadium. Once

375

I arrived in Cardiff it was great to be surrounded by Barnsley fans and their unique dialect I'd come to love twenty five years earlier. Dressed in my Barnsley shirt and with my 'Super Tykes' scarf draped around my neck, I felt at home amongst the 'red' end of the Millenium Stadium…high up in the middle tier to the left of the goal. After ninety minutes of end to end football and a roller-coaster of emotions the score was 2-2 and extra-time was now waiting for both teams. Swansea were by far the better team in extra time and Barnsley were hanging on, as Lee Trundle came at them time and time again with mazy, marauding runs…it was true backs to the wall and nail-biting time for us Barnsley fans. Thankfully the referee brought our anguish to a temporary end when he blew the whistle that signified the end of extra-time with the scoreline still 2-2…the anguish would start again shortly as the match would have to be decided by penalties. This was a nervous time for both sets of fans, made worse by the hush that swept over the stadium as the first penalty was about to be taken. After eight penalties Barnsley were winning 4-3, as the Swansea player Tate stepped forward the whole stadium knew that he had to score to keep Swansea in the penalty shoot-out…if he missed, Barnsley were going to the Championship. Tate looked nervous and it was a weak penalty, easily saved by Colgan in the Barnsley goal…Barnsley had done it, they were going back to the Championship. The celebrations started as Colgan ran out of his goal, immediately starting a mass exodus of the Swansea fans, leaving us Barnsley fans eagerly awaiting the cup to be presented. When the trophy was finally lifted by Paul Reid, the Barnsley skipper, the whole 'red' end erupted and there were grown men crying everywhere, including me, such was the emotion of the occasion…when they played *Glad All Over* by the Dave Clark Five, the sound of around twenty thousand Barnsley fans singing and stamping their feet, at the appropriate time during the chorus, it was a sight and sound to behold…the atmosphere was electric. To be a part of that day was very special, but trying to get hold of my father (a Swansea City fan) to share the good news was very difficult and it took four or five days before he answered the phone!

Being a Barnsley fan has been a roller-coaster of emotion with the highs of promotions and the lows of relegations. There have been a couple of good F.A.Cup runs that we have enjoyed, firstly in 1997 when we defeated Bolton Wanderers, Tottenham Hotspur and Manchester United before losing the quarter-final against Newcastle United. Then in 2008 they beat Blackpool, Southend, Liverpool (at Anfield) and Chelsea before losing a semi-final at Wembley 1-0 to Cardiff City...did I get some stick in work for that one! In recent years we won another League One play-off final against Millwall 3-1 in the 2015/16 season, after winning the Johnstone's Paint Trophy a few weeks earlier against Oxford Utd...3-2.

Despite all the highs and lows the funniest memory has to be the day I met Mick McCarthy at Elland Road in 2001, when Barnsley played Leeds United in the 3rd Round of the F.A.Cup. Paul Watson (Nuaire, Sales Manager for Yorkshire) had arranged for me to attend the game as a guest of Nuaire...free drinks, three course meal etc at the banqueting suite at Elland Road. After a dour first half, we made our way back to the banqueting suite for a half-time buffet...and more drinks. But first, we had to make a visit to the toilet...the beer we'd drank prior to the game was now ready to leave our bodies!! I was the last one to leave the toilet and when I came out Paul was waiting for me at the entrance to the banqueting suite, but there was one other person in that foyer area...Mick McCarthy, Barnsley legend. It was too good an opportunity to miss and I shouted;
"MICK" and ran over and started to shake his hand furiously whilst spurting out a string of slurred I love you, what a great player you were and a great manager etc. Then as quickly as I'd approached him and started shaking his hand, I stopped, let go, turned and walked away leaving a totally bemused Mick McCarthy wondering what the hell had just happened. A minute or so later Paul walked into the banqueting suite laughing and told me that when I turned and left, Mick McCarthy look at me and mouthed;
"Who the fuck was that?"
Classic moment of being star-struck...me, not Mick.

I will follow Barnsley until my last breath and intend on making a couple of visits to Oakwell this season (2018/19) as we attempt to bounce back into the Championship following another relegation last season...CUMON YOU REDS!!!

The Summer Olympics

Despite my love of football and rugby I love the Olympics...it is my favourite sporting event and something I eagerly look forward to every four years. I have watched hours and hours of the Olympics since becoming addicted as a nine year old during the Munich Olympics in 1972. My first crush wasn't a pop singer, or a film star...it was a Romanian gymnast, fourteen year old Nadia Comaneci, who took the world by storm at the Montreal Olympics in 1976. She was the first gymnast to score a perfect ten...and I loved her! The Olympics has provided so many memorable and emotional moments across so many different sports and to list them all here would be impossible, but I have picked out a few stand-out memories and needless to say...Nadia leads the way!!!

The Romanian gymnast, Nadia Comaneci, was my first crush and I fell in love with her during the 1976 Montreal Olympics...so much so, I struggle to remember anything else about the rest of those games in 1976. Nadia's performances were majestic and I was captivated by her flawless displays in the various gymnastic disciplines, her lithe body, beautiful smile and single pony tail of dark brown hair...Oh Nadia! She was the first gymnast in Olympic history to score a perfect '10', a feat she repeated another six times as she won three goal medals...and another unofficial gold for capturing my heart. She went on to win another two gold medals at the 1980 Olympics in Moscow...she was a truly great gymnast, and so pretty.

However, the first Olympic Games I can remember watching were the 1972 Olympics, but for all the wrong reasons...terrorists had stormed the Olympic village and taken a group of Israeli athlete's hostage. These horrific events unfolded on T.V. but I was nine years old and couldn't understand why all the great sport had stopped!! It would be much later that I would come to understand the enormity of those tragic events, that would eventually result in all the hostages and the terrorists being killed when the German authorities authorised a rescue attempt, when a bus they were on arrived at the airport...it was complete carnage and a very, very sad day for the families of the Israeli athletes who lost their lives, the Israeli people and for the Olympic movement itself! The death of the Israeli athletes understandably overshadowed the achievements of some great individual performances, but our Mary Peters was rightly lauded on her return to Britain after winning the Heptathlon gold in 1972.

I remembered some of the great rivalries that came out of the Olympics such as the one between British middle distance runners Steve Ovett and Seb Coe, and in 1980 it produced two great finals with Steve Ovett winning the 800m final (Seb Coe came second) and Seb Coe winning the 1500m (Steve Ovett came third). Carl Lewis and Ben Johnson produced another famous rivalry at the 1988 Olympics in Seoul, when in the 100m final Johnson won the gold in a world record of 9.79 seconds with Lewis suggesting some athletes were winning via illegal 'help'...Johnson was later disqualified as a drugs cheat...drugs have been and continue to be a major problem in Olympic sport as more and more athletes have tested positive for performance enhancing drugs.

I have been lucky enough to have witnessed the great British rower Steve Redgrave winning gold medals in five consecutive Olympics from the Los Angeles games in 1984 through to the 2000 Olympic Games in Sydney. Also, the unusual but successful style of the American athlete, Michael Johnson, who won four gold medals (4 x 400m at Barcelona in 1992, 400m and 200m in Atlanta in 1996 and 400m in Sydney in 2000) with a style of running that defied logic...but what an athlete. I have enjoyed watching the Decathlon triumphs of our own Daley Thompson in 1980 and 1984, GBs mens hockey triumph in Seoul in 1998 and the GB womens hockey team bringing home the gold in 2016.

My favourite all-time Olympic memory though has to be the performances by Kelly Holmes in winning the middle distance double of 800m and 1500m at the 2004 Olympics in Athens. Kelly had been an athlete with great promise, but had suffered from injury problems throughout a career which had stopped her achieving her full potential...she came into the 2004 Olympics as a 34 year old with little expectation and obviously in terms of Olympic medals this was 'last chance saloon'. The grit and determination she showed in winning both races are the stuff of legends and the realization and instant elation she felt at realising she was a double gold medalist was a very emotional moment and probably one of the most emotional moments I have ever witnessed in watching sport...a close second was Andy Murray winning Olympic gold in the mens singles Tennis finals in 2012 and 2016, and super Saturday, when Greg Rutherford (mens long jump), Jessica Ennis-Hill (Heptathlon) and Mo Farrah (10,000m) all win gold in the space of 46 mins at the 2012 games in London. Who can forget the incomparable Usain Bolt, undoubtedly the best sprinter the world has ever seen, who completed a treble of double victories in both the men's 100m and 200m events at the 2008 (Beijing), 2012 (London) and 2016 (Rio de Janeiro)...a feat that is unlikely to ever be repeated.

Over the years, I have also been lucky to watch great cycling events (especially the dominance by British cyclists such as Sir Bradley Wiggins Sir Chris Hoy, Jason Kenny, Laura Trott (now Kenny), Victoria Pendleton etc in recent Olympics), rowing, equestrian, sailing, shooting, archery, canoeing, fencing, marathons, triathlons, rugby, Judo, Taekwondo (especially double-olympic champion Jade Jones), beach volleyball, golf, football and many, many more. Lastly, I have witnessed amazing performances in the swimming and diving pools, and this is where the greatest ever Olympian, Michael Phelps, delighted us by winning twenty-eight medals across four Olympics in 2004, 2008, 2012 and 2016. Yes, the Olympics have provided me, and millions of others, with amazing memories of great sporting heroes and controversial and emotional moments. The great joy with the Olympics is that over two weeks you can watch so many different sports and as a sports lover for two weeks every four years I am in seventh Heaven.

World Cup Football & Rugby

Another great sporting event is the football World Cup and this is another event that is played every four years. Whilst I have flashes of memories from the 1970 tournament in Mexico it was the 1974 tournament that provided me with my first great memories...the great Dutch side that included Johan Cruyff and Johan Neeskens narrowly losing to a West German side with Franz Beckenbauer and Gerd Muller. A great final! There have been many great players and teams that have graced the World Cup over the years, but sadly I have never been lucky enough to see Wales in one…who knows perhaps next time in Qatar in 2022! Again, there are too many memorable games, moments and goals to list here and I have just picked out some of my favourite memories! Additionally, rugby has provided some great World Cup moments. In 1987 the first World Cup tournament was played and Wales came third, but in the World Cups that have followed we have never improved upon that first one. With exception of England winning the 2003 tournament the Southern Hemisphere teams of New Zealand, Australia and South Africa have dominated World Rugby, not just at the World Cup, but in every sense!! There have been wonderful players that have graced the rugby field over the years, but the stand-out performances of Jonah Lomu at the 1995 World Cup in South Africa are still difficult to comprehend, a player who was 6ft 5in and 120kg and played…on the wing. Yes, on the wing!! Sadly, Jonah is no longer with us, a gentle giant who was loved by everyone who met him, but who succumbed to a cardiac arrest following years of trouble with his kidneys. Nevertheless, he and many others have provided us with great memories, but it is with that third/fourth place play-off between Wales and Australia in 1987 that will provide the first of my great memories from the rugby World Cups I have seen!!!

As with the Olympics, the World Cups in both football and rugby are played every four years, and they also provide exciting sporting occasions, again littered with great players, controversy and the odd surprise. I have just enjoyed watching the 2018 World Cup in Russia, and as Wales had again failed to qualify, I decided to whole-heartedly give England my full support…the tournament didn't disappoint and neither did England who were unlucky not to make the final. Thankfully, the rugby and football World Cups are not played in the same year, and this means that next year I can look forward to watching the 2019 World Cup in Japan…again hoping that Wales will do well. The football World Cup has been played a lot longer and the first one I remember watching is the 1974 World Cup in Germany. Whereas, the inaugural rugby World Cup was in 1987, and it provided historic memories of that first tournament.

The football World Cup normally has the same favourites every four years; Germany, Brazil and Italy with one of the occasional 'others' such as France, Spain, Holland and Argentina getting a mention. There are sometimes those 'dark horses' that shine through such as Croatia, as they did in the recent World Cup in Russia when they made it all the way to the final. Everyone always talks about the 'flair of the Brazilians', the 'machine-like work of the Germans' or the 'Italian defences' and the 'possession football of the Spanish' and in recent World Cups there is always the expectation that an African team will do well. England always gets a mention…by their own press and normally they fail to deliver and embarrassingly and spectacularly leave the tournament on the back of some bad results. However, this year, without a great deal of expectation, they did make it to the semi-finals, narrowly losing 2-1 to Croatia after extra time. But for me it was their performances in 1990 that still rank as one of my highlights from all the World Cups I have watched over the years. After scraping through the group stages with draws against Ireland and Netherlands and a narrow 1-0 victory over Egypt they made it into the last sixteen. In a very tight match against Belgium it was left to David Platt to score the winning goal toward the end of extra time that took them in to the quarter-finals where they met Cameroon. England had to come from behind despite an early lead from a David Platt goal and two Gary Lineker penalties, the second in extra-time, in a frenetic game that saw England beat Cameroon 3-2…next it was the Germans in the semi-final. This was a fantastic game and was decided by penalties, but it will always be remembered for Paul Gascoigne trying to hold back the tears when he was booked in extra time which meant that if England won he would miss the final. As it was, Germany won the penalties 4-3 and the England dream was over, but for excitement Italia 90 still remains my favourite World Cup…with exception of the final between Germany and Argentina, as all the Argentinians wanted to do was kick Germans up in the air, very poor final but deservedly won by Germany 1-0. I also have a soft spot for the 1974 World Cup as it was the first one I remember, and because of the great Netherlands side that included one of the greatest players to ever grace a football field, Johann Cryuff…I was gutted when Germany beat the Netherlands in the final 2-1. Another memorable game was when France beat Brazil in 1998 to win the World Cup for the first time, and lastly we won't dwell on a certain incident that has been talked about again and again and again, I'll just say…'the hand of God'.

There have been many great moments in World Cup rugby but for me the most memorable are Wales winning third place in the inaugural World Cup in 1987 against Australia following a last minute try by Adrian Hadley and a touchline conversion by Paul Thorburn to win 22-21; Japan's last minute win 34-32 against South Africa in 2015…the stuff of dreams and another classic; another I enjoyed was England's World Cup win in 2003, when Jonny Wilkinson scored the extra-time drop-goal to win the game 20-17. But the most memorable World Cup has to be the 1995 World Cup in South Africa, memorable for two reasons. Firstly, it was the World Cup that introduced a certain Jonah Lomu to the world…he produced devastating displays of speed and strength that resulted in Will Carling referring to him as a 'freak', but in a complimentary way…he was an outstanding player, a true gentleman and an outstanding ambassador for rugby. It was a sad loss for his family, for New Zealand and for rugby when he sadly passed away in 2015…a great, great man. Secondly, the other memory is not so much to do with rugby but a political situation that saw the 'Birth of a Nation'…when Nelson Mandela, the new South African President, walked out for the final wearing a Springbok shirt it unified a nation…to wear a shirt that had long been a sign of white supremacy in South Africa was a brave move and without a doubt the reason South Africa defeated a great New Zealand team, which included the All Black legend, Jonah Lomu, 15-12…a truly remarkable day!

The rugby World Cup just gets better and better and some of the rugby witnessed is breathtaking…it is also refreshing to see so called 'lesser' rugby countries such as Georgia and Uruguay making their mark on the world stage, but it is New Zealand that are still the team to beat and who everyone sets out to emulate!

Watching my children play sport

*I have been lucky enough to see all my sons play football,
however 'K', the eldest, admittedly only played a couple of
times. Additionally, 'A' played a few games with 'Rh' when
they were in the U'8s and playing mixed football. But I
watched my sons 'G' and 'Rh' regularly from U'8s all the way
through to U'16s...I coached 'Rh' from U'8s to U'10s and
again U'14s to U'16s when he returned from Middlesbrough.
I have also watched Amy play rugby for the Caerphilly
Chargers girls team U'8s.*

It's a strange phenomenon watching teams that you could be
playing in yourself and I openly admit...I hated it. But
watching your children play sport and watching them develop
comes a very, very close second to actually playing
yourself...in some respects it's better, and on one occasion it
was very emotional. As I said, 'K' did start to play in a team,
but soon gave it up saying he was bored and didn't like it...I
didn't push him. I've tried to let my children make their own
decisions as to the sport they want to play. Some people have
asked me why I didn't push any of them to play rugby,
knowing how successful I'd been, but this wasn't about me, it
was about them and what they wanted to do. I encouraged and
supported them, and with 'G' and 'Rh' this brought a lot of
proud (and bizarre) moments and I knew how important it was
to them, for me to be there week after week watching them
play...win, lose or draw, and providing an honest appraisal of
the way they played...good or bad. I knew it was important as
I had wanted my parents to be there watching me...but I could
count on one hand the amount of times my parents had seen
me play football and rugby. With my children, I don't think I
have missed many games (with exception of when 'Rh' and
'A' were living in Middlesbrough), and collectively, I have
probably watched them all play in excess of a hundred times.

'G' and 'Rh' were very different players with exception of one
aspect of their game; they were both fearless in the tackle and
were scared of nothing. However, 'G' may have lacked the
speed 'Rh' possessed, but his vision was way ahead of his
years...his ability to pick out a 'killer' pass was exemplary.
'Rh', on the other hand, was the 'star of the show' when he
played six-a-side up to the U'10s; scoring from corners,

shooting and passing with both feet and he had electrifying pace. I have seen them both score outstanding goals, and believe me there is nothing better than seeing your son score any kind of goal, but when it's a 'special' goal from outside the box or a volley, then it's very emotional. The most emotional goal I witnessed was when 'Rh' returned from Middlesbrough (I hadn't seen him play for three years and when his mother took them to live in Middlesbrough I didn't think I'd ever see him play again, let alone score). However, in a game at Cilfynydd when the score was 1-1 with about ten minutes left, 'Rh' ran onto a through ball and slid the ball under the advancing Cilfynydd keeper to score and make the score 2-1. It was the first goal I'd seen him score in over three years and it was extremely emotional and tears welled up in my eyes, and it was difficult to focus for a moment, which was a bit of a problem…I was the referee. I managed to compose myself and eventually 'Rh's team would go on to win 3-1.

The most bizarre moment came in a cup game 'G' played for Caerphilly Cavaliers U'15s in a cup game in Merthyr Tydfil. It was a fairly easy game for the boys and with five or so minutes left they were winning eight or nine nil. 'G' hadn't had a particularly good game but was determined to get on the scoresheet. Dribbling into the box however, he tried to beat one too many of the defenders and shot wide…there had been an easier pass into the middle where a team mate was unmarked. Following the miss and the abuse he received from his team mate, 'G' walked off the field and sat on a tump of earth close to a field where an old horse was grazing…the coach looked at me and I shrugged my shoulders. I then walked to where 'G' was sitting with his arms folded and said; "You've just made yourself look like a cunt!" (I understand that calling your fifteen year old son a 'cunt' is more than a bit harsh, but sometimes you have to be brutal and talk to them in the only language they understand…I am not naïve and knew that he and his mates were using that language and I can honestly say I didn't make a habit of swearing in front of my children). I didn't stay to discuss his actions, I immediately walked away and left him stewing in his own pity. But I talked to him again on the way home in the car explaining calmly that he'd let himself down, but more importantly, he'd let his team mates down…fair play to him, he understood he'd been

385

an idiot and took it upon himself to apologise to everyone at training the following week.

I know they are my sons but my only wish for them was that they enjoyed playing. Yes, there is always a competitive edge when playing any sport, but ultimately it is only a game and to continue playing any sport you have to enjoy it…once the enjoyment is not there, it's time to give up. Thankfully, they are both still playing for local teams…and over the years I have enjoyed watching them both play, and briefly watching 'K' and 'A' play.

My youngest Amy, did provide me with some hope on the rugby front when she played touch rugby for a season with Caerphilly Chargers U'8s. But after a season she'd retired from rugby…it wasn't for her, but I supported her as I had supported the others, but again not in a pushy way. One thing I have never been is a 'pushy' parent…if my children wanted to play I supported them…if they didn't, I also supported that decision aswell. 'R' didn't play sport but I supported her in her chosen activity…dancing, and went to see a couple of shows at the Blackwood Institute, where her and her friends were excellent. Another proud father moment.

Welsh Rugby (Part 2)

Since returning to Wales I have had some memorable days watching Wales play rugby, absolutely fantastic days watching games in the stadium or in the pubs and clubs around Caerphilly and Cardiff. I have created great memories and shared historic rugby and funny moments with family and friends such as Stuart and Becky Robson, Warren Evans and Jag (James Gardiner). We have watched Wales win the Grand Slam and win some memorable games against the 'old' enemy, England…these great days have normally led to some great nights…who can forget 'Flares' and that famous dance…eh Warren. There have been some days that stand out more than others and for that reason I will be have to be selective and start with the Wales v England game in 1999, then 'Flares', the day/night we beat France to win the Grand Slam in 2012 and the day we celebrated my 50th in 2013 and watched a great Wales v England game…well, great if you were Welsh that day!

Wales v England – Wembley 1999

We all sat in the 'big' room at the Buffs Club in Abertridwr
eagerly waiting for kick-off in another Wales v England
clash…the signs weren't good, Wales had received some
heavy beatings from England in recent games. But there was a
simmering air of confidence (as there always is when Wales
play rugby) that this year was our year! The confidence levels
increased as Tom Jones and Max Boyce belted out the classic
Delilah and *Hymns and Arias* respectively, whipping the
crowd at Wembley (and in the Buffs club) into a frenzy of
unbounded expectation. Once the national anthems had been
sung everyone was ready for the kick-off. England dominated
the first half and scored three tries, but indiscipline cost them
dearly and the Welsh kicking machine, Neil Jenkins, kicked
six out six penalties to keep them within touching distance at
half-time as England led 25-18. Soon after the restart a Shane
Howarth try and conversion by Neil Jenkins brought the sides
level at 25-25…there was a simmering level of expectation
growing in the crowd at the Buffs, but England edged in front
with two penalties from Jonny Wilkinson making it 31-25 and
the Grand Slam was in sight for England. As injury time
approached, a dubious penalty decision gave Neil Jenkins the
opportunity to kick for touch and to push the Welsh deep into
the England half…his kick was excellent and resulted in a
Welsh line-out on the edge of the English twenty-two. Garin
Jenkins threw the ball into the line-out and it was caught by
Wyatt who then gave it to Howley, who then threw the ball
out to Scott Quinnell, who, after a slight juggle, gave a short
pass to Scott Gibbs on the angle, who burst through the
gap…people started to stand-up shouting at the TV;
"GO ON GIBBSY BOY…GO ON SON!!"
Gibbs stepped outside the England full-back, Matt Perry, and
then to the right of the English winger, Steve Hanley, he was
over the line…TRY!
Wembley erupted…the Buffs erupted, there were people
jumping around, beers going up in the air, people hugging
each other, people punching the air in delight and the familiar
chants of;
"WALES, WALES, WALES!!" filled the air. Then there was
the realization that Wales were still losing 31-30…they still
needed to kick the conversion to win. Who would you want in
this kind of pressure situation?…yes, Neil Jenkins. Who did

Wales have?...yes, Neil Jenkins. As Neil Jenkins prepared to take the kick, someone ran out in front of the TV and told everyone to "SHUSH" and put his finger over his mouth to emphasize the point. I thought to myself;
"We are in Abertridwr...Neil Jenkins is unlikely to hear us from Wembley" and chuckled to myself as the room fell silent. Neil stepped up, and cool as you like, kicked the ball high between the posts, and turned as if it was never in doubt...Wales were now in front 32-31. The room erupted again and was still celebrating, shall we say, 'enthusiastically' when the final whistle was blown...what a game, what a day and what a hangover I had the following morning!

Flares

Warren and I left the stadium after watching Wales beat the Pacific Islanders 38-20, in a game boasting eight tries, and headed for the bright lights of Cardiff for a few cheeky refreshments...a standard procedure for post-match entertainment and who knew where the night would lead! It was still fairly early when we walked into 'Flares' on St Mary Street, a bar that specialised in 1970s music. As you walked through the door the dance floor was directly on your right with an open end to walk into, and with a ledge-like shelf and stools all the way around the dance floor to a big pillar that stood opposite the bar. As we walked in we could see the bar 7-8 metres in and which ran down the left-hand side of the room. We bought our drinks and went to sit on two stools the other side of the big pillar and which overlooked the dance floor. Warren sat on the inside and the pillar obscured his view of the entrance, whereas I had an excellent view of the entrance. Warren and I were generally chatting, mainly about the game, when I noticed a women coming in and who stood immediately to the right of the entrance with another woman and a man...Warren had no idea they were there and certainly had no idea what I was about to do! Now I'm certainly no oil painting and I am an excellent example of imperfection...on many levels. But this woman was a...should we say, large...no, no, no...a rather large...no, no, no...she was fucking huge, and not blessed with super-model features. I, shall we say, seized the day and said to Warren;
"I've just seen a girl walk in...I'm going to go and ask her to dance" and I jumped off the stool and headed toward the

target…I mean lady. Warren had no idea where I was or who I was about to talk to as he couldn't see a damn thing. I introduced myself to the lady and her friends and politely asked if she would like to dance…she smiled and said "Yes"! So I made my way on to the dance floor…backwards, giving it all my best moves with my new friend and as we shimmied and stepped backwards I came into Warren's view and smiled. Warren at this point could see me dancing but still had no idea who I was dancing with. I kept slowly edging backwards smiling at my new dance partner…looking across and smiling at Warren…who was eagerly waiting for his first view of the mystery woman!...as we edged backwards…a little further…one more step…perfect. I looked across at Warren and I knew he could now see my new dance partner, as he was laughing hard and had started to slide off the stool. A couple of minutes later the song ended and I escorted the lady back to her friends, chatted for a few minutes and thanked her for dancing with me. I returned to Warren, who was still laughing, so much so, that he had tears streaming down his face and he was struggling to string two words together…it appeared that I had made two people happy with the one dance, the mystery lady and Warren!

Beating France to win the 2012 Grand Slam

I was out with Stuart, Becky, Jag (James Gardiner), Aaron (Dynes) and Rhys (Davies) for the French game in 2012. We had met up in Cardiff and the atmosphere was electric as the pubs were overflowing onto St Mary Street with rugby fans enjoying their pre-match drinks. Walking past the Brewery Quarter and looking down St Mary Street all you could see was a sea of the red and blue of Wales and France…Cardiff on Welsh rugby match days was a site to behold and you could feel the expectation in the air of both sets of fans. Despite not having tickets for the game we all wanted to experience the atmosphere in Cardiff that day as we all knew that if Wales beat France they would win the Grand Slam and be the Six Nations champions for 2012. We became separated for the game, as Becky, Stuart and I stayed in the Owain Glyndwr, where a good match day atmosphere was already in full swing. We had a great view of the TV and good access to the bar, so all was good. The game itself was a tense affair and Wales eventually edged a tough contest 16-9…Wales had done it…they had achieved their third Grand Slam in eight seasons. When the final whistle sounded we jumped up, hugged each other and the whole pub was chanting "WALES, WALES, WALES!" at the TV. We quickly drank our drinks and made our way to Kitty Flynn's where Jag and the boys had watched the game (we wanted to get there before the stadium emptied). After queuing for five or ten minutes we finally made it inside, where Jag, Rhys, Aaron and Llyr were waiting for us…more hugs, as we celebrated our county's success with copious amounts of BEERS (with exception Aaron and his two mates from home who were muttering something incoherent about the English who were beating their beloved Ireland). We had a great night in Kitty Flynn's, and the French fans were more than gracious in defeat…they were enjoying the night as much as we were!! My abiding memory of that day was not Wales winning the Grand Slam or the drunken celebrations after the game, nor the majestic scenes before and after the game of intermingled Welsh and French fans. No, it was Jag with his arms around two French fans belting out the French national anthem…well the version I'd taught him – "OU EST LE PAPIER". Jag singing at the top of his voice with two Frenchman looking bemused as he sang in French "WHERE IS ZE PAPER?"…priceless, and we still laugh about it now, six years later.

Wales v England – 2013 (and my fiftieth Birthday)

It was March 16th 2013 and I met Warren for breakfast in the Malcolm Uphill (Wetherspoons) in Caerphilly before heading in to Cardiff for, hopefully, a double celebration…my fiftieth Birthday and Wales beating England in the Six Nations game. There would be no Grand Slam or Triple Crown this year, but this was England and therefore, a must win game. As Warren and I were sitting eating a full English breakfast (the only good thing about England that day), in walked Paul Williams, Martyn Price followed shortly by my son, 'G', it was at this point that Warren gave me a present, I opened the bag…deep joy (not), it was one of those horrendous 'leek' hats you see in the crowds at Welsh games! Apologies, for sounding ungrateful, but it made me look like more of a bell-end than I normally do and it was fucking boiling…after the obligatory photos it came straight off and went into my pocket were it stayed for the rest of the day.

We made our way to Cardiff and to the Revolucion de Cuba bar, where we were soon met Stuart and Becky and Alun Thomas and his brother. It has to be said the management of Revolucion de Cuba got it absolutely right that day…they resisted the temptation to cram as many people in as possible (a crime of many other bars in Cardiff on match day), and everyone had ample room to move, it was easy to get to the toilet and there were no long queues at the bar…hats off to them, absolutely spot on! Plus, there was live music before, at half-time and after the game had finished providing a real party atmosphere around the room. If England had beaten Wales that day they would win the Grand Slam, but the difference between this game and the game at Wembley in 1999, was that a good win by Wales would mean they would be the Six Nations champions for 2013…it was nicely poised for a classic, but no-one could have predicted the final score that day as it was too close to call. The atmosphere was building in the bar and just after the national anthems had been sung a small group of English fans provided a great rendition of "Swing Low, Sweet Chariot" which was given the respect it deserved, by the mainly Welsh dominated crowd in the bar, before us Welsh responded with an ear-deafening "Bread of Heaven"…it would be the last time the English fans were heard that day as Wales dominated the game, physically battering the English in every contact, including the scrums. At half-time Wales led 9-3, but by full-time the final score was Wales 30 England 3…handing Wales a resounding victory and the Six Nations Crown. What a brilliant way to celebrate my 50th Birthday, a great day had by all…unless you were English of course.

Other sports

I have enjoyed watching many other sports such as cricket, boxing, tennis and even ice hockey, and even one event from the horse-racing calendar…The Grand National. These spectacles have almost entirely been watched from the comfort of my own living room, but nevertheless I have enjoyed them all the same!.

Cricket cannot be described as the most exciting of sports, but it can still be enthralling to watch and I have watched cricket, mainly test cricket, for many years. But for tension and excitement none can compare with the Ashes Test Series in 2005 when each test was on a knife-edge and the margins between victory and defeat were miniscule...England, with the likes of Flintoff and Pieterson, won the Ashes against an Australian team that included Ricky Ponting and Shane Warne, with a 2-1 series win. It was a credit to both teams and a great advert for Cricket and probably the best series of test matches I had ever seen...it was also funny seeing the human side of the players as their celebrations were televised as much as the matches, but why shouldn't they celebrate a great sporting achievement!

I have also been lucky in my lifetime to have witnessed some classic boxing matches such as the 'Rumble in the Jungle' between Muhammad Ali and George Foreman and I have also seen, over the years, many other great international boxers such as Mike Tyson, Joe Frazier, Evander Holyfield, Marvin Hagler, Sugar Ray Leonard, Tommy 'Hitman' Hearns, Roberto Duran, Manny Pacquiao, Julio Cesar Chavez, Marco Antonio Barrera and many, many more. I have also watched many of our home-grown talents as Britain has also produced its fair amount of good boxers such as Joe Calzaghe, Lennox Lewis, Anthony Joshua, Amir Kahn, Joe Conteh, Duke McKenzie, Sir Henry Cooper, Naseem Hamed, Barry McGuigan, Ricky Hatton and many, many more. However my favourite era was the late eighties/early nineties when Britain produced some great middleweight boxers such as Nigel Benn (The Dark Destroyer), Chris Eubank, Michael Watson and Steve Collins and collectively they produced some unbelievable boxing matches which made for compelling viewing...sadly, one fight resulted in Michael Watson collapsing toward the end of the 11th round in a tough, uncompromising fight with Chris Eubank, resulting in him almost dying. As the scenes unfolded on T.V. it became obvious that Watson was in trouble, but although he pulled through, he only partially recovered and was left a shadow of the man he once was as the blows he had taken that night resulted in him being left with brain damage...although boxing provided wonderful sporting spectacles, this was the darker side of boxing. In 1995, Nigel Benn knocked out American Gerald McClellan, with similar results, that would ultimately affect both boxers, but in different ways! However, despite tragedies such as those mentioned above boxing remains compelling viewing.

Tennis is a game I loved playing, but a game I also loved watching. I have watched highlights from the four 'Grand Slam' tounaments (Australian Open, French Open, Wimbledon and US Open) and also the Davies Cup, but one tournament I can watch for hours and hours is Wimbledon. I fell in love with Wimbledon in 1971 when watching the antics of Ilie Nastase, the Romanian clown, sadly he lost the final that year in a classic five setter against the American, Stan Smith. In my time watching Wimbledon I have seen many great players such as Jimmy Connors, Chris Evert, John Mcenroe, Martina Navratilova, Bjorn Borg, Steffi Graf, Andre Agassi, Pat Cash, Jana Novotna, Monica Seles, Pete Sampras, Martina Hingis, Roger Federer, Rafael Nadal, Gabriela Sabatini, Novak Djokovic, Garbine Muguruza, Venus and Serena Williams and many, many more. Like many British tennis fans I spent years waiting for a men's British champion…hoping and praying every year that this would be the year. But year after year the chance would go despite the efforts of players such as John Lloyd, Jeremy Bates, Andrew Castle, Greg Rusedski and Tim Henman. Finally, in 2013, Andy Murray achieved the dream of winning Wimbledon when he beat Novak Djokovic in straight sets 6-4, 7-5, 6-4…that was a very emotional day when a Brit at last won the men's title, there is a God! Wimbledon is an iconic tournament and in addition to the tennis it's as famous for its strawberries and cream, its famous fans and even Cliff Richard giving an impromptu performance during a downpour. Everything about Wimbledon is fantastic and providing the weather is kind it's a wonderful sporting event, and it's a date in the sporting calendar that I look forward to every year.

Other sports I have watched over the years are ice hockey, mainly for the fights and the level of violence on display…a sport I would much rather watch than play, and the Grand National where I will have a £2 each way flutter on a horse with a grand name that normally falls at the first couple of fences, but I can't watch any other horse racing event…it's so boring. I also detest motor racing in any form such as the Grand Prix or Super Bikes…I can't even watch the condensed headlights on the news. However, I have enjoyed speedway racing in the past but it's not something you tend to see any more.

Sport is fantastic and the great thing about it is that everybody likes at least one sport or a sporting event…there is literally something for everyone. Admittedly, to a sports buff like me, I love watching most sports, but as you have seen in Chapter 6 and this chapter, football and rugby are my favourites, always have been and always will be!

Chapter 8 – Love, Loss and Tragedy

Life is not all joy and happiness and to some extent, when we are younger, most of us are protected from the harsher things in life such as illness, heartache and death! However, as you have already seen in previous chapters, there have been good times and bad times, and despite my parents divorcing when I was five, seeing my friend Adrian being hit and killed by a car and experiencing the sudden loss of a family member, at the time I still believed my childhood was idyllic!! I never wanted for anything and my grandparents (both sets) provided the stability every child needs!! However, it's only with hindsight that I can see my childhood wasn't idyllic, it was disjointed and could have been the catalyst that led to my decision to join the army…a form of escapism perhaps!!! Despite my grandparents providing the stability of a good home there were many reasons why I now believe my childhood was disjointed such as; following my parents' divorce my mother and I stayed with Nan and Grampa Henson and within a short while I didn't see my father for approximately three years. When I did start seeing my father again he re-married and moved to London, and around the same time my mother, who also had a new boyfriend, moved to a flat on the other side of Bridgend leaving me with Nana and Grampa Henson. When I was thirteen my maternal grandfather suffered a series of debilitating strokes and I watched him change overnight; sadly, gone was the happy grandfather who had tried to teach me to drive, would take me places and who played football and snooker with me – as a thirteen year old I didn't know how to deal with this and I didn't understand the frustrations my grandfather was experiencing! Later, the same year my paternal grandfather died suddenly – I was devastated, within six months I had lost the two male role models in my life! I was also travelling to London and Norfolk to spend holidays with my dad and step-mum…however, my dad was always working and I didn't see him much. Lastly, throughout school I cannot remember any of my friends having parents that had divorced, therefore I had to deal with the stigma associated with having divorced parents and the lies that came with it). In some respects, I felt slightly detached from my family, and sadly, in some respects, I still do today (with exception of my own children and grandchildren), which made the decision to join the army an easy one. The above is a reality, but the childhood of any individual is 'the norm' and mine was no different...that's why, to me, my life seemed idyllic, and yes, throughout my childhood there was laughter, great times that resulted in great memories which far outweighed any sadness! But collectively, the good and the bad are integrated and shape the person we become and the personalities we develop as individuals. Looking back, I can smile about a lot of the adverse situations I experienced as a child and also those I experienced as an adult, such as the treatment I (and others) experienced as an army recruit (as shown in chapter 2), dealing with bereavements or the ending of relationships. In hindsight, I now understand that as human beings we are a complex mix of feelings, emotions and personalities, and we all have our own coping mechanisms. Unfortunately, these coping mechanisms are sometimes insufficient and we are unable to cope with some of the things life throws at us...sadly, I have first-hand experience of situations when this is the case! Thankfully, the majority of people are stronger than they think, and as a result, whilst we push the bad experiences to the back of our minds, we tend to remember the good times and will re-live and re-tell the funny episodes in our lives, time and time again!!! In this chapter I try to re-live those low points and high points that have the shaped the man that is writing this...I am happy and content with life and I appreciate that who I am today has been shaped by my own experiences and by those who have been a part of my life up to this point!!!!

■■

<u>Idris and Stanley...great men!</u>

The first time I realised that the good things in life shouldn't be taken for granted was in 1976 when I was thirteen years old...I was taught a harsh lesson about the fragilities of life when my maternal grandfather (Stanley), weeks after his retirement in April, suffered a series of strokes that left him severely disabled. The smiling gent I had loved was gone and was replaced by a sad, frustrated, angry and bitter man...difficult for a thirteen year old to comprehend! Within six months, I would experience the bereavement of a loved one for the first time, when my paternal grandfather (Idris or 'Eddie' as he was affectionately known) collapsed and died suddenly following a brain hemorrhage...I was devastated!

Within six months I had effectively lost the two men who had been major influences in my life to that point, absolute heroes who I loved and admired and still do to this day!!

Grampa Thomas (William Idris Thomas)

I walked into the bungalow carrying my new football boots…I was excited and couldn't wait to show Grampa Henson. As I stepped into the kitchen Grampa was standing at the opposite side of the kitchen precariously balancing on his walking stick and a pained expression on his face…nothing unusual about this given his frustrations with his disability. I shouted over to Grampa, as my mother stepped into the kitchen behind me;
"Everything OK Grampa?"
"You OK Dad? My mother asked.
He stood there wanting to say something for a few seconds and then said;
"I…I have some b…b…ad news…H..Huw" he stammered
"What's the matter Dad?" my mother said, concerned.
"H..Huw…your Uncle I…Ivor called when you w…were out, it's your Grampa T…T…Thomas…he…p…p…passed away earlier today…I'm s…s…sorry"
I could hear my mother's and Grampa Henson's voices, but I had no idea what they were saying, as I was trying to process what I'd just been told. I burst into tears and ran to my bedroom quickly followed by my mother who tried to comfort me as I sat on the edge of my bed sobbing uncontrollably with a multitude of thoughts and questions running through my head; what happened to Grampa Thomas? It can't be true, can it? He was so strong…it must be a mistake. Where did he die? What time did he pass away? Where was Nanny Thomas? Does my father know? He was fine when I saw him a few weeks ago?...and many more. I was thirteen years old, and it was the first time I experienced losing someone so close, someone I had idolised. I was struggling to comprehend the situation as I naively thought my Grampa would last forever.

It was Sunday before I could face going to Tondu to my Nan's flat. I turned the key hanging in the door (this was a time when you could leave the key in your front door so people could let themselves in) and climbed the stairs to the hallway (my granparents flat was an upstairs flat in what looked like a semi-detached house from the front) and headed for the kitchen…I knew that's where Nan would be. Just before I stepped into the kitchen I glanced to my right and could see my Grampa's Dai cap hanging in its usual place, on the hook of the coatstand in the hallway. I swallowed hard and walked into the kitchen, I could see my Nan continually washing the same plate and staring out of the window at nothing in particular.

"Nan…I…"

She turned, her eyes red from the many tears she had obviously cried.

"Oh Huw…oh Huw…" and she held out her arms.

We both immediately started crying, I walked over and she wrapped her arms around me and repeatedly said;

"Huw…Huw…Huw…" as we held each other and wept uncontrollably for a good few minutes. Eventually, we sat at the kitchen table as we had many times before and would again many times in the future and once she composed herself my nan told me what had happened to grampa…and that it happened there in the same room we were sitting in and that my cousin Deborah was with him. I remember thinking at the time, "how terrible that must have been for Deborah?" she was only twelve. My nan continued to tell me that grampa and Deborah had been stood looking out of the window and waving at her and auntie Jean as they came back from the shops and grampa said to Deborah;

"I'll put the kettle on" and turned away from the window. Deborah was still waving furiously when she heard a loud "T-H-U-D!!!" She turned and saw Grampa lying prostate on the floor, a nasty cut on his forehead and his glasses in pieces all around him. Nan said;

"At least it was quick Huw…he didn't suffer…the doctor said he was probably dead before he hit the floor" and she wiped away the tears.

I nodded with tears streaming down my face and immediately thought of my grandfather. I was struggling to comprehend that there would be no more walks with Grampa and Wag (his mongrel terrier and best friend), no more helping him feed his beloved birds (budgies and parakeets) that he bred in a purpose built shed in the garden, and no more sitting on the wall and watching him sawing and hammering for hours making nothing in particular, just keeping me occupied and no more listening to his wonderful ghost stories. I loved him so

398

much and I was trying to come to terms with the fact that I would never see him again.

Grampa's funeral was the first I'd ever attended but it would be the only one that I'd attend where the women didn't go to the crematorium (still tradition at the time in Wales in the mid Seventies). It was a difficult day, made moreso by the journey of around fifteen miles the funeral cortege had to make from Tondu to Pontypridd (where Glyntaf Crematorium was located) and back again…my grandfather was going home. It was a sombre affair, and I can still see the image of my grandfather's coffin disappearing behind the curtain as we all sang "The Lord's my Shepherd" far worse than any choir could have managed, but with enough gusto to give him a good send off. The tears welled up in my eyes when the time came to leave, but thankfully I was flanked protectively by my father and uncle Ivor as we made our way out of the chapel into the throng of people I'd never seen before, and who told me how sorry they were, the connection they had to my grandfather, what a great man he was and it was such a shame, a sad loss (it's only years later that I realised that the same things were said at all funerals…hopefully it'll be the same at my funeral at some point in the future). My last abiding memory was when we drove out of Treforest on the opposite side of the valley, and I looked out of the window of the limousine at the crematorium on the other side of the valley…I could see the whisps of smoke drifting into the grey autumn sky from the chimney and I mouthed in its direction a mute "goodbye Grampa…I love you".

Grampa Henson (Stanley Henson)

When I joined the army in October 1979 grampa Henson had already been diagnosed with terminal bowel cancer. The series of strokes in 1976 had already reduced my grandfather's mobility and created an emotional and frustrated man out of somebody who used to be so hardworking, jovial and proud. He used to be a joy to be around and everyone always commented on what a gentleman he was…so, so sad to see him reduced to the broken man I remember in my mid-teens. In some ways, we all saw the cancer as a blessing, an early release from the living nightmare my grandfather was now experiencing. The last Christmas he was alive in an attempt to cheer him up I brought my uniform home so he could see me dressed as a soldier, as he had been too ill to attend my passing-in parade at Dover a few days earlier…he was extremely proud of me and despite the obvious pain he was in he gave me a huge smile, and for a moment, there was a glimpse of the happy grandfather I'd known and loved. Sadly, that Christmas would be the last time I saw him alive. He passed away at Easter in 1980 and was finally at peace after four miserable years…it was a blessing in the end. I don't remember much about the funeral itself, my only two vivid memories were finding out from my grandmother that my grandfather had passed away, and the moment the hearse pulled up outside our bungalow at 30 Longfellow Drive on the day of the funeral.

It was Easter and I was on leave, staying with my cousin Stuart in Pucklechurch, nr Bristol. It was around lunchtime a couple of days into my leave when Stuart and I could hear the phone ringing in the hallway…we were sat on the settee talking and didn't give the phone a second thought as we knew Alan (Stuart's dad) had answered the phone. A few moments later Alan popped his head around the door and said;
"Huw…it's your grandmother on the phone"
I stood up and looked at Stuart and said nonchalantly;
"My grandfather has passed away"
I made my way to the hall and Alan passed me the receiver;
"Hello…Nan"
My grandmother being an ex-nurse was very calm, direct and in some respects quite 'cold' as she said;
"Huw…your grandfather passed away earlier today…we'll let you know when the funeral will take place…OK…bye…see you soon"
I didn't get the chance to say anything as I heard the clicks of my Nan replacing the receiver at her end of the line. I remember standing there for a moment and thinking my gran must be so relieved that Grampa had passed away as she had nursed him for the last four years…it just seemed so cold and calculated the way she told me. My opinion would soon change on the day of the funeral when my nans reaction would shock me and force me to re-evaluate my grand-parents relationship.

When I returned from Bristol a few days later and went to see my nan she was still very cold, unemotional and 'matter of fact' about grampa Henson's passing. But on the day of the funeral I remember my nan sitting in her normal chair that faced the window of the living room, and other close family members including my mother and I sat with her waiting for the hearse to arrive. We didn't have to wait too long, no more than five to ten minutes, but nothing prepared me for my Nan's reaction when the hearse, carrying my grandfather's body, came slowly into view and parked directly in front of the window. My nan became hysterical...sobbing...screaming;

"STAN...STAN...OH STAN...STAN...STAN...!!!"

I had never seen my nan so emotionally animated, she was always so calm, so 'in control' of her emotions to the point of being emotionless, some may say typical of a generation of women that had known so much suffering. In that moment, I realised how much she loved my grandfather and that 'love' wasn't about open displays of affection, it was much more profound. I now thought of the times when my grandfather had been ill and now remembered how my grandmother had caringly washed him, shaved him, help dress him and even simple tasks as wiping his mouth...I remembered how they looked at each other and the patience my grandmother displayed to her husband...my grandfather. I thought to myself that is love right there and the emotion my nan showed that day was her showing how much that love between them had meant to her. I had a renewed and deep feeling of love and utter respect for my grandparents on that day of Grampa Henson's funeral.

What did you say? (Linda Hutchinson, my first real love)

People often ask me "Why do you support Barnsley F.C.?" Well, it's a long story and involves a girl, Linda Hutchinson. Buckle up and enjoy this emotional ride as I open this little box of heartache that was hugely significant and life-changing...

It has been said that you never forget your first love...for me this is true, as I have never forgotten Linda and what we shared during our short time together. It could be considered that a 'love' is a conundrum; do you love the other person

401

because of the way they make you feel? Or is the depth of feeling a result of the personality and looks of the other person? For me it was a mixture of both, and I consider myself blessed for experiencing the depth of love I felt for Linda...she certainly captured my heart and soul!! Knowing what I experienced with Linda, I feel for those that may never experience being in love and that is such a shame as they are missing out on so much joy...admittedly, there is the flip side of losing a loved one, for whatever reason, and that is extremely painful, as you will see and sometimes very difficult to come to terms with and to find love again! But as it has been said, 'better to have loved and lost than never to have loved at all'. As you read this there may be some of you who may criticise the love that Linda and I shared, but please try and understand there are times in life that we can't help who we fall in love with or the circumstances in which the love unknowingly blossoms...and we were only nineteen (me) and seventeen (Linda) respectively. I have a very good memory, but even I struggle to remember conversations word for word so, as with the rest of the book, the conversations are as close to how I remember them. I also understand that others may remember things differently or remember things that I can't, but the events surrounding Linda from 1981 up to 2001 have been replayed in my mind time and time again. As a result, I remember them as if they only happened last week.

The first time I met Linda she was the girlfriend of one of my then best mate's, Eric Gothard, who came from Barnsley. I met Eric when we found ourselves in the same four man room together during our combat engineer training at 1&3 Training Regiments near Farnborough, and I met Linda during a couple of visits to Barnsley with Eric. I even went on a double-date with her and Eric and her best friend Debbie...but nothing developed further between Debbie and I! At this point I believed Linda was nothing more than the girlfriend of a friend, but looking back that may have not have been the case...more on this later. When our training finished, Eric was posted to 22 (two two...once you get past twenty with regiments and squadrons in the army, it's two two, three nine etc) Engineer Regiment at Tidworth and I was posted to 39 Engineer Regiment at Waterbeach...we soon lost touch in those days before mobile phones.

My time at Waterbeach was cut short after a couple of months when, out of the blue and much to my dismay, I was posted to 24 Field Squadron at Chattenden in November 1981..."it's because of rugby" explained the OC "I knew you'd want to go". So I headed to Chattenden Barracks and the start of my time at 24 (two four), and for the next 6 months it felt as if I was on a rugby merry go round, playing for the squadron, Army U'19s, Combined Services U'19s, The Corps (Royal Engineers) and even Bridgend Youth. In July 1982, the first of a coincidental chain of events happened that would eventually lead me back to Barnsley...and to Linda! One evening I was trying to find my passport and I had emptied my personal drawer (a compartment in an army locker that could be secured with a padlock and where important documents, letters, photos etc could be kept). During this search I discovered a small unfamiliar photograph of two girls dressed as clowns! I stared at this strange photograph for a few seconds before turning it over and discovered writing on the back, 'Thanks for a fantastic weekend love Debbie...and there was a phone number and three small kisses'...as much as I tried to remember, I just couldn't think who the girls were or where the photograph came from. I was completely mystified and in frustration I tossed the photograph onto the bottom shelf next to my bed! Later that evening I picked the photo up again and almost immediately the 'penny dropped' and I realised the clowns were Debbie and Linda (following the weekend I had met Debbie, Eric had found the photograph and for a laugh wrote on the back to make out to the other lads in the troop that I'd met a girl during my weekend in Barnsley!). The day after finding the photograph I decided to ring the number on the back, not even knowing if it was real or whether Eric had just made it up! I made my way to the pay phone that was located outside the Duty NCO's bunk on the ground floor of our accommodation block. I patiently waited my turn as there were two people in front of me, and after about twenty minutes I was at the payphone with a 10p perfectly poised over the slot. Holding my breath, I slowly and nervously dialed the number on the back of the photograph...once I'd finished dialing there were a few distant clicks as the connection was made and then I could hear the phone ringing at the end of the line. Suddenly, in a deep, South Yorkshire accent I heard "Hello!", it was Debbie's dad...this prompted me to push the 10p into the slot and I excitedly *explained, in a continuous stream of words and without breathing, who I was and why I was calling? By the time I'd put the phone down I was holding Linda's phone number in my hand, and I thought, "Brilliant…I'll be able to get hold of Eric again!" Halfway back to my room I looked at Linda's number again and thought, "I might as well ring her now". I made my way back to the pay phone and again waited patiently for my turn (this is how it was in the pre-mobile phone days of the early eighties). When I was next in line it was obvious that the lad now using the phone was talking to his girlfriend as he turned away from us all and spoke in hushed whispers. After about 10-15 minutes we could tell the call was ending as we heard the recognizable, but whispered, "Yes, I love you too…yes, I miss you too…" - the poor lad had opened himself up to a torrent of abuse and ridicule (which included mocking "I love you's") from those waiting to use the phone…myself included!! It was soon my turn and I dialed the number and went through the same process as before with the 10p. I immediately recognized Linda's voice when she picked up the phone, pushed the 10p into the slot and said "Hi Linda, its Taff"…I could hear her shouting to her mother and father, Jean and Roy, "It's Taff…it's Taff". We talked for about twenty minutes and she told me Eric was in the Falklands and due back at Christmas. She took my address and told me she would write and forward Eric's address so I could write to him. We said our goodbyes and I was happy that I would be able to get in touch with my good old mate Eric again! A few days later, and true to her word, I received a letter off Linda with Eric's address…that evening I wrote two letters, one to Linda thanking her for her letter and one to Eric. Over the course of the next six weeks, Eric, Linda and myself had arranged that we would meet up in Barnsley for New Year (following Eric's arrival back from the Falklands)…we were all looking forward to it and eagerly made plans of how we would spend New Year's Eve. But it never happened…I would receive news that resulted in the plans being cancelled.*

In early September a squadron parade was ordered by our OC (Officer Commanding), Major Owen, and it was announced that we were going to the Falklands in late October/early November…a six month (door to door) construction tour – the first thing I thought about was rugby as I had been asked to

play for London Welsh...unfortunately, that didn't happen.
The following week I was on a B3 Clerks course at Blackdown
Barracks in Deepcut, nr Camberley...this was where a
catalogue of events spiraled out of control!! As if by destiny,
there were three fellow Sappers on the course who all came
from various parts of West Yorkshire...they had already
arranged that they were going back to Yorkshire that coming
weekend. I asked them if there was any chance of a lift to
Barnsley if I could arrange for somewhere to stay. I rang
Linda and explained about the Falklands and that I had an
opportunity to come to Barnsley...I thought it would be great
to see them all before I left for the Falklands...I told Linda
that I wanted to return the money her parent's had paid for my
train ticket back to Barracks when I had been hospitalized a
year earlier with blood poisoning (Chapter 2). Linda's mother
Jean said I was more than welcome to stay with them and
Linda told me to bring trousers, shirt and tie and smart shoes
as she had a presentation evening planned with Barnsley Road
Runners (Linda was an excellent long distance runner and ran
competitively in and around Yorkshire) and her and her
friends were planning on heading to Rebecca's (a nite club in
Barnsley town centre) later on in the evening. That weekend I
headed to Barnsley in the shared car and was very much
looking forward to seeing Linda, Jean, Roy, Andrew and Lady
(a beautiful but typically jealous jack russell terrier)
again...and hoping that Jean had made some of her legendary
'mint crisp' (crushed digestive base, mint cream and a milk
chocolate topping). It was a fantastic weekend. As a
hairdresser, Linda worked on Saturdays, so I took her brother,
Andrew, to watch Barnsley F.C. in a fantastic game against
Fulham which Barnsley won 4-3 (I've been an avid Barnsley
fan since that day – see Chapter 7), and I even got to speak to
Eric on the phone when he rang Linda's house from the Cable
and Wireless building in Port Stanley. However, something
changed that weekend between me and Linda...when we
returned from Rebecca's we stayed up until around 5 o'clock
on the Sunday morning talking about anything and everything,
and she even told me that things weren't good between her
and Eric, but at the time I didn't think anything of it! Why
would I, we were friends (and she was the girlfriend of a good
mate), but it was good to talk to Linda and to get to know her
better! That Sunday evening after Linda and I had spent an
hour or so together in The Outpost, Roy and Linda dropped

405

me to the car park adjacent to the town hall, and within a few minutes I was sat in the back of my friend's car, waving frantically to Linda and Roy as we drove away.

Back at Blackdown Barracks Linda dominated my thoughts and what she had said about her and Eric, and as the days passed I couldn't get Linda out of my head and it was becoming obvious that, as much as I tried to fight it, I was beginning to develop feelings for this pretty, elfin-like Barnsley lass or had these suppressed feelings already been there longer than I'd realised. I was also struggling with my own conscience due to the developing complexity of the situation...how could I fall in love with my friend's girlfriend? This was becoming a fucked up dilemma! That next weekend I returned to Yorkshire, staying with one of the Sappers at his family's home in Heckmondwike, nr Leeds. I called Linda late on the Friday night and we talked...and talked, and eventually I remember her saying;
"This line is clear Taff, where are you?"
(In the world of pre-mobile landlines you could tell if a call was local or whether it was long distance!)
"I'm in a place called...Heckmondwike" I said coyly.
"Aww Taff...you are near Batley...that's great...is thee popping to Barnsley to see us" she asked excitedly.
"I...I don't know Linda...I...I...don't think I...I should" I stuttered.
"Why...what's wrong Taff?"
"I just don't think it's a good idea...I..."
"What's appened Taff?" she said
"Nothing...well...it's just that..."
"Cumon Taff...Thy's worrying me nar!"
I sighed, paused and took a deep breath!
"Linda...I don't think it's a good idea... I'm...I'm starting to think of you...to think of you as being more than just a friend...my feelings for you are...are changing...I'm...I'm sorry, so, so sorry...I..." Before I had a chance to finish she said firmly;
"Taff don't apologise...come over tomorrow and we can talk about it"
"I don't know Linda" I said quietly, but she wouldn't take no for an answer.
"Please Taff" she pleaded
"Are you sure Linda...cos I'm..."

"Yes Taff" she interrupted
"We can talk...don't worry, everything will be ok...just tell me thy'll come and see me...I need to see you..."
"Ok Linda...OK...I'll see you tomorrow...why do you need to see me?" I said intrigued
"Tomorrow Taff...see thee...and don't worry...neet Taff"
I heard the click as Linda put down the phone and I was left with one thought...why did Linda need to see me? I drifted off to sleep comforted by images of Linda as I slipped into a world of dreams.

The following day I went to Barnsley and met Linda and we talked...and talked...and talked, and by the Sunday evening it had become clearly evident that we both felt the same way about each other. It also explained why she had said "I need to see you" when I had phoned her on the Friday evening. The depth of feelings we had for each other grew quickly, and eventually became too strong to ignore, and as we were young we were initially blinkered to anything else...sadly this included Eric! However, this did change after a week or so and we started to think of the impact on others, especially Eric! We talked about the best way of managing the situation, and agreed that she would tell Eric they were finished when he returned at Christmas (we both agreed that he deserved to be told face to face and not in a letter), and we also agreed to be sensitive about open displays of affection so as not to advertise our love until the 'Eric' situation had been resolved. In hindsight, I believe we probably made the wrong decision about telling Eric in person, but we thought we were doing the right thing at the time. Over the next two months Linda and I become insanely close, and even jokingly talked about travelling to Gretna Green and getting married...perhaps we should have! Unfortunately, the day arrived that I had to leave Linda and Barnsley...Tuesday the 9th of November 1982 is etched in my memory and every year it serves as a painful reminder of what might have been! We met for lunch and enjoyed a last drink together, but inevitably the hour passed quickly and the time came for Linda to head back to work at the Clip Joint on Sheffield Road. We headed down the subway to the sunken open area in the middle of the Alhambra roundabout and started to say our farewells...I held Linda close to me and soon became aware that she was sobbing. I pulled away slightly and lifted her head, I could see the tears streaming down her face and I caringly and gently wiped them away, but they were quickly replaced by new ones...she looked at me despairingly one last time, her eyes pleading 'don't go!', then she pulled away completely and ran in the direction of the subway that would take her up to Sheffield Road. I called after her "Linda...Linda...stop...come back", but she disappeared from sight and I was left there alone with my rucksack and suitcase...my only company were a handful of pigeons and an old fella sitting on one of the benches who shouted "Everything Ok lad". I nodded dejectedly, wiped away developing tears and sat on my suitcase hoping Linda would return, but she never did, and overwhelmed by sadness and a heavy sense of loss I headed to Roy's work as he was giving me a lift to Doncaster Railway Station. I spent the entire journey back to Chatham thinking of that image of Linda crying and running off and it was so painful...really painful! It was a pain I'd never experienced before...an ache that couldn't be treated with medicines, an emptiness that could only be filled with Linda's presence, but sadly it was a yearning for a love that I didn't know was already lost. That evening when I got back to Chattenden I rang Linda and she apologized for running off crying, and explained that she was so upset that I had to go back to camp...she said she didn't know what to do and just ran back to her work. That night when I was lying on my bed in the silence of my room, I knew that I was so in love with Linda, as the feelings were stronger than I'd felt for another human being in my entire life up to that point. But little did I know, that the love I held inside my heart for Linda would haunt me, along with those images of her crying and running away that day, for a very, very long time...as sadly, it would be almost 20 years before I saw Linda again.

The short story below is not directly about the events of 1982, but of a return visit I made in 1991 when I visited Jean. The visit to Jean that day was when I found out for the first time what had really happened when Eric returned from the Falklands! In an attempt to come to terms with the devastating news I had heard, I left Princess Street that day and again returned to the Alhambra roundabout (as I had done in 1984 and 1985), the last place I saw Linda in 1982, and re-lived those wonderful memories (and the heartbreaking image of Linda running away crying) from the Autumn of 1982 and the

love I shared with her…it was a place that in some perverse
and strange way still made me feel close to Linda.

It was the summer of 1991 and I was driving down the M1
from Leeds, where I'd just installed a fax/answer machine in
the house of a Raleigh sales rep, when in the distance and to
my left, I could see the familiar sight of the clock tower of
Barnsley Town Hall. The Portland stone of this impressive
building was glistening in the afternoon sun, and this alluring
image was 'calling me home'. Within minutes I was
approaching junction 37 and made the impulsive decision to
'pop in and see Jean!' not knowing that I would soon hear
news that would leave me feeling guilty, angry and
emotionally devastated. It had been six years since I last saw
Jean, Roy and Andrew (and almost nine years since I'd seen
Linda) and it was too good an opportunity to miss. As it was
the middle of the day I took the gamble that Jean would
probably be on her own in the house. I indicated and pulled off
the motorway, and I was soon driving down Park Road where
the familiar sites of *Locke Park* and the huddled terraced
houses of coursed dressed sandstone welcomed me like an old
friend!! I slowed down as I pulled alongside *The Silkstone*
pub, indicated left and turned onto Duke Street, after around
fifty metres I turned left onto Wood Street and within seconds
I could see Princess Street in the distance. A few minutes later
I was parked up outside 92 Princess Street and I smiled as
memories flooded my mind and fought for their own
prominence…it was strange, despite all the places I had lived,
I always felt happy in Barnsley, and Princess Street always felt
like I was going home! I stepped up to the front door, paused
as I looked up and down the front of the house, took a deep
breath and knocked on the glass…momentarily I poignantly
ran my finger over the nine and two of the number plaque
before seeing the image of Jean through the frosted glass.
When she opened the door and realised who I was she
shouted,
"TAFF…OH MY GOD, WHAT'S THY DOIN ERE…GET
YOUR SEN IN LAD!!"
I stepped into the house, closed the door behind me and
followed Jean through a living room that held so many happy
memories and into the kitchen, explaining that I'd been to
Leeds with work and thought I'd pop-in to see her on my way
back to Nottingham.

"Nottingham!" she said inquisitively.

"Yeah…I'm out of the army and living in Long Eaton…with my wife and three children"

"Well I never…sit your sen darn thear and I'll pop kettle on" and gave me a big smile.

We talked for an hour or so…firstly catching up with what I was doing and then she brought me up to speed with what Roy was doing, how Andrew was getting on and finally the subject came round to Linda! It started quite normally and I was genuinely pleased (and probably a little jealous, but I didn't let it show) that Linda was in a relationship, living in Higham and was now a mother. However, Jean started to tell me how Linda had changed and why…it appeared that the 'happy-go-lucky' Barnsley lass I had known had now been replaced by a strong-minded young women with a steely demeanor due to the events she and her family had been through! As I listened to Jean, I felt an overwhelming sense of guilt and anger sweep over me and I felt myself sink into the chair in horror as she continued!!!

Jean told me that when Eric returned from the Falklands he had been diagnosed with having a cyst or some sort of non-malignant growth on the brain. Following the operation to remove the 'cyst/growth' and the subsequent recovery period something about Eric's personality had changed!

"What do you mean Jean…his personality had changed?" I was shocked by this revelation. "Hang on Taff…I'll make us another cuppa…does thy want some parkin?"

"Oh yes please Jean" and smiled, but I sat there pondering on where the conversation was leading and what had changed about Eric?

Armed with fresh cuppas Jean continued…I couldn't believe what I was hearing;

Emotional blackmail…(I sat there wondering if Linda had tried to finish with Eric when he came back from the Falklands, as we'd agreed, and he'd used emotional blackmail to make her feel guilty to stay with him!)…

Theft…(Eric had stolen money from all of them)…

Split personality…(I thought of a phone call I had received from Eric in the summer of 1983 when he spoke to me as if nothing had ever happened between me and Linda, and he had

even invited me to Barnsley…it all made sense now and I should have contacted Linda after that phone call!)…
Debt…
Dishonorable or medical discharge from the army…(not sure which one).
False holiday…(Jean told me that Linda was packing for a holiday to America; when Eric asked her what she was doing? Linda said "we are off to America tomorrow". Eric had no idea what she was talking about!…Jean said Linda had been giving money to Eric for months and months towards that 'imaginary' holiday!)…
And finally…Eric began stalking Linda after she'd finished with him…

I began to feel angry with myself for not returning to Barnsley when I came back from the Falklands. I looked at Jean and shook my head in disbelief;
"I'm sorry Jean…I'm so sorry…this is my fault" and put my head in my hands.
"Taff, thy can't blame thee sen"
"But Jean…I put Linda in a difficult situation before Eric returned from the Falklands…and I feel as if I let Linda down…I let you all down…!!"
This wasn't the first time I'd apologised to Jean about what had happened between Linda and I back in the autumn of 1982. I had written a letter to her and Roy in February/March 1983, after Eric had found out about me and Linda. I remember apologising and telling them that I'd betrayed their trust and friendship for allowing myself to fall in love with their daughter! However, Jean wrote back telling me that her and Roy had known what was happening between Linda and I and spared me from any blame, saying that we were young and we were living our own lives…and beside the point, they could see we were both so happy. Once again, Jean moved to dismiss any guilt I felt,
"Taff, it wasn't your fault…you and our Linda didn't have a chance to…"
Her words drifted away as I felt an overpowering sense of anger at what had happened to Linda, Jean, Roy and Andrew, and at my own stupid decisions not to call Linda or go to Barnsley in mid 1983, and there were now a multitude of thoughts and questions running through my head;

411

Why hadn't I stayed in touch with Linda?...
I should have been there for her...and for Jean, Roy and Andrew...
I felt that I'd abandoned Linda...she needed me and I wasn't there...
How could Eric do what he had done?...
Was he ill or was that an excuse?...
I wish I'd known, I could have done something...
Why didn't Linda tell me?..
Did she think I didn't care?...
But what would I have done?...
I shouldn't have stayed in the army...
When I came back from the Falklands I should have gone straight to Barnsley and spoke to Linda and showed her how much she meant to me...

I whispered to myself "I'm so sorry Linda..."

I suddenly felt ashamed that I'd felt sorry for myself back in 1983 when, at the same time, Linda and her family were being put through hell!
These futile thoughts and questions, of a past I could not change, continued. It was this harsh realization that made me look up and I then heard Jean saying;
"...Linda finished with Eric, but then he wor waiting for our Linda to finish work every neet and arrassing her!"
I looked at Jean and my tormented but hushed voice whispered angrily; "I should have been there for Linda...I should have been there Jean...she needed me and I wasn't there...I should have..."
But Jean interrupted me, "...Nay Taff, thee didn't know whot wor going on!"
I struggled to hold back the tears and tried to argue;
"I loved her Jean...I loved her so much...I st...!" I stopped myself and again lowered my head. I don't know if Jean heard the last part...if she did, she didn't let on!
"I know Taff...I know thee did...unfortunately, that's life Taff...it's ard!"
Jean then told me that it was during this period that Ken stepped in to help Linda; he worked at a motorbike shop close to where Linda worked at the Clip Joint on Sheffield Road and started bringing Linda home and taking her to work, their relationship developed from there! Whilst I still believed I

412

should have been there for Linda, I was genuinely happy that Ken had been there for her and that they were now happy together!

Despite what Jean had told me about Linda and Eric, it had been fantastic seeing her again...Jean and Roy had always been very good to me, and I had never forgotten how they took me in and treated me like one of their own...amazing people! I drank the last of my tea and ate the last mouthful of parkin, and said my farewells to Jean. A few minutes later Princess Street disappeared behind me, but I wasn't ready to go home...there was something I had to do! Ten minutes later I was sat on a bench in the middle of the Alhambra roundabout, facing the subway that led to Sheffield Road...the last place that I'd seen Linda on that fateful day in 1982. This wasn't the first time I'd been back to this spot, a place that provided me with mixed emotions. I'd sat on the same bench in the summers of 1984 and 1985 to remember Linda, but despite the sadness associated with that day in November 1982, I drew comfort from the fact that it was the last place I saw her...it was a place I used to try and exorcise the ghosts from the past, but also remember the happy times we had spent together and the many memories we had made!

I again sat there on that bench, stared at that sad space for a few minutes, reflecting on what might have been, and slowly closed my eyes......

Almost immediately the memories came flooding back complete with their own unique soundtrack that created a nostalgic and touching tribute of our time together...it was similar to watching the trailer of a romantic 'chick flick', with Linda and I as the stars! The first image that greeted me was Linda visiting me in hospital on the day of the 'Barnsley 6' back in 1981...I wondered for a moment "had our feelings unknowingly started back then!" Then the images fast-forwarded to Linda and I at the presentation evening a year later where we were joining the already crowded dance floor for the sixties classic *'Hi ho silver lining'*, still a great song and there were plenty of hands waving, pointing and singing along as we faced each other...blissfully happy with not a care in the world. I smiled to myself as the images continued to Rebecca's later that evening, where we would have our one

413

and only slow dance! I then remembered my short-lived excitement when we came out and I saw a burger van on the other side of the car park, I sprinted across to it, only to be disappointed to find it wasn't a burger van…it was a 'pie and peas' van…a 'pie and peas' van…bizarre, never seen one before or since!

I briefly opened my eyes and sniggered quietly to myself……

Shutting my eyes again the video of my memories played on in my mind to where we were back in the kitchen at Linda's house that same night, the same kitchen I'd just left, where we innocently talked and talked and jokingly messed around…tickling each other, which prompted Lady to continually force herself between us, growling a friendly but jealous warning for us both to stop!

I laughed again, opened my eyes, stood up and walked a few paces to roughly the spot I last held Linda…I winced at the painful memory of her running away, turned and walked back to the bench. I sat back down, raised my head to stare at the cold, grey sky which had now replaced the sunshine of earlier, and returned to the happier memories as Dire Straits *'Romeo and Juliet'* became the new soundtrack in my head, and the lyrics of that iconic song took me back to a place and time I wished I'd never left ……

I remembered the nights in *The Vine Tavern* where we would talk about absolutely anything…a place where we became so lost in each other, and being on our own away from everybody else we could be ourselves, huddled close to a roaring open fire we would hold hands, kiss and be openly affectionate with each other. It was here we plotted and mapped out our lives together; marriage, children, childrens names, where we'd live, and even the colour of each room, pets, holidays etc…all the plans couples loved to share with each other. Additionally, knowing I was leaving the army in March 1984, I remembered that I had made enquiries to join South Yorkshire Police, South Yorkshire Fire Service and West Yorkshire Fire Service…Barnsley was where I'd wanted to live, and with Linda. As Dire Straits continued to sing in my mind, I smiled and remembered us singing *Romeo and Juliet* as we came back from *The Vine* one night…singing at the top of our voices as we walked hand in hand down the centre of the road on Princess Street…young love at its carefree best.

I laughed out loud and a passer-by gave me a strange look before hurrying toward the town centre, and Dire Straits sang on, twisting my emotions with their mixed lyrics of the joy and incredible sadness of being in love, and lyrics which sadly seemed to mirror what happened to Linda and me nine years before. The smile quickly slipped away, as I again remembered what I had lost……

I remembered the phone calls, the letters we wrote with the outpourings of love, hopes and dreams, and the little pictures Linda drew in her letters to me and the letter which included her teardrop stains. I remembered the small *smurf* keepsake I bought her with 'I miss you' on it. I remembered Linda having a photograph taken with the smurf and sending it to me in the Falklands. Sadly, I also remembered my mate Jack Sutton taking that same photograph out of my wallet in 1985 and ripping it in half and burning it. Yes…I still carried her photo in my wallet in 1985. It was the small things, the simple things that made our love so perfect. Standing alone in that spot nine years later I realised I missed those simple tokens of our love, the warm affection we shared with each other…it immediately dawned on me that my love for Linda had not waned with the passing years and I still missed her more than ever. I remembered never being happier than that autumn of 1982, my eyes welled up as a feeling of incredible loss swept over me…and in my mind Dire Straits 'Romeo and Juliet' came to an end, and this simple, 'lovestruck Romeo' sighed at the thought of a lost love that once meant everything.

I opened my eyes, wiped my eyes and smiled again as images of Linda flooded my mind, and an old lady passing by with a shopping trolley thought I was smiling at her…and smiled back. I chuckled to myself, closed my eyes and returned to another trailer of memories and Chicago accompanied the new images with 'Hard to say I'm sorry', the record I remember buying for Linda…for me it said it all. Little did I know that when I watched Linda disappear from view through that subway in November 1982, that the 'little time away' that Peter Cetera (lead singer of Chicago) sang about would turn into nine years, I sighed heavily……

415

My thoughts turned to Linda herself...to me she was perfection, everything I had ever dreamt of in a girl. Being a hopeless romantic I had this image of love, and with Linda...I lived those dreams. I remembered that every time we kissed, touched or I looked into her eyes my body tingled with excited expectation and emotion, and every time she left the room my heart ached until she returned...she was my world. I remembered struggling to comprehend feelings I'd never experienced before, but there was a sense of realization they were because of Linda, a girl who unknowingly taught me the meaning of love and all the joy it brings, and who probably never fully realised how much I loved her and how happy she had made me. I knew standing there at that exact moment, enduring the incredible feelings of pain, meant our love had been so very real. I also remembered that apart from saying 'I love you' the thing we said to each other more than anything was "What did you say?" It was a standing joke between us because of our different accents and dialects, and was included in the letters we wrote, Linda even incorporated it into the drawings she drew in her letters to me. She was a beautiful, petite, funny and caring Barnsley lass who lit up my world, but who now only existed as an image in my mind, and Chicago sang on. I thought of Linda the athlete...she was a fine long distance runner and I had enjoyed watching her race, particularly at an event in Hillsborough Park and also in the Rowntree 10 in York. As a sports lover it made me immensely proud to support her and I even trained with her once...it would have been nice if it had been more and I know she would have supported me in the same way, unfortunately, she never got the chance to see me play rugby or football. I remembered returning from the Rowntree 10 with Linda, sat in the back of Roy's car where we secretly held hands as our love continued to blossom. I remembered the nights at Barnsley Road Runners (behind Oakwell), the day we spent in Sheffield together and the following day that we were together in Leeds, where, during a visit to the bank, the bank teller tried to attract my attention, but Linda and I only had eyes for each other and were oblivious to anything or anyone else around us...it took several attempts by the bank teller to gain my attention before I walked over red with embarrassment, apologizing repeatedly. I smiled as I remembered Andrew catching us kissing as he looked in on us through the window into the

416

living-room of the house in Princess Street…I think Andrew believed us when we denied it!

I remembered all these things as Chicago continued to sing 'our song' in their own unique and haunting style;

The memories just kept on jumping into my mind, whilst they may seem meaningless and trivial to others, to me they were everything…they were all I now had! I remembered the time I embarrassed myself at my first Sunday dinner at Jean and Roy's! I was in the living room putting a model plane together with Andrew, when Linda popped her head around the door and said;
"Taff…Andrew, dinner's ready"
Andrew and I got up and followed Linda into the kitchen where it looked as if there had been a Yorkshire pudding explosion…they were everywhere, all different shapes and sizes. At one point I thought there was a hole at the back of the oven and they were being passed through from next door…I'd never seen so many Yorkshire puddings! I sat down and watched everyone getting stuck-in, it was frenzy of Yorkshire puddings and gravy but my plate was still empty and after a few moments Jean noticed my empty plate and said;
"What's the matter Taff…don't thee like Yorkshire pudding?"
"Yeah…" I said hesitantly, "…I don't want to appear rude but…where's the meat and veg?"
Silence…everyone stopped eating and looked at me and then burst out laughing, and Jean looked at me and said;
"This is Yorkshire Taff…we ave t'yorkshires first, it's tradition…then meat and veg…then cold Yorkshires with jam and custard for dessert!"
Jean stood up, rocked her head back and was roaring laughing as she fetched more Yorkshires and brought them to the table, shaking her head and saying repeatedly;
"Where's the meat and veg?" still laughing she looked at me and said;
"Eee Taff, Thy's so funny!"

This simple memory made me open my eyes and laugh out loud, frightening the two pigeons that had been strutting their stuff around my feet, and who then flew away to a safer part of the roundabout, further away from the mad, but sad, Welshman on the bench……

417

The weather had now changed, the sunshine was gone and the grey clouds began squeezing out a smattering of fine, but insignificant raindrops…but still the memories came and the soundtrack that accompanied them had changed to The Jam singing '*Bitterest pill (I ever had to swallow)*', a song Linda once told me reminded her of me as she knew I was a big fan of The Jam, and it was in the charts in that Autumn of 1982…despite the negative lyrics it now reminded me of our happy time together.

I again closed my eyes to the present and drifted back to my memories of Linda, and as The Jam sang on, I remembered the day Linda and I took Lady to Locke Park…it was midweek on a dark and cold November day and the park was almost empty…it was as if it had been opened just for us. The peace and quiet was beautiful, and as Lady excitedly trotted along between us, the setting provided a stunning backdrop for our thoughts, dreams and unbridled love. We were inseparable as we walked into the countryside adjacent to the park; even the mundane images of Dodworth in the distance and the M1 snaking its away south in the direction of Sheffield, had no impact on how we felt…the feelings would have been no different had we been walking on a sun-kissed beach of white sand…the location was irrelevant, we were just so happy….why wouldn't we be?...we were together and in love. I chuckled as I remembered the trip to the cinema to watch 'The Exorcist' where the main character, Regan, was projectile vomiting what looked like the mushy peas we'd had for tea with our fish and chips – not the best memory, but funny all the same, and the fact we watched it together was all that really mattered! I remembered bonfire night in Princess Street…great to see a community pull together to put on a firework display in a carpark behind the houses on Princess Street, there were even hot dogs, and it was great to share this community spirit with Linda! I remembered the trip to Sheffield train station later that evening, where the darkness outside the car window was continually lit up by fireworks in the night sky, and every year since, similar images have always served as a reminder of Linda. I also remembered sitting on the train that evening and looking despondently out of the window at Linda and the mirrored sadness etched on her face as the train pulled slowly out of the station. But I smiled as I also remembered the joy the following day when we were told we could go back on leave until Tuesday 9th November…I remembered calling Linda with the news, and returning to Barnsley, where she was eagerly waiting for me!

I opened my eyes and the smile slowly slipped away as I sat on that bench and remembered those last few days with Linda…we had become so, so close, and it became painful for us both knowing the distance that would soon be between us……a distance that, despite me clinging to a small thread of hope, I now realistically knew would sadly never be bridged!!.....

We slipped away on the last night to spend some time alone at the *Manor House*. I remembered that our heads were filled with so many hopes and dreams about our future together, and that our hearts were so full of love for each other. Sadly, I now remembered that neither of us realised at the time, but that night would be the last night we ever spent together. I remembered us slowly walking hand in hand back to Princess Street, even though we were together, we were also alone with our own thoughts and the silence between us was deafening as we both unknowingly tried to fight the inevitable! When we eventually got back to Princess Street it was still, but eerily welcoming, and the house was in, what seemed like, a scripted darkness. We entered the house and as the street lights peeped in through the curtains like nosey neighbours, we sat in the half-darkness and barely a word passed between us. We then lay on the floor and held each other tightly, neither of us daring to let go…and then made love for the last time, a final snatched togetherness where our bodies were entwined as one, in one final act of defiance to the impending separation. At that exact moment, I hoped that I would spend my entire lifetime providing Linda with a love that knew no boundaries.

Sat on that bench nine years later, I lowered my head and wiped away a solitary tear…as I sadly remembered Linda sobbing in my arms on that final evening in 1982 as we lay there in the stillness of the night for what seemed like an eternity……I never wanted that moment to end, and in my dreams it never has…to me that shared moment was the epitome of our love, a beautiful snapshot of a forbidden togetherness.

I stood up, sighed and looked up at the sky and slowly mouthed the words "Linda…be happy". I glanced across to that exit to Sheffield Road and as I had done nine years before, I paused and stared at the space hoping that Linda would appear and run back into my arms. Of course she never did, and with a heavy heart, I turned and walked away, immersed in sadness, but thankful for the memories Linda had given me. In a compilation of vivid images I had again watched our love grow in a crescendo of emotion and also re-lived that heart-rending final farewell…we were just kids back then, but kids that were so, so in love. Ten or so minutes later I drove up Park Street toward the M1 and a wry smile crept onto my face as I remembered Linda one last time…once again, Barnsley disappeared in the rear view mirror.

Post note:

Initially, writing this book has allowed me to reflect on events in my life, and I now understand the the events surrounding Linda were a pivitol time in my life where everything changed…my life path, my character and much, much more. I thought re-visiting my 'first love' would be easy and that in a day or two I'd have written about Linda, and enjoy re-living those happy days in 1982. Whilst I have enjoyed re-visiting those memories, it has been incredibly difficult re-evaluating the love I felt for Linda and realising that the love had remained as strong for more than twenty years. I had no idea how emotionally draining it would be re-visiting those very vivid memories from the autumn of 1982 and that day in the summer of 1991, when I popped in to see Jean and re-visited the Alhambra roundabout. I underestimated my depth of feelings for Linda and the impact she had on my life, and I can now appreciate that those events from the autumn of 1982 were a defining moment that influenced much of what followed. The army had brought us together, but unfortunately it also ripped us apart…I still curse the 'enforced separation' that ultimately left us both broken-hearted. Linda and I were still writing to each other up to March/April 1983, but the letters became less frequent obviously due to the reasons highlighted in the short story above from that visit to Barnsley in 1991. Linda and I have never had the chance to speak about what happened when Eric returned to Barnsley toward the end of 1982. Therefore, I don't know if Eric blackmailed Linda into staying with him or whether she decided to stay with Eric as she felt guilty about what happened between us. I don't think I'll ever know and that is one part of the story that Jean couldn't tell me back in 1991, all I do know is whatever happened, it absolutely broke my heart and changed me as a person. As I reflect, not only on the events of 1982 and 1991, but also on two smaller, and for me, significant events that happened in 1984 and 2001. These provide proof that Linda is an incredible, caring and compassionate woman, and justifies why I fell so deeply in love with her...body and soul. Firstly, at some point in 1984 I contacted Linda by phone and she was genuinely pleased to hear from me and we exchanged a couple of letters, but unfortunately after a few weeks her new boyfriend Ken understandably didn't appreciate Linda writing to me or us speaking on the phone, hence I received a very compassionate letter in which she wrote, 'It hurts me as much to write this as it will be for you to read it...'. I never forgot those words which I know were genuine and heartfelt, and yes it hurt but I respected her decision. Strange as it may seem, I never did ask her what happened when Eric returned from the Falklands and why she hadn't finished with him as we'd discussed...perhaps I was scared of what the answer might have been and as they say 'ignorance is bliss'. Secondly, there were two life-changing events in 2001 that I now understand that for me it hadn't ended in 1982, 1984, 1985 or even 1991, sub-consciously I was still very much in love with Linda up to that point. It was the first event in 2001 that I still consider to be a beautiful moment...it was a small gesture that had a huge impact on me, and again proved that Linda is a beautiful person. Over the years, I had remained in sporadic contact with Jean and Roy, but when my phone rang one Thursday night in the middle of 2001, I was shocked to hear the voice on the other end of the phone...it was Linda. Initially, I thought I was dreaming but sure enough it was her, she had rang me out of concern, and to check that I was ok following the difficult time I had been through after the messy divorce from ex-wife (Jean had obviously told her that I'd had a real rough time). We talked for about ten to fifteen minutes and it was great to hear her voice...it was an incredible moment. However, again, I didn't ask her what happened in 1982 when Eric returned...this time it didn't seem appropriate as she was calling out of genuine concern for my welfare. On reflection, I would like to think that the compassion shown by Linda in making that phone call meant that our love back in 1982 had been very real. When Linda asked me what my eldest daughter was called and I told her she was called 'R', she laughed and said she knew I would have given my daughter that name (well…it was a name we had discussed all those years before in The Vine). Linda saying that about 'R' made me think that perhaps, from time to time, she had thought about me and us. However, it also brought home the fact that, despite almost twenty years passing, my depth of feeling for Linda had not changed since 1982…I thought that I had moved on emotionally by the time I had returned from the Falklands, but having re-evaluated events I now accept that up to that point in 2001 I still loved Linda unconditionally…as my ex-wife had always suspected. Despite the relationship physically ending sometime in early 1983, in an emotional sense, the events in 1984, 1985, 1991 and 2001 made it clearly evident that I was still in love with Linda well into the 2000s. Additionally, I can now see that the reasons I had so many failed relationships after Linda was that I was still emotionally attached to her…if you love someone else how can other relationships work? It's impossible, and I was only fooling myself and others that I was over Linda. I'm not embarrassed to admit that there were many times over the years I hoped I would wake up back in Barnsley, back in 1982 or felt the sorrow of waking up after a night of vivid dreams, where me and Linda were still together, only to realise when I woke up, they were just dreams. Love is not something that just ends overnight, it's something that will remain buried deep inside, and every now and again a song, a memory etc will bring that love to the surface…and that's how it was with Linda. I don't think it was such a bad thing as it highlighted how special the love was at the time and it was a positive way of remembering her.

I returned to Barnsley in the summer of 2001 for Andrew's wedding evening and met Linda again…but on reflection, going to the wedding evening wasn't the right thing to do. However, although it felt awkward it did lead to the beginning of those ghosts of 1982 being partially exorcised. When you love someone as completely as I loved Linda their happiness is paramount, and everything else is irrelevant, even my own happiness. Therefore, seeing her in 2001 with her family (husband Ken and her two children Kenny and Bethany) and

422

after talking to Ken that same evening, I could see he was a good man and that he had obviously made Linda very happy…seeing her happiness that day was wonderful and my own emotional healing began. Up to that point the last traumatic image I had of Linda had been of a broken-hearted seventeen year old girl running away crying, thankfully this had now been replaced by that of a beautiful mother happily dancing with her daughter. The twenty years I had sporadically popped in to the edge of Linda's life was not only to catch up with Jean and Roy, who I loved dearly, but also to know that Linda was happy and well, and that weekend in Barnsley confirmed that she was, and more importantly for the first time in twenty years, I witnessed this with my own eyes. Since 1982 I had always tried to be sensible and allow Linda to move on with her life, but it meant a lifetime of battling my own instincts and not following my heart and doing something that would make Linda hate me…there may have been the odd indiscretion such as Andrew's wedding, but I hope I succeeded in not turning the love Linda once held for me into hate. I didn't just stop loving Linda when I walked away from Barnsley that weekend in 2001, it took a few more years to be able to manage those feelings. But eventually I was able to lock that love away into a corner of my heart…and from time to time, the door has been unintentionally unlocked and I've thought about those memories we made and the love we shared and it always makes me smile. However, it has been incredibly intense unlocking that love and re-living all these memories in their entirety and at the same time, of that time long ago in the autumn of 1982.

I think it's plain to everyone reading this that I loved Linda with everything I had, I kept nothing back and my soul was laid bare. We shared something incredible, something rare that may have only physically lasted through the autumn of 1982 and into the spring of 1983, but emotionally for me, there had been a far greater connection. It was a love, as I highlighted in my recollections above that was built on simple actions and gestures. The foundations weren't built on large sweeping romantic gestures or expensive gifts, it was a 'real' love that, had it been given the chance, I believe would have grown and developed into something unbreakable. We sadly never shared Birthday, Anniversary, Christmas or New Year celebrations together, no romantic dinners, there were no magical holidays, the joy of children, or buying our first home together etc. We never even experienced waking up together, and living that simple joy that the first thing you see when you open your eyes is the face of the person you love more than life itself. We never visited the seaside together or went to a concert, we never argued and as a result never had to make-up…I never even had the chance to buy Linda flowers. The really sad thing is that I can't even 'officially' say Linda was my girlfriend, but in my mind during that autumn of 1982 she was more than just a girlfriend…she was my soul mate and my future. Sadly, all those things we never shared, I have only experienced them in my dreams. I can only imagine how strong our love could have become had we shared those memories and added them to those simple memories we had already made. Admittedly, I am not naïve, I am a realist and I know there would have been arguments or disagreements, and I also know we never experienced the challenges in life such as illness, or the passing of a loved one, financial issues, difficulties with children or job losses, but given the foundations we had laid I believe we could have overcome them TOGETHER…I strongly believe that our love would have developed into that love I witnessed with my own grandparents, and that we could have afforded that same level of patience to each other during adverse times. What about the 'Eric' situation? I hear you ask, why couldn't your love deal with that? Well…that was a unique set of circumstances that I didn't know about until that visit to Jean in 1991, as I was eight thousand miles away when they began. But saying that, I should have made it my business to know when I returned from the Falklands. I don't normally do 'regrets' as I believe our characters are shaped by the decisions we have made in the past, and I hope you will begin to appreciate this about my character when you finish reading the book. But I should have contacted Linda and let her know "I am here for you if you need me"…that decision I made to stay away is the only regret I have from my life, as it ultimately proved to be an enormous life-changing decision. I've never felt any bitterness toward Linda…why would I? I have only felt love, as we never argued or purposely hurt each other. I met a girl that made me blissfully happy, and I am still happy today that we met, became so close and fell in love all those years ago. Therefore, my life has been richer with Linda having been a part of it, and as a result there's no room for any bitterness. I know that had I not told Linda how I felt about her, in that phone call back in 1982, my life could have been so different, but I also know that I would never have shared that love with Linda that brought so much joy. Therefore, I'm glad I made that decision to tell her how I felt as we went on to share a love that was very special, it was very real and something that not many people experience, and I'm convinced it would have been as strong today, had other events not interfered with our love and the life we had planned. Whilst I appreciate it is possible that our relationship may not have worked, I believe we should have been given a fair chance to try and find out for ourselves. Coupled with the 'regret' above, I have always 'beaten myself up' about not returning to Barnsley when my Falklands tour had finished. I have often thought that had I returned to Barnsley and met Linda and we had talked that perhaps things could have been different...I should have tried, but I didn't and that is something that I have had to live with for over thirty five years. I also believe I loved Linda for so many years as there were no negatives (i.e. arguments, struggles of life etc) to destroy the love and in some sense it could be described as 'perfect'. Could I have made her happy? I'd like to think so, but there is always that doubt that that wouldn't have been the case and that is why I think meeting and marrying Ken was the best thing that could have happened to Linda, therefore, it could be argued that Linda, Ken and I were all winners. I believe Linda and Ken love each other very much and have enjoyed a happy marriage in which they have raised two children...and I was able to continue loving Linda from afar and for many years without the fear of experiencing any additional hurt!

I don't know for sure if Linda's depth of feelings were as strong as mine or whether she felt let down that I didn't fight for her. She may have been waiting, hoping that I would get in touch back in 1983, I'll probably never know. But I would like to think that Linda also believed we had something special and that she loved me as much as I loved her back in 1982...for me, her intentions and actions (some unintentional) in 1984 and 2001 confirmed that perhaps, she had once felt the same about me all those years ago . Unfortunately, it wasn't meant to be, and as Jean said to me in 1991 "Life's 'ard Taff". Sadly, it's possible that Linda has forgotten much about our short time together in 1982 and I maybe now just a distant memory of somebody she once knew…as much as I hope that's not true, I have to accept it's a possibility. Today, Linda and I both have our own wonderful families and have created many new memories, albeit separate ones…this is the good that came from something that was once so wonderful, but became incredibly sad and difficult to deal with. But I still look back with fondness and over the years there have been many songs that have reminded me of Linda and exactly how I felt during our time together. But still, if I hear 'Hard to Say I'm Sorry' by Chicago (the record I bought for Linda in 1982) it has and always will 'stop me in my tracks' and take me back to that autumn in 1982 which we spent very much together.

Additionally, there is a Thai song I listen to by a little known group that has a few simple lines in it that now sums everything up;

"I still remember the stories, every second that I had you with me, creating dreams together,

I still miss you every time, when I open my eyes and wake from my dream,

Even though I know there will never be a day, I still secretly smile every time I think of you" (literal English translation)

I have been back to Barnsley many times over the years to watch Barnsley F.C. and I always make a point of dropping into Princess Street to see where it all began. Sadly, Jean passed away many years ago, and following a major family crisis (see Chapter 5) I lost contact with Roy around ten years ago. As a result, I don't know how Roy is or how Linda's and Andrew's families are getting on, but obviously I hope they are all well. But, in addition to visiting Princess Street, I always drive past the Clip Joint and the Alhambra roundabout and think what might have been. Sadly, the Vine Tavern and the Manor House pubs are long gone, but like the memories of Linda they still exist in my mind. And if I see something on TV, read something in a magazine, newspaper or anyone mentions Yorkshire or Barnsley, I immediately think of Linda and smile, I also think of Jean, Roy and Andrew…and of those happy times I spent with them all. I have spoken with my daughters, 'R' and 'A', about Linda and the love Linda and I shared, and they have expressed their understanding of how much Linda meant to me and their sadness about what happened. I would like to think that if Linda ever read this that she would take it as a compliment that I loved her so much and for so long, and that I never forgot her, our time together or the memories we created. As time passes by and before the fragility of life blows me that final fateful kiss, I would love to have the chance to sit down one last time with Linda and say…

"Thank you Linda for allowing me into your life and for helping to create wonderful memories and sharing a very special love during that autumn of 1982"

But I'll probably have to say it two or three times as I know Linda would say…

"What did thy say Taff?"

"Do you know what a woomfer is?"

The line above still makes me instantly laugh when I think of a certain girl, Lenora, a girl who was, simply, 'the one that got away' or to put it more precisely 'the one that I stupidly let go'. Despite my first love still being a joyous memory, it changed me and I now appreciate that it was a pivotal moment in my life that ultimately had affected me deeply, and affected my decision making when attempting to find love again. But I did find love again, with a great Cornish girl, Lenora Stupple, sister of a great friend, Michael Stupple,…she nearly saved me from myself…nearly! Unfortunately, I now understand that losing Linda had a profound effect on me and others as I struggled to maintain loving relationships with those that came after Linda. I still wanted the perfect relationship, a loving partner, but every girl was unfairly compared to Linda. Hindsight is a wonderful thing and I can now understand that we are all individuals, and it was unfair to try and compare other relationships with one that, sub-consciously, I missed so much. As you have already read I still loved Linda through the remainder of the eighties, nineties and into the 2000s, and coupled with the drinking culture I was embroiled in at 24 Field Squadron I became emotionally 'dead'. This resulted in me either being hurt or hurting others, either way it would always lead to me drowning my sorrows in drink. Therefore, sadly, every relationship that followed Linda was doomed to failure as I didn't realise that there was an underlying problem…sub-consciously I was still in love with her. This manifested itself as an irrational 'fear', and whilst I still tried to find 'love', I used the fear of being hurt as a coping

427

mechanism to end new relationships. Normally around 6-8 weeks into any new relationship I would make all sorts of excuses or purposely do something wrong (i.e. infidelity, not turning up, not calling etc) to make relationships end prematurely and often acrimoniously...and then I'd bury myself in alcohol with the lads. This was certainly the case with an ex (who later became my first wife in 1988 after two failed relationships in 1984 and 1985), Helen Beaulieu; Gaynor Jones; Jackie Sutton; Kerry Fleetwood and many other girls. I had changed from the loving person I was with Linda to someone who became very selfish, intent on self-destruction. To be brutally honest, to treat girls the way I did was abhorrent and it should never have happened, and the only person I blame is myself...I am ashamed of the way I behaved towards others and I apologise to each and every person that I hurt during those years in the eighties. If I could go back in time and speak to my younger self I would try and guide the young fool I was then, but would I have listened? Probably not. I don't believe anyone is capable of totally loving two girls at once and I was no different, but on one occasion I came close to breaking that emotional bond with Linda and had started to love another, Lenora. However, again it wasn't to be, and hence I do believe in Karma, and the way I treated others has re-visited me in abundance and is nothing more than I deserved. Nevertheless, we are shaped by events in our life, and despite being content with again becoming that caring, fun-loving person I was in 1982, I am still ashamed of the way I treated others in the distant past. One of those I hurt during this period was Lenora, a relationship that I fucked up and believe was a missed opportunity of finding true happiness!

A few weeks after Mick and Karen's wedding (Chapter 3) in the lead-up to Christmas, Lenora came to Chattenden to stay with Mick and Karen and to see Andy 'Scouse' Murray who she'd met at the wedding. I don't know what happened between Lenora and Andy as the mists of time have clouded the memory, but I do remember Jake Maiden and I looking after her in the stomp and in the NAAFI during her stay at Chattenden...not that Lenora needed looking after! This was the Christmas that Johnny Witchell and I decided that we were going to stay in the camp for Christmas and just get pissed, and on the day everyone went on Christmas leave Mick and

Karen invited us over to their pads quarter (army apartment) for a few drinks before they and Lenora left for Padstow the following morning. Following-on from the wedding and the great nights we'd all spent together in the NAAFI, I was really getting to know Lenora and discovered that she was a great girl with a huge personality and a huge heart to match. As the night wore on, it was becoming obvious to Mick, Karen and Johnny that Lenora and I were starting to flirt heavily with each other. This heavy flirting eventually resulted in Johnny making his excuses and going back to his room in the barracks and Mick and Karen making their excuses and heading off to bed, leaving Lenora and I alone…this eventually resulted in us spending the night together and getting to know each other a bit more (wink wink!). The following morning I said my farewells to Karen, Mick and Lenora and wished them a merry Christmas as they were heading back to Padstow that morning. I can't remember how I came to follow them either later that day or the following day, but I presume Lenora asked me if I would like to come to Padstow for Christmas. I didn't need convincing or asking twice…I wanted to spend more time with her as she was great fun to be around and I can honestly say I have never laughed as much as I did with Lenora. I remember thinking at the time that she could be the one who could bring love and happiness into my life, and I arrived at Bodmin train station filled with hope. When I left Cornwall to go back to Wales for New Year I honestly believed that I had found a girl I wanted to spend the rest of my life with. However, in true Thomas fashion I would break Lenora's heart because of my own fears and my own selfishness. And as I look back on the stupid decisions I made, I know that I messed-up a fantastic opportunity of a chance to spend the rest of my life with Lenora. A girl who I know could have provided a lifetime of love and laughter. I have been lucky enough to have had the opportunity to apologise to Lenora in the past couple of years for my appalling behaviour over thirty years ago and it was great to meet her (and to be re-united with my fellow usher Johnny Witchell and former rugby team-mates, Garth Hamley and Andy 'Scouse' Murray) again at Mick and Karen's 30th Wedding Anniversary…embarrassingly, I also got to meet Lenora's cousin Karen…again!!!

The train was twenty minutes away from Bodmin, and I stared out of the window as we sped past the charming little cottages, nestled in their haunting winter settings amongst the frosted fields of Cornwall; where the leaves had long fallen from twisted trees and kissed the ground with their autumnal colours of golds, oranges and various shades of brown. I thought of Lenora, and as if by magic, the image of her face appeared in the condensation on the glass, her tell-tell wicked and devilish smile gently drew me in. But as quickly as the image appeared, it was gone, but it made me think of this bundle of overflowing joy that I would soon be with…it was impossible not to be captivated by Lenora's vivacious and warm personality. As the train approached Bodmin I experienced a nervous excitement that I hadn't felt for a few years and I was convinced that Lenora was going to fill the void that no-one had managed to fill or even came close to filling since Linda…I had an overwhelming feeling that Lenora was 'the one', and the early signs of how I felt were more than positive.

The train was slowing to a halt and I made sure I had all my belongings and picked up my book, Walkman (for you youngsters out there…a portable tape player and headphones), cigarettes and lighter off the table and stuffed them in my ruck sack, and made my way to the door, pushed down the window and when the train finally came to standstill, I reached outside for the handle and pushed down, opened the door and stepped onto the platform;
"Shit…it's fucking freezing" I thought as the icy breeze bit into me and started gnawing on my bones. I shivered as I tried to get my bearings and then I saw Lenora…well heard her;
"ERE…TAFF…TAFF…OVER ERE!!!" she shouted in her unmistakable Cornish lilt.
I saw Lenora jumping and waving her arms in the air just behind the station-master, and I waved back and started walking towards her. I was really pleased to see her and that warm devilish smile, and when I was close enough we threw our arms around each other and after a huge hug our lips locked in a warm, welcoming kiss before we separated and Lenora let out that infectious laugh that I had quickly come to love and said;
"Welcome to Cornwall Boyo" and laughed that raucous laugh again.

Hand in hand we left the station, quickly found her mum, and were soon on our way to Padstow for a fantastic week together.

When we arrived in Padstow, our own purpose made chaperones, Mick and Karen, were there to meet us…for a week of unbelievable hospitality, amazing parties and even a visit to the church…but not for a wedding this time. I was humbled by the way I was welcomed into this close-knit family unit and immediately felt at home under the protection of my new guardian angel…Lenora, she really was a beautiful and amazing girl and so much fun to be around. Later that day we made our way down into Padstow for a few drinks in The Ship and The Golden Lion…places that would see a lot of us over the next four or five days. Back at Lenora's I found myself sleeping on a sofa bed in the living room and as everyone made their way to bed Lenora kissed me goodnight and gave me a wink…this told me that she'd be back. And came back she did, in what became a nightly ritual as we would make love, as the rest of the household was pushing out the zzzzzzzzzs…she was an incredible lover.

It was soon Christmas Eve and as usual we all headed down into Padstow for another night of drunken revelry…this time with a difference. Somebody, I am not sure who, thought it would be a great idea if we went to St Petroc Chruch for Midnight Mass…but there was a slight problem, the amount of alcohol we had drunk had not been factored in to this decision. This was not going to end well. Mick, Karen, Lenora and I staggered, giggled and shushed our way up Church Lane and eventually made it to the church…disaster, the service had already started a few minutes earlier. We stepped into the medieval church on our best behaviour, but the church was almost full. We were directed to a pew, one row behind the front pew (which was empty) on the right hand side of the church…in full view of a disapproving vicar who was stood no more than three to four metres away. I might be wrong, but I think we got away with it…standing, sitting, praying, singing all at the right times, right up until it was time for the sermon. This part of the service is where the vicar attempts to tie-up a current 'issue' such as drug abuse, to an extract in the Bible, and in an Anglican/Catholic church it is a staid affair and extremely boring. It could be argued that this element of the

431

service could put an insomniac to sleep…due to the alcohol intake of the evening, I was in trouble. As the vicar began I could sense an overpowering desire to sleep, enhanced by the facts it had been a long day and the assistance of the alcohol drunk that evening…I knew I would lose the battle to stay awake. Within a few minutes my eyes were getting heavier, and a couple of times my eyes closed and my chin sank to my chest and then jolted upright and looked around to make sure no-one had seen me…then I was gone, my eyes closed, my head dropped and the momentum forced my upper body to naturally tilt forward to the point of no return and…"T-H-U-D", fully asleep, I head-butted the back of the pew in front of me and the noise reverberated around the church. I woke up immediately, and did not dare look at the vicar who was probably damning me to an eternity in purgatory…I also sensed that Lenora, Mick and Karen were struggling not to laugh. Thankfully, despite the alcohol, and the watchful eye of the vicar, we managed to maintain a level of decorum for the remainder of the service. Eventually, we finally made it back to Lenora's where once again, as Padstow slept, there was a 'special' visitor to the Welshman on the sofa bed.

It was Christmas Day and following the opening of presents and visits from Lenora's family members we made our way to the Golden Lion for a couple of pints (pubs were only open for a two hours on Christmas Day back in the eighties) and it was here that Mick showed me his and Lenora's father…for those who don't know, Mick was a man-mountain, he was 6ft 3in and 18 and a half stone of prime Cornish beef with arms bigger than my thighs…but a gentle giant (unless you upset him) and loved by all who knew him. That lunchtime in the Golden Lion I can remember Mick saying to me;

"Don't look now, but the man behind you in the corner by the bar…he's my dad…but…we don't speak"

When the opportunity presented itself, I turned to go to the bar to get the next round of drinks;

"Fuck me…" I thought. "He's fucking huge". I was astounded and to this day I don't think I've seen anyone bigger…Mick's dad wasn't in the corner, he was the corner.

We were soon back in the house enjoying a fabulous Christmas dinner in fantastic company. It was a fairly relaxed afternoon and evening as Lenora and I were enjoying spending time together …I remember thinking "I am so happy", Lenora was so much fun to be with and as time went by I seriously began to think "I want to spend the rest of my life with this girl". Not only was I feeling loved, I hadn't laughed so much with any other girl as I had with Lenora…I remembered a joke she told me that provides a great example of her sense of humour and the fun girl she was and still is;

"Taff…do you know what a woomfer is?"

"A woomfer…a woomfer…hmmm…sorry Lenora…not the foggiest"

"It's the piece of skin between a women's cunt and a women's arsehole…cos if it woomfer that 'er guts would fall out" and she rocked her head back and laughed and laughed, slapping me and repeatedly shouting;

"COS 'ER GUTS WOULD FALL OUT!!!"

I initially nodded my head in dismay, but I was soon laughing with her, due to her raucous laugh…priceless moment. This is what I was dealing with and I knew that life with Lenora certainly wouldn't be dull. She was a tonic of infectious energy and being with her was like riding an eternal wave of unbounded joy…I was beginning to fall for this Cornish gal and damn it felt good. I also had an extra special Christmas present that night following another 'visit' from my 'midnight lover'.

The following day was Boxing Day and there was a surprise in store for me that evening…I didn't know Boxing Day in Padstow was also called 'Mummers Day' or 'Darkies Day' a pagan celebration to do with the winter solstice. I remember walking into the kitchen and Lenora's mum saying nonchalantly;

"We've got a dress for you to wear and the boot polish is on the table Taff"

"Come again" I said, confused. Lenora's mum repeated what she had said and I looked at her and said;

"I'm not falling for that one"

"But it's Darkies Day…it's tradition ere in Padstow"

I was still none the wiser and believed they were all winding me up and said, as a compromise; "If I see Mick in a dress with boot polish on his face…I'm in"

A few minutes later I was stood in the hall watching my fellow soldier and rugby player walking down the stairs in a blue chiffon dress and boot polish all over his face…I thought ;

"If it's good enough for Mick…it's good enough for me…go on, give me that dress".

433

Twenty minutes later we all walked into Padstow, Mick and I like a pair of hookers who had just finished a shift in a coal mine. Ahead of us was a great night in the Ship where, I'm sure, there was a disco…I believe there is photographic evidence of Mick and I dancing together that night in our beautiful dresses and faces covered in boot polish, but thankfully over the mists of time I think the photo has been lost…thankfully, no mobile phones in those days to catch the magical moment…thank God.

That night was the last night Lenora and I spent together as something happened between Lenora and Mick's mum and Karen…but it didn't stop Lenora making her 'special' visit to her 'sofa bed Romeo' after everything had calmed down and the house was quiet. The following day I left with Mick and Karen, armed with real homemade Cornish pasties from Lenora and Mick's grandmother…and they were ansome! We said our farewells and I promised Lenora that I would be back for New Year…as Mick and Karen headed back to London, I headed to South Wales to see my family. Unfortunately, I never made it back to Padstow for New Year and despite asking Lenora a few weeks later if she'd like to get engaged (which she happily accepted), I would spectacularly press the self-destruct button and end up breaking Lenora's heart...as the 'fear' factor again kicked-in.

Post note

I genuinely thought the world of Lenora and I know that had I followed my heart and not my loins I would not have made the stupid decisions I did when I returned to Chattenden at the beginning of 1986. As I have written above, I believed that Lenora was a 'keeper' in every sense of the word…she was beautiful, fun, caring, a good cook and I have no doubt she would have been an excellent wife and mother, and made me happy. I refuse to make normal excuses by saying: I was young, I was easily led, or it was the alcohol etc as they are easy 'get out' clauses for inexcusable behaviour and I am not proud of the person I was back then. However, hindsight is a wonderful thing, and what I have come to realise is that there were underlying emotional factors at play that, due to being in an army environment, could not be openly displayed or discussed. When I had returned from the Falklands in April

1983 these factors certainly began to have a bearing on my character and behaviour. I stumbled from relationship to relationship always expecting the worst from the outset that the girl would end the relationship, and if they didn't of their own accord, I would make sure they were 'nudged' in that direction by my actions! I would reach a point in a relationship where I would get scared that I would love a girl in the same way I loved Linda, and then get hurt and feel that same devastation I'd felt in 1982...and I never wanted to feel that way ever again. Therefore, forcing relationships to end was my way of protecting myself...my own sub-conscious coping mechanism. If I met girls from home or in other parts of the UK then I would always expect the 'Dear John' letters to arrive eventually, and more often than not, that's exactly what happened with the usual reasons for finishing such as "it's not you, it's me" or "I've met someone else" or my personal favourite "the distance between us isn't working" etc. Each time they arrived I would laugh with my mates and move on, but secretly it hurt like hell and being in the army in the 1980s the last thing you could show was emotion...it was seen as a weakness. This is in stark contrast to how I feel today, I now understand that showing emotion or expressing feelings is a sign of strength and not weakness, and as you have probably seen throughout this book I am not afraid to express my feelings and emotions and try to be brutally honest regardless of whether its negative or positive...if we can't be honest with ourselves, how can you possibly be expected to be honest with others! I am certainly not attempting to absolve myself of blame or lay the blame elsewhere...I take full responsibility for my actions and others were the victims, not me. With my ex-wife (girlfriend at the time) in early 1985 I fabricated an argument about wanting to join the police and then didn't contact her, within a couple of weeks the 'Dear John' letter arrived. In mid 1986 infidelity (from the time we were together in 1985) was used to end the relationship and again the 'Dear John' arrived with the statement 'a leopard never changes its spots' thrown at me. I again fabricated an argument and didn't contact Helen Beaulieu to make her end the relationship and with Jackie Sutton I just stopped calling her and she ended that relationship...and that's how I dealt with my irrational fear. I knew it was wrong to treat girls the way I did, but I couldn't help myself and I am ashamed of the way I was back then and there is no-one to blame but my

435

*younger self. Helen, Jackie and many others were lovely girls
and certainly deserved to be treated better, and potentially
they would have been ideal long-term partners had I not been
such an arsehole. Admittedly, I did marry my ex-wife in
1988...we met again and married within eight weeks, but even
then I had started to have doubts about whether marrying her
was the right thing to do.*

*Unfortunately, as much as I thought Lenora and I had a future
I eventually treated her in a similar way. I started seeing one
of the WRAC girls on the camp knowing that Karen and Mick
would find out, which they did and obviously told
Lenora...again I had purposely created a situation that would
end the relationship. Lenora was a wonderful girl and as with
my ex-wife (when we were courting), Helen and Jackie etc, she
deserved to be in a relationship with someone who wasn't
selfish, inconsiderate and emotionally scarred as I obviously
was at the time. Firstly, I have now come to realise that I still
loved Linda and struggled to love anyone else, although I did
try...I just couldn't get past those barriers I'd created to
protect myself from being hurt again (ironically, it was those
same barriers that resulted in me getting hurt again, again
and again). Secondly, as others hurt me I became emotionally
harder and my behaviour got worse resulting in me
reciprocating that hurt, and hurting those that I should have
loved. By the time I married in 1988 I was emotionally 'dead',
and my children have commented that they can never
remember seeing me crying when they were younger.
However, the only exception to this deadness was the love I
had felt for Lenora and the love I still held for Linda. I am
ashamed of my younger self and wish that I hadn't behaved
the way I did, but unfortunately I can't undo what has been
done in the past and I hope that all those I hurt went on to
have the loving relationships they deserved. During the period
above and during my marriage I was similar to a pressure
cooker, every time I got hurt or hurt others all the emotions
associated with those events were popped inside and the lid
put on. However, you can't just keep doing that, eventually
something has to give and events throughout the 1990s would
eventually blow the lid off the pressure cooker and ultimately
bring me to my knees...emotionally and physically.*

When I look back on that Christmas of 1985 it is with great fondness...Lenora was a very special person who, I am ashamed to admit, was treated appallingly. I consider myself to be extremely lucky to have had the opportunity to apologise to Lenora for the way I treated her in 1985, when we became friends on facebook. I also met her again at the 30th wedding Anniversary party of Mick and Karen back in 2015, and had the pleasure of meeting her daughters, Lauren and Sadie (Spud). Lauren's opening line to me that evening was;
"My mum told me you broke her heart"
"Yes" I admitted "I was an arsehole back then...but, on a brighter note, if your mother and I had stayed together you could have been shorter and ugly"
Thankfully she laughed. Happily, Lenora did meet someone else and has been happily married for many years, has two wonderful daughters, three beautiful grand-daughters and a grandson on the way. She is still the beautiful, bubbly, funny and caring girl I loved all those years ago...yes, I did love Lenora. Sadly, I just couldn't maintain relationships at that time and Lenora became another casualty of my actions and for that I am eternally sorry. The events of the late 1990s eventually helped me to re-build my character and personality to the place it was in 1982...I am again the happy, loving, loyal and caring person I was, and out of something bad eventually came something good. I try not to have regrets, I prefer to call them 'life experiences', and whatever happened along the way, Lenora and I will always have Christmas 1985, our first and 'Last Christmas' (see what I did there Lenora...those who know, know!) and nobody can take that away...thank you Lenora.

First born...Wow!

Witnessing the birth of a child is a wondrous event and thankfully I am from a generation of fathers that have been allowed...in fact, encouraged to play an important supporting role in the birth of their children. Despite having six children I have only actually witnessed the birth of two of them...my daughter 'R' and youngest daughter, Amy. My eldest son, 'K' was born before my ex and I got married and her first husband, was the biological father, but I did later adopt him (the subject of the next short story). My second son 'G' had to be rushed into theatre due to compilations that could have

437

endangered his and his mother's life, and was delivered via the use of ventouse. The twins, 'A' and 'Rh', were delivered by emergency caesarean section and which meant that I was unable to enter the theatre and witness their births…I was left outside pacing up and down the corridor. Finally, Amy was the only natural birth I witnessed. However, the births of all my children (and 'K's adoption) have all been very special events, but witnessing the birth of 'R' was very special, as it was the first time I had experienced the amazing and beautiful miracle of the birth of a child. Witnessing anything (i.e. a child walking and taking for the first time; a sunset; a sensational news story or a historical sporting moment etc) for the first time is always extra special and birth is the pinnacle of any special moment…the emotions you experience are very difficult to explain as you enter the realms of the unknown. It is exhilarating, but worrying at the same time and your emotions are caught-up in a mixture of intermingled highs and lows. As you will see, or may have experienced, there can also be a comedy element that can creep into the proceedings! Whatever your own experiences may be, I am sure that, like me, you have never forgotten the phenomenon of birth and the joy it brings! I hope my own experiences may prompt a forgotten memory from either witnessing a birth or even actually giving birth!!!

It was July 5th 1989 and my wife, son 'K' and I were in one of the delivery suites at the Queen's Medical Centre in Nottingham…my wife was ten days overdue and we had come to the hospital for a scheduled induced birth. 'K' was two years old, and as we were away from our families, there was no-one to look after him…armed with a colouring book and crayons and a couple of his favourite toys he had happily set himself up on the armchair in the corner of the suite, oblivious to everything going on around him.

I am not sure what they had given my wife that morning, but she had already 'shit the bed'…giving birth often results in all dignity disappearing and the midwife didn't seem the slightest bothered…she'd probably seen it all before;
"Don't worry my darling…it happens…we'll soon get that cleaned up…OK darling!"
Slightly embarrassed, my wife said under her breath
"OK…sorry…ungghhh…"

438

I said reassuringly stroking her head "don't worry"
She was as comfortable as could be expected, given the condition she was in, and the midwife had been popping in every ten or fifteen minutes to check the monitors She was wired up to and asking if everything was OK. This was all a new experience for me and I had no idea what was going on…I continually tried to reassure her, paced up and down, bit my nails, checked 'K' was OK and looked concerned every time the midwife came in and checked the monitors.

It wasn't long before I noticed a recognizable aroma developing in the suite, well more a stench…I gave her a knowing look and she responded with a half-smile and a shrug of the shoulders. As if by impeccable timing the midwife walked on all smiles and said;
"How's everythi…ooooo…right…I think it's time we opened the windows…getting a bit…stuffy in here…" Her face a contorted image of disgust as she obviously recognized the sweet smell of shit…yes, she had shit the bed again and as a result of the mixture of pain and pain relief, she really wasn't bothered anymore. The midwife cleaned up the mess, but unfortunately the smell remained like a guest outstaying their welcome at a party. Things were beginning to develop and my wife was in a lot more pain as the time between the contractions was getting shorter, and it looked as if the end was in sight…and 'K' was still happily playing in the chair in the corner.

She was becoming more uncomfortable as the pain increased and my levels of concern were also increasing…I felt so helpless, I wished I could take the pain away, but there was nothing I could do. There was a nagging vulnerability that enveloped me, and a multitude of emotions raged through my head: fear, anger, love and helplessness, as a doctor walked in and spoke to the midwife and hushed whispers. He looked up and could obviously see I was concerned and came over to the bed, cleared his throat and explained that my wife and the baby were showing signs of distress, and that she would need some help in delivering the baby. That didn't really calm me and he must have seen the panic in my eyes, he reached over, put his hand on mine and said;

"Don't worry…everything will be fine. We will use forceps to assist with the delivery…really, there is nothing to worry about"

My concern eased slightly until she let out a small scream and muttered something incoherently as another contraction swept over her…I turned around to check on 'K'…not a murmur…he was still colouring and not the slightest bit worried by the increased stress levels in the room.

The doctor and midwife were in position…and so were the forceps. The doctor barked out instructions and she let out a huge scream…'K', looked up, slid off the chair and trotted around to where the doctor was using his full body weight to pull the baby out…a quick glance from Keiran and he turned back around, trotted back to the chair and carried on colouring. In one swift moment (I remember thinking at the time, "Oh my God…he's going to pull the baby's head off!"), the baby was out…a few seconds passed, that seemed like an eternity, and then the joyous sound of a newborn baby's cry filled the room…at the same time tears welled up in my eyes as I heard the words;

"You have a beautiful baby daughter…congratulations to you both…and to you in the corner…" 'K' looked up briefly and then carried on colouring.

I looked at her and told her she was amazing, and I bent down and kissed her on the forehead. My new baby daughter was soon being held by my wife, as I attempted to grasp an understanding of what had just happened. I looked at the baby's little hands all stretched out like two small starfish, the pink skin and the little face with the tell-tale traumatic mark from the forceps…they had been inadvertently positioned over her one eye which was closed and slightly swollen…she looked as if she had just been twelve rounds with Mike Tyson. The doctor assured us it was superficial and would be fine in two to three days. To me, she was perfect and I couldn't take my eyes off her…attempts to get 'K' interested proved fruitless…he had one quick look but was soon back to his colouring. I finally got to hold my daughter and my heart melted as I lovingly stared at the wonder before my eyes…it was a beautiful moment and something I will never forget as the baby wrapped her tiny little hand around my index finger. I sat there, content looking at every small detail of the baby in my arms. It was a special, special moment and something I

440

feel blessed to have experienced. I looked at my wife and thanked her for giving me such an amazing gift…she smiled back and said;

"What do you think of your new daughter…'R'?"

I smiled and said; "She is so, so beautiful…I have never experienced such an emotional day…thank you!"

Soon it was time for me to take 'K' home and to make those phone calls home to let everyone know that the baby had arrived…I was so proud.

Sadness 2 v Joy 1 (Uncle Ivor, G and mum!!!)

1991 would be a year of very mixed emotions for many reasons, but losing Uncle Ivor (my father's brother), the birth of 'G' and the premature death of my mother were the major episodes in a very difficult year. However, there were other issues such as a job loss, Jean sharing with me the shocking news of Eric and how he had treated Linda and her family, leaving Long Eaton rugby club, temporary disappearance of my wife and the children, third hand news of my mother's brain tumour and a potential medical issue with 'G' that all contributed to 1991 being a very emotional and challenging year!!!

Uncle Ivor

"Make sure you come back to Wales to live" was the last thing my Uncle Ivor ever said to me…three weeks after that phone call he finally succumbed to the Cancer that had ravaged his body for the previous three years!

The weather deteriorated after Uncle Ivor had passed away, and living in Long Eaton at the time it was going to be touch and go on whether I'd be able to get back to Wales for his funeral…snow might deny me the opportunity to say farewell to a man that had become a surrogate father throughout my childhood, following the continued absence of my father, the death of Grampa Thomas and the strokes suffered by Grampa Henson. He had always been there for me through my early life: teasing me, advising me and generally keeping a watchful eye on me. He was a great man, great husband, great father, great grandfather, great son and a great friend…and at fifty

441

three years old, life's fragility showed its hand when it took Uncle Ivor far earlier than it should have.

Despite the snow, I managed to make it back to Maesteg in plenty of time for the funeral. I spent the day before the funeral with Auntie Glenys, my cousins Michelle and Nicola, Gran Thomas, Shirley and my father, as a steady stream of people came to the house to pay their respects to Uncle Ivor. It was difficult trying to console Michelle and Nicola on losing their father…they were only twenty-two and nineteen respectively, but I hope they took comfort from the funny stories being told about their father by the many people who visited that day. Strangely, the house was full of tears and laughter and it caused me to reflect on my own memories of a much loved man; the holidays in the caravan, his continual advice (and stories) about army life, his love of football, his continual teasing (a Thomas family trait), his pigs (for some reason he kept pigs on a farm in Llangynywd), his infectious laugh (and coughing) and my abiding memory of him continually scratching the beard I never saw him without, and many, many more. Despite his premature death he had certainly lived a full life considering he had been ill for most of it with chest problems!

My memories of the day are limited due to the passages of time, but I do remember consoling my Nan who was understandably devastated at losing her eldest son…I hope I never have to experience the despair of losing a child, I couldn't even begin to imagine what my grandmother was going through on that morning. But I tried to put my Uncle Ivor's premature death into perspective as I remembered my nan telling me years before that Uncle Ivor had been ill all his life and had been lucky to survive infancy. I loved my grandmother so much that it broke my heart to see her so upset that morning and I put my arms around her and said; "Nan, you told me many years ago that the doctor had said to you when Uncle Ivor was a toddler that there was nothing more they could do for him, apart from suggesting that buying a bike would be good for him when he was older" he's in God's hands Mr and Mrs Thomas". Well Nan, that little boy went on to join the army, get married, have children, which he saw grow up, and he became a grandfather…that is pretty amazing that that sick little boy grew up to do all those

things…try and hold onto those positives Nan and think of all
the things that Uncle Ivor done that no-one thought he would
do, and remember …I'm here and I will help you get through
today the best I can. I love you Nan" and I hugged her tightly
and kissed her on the cheek. She looked up at me and through
teary eyes her eyes glistened with love and she attempted a
smile;
"Thank you Huw…I love you too…God bless you". I
remember thinking to myself, "this is going to be a difficult
day".

Funerals are never easy…I suppose the easiest funeral we will
ever attend will be our own! This day was difficult enough
when you see your Auntie, cousins and grandmother
inconsolable as you witness them holding on to each other for
support and see they are emotionally in absolute pieces…and
there is nothing you can do to take away that pain at that
particular moment in time. The beautiful but most emotional
part of the service was having the Llantrisant Male Voice
Choir singing my Uncle Ivor's favourite song 'The Rose'…it
was one of those moments that makes the hair on your neck
stand on end and tugs at every emotion. It was a fitting tribute
to a man who loved life and loved his family with all his heart,
and needless to say there wasn't a dry eye in the house that
day. The hundreds that attended on that snow covered day in
Bridgend showed exactly how much my Uncle was loved and
respected…It was an honour to have said goodbye to my
Uncle Ivor in such a fitting manner.

'G's' Birth

It was early on a Sunday morning when my wife's waters
broke announcing that it was time…we didn't have a
telephone in the house (financially it had been difficult since I
left the army) so I had to run to the phone box on Briar Gate.
The funny thing about this was that as you turned left out of
our street (Bracken Close) onto Bracken Road and after
walking about 100m you reached a t-junction with Briar
Gate…the phone box was around 50m to the left, but 50m to
the right was the ambulance station! I couldn't go straight to
the ambulance station I had to ring the number given to me by
the hospital. I made the call and started running back to the
house…ironically, halfway down Bracken Road the

443

ambulance passed me and was parked up outside the house by the time I approached on foot. I laughed as I politely pushed past the paramedics and let them into the living room where my wife was struggling with another contraction. They asked a few questions and checked her over and didn't waste any time transferring her to the ambulance…within ten minutes of arriving at the house, they were on their way to the QMC (Queen's Medical Centre) in Nottingham. I'd had no time to kiss her goodbye and just shouted;
"I'll get to the hospital as quick as I can" and the ambulance doors closed and drove off with the blue lights flashing.

Within twenty minutes our neighbours Grace and Brian had agreed to look after 'K' and 'R', and I was on the way to the hospital in a taxi. Within another twenty minutes I was running through the entrance of the QMC with my wife's suitcase filled with nighties, underwear, change of clothes, toiletries etc and the essential 'baby' bag with baby grows, nappies, dummies and an array of Johnsons baby products etc. I finally made it to the reception of the maternity ward, managed to catch my breath before frantically asking where my wife was…problem, I had frantically asked in a fast incoherent Welsh accent which was wasted on the receptionist who looked at me with a pained expression on her face and said;
"Pardon!"
I apologised and repeated my request slowly. Within a couple of minutes I was off again and armed with the information that took me to where she had been taken by the paramedics. Two minutes later I was stood at the side of her bed trying to breathe normally after my mad dash and side-stepping display through the hospital…thankfully, I hadn't missed anything and she was fairly comfortable with exception of the contractions that were now becoming more frequent and more intense!

Half an hour later the doctor and midwife decided that to deliver the baby they were going to have to use ventouse as the second stage of labour was not progressing adequately. However, whereas I witnessed the birth of 'R' with the forceps a couple of years earlier, this would be different…five minutes later I was sat in the chair as my wife had been taken to a surgical area leaving me to wait patiently in the delivery suite. I use the term 'patiently' loosely, as with all Births it was a

444

mixture of sitting down, standing up, pacing up and down, repeatedly looking at the time, attempting to read the newspaper, asking the staff (every two minutes), looking out of the window, becoming anxious…calming down and then becoming anxious again (and repeat), more pacing…yes, it was a lovely hour that seemed to have lasted three days before I saw my exhausted wife being wheeled back onto the ward holding a little bundle of joy. At this stage I still didn't know the sex of the baby until the midwife shouted;

"Aye up me duck…congratulations…you've got a baby boy…7lb 4 oz"

The tears welled up in my eyes as I grasped the enormity of what the midwife had just said to me and I leant down and kissed my wife who was proudly holding our new son. No words were necessary…we just sat there looking at our beautiful addition to the family and a couple of minutes later she asked if I would like to hold him.

"You bet" and she passed him to me and straight away I said;
"'G'…John…William…Thomas, welcome to the world little man" But, I started thinking…"hang on, how do I know it's a boy?…I haven't seen any proof…they might be wrong…I'll have to check" and I started undoing the baby grow. She said inquisitively;

"What are doing Huw?"

"I'm checking it's a boy…they might have got it wrong…" She laughed "what are you like…checking to see if it's a boy…"

I managed to get to the nappy and pulled it slightly to the side…just enough and saw what I was looking for, looked at her, smiled and said;

"There it is!"

Putting the nappy back in position and doing up the baby grow I was now satisfied that I had a new baby son…and again the tears flowed as I sat there proudly with a huge grin on my face holding 'G' and just gazing lovingly down at his scrunched up little face.

Later that evening when I was back home my wife rang and told me that they'd found a heart murmur in 'G's heart, but she said they didn't appear concerned about it and said it would probably disappear in a few days…as you know from Chapter 4, it wasn't an innocent heart murmur!

Bye Mum!

The post had arrived and to my surprise there was a letter off
my father and Shirley…intrigued, I opened the letter and
starting reading and I have to admit I had to read it three or
four times before I grasped its content. They had heard that my
mother had a brain tumour…a brain tumour, she was only
forty-six years old!

The news was true and over the Easter weekend of 1991 we
went home to Wales and I visited my mother in
hospital…apart from looking a little tired she was still very
much the same person and was extremely positive about her
medical condition. My mother believed that she was winning
the battle with the rheumatoid arthritis that she had been
diagnosed with in 1976, and she also believed that this was
another battle that she would win…unfortunately, I found out
a couple of months later that this was a battle she wouldn't
win as she had been given six months to live back in February,
my mother had unknowingly given me false hope.

Despite her positivity, during those first weeks after she had
been diagnosed, my mother made sure that she had made the
necessary arrangements for my grandmother's care. My
mother had to break her promise that she would never put my
grandmother into a care home, but they hadn't foresaw that
my mother would become ill and possibly pass away before
her own mother…unfortunately, this now became a possible
reality. The receipt of a letter from my mother's cousin Beth in
June 1991 was when I finally realised that my mother was
dying…and she didn't have long. Beth suggested that I should
go and see her. A week or so later we headed back to Wales
and when we visited my mother we were in for a huge
shock…she was unrecognizable; gone was the smart, slim and
attractive middle-aged women of forty-six. In her place was a
grotesque, obese, balding and aged women, the only trace left
of my mother was her voice…the steroids my mother had been
prescribed had ballooned her weight and she was also now
becoming slightly confused as the pressure of the tumor on
either side of her brain increased. It was a difficult afternoon
for two reasons: Firstly, it was clearly evident that my
mother's positivity was not going to save her from an
inevitable premature death. Secondly, there was an incident

446

between my then wife and my mother when we came to leave that day. Back in October 1990 my mother and my wife had an argument which resulted in her forcing me to call my mother and say I would have nothing more to do with her (something even her parents felt wasn't right)…on the day of my nan's eightieth Birthday. When we came to leave my mother's house that day I kissed my mother goodbye and had given her a big hug, but when my wife leant in to do the same my mother pulled away and said venomously;
"I don't think so"
My wife's reaction to this was to start shouting at my mother. I was shocked and angry at this outburst and ushered my wife out of the door and back to the car.

The last time I saw my mother was a few weeks later and by this time she had been hospitalized and her condition had deteriorated greatly; she was now blind, very confused and despite only being forty-six years old, she looked as if she was the eldest patient on the ward. It was very emotional leaving the ward that day as I knew that, as we lived in Nottingham, this would be the last time I would see my mother alive.

When the call came a couple of weeks later, there were no tears, no angry shouts of "why my mother?" or "she was only forty-six". There was just a silent acceptance that my mother was gone…my immediate thoughts turned to my nan as she had been kept somewhat in the dark about my mother's condition to the point that she hadn't been told that my mother was dying. I had been sworn to secrecy by my step-father and therefore, my nan was unaware of how grave the situation was and when I visited her during my mother's illness I witnessed my nan's bitterness at my mother putting her into a care home. The tears came when I visited my nan in the care home a couple of days before my mother's funeral, and my tears were more for my nan as she was the one who had brought me up. The tears I cried with my nan were because I witnessed the utter devastation of my nan living with the pain that she had now outlived both her children (I would have had an uncle but he died as an infant before my mother was born). I felt so sad for my nan more than I felt sad for myself and I also felt sad for my children as I knew that my mother would now just be 'the woman in the picture on the wall'…due to their ages they would have no recollections of their grandmother.

447

It was a difficult day saying goodbye to my mother…watching my nan struggling to come to terms with losing a daughter she loved very much. As we sang "abide with me" I watched my mother's coffin sink from view and for a few moments, I glanced upwards and mouthed "bye mum". I listened to the sniffles amongst the well-wishers and comforted my nan as the last lines echoed around the room of that famous hymn.

Adopting 'K'

'K' is my then wife's son from her first marriage and he was only fifteen months old when I first met him, a beautiful toddler who everyone fell in love with when they first met him…including me! When his mother and I met (again) she was in the process of divorcing 'K's biological father, Brian, and shortly after the divorce came through we married and she and 'K' moved to Nottingham where I was based with HQ MWF. Early in the marriage we talked about the possibility of adopting 'K' (she also had to adopt 'K' due to the change in her surname to Thomas) and we started the process in early 1989. Thankfully, we had the permission of Brian (he had spoken to his priest who had advised Brian to allow us to adopt 'K') to proceed with the adoption process which made it more straight-forward, but by no means, a formality. It took almost three years of form-filling, vetting/police checks and interviews (together, separate, 'K' and my wife, 'K' and me etc) with the social worker who had been assigned to us, Theresa Andrews. This story isn't about the above process, but about the special day we enjoyed as a family on the day the adoption was finalised, and 'K' was issued with his new Birth Certificate. As with the Birth of any child this was a very special day, and I was filled with pride as 'K', who I considered as already being my son, now officially became a 'Thomas'!!

My wife, 'K' and I were called into the judge's chambers at Nottingham Crown Court, as Theresa, our social worker watched my daughter, 'R' and son, 'G'. It was daunting stepping into the judge's domain, but he soon put us at ease asking us to take a seat and saying how moments like these were special and how much he enjoyed this part of the job…this moment was the culmination of the adoption process

448

and had taken almost three years to reach. The judge called 'K' over and asked him if he'd like to try on his judge's 'wig'...'K' happily trotted around the large table to where the judge was sat and the judge carefully placed his wig on 'K's head...'K' looked adorable and gave us a huge smile from the opposite end of the table. The judge then removed the wig, issued 'K's new Birth Certificate to 'K' and said; "'K'...go and give this very special piece of paper to your mummy and daddy" and he smiled at us. 'K' trotted back to us and handed my wife the new Birth Ceritifcate, she quickly read it, smiled and then passed it to me. I read it and grinned broadly as I saw the words 'K' A THOMAS', it was a fantastic moment...'K' was now officially adopted by us both, and a huge weight had been lifted off both our shoulders. The judge finally reminded us that this decision carried a huge responsibility and then smiled and assured us that he believed we would be a happy family and wished us good luck for the future. We thanked the judge and walked out into the corridor where a smiling Theresa was waiting for us with 'R' and 'G'. "Daddy" my daughter, 'R', shouted and ran into my arms. We invited Theresa to join us at the café in Nottingham Castle for a celebratory coffee and cake...she happily accepted. We were determined to make this a 'special' day and had planned the day in advance. As a birth of a child is a 'special' day we believed this 'Adoption' day was equally important.

Following our coffee at the castle café, we took a few group photographs, which included Theresa...she had been on this journey with us from the beginning and it was only right that she was a part of the celebrations. Theresa was a genuinely lovely person as well as being an excellent social worker and the coffee and photographs were just a small thank you from us all for her help, sensitivity and sincerity. We eventually said our goodbyes with Theresa and made our way to the next part of the day that we had planned...a family meal at the *Bull's Head* in Breaston for a family lunch...and more photographs.

The day did not end there, once lunch was over we made our way back to Nottingham, to Highfields Park and boating lake on Nottingham Boulevard...a beautiful park in front of the university and previously part of the grounds that once belonged to Jesse Boot, the son of the founder of the Boots Company. The children played in the park having great fun on the swings and slides and as it was a school day they had the park to themselves. Following half an hour or so in the park we completed the day by hiring a rowing boat on the stunning lake adjacent to the park. We had taken a multitude of photographs throughout the day, but it was finally time to head home…the celebrations complete.

Later that evening when the kids were safely in bed, we sat down and talked about the day and agreed it had been a perfect way to celebrate 'K's adoption. My wife also had a fantastic idea that would be a perfect memory of the day…she said we should put a folder together of the day c/w the new Birth Certificate and photographs, in the style of a story book. I agreed that it would be the perfect celebration of a momentus occasion of 'K' officially becoming a 'Thomas'…'K' still has that folder today.

It's twins!!!

To say I was shocked when I found out we were having twins is an understatement as I hadn't planned on having more children after 'G'. Firstly, there was a five percent chance that any future children we had could also have the same medical condition (coarctation of the aorta) as our son 'G'. This was a major concern, as I didn't want to have to go through the same emotional roller coaster again (see chapter 4)…I can't speak for my then wife, but I certainly was adamant that we had three children and that added risk categorically meant that I did not want any more children. Secondly, financially we were struggling with three children, how could we possibly manage with another child? My wife talked me round to trying one more time and I guess the fact it was twins was an unusual example of karma for daring to deny my wife another child!!! On reflection, having twins was a blessing as there are those who never know the joy of having children or may have gone to great expense via either IVF or adoption to fulfill their dreams of becoming parents…I am convinced she became pregnant when we talked about having children!!! Once we got over the shock that we were having twins (she came to terms with the news far easier than I did) we played the waiting game! We had no idea of the sex of the twins, but we knew they would probably arrive earlier than the normal forty weeks (36 weeks tended to be the norm!). True to form, it had to be a Saturday that she went into labour…eleven days

450

before Christmas, resulting in me missing my one and only
rugby match of the season. We made our way to Cardiff Heath
Hospital (they had monitored the twins throughout the
pregnancy, due to 'G's medical condition, hence why they
weren't born in the Miners Hospital in Caerphilly), where the
fun really began. It was here I jokingly said (taking my life
into my hands) to her, "you'll do anything to stop me playing
rugby!" – understandably, between contractions I was given
'the look'!!

I packed my rugby kit into my sports bag and strategically
placed it near the front door ready for the big game later
on…It was the local derby against Nelson and I had been
looking forward to this one since I'd seen it on the fixture
list…there is always something special about playing in
derbies and I knew this would be no different.

Twenty minutes or so later, I was in the kitchen washing the
last of the breakfast dishes when I heard my wife shouting;
"HUW…HUW…!"
I ran up the stairs and into the bedroom where I found her
lying on the bed.
"Everything OK…what's the matter?"
She gave me that look I'd seen before;
"It's time" she said and smiled.
I thought "there'll be no rugby today…damn!" and then
replied;
"OK…I'll ring your mum and dad…'R', COULD YOU
COME HERE PLEASE LOVE?"
'R' walked in the bedroom;
"Yeah Dad"
"Can you please stay with your mum…it looks as if the twins
are on their way…I'm going to ring nan and bamp Jenkins"
"Yes" whispered 'R' and punched the air.
I ran downstairs to the phone, started dialing…
"cumon…cumon…cumon…pick up the phone…" I thought,
and then I could hear my father-in-law on the end of the line
"Hello"
"Dad…it's Huw…it's time…can you come over so I can take
your daughter to hospital" I blurted out.
"Ok Huw…we'll get our shoes on and leave now in a
minute…see you in a bit Butt"

451

"Ok...bye" and I replaced the receiver and ran back upstairs to my wife and daughter 'R'.

"I've spoken to your Dad...they should be here in about half hour...do you want to go downstairs now or stay here? She looked at me, grimaced, pointed to the bed and said;

"I'll stay here"

"Ok...I'll get everything ready". I went to the wardrobe where the 'special suitcase' was being kept and lifted onto the bed and opened it and quickly check the contents...despite the fact that it had already been checked forty-two times in the last three days! I took the suitcase downstairs and picking up my sports bag I placed it in the same place by the front door...I briefly looked at my sports bag and thought "I was really looking forward to that game today" before taking my bag and placing it in the cupboard under the stairs...grabbing our coats I passed 'K' and 'G' who were oblivious to what was going on as they were engrossed in the normal Saturday ritual of watching WWF wrestling. I shouted;

"OK boys...looks like the twins are on their way"

Without looking up the said in unison

"OK Dad". I laughed and ran back upstairs and waited with my wife and 'R'. My wife struggled to get comfortable...she was only 5ft and a fag paper and as she was carrying twins and she was huge, over the last couple of weeks she had struggled to get comfortable when she was standing, sitting or lying down. We soon heard the front door and then heard my mother-in-law's trademark Welshy, high-pitched "hiya". I shouted down;

"UP HERE MAM...WE'LL BE DOWN NOW"

'R' and I helped her up and it took around ten minutes to get her down the stairs and out into the car. I rushed back in to get the suitcases and coats (well it was December) and said to the boys:

"I'm taking mum to hospital now...nan and bamp are here!"

But they were still oblivious to everything as Triple H hit The Undertaker with a forearm smash to the face...they both shouted "YES" and then without looking away from the TV again said in unison "Ok dad...bye"

I left the house and got into the car, and as we pulled away my father-in-law shouted;

"GIVE US A CALL LATER...WE'LL BRING THE KIDS TO THE HOSPITAL...SEE YOU LATER!"

452

"OK" I shouted back and then drove down Bryngelli Terrace, turned left onto High Street and headed for the Heath Hospital in Cardiff.

Thirty minutes later we were parked up outside the entrance to the maternity wing of the hospital, and I was helping my wife out of the car. After admission she was lying on a bed in a general waiting area when I said;
"You OK?"
"Yeah…a bit uncomfortable, but I'm OK" I looked at her, tutted and said;
"The things you'll do to stop me from playing rugby!" She said nothing and just glared at me…I laughed.
"Only joking…anyway I've got to go and move the car…I won't be long" I thought to myself "that was close…quick…get a move on". I smiled and then kissed her forehead.
"I won't be long."

Ten minutes later I was back by my wife's side and then around half hour later we had been moved to a room adjacent to the theatre. The plan was that she would have an epidural and then we would be transferred to theatre for a scheduled caesarean. However, because she was so big they couldn't get her body into the right position for them to administer the epidural. Therefore, the decision was made to give her a general anaesthetic which meant I wouldn't be allowed into theatre, and that I would have to wait outside in the corridor adopting the normal role of father of perfecting the pacing up and down the corridor, continually looking at my watch, praying that everything goes well, and finally listening for the telltale sign of the birth…a crying baby. It wasn't long before I heard the first cry ('A') and tears started welling up in my eyes and then around two minutes later there was the second cry ('Rh') and now the tears of joy flowed in abundance. A nurse popped her head around the door to the theatre and said;
"Mr Thomas…" I nodded and tried to focus through the tears,
"…you have a beautiful baby girl and a beautiful boy" she smiled.
"Thank you…is everything ok" I asked tentatively.
"Yeah…everything's good, they are both doing well and mum is fine too". I nodded and wiped away the tears and waited

patiently to see the new arrivals to the Thomas clan…I now officially had a five-a-side team!

Finally, I was able to see our new baby daughter and son and they were beautiful in their separate hospital cots which were side by side, my new daughter 'A' being easily recognisable with her mass of dark hair…my wife was still in theatre, but soon joined as, albeit still asleep from the anaesthetc. The joy of birth provides different emotions and each Birth is generally a contrasting experience…the Birth of the twins was different, in that we were back in Wales and were able to share that joy with our families…a new experience for me as 'R' and 'G' had both been born in Nottingham. I rang the house and 'R' picked up the phone and excitedly asked;
"What's happened dad?" I explained everything to 'R' and she let out whoops of delight and I heard her shout;
"NAN…NAN…THE TWINS ARE BORN…THE TWINS ARE BORN…" My mother-in-law came to the phone and I provided the normal details of times and weights and that everything was fine with both the twins and my wife. My mother-in-law said they would leave shortly for the hospital so that 'K', 'R' and 'G' could meet their new sister and brother. By the time they all arrived at the hospital my wife was awake and was now seeing the twins for the first time…her emotions were in check as she was still a bit groggy. It was wonderful sharing the joy with family, and as it was twins, there was double helping of joy and plenty of 'baby swapping' as everyone took their turns in sharing the happiness. It was an amazing day, full of emotion as the birth was shared by my wife and I, their siblings and maternal grandparents…having twins was certainly different. For those of you who are interested, Senghenydd lost the derby game with Nelson so I didn't miss a great deal!

Devastation in 12 months

My two grandmothers were much more than the name suggests…they were also surrogate mothers and huge influences on my life and losing them both within a twelve month period was devastating. They both succumbed to the dreaded 'C' (cancer); a group of genetic diseases that arguably touches all families in some shape or form. My grandmothers were remarkable women, but in very different

454

ways…both excellent cooks and totally unselfish, as they
always put the needs of others first. They say that women are
the stronger sex and whoever first made that statement must
have modelled the idea on my grandmothers. Nan Thomas
passed away first in August 1997, followed by Nan Henson
almost a year later. Between them they brought me up, but
Nan Henson played the bigger role as she was the constant in
my life right up to the time I left school at sixteen. She lovingly
took on that role following her retirement as a psychiatric
nurse in 1970 (when I was seven), and showed her strength
when she later cared for my grandfather following a series of
strokes that left him partially paralysed…I was thirteen at the
time and not once did I ever hear her complain! She took it all
in her stride! I have fond memories of both my grandmothers,
some of which you have already read, and of all the people
I've lost in my life it's my grandmothers that I miss the most!!!

Nanny Thomas (Iris Thomas *nee John*)

It was a Friday and I was looking forward to the weekend, but
I hadn't been in work long when my phone rang. I sighed and
picked it up and provided the normal cheery greeting;
"Huw Thomas…Nuaire…how can I help you?"
"Huw…it's dad…it's nan…she's in hospital…" He quickly
filled me in with the details and after putting down the phone,
I initially sat there in shock for a few moments before telling
my manager, Alun Morton, who kindly arranged for me to
have the use of a pool car (we didn't own a car at the time).
After calling my wife with the news I was soon driving down
the M4 in the direction of Bridgend…and my grandmother.

Arriving at Bridgend's Princess of Wales Hospital, I found a
parking space and was soon nervously walking through the
hospital, not knowing quite what to expect. I walked onto the
ward and found out where nan was located and was soon
walking into a private room where my father, Shirley, Auntie
Glenys, Auntie Jean and my cousin Deborah were all sat
around the bed where I could see my nan lying, her eyes wide
open staring into space and it appeared she was continually
blowing raspberries, as bizarre as that sounds…my father
explained that despite her eyes being open she was, in fact,
unconscious. It was a little unsettling, and nan remained this
way for the next few hours. Even though she was unconscious,

we continually spoke to her of our own personal and collective recollections, we also spoke amongst ourselves in a similar vein, and as the hours passed nan started to become calmer, her eyes closed and the raspberry blowing action stopped, and I can remember my father every now and again saying; "Come on mam let go…you don't need to fight anymore…just let go". It wasn't nice seeing nan this way, she'd beaten cancer twice before but it had returned with a vengeance and there would be no beating it a third time…the cancer had spread to other vital organs and her body was just gradually 'shutting down' as the hours passed. Late at night as the ward began to settle down to hushed whispers of the staff, occasional coughs, alarms and even snoring, we kept our vigil at my nan's bedside all determined to keep her company during her final hours. By the time Saturday morning came round nan's breathing had started to become shallower and the signs were there that we were losing her as she started slipping away…it's not easy watching someone you love, someone who was full of life and someone with whom you shared so many happy memories, becoming so helpless, and it's extremely painful watching their life ebb away.

Eventually, nan slipped away quietly and she was now free of any pain…it was a relief in the end but also very surreal. She passed away during the funeral service for Princess Diana. As everyone was watching the service on television, my nan was taking her last breaths as the ward was filled with choir music, people crying and hymns from the funeral. It was strangely calming and pleasant, given that my nan was very religious it seemed a fitting time for her to pass away, and knowing my nan the way I did, I thought she would have been smiling inside at the irony. I rang my wife and broke down on the phone…my nan had been a huge part of my life for well over thirty years and now she was gone.

The funeral itself was the most poignant I'd ever attended, mainly because it was held in St John's where my mother and father had married (just before I was born) and where my nan was a parishioner, and therefore the vicar was speaking from the heart as he personally knew my nan…it was a genuine service and I still remember the advice he gave to my nan's family and friends; "even though it's a sad time…remember all the good times, all the happy times, the funny stories because that's exactly what I will be doing and I know that is what Iris would want you to do". I have many fond memories (some of which you have seen in earlier chapters) of a nan who was full of love and life and I think of her often and its always with a smile on my face.

Nanna Henson (Margaret Aileen Henson nee Leyshon)

I sat with nan Henson and held her hand as the doctor explained that she had throat cancer and that any treatment she received would only prolong her life by a month or two…he asked her directly, not through me, but directly, treating her as the intelligent adult that she was despite being eighty-seven years old; "Do you want the treatment Margaret?" It restored my faith in humanity that the doctor treated my nan with humility and sensitivity and spoke to her as an equal and not like a child. I admired him greatly for the way he dealt with my nan that day, and it made me resent the manager of the nursing home who attempted to make decisions about my nan's future at Cae Bron without my nan being in the room…I refused to speak to him until they brought my nan into the meeting. She may have been physically disabled following a stroke, but she was mentally as sharp as she had always been. The doctor knew this and that's why he spoke to her and not to me. My nan used to be a nurse and she knew that the treatment was futile, there was a silent acceptance by my nan that day that she would soon be joining my mother, Grampa Henson and the infant son she never spoke of…I respected her decision and when she said "no" I didn't try to interfere or influence her as I felt I would be denying my nan her dignity. As much as I didn't want my nan to pass away, I was wise enough to realise that it would be selfish and unfair of me to try and make her change her mind…I had to let her go.

Over the next few months my nan's health deteriorated and eventually she was transferred to the 'Y Bwthyn Newydd' hospice in the grounds of the Princess of Wales Hospital where they would make her as comfortable as humanely possible during her final weeks. I took the children to see my nan one last time before her appearance would be too upsetting for them, and obviously my nan shed a few tears as she probably knew it would be the last time she would ever see them. When it was time to go, one by one we kissed her goodbye, but as we were leaving the ward she called me back…telling 'K', 'R' and 'G' to watch the twins, I returned to nan's bedside. I leant down and she put her hand on mine, looked me in the eye and said;

"I wish I'd had a large family!" I could see the sadness in her eyes.

"Oh nan…you have got a big family" I knew what she meant, but didn't know what to say. What could I say to the woman who had lost both her children? I kissed her goodbye and hurried off after the children. Driving back to Caerphilly that day I thought about what my nan had said to me earlier. This was the same woman who thought one child was enough for any family, who's thinking influenced my mother, but not me…I was too independent, I made my own decisions. There she was telling me she wished she'd had a large family…I felt sad for my nan that she was thinking like that when it was too late. I looked at my children and realised I had been blessed and I think my nan could see that, and in some small way she was telling me that the choices I had made in life were correct…it was a bittersweet moment.

A week or so later, I made the trip to the hospice, for what would be the last time, and my nan was now in a single room for her privacy and dignity during her final hours. I walked into the room and she was lying prostrate on the bed, a shadow of her former self, due to being unable to eat. I came over to the bed and she looked at me and tried to say something, but sadly to this day I don't know what she said…they were her last words as shortly afterwards she slipped into unconsciousness. Similar to those final hours with Nan Thomas less than a year earlier, Den (step-dad) and I played the waiting game, staying up all night at my nan's bedside to guide her through those final hours. It is very painful seeing a loved one fade away…it is cruel and probably why it's such a blessing when someone suffering from a long-term illness finally passes away and is finally at peace.

When my nan finally took those last shallow breaths, I'm thankful I was there, as she had been there for me throughout her life. When I was young she provided the guidance I needed and there was nothing she wouldn't do for me. Later that day, I collected her belongings from the care home…it was sad to see that someone who had worked hard all their life, owned their own house etc, that everything they now owned fitted into the boot of my car…very sad. Back at the house I looked through my nan's photographs and found a picture of me as a baby lying in my pram in the garden at 43 Parcau Avenue, and my nan lovingly looking down on me…a beautiful black and white photograph, and I thought it was ironic that the image had been reversed today, when I spent those last moments looking lovingly down on my nan.

Of all the people I've said goodbye to I knew this would be the hardest, my nan Henson was a very strong and determined woman who had almost single-handedly brought me up and during the service I couldn't hold the tears back …it was the first time my children had seen me cry, cry the tears for a nan who had provided me with an unequivocal love.

Third party sufferers of child abuse!!!

Child abuse is an abhorrent crime and thankfully, I was never sexually abused as a child, and as a result, I couldn't even begin to understand what someone who has been abused has gone through and is probably still going through! I could only imagine that the psychological effects of being sexually abused are extremely profound and would include emotions such as anger, fear, hate and mistrust etc. However, I have seen the destruction that child abuse can cause, not just to those that have been abused, but to family members and friends. Again, I cannot speak for others as the experiences of anyone living or knowing someone who has been abused would be different. There may be some similarities, but the dynamics of the relationship between a husband and wife are different to those between a parent and child. Therefore, it would be unfair to speak on behalf of other 'third party' sufferers as I cannot and shall not attempt to tell you how others feel. How sympathetic they may be? Or even how angry they may be? I consider myself to have had a relatively happy childhood, growing up with loving parents and grandparents and was therefore protected from such horrendous behaviour and it may be hard to understand that I was twenty one before I became aware of child abuse for the first time and that it was quite commonplace! You may think that is naïve, but how would you know if this sort of thing never happened in your family…you don't watch the news as a child so why would you know! I

459

found it very difficult to comprehend that adults sexually abused children...and still do as it is such an abhorrent act!! My aim here is not to try and understand the abused or the abuser, but to hopefully, through relaying my own experiences as a 'third party' sufferer, provide some sort of guidance on the difficulties of living with someone who has been abused, and how best to deal with the problems and turmoil that it can cause within the family unit. Child abuse is more commonplace than we think, for example at the time of writing, the current NSPCC statistics claim that 58,000 children in Britain need protecting from abuse. That is an extremely high figure and it could be argued that the figures of 'third party' or indirect sufferers of child abuse could be ten times that amount or more which highlights its destructive powers. But despite searching, I could find no actual statistics that confirm the figures for 'third party' sufferers!!! We should all work together to try and reduce the above figures, which appear to have got worse since the high profile cases of Jimmy Saville, Rolf Harris, Stuart Hall, Gary Glitter etc hit the headlines...especially as the amount of convictions has risen by sixty percent in recent years!!!

I once lived with someone who had been sexually abused, but I had absolutely no idea of the impact it had on her and how it had affected her...as a result, I certainly could not forsee the impact it would have on me. I am now looking back on a relationship with the benefit of hindsight, and the effects from the abuse are much easier to analyse than when I was living through them.

In my humble opinion and in my experience, one of the major issues that an abused person understandably struggles with is 'trust'...when you consider that an abuser is normally someone close to the abused person, it should be someone that can be trusted 100%. Therefore, abuse results in 'trust' being completely destroyed resulting in the abused person trusting NO-ONE, and I mean NO-ONE! Closely coupled with 'trust' is the feeling of being 'let down' by someone who should be providing protection and love. Therefore, anyone (parents, siblings, partners, children, other relatives, friends, work colleagues etc) in an abused person's life would have to be 'squeaky clean' a hundred percent of the time to ensure that trust is maintained. Unfortunately, the reality of life is that that level of trust is difficult to maintain when you are dealing with someone who is always expecting people to let them down, and therefore there is continual conflict between any relationship in the life of an abused person.

I started to realise early in the relationship that something wasn't quite right, as there were continual bouts of irrational behaviour, exaggeration, fabricated accusations, depression, battles with my involvement in rugby, my friends and so on. Added to the lack of money and my emotionless character it quickly became a toxic relationship that enjoyed brief moments of happiness. Thankfully, there was no violence in the relationship and as far as I'm aware there were no affairs when we were together. However, she did sleep with someone else toward the end of the relationship, but we were separated at the time – it was her way of ensuring that our relationship had ended! But during those early stages I couldn't say her behaviour was because she was abused, that realisation would come much later…in the early years I just put her behaviour down to her just having a 'bad day'. The impact on me wasn't something that happened overnight, it took years before it affected my character and well-being. I now believe that the route of what she suffered from and what she is suffering from now has to be as a result of the abuse she endured as a child. Therefore, it effectively destroyed her trust, confidence, self-belief, self-worth etc, however, that abuse also played a part in the destruction of our relationship. I found the 'mood swings' incredibly difficult to deal with and I can only describe how I felt going home in the evenings not knowing if 'she would throw her arms around me in a loving embrace or whether she would just stick a knife in my chest'…they were the two extremes. I would go home and a meal would be ready and the house tidy. The alternative was her curled up on the settee in the fetal position and the house looking as if someone had lobbed a hand grenade into the house and shut the door. There were the accusations that I was always having an affair, accusations of lying, the exaggerations of what somebody has said, the arguments with other family members or friends…all of which turned to mistrust and the continual feelings that she was always being let down by EVERYONE around her. Abuse was definitely at the route of all this negative behaviour, and it is terrible that someone has had to live their life this way and for so long. Unfortunately, the abuser doesn't

461

just affect the life of those they have abused…there is a knock-on effect that has an impact on family and friends and one single act of abuse can, in turn, create problems for scores of people.

The behaviour of the victim of abuse is not something that happens now and again, this is constant, and living on this never ending roundabout of misery has terrible long-term effects on others. I lived with this behaviour a fairly long period and the impact on my relationships with others and on my health were profound…I had gone from being a very sociable person with many, many friends, to a person too scared to argue with her (there was always the feeling that I was continually walking on eggshells), low in confidence, short-tempered and somewhat of an introvert. Admittedly, being emotionally hard from years in the army, living with someone who had obviously been affected by what had happened to her as a child and the stress I was experiencing at work and at home, something had to give. The breaking point came when I was travelling back from Scotland with work, I was driving down the A470 around midnight when I pulled into a layby just before Cilfynydd…I didn't want to go home! I sat there for twenty minutes dreading the thought of being in the same house as her. Eventually, I did go home, but the following day was the beginning of the end for us…that evening I told her I didn't love her, I couldn't take anymore. In hindsight, it wasn't her fault that I felt like this…it was a mix of my issues and the abuse she had suffered as a child that resulted in her abnormal behaviour that had eventually brought us to this point. Any love and respect that had been there had been destroyed by the cancer that is 'child abuse'. It could be argued that although it is a very different issue, in some respects 'child abuse' has similar destructive capabilities that affect relationships as alcoholism, drug addiction and gambling. Yes I had problems, and yes they played a part in my nervous breakdown and the attempt to take my own life, but 'child abuse' definitely played an influential part in my health deteriorating to the point that my mental well-being was deeply affected.

It is difficult to provide an explanation on the best way to try and deal with someone who has been abused, as each case of abuse would be different and the levels of impact would be different. However, in simple terms, there has to be a level of understanding that the behaviour of the abused person is as a result of the abuse they have suffered…it is not because they are purposely trying to make your life difficult or miserable. Be honest, whatever you do…don't lie, this will immediately increase the levels of mistrust that already exist (during times when we had little money I would tell little white lies to say I'd paid a bill as I was 'robbing Peter to pay Paul'…big mistake). Don't try and force an abused person to have counselling…that must be their decision as it is an extremely difficult subject for them to talk about. Additionally, if they do 'open up' to you about what they have experienced…don't probe too deep, let them tell you in their own time – remember, it is a very painful experience that they are re-living…be sensitive. Correct diagnosis of any mental condition is critical, as correct diagnosis provides correct treatment…this is a difficult one, it might be worth making a note of any erratic behaviour (e.g. sleeping for long periods, self-harm, false accusations etc) and discussing them with your doctor if you have any doubts. Lastly, remember, as there is a likelihood that there is a probability an abused person may now have a form of mental illness (i.e. bi-polar, depression, anxiety etc). If this is the case, then it is important to remember that their thought processes will be different to yours, therefore, a level of understanding is required. I can say all of these things, as I didn't do any of them and watched the destructive force of 'child abuse' (with my own issues) help destroy the relationship…I didn't understand, I wasn't sensitive, I unfortunately lied (financial matters), I probed, I was frustrated, impatient and accepted the erratic behaviour as the norm and lastly, the diagnosis of her mental state appears to have been incorrect during our marriage!

Eventually, I was able to re-build my health, my confidence and my life despite a second bout of reactive depression. The fact of the matter is that 'child abuse' is extremely destructive, not just to the abused, but to the relationships the abused has with everyone they come into contact with…it is fair to say that each act of abuse affects not just one person but probably hundreds of people. This is unacceptable and if we re-look at the 58,000 children that the NSPCC claim need protecting from abuse and think outside the box we can determine the figures of people who are 'third party sufferers' of child abuse.

463

If you take each individual and apply a conservative estimate of that individual having relationships with fifty people (family, friends, work colleagues etc) the figure of people that have been indirectly impacted by child abuse increases to 2.9 million…that is a shocking statistic and somehow this has to be reduced as this must impact on divorce rates, increased medical and benefits costs and social structures in our society.

Ada and Amy!

When I met Ada in 2009 I had no idea where our journey would lead us. Ada is an incredibly beautiful (both inside and out) and strong person, and she thinks of others far more than she thinks of herself, something I have witnessed time and time again, both here and in her native Thailand. She is fiercely independent and doesn't like the word 'no' (as I have found out on many occasion). We have a fantastic relationship (when I listen) and she is so much fun to be with and despite the initial language barrier it has never really stood in the way of our love, in fact, it's produced some funny moments such as I remember early in the relationship I sent her a text saying 'I miss you', the text I had back said 'I am not missing I am here' – yeah, we certainly laughed about that one. There have been a few differences due to our cultures clashing but nothing we haven't been able to deal with and we are partners in every sense of the word. We discuss everything as all couples should and I love her so very much, and she is the best thing to have happened to me since I left my teens and the times my children were born. She makes me extremely happy and gives me the strength to want to succeed in life more than I ever did before…the drive, determination and unbelievable mental strength has enabled me to gain a BA Honours degree from the Open University and have already qualified as a TEFL teacher. I have witnessed the work she has put in to passing her driving theory (in English) and 'Life in the UK' tests. She is an amazing, caring and warm person and I feel I am very blessed to have met such an amazing person at a time in my life where there had been so much turmoil and sadness. We have enjoyed nights out with friends and day trips out to various places and we both love our trips into Cardiff for coffee and a look around the shops…Ada loves shopping and she has mastered the art of disappearing in shops if I turn my back for one second! I have tried to learn the language of

Isaan Thai which differs slightly to Central Thai mainly so I know what she's saying when I have done something she doesn't like and then proceeds to abuse me in her own language...yes, we laugh, laugh and laugh and I feel honoured to have found love after so many years of not being able to love someone for reasons already mentioned earlier in the chapter. It's not all chocolate and roses, we do have our disagreements but it's normally I am the one that's wrong...so she tells me, and a word of advice; "Don't ever cross a Thai woman". The Buddhist way is simple and that is how they look at life, for example, Ada tells me that she shouts at me because she loves me, it's the women that are quiet you have to be scared of, like a dog that doesn't bark...they bite! I wouldn't change her for the world and I love everything about her.

I thought that when the twins were born that grand-children would be the next big addition to the family. However, meeting Ada would change that! Ada had sacrificed so much for her family providing financial support and paying for the family home in Ban Sam Rung, nr Khon Kaen to be re-built, that she never married or had children before I met her. We never discussed having children, but we never discussed not having children...I think due to our ages we would just let nature take its course. I certainly wasn't going to deny Ada a child if that was what she wanted as she had already sacrificed so much in Thailand. I was forty-seven when we found out Ada was pregnant and she was forty-two, as a result, we were in the high-risk group for downs syndrome. But Ada wasn't interested in having a test to confirm whether the baby would be born with downs syndrome, she was happy to continue with the pregnancy without knowing due to the risk that she could miscarry if she had the test (she had already mis-carried a few months before becoming pregnant again). Despite being the age I was, I thought it would be unfair to deny Ada the opportunity to have a child, especially as she had thought the opportunity had passed her by! I was there with Ada for every hospital appointment, doctor's appointment and scans and we also attended the antenatal classes at Caerphilly Miners Hospital. It was a wonderful period and I saw the new arrival as a second chance of happiness having missed out on so much with the twins ('A' and 'Rh'), following their removal to Middlesbrough. I discovered from Ada that in Thai culture it was important that they gave birth to girls, so the scan that

465

can determine the sex of the baby was a crucial moment as
Ada wanted to know the sex of the baby. When they told Ada
that we were having a girl I could not even to begin to
describe the smile that appeared on Ada's face...she has a
huge, warm smile normally, but this was something special. I
just wish I could have filmed that moment...priceless.

It was around midnight when Ada shook me awake and said
that her water's had broken...I was immediately wide awake,
getting dressed and gathering the necessary essentials to go to
the hospital. No more than fifteen minutes later I was helping
Ada into the car and throwing the suitcase etc into the boot,
and driving through the deserted streets of Caerphilly,
Trethomas and Machen on-route to Newport and the Royal
Gwent Hospital. Despite the contractions Ada was having and
my blind panic I managed to arrive safely at the door that led
to maternity at the Royal Gwent...stopped the car and then
helped Ada into the lift. We made our way to maternity, rang
the bell and waited for someone to answer...within a couple of
minutes we were on the maternity wing and Ada was lying on
a bed with midwives checking the normal blood pressure level
etc and asking questions to find out what they could about
Ada's condition. Between Ada and I we managed to help the
midwife build a picture of Ada's condition. We spent an hour
or two in this 'holding' area of the maternity wing until a
delivery suite became available...which was 'bang on time' as
the time between the contractions was starting to decrease. It
was now roughly between 4-5am.

Initially, things were fairly calm and Ada was coping very
well with the contractions and despite the time between each
contraction gradually decreasing she hadn't reached for the
gas and air that the midwife had pointed out to her and showed
her how to use. But that would soon change a couple of hours
later as the contractions became stronger...the gas and air then
became Ada's best friend. Sometimes, it's incredibly
frustrating for us men in a delivery suite as sometimes you feel
useless or in the way...even when you are being supportive
you sometimes get 'the look' from your wife or girlfriend that
basically says "look what you have fucking done to me you
bastard...I'll get you back for this", but thankfully they have
no memory of the incident once the baby is born. I can't
underestimate how incredibly strong Ada's pain threshold

must be as she didn't scream or cry out once…she gritted her teeth and with a steely determination just got on with it, but her new best friend 'gas and air' certainly helped. The five to six hours we had been in the delivery suite had flown by and we were now approaching the delivery itself as the midwife was now at the 'business end' and directing matters from there with commands such as "push…push…push" and "stop pushing". It's hard to believe that this would be my sixth child, but it would be the first time I'd seen a normal delivery.

In a final, teeth gritted grunt from Ada, Amy was born just after 10am on 29th April 2010. Unfortunately, whilst Ada was able to deliver Amy normally, they couldn't remove the after-birth etc and Ada had to go to surgery to have it all removed leaving me with our new daughter. I took a couple of photographs of her in the hospital cot and could immediately see the tell-tale Essan nose and eyes in her facial features…she looked absolutely gorgeous and I sent a text with the photographs to all family and friends (oh how things had changed since my other children had been born…no mobiles in them days, everyone had to wait until they physically saw the new arrivals). We had a good couple of hours together before Ada returned from surgery battered and bruised and in a lot of pain, but at least she was safe from possible infection. As I mention above, Ada was amazing during the birth and had produced a beautiful baby girl and to see her holding Amy and gazing lovingly at not just a baby she thought she would never have, but a baby 'girl' she thought she would never have. To see that joy on someone's face is a gift in itself and I believe I was right in not denying Ada that chance of having a child…she thought that the chance of having her own child had long passed her by due to the sacrifices she had made back in Thailand through her twenties and thirties. This truly was an amazing moment.

Later that day, my father, Shirley, daughter, 'R' and son, 'G' came to the hospital, all taking it in turns to hold their new grand-child and sister respectively. It was a very special day and something I will treasure for a long time…as I do with the births of all my children and the adoption of 'K'. Life can be full of joy and it appears in various guises…love for a partner, a family member, a friend, an academic achievement, a sporting achievement, passing a driving test and so forth, but the birth of children and grand-children etc, for me, is the pinnacle of happiness.

You're a Grandad!!

Early in 2011 my daughter 'R' and her partner Gareth announced that they were expecting a baby...I was going to be a grand-father eighteen months after becoming a father again. I was so pleased for 'R' and Gareth when Alexa was born in October 2011 and it was fantastic to be a grand-father...I felt more relaxed as a grand-father than I had been when I became a father for the first time. With there being only eighteen months between Amy and my grand-daughter Alexa they are extremely close (even though they are auntie and niece), but 'R' and I, despite living 50m apart, only allow the girls to see each once a week and it means they both look forward to seeing each other! Approximately, 20 months ago 'R' and Gareth had a second daughter (and second grand-daughter for me), Louisa, who is totally different to the sensitive and studious Alexa...she has a huge temper and I can see trouble ahead (like her mother was growing-up...good luck 'R'!). I love my grand-daughters so much and I'm sure that as I have five other children there may be a few more grand-children on their way in the future!!!

The Birth of my children was amazing on many levels, and the Birth of grand-children is no different. With exception that as you are not directly involved, it is a more relaxed affair, despite the worry that everything obviously goes well. On both occasions, the worry was from a distance, either in work or at home...it was somebody else's turn to pace the corridor and provide the support.

When Alexa was born back in 2011, it was my ex-wife who provided the support to 'R' and Gareth, which would have been good for her to see it from the perspective of seeing someone she loved giving Birth, as opposed to being the one that was actually going through the painful experience of actually giving Birth. 'R' had opted for a water birth which was never an option when my children came along twenty or so years before. It was strange waiting for the phone to ring to hear the news that I was a grand-father for the for first time...when it came it was almost as emotional as being there

468

and watching the delivery…it was also a relief to know that everything had gone well and both 'R' and my new grand-daughter Alexa were both ok. That night after work Ada, Amy and myself made the trip to see 'R', Gareth and Alexa at the University of Wales Hospital (The Heath) in Cardiff. It was lovely seeing that everything was ok with your own eyes, it puts your mind at ease and it was amazing to see my beautiful grand-daughter, and Ada and I both got to hold Alexa…those memories of holding 'R' as a baby came flooding back and it was hard to believe that had been twenty-two years before. Amy may have only been eighteen months old herself, but she was so excited seeing her niece (even though she didn't know what the word niece meant!) and it's possible that her seeing Alexa that night might be part of the reason that they are so close today.

We have been lucky enough to watch 'R' develop as a mother (I never had any doubts she wouldn't be a good mother as she had always had strong motherly instincts) as our houses are only fifty yards apart, and also watch my grand-daughter blossom into a beautiful, well-balanced, caring and intelligent little girl. Alexa and Amy couldn't be closer if they tried and are so easy to look after when they are together. But I believe that this is because 'R' and I make sure that they only see each other once a week (twice at the most) and it enables their excitement to see each other to remain. Alexa loves being tickled…not, and it is a standing joke between her and me when it is time to leave that when I go to hug and kiss her that she scrunches herself up and says "don't tickle me". I love her with all my heart, and like 'R' was the first child I saw being born, Alexa has the honour of being my first grand-child.

When 'R' announced she was pregnant a second time early in 2016, we were obviously delighted…it would be a nice age gap and the new baby would have a big sister that would help look after it. When the appropriate time came the scans showed that 'R' and Gareth were having another daughter, and it was decided that when the time came we would have Alexa with us when 'R' went into hospital…she was familiar with the surroundings and as she was so close with Amy it would take her mind off worrying what was happening with her mum at the hospital.

469

The day finally arrived when I received the call from R that it was time…it was about five thirty in the evening and it was already beginning to get dark. I left work, picked up Ada and Amy from Caerphilly and made our way to Abertridwr. After parking the car I went straight to 'R' and Gareth's house with Amy to collect Alexa, whilst Ada let herself in to our house. 'R' told me that after calling me she'd walked down High Street to the 'Square Chip Shop' and bought some chips…"I was hungry dad!". Wishing them luck and telling them to text me when they have any news, Alexa, Amy and I left 'R' and Gareth to make sure they had everything they needed before they left for the hospital in Ystrad Mynach…and another water birth.

The following morning I woke to a text from 'R' that grand-daughter number two had arrived…I sent a text back with our congratulations and letting her know that I would bring Alexa to the hospital once we'd dropped Amy off at school. I told Alexa and Amy that the baby had arrived and they were super-excited and were screaming and jumping around the living room like two demented chickens shouting "the baby is here…the baby is here…". After everyone had calmed down, got washed and dressed, had breakfast and brushed their teeth we were on our way to Caerphilly. We dropped Amy off at school and then I took Alexa to buy a card and presents for her new baby sister…she was so excited and soon picked out a card and two cuddly toys to take to the hospital. Twenty minutes later we were heading up the valley toward the hospital and we were soon parked up, climbing the stairs and pressing the bell outside the maternity wing of Ystrad hospital…Alexa could hardly contain her excitement and it was lovely to see that she was so looking forward to seeing her new baby sister. 'R' and Gareth had got it right in the age gap between the two children. As we waited to be let into the maternity wing I text 'R' to let her know we were outside. A midwife let us in and as we approached the nurses station I could see Gareth standing at the end of the corridor; "Look Alexa…there's daddy"
"Daddy" she shouted and ran into his arms. I told Gareth that I would wait here and let Alexa meet her baby sister before coming down…tell 'R' to let me know when it's ok. Gareth nodded and then walked around the corner with Alexa and out

of site. The two nurses (probably midwives, given it was maternity) said to me;

"Awww…that's such a nice thing to do…letting her meet her baby sister first". I smiled.

"My daughter wanted Alexa to be the first one to meet the baby, and I think that's a lovely gesture…anyway, there's plenty of time for me to see my new baby grand-daughter". Five minutes later I was 'summoned' and I quickly got up, smiled at the two nurses and said;

"My turn" They laughed as I headed for the room where 'R' and her little family were waiting. I walked in gave 'R' and Alexa a big hug, shook Gareth's hand and was soon sat on the bed holding another bundle of joy…it was another special, special moment as I looked down on another beautiful grand-daughter.

At the time of writing, Louisa is now twenty months old and her little character is developing, and to say she is different to Alexa is an understatement…it appears she has inherited her mother's fiery temper as she head-butts everything, throws herself around or throws things whenever she hears the word "NO!"…I can see trouble ahead and more often than not I give 'R' a knowing smile that she's going to have a work cut-out with this one; she is very independent, loves her food and beginning to show Alexa who is the boss! She is now beginning to talk and already has quite a vocabulary with her favourite phrase being "Oh no". She's another beauty with her red hair and mischievous, but loving nature.

I love my grand-daughters and see them every week, and I am sure there will be a few more grand-children in the future…well, with six children I think that's a safe bet!

Family Secret

A few years ago at a family gathering I found out a deep, dark family secret that I believe I should have been told when I was around eighteen. However, that didn't happen, but I'm hoping that at some point in the future that this secret will be revealed and I will be armed with the information I need to enable me to try and put right the wrongs this secret has caused. Watch this space!

Chapter 9 – Thailand (and Laos)

In 2011 I had the opportunity to travel to Thailand and not knowing quite what to expect I was filled with mixed emotions of excitement and trepidation! I had always wanted to travel to SE Asia and this was a dream come true for me and I soon discovered that Thailand is a beautiful country on many levels. I have been lucky to have seen amazing sights both famous and not so famous...but it is the sunsets and sunrises that always leave me speechless, they really are a sight to behold. Many of you may be familiar with images of Thailand and its tourist destinations such as Bangkok, and the beach resorts of Phuket and Koh Samui or the mountains around Chiang Mai, but there is so much more to Thailand, and I can confirm that although photographs of Thailand highlight its beauty, this beauty is increased tenfold when you witness it in person. The Thai people are so friendly wherever you are in Thailand and as I have discovered, family is an important part of Thai culture and Thai life, although very hierarchical, respect is evident at all levels of Thai society. Thai people are also deeply religious and deeply spiritual with 97% of the population being Buddhist, but they are also deeply superstitious and I discovered there are many things they believe are lucky, but also many things that they believe are unlucky such as having your haircut on a Wednesday. I have travelled all over Thailand during my trips and always try to see something different each time I travel, but I always enjoy visiting my Thai family in a small village called Ban Sam Rung, around twenty kilometres from Khon Kaen in Northeast Thailand...it is a pleasure to leave the 'rat race' of western society behind and enjoy a peaceful and simple life in a Thai village, and this is where we spend the majority of our holidays. Whilst I have visited many of Thailand's great tourist sites, I have also been to funerals, played in a football tournament, been to parties where a friends son is joining the army, religious festivals, family parties, Thai New Year (Song Kran), Thai barbecues, watched morlams (live Thai music/dancers – stage set-up in village temple grounds), travelling cinemas and generally watching and interacting in rural Thai life. It is a fascinating part of the world that is filled with contradictions...just when you think you understand a local custom something will happen that will tear your understanding to shreds...that is not a criticism, it is part of

472

the magic of Thailand. It is a country with a rich and colourful history and a constitutional monarchy which has some of the strictest 'Lese Majeste' laws in the world, and you might not know that as a result, the Yul Brynner film/musical 'The King and I' and the Jodie Foster film 'Anna and the King' are both banned in Thailand as they both suggest that Anna Leonowens had a relationship with King Mongkut...something the Thais will not accept or tolerate. A country that has never been occupied by a Western power...a unique and interesting fact when you consider that, with exception of Thailand, all the countries around them have been controlled by European nations, for example Malaysia, Myanmar (Burma) and Singapore were controlled by the British; Laos, Cambodia and Vietnam by the French and Indonesia by the Dutch. Even during World War II when the Japanese invaded and controlled SE Asia, The Philippines, Korea and Hong Kong etc, Thailand was the only country not invaded...they signed a 'Treaty of Accord' which allowed the Japanese to peacefully enter Thailand, hence it is alleged that no Thai person died building the 'Death Railway'. A shrewd and clever country that, under King Mongkut (of 'The King and I' fame) and his son King Rama V, played the Western Powers off against each other, maintaining the independence of the former Kingdom of Siam, that later became Thailand. In addition to the customs, beauty and history of Thailand there is a wonderful array of wildlife such as tigers, Asian elephants, sun bears, gibbons, macaques (a breed of monkey), various snakes (King Cobra, Burmese and reticulated pythons etc), various lizards and an abundance of different birds (over a thousand different breeds) and insects (bird eating spiders, giant centipedes, mosquitoes). Another thing Thailand is famous for is 'food'...there is an amazing variety of dishes which are spicy, sweet, sweet and sour such as kapow gy, red curry, green curry, masaman curry, papaya salad, tom yum soup etc all served with a wonderful range of vegetables, fish, boiled fragrant rice and the famous 'sticky' rice. Additionally, there is large selection of fruit and wonderful desserts...my favourite being a mix of both...mango and coconut and condensed milk covered sticky rice. However, there are other things to eat that you may think "Whoa, I'm not eating THAT" such as grasshoppers, beetles, rat, mealworms, frogs (not just the legs, but the whole frog), buffalo blood and chilli...as a dip and my personal favourite...ants eggs. I have tried to integrate myself into Thai life and I have attempted to learn Isaan Thai which is a language similar to Laos, but also uses many words from Central Thai. Whilst I can ask and answer simple questions and have a wide vocabulary, I still haven't mastered it to a conversational level but I can get by, both in the village and the wider community (Kohn Kaen - Ada's city)...family and friends seem to appreciate my efforts. There is so much I could say about Thailand, but I will hold back on saying any more in this introduction and will open up more in the stories/travel journals below. I hope you'll enjoy learning about Thailand as much as I did during my trips there...it really is as the adverts suggest...'Amazing' Thailand (as you are reading through these stories/travel journals why not google the places I mention and give yourself a visual of these mystical but beautiful places).

■■■

2011 – Phimai, Khon Kaen, Ban Sam Rung, Ban Chang, Ayutthaya, Kanchanaburi, Jomtien and Bangkok

My first visit to Thailand was special for many reasons, the main reason being that Ada and I had a wedding ceremony in Ada's village, Ban Sam Rung. An unbelievable experience and something I'll never forget...the whole event (organizing, ceremony and party) was a stunning spectacle of a typical traditional Thai wedding in a rural village in Thailand...it was something of the like that I'd never witnessed or experienced before and was certainly a 'special' heartwarming occasion and a great insight into the cultural side of Thailand and its sense of 'family'. I am sure we could all think of holidays or places we've visited that have provided jaw-dropping sights of beauty, horror, shock or even amusement. Thailand, for me, has been no different as I have seen the charming temples of reds and golds of various sizes, animal encounters, breathtaking scenery and beaches, hustle and bustle of its cities, glimpses of its historical past, the famous Thai 'smile' and the friendliness of its people have been a joy to behold. There were many times during that first trip, and the trips that followed, where I witnessed or experienced something such as an iconic historical landmark or an event or even an image of spectacular beauty that it drew an immediate 'wow', similar to those moments of wonderment when, as a child, you witnessed or experienced something for the first time, and in Thailand

474

they were nothing short of incredible. I have many
photographs from our trips to Thailand, and whilst they
capture its amazing beauty and my wonderful experiences, it's
not the same as seeing them first hand, and I hope I can do
them justice in the descriptions of those images and
experiences below...buckle up, we are off to Thailand for our
first trip to the 'Land of Smiles' to discover the historical sites
of Phimai, Ban Chang and Ayutthaya, stunning beaches of
white sand and crystal clear water, the sadness and beauty of
Kanchanaburi, chaos of Bangkok and the spectacular 'Grand
Palace'. Additionally, there were a few animal encounters on
this trip which I'm sure will make you all envious.

It was early evening when we arrived at Suvarnabhumi
Airport near Bangkok, a futuristic airport of gigantic
proportions and a hive of activity as a mixture of foreign
tourists and Thai airport workers intermingled in a multi-
cultural interaction of international discourse...with a mixture
of different languages, including broken English, and an
unofficial international sign language that included a great
deal of pointing which laughingly mimicked a game of
charades. These common scenes were comical as we walked
through the airport toward the connected car park where Ada's
4 door Toyota Hilux pick-up had been parked by Ada's
nephew, Pet. Stepping out of the air-conditioned airport the
first thing I noticed was the heat...despite being early in the
evening you could still feel the intense heat of the day...'how
will I cope?' I thought.

It was dark by the time we left the airport and headed for
Korat (now known as Nakhon Ratchasima...for ease I will
refer to it as Korat throughout this text) where we planned on
staying the night before heading to Ada's home city of Khon
Kaen. I was impressed with Highway 2, the main highway that
takes you to Northeast Thailand and onto Laos and our route
to Khon Kaen. I was also relieved that in Thailand they drove
on the left hand side, as we do in the UK, but the lack of
roundabouts (well none that I have ever seen) and the
unfamiliar use of the common 'U Turn' lanes was a little alien
to me at first. Due to the darkness, it was difficult to form an
opinion and my first impressions were fairly neutral that first
night. I couldn't really see what the Thai countryside was like,
and I was only able to see what, I now know, are the common

and traditional wooden two-storey houses with corrugated tin roofs or the faint lights from a distant village. When we eventually arrived in Korat I finally got a glimpse of a mix of aged and modern Thai architecture typically found in Thai cities…I was suitably impressed by what I saw, but couldn't wait for the light of day to see Thailand properly for the first time. It was about 10pm when we found a hotel and we were soon in a room high on the eighth floor and I could see the flickering lights of the city sprawled out before us and couldn't wait to greet the dawn of a new day. It wasn't long before we were all tucked up in bed and sleeping, given the twelve our flight from the UK and the four hour drive from Bangkok.

The following morning I woke up, jumped out of bed like an excited child on Christmas morning, and opened the curtains…I was excited and eager for my first proper look at Thailand. I had no idea what to expect, but I did have some pre-conceived ideas of how I thought it might look based on images and films/documentaries I had seen on Vietnam, but I was pleasantly surprised by what greeted me from our high vantage point on the eighth floor of the hotel. I surveyed the scene below me, watching people going about their daily business and carefully assessing the details of the buildings in front of me. Whilst there were some similarities with some of the older buildings, they were without the heavy influence of the French colonial style found in Vietnam, Cambodia and Laos. But it was the sophistication and style of other buildings that took me by surprise…mixed with the reds and golds of the several Buddhist temples (Wat) were the buildings (schools, hospitals, administrative buildings etc) that represented modern Thailand and my first impressions were positive as my eyes darted left and right and absorbed every detail such as the clothes people wore and the vehicles being driven, as Korat came to life before my eyes.

An hour later, after breakfast and checking out of the hotel, we were in a large square in the centre of Korat, and I had my first taste of the rich Thai history when we were stood in front of an impressive set of bronze statues of warriors wielding swords/knives, but there was something different about these statues…on closer inspection, these warriors were women. Intrigued, I asked Ada what story did these statues represent and she told me it represented a Thai heroine called Thao Suranari, wife of the Governor of Korat, who, with other women, harassed a Laotian army who had attacked Korat in 1826. On a single plinth in one corner of this impressive square was a single bronze statue of Thao Suranari, standing proud in a resplendent traditional Thai dress from a bygone age, cropped hair and holding a sword in her right hand that defiantly pointed to the floor. The stance befitting of this legendary figure in Thai history, as she appears to still stand guard over Korat and its people, and the statue acts as a shrine to her bravery. The base of the statue is adorned with garlands in a mix of bright colours, and I witnessed many people paying their respects to this great woman with offerings of fruit, flowers, candles and incense sticks. I felt it was appropriate, as a visitor to this great city, to also pay my respects to this brave woman from Thailand's past...the first of many acts of respect to shrines and Buddhist images/icons on my trips to Thailand...follow and copy the locals and you won't go far wrong.

We were soon driving out of Korat and heading northeast on Highway 2 toward Khon Kaen, and I was enjoying my first views of rural Thailand...it was not what I expected. Whilst we passed typical Isaan villages of wooden, single and double storey houses of various styles and sizes, and a continual patchwork of a mix of already harvested and still growing rice fields that littered the slightly undulating landscape of the Korat plateau (that Isaan was otherwise known as), and small herds of cattle or buffalo and the occasional farmer...I was expecting to see a more tropical countryside. But what I was seeing were sporadic pockets of the sort of deciduous trees seen in Europe and this rural mix of autumnal colour of greens, yellows and browns portrayed images similar to an area that was experiencing a severe drought...it was dry, very dry and it looked as if one match would set the whole of Thailand ablaze. Around an hour after leaving Korat we saw the signs for Phimai Historical Park, a place I was keen to see, and we turned off Highway 2 and no more than five minutes later we were parked up outside the impressive Prasat Hin Phimai, a temple similar in style to Angkor Wat in Cambodia as it was built by the same dynasty. It was nestled amidst an array of trees including the common Billimbi or cucumber tree, and this eleventh-century temple had been built from a mix of beautiful dusky pink/grey/white sandstone which over the centuries had been weathered to a smooth and strangely calming appearance, gone were the harsh, straight edges you would associate with European castles. Additionally, the weathering process had reduced the imposing nature of the carved lions and snakes that appeared to stand guard over the temple entrances, giving them a more approachable appeal. The main focal point of the temple were the spectacular, but intricately carved spires that punched the skies in an adorned explosion of power arguably representing the great Khmer Empire that had built this temple in the early Middles Ages, and it was a great example of a site built in the same style as its parent temple complex at Angkor Wat in Cambodia. It was in the grounds of this charming, but mystical temple that we had lunch from a simple open air restaurant that consisted of an eating area of many brightly coloured Thai style reed mats (no table and chairs), two large trestle tables with silk table cloths that were covered with an array of ornate silver tureens with various Thai dishes of home-cooked delights, and boiled rice, noodles and sticky rice. In the welcome shade provided by the trees, offering protection from the midday sun, we sat on the mats in this prime position enjoying our lunch...gazing at the wonder before us that is Prasat Hin Phimai. After lunch and visiting the small but informative museum building, we were again on Highway 2 heading northeast to Khon Kaen.

It was early evening when we reached Khon Kaen, and after dropping in to Tesco Lotus to buy provisions (water, vegetables, fruit, meat etc) for Ada's family, it was again dark as we turned off the main highway and headed for Ban Sam Rung. After driving for around fifteen minutes and passing through a couple of villages, one of which was Ban Kohk Si where Ada told me she went to high school...as we passed the school she pointed, but in the dark there was nothing to see except the perimeter fence. We arrived in Ban Sam Rung and were soon pulling into the drive of Ada's parent's house where there were many of Ada's family and friends waiting to greet us. There was mum and dad, sisters, nieces, nephews, cousins, friends etc it was all overwhelming especially as they didn't speak English (apart from the odd word) and I didn't speak Thai...none, zilch zero...not even one word, this was going to be interesting. But they all wanted to see Amy, as they still didn't believe that Amy was Ada's daughter, she'd never

478

married in Thailand and never had children, so given her age no-one believed Amy was her daughter…it was quite comical and I soon learnt that the Thai people had a wicked sense of humour, as even producing the photos of a pregnant Ada didn't convince them. They all made a great fuss of Amy, and Ada's sixteen year old niece, Tong, immediately formed a bond with Amy that was evident throughout our time in Ban Sam Rung. It dawned on me that it was Saturday 12th February, the wedding ceremony was in four days (16th February), and nothing had been arranged other than the date, as dictated to by the Buddhist monks from the village temple using some sort of chart/calendar, they had determined that the 16th February was lucky (as I stated in the chapter introduction, the Thai's are very superstitious and their lives revolve around good and bad luck)…and I mean nothing had been arranged, absolutely nothing and I thought, "how is this going to happen? Surely it can't be feasible to organise a wedding in three days". Watch this space…Ada assured me it would be fine and the organization would start tomorrow.

My first morning in Ban Sam Rung was an interesting one as I was awoken by a combination of unfamiliar noises…cockerels crowing (in fact, they have no concept of time and crow all night from different parts of the village), dogs barking, monks chanting (made worse by the fact that the family home was directly opposite the temple) and the strangest of all was a man with a microphone who, via a tannoy system, was announcing events (as Ada explained) that were happening that day in Ban Sam Rung…in Thai of course. If that wasn't enough there appeared to be a loud argument developing in front of the house between two villagers…I asked Ada if everything was ok and what were they arguing about and she just laughed and said, "that way we talk…this Isaan…everybody shout loud". I thought to myself "this is going to take a bit of getting used to". My next challenge was to shower…I use the term 'shower' loosely…in Ban Sam Rung the water supply to each house was only turned on for an hour each morning which allowed people to fill various receptacles (bowls, tin/plastic baths, plastic bottles etc) used mainly for washing themselves, clothes or dishes. However, in Ada's house there was also a simple tiled wet room slightly sloping with a drainage point, and in this space was a tiled 1m cubed bath that was filled with cold water and used by everyone (not at the same time) to shower…the idea is to stand outside the cubed bath on the tiled floor, take a plastic bowl and scoop the cold water out and pour it over your head and body, wash yourself with shampoo and soap, and then using the same method with the plastic bowl, rinse away the soap/shampoo. Voila, Thai shower…but God is that water cold.

The next three days with the guidance of Ada's nephew (now niece), Namphon (yes, he's a ladyboy and only a week earlier his mother, Ba (Ada's sister), had paid for him to have breast implants) we hired the wedding clothes, flowers, hairstyling and make-up, bought invites and sent them out to guests, bought the wedding rings, food and drink ordered and paid for, plates, utensils, tables, chairs and gazeebos signed out from the temple (ingenious…the temple held this stock for the whole village, whenever needed it was signed out, free of charge, and then signed back in – used by the whole village for all parties; weddings, funerals etc), live music booked and in true Thai tradition we even bought a new bed for the happy couple…us. Additionally, the headmaster of Ban Sam Rung primary school made a banner with our names on it (approximately six foot high and twelve foot wide) and it was hung on the wall in the main room of the family home, where the wedding ceremony would take place. By Tuesday evening everything was ready with exception of the food…this wasn't a problem as about ten to fifteen village women (friends of the family) stayed up all night to prepare all the food. I don't believe you would ever find a greater demonstration of 'family' and a 'sense of community' than what I witnessed over those three days in Ban Sam Rung…it was nothing short of amazing, and I can't think of anywhere that could arrange a wedding on this scale with a minimum of fuss. I felt truly honoured and humbled to be in the company of such wonderful people and I couldn't think of a better place to have a wedding. It was during this hectic three days of organizing, during a visit to Khon Kaen to buy the wedding rings, that I experienced my first animal encounter in Thailand. We had just parked in a car park in front of the main police station in Kohn Kaen, and were waiting to cross the road to the shopping centre (where the gold shop was located) and large market across the street. Something caught my eye and I thought, "Nah…can't be", I looked again and immediately had to do a double take, there was a man riding an elephant down the street, a main shopping centre in the city…to put this into context, imagine the busiest street in a city close to where you live and picture a man riding an elephant down that street, but this was Thailand…land of the unexpected. We crossed the road as the elephant approached…I was like a kid in a sweet shop, to get this close to such a magnificent animal was absolutely breathtaking and the stuff of dreams. I was soon feeding the elephant a bag of sugar cane I had bought from the woman walking behind the elephant, not just feeding but touching and patting this gentle giant, an animal I had only seen from a distance or on TV…and here I was experiencing a truly emotional moment of pure joy.

It was an early start as the monks were arriving at 7am…and awaiting their arrival was an abundance of different dishes and also the wedding guests, some of whom I recognised and others that were completely unknown to me. Additionally, the covered tiled patio area at the front of the house was an explosion of different pinks as floral bouquets were strategically placed for maximum effect, and there was also a pink and white silk backdrop heavily adorned with more pink floral bouquets, providing a great place for people to take photographs. There was also a heart shaped arch with more floral bouquets in front of the house…it all looked stunning. The dress code for the main protagonists was 'chut thai' (traditional Thai costume), therefore, I was wearing a gold and black patterned chong kraben (traditional Thai silk short pants), a white Nehru-style jacket with a patterned silver sash decorated with a smattering of small red diamonds, whilst Ada wore a traditional Thai cream blouse adorned with ornate gold and silver belt and necklace and on the lower half of her body a patterned pha nung (long skirt) in mix of blues, purples and black…she looked absolutely stunning. The monks arrived and as they filed into the house there were respectful wai greetings from everyone present, myself included, and with their saffron robes and shaved heads they exuded an instant serenity, fascinating and magical image to a foreigner like me as they sat cross-legged against the interior wall to the left of the door…the remainder of the large communal area of the house was filled with family and friends who faced the monks, all sitting cross-legged each offering a respectful wai and chanting the original Pali texts…I still had no idea of what

481

was happening and muddled along as best I could, copying Ada in offering the monks food from the many dishes so they could fill their large silver goblet style tureens, adorned with saffron sashes. This haunting chanting and Buddhist ritual was like nothing I'd ever seen, and this powerful, yet sensitive occasion was enchanting. Eventually, we received their blessing when they each tied a string bracelet on mine and Ada's wrists. When the monks eventually left there was a lull in proceedings before the actual wedding ceremony so we used the time to take a few photos with our bridesmaids, Tong and Ker (Ada's nieces), who were wearing beautiful pink sabai costumes.

Before returning outside, I swapped the traditional chong kraben short pants for a pair of long white trousers that matched the Manchu style jacket I was wearing. When I showed my face outside I was immediately grabbed by a shouting Nang (Ada's sister) and another lady, who led me out onto the road and with twenty or thirty others in tow we walked about a hundred metres down the road, and when we stopped I was given two envelopes, each containing 20 baht (Thai currency)…again, I had no idea what was happening, what I had to do next? Or what surprises were coming next? Then the music started, loud and upbeat Thai music which prompted many "whoops" from the people around me, who then started to move slowly toward the house whilst twisting their hands and arms in a dance type movement that is synonymous with Thai dancing…what to do? I just copied them all, even joining in with the occasional "whoops", and just rolled with it. Eventually, we reached the entrance at the front of Ada's parent's land, but there were two people holding a ribbon across the entrance stopping us from entering…Nang put her arm across my chest and with her other arm motioned for me to stop, and then, looking at me, she pretended to take one of the envelopes and give it to the people barring our way. I understood what Nang meant and I passed over one of the envelopes…they both smiled and let us through, this was then repeated at the doorway into the house…absolutely fascinating. Re-united with Ada, the wedding ceremony continued with the ritual of the 'dowry' being presented to Ada's parents and all the guests took it in turns to tie the string bracelets onto our wrists…another symbol of good luck. The ceremonial part of the wedding had come to an end…now it was party time.

I came to learn very quickly that the Thai people love a party and it wasn't long before everyone was tucking into the masses of food that had been prepared and cooked…I even got to try a lovely dip of buffalo blood and chilli…mmmm! The Chang and Leo beers were also being cracked open as the beer flowed, but served with ice…due to the intense heat of the Thai summer. Two of Ada's brothers, Kian and Sunya had a little too much and toward the end of the afternoon both could be seen being heavily scolded by their respective wife's …I didn't need to speak Essan Thai to understand that. The party also included 'live' music that came in the guise of two singers (who took it in turn to sing, one young woman and one young man) and two female dancers, performing off the back of a flatbed lorry with huge speakers and a suitable backdrop…ingenious, and they were excellent, entertaining the crowd with loud Thai pop music which got most people up dancing…including me. Ada and I, the family and all the guests were having a great time, dancing, eating and drinking…it was a great day. The day finished with another Thai tradition…remember the bed? It had been set-up in the small room off the main communal area (where the wedding ceremony had taken place earlier), and everyone who was still at the party had gathered around the entrance to the room as the cajoled and pointed for Ada and I to go in…more "whooping" and "laughter" as we shut the door for our first night as a married couple. It had been a fantastic day experiencing all the elements that made up a rural Essan Thai wedding and something I'll never forget.

It was relaxing for me in Ban Sam Rung and I'd often be found sitting on a chair in the shade of the tiled patio at the front of the house, reading or watching the family go about their business or generally just watching village life unfold throughout the day…trying to understand their routines and customs. I felt very humble witnessing the happiness of a people who lived a frugal life, and I reflected on the 'rat race' I had left behind in the UK…these Thai people lived for today, they let tomorrow take care of itself. I'd watch people come and go and at mealtimes people walking by would be invited to eat with the family from the various array of dishes on offer at every mealtime. Additionally, there would always be someone selling something such as fruit, fish, honey, vegetables (all fresh), mats, pots and pans, mosquito nets etc…it was amazing to watch the simplicity of Isaan life and there was a jealous sense of respect growing in me for these wonderful people and their way of life. Additionally, to spending time in the village we would visit Khon Kaen and we also visited many other places during our time in Ban Sam Rung including the Sala Mai Thai Silk Museum in Chonnabot, Wat Nong Wang in Khon Kaen, Ban Chiang, Ubol Ratana Dam and my favourite, and a truly enthralling and hair-raising place, Ban Khok Sa-Nga…otherwise known as 'Snake' Village.

An hour south of Khon Kaen on Highway 2 is Chonnabot, famous for its silk museum and workshops. Around fifteen of us crammed into Ada's truck (as she called it) and made our way to 'Silk Road' in Chonnabot. It was Sunday and therefore it was fairly quiet, but we still managed to get into the Sala Mai Thai (Silk Museum) and it was intriguing to learn how silk is made and to see and touch the various elegant and detailed patterns in an array of rich and stunning colours. Silk Road itself was fairly quiet but we did witness a couple of shops making silk garments in the old traditional way, simple but labour intensive. However, seeing the simplicity in these workshops gave the silk garments being made a personal and loving touch that mass production would never be able to replicate. From Chonnabot we headed back to Khon Kaen, to Wat Nong Wang, a stunning temple, similar in shape to a pyramid, which dominates the skyline that surrounds Bung Kaen Nakhon Lake…this beautiful red and gold, pyramid like, temple still remains a favourite of mine. Made of eight floors that decrease in size as you climb the stairs from one floor to the next, finally finishing with a gold spire piercing the skies above the city. There are many windows on each floor, each with individually carved red shutters…the detail is intricate and beautifully crafted. Around the outside of the ground floor there is a wide walkway and on the outside edge of each corner there are small three metre square buildings with triangular roofs which are identical smaller versions of the temple itself…nothing has been spared in the attention to detail. The whole area is set in a beautifully cared for gardens where there are a mix of symbolic statues/ornaments such as

484

white elephants, a large ceremonial gong and the handrails on the sides of each set of steps are the ornate serpents (nga's) that you see protecting all Thai temples. When we arrived that day there was a Buddhist celebration in full swing and we were all soon dancing around the temple...the obligatory three times (for good luck), and in the customary Isaan style. These joyous events in Thailand are infectious and you can't help but get caught up in the unrelenting happiness of the Thai people...I was beginning to understand why Thailand was known as "The Land of Smiles".

Ban Chiang, a village in Udon Thani province (around 2 hrs drive from Ban Sam Rung), was another interesting trip. It is a UNESCO World Heritage Site that boasted remains of what is alleged to be the oldest civilization (360BC) ever found in SE Asia...a bizarre but advanced civilization, and the major representation of Ban Chiang is its famous attractive red painted pottery of differing shapes, sizes and designs/patterns. Burial grounds were found with this pottery either being buried with the adults or morbidly with infants inside the larger pots. The village includes an outstanding museum, a large two storey building set in beautifully maintained gardens awash with an array of colourful shrubs and carefully manicured lawns. Across the road from the museum are a row of souvenir shops offering a selection of charming miniature and lifesize copies of the original pottery, t-shirts, key rings etc. A typical burial site can be found toward the back of the village, in a temple complex, and includes another informative museum type building. For a history buff like me it was a brilliant day out made better when, during lunch, I tried 'ants eggs' for the first time...they had arrived wrapped in a leaf and have to say they were exquisite and I could see why they were considered a delicacy in Thailand. Whilst the grasshoppers I'd eaten the previous evening were very nice, the ants eggs remain my favourite of the 'unusual' food I've eaten on my travels throughout Thailand.

Another trip, that still remains my favourite, is to a village with a fearsome reputation, the village of Ban Kohk Sa-Nga (a village you may know from Karl Pilkington's visit to Thailand for 'An Idiot Abroad'), and I found out why on my first visit to this unusual, but iconic, tourist attraction...it was here I saw the infamous 'King Cobra', a snake that has a bite that can bring down an elephant. This is a place that I find really enthralling, but equally terrifying, and I have a huge respect for both the people and the snakes from this village. It was no more than a twenty minute drive from Ban Sam Rung, and throughout the journey I was unsure of what I would see when we arrived in Snake Village. We arrived in Ban Kohk Sa-Nga and were soon parked up on a large open space adjacent to a row of tented shops selling souvenirs such as t-shirts, children's toys (mainly to do with snakes), Thai whiskey bottles with snakes 'embalmed' in the whiskey and many other standard souvenirs (key rings etc)…in true worldwide tradition, wherever there are tourists there are souvenirs and Thailand was no different. We made our way to an arena which had a square raised platform, similar to a boxing ring but without the ropes etc, four tiers of bench seat on three sides, and on the fourth side there was a booth (more on this later) and this was all covered by a corrugated roof on stilts. We all sat on the bench seating opposite the booth…Pichar, Ba, La, Toy, Gaer, Gy, Tong, Ker, Lair, Namphon, Daling, Pa, New and others, along with Ada, Amy and I, as we waited for the show to begin. Whilst we were waiting I could see a collection of wooden boxes on the stage which, judging by the small holes in the top of the boxes, I presumed was where they kept the snakes. A few minutes later I quickly discovered what the booth was for as a woman started speaking (in Isaan Thai) into a microphone…it was a commentary box, she was shouting, what I presumed was, an announcement for the next show, and almost immediately five young girls in their early teens ran up the steps onto the raised platform in front of us. They positioned themselves in two rows (three at the front and two at the back) roughly equidistant apart, music started playing and I recognised the now familiar Isaan Thai style of song and the corresponding dancing of the girls…a few minutes into the routine five men came onto the stage each carrying a python which they placed around the shoulders of each of the young girls. The girls continued to dance and at one point put the head of the python they were each holding into their mouths…wow, braver than me. The girls finished their routine and quickly disappeared off the stage, but were quickly replaced by a young boy of about seven or eight years old and a man (possibly his father), the boy stood there expectantly as the man opened one of the boxes slightly and brought out what I now know to be a rat snake, a non-

486

venomous, but aggressive snake, and placed it on the floor in front of the boy who then began to annoy the snake by gently tapping on its tail before attempting to avoid the agitated and striking snake, not always being successful…all this was happening to the sound of the frenzied rantings of the woman in the commentary booth. Another couple of boys repeated the performance of the first boy…what next? I presumed it would be the men. I wasn't wrong, a man climbed the steps onto the stage and gave a wai greeting to the crowd, as other performers had done before him…I wasn't prepared for what happened next, another man opened one of the boxes slightly and brought a 'King Cobra' using a special stick with a curved metal piece on the end and placed it in front of the other man…it was huge, around four to five metres long, and it immediately went in to the familiar cobra striking position, the upper part of its body standing vertically erect with its head in the famous hooded pose associated with a cobra, appearing to watch the every move of the man bobbing and weaving, and when the snake turned to move away the man would gently tap the tail of the snake, and it would, in an instant, return to its terrifying striking position…absolutely mesmerizing…the woman in the booth was inciting the crowd with her 'edge of the seat' commentary. Another two men followed, one of which, during his performance, as the cobra was in its striking position, moved closer and closer to the snake in slow movements until he was hovering inches above the snake…he then kissed the top of the snake's head…unbelievable, it was difficult to comprehend what I was watching, I was nervous and I was sitting in relative safety on the fourth tier of seating. What makes it more remarkable is that I have since found out that in similar shows in SE Asia, snakes have had their venom sacs removed or their mouths glued for the show. But in this show in Ban Kohk Sa-Nga the cobras are 'fully loaded' and one bite from one of these snakes would mean you would be in serious trouble, and I know that in the last ten years four men have died from King Cobra bites during this type of show in this famous village. The men then finished the show by dancing with the pythons, similar to the young girls at the beginning of the show, but with the additional 'party' trick of putting the snake down the front of their shorts. When the 20-30 minute show finished, a couple came out with a python into the crowd so people could have their photo taken with the snake for a small charge of one hundred baht (around £2). Ada and her family quickly stepped back, and you could see the fear in their eyes, so the couple with the snake headed for the crazy farang (foreigner)…me. I soon had the python draped around my shoulders and was even encouraged to put the snake's head in my mouth (which I did) but there was no way the snake was going down the front of my shorts…absolutely no way. This was a day that had been filled with a range of different emotions…fear, happiness, surprise and even anxiety.

Before we left Ban Sam Rung we visited the Ubol Ratana Dam near Khon Kaen, but despite the huge expanse of water, the dam and the beautiful gardens, it was the gigantic white Buddha at Wat Phra Bat Phu Pan Kham, set high on a hill with its back to the lake and appearing to oversee the inhabitants of the flat plateau that spread out below in a continuous patchwork of villages and rice fields, that impressed me. There are large Buddha's all over Thailand, but this one is particularly majestic from its elevated position and also includes a long, steep staircase on the eastern side which is equally impressive. Another breathtaking vision of immense beauty…Thailand just kept providing "wow" images.

The following day we left Ban Sam Rung with tearful farewells all round, in the short time I'd spent there I'd been well looked after by everyone and it was sad to leave my new family and the friends I'd made there, and it would be impossible not to miss them, their kind and their welcoming smiles. It was a wonderful experience that gave me a respect for rural Thailand, and I was slightly envious of their simple outlook on life and their immense gratitude for even the smallest of gestures. The truck was loaded and we were soon on our way with Gaer, a Buddhist monk…seven or so hours later we dropped Gaer at Rangsit train station before going to Ada's condo (condominium or apartment) in Rangsit where we stayed the night before travelling to Jomtien, to the east of Bangkok close to the hedonistic city of Pattaya.

In Jomtien we stayed in the Hotel Ambassador, possibly the largest hotel I have ever seen and a hotel Ada worked in when she left college when she was twenty years old. It consisted of four large blocks with a total of over 4,000 rooms. It appeared that we were the only family from the UK…the entire hotel was full of Russians. I had never experienced being in the same vicinity as any Russian before, and it may have been the harshness of their language that made them seem rude and brash…I know the Thai waitresses in the hotel were treated appallingly by my fellow Europeans, which saddened me immensely given the positive experiences I was having with the Thais. It was as if someone had got all the inhabitants of a government housing estate and said "Come on, let's all go on holiday together". I'm sure that individually they are fine people, but as a collective their behaviour left a lot to be desired. I didn't let it spoil our few days in Jomtien as we visited the Million Years Stone Park and Pattaya Crocodile Farm, Koh Lan, Pattaya Aquarium and Buddha Mountain (Khao Chi Chan) near Sattahip.

The crocodile farm was an unusual place in that I have never seen so many crocodiles in one place, there were hundreds of them a lot of which were easily larger than 10ft long, there was even a fenced platform at the side of the lake, where these crocodiles were located, where you could feed them with waste meat and fat etc that you could buy from the small shop/kiosk on the platform…bizarre, but this is Thailand where it was seen as perfectly normal. The shop would give you a stick/pole with short line and a large hook on the end where you could hang the meat. Then you would dangle the pole over the water where the crocodiles would jump vertically out of the water and grab the meat, with jaws that can bite at insanely high pressures (+3000 pounds per square inch), and everyone's happy, even the crocodile…I didn't have a go as it had 'tragic accident' written right through it and anyone involved in Health and Safety in the UK would have recurring nightmares about how to write a procedure for feeding crocodiles. But the crocodile show was even more of a Health and Safety issue with the Thai handlers in nice silk outfits putting their heads in the mouths of crocodiles…no thanks. But this park also doubled as a zoo and there were the normal mix of tigers, giraffes, monkeys, bears etc that could also be seen. It was here I would have my next animal encounter. We had just finished looking at a beautiful white tiger in its enclosure, and as it was lying close to the edge we were able to get some good photos with Amy in the foreground whilst sitting in her pushchair staring at this majestic cat. As we left the enclosure the path sloped away in front of us to an open fronted building, where toward the back I could see a tiger lying on a raised platform, about two feet in height, of polished pebbles and stone…it looked as if it had been purpose built for the tiger. Intrigued, we walked down the slope where I also noticed to my right there was a sun bear…it then dawned on me that you could have photos with these animals. "Yes…" I thought, but as I got closer I realised how big this tiger actually was, it was huge and I could now see the chain that was fixed to a ring on the plinth and to a collar around the tiger's neck…when you watch a wildlife programme in the comfort of your own living room, you have no concept of how large these tigers are, and this one was an impressively large beast and I swallowed hard as I got closer. I approached one of the Thai handlers and he ushered me to the side of the tiger and pointed to where he wanted me to sit…I now felt totally insignificant next to this majestic animal. I nervously sat next to the tiger and the handler placed my hand on its back, the fur was very coarse and a thick mix of black, deep orange with a white underside…adrenalin and nervous excitement were reaching heights I'd never experienced before, but I made sure I was sitting ready for a quick getaway if anything went wrong. The photographer (and Ada) took a few photos and then the handler placed my hand on the enormous head of this tiger, a head that was probably bigger than my torso, he then said something to the tiger in Thai and the tiger tilted it's head back and let out a loud roar…the photographer snapped away, whilst my heart skipped a beat and I nearly shit myself…what an experience, such a majestic and iconic animal. I often look at the official photograph I had taken that day of me sitting with that tiger and the power of that wonderful animal is there for all to see…each paw is probably eight to ten inches in diameter, the whole beast oozes 'strength', its unique markings and powerful jaws and teeth…a magnificent mix of stealth, strength, agility and dominance. It was an absolute honour to sit next to such a beautiful and iconic beast.

The following day we took a boat trip to Koh Lan, a tropical island off Pattaya, and it was mine and Amy's first experience of visiting a Thai beach. We moored a few hundred metres offshore and were all transferred to an open top boat that took us in closer to the beach where, in about two and a half to three feet of water we waded ashore…made a tadge more difficult by the fact I was carrying Amy who was still only ten months old. It was a beautiful beach of pristine white sand and warm clear water and it was ideal for Amy, but we had to be careful as the sun was fierce and luckily at the back of the beach were sunbeds and parasols so we could keep Amy in the shade as much as possible…just nipping on to the beach or into the warm water for short periods. But we took some great photographs for the family album of Amy's first time on a beach and what a stunning place to do it and create those memories. Around 4pm it was time to leave and we waded into the sea, climbed onto the open top boat and were taken back to the boat that would take us back to Pattaya harbour…the sun glistening and shimmering on the ocean as Koh Lan faded away into the distance.

The next day we visited the excellent Pattaya Aquarium and Khao Chi Chan (a gold outline image of Buddha on a cliff face) at Sattahip before heading back to Bangkok and the Grand Palace…if there is somewhere you have to see if you visit Bangkok, this is it and there are not enough superlatives to describe its magnificent beauty. Be warned, to visit the 'Grand Palace', as with any other Royal residence in Thailand, you have to wear long trousers (men) or long trousers/skirts (women) and neither should wear sleeveless tops, dresses nor vests and if you wear sandals or flip-flops you will have to wear socks, therefore, sensible shoes/trainers are advised. The Grand Palace is set within a white external wall that stands about fourteen to sixteen feet high and resembles the battlements seen in European castles. The palace is made-up of three areas: Firstly, the Outer Court' which houses buildings that were once the administrative seat of government, Thai War Ministry, state departments, mint and the most important temple in Thailand, 'Wat Phra Kaew (Temple of the Emerald Buddha – the emerald effigy of Buddha in the temple was carved from a single block of jade in the fourteenth-century). Secondly, the 'Central Court' was where the residences of the king were located along with halls used for conducting state business. Thirdly, the 'Inner Court' was where the king's royal consorts and daughters lived. These areas in this walled palace are a testament to the skills of Thai artisans with stunning intricate detail wherever you look, be it in the buildings, statues or gardens…it is awash

491

with outstanding beauty and magnificence. This is the palace that housed King Mongkut or Rama IV, the king made famous by Yul Brynner in 'The King and I' which is, as mentioned in the chapter introduction, banned in Thailand.

Visiting historical sites is a favourite hobby of mine, as I appreciate that I am walking in the footsteps of iconic historical characters, and I find that incredible. When we walked into the area where the 'Temple of the Emerald Buddha' is located it is overcrowded with other buildings of various styles, sizes and wonderment, of statues and excellent examples of topiary, all surrounded by a covered walkway which houses a series of murals using gold leaf that depicts the epic story 'Ramayana'. The intricate detail of all the buildings captures the attention, as the use of vibrant colours such as gold, red, green and various blues, compliments each other in a strict co-ordination of stunning beauty…even the giant-like fearsome statues standing guard throughout the complex are spectacular, and epitomize the Thai architecture known throughout the world which is also copied in other temples found all over Thailand. This temple and palace complex is the heartbeat of Thailand and its very own Shangri-La. The building that is the former residence of the Thai kings up to 1932, is European in style, but the roof is definitely in line with Thai style architecture with the gold décor and red and green roof tiles that match the other buildings that surround it. The Grand Palace is a breathtaking, must see piece of Thai history and culture that every visitor to Thailand or, in particular, Bangkok must make an effort to see.

With only two days left in Thailand time was precious, and therefore, the following morning we were driving to Kanchanaburi, a place of outstanding beauty that is unfortunately associated with horrific events from World War II…following the surrender of allied troops at Singapore, many of the captured troops were used by the Japanese to help build the 'Death Railway', a supply line from Bangkok to their armies in Burma fighting the British/Indian forces, including the Chindits (Long range penetration groups fighting in Burma). Due to malnutrition, ill-treatment/torture, disease (malaria, cholera, beriberi, tuberculosis, tropical ulcers and many others) and even fatigue, resulted in the death of over 12,000 allied prisoners of war and 90,000 southeast Asian civilian labour (mainly Burmese and Malays) building the Thai/Burma Railway. As we approached Kanchanaburi the arid images of Northeast Thailand became a distant memory as the scenery of Kanchanaburi province revealed itself as a mix of lush greens of various shades. As we drove through Kanchanaburi city its buildings were similar to those in other cities of Thailand, but as we passed the railway station we passed a sign indicating that Kanchanaburi War Cemetery was just ahead and there was also a sign for the world famous 'Bridge on the River Khwae (or Kwai, as we know it)'. A few moments later we were parked up in front of the War Cemetery and for a few moments I stared at this beautifully maintained resting place for many brave souls and thought "wow…what an image of tranquil sorrow…it's so beautiful, and a stunning final resting place for many a young man". I opened the door and stepped out of the truck and you can't help but become immersed in feelings of sadness, and I was mesmerized by the serenity and how well maintained the grounds were. Whilst there was, ironically, a barbed wire fence around the perimeter of the cemetery, it was hardly noticeable compared with the disorderly and sporadic lines of trees dotted around the cemetery at irregular distances apart. The cut of the plush green grass was so short it resembled the surface of a snooker table, and the rows of angled plaques of the 6,982 dead were intermingled with various shrubs of similar size but in an array of bursts of differing colours…just a beautiful, simple and perfect field of remembrance. The entrance is a simple three arched building of white stone with the words 'Kanchanburi War Cemetery – 1939-1945, and as you walk through this building you are immediately drawn to a simple white cross that stands around twelve to fifteen feet high and is toward the top of the cemetery at the head of an avenue of grass that dissects the memorial plaques. It was very poignant walking amongst the plaques that identified the remains of so many young men…the average ages of these soldiers seemed to be early to mid-twenties, soldiers who, at one time, would have had similar dreams to us of getting married, having children and growing old…but sadly those dreams were ripped from them, and one plaque, in particular, drew my attention; 1924664 Sapper G.R. Perriman, Royal Engineers who had died on 1ˢᵗ June 1945, age 25…as an ex-Royal Engineer myself it saddened me to think he had passed away just a few weeks before he would have been liberated.

The message on the plaque simply said 'Peacefully sleeping. In God's own time we will meet again', I remember thinking that when an ex-Sapper passes away and it's posted on Facebook, there are a ream of messages of comfort that simply say, R.I.P. Sapper…Your duty is done…See you in the Squadron Bar one day', and I remember saying to Sapper Perriman as I stood in front of his final resting place "R.I.P. Sapper Perriman…thank you for your sacrifice, I'll buy you a beer when I see you in the Squadron Bar". This was the first time I'd visited a war cemetery anywhere in the world and it was emotional and thought provoking. It is sobering to think that these men probably died agonizing deaths from one of those causes listed earlier in this paragraph and not as a result of a true act of war…tragic and very, very sad. Adjacent to the cemetery is the 'Death Railway Museum and Research Centre', a small two-storey building that provides and informative and tasteful, but tragic, history of the ' Death Railway' and the cruelty, working and living conditions the prisoners of war were forced to endure. Let's not forget the civilian labourers (over 100,000 Malays and Burmese etc) who are buried in many unmarked graves along the route of the railway…unknown forgotten casualties with no pristine war cemetery or memorial as their final resting place.

Leaving the cemetery, we followed the signs to the famous bridge that spanned the River Khwae and were soon parked up close to the river and the bridge that can both be considered as a monument or symbol of the 'Death Railway'. At one time there were two bridges that spanned the river on this site that stood a couple of hundred metres apart, the original wooden bridge and the newer steel bridge, but both were successfully bombed on the 24th June 1945 by a R.A.F. Liberator Squadron. The wooden bridge has long since disappeared, but the new steel bridge was repaired and this is the iconic bridge that spans the River Khwae Noi (Little Kwai) today…the two original curved spans damaged by the bombing raids have now been replaced by angular truss spans, allegedly provided by the Japanese as part of the reparations they were forced to pay. Tourists can walk on the bridge, but beware this is still a working railway and trains to and from the station at the end of the line, Nam Tok (you can catch a minibus from here to 'Hellfire Pass', so named as it resembled hell when the POWs were working through the night to forge a gap through the rock) will periodically cross the bridge. But on this short visit to the bridge we took a ride on a purpose built slow train that takes you over the bridge and a few hundred metres along the line on the other side of the river before stopping and coming back over the bridge to the bridge station. Following the mini train ride we took a short walk to the Jeath War Museum, passing shops and restaurants along the way. About fifty metres along the road I just happened to glance in to an open fronted large restaurant, and I saw something that made me do a double-take...I stopped, looked again and saw a leopard sprawled across a large, highly polished wooden table. I took a few photos and this beautifully marked cat seemed oblivious to the attention. One of the handlers motioned me to sit next to to the leopard, which I was happy to do...compared to the huge tiger I'd sat next at the Crocodile Farm the previous day, this cat was like a housecat. I sat on the table next to the leopard and the handler/keeper took my hand put cooked chicken onto it...this alerted the leopard who was now more attentive and it started to gently eat the chicken out of my hand...stroking the back of this sensational feline the fur was like velvet. Another awesome animal encounter, made complete by Ada and Amy joining me so we could have photographs with this magnificent animal. Leaving the leopard, we finally reached the 'Jeath War Museum', a bizarre collection of weird wartime antiquities that is well worth a visit...it even houses a rusting steam engine that was allegedly used by the Japanese on the 'Death Railway' to transport arms to their soldiers in Burma. Before we returned to Bangkok we also visited the Chungkai War Cemetery, a short drive of about 2-3 km from Kanchanaburi War Cemetery, another beautifully presented place of rest for 1,400 Commonwealth and Dutch casualties...the majority of whom died in the hospital that was once sited on the site of the Chungkai base camp...another moving experience, but I remember the sadness of seeing such a memorial of horror in an area of such natural beauty.

Our last day in Thailand was spent visiting the ancient, and former capital of Siam (the former name of Thailand), Ayutthaya, where we fed a boisterous and unruly baby elephant and endured an elephant ride...I won't say 'enjoyed' as it was not the best experience I've had, holding Amy with one hand and holding on for dear life with the other, and knowing what I know now that riding an elephant is detrimental to its health, I have not ridden one since. The new city of Ayutthaya has been built amongst the ruins of the old city that was 'sacked' by the Burmese in 1767, and this mixture of old and new is evident throughout the area. It was a sad sight to see the crumbling temple and damaged statues (the heads had been callously removed off Buddha statues by the Burmese in acts of wanton damage) of Wat Si Samphet, but it was an honour to see the prominent and iconic stupas still standing defiantly in a sea of devastation. Before we left this mystical city we visited Wat Lokayasutha where a 'reclining Buddha' statue is sited, over thirty metres in length…an impressive effigy, but we didn't hang around too long as there were too many abandoned dogs in the area, always a worry in Thailand due to the threat of rabies. On the drive back to Rangsit the sun was setting, not just on the day, but on our trip to Thailand, a beautiful sunset that epitomized the stunning beauty I had witnessed throughout our visit…the country, its people, its food, its animals, its sunsets and sunrises…I could go on, but it's a land full of surprises, a gift that keeps on giving.

2012 – Pattaya, Khon Kaen, Ban Sam Rung, Dan Sai (and Laos), Chiang Mai, Phitsanulok, Sukhotai and Bangkok

The second trip was the first time I experienced 'Songkran' the celebrations surrounding the Thai New Year…as more and more people have travelled to Thailand in recent years this is something that many of you will have heard of or even experienced yourselves. However, as we were staying in Ban Sam Rung I not only enjoyed the fun of the water pistols and the playful water fights, and playing football in a tournament involving other villages…I also witnessed and was involved in the tender moment as all the children (including Ada and me) washed Ada's parent's feet and hands in a touching ritual associated with the Thai New Year celebrations…another example of how important 'family' is to the Thai people and a touching tribute to the love Ada and all her brothers sisters held for their parents. But the first place we visited during this trip was the hedonistic city of Pattaya…not a city I enjoyed or a city I would ever return to as it is just not my cup of tea. However, I could see why it had such an appeal for single men, but as a family man I felt its seedy image was how many

*people sadly perceived all of Thailand was is so far removed
from the truth. This could be considered as being unfair as the
majority of the city is no different to any other city in
Thailand…but more on Pattaya below. This was also a trip
that we visited Dan Sai near Loi and actually spent around an
hour in Laos and where we would go on to experience the
beautiful sights of Northern Thailand as we travelled to
Chiang Mai and enjoyed the famous 'night market', visited the
pandas at Chiang Mai Zoo, stood on Thailand's highest point
at Doi Inthanon and visited the temple at Doi Suthep that
overlooks the city. We also visited the cities of Phitsanulok
and Sukhotai, where we visited the ancient ruins of the old city
that had been 'sacked' by the Burmese in the sixteenth-
century. We finished up in Bangkok with another visit to the
Grand Palace, Wat Pho and Dusit Zoo. My love of Thailand
was growing…I was captivated by every aspect of this nation
of wonder and its culture, outstanding beauty and of course
the beautiful Thai people. Another wonderful holiday, and
where we also celebrated Amy's Second Birthday in Ban Sam
Rung with her Thai family. Follow me on another journey of
wonderment and enjoy more animal encounters.*

We arrived at Suvarnbhumi Airport at around 7am, once
through immigration Ada found a phone shop, bought a Thai
SIM card and contacted her sister, La, telling her we'd arrived.
No more than ten minutes later we were met by La and Ada's
nephew, Pet, and within twenty minutes we had loaded Ada's
truck and we were on our way to Pattaya. I wouldn't say I was
looking forward to this part of the trip, as Pattaya's reputation
was not a positive one and it wasn't the Thailand I wanted to
experience…but there was also a curious intent to discover the
darker side of this hedonistic city to discover why it was such
a magnet for single men from all over the world. Despite its
negative reputation in the 1950s, the city was once a quiet
fishing village, then the Americans became embroiled in a war
in Vietnam that escalated during the 1960s…this was the
catalyst that created the booming city seen today, a city that
had grown as a R&R destination for American GIs escaping
the horrors of the first televised war. I had made a conscious
decision to reserve my own personal judgement on Pattaya
and give it a chance to prove the doubters and sceptics wrong.

After stopping at a large service area near Chonburi, it was late morning before we arrived in Pattaya and my immediate thoughts on Pattaya was its size, It was a huge city a mix of older 60s/70s style shop buildings toward the back of the city, and the nearer you got to the beach, the buildings changed to modern high rise tower blocks filled with apartments or condos, as they were called in Thailand, and high end hotels. Additionally, due to its sprawling size, the hectic chaos of traffic and impatient drivers honking their horns in frustration became the norm, as it is in any Thai city. Stuttering our way through this typical carnage, we eventually made it on to the beach road and the real appreciation of Pattaya being a popular holiday destination hit home. The beach front was typical of many places around the world, a mix of hotels, restaurants, bars, coffee shops, shopping malls, souvenir shops and stalls, street food sellers, and the large crescent moon shape of Pattaya's beach front was pretty impressive. We were at the north end of the beach and immediately after The Royal Cruise Hotel (a hotel in the shape of an ocean liner) we turned left onto Pattaya 3 Alley and found a small boutique hotel, and it was only about a hundred metres from the seafront. After booking into the hotel, we transferred the luggage to our rooms, showered, changed and generally relaxed, before the five of us (Ada, Amy, La, Pet and me) ventured out for something to eat. We soon found a restaurant and enjoyed our first meal back in Thailand, but as we had been travelling for almost twenty hours, after our food we decided to walk back to the hotel and pay a visit to the beach. After a short walk on the sand, some cool snaps of Amy, and a cooling dip in the sea, we could see that the colours of the sky were changing from a clear deep blue into a kaleidoscope of yellows, oranges, purples, pinks and reds as the sun appeared to be falling into the ocean. We called it a day before it got dark and headed back to the hotel.

The following morning after a mix of an American and Thai style breakfast we thought we would take a walk onto the beach and generally have a look around. There were many families on the beach with children of various ages enjoying the normal beach activities of building sandcastles, playing ball games or spashing around in the sea. You could hear the sound of happiness all around…even the squawk of the seagulls sounded as if they too were laughing with joy. In the bay there were people on jet skis or paragliding high above the sun kissed ocean. As we stepped off the beach we walked toward the south end of the bay on a meandering path that ran parallel with Beach Road, protected by the shade of palm trees. We passed more families, food sellers and even a few 'odd' couples whose behaviour resembled lovestruck teenagers when, in fact, there were clearly unhealthy age gaps between the elderly western tourists and their young Thai girlfriends etc. However, as we only passed one or two couples with this age difference, I dismissed it almost immediately, as judging by the amount of parents with young families perhaps Pattaya was being unfairly judged and its reputation was nothing more than myth. By late afternoon, after another dip in the sea, we were back in the hotel getting ready to go out for the evening.

It was still light when we headed to a seafood restaurant we'd seen earlier in the day, and as we sat in that restaurant, as with the previous evening, there was another explosion of colours in the sky, as the sun set over the bay…but as darkness fell and we sat there eating, we were unaware of the changes taking place in Pattaya. It was completely dark when we left the restaurant an hour or two later, and now we were headed for the world famous 'Walking Street', a street of go-go bars and night clubs/discos that I'd seen on TV, and it looked like 'Soho on speed'. Now Ada, La and Pet had been to Pattaya before, visiting Ada and La's niece, Noot, and they had seen Pattaya at night…whereas, I was like a child seeing something for the first time, and oblivious to what I was about to see. We crossed the road and were again on the path that meandered between the palm trees between the beach and Beach Road…Ada suggested I walked ahead, I asked "Why?" and she smiled, motioned with her hand for me to walk ahead saying "You see soon…go…go…leao leao (quick quick)". They stood still with Amy sat in the pushchair, as I walked on ahead, and I soon lost sight of them in the darkness with the twists and turns of the path, palm trees and other walkers. As I continued walking, I was surrounded by familiar sounds, such as car horns, the now familiar Thai language in shouts and whispers, music from bars and the bewitching sound of the ocean. There were also familiar smells such as the salty sea air, Thai cooking, exhaust fumes and cheap perfume…"hang on…cheap perfume", it was then I realised I had been walking past girls, sometimes on their own, their faces lit up from the glow of the screen as they scrolled through their phones or sometimes they were in groups of two's and three's chatting. I stopped and looked around, and realised that the girls I had been walking past were all wearing high heels, short mini-skirts (and I mean short), vest type tops or a various array of different coloured or patterned cocktail type dresses...The penny dropped...they were prostitutes or 'freelancers' as they were called in Pattaya, chancing their arm on the Beach Road as opposed to paying bar owners extortionate prices to sit in the bars of 'Walking Street' hoping they'll be picked by a tourist for 'fun in the sun'. "Ouch", something had just bitten me on the underside of my upper arm...I turned and quickly realised that it wasn't an insect...one of the prosititutes had pinched me, it was their way of getting your attention. She smiled at me and said "hello handsome man", I knew instantly this was no woman, this was a ladyboy...I gulped and said "hello" before swiftly moving on. Every now and then I would stop, look back to see if I could see the others, get pinched by a prostitute...they'd smile...I'd smile...I'd gesture 'no' with my hands and carry on walking. I came across an area that wasn't particularly well lit and there was only one prostitute here, sat on a bench looking as if she wanted to be elsewhere. I approached her, pointed to my camera and asked "Tai Loop (photo)", she shook her head and without smiling said "Bor (no)". Rightly or wrongly, I put my hand in my pocket and pulled out a 100 baht (about £2) note and offered it to the girl whilst again pointing at my camera...she nodded and said "OK". I took a couple of photos and said "Korp Kun Cap (thank you)", she again nodded, and tried to force a smile but I could see it was difficult for her, I smiled, nodded and carried on walking, looking back once, I immediately felt sorry for her as she cut a lonely figure there in the semi-darkness and I hoped she'd be ok. As I walked on I began to feel guilty and thought more about the girl I'd just left...there was little emotion in her eyes, they just appeared to be pits of darkness, a sorrowful stare. I wondered what her name might have been?...Where did she come from?...What was her story?...How old was she?...I thought "at a guess, possibly mid to late twenties or early thirties, but she could have been younger...she could have been older, it was difficult to tell". It felt wrong that I'd given her money for a photograph, but the only comfort I got from that 'transaction' was that even if she didn't attract a 'customer' that night, the money I'd given her would at least enable her to eat. I started to feel sorry for her and wondered how she had ended up in this sorry position…it was sad, very sad and it made me realise that Pattaya's reputation appeared to be accurate, and on the evidence of what I'd witnessed it must be the 'graveyard of dreams' for many a Thai girl. I finally reached the end of the meandering path and was now stood about twenty metres from the entrance to 'Walking Street', the giveaway being the large 'Walking Street' sign, lit by a continual flashing of different coloured lights. I turned to wait for Ada, Amy, La and Pet, who I could see were about fifty metres away, a few seconds later, as they got closer, I felt one of those now familiar 'pinches' on the underside of my upper arm, I turned to face three Thai girls who were stood behind me, the middle one who was stunningly pretty with that beautiful Thai smile said "hello falang". I smiled back, turned and stepped back and pointed to Amy in her pushchair who was now about three metres away with Ada, La and Pet. The girl immediately and repeatedly apologised, "sorry…sorry…sorry". I gestured that it was ok and smiled again…she gave me a wai and another smile, and as we walked away I heard her shout "sorry mr falang" one more time. We walked into "Walking Street" for a couple of hundred metres, turned around and then walked straight back out again, I'd seen enough…the scantily clad bar girls, the leering men of differing ages, sizes and nationalities were something I was finding difficult to comprehend, but the obvious exploitation of women was everywhere, and it sickened me, it was the Thailand I didn't want to see, but strangely was glad I had…I swore I'd never visit Pattaya again. I was relieved when we finally reached the hotel…I felt dirty, saddened and angry by what I'd seen and couldn't wait to leave Pattaya, and in an attempt to wash Pattaya out of my skin I headed for the shower.

After breakfast we left Pattaya, and around seven hours later we were approaching Ban Sam Rung…I was pleased to be away from 'Sin City' and to be back in Isaan where I could renew my love affair with village life in rural Thailand. The Songkran (Thai New Year) was due to start, and the day after our arrival we were heading out for a water fight…we fitted as many people (Nang, La, Pet, Toy, Tong, New, Nat, Ker and many others) as we could in and on Ada's truck…along with an empty oil drum. Before we headed for the first village we found a small river, Pet jumped in with a bucket and started passing full buckets of water out and in no time at all the oil drum was full…we were ready. We went on a tour of nearby villages such as Ban Non, Ban Kham and Ban Kohk-Si, where we were greeted by families outside their houses with large washing tubs full of water…and the fun began…we'd throw water at them…they'd throw water at us…they smeared talc on our faces…it wasn't long before everyone was soaking wet which was quote refreshing in the fierce heat of the afternoon…too cooling when water hit you from some groups who had put ice in with the water. It was a great afternoon…great fun and being continually wet was a recurring theme of the next few days with more sporadic water fights in and around Ban Sam Rung. The day finished with football training (a kickabout) on the football pitch at Ban Sam Rung School…I had been asked if I would help sponsor a football tournament which meant I had my very own football team, Ban Sam Rung United. The following day (the day before the football tournament) Ada and I went to Central Plaza in Khon Kaen, huge, modern shopping centres found in every city in Thailand…everything under one roof, and I mean everything, banks, clothes, shops, mobile phone shops, electrical stores, pharmacies, dentists, slimming centres, restaurants, bookshops, opticians, coffee shops (including Starbucks), market stalls, cinema, children's play area and amusements, karaoke, roller skating, gymnasium, gold and watch shops, sports shops, shoe shops, free parking, Robinson's department store (similar to Debenhams) crammed with designer labels and many, many more, you could even buy houses and cars. But I was only here to buy footballs for the tournament, which I found in the sports department in Robinson's. We also went to one of the many markets found in Khon Kaen where we bought a collection of different patterned colourful flowery shirts for all the family and friends…apparently it was customary to wear this style of shirt for Songkran…hence where my love for colourful and loud flowery shirts begun.

The day of the football tournament had arrived and it started with a short friendly match against a team of the village women who were all wearing a mixture of white or pink t-shirts, pleated, two-tiered and patterned skirts (similar to a tartan skirt but with brighter colours) and traditional Thai reed hats that you'd see women wearing when they worked in the fields…not the best football kit in the world, but better suited to what I saw them doing when the football tournament started properly later that morning. The game was played in the right spirit and ended in a draw, 2-2…but God was it hot, and it was only 10am. I met the team properly with a lot of wai geetings all around and we had a couple of team photographs taken (I made sure I had blown up copies made of a team photo and gave it every member of Ban Sam Rung Utd…my own photograph is framed and proudly displayed at home to this day). Our first game was against Ban Khok-Si at mid day and it was fair to say, due to my age and the intense heat, I was the weak link in the team. I was subbed five minutes into the second half…the heat was unbearable and had taken its toll, I was lead to the relative safety of the shade under the gazebo, where the head of the primary school was providing a microphoned commentary of the game, and Ada and the other girls were pouring water on me and in me in attempts to get my body temperature back to normal. We eventually lost that first game 3-2 but won our two remaining games that day, which meant we were in the semi-final. The following day we again made our way to the school pitch but lost the semi-final 2-1 to Ban Khok-Si. After the final had been played all the team came back to the family home where they were fed by Ada's family and I provided the Chang and Leo beers…great set of lads and a great way to integrate myself, even more, into village life. A word about Thai football…although a little 'raw' it was not vicious, despite there being plenty of full-blooded tackles there were some highly proficient and skilled football players, but they played more as individuals than as a team. However, it had been a great experience having the chance to play football with them and the framed photo in my house I consider to be another proud moment in my sporting life…not necessarily my best moments on a football pitch, but certainly a great experience.

The next two days were spent in a party atmosphere as the Songkran celebrations continued and there were Buddhist ceremonies, singing, eating, drinking…more water fights…again…again…and again. I don't think anyone was dry for long over thoses two days. There were also processions through the village to celebrate the beginning of the Thai summer with everyone holding the famous yellow Khon Kaen tree flowers, and also processions to raise money to help build a temple in the ancestral family village of Ba's husband (Thom – pronounced 'Tom') near Dan Sai in Loei province (northwest of Khon Kaen) that borders Laos, and after a four hour drive on the day after the Songkran celebrations had ended, around thirty of us, including Ada's mother and father, arrived late into the night at Dan Sai.

Waking up in the morning and stepping out of the hundred and fifty year old, traditional Thai wooden house, built on stilts, there was instantly a sense of beauty about where we were which had been hidden from us by the darkness of the previous night. Behind this small village the mountain rose up almost vertically, a wall of deep green foliage that eventually met the equally deep blue and cloudless sky. To the side of the village was a stunning view, which could be seen from the raised and open kitchen area Thom's brother's home, a slight incline from the lower end of the mountains that swept majestically downward to a level patchwork of colours of the rice fields that led you to the town of Dan Sai about two to three miles away in the distance. After breakfast it was decided that we were going to Laos…a casual decision it seemed, but there was a small village that bordered Laos, about twenty kilometres north of Dan Sai, called Ban Na Kha and with written permission (a 'pass'), you could cross the border by crossing the Hueang river into a small village in Laos…why not? So, off we went to Ban Na Kha, obtained our passes for a small fee of around thirty baht, walked down some steps toward the almost dry river bed, walked across a long thin boat being used to bridge what water was in the river and then, once on the other side of the river bed, walked up a slight incline onto a hardened red clay road, lined with similar wooden houses to those seen in Thailand, but there was a sense that the poverty was much greater here than their Thai neighbours across the river as although similar, the houses were much older and in much need of repair, and there was no evidence of any motorized vehicles or tarmac. This little corner of Laos was a mass of lush forest and much different to the obvious deforestation evident in Thailand to make way for rice fields and other forms of agriculture. We wandered around this semi-paradise for around twenty to thirty minutes before buying ice-creams in the sole shop and then returned back over the river into Thailand…quite unremarkable, but yet very bizarre. From Ban No Kha we drove to Dan Sai, bought some food from a street vendor and drove across the road to Phra That Sri Song Rak, where we ate our lunch before exploring this important landmark. Phra That Sri Song Rak housed a mortared brick pagoda built in 1560 to commemorate the alliance between the Kings of Ayutthaya (Thai) and Vientienne (Laos) in their fight against the Burmese. It's not fantastically impressive, but its historical importance to both Thailand and Laos was significant. Additionally, Dan Sai is an interesting town and every July it has a 'Ghost Festival' where you will see a wonderful array of locally made masks (I saw examples of these wonderfully detailed masks outside a shop in the town) and costumes on parade through the town.

That evening Thom's ancestral village organized a party for their guests (us) from Ban Sam Rung, and it was a great night (as a party always is when it's been organized by Thai people) with excellent food, a choice of alcoholic and soft drinks and the normal mix of Thai music and dancing. I was even lucky that the village drunk introduced himself to me (much to the annoyance of the village elders), but I'd like to think I calmed the situation down by not antagonizing him, as I happily shared the 'see-sip' rice whiskey bottle he kept thrusting in my face with shouts of "gin…gin…gin" (the 'g' in 'gin' is pronounced the same as 'g' in 'garden' and means 'drink') up until the point the village elders half convinced and half dragged him away from the party and away to his bed…it is difficult listening to the incoherent ramblings of a drunk, but to listen to the ramblings of a drunk speaking incoherent Isaan Thai was a whole new level of difficulty. Despite learning the basics of Isaan Thai, I had no idea what he was talking about, sadly he had drunk so much 'see-sip' he must have thought I could understand everything…he didn't realise or care that I was just nodding and smiling at appropriate moments. Thankfully, the rest of the evening passed by uneventfully, and when it was time to head off to bed we were told we were sleeping in Thom's auntie and uncle's house across the road from where we had slept the previous evening…this was a bonus as we had our own room (c/w air conditioning) in a house that was more akin to a European style house than a traditional Thai house…we had a good night's sleep that night.

The following morning, there was a procession from the edge of the village toward the village community centre that doubled as the village temple building...and I was at the front driving Ada's truck with the money 'trees' (open display of the money raised, folded notes displayed on sticks pushed into a pineapple) on the back with Ada's mum and dad. I had to drive really slowly as the procession of both sets of villagers walked and danced behind me...you may stumble across a Thai procession as a tourist, but it is a fantastic honour to be involved in one. Once we arrived at the makeshift 'temple' the monks were there to meet us, and the money, and the Buddha effigies that Ada had bought, were handed over in an intriguing ceremony of blessings, that I was now becoming accustomed to seeing . Once the ceremony had ended and after having something to eat, Ada, Amy and I said our farewells as we were heading off to Chiang Mai for a few days...and we had a long drive in front of us.

It was still light when we drove through the cities of Phitsanulok and Uttradit, and we passed through some illuminating countryside that provided more striking images of this charming country. The flat plains of the rice fields, the bread basket of Thailand, had long since disappeared behind us, replaced by forested mountains, winding roads and breathtaking views. On one such road we stopped for a drink and stretch of the legs at a large service area high on a mountain and the colours provided by the setting sun, not just on the disparate purples that filled the sky, but also on the sun kissed greens of the forested hills that shimmered and glistened on the gentle breeze, an orgy of colours that melted away into a distant pastel haze of sensuous radiance. As we continued, the light started fading and it was completely dark as we drove through Lampang and the last hundred kilometers of our journey were spent climbing and descending mountains, an endless route of continual twists and turns and warnings of wild elephants...there was a real need to maintain a high level of concentration on this dangerous mountain highway, heightened by the additional possible dangers posed by wild elephants. Eventually, approximately two hours after leaving Lampang we could see the lights of Chiang Mai in the distance, on its elevated plateau high in the Northern hills of Thailand...once known as the Lanna Kingdom and under Burmese control until it was captured by the Siamese forces of

506

Taksin the Great in 1774. It remained a vassal state of Siam until 1899 when it was annexed with Siam under the policies of King Chulalongkorn (RamaV) in 1899. Around half an hour later we had arrived in this historic city and had booked into the Chiang Mai Plaza, a stunning hotel just around the corner from Chiang Mai's famous 'Night Bazaar'.

Fully refreshed after a good night's sleep and a hearty breakfast we made the short drive across the city, passing the grand moats and stately red brick walls and gateways of the original city walls, to Chiang Mai Zoo which was situated toward the back of the flat plateau of the city, beneath the imposing mountain of Doi Suthep, the guardian of Chiang Mai. This was an impressive zoo which gave wonderful close-up experiences with many of its inhabitants such as the giraffes, elephants, koala bears, hippos, ostriches and crocodiles. Additionally, they had a wonderful panda enclosure and an excellent aquarium. Despite it being located at the beginning of the steep slopes that lead to Doi Suthep, there was a bus service that made it easier to get around the zoo, without it and in the heat, it would have been difficult to get to the top parts of the zoo, but it was an excellent zoo and a place I'd recommend visiting as children would be enraptured as Amy was with feeding the giraffes and elephants, especially the baby elephant that was there that day.

After leaving the zoo it was back to the hotel to shower and change, the air conditioning and cool shower was a welcome relief after the heat of the day. A word about the Chiang Mai Plaza Hotel…it was luxury beyond words and its elegant and large foyer/reception area was dripping with opulence that resembled images of stately homes in the UK, but with subtle Thai influences such as the ornate, decorative arches around the doors and windows and splendid ornaments. When we walked in after our day at the zoo, to complete this palatial setting, there were two young Thai ladies in traditional costumes sitting on a slightly raised carpeted platform, playing instruments I'd never seen before that produced a magical but haunting tune of serenity, traditional to the region…it created the perfect ambiance, and as we walked in from the humidity and heat of Chiang Mai we immediately felt relaxed in this cool, but spectacular space.

A couple of hours later we walked the short distance from the hotel, and around the corner onto Changklan Road where the firsts stalls of the 'Night Bazaar' began, and where we greeted by a cacophony of noise, the pleading shouts of the market traders attempting to attract buyers for their wares; a mishmash of Thai and popular western music; traffic (including horns); the murmurings of different languages from many tourists and backpackers in the market; and the faint fluttering of bemused moths constantly bouncing off the multitudes of lights throughout the market…it was a real hive of activity. The closer we got to the hub of this bazaar, a large open space behind the main thoroughfare of stalls, the noise intensified, and as we entered onto a large square our senses were overloaded with the mix of noise, incredible sights and an explosion of aromas from the many food stalls selling popular Thai dishes such as red and green curry's, pad Thai, spicy sausages and the Chiang Mai dish 'Khao Soi' (a soup flavoured yellow curry, coconut milk, boiled and fried crispy noodles), Thai desserts (beautiful colourful cakes and my favourite…mango and sticky rice with coconut milk). Around the perimeter of this square were many bars and restaurants, and there was even a ladyboy show…a parody of mimed songs and spectacular costumes. It was a fascinating evening, made more enthralling when visiting the many craft shops where intricately hand carved wooden objects could be found such as elephants, various styles of bowls, Buddha's, ornate animals and birds, flowers, scenes of Thai life and furniture…they really are spectacular and incredible pieces of art (google 'Baan Tawai Village' to see examples of these wonderful objects).

The following morning we drove to Doi Inthanon in the Shan Highlands …the highest mountain in Thailand. We drove southwest from Chiang Mai for about fifty kilometres before turning right onto the road that would take us to Doi Inthanon. We immediately started to climb into the forested hills and about fifteen minutes in we approached our first destination which was the Wachirathan Waterfall, despite it being the height of Thai summer this was still an impressive waterfall, close to the falls was quaint little coffee shop that provided us with well needed iced coffee's. The backdrop of the falls provided a great photo opportunity which we took full advantage of…the wall of rock provided a drop of around fifteen metres where one main fall of water, around two metres wide, and there were several smaller trickles flowing down the rock in various places...a hidden gem and a truly beautiful sight and with lush green forest on either side. Back in the car we continued our journey, passing beautiful mountain villages, small deforested areas that were used for growing an array of fruit, including strawberries, and vegetables and one such area had a long row of tented shops (similar to a market) selling this wonderful produce. We continued to climb until we approached two magnificent chedis built in 1987 to commemorate King Bumipol's 60th Birthday. The chedis are surrounded by beautiful, well managed gardens, a plethora of aromatic flowers and plants that resembled a palette of differing colours in a carpet of luxuriant green forest. A stunning place with breathtaking views of the Shan Highlands, and after lunch, visiting the two chedis and wandering amongst the beautiful gardens we drove the six hundred or so metres to a car park near the Royal Thai Air Force Weather Station we walked the hundred meters to the summit of Doi Inthanon, where there is large wooden sign that provides another great photo opportunity as you stand on the highest point in Thailand...2,565m above sea level. The interesting fact about this mountain is that it is named after the last vassal King of the old Lanna kingdom, King Inthawichayanon (shortened to Inthanon), and as he was keen to preserve the forests of the north, he ordered that his remains were buried there after he died. As a result, you can also visit a shrine near the summit that marks his final resting place...a fascinating tale of a magnificent mountain. After a visit to a sole souvenir shop, we made our way back to Chiang Mai where we enjoyed another evening wandering around the 'Night Bazaar'.

On our last day in Chiang Mai we drove up to Doi Suthep Temple, a resplendent temple that overlooks Chiang Mai from its high vantage point on the city's guardian mountain. Everything about this temple is strikingly beautiful, the panoramic views over a hazy Chiang Mai, the glistening large golden chedi at the heart of the temple, the intricate details on the now familiar golds, reds and blues of the temple buildings, the golden Buddha statues and shrines, beautiful paintings, the long stairway from the temple (down to the area where the food and souvenir stalls and car park) included a decorative

and colourful seven headed serpent (Buddhist Naga) on either side of the steps and the
guardians of the temple, the ancient gongs and bells and many other splendid artifacts. On entering the first tier of the temple complex there were three beautiful young Thai ladies about to perform a dance, they were barefoot, each dressed in a long, slim, gold, black and dark red patterned silk skirt, a rose pink collarless Thai blouse with a red sash adorned with gold jewellery and accessories, with their hair tied in a traditional Thai top bun decorated in a large flower and large decorative golden hairpins and adornments…they looked absolutely stunning, and they epitomized the picture postcard image associated with traditional Thai female dancers and their costumes. They were holding a vessel similar in shape to a huge egg cup type bowl that was filled with yellow and white petals. When they started dancing the deliberately slow hand and leg movements, to the equally slow music provided by the five musicians on a small wooden platform behind them, was entrancing. They captured the audience with each choreographed and synchronized movement of this typically Chiang Mai style of dance, eventually culminating in them kneeling on the floor, their backs and heads arched backwards as they held the vessels/bowls of petals above their arched bodies but parallel with the floor, and they then started sprinkling the petals behind them on the tiled terrace. The bewitched crowd watched in a stunned silence at this elegant, and arguably the most seductive and beautiful display of dance I had ever seen. After exhausting every corner of this magical temple, we enjoyed some lunch before driving a little further up the mountain to Bhuping Palace, the summer residence of the Thai Royal Family. We were driven around the site by a guide in a golf type buggy to see the beautiful collection of individually styled buildings, a mix of Thai and European alpine style chalets, all in beautifully manicured gardens and pristine lawns. It was only a flying visit to this unique palace as we left Chiang Mai and headed south to Phitsanulok.

Following an overnight stay at Rattana Park in Phitsanulok we visited Wat Phra Si Rattana Mahathat (known as Wat Yai 'Big Temple') in the city…judging by the crowds this was a popular temple amongst Thai people. It is easy to see why, as the golden Buddha image is one the most revered images in Thailand, therefore, it is an important pilgrimage site for Thai

Buddhists and tourists. As with most Thai temples there are several buildings within this beautiful temple complex, but it is the main 'hall' where this beauty is most evident. The large room is a complex array of extravagance, from the exposed golden beams in the high ceilings, the chandeliers and the blue and gold patterned pillars that create an avenue effect that immediately directs your vision to the 3.75m high golden Buddha image with aureola (flames) surrounding it, and this stunning and majestic image is directly opposite the entrance into the building. The history behind this Buddha is astounding as it was originally cast in bronze in the late fourteenth-century and then plated with gold in the seventeenth-century. We left this majestic temple and travelled to the historical ruins of Sukhothai (literal meaning 'the dawn of happiness'), the thirteenth to fifteenth-century capital of the Sukhothai kingdom and the first capital of Siam, before it was annexed into the Ayutthaya kingdom.

When we arrived at Sukhothai we had some lunch before we explored parts of this impressive city. The whole area is a collection of historical sites that provides a glimpse of the former glory of the kingdom of Sukhothai. There are palaces, Buddha statues of various styles and sizes, temples, network of dykes and lily ponds within the central zone that we visited, however, the whole historical park covers an area of seventy square kilometres and is spread over five zones (central, northern, eastern, southern and western). Using my imagination whilst looking at the ruined temples, palaces and buildings, I could envisage the grandeur of this kingdom and how magnificent the temple and palace buildings must have been at the height of the Sukhothai kingdom. Such is the beauty of the area, it offers great photographic opportunities, and we have some brilliant photos of our time is this magnificent old city. One such area was where the monument of King Ramkhamaeng the Great (reign: 1279-1298), a king who turned the relatively small kingdom of Sukhothai into a much bigger concern via clever diplomacy, well-chosen alliances and successful military campaigns...his influence stretched from Vientiane and Luang Prahang in Laos, west to the Indian Ocean of Burma and south to the Malay Penisula. He additionally united the region under the religion of Theravada Buddhism...he must have been an incredible monarch to maintain rule over such a large area, and it would be fair to say the Thai people owe a debt of gratitude to the third king of the Sukhothai kingdom, and the beautiful monument of King Ramkhamaeng in all his spendour sitting on a bench, guarding the central zone of this stunning site is a fitting tribute to this great monarch…arguably the ancestral 'grandfather' of Siam (now Thailand). We were only here for a few hours, and in the future I hope we can return to this historical site, hire bicycles and spend a few days exploring these beautiful, ancient ruins of old Siam. But for now we headed back to Khon Kaen…after a four to five hour drive, part of which was a torturous drive, in the dark, through the mountains of Nan Nao National Park...it was late as we approached Chum Phae and we decided to stop there overnight.

Before heading back to Ban Sam Rung the following day, we visited Phuwiang Fossil Research Centre and Dinosaur Museum, an impressive little museum that provides and informative look at the regions dinosaur 'finds' that includes evidence of the formidable Tyrannosaurus Rex. We also dropped into 'Pattaya 2', a beach 'folly' on Ubolrat Lake…a host of bamboo restaurants providing stunning views across this impressive lake. When we finally arrived back in Ban Sam Rung it was late, and after a fairly quiet evening, following a long and busy week, it was an early night for us all.

Over the next few days we spent time relaxing with the family in Ban Sam Rung, enjoying the relative tranquility and simplicity of village life in Isaan, reading, eating and watching the 'comings and goings' of friends and/or other villagers selling something (i.e. fish, vegetables, fruit etc). During this period we took the family to a Thai 'barbecue' restaurant (these are popular in Thailand and are large restaurants catering for hundreds of people where you cook your own food on table top mini-Thai barbecues and they highlighted the Thai sense of family perfectly)…a great night with great food, drink (alcoholic and non-alcoholic) and entertainment (live music for the adults and a mini fairground for the kids). I returned to 'Snake Village' where I again watched this intriguing but scary show…I filmed the entire show, but was a little too close to the action and when a King Cobra tried to make its escape it came straight at me and was half off the

512

stage and about one metre from my face before the handler pulled it back onto the stage. All part of the show, but I did give me a bit of a scare which is evident in the film, as there is a slight 'shake' in the action at that point. I also had my photo taken with an albino python…this village and its love for King Cobras is both fascinating and slightly disturbing. There was also a quick visit to Nong Khai where we stood on the Friendship Bridge that crosses the mighty Mekong River into Laos, a bridge that was a gift from the Australian people to the Kingdom of Thailand and Laos PDR (Peoples Democratic Republic). Additionally, we also had lunch at a boat moored on the Nong Khai side of the Mekong River…a seriously impressive and major river in SE Asia, flowing from Tibet and through Burma, Thailand, Laos, Cambodia and Vietnam before entering the South China Sea. Two days before we left Ban Sam Rung there was a slightly scary animal encounter as we visited 'Monkey Village'. A town near the city of Maha Sarakham, about thirty kilometres from Ban Sam Rung, and a place that is shared by the people and a large group of macaque monkeys, the badass of the monkey world, aggressive and unpredictable and who are not afraid to take whatever they want – a word of warning, don't try and feed them by hand, THEY WILL BITE and as they have been known to carry rabies, not an animal you want biting you. However, I did manage to get some good close-up photos with these 'primates with attitude'. Finally, the day before we left Ada's village we celebrated Amy's second Birthday with her Thai family…balloons, cake and the singing of 'Happy Birthday'…in English, which was amusing, considering most of them didn't speak English. A wonderful evening and seeing the joy on so many faces was worthwhile, and it was great to take photos of Amy with her grandparents, aunties, uncles, cousins and friends on a special day…which also involved another Thai 'barbecue' but this time at the family home. There was even a strange but funny custom of rubbing cream from the cake on each other's faces, resulting in a few comical photos. It was also the night I finally caught a 'chigium' (a small gheko type lizard) that was part of an army of lizards that attempted to keep the insect population down to a minimum and you could continually see them shuffling and darting across walls and ceilings to catch they prey… I had been trying to catch one for the previous couple of weeks, but they were so quick.

The day we left Ban Sam Rung we were involved in another special, but strangely weird ritual, and its main purpose was to provide us with luck on a journey back to the UK. It was an unusual ceremony carried out by an elder from another village and involving a receptacle that was around fourteen inches square made by Ada's sister's Ba and Pa from banana leaves, and consisted of nine equally proportioned compartments each filled with different foods. There were also nine thin sticks, each around fourteen inches in length (one on each corner, one in the middle of each and one in the roughly in the middle of the receptacle). String was then fed, from in front of the man, around each 'post' (stick) and then passed through mine, Ada's and Amy's hands which were clasped together in a wai (prayer like), over an item of clothing belonging to me, Ada and Amy and then passed back to the man forming a continuous loop of string through all the relevant parties/items. Additionally, there was a silver ceremonial bowl filled with water on the right had side of the man and in the receptacle in the middle compartment on the left hand side (right hand side as we looked at it) was a lit candle. I had no idea what was going to happen, but as I did with all ceremonies/rituals I just rolled with it…I could tell he'd started as there was a great deal of incoherent whispered prayers and chants, throwing of rice grains and I soon found out what the bowl of water was for when he took a mouthful, mid chant, and then proceed to spray us in the face with the water…straight from his mouth. This happened two or three times and we were soaking. After ten to fifteen minutes he finished by taking the candle and breaking each link by burning each section of the string between the sticks and between Ada, Amy and I. We finished with three wai's to show our respect. As strange as it seemed, I embraced this cultural ritual and felt blessed that I was included in this cultural ceremony of 'luck'. It was finally time to leave Ban Sam Rung and head to Bangkok for a couple of days before we travelled back to the UK. The attachment to Ada's family had grown strong during the visit, and it was another emotional farewell and upsetting for everyone as we paid our respects to Ada's parents and all the family, and with my new found basic understanding of Isaan Thai I said to everyone "Koy hak moo jow, koy hak Ban Sam Rung (I love you all, I love Ban Sam Rung)'. As we drove away I couldn't bear to look back…eight or nine hours later we were in a beautiful hotel room at the Royal Princess in Bangkok.

After breakfast Ada dropped Amy and I at the Grand Palace…the previous year it had been a rushed visit, therefore, I was looking forward to returning to this magnificent palace, and to Wat Pho. On this visit, I was able to fully appreciate the intricate details of the painted adornments and the mosaic like decorations of the temple buildings, the strange 'ugly' (Thai 'Yuks') protectors (statues) that were there to scare away unwanted visitors. There were also golden chedis, numerous golden Buddha's of various sizes that adorned the buildings…it has to be the most amazing display of beauty, in one area, anywhere in the world. Each corner you turn, each building you enter provides more stunning images. It is a truly breathtaking place, steeped in the history of the Thai Royal family that is revered to a level I'd never seen…there are people who love their Royal Family in places all over the world, but nothing like the love the Thai people have for their Royal Family and especially King Bhumibol Adulyadej (Rama IX)…a great and much loved Monarch that created so much for Thai people (sadly, he passed away in 2016…more of this in the last story of this chapter). From the Grand Palace we took the short walk around the outside of the palace walls to just behind the Grand Palace where Wat Pho was located. Wat Pho is another complex of beautiful temple buildings, ornate chedis, statues, well-manicured gardens, golden Buddha's and even…a Welsh flag. But the outstanding feature of this temple is the golden 'reclining' Buddha, forty six metres in length and five metres high and covered in gold leaf, with mother of pearl covering the soles of its feet in intricate illustrations of favourable characteristics of the Buddha. What I couldn't find out is how they got this huge horizontal statue in to the building, I didn't know if it was many parts taken into the building individually and then put together or whether the building was built around it…but it is a magnificent image and epitomizes the beauty found in the rest of Wat Pho. It was very hot and humid that day and we caught a taxi back to the hotel and the sanctuary of an air conditioned building.

Our last day in Bangkok was spent at Dusit Zoo, which is Thailand's very first public zoo, opened in 1938, having originally been built by King Chulalongkorn (Rama V) in

515

1895 as a private garden that included wild animals. We saw a variety of animals in this zoo such as pygmy hippos, otters, meerkats, zebras, elephants, giraffes, tigers, white tigers, sun bears, leopards, gibbons, various birds, tortoises, hippos, deers, various reptiles and many more species. It was all set in beautiful gardens with a large lake, childrens play areas…there was even an air raid shelter and museum, and overlooked by Ananta Samakhom Throne Hall in Dusit Palace grounds, a two-storey white marble building built in a European style with Thai influences and used for Royal celebrations, a magnificent example of Thai splendour mixed with Western influences and it's a permanent exhibition to Thai arts and crafts. Amy and I finished our day at the zoo watching a Kenyan acrobat team and the elephant show which included the elephants playing football…it was a great day out and a great way to end our second visit to Thailand.

2013 – Khon Kaen, Bangkok, Ayutthaya, Phuket, Phang Nga Bay and Vientiane (Laos)

This trip was a bit different as Ada and Amy travelled out a couple of weeks before me and returned a week after I'd returned. Unfortunately, Ada's dad had passed away between this visit and our last visit and there had being a low key funeral at the time of his death, but during this trip there was a huge celebration of his life. I witnessed an astonishing celebration that was held over 2-3 days, and in particular, there was one part that I found truly astounding and emotional on many levels…another reminder of the respect shown to a parent and elder member of, to an outsider, a complicated and hierarchical Thai society. This would also be the trip where we would take Ada's mother and two of her sisters (La and Nang) on a five day holiday to Phuket where there were more animal encounters and where we would visit the wondrous, breathtaking beauty of Phang Nga Bay, Wat Chalong, Simon Cabaret (Ladyboy show in Patong) and where we went snorkeling for the first time off Coral Island. The journey to Phuket involved us travelling to Bangkok by Ada's pick-up truck and then taking an aeroplane from Bangkok (Don Muang Airport) and this was the very first time Ada's mum and sisters had flown. The journey was interesting as it involved a car accident in Phuket and after the return flight to Bangkok, a train/bus journey from Rangsit (an area North of

Bangkok) back to Khon Kaen…interesting trip which gave me another view of Thailand. We also took a trip to Vientiane in Laos which would have ramifications when we all came to leave Thailand and come home to the UK.

Ada and Amy had already been in Thailand for two weeks when I landed in Bangkok and it was a mad rush as I only had just over an hour to get through immigration and catch my connecting flight to Khon Kaen. Thankfully, I managed to get to the Thai Airways gate for my connection to Khon Kaen with about ten to fifteen minutes to spare…just over ninety minutes later I was walking through the exit gate at Khon Kaen airport my eyes darting left and right looking for Amy and Ada. I finally saw them and attempted to run towards them, but with the throng of people, a large suitcase and my hand luggage it was proving difficult. I reached Ada, dropped my suitcase and threw my arms around her and gave her a huge hug, whispering in her ear "Hi love, I missed you so much"…I
looked at Amy who was clutching Ada's leg and looking at me sheepishly, I crouched, put my arms out and said "come to Daddy" but she stayed where she was and she was little distant, wondering where I'd been for the past couple of weeks and was probably annoyed with me. I thought "leave it, she'll be ok…don't force it" and I stood up and just ruffled her hair. It was dark as we drove through Khon Kaen and initially I couldn't get my bearings until we turned on to the Kalasin road…around ten minutes later we had pulled off the main highway and were driving past Khon Kaen Provincial Sports School and approaching Ban Khok Si. I was excited that I was heading back to Ban Sam Rung, but there was also a tinge of sadness as there was a very special celebration that would start tomorrow for Ada's father…since we had last been in Thailand Ada's father had sadly passed away, and we were about to start a two day celebration of his life. I was thankful that I had spent time with him on the two previous visits and that he'd met Amy…luckily we had videos and photographs of Amy with her grandfather. I had no idea what the next 48 hours would entail…it was my first experience of this kind of 'celebration', in some perverse way I was looking forward to experiencing another Thai tradition, albeit a sombre one. After something to eat I was exhausted and it was time for bed.

I was up and about early...not that I had much choice, as there was a lot of additional noise and commotion to the normal everyday sounds of dogs barking, monks chanting, cockerels and the 'microphone man' or village announcer. I went downstairs and there were people everywhere, all busy doing something, whether it was preparing food, cooking, washing dishes, sweeping the floors, ferrying food one way and plates the other, eating, drinking, moving furniture...whichever way I looked it was a hive of activity. The children were being ordered to do this and to that...I just stood there for a moment and watched the scene before me, and what seemed like utter chaos was a typical Isaan well-oiled machine. It was then I recognised our nephews, Pet and Lair, they were sat on chairs in the middle of the large indoor sitting/play area and people were taking it in turns to cut off a piece of their hair...La saw me and beckoned me over and passed me the scissors and was encouraging me to cut off a piece of their hair. I wanted to get involved and took my turn at this hair-cutting event...even though at that point I had no idea why. I found Ada and asked why people were taking it in turns to cut their hair...it transpired that as a mark of respect they were becoming monks for a few days and this was part of the process they had to go through before they became ordained. Additionally, it also involved a procession through the village and I was the driver of the vehicle carrying Pet and Lair. Sitting in the back, they threw sweets to the excited children running alongside the truck, and with family and friends walking/dancing behind the truck in a long trail of community togetherness. The procession ended on the other side of the village, behind the village school...the final part of the process was where they received their saffron robes at a ceremony in the temple at Kham Kaen (the next village to Ban Sam Rung). I enjoyed my involvement in this important ceremony and it made me feel part of this close-knit community. This ceremony was common practice for this type of celebration, and sons, nephews etc would be ordained as monks for a few days or weeks and they would live in the village temple and dress as monks for the duration...fascinating. Over the next two days the house was filled with people and with laughter, sombre ceremonies involving the monks and the normal chanting of the pali texts, sermon-like wisdom from solitary monk's...everyone dressed in their best Isaan clothes, it was a festival of bright colours, from the saffron of the monks robes

518

to the flamboyant and garish colours worn by everyone there, as you looked across the sea of people sitting cross-legged in front of the house it resembled a painter's palette. Despite the occasion, the laughter and idle chat was respectful and my love for the customs of these amazing people was growing with each visit…I believed I was reaping the benefits of immersing myself in Isaan life. I paused to reflect on the respect that was being shown to Ada's father, which was reinforced by the 'shrine' that had been arranged in his memory on a table at the front of the family home, a table that included a large framed photograph of Hom Nonthing (Ada's father), beautiful sprays of flowers in vibrant yellows and pinks, food offerings and incense candles. I could see that Ada's father must have been well loved by the family and judging by the people there paying their respects he must have been a well-respected member of the community. I paused in front of this 'shrine' for a moment and pondered my own death and hoped that family and friends would afford me the same level of respect as Hom when I eventually passed. I believed this celebration of life was a much better way of being appreciated and remembered than the sombre and depressing way we remembered our dead in western society. My wish would be that my life is celebrated in a similar way…with laughter and song and not with tears and sadness. If there is something you have to appreciate about Thai people it's their love of life and their wicked sense of humour that, similar to our working class sense of humour in the UK, enables them to deal with hardships such as loss of a loved one, drought and life threatening storms to name but a few…I was about to witness this sense of humour in an unlikely but beautiful way. My pensive mood was intrigued when I saw some of the menfolk bringing three unusual throne style red and gold chairs to the tiled area at the front of the house, and they placed them facing each other in a sort of triangle, each being about three metres from the other two. The arms and backs of these strange chairs were ornately painted in gold carved naga (snakes) with Buddha and other religious images. It was then I saw three monks approaching the house from the decorative arch that led to the grounds of the village temple (the temple complex was directly opposite Ada's family home), I presumed that these three monks would soon be the occupants of the three grand chairs…my senses heightened as I also witnessed a growing audience developing in front of the three chairs to whatever was about to happen. The chairs were predictably occupied by the three monks, each sitting cross-legged on their respective chairs, and each holding a microphone…what was I about to see? One of the monk's slowly brought the microphone up to his mouth, and in anticipation, I had set my smartphone to record…I felt something amazing was about to happen and I didn't want to miss anything. Then it began…and I wasn't wrong, after an initial 'staged' argument between the three monks which brought occasional laughter from the expectant crowd, one of the monks started to sing, a beautiful but haunting melody of rising and falling elongated tonal utterings, there was no musical accompaniment, just the monk's voice, and a hushed silence fell over the house as everyone stopped to listen to this incredible sound, it seemed as if the birds had fallen silent and even the familiar sound of the 'gap-gair' (lizard), from the trees in the temple grounds, couldn't be heard…it's as if the whole world had stopped to listen to this melodic and phenomenal singing. "Wow…" I thought, "…this is extraordinary…I've never heard anything like this", but what I didn't know was what he was singing about or what the 'staged' arguments were about. But judging by the occasional laughter from the crowd there must have been a comical element to it. Each monk sang a solo, each as good as the other but in their own unique voices, I felt privileged to have witnessed this amazing event, and laughed when Ada told me what they had been singing/arguing about…they were telling a story with one monk as the narrator, another monk as the wife of a man who has died, and the last monk playing the mother of the man who has died. The arguments were mainly between the wife and mother, the wife wanting to keep the life insurance money for herself and just have a quiet, inexpensive funeral. Whereas the mother wants to spend all the money on an extravagant funeral ceremony…the singing parts were the 'pleas' of the wife and mother, with the 'narrator' seeing both sides of the argument and providing the comedy. Experiencing rural Thailand and its customs was the Thailand I wanted to see, and my involvement and what I witnessed during this celebration was beyond my expectations…not something I'd see in Pattaya or the busy resorts of Phuket, Koh Samui, Phi-Phi or Ao-Nang.

A couple of days after the celebration for Ada's father we booked flights to Phuket as I had already booked two hotel rooms in Kata…we were taking Ada's mother and sisters, Nang and La, for a well-deserved holiday. We left Ban Sam Rung and drove to Ada's condo in Rangsit, arriving early evening, after something to eat we were all early to bed…but it was difficult to get to sleep as there was no air conditioning in the condo and with no mosquito nets we had to keep the doors and windows closed, it was so hot and a lot more humid in the built-up area of Rangsit, than it was in Ban Sam Rung, and six of us sleeping in the one room made it more uncomfortable. It was a welcome relief when morning came and we could all freshen up with a cold shower and something to eat, before venturing out to the 'Big C' supermarket. The plan was that after we'd been to the 'Big C' we'd take a drive to Ayutthaya.

Two or three hours later we were parked up close to the elephant kraal and show in the centre of Ayutthaya Historical Park and close to Wat Phra Si Sanphet…majestic ruins of the royal palace temple including three prominent chedis which provide great views of the surrounding area. But first, in true Thai tradition, we had something to eat…as if by magic, the saht (mat) was laid out on the grass in the shade of a small tree, and a variety of dishes were pulled from, what appeared to be, a bottomless bag. Fully replenished we made our way to the elephant kraal where we watched the show, fed the elephants, including a naughty and excitable baby elephant nudging everyone who got close. Luckily we took some great photos, group and individually, with an elephant adorned with a large red and gold patterned silk blanket draped across its back, and red, green and gold rosettes tied to its tusks. From there we drove the short distance to a car park close to Wat Phra Si Sanphet, but before entering the beautiful ruins of this former palace temple we visited the impressive Wihan Phra Mongkhon Bophit, a modern temple with a large, gilded statue of Buddha in a cross-legged sitting position…in true Buddhist tradition, we all paid our respects to this stunning and popular statue, and captured it's serene splendour with a few photographs. After buying tickets to enter Wat Phra Si Sanphet, we made the short walk to a small entrance through the exterior wall of this historical wonder…whilst we could see tops of the three chedis from outside the temple wall, seeing them in their full glory from inside the temple walls was a wonderful sight. As we walked around the iconic grounds, on what would have been, grand walled avenues, the beauty of the palace became more evident as the bases of smaller chedis could be seen at equidistant points around the inside of the exterior walls. The modern magnificence was exploded by the planting of random trees in the grounds, and their twisted chaotic branches created a mysterious but atmospheric setting…it brought the ruined palace temple to life, and the true size of the three main chedis provided the main focal point, as they dwarfed the visitors climbing its steps to enjoy the views of both ancient and modern Ayutthaya that surrounded Wat Phra Si Sanphet. A truly wonderful and humbling experience, and we added more great photographs for the family album, including some great photos of Ada with her mother. After leaving Ayutthaya we thought we'd pop into Bang Pa-In Palace, summer residence of the Thai royal family and associated with a sad story that highlights the extent of the old 'lese majeste' laws in Thailand. In 1880 the pregnant wife and daughter of King Chulongkhorn (Rama V), Queen Sunanda Kumariratana and Princess Karnbhirn Bejraratana, were travelling by raft to Bang Pa-In Summer Palace when tragedy struck…the raft capsized and the queen and princess fell into the river. Unfortunately, this was during a time when touching a member of the royal family was punishable by death, resulting in no-one helping them and both the queen and princess drowned. Thankfully, whilst the 'lese majeste' laws in Thailand are strict, as a result of this accident, this law was changed by King Chulongkorn. Unfortunately, our attempt to visit this spectacular palace ended in disappointment as we arrived ten minutes before it was due to close, therefore, we carried on to Rangsit where we had something to eat and another early night…we had to get up early for our flight to Phuket from Don Mueang, the old international airport.

It seemed like the middle of the night when we got up and made our way to Don Mueang and there was a fair amount of waiting around before we caught the plane to Phuket. By mid-morning we were loading up the hire car in Phuket and heading off to Kata and our hotel for a four night stay…but after driving for about fifteen minutes I was ordered to pull in to a Tesco Lotus superstore for something to eat (Tesco have a food hall where they operate a ticket system, and then you order your food from one of the stalls who will cook your customized order in front you…it's normally a struggle to spend a 100baht (about £2) in here you can even buy a dessert and a bottle of water and still have change. The food is good and whatever tickets you have left you can change for money back). After this customary food stop we carried on to Kata. However, a couple of kilometres from Kata, disaster…in trying to avoid a moped that pulled out in front of me a minivan slammed into the back of us. Thankfully, everyone was ok and Ada rang the car hire company and within ten minutes there was a representative of the insurance company at the scene joined a few minutes later by an insurance representative of the other vehicle. They collectively assessed the damage, blame was apportioned to the other driver…all sorted, with minimal fuss and we were on our way and no more than ten minutes later we were parked up in front of the hotel in Kata.

After booking-in to the beautiful 4-star Alpina Phuket Nalina Resort and Spa in Kata and being shown to our luxurious rooms, we decided to take a look at Kata beach. Ten minutes later we were walking on the tropical white sandy beach and admiring the deep turquoise ocean and stunning hotels that littered the hillsides of the outcrops of land to the left and right of this stunning beach. It was late afternoon and the sun was lying low in the sky, and the sunlight caused an almost silver shimmering effect over the water in the direction of Ko Pu (Crab Island), a small islet out in the bay. This idyllic beach was a little piece of paradise and the calm ocean and gentle breeze provided an ease of serenity, it was hard to imagine that this beach and the other beaches on the west coast of Phuket were victims of the infamous 2004 Tsunami that killed over 230,000 people in fourteen different countries. With exception of a few small 'escape route' signs, in the event of a tsunami, there was little evidence of the carnage and devastation caused in 2004, highlighting the resilience of the Thai people and their ability to 'bounce back' from the edge of despair.

Our first full day in Phuket started with a short drive to Wat Chalong, another beautiful but unique temple, and considered the most important temple in Phuket. There are a series of stunning buildings, including the tallest one (60m) which has a

523

stupa (chedi) that includes a bone fragment of the Buddha, and really is a magnificent building inside and out. It's a difficult building to describe as its first two floors are fairly square with gold painted ornate decorative windows and doors and pink marble effect walls, then there is a smaller white and gold third floor with an outside viewing area that has a gold decorative safety rail and barrier (small gold pillars 4-5 inches apart). Finally, there is a gold and white stupa that rises up into the sky above Phuket. Internally, it is a decorative ensemble of marble pillars and floors, gold Buddha's of various sizes/poses, flower arrangements, stunning paintings of important events in the Buddha's life and also paintings of members of the Thai royal family. The outside gallery on the third floor provides stunning views over the immaculate temple grounds, and a great view of the 'Big Buddha' high on the Nakkerd Hills that overlook most of Phuket…our next destination. It was again a short drive from Wat Chalong up to the 'Big Buddha', and the winding hillside road twisted and turned its way up the hill passing an elephant 'wrangling centre'…and nearing the top, a few roadside restaurants. After parking and making our way to a large, paved area below the base of this immense 45m tall statue made of reinforced concrete, but layered with beautiful Burmese white Jade which glistened in the afternoon sunshine. From this high vantage point we enjoyed fantastic views over Phuket Town, and other areas of eastern and southern Phuket including the many yachts off Rawai beach, dotted on the sea like flecks of coconut on a turquoise iced cake…they really are spectacular views and it is easy to see why the 'Big Buddha' had been built on such a perfect site. It was another great place for photographs and we took some great family shots, creating fantastic memories, with the backdrops of both the 'Big Buddha' and the excellent views over Phuket. Leaving this amazing place we were all hungry and dropped into a restaurant with more breathtaking views over Kata and Karon beaches. The food they brought to the table looked delicious, all presented in vibrant colours of greens, reds and yellows, and included a large dish of fried rice… all these wonderful dishes were cooked to perfection and by the time we'd finished we were so full not a single grain of rice would have been able to have been eaten by any of us. Later that evening whilst Amy stayed with her grandmother and aunties, Nang and La, Ada and I walked into the centre of Kata and looked

524

around the various shops before enjoying a couple of drinks in a quiet bar. We also met a baby elephant and its owner in the shopping precinct, providing another great photo opportunity which included the elephant kissing me on the cheek with its trunk…bizarrely, a work colleague Keith Graham and his wife Jodie, also had their picture taken with the same elephant around two weeks later…small world.

The next day we were up early as we were being collected for a day trip out to Phang Nga Bay, and I was really looking forward to this one…I had seen images of this area and it looked spectacularly stunning. Although an Island, Phuket is connected to the mainland by the Sarasin Bridge, and therefore, it only took us about ninety minutes to get to Krasom where we were would meet the boat that would take us out into Phang Nga Bay. On arrival, at this typical hive of tourist activity, we were hurried out of the minivan, and after putting our life-jackets on, we were ushered to a Thai longboat. We were soon on our way and travelling down a wide avenue of water with mangrove swamps on either side that protect coastal areas from erosion…and not where mangoes grow Jag. As we sped across the water, splashes of water occasionally caught you in the face, creating a well-appreciated cooling effect from the heat of the day, and in the distance dark shapes were beginning to emerge, the outlines of the famous limestone rock cliffs/formations/islands found in Phang Nga Bay. There were many formations of various shapes and sizes and it was soon obvious that this was an area of outstanding beauty of the like I'd never witnessed before, the green foliage and the limestone cliffs and rock formations appeared to be bursting out of the water in a chaotic jumble…a jumble of large, stunning islets and not one the same as another as if the they had been hand carved by a mythical giant, placed lovingly in the bay and decorated with vivid greens of different shades. As the mangroves disappeared behind us the bay opened out and we were soon passing Koh Panyi, where a Muslim fishing village built on stilts with the backdrop of a sheer limestone cliff…amazing and where we would be having lunch a little later. Around five to ten minutes later we pulled up alongside a larger boat, moored in the middle of this heavenly beauty, where refreshments were available and where those who had paid for it, went out in canoes to explore the natural caves that could be seen in some of the rock formations, caves that were just high enough to canoe through. We, however, relaxed on this boat with our drinks and used the opportunity to take more family photos on the deck with the stunning backdrops of the limestone rock formations of Phang Nga Bay. After about thirty minutes it was back on the longboat and we headed to our next destination, Koh Phing Kan or James Bond Island, made famous by the film 'The Man with the Golden Gun' as the luxurious home of the film's villain, Scaramanga. Despite being busy and a tadge commercialized with stalls selling souvenirs, it was still a wonderful experience to step onto such an iconic island and see the smaller islet of Khao Tapu, famous in the film for housing some sort of solar lazer in the rock. It was certainly an unusual but interesting island, and again, another great photo opportunity to create more wonderful memories. After twenty minutes it was back on the longboat to head to Koh Panyi…and some lunch. As we approached Koh Panyi we could see the large huddle of around three hundred and fifty houses, all on stilts and it was an impressive feat of engineering that included a mosque and a floating football pitch…just don't kick the ball into touch. The population of Koh Panyi is about sixteen hundred and they are the ancestors of two seafaring Indonesian families. We had a wonderful lunch and a wander around this amazing structure before heading back to dry land and a quick visit to Wat Suwan Khuha or 'Monkey Temple' as it is also known…a temple in a cave which includes a reclining gold Buddha and other gold Buddha statues, and my favourite (not), a large troop of macaque monkeys that dominate the temple scavenging for food from the many visitors and Buddhist monks that live in the buildings alongside the temple. But, in their defence, these macaques were relatively calm compared to other places I'd visited and encountered these 'aggressive' primates. We were soon on our way back to the hotel after an absolutely wonderful day, If visiting Thailand and especially this part of Southern Thailand I would highly recommend visiting Phang Nga Bay…it is an area of outstanding and spectacular natural beauty, and despite the photographs not giving the area the justice it deserved, it doesn't detract from the fact it is one of the most beautiful places I've ever seen.

After another hearty breakfast we headed to Phuket Zoo, and we were going for one reason, to meet Billy…an orangutan.

Whilst researching 'things to do in Phuket' I discovered photos of Billy being photographed with tourists in various humorous poses. However, reviews of Phuket Zoo were fairly mixed, some of which were negative and scathing about the conditions of the animals and of the enclosures they were kept in. The exploitation of animals is not something I agree with and I'm certainly not comfortable seeing animal cruelty of any kind. But there was something intriguing about meeting Billy and seeing the zoo conditions for myself as my experience told me that some people are never happy and reviews can reflect this and sometimes have to be taken with a pinch of salt. I'd been to zoos on our previous visit to Thailand, at Chiang Mai and Dusit, but these were national run zoos with encouraging breeding programs of endangered species and the zoos were clearly maintained and the animals in these zoos appeared to be well treated. But Phuket Zoo was a privately run zoo so there was a possibility that things could be different. It was only a ten minute drive from the hotel and was close to Wat Chalong, and when we arrived and paid our entry fee at the impressive entrance, first impressions were good. But my attitude soon changed as we walked around the zoo, with exception of my views on what I saw in Pattaya, I believe I have rightly been very positive about my experiences in Thailand and its people. But there were many negatives about Phuket Zoo and it appeared that some of the reviews I'd read had been accurate and reflected the horrendous conditions at the zoo. As we walked through the zoo there were many empty enclosures and it was abundantly clear why they were empty…they had been badly maintained and their dilapidated appearance meant that animals wouldn't have been able to be kept in them as they were unsafe and beyond repair. When we did pass enclosures where animals were kept, the animals were clearly distressed and in poor condition with very little evidence of any food or water being available to them. We sat and watched the elephant show, which was ok, but where five tourists were exploited aswell as the elephants. After the enclosures I'd seen, I couldn't help wondering how the elephants and other animals were treated away from glare of a tourist's camera. Ada and I met Billy and we had some amusing photographs taken with him, including one where the three of us were stood with our arms folded and all wearing sunglasses. The crocodile show was cancelled because of an accident the previous day and the remainder of the zoo was no different with empty enclosures and animals in poor condition. Eventually we approached the exit, but before we left Ada, Amy and I had our photograph taken with a tiger, a tiger that was a shadow of the impressive animal I'd had my photo with on our first trip…this tiger appeared slightly emaciated and was clearly drugged/sedated. It was a sad vision of neglect that epitomized the sad zoo, and it was a relief to walk out of this appalling place and drive away. I immediately felt sorry for **ALL** the animals I had seen that morning and felt angry and ashamed that I'd given money to a place that was clearly built for profit and not for animal welfare…a place with little or no understanding of how to treat animals and by far the worst zoo I had ever seen, not just in Thailand, but anywhere I'd travelled.

After the shock of Phuket Zoo we decided to head to Promthep Cape at the southern tip of Phuket, which offered some outstanding views across the bay toward Ko Man. There was a small promenade, the old lighthouse and a shrine which included small statues (3-4 ft high) of elephants…it was a beautiful area with stunning panoramic scenery. From here we headed back to Kata to have lunch at one of the roadside restaurants. We found the perfect restaurant with stunning views over Kata Noi and the meal was equally as good as the beautiful views from the restaurant built precariously on stilts, high on the hillside above Kata Noi. The views down the hillside were spectacular, as the contrast of the orange tiled hotel roofs nestled among the vibrant and vivid greens of the trees that covered the hillside…this breathtaking image was enhanced as it swept away into the distance and down toward the calm turquoise ocean…it was bewitching and I could have gazed at these views for hours. But Amy wanted to go swimming in the hotel pool and once we'd finished our lunch we headed back to the hotel where Ada, Amy and I spent the afternoon splashing around in the beautiful hotel pool…we were off out that evening to the world famous Simon Cabaret show in Patong, so it was nice to relax by (and in) the pool.

It started raining just after we'd finished at the pool and by the time the minivan picked us up to take us all to the Simon Cabaret in Patong it had turned into a tropical monsoon. Thankfully, by the time we got to Patong the rain had eased off and we didn't have to worry about getting beaten to death by the intensity and power of tropical raindrops. It was busy outside the theatre with minivans arriving from all directions and a throng of people being ushered across the car park and into the theatre…and the people from the previous show were pouring into waiting minivans before speeding away into the night. The marshals/attendants took it all in their stride and even in the midst of this chaos the whole operation worked liked a well-oiled machine, and we were soon sitting in our seats patiently waiting for the show to begin. For those who don't know (as I didn't before I booked the tickets), the 'Simon Cabaret' is a 'Ladyboy' show…I had no idea what to expect, but looking at the leaflets and the posters in the foyer, this was going to be a flamboyant and spectacular show. The room soon filled up, and you could sense the excited anticipation of an expectant audience…then a hush swept over the room as the lights dimmed and the stage curtains started to open.

What a wonderful show…it was good old fashioned Saturday night cabaret, the kind we watched on UK television in the 1970s. It didn't matter that the singers on stage were only miming, it was presented as a spectacle and it wowed the audience in every sense…the costumes, the dancing and even the comedic elements were spectacular. It was strange to think that all the beautiful women on stage were in fact all 'men', it was like watching a large group of very attractive Danny La Rue's. It did mess with your head, you'd think 'oh, she's a pretty girl', then it would dawn on you that it wasn't a lady, it was a man…then you'd feel ashamed and dirty. Seriously though, it was an excellent couple of hours entertainment and well worth the price and I would highly recommend anyone, if they visit Phuket, to go along and see the show. When it finished we left by a side entrance, where a handful of the performers were waiting…we had quite a few photos with them before we were quickly ushered into our waiting minivans, and before we sped away I noticed there was another audience being ushered into the theatre for the next performance. Those performers certainly earned their money as there were three or four performances a day.
The following day was our last day in Phuket and we were booked on a snorkeling trip to (Ko He) Coral Island. After driving to the car park near Ao Chalong Pier we found the speedboat that would take us to Coral Island and were

immediately issued with life jackets. We waited around for about ten minutes when, along with about twenty other tourists, we climbed aboard our speedboat. We set off, slowly at first until we'd zig-zagged our through a number of boats moored off the pier, and when we were in open ocean the pilot opened the throttle, and we bounced across the fairly calm water with Ko Lon to our left and the smaller Ko Bon to our right. In the distance we could see Ko He (Coral Island), and at the speeds we were travelling it was getting bigger all the time…considering Ada's mother was eighty-two she was having the time of her life. A few minutes later, as we got closer the pilot relaxed the throttle until it was just the momentum driving us toward the beach. About ten metres from the beach, the engine was pulled out of the water and the anchor dropped…after receiving our mask and snorkel we then filed out with me carrying Amy, into a couple of feet of water and on to the white sand of the of a beautiful beach. We made our way toward a small square wooden table and a group of brightly coloured deck chairs. This was the life…a real tropical paradise, warm sea, white sand…life couldn't get better than this. We stepped into the clear, warm sea and we immediately saw groups of tropical fish. It was fascinating swimming alongside these colourful fish who didn't seem too phased by the small invasion of humans now swimming amongst them. With exception of one breed of fish, the 'clown fish'(a small orange fish with a thick white stripe around the middle of its body outlined by a thin black line either side, this is repeated behind the eye and on the tail, and the tail and fins are black tipped), made famous by Disney's 'Finding Nemo' they darted left and right in their own frantic attempts to escape from the alien beings (us) swimming in their ocean playground. It was a fanstastic two hours spent either relaxing on the deck chairs, swimming in the sea or walking on the white sand. It was a perfect way to end our short trip to Phuket and after returning to Ao Chalong Pier by speedboat, it was back to the hotel to pack. A few hours later we were back in Don Mueang airport where Pechar was waiting for us to take us back to Rangsit.

We were up early the following morning and after a seven hour train journey back to Khon Kaen, and a meal at the 'Barbecue' restaurant we were back in Ban Sam Rung…where there was another celebration happening, as the village temple looked like a fairground with lights draped around the temple itself and patterns of fluorescent tubes arranged at various points around the grounds...it looked beautiful. Over the next few days there were Buddhist celebrations, a film (an outdoor cinema had been set-up in the temple grounds and it looked as if the whole village was there) and late at night you could hear the melodic and catchy tunes and sounds of the old style Isaan music, which consisted of a man and woman appearing to half sing/half speak a series of rhyming lyrics...a sort of twist on American style country music. It was really enjoyable and addictive to listen to, a style of music I'd never experienced before. There was even another 'charity' event as we danced our way around the village temple the obligatory three times for luck with 'money trees' raised from people in the village. Throughout the temple grounds there was an obscene amount of brightly coloured bunting everywhere, and miles and miles of a strange network of string throughout the entire area...I've never seen anything like it before or since and I tried to find out why, but no-one could tell me, all Ada would say is "it's a celebration". I gave up in the end and just enjoyed the general happiness that filled the air.

Ada, Amy and I were up early on our fourth day back in Ban Sam Rung so we could drive to Nong Khai...we were crossing the border into Laos, as were going to Vientiane for the day. After a two hour drive we arrived at border control just before the Friendship Bridge that crosses the Mekong River into Laos. It took another hour or so to sort out the visas (and the dollars...the sweetener for the Laos border immigration officer) and then we crossed the Friendship Bridge into Laos...once the formalities of passport stamps and checking of paperwork we were waved through and headed for Vientiane, which was only about 20km away. As we turned onto the main highway that leads into Vientiane we hit a slight problem...crossing the dual carriageway onto the left hand lanes we faced a bit of an issue...there were cars driving straight toward us (mental note to self: Laos is a former French colony, therefore, they drive on the opposite side of the road to Thailand), Ada quickly pulled off the road, we looked at each other and laughed, waited for a lull in the traffic and crossed into the right hand lanes and continued our journey. Fifteen or twenty minutes we were almost in the centre of Vientiane and could see the Patuxai Victory Gate, an

531

impressive arch that is similar to the Arc de Triomphe in Paris, and was built to commemorate Laos's independence from France and to those who lost their lives in that struggle. One of the avenues that led to this symbolic structure was reminiscent of the Champs-elysees and the Patuxai Victory Gate dominated the distant skyline, and as we got closer it became more impressive…skirting around to the right hand side of the gate and after a couple of hundred metres we found a car park. After parking the truck we hopped into a tuk-tuk and found somewhere to eat (and a pair of sandals for Amy…she had left hers in Ban Sam Rung). I was eager to get back to the Patuxai Victory Gate and see its magnificence close-up, the beautiful gardens and fountains that formed the approach to the gate and softened the harsh concrete structure, and the mix of these contrasts created great photo opportunities. The beauty of this Victory Gate was enhanced by the afternoon sun, and as the shone on the cold concrete it created a sandy coloured structure of warmth. The design of the gate could now be seen properly, and the Laotian detail gave it its own identity, firstly with the ornate decoration around the arch on either side, and the five towers atop the structure (one large ornate central tower and four smaller ornate towers on each corner) symbolize the five Buddhist principles of amiability, honesty, prosperity, flexibility and honour. It's not until you are inside the structure do you see the simplicity and untidy harshness of this concrete structure, but all that is forgotten when you climb out onto the external viewing gallery at the top of the structure…the views over Vientiane are spectacular, and these views were worth the hassle of crossing the border on their own. After leaving the Patuxai Victory Gate we made the short drive to Pha That Luang (Great Sacred Stupa), an impressive sixteenth century central stupa standing 45m high and surrounded by smaller crowned pillars, all set on an approximate 20m square plinth, and all coloured in gold which, as the sun was now sitting lower in the sky, was glistening in regal glory. In front of this stunning structure was the grand statue of its creator, King Xaysetthathirath, who had the stupa built in 1566 (six years after declaring Vientiane the capital of Laos) over an original smaller stupa that held a small fraction of the ashes of the Lord Buddha. There were other suitably impressive temple buildings in this iconic area, an area that could be considered the spiritual heart of the Laos nation. We left Pha That Luang and headed out of Vientiane and we were soon passing through Laos border control and crossing the Friendship Bridge back in to Thailand…the sun was beginning to sink lower in the sky creating a wondrous orange and purple haze high above the grandness of the Mekong River snaking its way into the distance on its long journey to the South China Sea. After staying overnight in Nong Khai we took a leisurely detour through rural Isaan back to Ban Sam Rung.

Back in Ban Sam Rung preparations were beginning for the Songkran celebrations, but I couldn't resist visiting 'Snake Village' again, much to Ada's protestations. It was during this visit that I met and spoke to the Thai man that Karl Pilkington had met and filmed with when he went to 'Snake Village' during his visit to Thailand to film 'An Idiot Abroad'. A fascinating elderly Thai who bore the scars of his lifelong relationships with the King Cobra…missing fingers following bites from this incredible and powerful reptile, leading to immediate amputations to stop the fatalistic cobra venom from spreading. The show still followed the same format as it had on my previous visits, but it didn't detract from the dangers posed by the unpredictable King Cobra, but it was so mesmorising…the battle between the defenceless human relying on speed of thought and anticipation to stay safe from the King Cobra's own striking speed. The snake's intimidating striking pose a warning to its handler to 'proceed with caution' in this compelling game of 'chess'. It really is a fascinating 'stand-off' between man and reptile which provides a fearful excitement from the expectant audience who relish the danger, but at the same time, want the handler to remain safe. There was another first as Amy, Ada and I rubbed a 20 baht note down the entire length of the largest python I've ever seen, for luck…my immediate thought being "lucky that it didn't latch-on and squeeze the life out of us". With each visit to this remarkable village my respect and admiration for both handler and snake continued to grow.

That same afternoon when we returned to Ban Sam Rung, around twenty to thirty of us headed to Bueng Khan Nakhon Lake in Khon Kaen in Ada's and Ba's trucks, for the Songkran celebrations. However, to get to Khon Kaen we had to 'run the gauntlet' through the villages (Ban Non and Ban Khok Si), and as a result, we were all soaking wet by the time we arrived at the lake in Khon Kaen. The only way to describe the scene around the lake was it was like one huge, but happy, water fight as trucks, overflowing with people possessing a fine array of water pistols, spraying others with an equally impressive selection of water pistols travelling in trucks in the opposite direction around the lake. We found a spot to park and started to walk, this resulted in us getting soaked by anybody and everybody with the occasional person running up and wiping talc in our faces…we all looked as if we wearing face packs. Most people were wearing the traditional 'flowery' shirt, a symbol of the carnival atmosphere created by the Songkran celebrations…it was a friendly, happy event with smiling faces everywhere and everyone enjoying themselves regardless of age. It was a pleasure seeing so much happiness, so much colour, and not a dry person to be found anywhere…tremendous fun. I consider myself extremely lucky to have been part of such a joyous occasion…your worries pale into insignificance as you enjoy this amazing festival with family and friends.

Another Thai trip was coming to an end, and on my last day in Ban Sam Rung we visited the important temple at Kham Kaen, about two to three kilometres away. As part of the Song Kran celebrations there were many visitors paying their respects at a temple that is believed to contain certain relics of the Buddha. There were food stalls and also a stage where live music and dance was being performed…I sat on the back of Ada's truck watching, not only the live entertainment, but also the many Thai families that were enjoying the music and picnics in the midday sun. I reflected on another enjoyable visit to this incredible country…I felt blessed that I was experiencing the rich, deep and meaningful culture of Thailand and its simplistic glory. The Thailand I was experiencing was far removed from what a normal tourist experienced…yes, I visited popular places or tourist attractions, but the time spent with my Thai family in Ban Sam Rung is, and always will, remain precious.

After flying from Khon Kaen to Suvarnabhumi Airport, there would be a slight drama to worry about at passport control…the officer checking my passport kept flicking through the pages whilst continually looking up at me, I thought something is wrong. I was right…he eventually called his superior over, a sullen and stern individual who looked as if he had never mastered the art of smiling. He repeated the action with my passport of flicking through the pages and looking at me until he finally closed the passport, looked at me and said "you in big trouble…where stamp showing you come back Thailand from Laos". I shrugged my shoulders and said "I don't know". After first seeing his manager, he escorted me back to the British Airways flight desk, where a stern conversation ensued. After a few minutes, he looked at me and said "come", I followed him back to the same officer who was originally checking my passport. My passport was checked (again), stamped and I was ushered through with one last stern glance from 'Mr Happy'. I walked around the duty free shops relieved that I wasn't being put through a body cavity search or being 'entertained' in a Thai prison. There was a sigh of relief when the plane finally left the ground a couple of hours later and headed back to the UK.

2014/15 – Bangkok, Khon kaen, Roi Et, Ubon Ratchathani, Buriram, Nakhon Pathom, Prachuap Khiri Khan, Baan Grood and Hua Hin

This would be our longest trip…six weeks. And it would also be a trip that involved a lot of driving. Initially, we stayed with Nang (Ada's sister) in Bangkok for a couple of days allowing us to visit Chatuchak market, a market with approximately 15,000 stalls…yes, that's correct 15,000 stalls. For this trip we left the UK in early December and came back to the UK in mid-January. It was a bit strange being away for Christmas, and it was the first time I'd been away for Christmas since my tour of the Falkland Islands between November 1982 and April 1983. But on the other hand, it was nice to leave all the drama and pressure of Christmas behind us…in all honesty, I would do it again, as it led to a stress free Christmas, no mad last minute shopping, worrying about who was visiting who and when or arguing over what TV programmes to watch. As a Buddhist country Thailand doesn't celebrate Christmas, but that doesn't stop them putting up Christmas trees in shopping centres or hotels etc as they accept that many foreigners living or visiting Thailand are Christians who celebrate Christmas…such is the tolerance and understanding of Buddhists towards other religions. As we were in Thailand for 6 weeks we made two trips during this holiday, one in the middle and one toward the end. The first, between Christmas and New Year, saw as travel from Khon Kaen to Roi Et and then on to Ubon Ratchathani, where a surprise was in store. From there we travelled to the Khmer temple at Prasat Phanom Rung and then onto Buriram before returning to Khon Kaen. Finally, we drove all the way to Ban Krood, stopping in Nakhon Pathom and Prachuap Khiri Khan on the way, on the return leg we stopped in Hua Hin before spending the last two nights in Bangkok. There were more animal encounters on this trip, but one was memorable for the wrong reasons.

Pechar, Ada's brother, met us (me, Ada, Amy and Sian Newton's Christmas wooden countdown board in a Santa shape/image…there would be plenty of photos of 'Santa' over the next six weeks) at Suvarnabhumi airport and we were soon on our way to Thailand's Amway (an American multi-level marketing company that sells health, beauty and homecare products) headquarters to meet Mr Racop and his wife (Ada had started selling Amway and Mr Racop had stayed with us a couple of times to help Ada get established). After touring the impressive headquarter's and learning of Amway's history in Thailand we headed to Mo Chit (an area in Bangkok) where Ada's sister, Nang, lived. It wasn't an easy place to get to as the huddle of small unique dwellings, that collectively created a tight community, were huddled below a huge concrete bridge that was part of the new motorway system, being built to alleviate the horrendous traffic congestion in Bangkok. And next to a busy rail network, a multitude of parallel and crossed lines that cut a swathe through urban Bangkok, dissecting the area between Nang's village-like community and Mo Chit Bus Terminus (Bangkok's main bus station), before splitting off and heading to West, North, Northeast and East Thailand…it certainly was a busy area. But once we, and our luggage, were safely in Nang's quaint and tidy little home it was as if we were in the middle of the Thai countryside…the hustle, bustle and insanity, of a city that never appears to sleep, was firmly shut outside Nang's little piece of domestic tranquility. Over the next few days we visited the Baiyoke Sky Hotel (once Thailand's tallest building), The Siam Paragon Shopping Mall (probably Thailand's premier shopping centre) and the impressive Chatuchak Weekend Market…a market where you could buy almost anything, which is hardly surprising when it has over 15,000 market stalls.

The first place we visited was the Baiyoke Tower, an impressive building that dominates Bangkok's skyline. Rising eighty-eight floors into the Bangkok sky, it really is spectacular when you stand close to the base of this monstrous tower and attempt to gaze up vertically as it thrusts skywards. But it is the approach to the tower where its sheer size is displayed in all its glory…it's a powerful image that resembles the famous Saturn V rocket being prepared for launch. And it's at night that its full beauty is revealed as it joins other buildings to create a scintillating assortment of twinkling lights, akin to glistening precious stones, against the velvet black backdrop of the night sky. But it was now the middle of the day and we were all eager to enjoy the views of Bangkok from the viewing platform at the top of the Baiyoke Tower. Considering its eighty-eight floors, it didn't take long to get to the internal viewing area which gave a partial all round view of Bangkok. But when we reached the external viewing platform…wow, such breathtaking views as Bangkok stretched away in all directions, and in the haze of the morning heat the countryside at the periphery of this sprawling city could not be seen. There were perfect views of central Bangkok and its array of modern skyscrapers, and the iconic buildings of famous landmarks such as Dusit Throne Hall, Wat Arun and the Grand Palace could be seen in the near distance, and in the distance, looking toward the Gulf of Thailand, the spectacular Bhumipol Bridge could be seen crossing the shimmering water of the Chao Phraya River that meandered its way through the urban landscape. The only other time in my life I experienced similar views was when my mother took me to Paris, when I was fifteen, and we enjoyed the panoramic scenes of the city from the Sacre Coeur in Montmartre. That same afternoon we visited the Siam Paragon Shopping Mall, easily the most impressive shopping mall I have ever visited, putting shopping centres in Britain to shame…you don't normally see car showrooms in a shopping centre, but there were quite a few car showrooms in the Siam Paragon, not filled with your everyday family cars, these were high-end car showrooms filled with top of the range cars such as Bentley, Maserati, Rolls Royce, Porsche, BMW, Jaguar, McLaren, Aston Martin and even Lamborghini. I could not believe what I was seeing…this was pretty impressive. It was a huge, multi-level shopping mall filled with designer stores and department stores, it also included ten pin bowling, cinema, colleges, language school, dance studio, dentists, banks, restaurants and in the basement was Bangkok's premier aquarium…Sea Life Bangkok Ocean World. This was luxury at its best and it was an eye opener wandering around this unbelievable shopping mall. The external façade was equally impressive with its glass fronted entrances that extended to the entire height of the building, and the outside space was littered with palm trees and modern fountains…and as it was approaching Christmas, there was even a large, modern Christmas tree, around 10-15m high, patterned with, what looked like, snowflakes, and this beautiful tree also changed colour every few minutes. It wasn't something I expected to see in a country where the majority of the population is Buddhist, but it just goes to show the tolerance of Buddhism toward other religions, and the understanding that many of the visitors to Thailand came from predominantly Christian countries. To finish this wonderful day we walked fifty metres to the BTS station and caught the busy 'sky train' back to Mo Chit…a train that, as the name suggests, is around 30m above the ground, and is the quickest way to get around Bangkok. Once back at the tranquility of Nang's house, and after something to eat, Amy and I were in bed, shattered by the heat and humidity of Bangkok.

The following morning, after a day spent at an Amway convention, Ada and I went to Chatuchak Market…I knew it was big, but nothing prepared me for actual size of this quintessential market. I didn't appreciate the sheer size of the area, as when we first walked in it looked like many other markets I'd visited in Thailand, it wasn't until we'd had something to eat and started to venture further in to the market that I started to discover the extent of this retail paradise…with exception of cars and property there was very little you couldn't buy in Chatuchak. It was an incredible market, and when we had walked about thirty metres in to one of the many corridors of stalls, in this permanent indoor market area, the sheer size of the place was revealed in all its glory. Built on a sort of grid system meant that every ten to fifteen metres you would stumble across one of the hundreds of 'crossroads', and whichever way you looked it appeared as

538

if each corridor was endless…very disconcerting, and it was easy to become disoriented in this maze of stalls. There were restaurants, food stalls, clothes, souvenirs (t-shirts, key rings, fridge magnets etc), ornaments, kitchenware, household goods, shoes etc…there were even pets…if you couldn't buy it here, you probably couldn't buy it anywhere. Sadly, some of the pet shops in the main market had puppies and kittens in small cages who were struggling with the heat and humidity of Bangkok. Thankfully, there was an adjacent building next to the main market which was air conditioned and housed a large pet section with many pet shops, the conditions for the puppies, kittens, birds, rabbits, reptiles etc being sold here were much better. This building also housed an area that can be described as 'arts and crafts' where there were excellent examples of Thai art (carvings, metal work, painting, sculpture, furniture and ornaments etc), which were absolutely breathtaking…the attention to detail in some pieces was exceptional, these were not 'knocked up' in a factory, these were made in the workshops visible in each shop and were obviously crafted by highly-skilled individuals. The sights, smells and noises in Chatuchak abused your senses and left you begging for more as you become lost in its insane chaos…it appeared to be an 'all consuming' experience of retail overload. It wasn't a case of 'buy…buy…buy', you didn't leave the market weighed down by bags of anything and everything, it was quite the opposite…you left Chatuchak with one or two items, and you felt 'cheated' that you hadn't bought more. Perhaps, because of its immense size, we felt overwhelmed, and that resulted in us treating Chatuchak more as a tourist site than as a functional market. There was so much to take in, not just the amount of things you could buy, but because it left us bewildered, but wanting more. It was a surreal, but unique experience that left us drained.

Despite the great time we'd had in Bangkok, staying with Nang, it was time to head to Khon Kaen. With everything loaded onto the truck and Ada, Amy, Nang and I sat in the back, Gaer in the front with Pechar, who was driving, we started the long journey back to Ban Sam Rung. It was a relief to leave the bedlam and intense heat and humidity of Bangkok, and whilst the journey is long it was great to kick back and enjoy the scenery of Thailand flashing past the window. We were soon passing Luntakong Lake, between

539

Saraburi and Korat (Nakhon Ratchasima), a stunning but huge expanse of water situated on the left hand side of highway 2, an impressive landmark as you climb from the low lying plains of Central Thailand and climb toward the Korat Plateau and Isaan. Once we were the other side of Korat we turned off highway 2 and headed toward the parent's house of Ada's friend, Bunta…we met Bunta's father and Ada gave him the money that Bunta had given her back in the UK. Our good deed done we headed to Chaiyphum, where we had lunch, before carrying on our journey to Khon Kaen…we re-joined highway 2 just south of the town of Phon. A couple of hours later we were driving past Khon Kaen Provincial Sports School heading toward the familiar village of Ban Khok Si. Twenty minutes later we were sat on the tiled frontage of the family home in Ban Sam Rung greeting family and friends with the traditional and respectful Thai wai greeting…it was great to be back in Isaan amongst my Thai family and friends.

Over the next few days we generally relaxed in or around the family home in Ban Sam Rung or drove into Khon Kaen to shop in the markets or drop into the Central Plaza for a coffee and a stroll around the shops. During one of these visits Ada dropped me and Amy at Wat Nong Wang, the beautiful pyramid like temple in Khon Kaen. Amy and I explored this wonderful temple and its internal treasures such as the murals on its walls depicting the story of the beginnings of Khon Kaen or the impressive shrine on the ground floor with its Golden Buddha, and even the historical displays on various floors, and the views of Khon Kaen from the 9th floor external viewing area are amazing. We enjoyed the panoramic views of the lake, city and the surrounding areas from this elevated viewpoint…they were really spectacular and we took some wonderful photographs of the views and also of other parts of the temple. It really is a beautiful and serene place to visit and one of my favourite places in Khon Kaen.

We visited Khon Kaen Zoo the day after the visit to Wat Nong Wang…when I say 'we', I of course mean as many people as we could fit on and in Ada's truck. The Zoo is located roughly half way between Khon Kaen and Udon Thani, off highway 2, and overlooks Khao Suan Kwang district, from its elevated position on the hillside. Before we explored the zoo, the reed mats (saht) were laid out and everyone started eating…breakfast (Ada told me everyone had missed breakfast). I was used to seeing this Thai obsession with eating and just shrugged my shoulders and laughed. Thankfully, it was another state zoo which was very expansive and we had to rely on a 'shuttle bus' system of transport to take us to the various parts of the zoo, where we saw sun bears, rhinoceros, lions, white tigers, hippopotamus, orangutans, camels, meercats and many other small animals/reptiles, and we even fed the Barking Deer before returning to the main entrance and the souvenir shop. After the zoo we drove to the water park at the top of the mountain/hill (the entrance fee also included entry into the water park), and despite the slides being closed for maintenance, we had a great afternoon in the large pool and the lazy river. It was a great way to escape the heat of the day…and the views from this hilltop paradise were spectacular, as the Isaan countryside rolled away into the distance. Before we headed back to Ban Sam Rung, we grabbed a great photo opportunity at the impressive entrance to the zoo with its large 'Khon Kaen Zoo' sign, statues of several jumping deer, a large gold framed portrait of King Bhumibol, Thai flags, fountains, beautiful gardens and a stone cliff as a back-drop.

The same evening, a few of us settled down in front of the TV to watch the second leg of the ASEAN Championship Cup Final between Thailand and Malaysia…we had already watched the first leg which Thailand had won 2-0. The return leg was in Stadium Shah Alam in Selangor, Malaysia. With thirty minutes to go Malaysia were leading 3-0 on the night and 3-2 on aggregate. It was looking like it wasn't going to be Thailand's night…but in the 82nd and 86th minutes Thailand scored two goals, and even though they were losing 3-2 on the night, they were leading 4-3 on aggregate. Thailand held on and we were mightily relieved when the final whistle was blown…Thailand were ASEAN Champions.

Christmas Day started with a video…Amy and I made a short video wishing family and friends a 'Merry Christmas' and posted in facebook, and we spent the remainder of the day in Khon Kaen at the Central Plaza. It was surreal, but nice, walking around a shopping centre and not enduring the usual stresses associated with Christmas Day in the UK. However, this was the year that Disney's 'Frozen' was a huge global hit and its music was everywhere…and when walking around the Central Plaza I could hear the inimitable sound of 'Let it Go'. Amy and I quickly found the source…there appeared to be a concert happening in one of the open display areas and luckily we were there in seconds and found a young girl of about ten, dressed as Elsa from 'Frozen', belting out 'Let it Go' and fairplay she was brilliant. When it ended a teenage boy stepped onto the stage, sat at the piano and started playing…guess what he was playing? Yes, absolutely correct…'Let it Go'. Then two girls stepped on stage, again dressed as Elsa…at this point, I stood up and said to Amy "Come on Amy, let's find mummy and have a coffee", and as we walked away I could the duet singing 'Let it Go'…again. Brilliant performances by all those taking part, but a little bit repetitive.

Around 1pm the following afternoon, we (Ada, Amy, Pa, Pechar, Gaer and I) were heading off on a three to four day round trip to Roi Et, Ubon Ratchathani and Prasat Phanom Rung. I was looking forward to this little trip as it provided another chance to see parts of Thailand we hadn't seen before. After driving through challenging back roads laced with varying sizes of pot-holes it wasn't long before we were on the outskirts of Maha Sarakham and heading toward its famous university, and around an hour later we were heading toward Wat Burapha Phiram in Roi Et to visit what we could already see from a distance as we approached the city…the 60m tall golden Buddha and the most prominent feature in the town. It wasn't until we drove into Wat Burapha Phiram did we appreciate the actual size of its standing Buddha…such was its immense size, it was difficult to find a place in the temple complex where you could take a photograph that would include the entire statue. It was truly impressive and was rightly the outstanding feature of Roi Et's skyline, a protuberant Buddhist figure that pierced the blue sky above the city with its religious greatness. As we drove away from the temple, the statue's eminence appeared to follow us, whispering its importance until it disappeared in the rear window as we continued our journey to Ubon Ratchathani. Before we left Roi Et province we visited Wat Chai Mongkol where the large and beautiful Phra Maha Chedi Chai Mongkol (The Great, Victorious and Auspicious Pagoda) is found, a huge chedi that is 101m long, 101m wide and 101m high which is significant as 'Roi Et' literally means 'one hundred and one'. Set in a stunning walled garden, which is entered via an elaborately gold painted entrance, and includes splendid gardens that create a serene paradise for visitors. The centerpiece is the magnificent chedi which is painted white with elaborate gold decoration which is mirrored in the gardens with the gold Buddha's, familiar seven headed mythical serpents (Naga or seven headed King Cobra) and the ornate gold trimmings of the fountains and ponds…it was an area of palatial oppulance. Amy and I climbed the internal stairway of the chedi to the outside viewing area which was below the important top part of the chedi that housed Buddha relics and is finished with a finial of pure gold. From this idyllic viewpoint we witnessed the beginnings of an amazing sunset as the colours of the sky danced in a merged collection of oranges, blues and hazy mauves…from this hilltop paradise the view across the entire area was glorious as the shadow of the setting sun chased away the warm glow of another day. The sun was setting fast as we drove away from this beautiful chedi and temple and it was soon dark. A few hours later we entered Ubon Ratchathani, and the birthplace of my favourite Thai singer, Tai Orathai.

After a restful night and a fairly simple breakfast at a resort on the outskirts of Ubon, we set off to see if we could find our great-niece, Sunny, the grand-daughter of Ada's deceased sister, Sum (pronounced 'Soom')…I sadly never met Sum as she passed away in 2009, just after I'd met Ada. Pechar knew roughly where Sunny was living, with the parents of Ada's niece's boyfriend, and we hadn't seen her since Ada's brother-in-law (Sum's husband) had forcibly taken her from La's house in Ban Sam Rung…if we found her, I had a feeling this would be an emotional reunion. The area where Sunny was living was about twenty to thirty kilometres outside of Ubon Ratchathani, but we were relying on Pechar's memory of how to get there. Initially, we found the village that Pechar remembered but, he was having difficulty remembering which house…eventually we stopped, and Pechar got out to ask someone who pointed us to a house, but the person was sure they had moved to another village. On checking with a neigbour, they confirmed that Sunny's carers had indeed moved to another village and they gave Pechar the details. Around fifteen minutes later we had parked up and were walking to a smart little house adjacent to a dried-up rice paddy where an old man was sitting on the front porch. Pechar approached the man and spoke to him...I saw the old man nod, turn and he shouted something in Isaan through an open door of the house. A few moments later the man's wife appeared holding Sunny's hand. Pa immediately started wailing and the rest of us were choking back the tears...it was fantastic seeing Sunny and her huge innocent smile again, she certainly filled us with so much joy with her infectious happiness. The reunion was made more special by the fact that she appeared to be really pleased to see us and our tears were quickly replaced with matching smiles. A word about Sunny...she was around seven or eight years old, and as I understand things, she had been starved of oxygen during her birth resulting in brain damage and a probable stroke that had left her partially paralysed, but it didn't dampen her happy nature. It was an absolute pleasure to spend time with such a joyful child, playing and having photographs taken with her...I've seen many beautiful things on my travels to Thailand, but nothing more beautiful and heartwarming than Sunny's beaming smile. It was difficult saying goodbye, and I'm not ashamed to say, we all shed a tear as we left, and as Pechar drove us back to Ubon there was a hushed silence in the truck, a sadness that needed no words as we all wished we could have taken Sunny with us back to Ban Sam Rung and her surrogate mother, Ada's sister, La.

That afternoon we visited Wat Phra That Nong Bua, the site of Sri Maha Pho Chedi, a 55m tall stupa, loosely based on the Mahabodhi stupa in Bodhgaya, India. It is a stunning white and gold stupa that is housed in beautiful walled gardens, the centerpiece of the temple complex...another example of exquisite Thai architecture, and its ornate decorative gold finishes are breathtaking both inside and out., and it is difficult not to be impressed by the detail. The extensive gold coverage provides a stark contrast to the white, and as a result, it transforms the images on the white areas, bringing them to life and it is the white areas that stand out and not the gold...it is a remarkable transformation and another splendid temple complex that provides more 'jaw-dropping' images...even moreso in the night, as we had seen the stupa the previous evening when we arrived in Ubon, bathed in light it appeared to be shining like a beacon of hope in the blackness of the night. From Wat Phra That Nong Bua we went to a river restaurant (a collection of open-sided floating huts), where a series of raised wooden gangways took you to an individual hut where you would sit on reed mats and listen to the gentle and clear waters of the Mun (pronounced 'moon') River swept silently past to join the mighty Mekong River, around 50km downstream. We enjoyed a fabulous meal, made more spectacular by the sunset that turned the sky and shimmering water of the Mun River into a tangerine abyss, creating a scene that would be the envy of lovers everywhere. Our busy, but enjoyable and emotional day finished with a trip to a night market before we returned to the resort...and bed.

We said goodbye to Gaer after breakfast the following morning...he was returning to Bangkok. We then left Ubon Ratchathani and headed for Preah Vihear Temple...a khmer temple from the Angkor dynasty, a temple that is actually in Cambodia, but due to its elevated position on an escarpment, it could only be accessed via Thailand. It was once used as headquarters by the Khmer Rouge, and as a result, the area was heavily mined and to this day it is still considered to be too dangerous to wander outside the designated 'safe' areas. The problem with this temple is due to its position and border tensions between Thailand and Cambodia it isn't always accessible to the public...when we arrived in the town of Kantharalak and made some enquiries we discovered that today was one of those days when it was closed to visitors. Therefore, we turned around and continued our journey to our original destination...Prasat Phanom Rung, allegedly the most impressive example of an Angkor temple outside of Cambodia.

Around two hours later, after driving across the flat terrain and repeated landscape of the Korat plateau, a single hill could be seen in the distance...the extinct volcano and site of Prasat Phanom Rung, and twenty minutes later we were parked up in the car park that served this historical gem. But we still hadn't seen any sight of the famous Khmer temple as it was hidden amongst the trees at the top of the extinct volcano. After something to eat in one of the many restaurants adjacent to the car park, Amy and I started to explore the row of tented souvenir shops that line the opposite side of the car park, which marked the inclined route that led to Phanom Rung.

After passing the last souvenir shop, the ancient mix of avenue and steps stretched away up the hill in front of us, up a now steep incline. Interestingly, the power of nature could also be seen, as trees had forced their way through the neat avenue of stone slabs/steps, lifting the dimensionally equal paving stones, creating a landscape that epitomizes the continual battle between nature and man-made objects. As the incline began to steepen we entered the small, but interesting, museum for Prasat Phanom Rung, before continuing on up the series of neat steps. I paid the entrance fee and paused to read a sign that provided a brief history, in Thai and English, of Prasat Phanom Rung…telling of the 900,000 year old dormant volcano that housed the relative newcomer in the eleventh-century temple. As we approached the top of the steps there was an excited expectation building as to what we would see, but despite seeing photographs of this majestic temple, nothing could have prepared me for the stunning beauty I was about to witness. I took a deep breath and took the last step to where I would be able to see Phamom Rung for the first time…It was breathtaking and another 'wow' moment in my growing list of Thai 'wow' moments. I was finally stood on a slabbed platform, on what was probably the rim of the extinct volcano, and I let my eyesight take in the unbelievable vision in front of me…from where we were stood, steps led down to a 160m avenue lined on both sides with ornate stone pillars around 4ft in height, that led to another series of layered steps that led to the walled temple that housed the main tower, the centerpiece of this incredible site which was built in the similar pink sandstone used to build the temple at Phimai.

Phanom Rung is a Hindu temple and the literal translation is 'stone castle', and its impressive main tower symbolizes Mount Meru, the Hindu centre of the universe, the symbolic ponds found in and around the site were the oceans that surrounded Mount Meru. The Naga bridge at the end of the avenue and at the top of the main stairway are where you pass from the mortal world into the world of the Gods. It is a truly magical place and when a large group of Buddhist monks arrived, their saffron robes added a warmth of colour to the weathered pink and grey stone, and the many shades of green from the many different types of trees and grass that in places had been harshly scorched by the fierce sun. It was mesmerizing and humbling strolling around this wonderful complex of symmetrical rooms and open doorways of equal size, all in a perfect line with each other, meaning you could look straight through the main tower building from one side of the exterior wall to the other, and the temple was brimming with decorative carved stonework of Hindu Gods…a treasure hidden from view until you reach the top of those first steps, when it reveals its full glory. We eventually left Prasat Phanom Rung and drove to a small village at the base of the extinct volcano where Prasat Muant Tam was located, another Khmer temple equally as beautiful as its famous cousin on the hill. The fading light of the day played tricks with the colour of the stone…it turned the stone a deep terracotta colour when bathed with the light from the setting sun. The temple adopted a surreal, almost eerie, feel as the setting son emphasized the pink sandstone and heightened the beauty of this amazing complex. We left as the sun hovered gently above the horizon. Taking one last look before it disappeared and darkness replaced the last glowing embers of another stunning sunset. An hour or so later we were booking into a hotel in the centre of the city of Buriram.

The hotel (Theprakorn Hotel) we stayed at consisted of two buildings, the original hotel (probably built in the 1980s) and where our rooms were, and a newer building where breakfast would be served. It was Christmas time and in an attempt to please any foreign visitors there was a decorated Christmas tree and a lifesize santa in the reception of the older hotel…however, I have never seen santa wearing an imitation leopard-skin fur jacket (c/w matching cape) and a red hat with a matching leopard-skin fur trim…it looked as if a 'cross-dressing' santa was in town. But it got worse…when we went for breakfast the next morning to the newer building there were two santas' in the foyer, one wearing the same hat as the one in the older hotel, and a red jacket covered in white stars with the same leopard skin trim and matching fur slippers…and he was holding a saxophone. The other santa was wearing a patterned sky blue silk dress, with a long red coat with a white fur trim, matching hat and holding presents and a parrot. You have to take your hat off to the Buddhist Thai people for their brave efforts in trying to make foreigners feel at home with the Christmas theme, but I've got a sneaky feeling the staff at this hotel may have been advised about Santa's dress code, by an ex-pat with a wicked sense of humour. After breakfast we visited the Big Buddha at Buriram, another of the many 'Big Buddha's' seen all over Thailand. This one, similar to Prasat Phanom Rung, is located at the top of an extinct volcano (Khao Kradong volcano), and to reach the top you either drive or climb the 297 steps...I foolishly chose the steps, but it was worth it, as when I reached the top the views over Buriram were stunning. One of the best images was the impressive stadium, 'Thunder Castle', the home of Buriram United F.C....with a name like 'Thunder Castle' visiting teams must have felt as if they were a goal down before the even game kicked-off. The 15m high gold Buddha, gazing protectively over Buriram, glistened in the midday sun from its elevated position...a very impressive and beautiful sight. There is a tree found here that is only found in extinct volcanoes, called Yoni Pisat (Devil's Vagina) Tree, and I'm not going to even begin to try and explain the reason for its name. Before we headed back to Khon Kaen we dropped in to Thunder Castle, and by a stroke of luck, the club shop was selling the new shirts for the up and coming season...needless to say, at £10 each, Ada, Amy and I were soon sporting the fabulous football shirts of the current Thai football champions. A few hours later, after flying visits to a couple of more modern temples, we were back in Ban Sam Rung.

Over the next week we enjoyed a huge flower show in Khon Kaen, visits to the Central Plaza in the city and a fantastic New Year's Eve party with great food, drink and even fireworks. New Year's Day was spent at my favourite place...'Snake Village', and there had been some improvements to the small collection of enclosures behind the arena used for the snake shows. The show itself was still the same, but the 'danger' element still created an air of uncertainty, intrigue and unpredictability. But as it was the last day of the New Year's holiday there were large crowds and as a result good photo opportunities were few and far between. Therefore, Amy and I returned the following day and I am glad we did as the crowds had disappeared and there were only a few other people there...as a result, I experienced possibly the greatest animal encounter I have ever experienced. On the opposite side of the arena I could see a woman taping closed the mouth of a large King Cobra, she then started to walk over to our side of the Arena. A few minutes later I had this magnificent, but dangerous snake, draped around my neck and with my right hand I was holding its tail and my left hand was holding it about twelve inches behind its head…whilst it was the scariest and most amazing feeling, it was an absolute honour. Despite the snake having its mouth taped with a single piece of insulation tape, I was holding a snake with so much power that its venom could bring down an elephant…it was a unique experience and one I will always treasure. When I got back to Ban Sam Rung everyone else didn't quite see it that way and there were looks of disbelief and murmers of "ting-tong farang" (crazy foreigner). A few days later it was time to leave Ban Sam Rung and head south for a week or so at the beach.

It is always sad leaving Ban Sam Rung and this time was no different, and after the usual visit from the 'lucky man', as I called him…who bestowed luck for our future journey and return to Ban Sam Rung. There were the usual family tears and finally another visit to Ban Sam Rung had come to an end, and we set-off on the, now familiar, drive to Bangkok. Seven or eight hours later we paid a flying visit to Nang to drop Ada's mother off before continuing our journey to Nakhon Pathom…we would stay the night there before heading to South Thailand and the town of Prachuap Khiri Khan. It took around an hour to get to Nakhon Pathom, home of the largest chedi in Thailand, and it was very late before we found a hotel for the night. We got up the following morning, and on opening the curtains, we could see that Wat Phra Pathom Chedi dominated the skyline of the city, and after breakfast and booking out of the hotel, Ada dropped Amy and I at this gigantic Lanka-style bell-shaped chedi and its temple complex. The pale orange and terracotta coloured chedi houses another of Buddha's relics, and is 120.5 metres high and at its widest point has a perimeter of 233 metres…it was an impressive structure and not something I'd ever seen before. The usual beauty associated with Thai temples was also evident here, first with the views of the city, the wonderful array of Buddha and other statues, nagas, small ornate buildings that housed bells, beautifully pruned trees and a central shrine with a large Buddha statue made for a very special and peaceful place. From here we took a short drive across the city to Sanam Chandra Palace…a complex of five buildings commissioned by the Crown Prince Vajiravudh and

549

was completed in 1911 a year after he became Rama VI. The buildings of this palace complex are situated in an idyllic park area with mature trees, beautiful gardens and man-made waterways/lakes...considering it's in the middle of a busy city, it is a peaceful and splendid setting. There is a building that looks like a small European castle/mansion house, linked traditional wooden Thai style houses built on stilts, a large main palace which is fascinating to walk around, as it is very informative about the displays (furniture, personal items, photographs etc) in the building and of King Rama VI (the former Crown Prince Vajiravudh) and his family. Additionally, there was a walkway that provided access to a traditional Thai temple. It was a joy to visit this wonderful, but unique, Royal Palace and its majestic setting. It is really a hidden gem that I had not seen in any tourist books I'd read about Thailand...probably a little way off the normal areas that tourists visited. By mid-afternoon we had exhausted the exploration of this charming palace and its picturesque grounds, and we set-off for Prachuap Khiri Khan. I was excited about this leg of the trip, due to the photographs I'd seen of the stunning sunrises in Prachuap's spectacular bay. After a three to four hour drive we arrived in darkness at the town of Prachuap Khiri Khan, and as we drove along the beachfront it couldn't reveal the wondrous beauty of its bay. We booked into our hotel (the 3-star Hadthong Hotel), which faced the ocean, and then strolled along the front to a busy open-air restaurant, a sure sign of good food...we weren't disappointed, and after a wonderful meal we headed back to our hotel and bed. I made sure I set my alarm for four thirty in the morning, a time when I knew it would still be dark...I didn't want to miss the sunrise. Our room was at the front of the hotel on the second floor...we had a perfect view of the bay from the room and balcony, but as excited as I was, I eventually drifted off to sleep.

Despite the time, the sound of my alarm was a welcome sound, and I excitedly, but quietly, got out of bed, so as not to wake Ada and Amy, showered, got dressed and slowly slid open the door to the balcony, stepped out and slid the door shut behind me. The warmth of the sea breeze was a welcome change to the icy air conditioning of the hotel room, and I sat down on one of the two chairs on the balcony, placed my phone and digital camera on the table beside me...and patiently waited for the darkness to be lifted by the beginnings of a new day. It seemed like the darkness was here to stay and my excitable patience was wearing thin, but about forty minutes after stepping onto the balcony, chinks of light started to appear, revealing a not so perfect sky as there was broken cloud on the horizon, a large uneven band of clear sky followed by more broken cloud. The colours in the sky and across the calm waters of the bay were morphing before my eyes…initially, the clouds appeared dark grey, as did the reflections in the ocean of three silhouetted islands on the right hand side of the bay. The warm yellow glow of the sun started to turn the sky from yellow to orange, and the band of clear sky between the broken clouds started to reveal its creamy blueness to an unseen audience. It was then I could hear a faint, but continual "chug, chug, chug…", as a small, but distinct, silhouetted shape of a fishing boat could be seen crossing the bay from left to right…the only sound that could be heard in this heavenly and serene scene playing out before me. The colours became more intense as the sky above the outer island of the chain of three (I later found there was a fourth island sitting behind this island) was ablaze in a stunning fireball that broke through the cloud on the horizon, and a few minutes later it appeared as if this fireball was projecting across the water directly toward me…it was like a lazer cutting through the ocean, and the "chug, chug, chug…" of the fishing boat faded with the darkness as the entire bay came out of hiding to welcome another day. I had the best seat possible to witness this breathtaking sunrise, and it was an unbelievably beautiful sight. Despite the amazing things I had seen on my Thai trips and also seen in other places I'd visited, I had never witnessed something as spectacularly magical as the sunrise over Prachuap. I could now hear Ada and Amy stirring in the hotel room and thirty minutes later we were having breakfast on an open veranda adjacent to the hotel restaurant, and watching the sun continue its journey into the sky. There was another memorable moment that morning…I had my first taste of 'rice soup' as I watched another fishing boat "chug, chug, chugging" its way across the bay and I thought "what a stunning place…I want to be a fisherman ON THAT BOAT". I continued eating my breakfast and looked through the photos I had taken of the most impressive sunrise I think I'll ever witness…it was spectacular and made even more special by the huge 'horseshoe' shaped bay and its islands at Prachuap Khiri Khan.

Another memorable episode in Prachuap was memorable for all the wrong reasons…there was a single hill roughly halfway around this beautiful bay which houses a small temple, Wat Thammikaram Worawihan, right at the top of the hill. This temple could only be accessed by a set of 396 steps, close to the City Hall and opposite the City Pillar Shrine. But there was a problem…to climb the steps to the temple you had to negotiate your way through a large troop of macaques that lived on the hill…nasty, aggressive macaques…with attitude, as it turned out. Ada, Amy and I had every intention of visiting this temple, but after taking some photos in front of a fountain at the foot of the hill, a fountain that included two large stone statues of macaques, which incidentally, had two real macaques sitting on them…young macaques…they looked cute, but they were full of impish mischief. As we walked around the corner toward the steps, there were a couple of young ones, but with an adult macaque which I presumed was the mother…as it turned, I was absolutely correct. We made no attempt at approaching these macaques, but that didn't stop the mother from charging at us, I quickly stepped in front of Ada and Amy and the macaque stopped a couple of metres away, as I shouted "YES, YES…", thankfully it backed off and went back to its young…I guess she was only being a protective mother, but it was enough for Ada to decide that she wasn't going up those steps. It was then that a local woman came over holding a large stick, and started speaking to Ada and started walking and tapping the floor with the stick, left and right "tap, tap, tap…" . I think I got the gist of what she was meant, and Ada confirmed what I thought, that we should walk up the steps tapping the stick in front of us, and the macaques would move away…so I took the stick off the woman and Amy and I started to climb the steps, and sure enough…the female macaques and younger ones moved away, with exception of the occasional youngster that held its ground and hissed its defiance. However, the male macaques were totally disinterested in us and the stick, and just continued to preen themselves or yawn their disapproval at the 'hissing' youngsters. After about ten minutes, we reached the top, and passed a monk sweeping the floor, totally oblivious to the macaques…in a sort of harmonious understanding, he didn't bother them and they didn't bother him. We sought sanctuary in a sort of shrine or shelter that overlooked the bay, and the views over the bay and the city of Prachuap were pretty special, and the full appreciation of this impressive natural phenomenon was now in full view. However, this vantage point gave me an ideal view of the dark clouds building-up beyond the group of small islands on the right hand side of the bay. After taking a few photos/selfies of us both, maximizing the fantastic back-drops of the bay, temple and city, we headed back down the hill, but this time in the middle of a group of others who had braved 'macaque alley', and at the same time the dark clouds continued to build over the ocean. We were about a hundred metres from the pier when we noticed the islands to our right could not be seen…a wall of tropical rain was heading our way and quickly. Amy and I crossed over the road and sought refuge in a café just as the squall hit us…my God, when a tropical storm arrives you need to be under cover, the temperature dropped and the rain was bouncing of the pavement and road, but as with all tropical storms, it passed quickly, and ten minutes later we were walking back to the hotel as the warm evening air returned.

After another stunning sunrise, breakfast and taking some family photos of the beautiful beaches near the Royal Thai Air Force base, home of 'Wing 5' in Prachuap, such as Ao Manao, we set off for Baan Grood…around sixty-five kilometres south of Prachuap. We drove through a beautiful landscape and I was now seeing the type of scenery I expected to see when I first visited Thailand in 2011. A little over and hour later, and driving through miles and miles of coconut groves, we arrived in the stunning Baan Grood Arcadia Resort and Spa, directly opposite Baan Grood beach, a beach of white sand that stretched a couple of miles in both directions…it was almost deserted when we got there, we had found a piece of paradise. The deluxe bungalow I'd booked turned out to our own piece of luxury in this paradise, situated in beautifully manicured gardens with an array of different trees and shrubs, and only about twenty metres from the pool. In true Thai tradition the first place we headed was to a beach restaurant for something to eat, and then we went back to the resort and Amy and I spent time in the splendid pool…considering it was tourist area it was very quiet and we all felt relaxed in this wonderful resort in a stunningly gorgeous part of Thailand, almost untouched compared to places I'd previously visited such as Phuket, Pattaya and Jomtien.

It was a fun few days in Baan Grood, stunning sunrises, relaxing poolside and also having fun with Amy in the pool, walks along the almost deserted beach, great food and drink…it was a very peaceful area and thus very enjoyable. But we didn't go in the sea, purely because the ocean floor dropped away quickly from the beach, and the waves violently crashed onto the beach, and we felt it was too dangerous for small children, hence we only used the pool at the fabulous resort. During our three day stay we visited Wat Tang Sai on a headland about two miles south from the resort. A magnificent temple (too difficult to describe) with stunning gardens, demon guardian statues and its own 'Big Golden Buddha'. The temple had been built in 1996 to mark King Bhumibol Adulyadej's 50th year on the throne. But it is the views that are also spectacular, from different parts of the temple you can see miles of sandy beaches and coconut groves to the north, and also miles of beaches heading south…looking toward Baan Grood it is difficult to see any of the buildings of the village as they are well hidden in what appears to be one continual coconut grove that stretches as far as the eye can see. You can also see the beautiful, but imposing, Tenasserim Hills, a 1700km mountain range stretching from Central Thailand where it forms a natural barrier between Thailand and Myanmar and heads south to the Malay Peninsula. It is a truly beautiful place and I hope it stays that way as there enough over populated, hectic resorts in Thailand in areas such as Phuket, Koh Samui, Pattaya etc, therefore, this paradise at Baan Grood was heavenly…provided you avoid visiting at weekends and Thai holidays. It was sad to leave Baan Grood, but as part of our journey back to Bangkok, we headed to the popular holiday destination of both Thai's and 'farang' (foreign) tourists…Hua Hin. And a couple of hours later we were booking-in to Escape Hotel, Hua Hin, another beautiful hotel…a series of two storey buildings painted in a dusky salmon pink, including an open-sided restaurant, all facing a central pool area c/w sun loungers, parasols and an open-sided Thai massage area…and finished with palm trees, other shrubs and manicured lawns. It was sandwiched between a busy road and the beach, but when inside the restaurant and pool area the tranquility was deafening…it was another hidden gem, and ideally located. It was here we met Egil Nordby and his Thai wife, Rattiya, a lovely couple and for the three mornings we were there at Escape we had breakfast together. Hua Hin was livelier than Prachuap and Baan Grood, there was a lively night market in the centre of the city with great restaurants and a few small bars, and live music and great food in front of the Market Village (a shopping centre a short distance from the hotel). We'd also walk along the busy beach from the Escape up to where the Hilton Hotel was located on the edge of the city centre, and around a two kilometre walk past an array of stunning high quality hotels and beach front condominiums of various sizes and styles. The beach was busy with the 'traffic' of power-walking pensioners with tanned leathery skin from too much exposure to the sun, and sporadically littered with families whose children were happily playing in the sand. In the pristine blue sky above the beach you could see the tell-tale parachutes of people enjoying the thrills associated with parascending, as their accompanying speedboats and those on jet skis darted at varying angles across the ocean. There were also a few Thai massage areas set-up on the beach and occasionally one of the famous Hua Hin white ponies would trot past, being led by its jogging handler, and carrying a laughing child clearly enjoying his or her pony ride on the beach…twice we paid for Amy to enjoy a pony ride on one of these pretty white ponies, and the joy written on her face as the pony trotted off down the beach, with its jogging handler, was well worth the 200baht fee. The highlight for Amy and I (Ada went shopping at a local market) was a visit to a fantastic water park (Van Nava Hua Hin). Amy had a brilliant time at the 'Rain Fortress' where there were slides and different water sprays etc and every ten minutes or so a large barrel, at the top of this fun structure, would fill with water before tilting forward, and tipping its contents (via a short downward facing board that spread the water) over an expectant and excited crowd of children below who let out screams of delight as they all got soaked. There were a lot of activities (wave pool, surfing, lazy river etc) and larger slides for older children/adults, and everything was well supervised…it was a great way to spend the day. Before we left Hua Hin we made a visit to an interesting sight and not something you'd expect…the railway station. The station is unique in that it has a pretty little building on the platform in a Thai style with ornate red decorative trimming, and cream panels with a yellow trim. Additionally, the platform is well kept with beautiful gardens and manicured lawns and an ornate red sign with 'Hua Hin' in black on a white background. It really is a lovely little station and unusually a popular tourist attraction...google 'Hua Hin train station' and see for yourselves.

After four days in Hua Hin it was time to head back to Bangkok...our six week stay in Thailand was sadly coming to an end. Our last couple of nights in Bangkok would be spent at the Royal Princess in Lara Luang...a hotel we'd stayed at before and the perfect place to finish our holiday, close to many top tourist attractions. On our penultimate day we drove to Nang's house in Mo Chit and picked up Ada's mum and niece Ker...the plan was to visit Vimanmek Mansion (we'd tried to visit this mansion at the beginning of the holiday but it was closed), a palace that was originally in Chonburi, but in 1900 it was dismantled, moved to Dusit Garden and re-assembled, and in 1901 it was used by King Rama V for five years, and is still used for state functions today. It is an unusual palace in that it is not built of stone or brick, but was constructed from teak, which, it could be argued gives it its majestic beauty. Situated in mature gardens, the 72 room mansion/palace oozes spendour and the tour around its grand rooms is a delightful glimpse into the life and rule of probably one of Thailand's most influential monarch's and one of the most revered...for all you film buffs, King Rama V is the eldest prince of King Mongkut in the film 'The King and I' (banned in Thailand for suggesting that King Mongkut was a buffoon and that he had a 'romantic' involvement with Anna Leonowens...King Mongkut was an able and excellent monarch and a relationship with a western commoner would never have happened in the strict hierarchical society of old Siam). It is important to note that, as with all royal residences in Thailand, shorts and sleeveless tops are not suitable attire as the legs must be covered to just below the knee, and shoulders are not allowed to be exposed. Additionally, cameras, bags and mobile phones must be locked in lockers before you enter the area where Vimanmek Mansion is located, but once the internal tour has been completed you can retrieve your belongs and take family photos in front of the palace. There are other smaller buildings in the palace complex that house a fantastic exhibition of photos taken by King Bhumibol (Rama IX) and another large building exhibiting many different kinds of Thai crafts. After something to eat, Ada and I went to Ananta Samakhon Throne Hall to look at the Thai handicraft exhibition…this was exciting for two reasons. Firstly, the throne hall was only open to the public for two weeks in January each year and the chance to see the interior of this beautiful and iconic building was too good to miss. Secondly, the art being exhibited was equally as magnificent as the breathtaking building, the elite collection of Thai art consisted of painted, embroidered and carved wooden screens, gold throne chairs (yes, real gold), gold covered palanquins, models of royal barges (again, in gold), and elegant ornaments of mythical creatures, ships, bowls etc. The Throne Hall is a suitable venue for this exhibit, as the exquisite interior of the palace, mirrors the elaborate designs of the sensational and finest examples of Thai art. It was an extremely privileged experience to enjoy this exhibit in such a majestic building.

That evening we saw a different kind of Thai culture, but equally as fascinating…we took a tuk tuk to the bustling chaos of Khao San Road. This area is 'backpackers paradise', teeming with cheap accommodation/hostels, great street restaurants, popular bars, shops and market stalls…selling anything and everything you could associate with backpacking or tourism. It is an excellent place to visit and is a great demonstration of the hectic pace of Bangkok, the 'in your face' hundred mile an hour pace of life in a crazily busy city. As the tuk tuk stopped at the top of Khao San Road, there was a sea of people stretching away into the distance, illuminated by the numerous neon signs that lit up this hedonistic street like a Christmas tree. The swarm of bright colours played tricks with your vision and it was difficult to focus on any given point, and whilst it was children friendly, in the sense there were no Go-go bars and the like, it is extremely busy and we had to keep Amy very close…holding her hand at all times. The sounds in Khao San Road confused your senses as you walked around a chaotic area that was filled with the reverberation of contrasting languages and differing English dialects. Additionally, the sights and smells compounded the confusion, as the different smells created a melting pot of aromatic befuddlement, and equally, the psychedelic images created a drunken haze of uncertainty. Whilst it was a place of continually contrasting images it was a fantastic place to visit, a 'must see' experience, and the only place I know where you can buy 'Pad Thai' and fried 'scorpion's on a stick' within a couple of metres of each other...it was also a great place to purchase those last minute souvenirs or presents.

Our last day started with a visit to Wat Saket or 'Temple of the Golden Mount' as it is more famously known, one of the oldest temples in Bangkok that was also once the highest point in the city before modern skyscrapers became commonplace. As a result, when you get to the top, it offers spectacular views across Bangkok where other tourist sites can also be seen such as the Grand Palace, Democracy Monument and Loha Prasat (Iron Castle). It was also used as the main crematorium during eighteenth-century plague and cholera epidemics and it is estimated that the ashes of 60,000 victims are buried in the base of this stunning elevated temple. Cremations were normally carried out outside the city, and in those days the exit gate out of the city was next to Wat Saket, therefore, the bodies being dumped there were either cremated or fed to vultures, and the neighbourhood surrounding the temple became known as Phratu Pi (Ghost Gate). As we walked up the mound, via 318 steps of a spiral staircase, we came across a macabre memorial to those that lost their lives in the cholera epidemic (reported to be 1 in 10 of the population of Bangkok)...the emaciated victim statues and the vulture statues picking at the statue body of another victim could be considered as graphic, but it is a realistic visual of what conditions would have been like at the time. The remainder of the mound includes beautiful gardens, fountains, golden Budda and other statues, many bells and gongs, and at its peak is a shrine room and a golden chedi...Wat Saket really is a fitting and beautiful memorial to the victims of the eighteenth-century epidemics.

After driving to Chinatown to buy Ada's Christmas present...a gold bracelet from one of the many gold shops on Yaowarat Road, we took a short drive to a car park adjacent to Wat Pho and next to the Chao Phraya River...Ada and her mother stayed with the truck whilst Amy and I took a short walk to catch a river taxi across the Chao Phraya river to Wat Arun (Temple of Dawn)...one of the most iconic images of Bangkok, especially when it is lit-up at night, a truly stunning image in Bangkok's eye-catching skyline. The cost of the river taxi was 19baht each and within about five minutes we were stepping off on the opposite bank (west bank at Thonburi) and straight into the grounds of Wat Arun. It was surprising how big Wat Arun actually was when you got close to it, and the other amazing feature of this iconic structure was how it had been decorated…thousands of pieces broken china had been cemented to its spires. We walked up very steep steps of two sections, but coming down was not as easy, but again the views over the city and up and downstream of the river were very impressive. Again, there were beautifully manicured gardens around Wat Arun, and it also included some beautiful functioning buildings within its magnificent temple complex. We even managed to get some stunning photographs of this iconic temple which included Amy dressed up in traditional Thai costume. After an hour or so we caught the river taxi back across to the east bank and strolled around the souvenir shops before heading back to Ada and her mother. From here we drove to Mo Chit, to drop Ada's mother back to Nang…we spent a few hours at Nang's having something to eat and chatting, as the sun set over Bangkok and on another wonderful Thai adventure. That evening we drove to our usual hotel, the Orchid Resort in Lat Krabang…only a ten minute drive to Suvarnabhumi Airport.

2017 – Kanchanaburi, Phitsanulok, Khon Kaen , Ban Sam Rung, Khao Yai National Park, Koh Chang, Bangkok

At the beginning of this trip we returned, in my opinion, to one of the most beautiful parts of Thailand…Kanchanaburi, such a shame it is associated with the horror that surrounded the 'death railway' engineered by the Japanese during World War II, and built by prisoners of war and Malays. We took an emotional rail journey to Hellfire Pass, and also revisited the military cemetery at Kanchanburi. We then travelled to Bangkok for one night, followed by one night at Phitsanulok, staying overnight before travelling to Khon Kaen and Ban Sam Rung. It was here we would enjoy another Songkran festival, but this time we also travelled into the centre of Khon Kaen for the huge city celebrations (go to You Tube and search 'songkran Khon Kaen'…you won't be disappointed). Once the Songkran celebrations were over we travelled south to Khao Yai National Park (the largest national park in Thailand) before heading to the beautiful island of Koh

559

Chang, Thailand's third largest island behind Phuket and Koh Samui just across the water from the city of Trat on the Thai/Cambodian border. We again headed to Bangkok for the last couple of days.

It was around four in the afternoon when we landed at Suvarnabhumi Airport and we managed to get through immigration fairly quickly, and it wasn't long before we were met by Pechar and were travelling in Ada's truck toward Bangkok...slowly, as we were caught up in the rush hour traffic, not that there's any let-up in the traffic in and around Bangkok. Luckily, it only took about an hour to get through this crazy city, using the motorway and toll-booths, and it wasn't long before Bangkok was behind us. It was now getting dark, but at least we were well on our way to our first destination...Kanchanaburi. It gets dark very quickly in Thailand and we were soon driving through badly lit villages and the occasional town, but thankfully the traffic was fairly light and at around seven thirty we had reached Kanchanaburi. After driving past the war cemetery we turned onto the road that headed toward the iconic Bridge on the River Kwai...we approached the bridge, but it was difficult to see it in the dark, and a few minutes later we were parked up at our resort...Good Times Resort. First impressions were very good, and despite the darkness it looked like a quaint place next to the Kwai River. We booked in and were shown to our rooms which were very good, and after dropping off the luggage we headed out to get something to eat. After a short walk we decided on good old 'street food' and sat at one of about five tables and watched our food being cooked in front of us...the only way to eat in Thailand, cheap and fresh. After our food we headed back to the resort, had a small glass of beer on the veranda and listened to the river flowing past, and occasionally lapping against the riverbank...it had been a long day and it wasn't long before we were all tucked up in bed.

When we woke the following morning and opened the door from our room and saw the resort in the light of day it was a pleasing sight...there were large ponds, beautifully manicured gardens awash with lush greens and bright yellows and oranges. Additionally, the breakfast tables were on a terrace just a few metres from the Kwai River...it was idyllic and a great way to enjoy our breakfast and begin another Thai adventure. After breakfast we drove to the Bridge Railway Station, located just before the bridge itself (hence the name)…we were heading to 'Hellfire Pass' which involved a train journey to Nam Tok station (the end of the line) and then the remainder of the journey would be via a taxi or hired mini-van. Ada bought our tickets and we patiently waited for the train, and it wasn't long before we could see the train trundling down the track toward us through the haze of the morning's heat. It gently pulled alongside the platform and eventually came to a standstill, we made our way to one of the open entrances, waited our turn and then climbed aboard, and headed to the nearest carriage…unfortunately, it was extremely busy and initially it was standing room only. We heard the screech of a whistle and immediately sensed the train pulling forward and it headed over the iconic 'Bridge on the River Kwai' and immediately sped up. Despite standing, the discomfort was made bearable by the views from the window…Kanchanaburi is a beautiful part of Thailand, and as we headed west this was exemplified by the Kwai river, an abundance of lush green foliage on either side of the track, and a backdrop of the imposing Tenasserim mountain range in the distance. After a few miles a more familiar landscape emerged as we crossed a flat plain of rice paddies, which didn't seem as featureless as it does in other parts of Thailand, due to the stunning silhouetted backdrop of the mountains to the west…where 'Hellfire Pass' is located. Ten to fifteen minutes after leaving Kanchanaburi we found a carriage with empty seats and were able to relax more now that we could sit down and enjoy the scenery flashing past the window…the train was clean, comfortable and functional and thererfore, couldn't be described as luxurious. Around an hour later we had started to enter the foothills of the Tenasserim Range, and the lush greens of the variety of trees enveloped the train, and in this picture perfect paradise, the train began to slow down…we were about to cross the Wampo Viaduct. A viaduct that was built by British, Australian and New Zealander POWs (prisoners of war) and Malay/Burmese forced labour. It was about half a mile long, and tucked into a vertical rock face, that for most of its length, ran parallel with The Khwae Noi (Small Kwai) River…it is an unbelievable piece of engineering, created by the unmistakable fortitude of the POWs and civilian labour, and in harrowing conditions (heat, beatings from the Japanese soldiers, lack of food and water, injury, disease etc). The fact it's still standing and still in use over seventy years after it was erected is testament to the skills of those soldiers/civilians, and it is sad to realise and very sobering that they certainly wouldn't have enjoyed it the way we were enjoying it today. The location of the Wampo Viaduct is filled with natural beauty, the lush green forests, through which the Khwae Noi flows, and the rolling hills that herald the beginning of the Tenasserim Range, which acts as a natural border between Thailand and Myanmar…it is an incredibly charming area of Thailand, that even its recent tarnished history can't detract from its natural pulchritude.

Around half an hour after crossing the Wampo Viaduct we pulled in to Nam Tok station, and from here we hired a driver and his mini-van to take us to 'Hellfire Pass'…a twenty minute roller-coaster of a journey on a twisting road through forested hills that eventually led us to a car park adjacent to a small, but modern, visitor centre. The first thing I realised when I stepped out of the air conditioned mini-van was the intense heat and humidity. I immediately empathized with the POWs and civilian labour that had toiled in this cauldron of heat, working up to 12-14 hours a day…emaciated, riddled with disease and with little food and water. I looked at myself…I was a reasonably fit man, who had access to water, proper footwear, protection from the sun etc who had been brought to this 'tourist attraction' in an air conditioned van and I was immediately struggling with the same heat…I cannot even begin to appreciate how they coped or survived, and sadly so many didn't. Even Ada and Pechar were struggling with the intense heat and humidity, and they are Thai and more acclimatized to these conditions, therefore, I have no idea how any of the POWs and civilian labour survived…what they were put through was relentless, barbaric and inhumane and no human being should suffer as they suffered at the hands of other human beings. It was extremely sobering and humbling realizing what these people had sacrificed for the freedom of others. We headed for our final destination, on foot, on an undulating path around 2-300 metres long, and eventually we dropped down into 'Hellfire Pass', via a series of steps…named by the POWs that worked there, as at night flamed torches would create a scene straight from 'HELL', with flickering flames, dancing shadows and the continual "ching" noises of metal hitting rock. There are many reminders of the past in this man made ravine such as an old rusting mining cart that would have been used to remove the blasted rock, marks and evidence on and in the rock faces from the 'hammer and tap' men who created the holes for the explosives, memorial plaques (the most moving being the one dedicated to Sir Edward 'Weary' Dunlop and his medical team who dedicated themselves to helping the sick and dying POWs and Asian civilians...when he died in 1993, some of 'Weary' Dunlop's ashes were scattered near 'Hellfire Pass', re-united with many of the soldiers he had tried to help), part of the tracks of the old railway line and many wreaths, small wooden crosses and messages from loved ones who had lost a husband, father, brother etc in this beautiful corner of Thailand. 'Hellfire Pass' is only part of the story of the 'Death Railway' (otherwise known as the Burma-Siam Railway), but whilst most of the old railway has disappeared, the cutting through the rock at 'Hellfire Pass' will always stand as a permanent memorial to those who lost their lives during the building of the entire length of the 'Death Railway'. It will be an everlasting scar in the unforgiving heat of this part of Thailand long after the 'Bridge on the River Kwai' and Wampo Viaduct have long gone. As an ex-soldier, I found the experience of visiting 'Hellfire Pass' extremely moving, and despite the 'cutting' appearing to not be very impressive from a distance, it is quite overwhelming when you stand in the middle and realise its actual size...you quickly become dwarfed by the high scarred sand coloured rock on either side. It is then that you begin to appreciate the enormity of the task that faced the POWs and civilian labourers at 'Hellfire Pass'...a task that was completed using hand tools and explosives. As with 'Wampo Viaduct', the famous 'Bridge on the River Kwai' and the remaining stretches of the 'Death Railway', 'Hellfire Pass' is another exemplary feat of engineering and human endeavour. But the human cost was a catastrophe, as it is estimated that about 90,000 Asian civilian labourers and over 12,000 Allied prisoners died building this railway. This is a sobering thought and one I mulled over as we walked back to the visitor centre, and the many steps we had to climb in the overpowering heat took its toll on us all. At the visitor centre Ada, Amy and Pechar watched the videos showing the emaciated soldiers being liberated at the end of the war...Ada and Pechar felt an element of shame that Thailand had signed a 'Treaty of Accord' with Japan, allowing the POWs and Asian civilian labourers to be treated so inhumanely by the Japanese...they had no idea and it was a humbling experience for us all. We headed back to Nam Tok, caught the train back to Kanchanaburi, and a few hours later we were again sat on the terrace next to the River Kwai having a wonderful Thai meal in the hotel restaurant...each of us pensive about what we'd seen earlier in the day.

Following another glorious breakfast experience on the terrace next to the river, and Amy and I enjoying a quick swim in the resort pool, it was time to leave the quaint Good Times resort. But before we left Kanchanaburi I wanted to take Amy to the war cemetery...she had been asking questions about the 'thin' men she had seen in the films at the 'Hellfire Pass' visitor centre. I wanted to answer them as honestly as I could, and in a way that a seven year old girl could understand...to help me, I felt the cemetery and the adjacent 'Thailand-Burma Railway Centre' (a museum and research centre) would be able to help. The cemetery wasn't far from Good Times Resort, therefore, despite the heat, Amy and I decided to walk...but we were soon standing in an air-conditioned 7-11 buying water...God it was hot. Visiting the Kanchanaburi War Cemetery again, especially after visiting 'Hellfire Pass', made this visit more emotional, more meaningful and more purposeful, as it helped me explain to Amy the events that occurred here over seventy years before. I don't know if it was a coincidence or whether it was because I was deliberately looking for fellow Sappers, but sadly there were a lot of Royal Engineer's in the cemetery...Sapper Mansfield (aged 24), Sapper Wall (aged 23), Sapper Clark (aged 25), Sapper Jenkins (aged 26), Sapper Walsh (aged 26), Sapper Smith (aged 23), Sapper King (aged 'unknown') and many, many more. It was as if by some sort of tragic fate that they would have been involved in the building of the 'Death Railway', and its now famous landmarks such as 'Hellfire Pass' the 'Bridge on the River Kwai' and 'Wampo Viaduct', probably due to their experience in construction and bridge building. Whilst I empathized with all those who lost their lives during this tragic episode in global history, I had an understandable special empathy for my fellow Sappers. The ages of those Sappers above, and others, highlight the fragility of life when the human body is pushed beyond its limits...a limit that was increasingly exceeded by the conditions they endured and by the vicious treatment meted out by their

Japanese captors. Amy, although only seven, seemed to understand the importance of the cemetery and the need to remember those who had died…she was combining what she'd seen at the visitor centre at 'Hellfire Pass', here at the cemetery and from what she saw in the Thailand-Burma Railway Centre, and confirmation of this was evident in some of the questions she was asking. Kanchanaburi is a beautiful place and yes, it is sadly associated with the horrific events that took place there during World War II. But despite its history it is still one of my favourite places to visit in Thailand, due to the allure of its lush forested hills and the magical draw of the famous River Kwai (Khwae).

Eventually, we left Kanchanaburi and headed back to Bangkok…over the next few days we visited Asiatique next to the Chao Phraya River in Bangkok, a great boutique shopping centre with great restaurants and waterfront bars. It also had a huge ferris wheel which Amy was keen to go on (I was reluctant due to my fear of heights despite the enclosed cabins), and I'm glad we did as the views over the city were spectacular. Despite the city being in darkness the twinkling lights from many high-rise buildings that made up the Bangkok skyline, and from the pleasure boats on the river, provided a magical scene. We also drove to Phitsanulok and again visited Phra Si Rattana Mahathat Temple and its iconic and historic gold Buddha, before driving through Nam Nao National Park, where we visited another stunning temple, stunning in more ways than one. Wat Pha Sorn Kaew, in some ways, is very unique and is built on a high vantage point, and there are two equally magnificent buildings which are also very different. The first sits on a man-made level platform which includes five Buddha's, the rear Buddha is a huge white figure and the remaining four Buddha's (all in white) reduce in size to the smallest at the front and there is a large viewing area that enables you to enjoy the fantastic views over the mountains and deep valleys of the national park. The other building is the main prayer hall that can only be considered as a 'work of art', a 'busy' building in that it is covered in modern mosaic images. To fully appreciate the beauty and full glory of this temple you have to google 'Wat Pha Sorn Kaew' and select 'images'. The sun was setting as we left this architectural masterpiece which intensified its magnificence and it could be considered Isaan's hidden gem. We carried on our journey to Khon Kaen and it was almost 11pm by the time we arrived in Ban Sam Rung, where we were greeted by an eerie silence as we drove into the village, broken only by the occasional distant barking of restless dogs. When we pulled on to the driveway of the family home only Ada's mother and our niece, Toy, were there as no-one had any idea that we were in Thailand…we wanted to surprise everyone, and Ada's mother (Yai) was shocked but pleased to see us. After paying our respects to Ada's mother, we followed Toy to La and Ba's houses (Ada's sisters)…there were "whoops" of surprise when they came out of their houses and saw me and Amy stood behind Toy, and it was great to see them all again, as it been just over two years since we'd last been in Ban Sam Rung.

The next couple of days were spent relaxing on the front veranda (covered and tiled area in front of the house and where everything happened…eating, chatting, parties etc) before we embarked on a family/friends trip to Ubolratana Dam…Ada, Pechar and Namphon, Ba's daughter (formerly 'son', if you know what I mean), had organized a day out on the water on a large, covered and motorized raft c/w karaoke and bar-b-cue with homemade briquettes. All we had to provide was the food and drink. The usual two trucks, filled with family, friends, food and drink, left Ban Sam Rung and headed to the dam…an hour later we were parked-up in front of many moored up rafts. Initially, there was a problem…Namphon and others were not happy with the raft we'd been given, in typical Isaan fashion there was a lot of shouting and disappointed faces. I sat there totally perplexed and asked Ada what was wrong, and she explained that this raft wasn't what they'd ordered…Namphon, Pechar and a couple of others, along with the raft's pilot, went to see the owner, and I was intrigued to see how this panned out and followed on behind. We found the owner at her property/business on the other side of the car park…a jovial, well-built woman in her fifties, who tried to impress me with her English (as I tried to impress her with my Isaan Thai), explained that the raft given to us matched the price agreed on the telephone…I didn't get directly involved in the negotiations between Namphon and the raft owner, but I did have a small input with suggestions that Namphon translated for her. After around fifteen minutes and an additional 2000 baht (around £40) everyone was smiling…half hour later we'd transferred to an upgraded raft (that pleased everybody) and heading out onto Ubolratana Lake, which has an impressive catchment area of 4,673 square miles. We joined two or three other rafts on the lake, but there was enough distance between us all that each raft couldn't hear the loud music blasting out from the other rafts. A handful of the woman had already got the cooking underway and the delightful smells of fresh fish, chicken and pork wafted across the raft to where I was sitting, immediately igniting pangs of hunger….the raft was now 'rocking' to some familiar and not so familiar Thai tunes, the karaoke had started and people were up dancing…the party was in full swing. Ada told Namphon that I liked a particular and famous Ying Lee song…and I soon found myself singing with Namphon Ying Lee's 'Kau Jai Tur Lak Bur Toh (Your heart for my number)'…well Namphon sang the verses and I sang the chorus, much to the amazed delight of everyone on board, including the pilot…bemused at the farang who could partly sing a popular Thai song. It was very relaxing on the lake, and the shade provided by the roof of the raft, combined with a slight, cooling breeze made it a pleasurable day, enhanced by the wonderful views across the lake…we even had our own guardian, as the large white Buddha of Wat Phra Phutthabat Phu Phan Kham watched over us from high up on the hill that overlooked the lake. Everyone had a great day, but as with all good things our great day on the lake came to an end, around 4ish the pilot guided the raft close to the shore and we all trundled ashore carrying what little food and drink was left over, boarded the trucks and headed back to Ban Sam Rung.

Ada and I headed in to Khon Kaen the following day, to 'HomePro'…Thailand's nearest equivalent to B&Q. I'd mentioned to Ada months earlier that I wanted to paint the family home during our stay in Ban Sam Rung…a sort of thank you for all the times we'd visited. As it was only about a week until the Songkran celebrations began it was a perfect time to do the painting, but as with all visits to a shop with a woman, we came out with far more than what was originally on our list, but at least we had the necessary paint, brushes, scrapers, rollers etc to get the job done…we had, however, spent twice as much as we'd originally planned.

I was up early the following morning, and after a cup of coffee, I was raring to go…as you looked at the house from the front I started in the far corner of the left hand side, on the wall that was next to the buffalo pen (a covered fenced enclosure that held the family's five buffalo). I was happily scraping any flaking paint or rough edges, but as I got closer to the buffalo pen I noticed there were dark bumpy flecks starting to appear on the wall which increased tenfold when I was alongside the pen…it soon became apparent that it was buffalo 'shit' and a fairly straight forward task become a lot more difficult. The buffalo had obviously shat in their pen and then kicked it up the wall in a sort of bovine 'dirty protest'. I spent most of the morning scraping that one wall and trying to think of ways we could protect the wall once it was painted from becoming covered in Buffalo shit again…as I got to the corner that led to the front of the house I noticed a dark fabric they were using at the front of the house as a sort of 'sun screen'. I called Ada over and explained to her that we needed to buy material, similar to the one being used to protect the children from the fierceness of the sun, so we could form a protective screen between the buffalo and the wall of the house…she called Ba's husband (Thom, pronounced 'Tom'), who was building a wall behind the buffalo pen and rice store between our property and Gy's (Ada's friend) adjoining property at the back of the house. He immediately knew what I wanted and where to get it…we immediately measured up and he told Ada that we could go and get it that afternoon, after food. He returned to his wall building and I carried on scraping the remaining walls. After a bite to eat…I drove Thom to a hardware and general store in Ban Bua Yai, a village around five or six kilometres from Ban Sam Rung, and the same village where we'd hired our wedding outfits back in 2011. Within an hour we were back in Ban Sam Rung and fixing the protective screen in place, creating a walkway between the wall of the house and the buffalo pen…when we finished the screen we called it a day and Toy went to the small village shop around the corner and bought three bottles of Chang beer for a few of us to share after a hard day's graft in the fierce Isaan summer.

We started painting in earnest the following day…I started on the exterior, already painted, concreted walls of the ground floor whilst Ba's husband and Ada's nephew, Lair, painted the

568

wooden walls of the first floor with woodstain. Over the next two days, Ba's husband, Lair and I painted the outside of the house and the main ground floor living area (horng nang len – sitting/living room). Ada's sisters and nieces made sure we were fed and watered, and they kept me cool by re-positioning the fan as I worked my way around the house with a roller and paint brush…between the three of us we had improved the appearance of the family home, and I was immensely proud at what we had achieved, and all done with a few days to spare before the beginning of Songkran (Thai New Year). The next day I was back in my second home, 'Snake Village', and was again mesmerized by another heart-stopping show of dare and nerve…albeit in a different arena. Despite 'Snake Village' becoming more commercialized since my first visit, for me it still hasn't lost its dangerous charm and I always enjoy every minute of my trips to this crazy, terrifying and hair-raising village…every time I leave this place, I can't wait to return to see what has changed. From 'Snake Village' we headed back to Ban Sam Rung for something to eat and then drove to Khon Kaen to watch Khon Kaen F.C. play Ubon Ratchathani in a Division 3 game…it was our first time watching Thai proessional football live. We missed the first 5-10 minutes, but thankfully it was still 0-0 when we sat down…the crowd was no more than a couple of thousand, but the noise from the Khon Kaen fans, who were singing their football anthems accompanied by a huge drum, was great fun, and relentless (they didn't stop throughout the whole game). About five minutes after we'd sat down, Khon Kaen took the lead which they doubled just before half time. During the interval we walked around to the club shop and I bought Khon Kaen football shirts for the three of us…they were fantastic quality and only £10 each. It wasn't long after halftime that Khon Kaen made it 3-0, but despite dominating possession, it was Ubon Ratchathani that scored a late consolation goal. After the game we met up with some of the family at a free concert in Khon Kaen…fantastic live music, and stunning costumes from the dancers/singers (a different one for each song)… great time was had by all, and it was a relief to get to bed that night after the busy day we'd had.

It was another early start as Ada, Amy, La, Pa, New and I travelled to Wat Kham Chanot…a temple in Udon Thani province, but one I had never heard of previously and had no idea what to expect. After a two hour drive we arrived at Wat Kham Chanot and it was complete chaos…it was similar to what I imagine the traffic to be at a music festival, there were vehicles and people everywhere, but we managed to find a parking space on a piece of waste ground adjacent to a village shop, that had been turned into a temporary car park for about fifteen cars. After parking up we were directed by a young car park attendant toward the shop, where the shop owner charged us 100 baht. But at least we had managed to park close to what looked like a tented village…a mix of restaurants and market stalls, and there were lottery sellers everywhere. For those of you that don't know, the Thai people have an obsession with the lottery, and you don't just pop into a shop and buy lottery tickets like we do in the UK, in Thailand lottery tickets are sold by individual vendors, which are found anywhere and everywhere, who display pre-printed tickets in a type of open briefcase, hung around their necks. I was still in the dark about this temple, as despite seeing a large gold standing Buddha, and a couple of typical buildings you associate with Thai temples, there didn't appear to be anything of note within this complex, and the only information I could get from Ada was something about a 'big snake' and 'good luck'. But, first things first, it was time to eat and almost immediately we found ourselves seated in one of the tented restaurants. Eventually, after food and buying lottery tickets, we strolled through an avenue of market stalls that sold drinks, t-shirts and religious ornaments/jewellery. We passed numerous lottery vendors who tried to sell as more tickets, but who then became amused at the 'farang' shouting back "SEU LEAO…SEU LEAO" (an example of reduplication in Isaan Thai which means "I've bought already"). We finally made it to an area where many, many people were removing their footwear and placing them in the racks provided, before heading down a walled walkway with a seven headed Naga on either side and their bodies heading off into the distance, but acting as brightly coloured handrails for the sea of people on the walkway, one group on the left-hand side walking across to an island in the middle of a large lake, and others on the right-hand side returning from the same island. After a two to three hundred metre walk we emerged into a forested area on the 'island' teeming with people, and which I presumed was the 'main attraction'…it was very chaotic and I quickly became separated from the others. People were paying their respects to

570

Phaya Naga (a mythical semi-deity) that is said to live on the island…the King of Naga gave shelter to the great Lord Buddha when he was in the midst of a long meditation, and before his enlightenment. I began to understand its importance to the Thai people, hence the temple's popularity…there was even an old, large tree with many of its roots above ground and people were pouring water or putting talcum powder on the twisted roots in the hope that they reveal numbers they can use as their winning lottery numbers….hence the high number of lottery vendors at the temple. The large crowds were a bit overwhelming in the intense heat and it was a relief to return over the bridge, put our shoes back on and head back to the car, after popping in to a local shop to buy well-needed cold drinks for everyone. We were soon on our way back to Ban Sam Rung, but the roads remained busy until we had reached the Khon Kaen side of Udon Thani…it wasn't a place I would be keen on visiting again, purely because of the crowds and I was happy to reach the relative calmness of Ban Sam Rung later that evening.

Songkran was upon us and the fun began, and leading the way was Ada's sister, Nang…soaking everything and everyone that came past the house, and encouraging the children to do the same…Nang is a wonderful person who has a big heart and the kids love her. Everyone was wearing various flowery (Hawaiian style) patterned shirts, traditional attire for Songkran and there was a definite party atmosphere in the air. That same afternoon around twenty of us climbed aboard Ada's truck and headed for Nong Wai Dam (a river a few kilometres north of Khon Kaen city and just off Highway 2). I was driving and was directed through the back roads, to avoid the villages and the inevitable soaking we would have had…not fair, as we had nothing to retaliate with (no barrel of water and bowls, and no water pistols). We reached the Nong Wai River about forty minutes after we'd left Ban Sam Rung, parked up and we all headed for the river…accessed through tented riverside restaurants. Eventually, we were all sat on rocks or paddling in the cool, shallow, but clear waters of the river and the children, including Amy, were having fun in the river (the older ones were riding down a gentle rapid on inflated inner-tubes…oh to be a child again. After an hour or so we headed back into Khon Kaen for the Songkran celebrations around the Central Plaza, City Pillar (the centre of a Thai city, and in this case the temple or 'City Pillar' was called Thewasathan Phra Mae Thoranee) and Sri Chant Road. Fifteen minutes later we had parked the truck next to Thanarak Arusorn Public Park, across the road from Central Plaza. It was hot, but overhead there were dark clouds gathering…it looked as if a storm was on its way. Ada and I left the others sat on the grass whilst Amy and the other children played in the park, but when Ada and I were in Sri Chant Road we were soon joined by Ker, Lair and their cousin (their father's sister's daughter) Toy…it was still light, but the crowds were getting bigger and wherever you looked everyone was happy, smiling and laughing, and it was fantastic witnessing such an abundance of joy. It was around this time that a Thai news team (36 PPTV) approached me and asked if they could interview me, I happily agreed…they asked me a few questions such as "where was I from?", "was I enjoying Thailand?", "what did I think of Songkran?", when they had finished I took a selfie with them and then they disappeared into the crowd. Ada and I briefly returned to the others in the park, but headed back to Sri Chant Road when it started to get dark…there must have been over 100,000 people in that central part of Khon Kaen. We were stood about one hundred metres from the main stage, where Sri Chant Road met Pracha Samran Road, ideally placed for the impending 'human wave' (at the time of writing the Songkran 'human wave' at Khon Kaen in 2019 is now the longest human wave ever as recorded in Guiness Book of Records…the 1.4km road was filled with people and 'wave' went back and forth five times). The excitement was building and looking down Sri Chant Road it was a sea people and staggered stages where bands played live music. The announcer started speaking and I sensed that the 'human wave' was about to start as people started to crouch down, so we joined them…you could feel the tension and anticipated excitement reaching a crescendo as the countdown started "Seep…gow…baet…jet… (10, 9, 8, 7…)" .When "neung (1)" was shouted out the 'human wave' started close to the stage and with perfect timing we stood up with our hands in the air and for a few moments stood there watching the 'human wave' disappear down Sri Chant Road. We, and everyone else, crouched down and a few minutes later the 'human wave' could be seen heading back toward us and then "WHOO" and up I jumped with everyone else, crouched down again, and almost immediately jumped up again and again watched the 'human wave' disappear down Sri Chant Road for a second time. As with most Thai celebrations there was a third 'wave' for good luck, quickly followed by two more. Once the 'wave' was all over, we walked into Sri Chant Road, and stood between the first two stages, and the live music and dancers were entertaining the crowds, we decided not to venture any further in to the melee as it was nigh on impossible to move. But everyone was still happy in this unbelievable atmosphere. We (Ker, Toy and I) decided to walk back to the Chang sponsored area in front of the Central Plaza…when we got there it was bedlam as an excellent band was playing on a central stage…Ker and Toy were soon dancing when the band started playing what was obviously a popular song, and they also joined in with many others singing along with the band. At that point the pretty promotion girls dressed in denim shorts and Chang beer vests and stood on strategically placed towers starting hosing everyone with water…it was carnage, there wasn't a dry person in the whole area, including me, by the time the song finished…it was great fun and I was wetter than wet, but we didn't care, it was bloody fantastic and the biggest party I'd ever attended. After getting drenched again we made our way back to the others in the park and were soon joined by Ada, the other Toy and Lair, and around an hour later we were back in Ban Sam Rung and completely dry…thanks to the heat of the evening…what an absolutely brilliant day.

The following day we again met the 'lucky man' and it was again an honour to be part of the ceremony to give us good luck on our remaining travels in Thailand and our journey back to the UK…even the part where he sprayed/spat water in our faces didn't bother me…it was the inevitable farewell that I wasn't looking forward to. Each time we left Ban Sam Rung it became more emotional than the previous farewell and I knew that I would genuinely miss my Thai family and friends…they were now a big part of my life and the farewell was always the part of the holiday I dreaded. With the 'lucky man' safely returned to his village, and the group photographs behind us, the pain of leaving had arrived and there were many tears, myself included…but it was time to leave, and as we reversed out of the driveway a wall of sad faces stared back at us and as we drove off I waved and shouted "KOY HAK MOO JOW…BPY GON DER" (I love you all…goodbye, I'm going now). I looked in the mirror one last time and whispered "koy hak moo jow…koy hak", turned the corner and a few minutes later Ban Sam Rung once again disappeared in the rear view mirror.

We were heading to Khao Yai National Park, the largest national park in Thailand, and located SE of Nakhon Ratchasima, but it was soon evident that we'd picked the wrong day to travel…it was the last day of the Songkran holidays and all those people that had travelled from other parts of Thailand (mainly Bangkok) to their family homes and villages, were now heading back to their jobs in Bangkok. Highway 2 was busier than I'd ever seen, even the additional lane they were using from the northbound side of the highway wasn't making much difference…we crawled toward Nakhon Ratchasima and a journey that should have taken around four to four and a half hours, took us around eight to nine hours…it was like travelling on the M25 in rush hour, but for five hundred kilometres. We finally reached our hotel, a stunning boutique hotel called Phuwanalee Resort, a resort hidden away in a jungle paradise.

After breakfast the following morning and visiting a few shops, we headed into the national park, and after paying the entrance fee, we stopped at a small shrine for around ten minutes before continuing up a long, uphill and winding road, surrounded to our left and right by thick and unrelenting vegetation, that led to a 'viewpoint' where the views were spectacular…you could see right down into the valley where the hotel and resort complexes were located, a world away from the jungle paradise we now found ourselves in, and the diverse animal life started to reveal itself with breeds of birds I'd not seen before in Thailand, macaques, barking deer and strange squirrel like animals. The forested hills of Dong Phayayen Khao Yai that surrounded us were stunningly beautiful, and as the shadows of the broken cloud rested on these forested hills it changed the lush green colours into dark grey creating a blend of wonderful coloured features, enhancing the beauty of the scenic views before us…charming and serene, but rugged and mysterious at the same time. We continued on, keeping an eye out for wild elephants, and after a couple of kilometres we drove into the park headquarters where there was a food court, small museum/exhibition centre and souvenir shop…it was approaching lunchtime so we decided to have some food. Once we'd had lunch, walked around the conservation museum and booked tickets for a night safari we headed for Pha Kluai Mai Waterfall. After parking up the truck, we were soon walking on an undulating path through the dense jungle…the first thing I noticed was the deafening noises of the hidden jungle insects. We could also hear the distinct sounds of toucans and gibbons, and whilst we did see a single toucan fly overhead, we never saw a single gibbon…this shy, but noisy, primate remained well hidden in this jungle abyss. Looking at the adjacent riverbed it was probably the wrong time of year to see waterfalls as it was the dry season, and apart from the occasional stagnant pool between large rocks, the riverbed was almost dry. However, walking down this jungle path was fascinating, but eerily scary at the same time…it was difficult to see any more than a couple of metres into the jungle as in places, on either side of the path we were faced with a wall of dense vegetation, and there was a continual sense that we were being watched. Allegedly, there had been no evidence of tigers living in Khao Yai for around twenty years, but it didn't settle the nerves completely, considering that tigers are 'masters' at staying hidden and the fact that there are still clouded leopards in the jungles of Khao Yai was a bit disconcerting. We came across a small clearing and there was a huge tree stretching into the sky above, angled over the path with a large vine hanging down and almost touching the floor…it was too good an opportunity to miss, we all had a go but I couldn't resist swinging on the vine and letting out a strangled 'Tarzan' like cry "AAAH-AH-AH-AH-AH…", great fun. We accepted the fact that we weren't going to see any waterfalls and turned around, walked back to the truck and returned to the hotel. After freshening up and popping for a coffee in a small, but unique, shopping centre that, for some reason, was styled on a Tuscany style Italian village called Palio Khao Yai…strange but very beautiful with its clocktower, narrow cobbled streets, individual shops and buildings in rustic oranges, browns and terracottas. It was almost dusk when we left and by the time we had re-entered the national park and parked up at the park headquarters it was completely dark. It wasn't long before we were sitting on the back of an open truck peering into the darkness and half-light, from a small search light that our ranger was using to find wildlife. Ocassionally, we would see

575

the reflection of many eyes as we passed a group of Barking and Sambar deer. We also saw a solitary wild elephant, a porcupine and various birds and an abundance of fire flies. It was a great experience, not so much for the animals we did see but for the expectation of the animals that we might, but didn't see. However, the highlight for me was when we returned to the car park and the ranger found, what the Thai people call, a 'jackadan', but is probably some type of cicada, and is probably the ugliest and loudest insect I have ever seen, the noise it made was horrendous. Once back at the hotel we had another wonderful meal and headed off to bed to have a good night's sleep for another long journey ahead of us to Koh Chang.

The following morning after another fine breakfast and loading up the truck we set-off for Koh Chang, an island close to the city of Trat, a border city close to neighbouring Cambodia. The quickest way to get to Trat was to cut right through Khao Yai National Park, but Ada was not happy that we had to pay (again), which was plainly evident to anyone within a hundred metre radius of the entrance booth, and also the office at the exit gate…it was not an auspicious start to our, what would become an 'eventful' journey. Around half way between Prachin Buri and Chantaburi we hit an unbelievable storm and when it rains in Thailand, my God does it rain…almost immediately, we were driving on roads that resembled shallow rivers, there must have been around 6-8 inches of surface water covering the roads. With the rain, rising water levels, the thunder and bolts of lightning, that were too close for comfort, it was a very scary experience, but thankfully as quick as it had started, it stopped and we continued on our journey as the the dark clouds gave way to clear blue skies and glorious sunshine. The final eventful part of the journey occurred about twenty kilometres before Trat as we approached another 'checkpoint' (we'd driven through one on the approach to Chantaburi), with armed police and soldiers. As we approached this checkpoint I slowed down and joined a short queue of three or four vehicles, almost immediately, it was our turn to drive through the checkpoint, but a police officer signaled for us to pull in on the right hand side behind another vehicle. The same police officer walked over to the driver's side of the vehicle and tapped on the glass,

I lowered the electric window and smiled at the police officer and said,

"Sawadee Kap"

Completely expressionless he replied with, "Licence?"

I reached for my wallet and pulled out my driving licence and handed it to him saying,

"It's an international driving licence"

"Without looking up he angrily said "You cannot use in Thailand" and without saying anything else he turned and walked away...with my driving licence. Ada, already angry was not having this and jumped out of the truck and set-off in hot pursuit of the police officer, shouting and ranting in Thai, as she approached a couple of senior officers sitting in the shade beneath a large gazeebo at the side of the road. Ada was screaming in unintelligible Thai and pointing at the CCTV cameras overhead...I honestly thought she was going to get arrested if she continued with this behaviour, but after a few minutes she was walking back to the car, occasionally turning, shouting and pointing at the police officers, and as she got closer I could see she was holding my driving licence and another piece of paper.

"What's that?" I asked

"Your fine for having no licence"

She passed me the piece of paper , but it was all in Thai...the only thing I could make out was the '90 baht', my fine for driving in Thailand without a valid licence was equivalent to around £2...no points on my licence or a hefty fine...£2. Ada told me that the policeman was hoping to make some additional money for himself, but she wasn't going to let that happen and demanded they write a ticket...Ada is a formidable person, as the policemen at that checkpoint could now testify. With Ada now behind the wheel, the police waved us on and I secretly think that ours was one vehicle they regretted stopping that day. We eventually made it to the ferry terminal, and thankfully, with plenty of time to spare. After a short wait of around thirty to forty minutes we were marshalled onto the ferry and heading to Koh Chang, whilst I stayed on the vehicle deck, Amy and Ada climbed the decks to the passenger deck and were soon waving at me from the highest point of the ferry. The sun was low in the sky as we crossed the short channel between the mainland and Thailand's third biggest island (Phuket is the biggest, with Koh Samui being the second biggest)...the reflection of the low sun shimmered across the ocean, and these silvery tentacles provided another idyllic sunset to add to many others we had seen on our many travels in Thailand. The crossing was only twenty to thirty minutes and the ferry was soon approaching the hard concrete standing of the landing port, and within minutes we were driving off the ferry and out of the ferry terminal. It was only around three kilometres to White Sand Beach, therefore, around ten minutes after leaving the ferry terminal we were parked-up outside our hotel, the Erewan. After booking-in to the hotel and quickly settling in to our room, we walked across the road and down a twenty metre path to an absolutely stunning beach of white sand and palm trees, that looked even more spectacular with the setting sun and the lights of various beachside bars and restaurants…the twinkling lights disappeared off into the distance in a blur of magical colours. The sun disappeared below the horizon, and the almost instantaneous darkness made it seem as if the ocean had extinguished the flamed setting sun.

We spent three great days at this wonderful hotel and after previously spending four days on the hedonistic island of Phuket, we found that Koh Chang was far more relaxed and less busy. However, we did ask if we could move to a room at the back of the hotel, as Ada was struggling to get to sleep due to the live music coming from the bar next door…the hotel staff were excellent as they reacted immediately and we, and all our belongings, were moved to a quieter room within minutes. Over the next few days we visited Khlong Phlu Waterfall, a beautiful waterfall that was situated in a stunning forested valley, spent time on the beautiful sun-kissed beach of white sand with its warm water and stunning views of the island and spent evenings in the hotel's rooftop pool or at the poolside bar watching the spectacular sunsets whilst sipping Singha beer. We also ventured out into the main, and only, street to browse amongst the market stalls and enjoy some wonderful food in one of the many Thai style restaurants…I love Koh Chang, it is a very relaxing and laidback place to visit and great for families to recharge their batteries before heading back to their hectic western lifestyles. On our last full day we spent the morning snorkeling off one of the smaller islands off Koh Chang as the previous evening we had paid for a snorkeling trip. The transport picked us up from our hotel and took us to Kaibae pier where a speed boat took us across to this little island…I have never seen waters so clear as they were off this small island and the views across the water back to Koh Chang were spectacular. The fish in this clear water were as intrigued about us as we were about them and they were soon nibbling at your legs and feet if you stood in one place for longer than a few seconds. We saw our first hermit crab on the beach and despite the fierce sun, there was a slight cooling breeze that made standing on the beach a pleasurable experience. It was a great morning out and a great taste of the paradise that is provided by Koh Chang and other islands in this part of Thailand…an absolutely stunning part of SE Asia, if it's a more peaceful holiday you are after then I would recommend Koh Chang over Phuket, Koh Samui, Koh Phangan etc. After returning to our hotel, having quick showers we headed out and drove to Kai Bae viewpoint…a place that provided great views over the island group we'd snorkeled at earlier, and was a great place to take family photos, with the backdrop of a huge 'TRAT' sign in the colours of the Thai flag and the ocean, islands, beautiful gardens and blue skies, it was perfect.

It was sad to leave Koh Chang, but our holiday was drawing to an end, and after catching the ferry back to the mainland and a three hour drive back to Bangkok, we were booking in to the Royal Princess…a stunning hotel close to all the sights and somewhere we had stayed before. We were soon joined by Nang, Pechar and Toy, and the six of us, somehow, managed to squeeze into a tuk tuk who took us the short distance to Khao San Road. This hectic and bustling street was no different to how it was on our last visit…a sea of nationalities browsing the market stalls for last minute souvenirs or enjoying a welcome drink in one of the many bars. Where Khao Yai was a jungle of dense vegetation, Khao San Road was a jungle of people, shops, food stalls, restaurants and bars and 'lit-up' signs advertising anything and everything. It was a street that not only confused the visionary sense, but the senses of smell and sound. Your nostrils are confronted with a range of aromas that melt into a fused sense of the unknown, both sickening and pleasing my sensory reception. And the confusion was compounded by the reverberating hum of noise that finally overloads your senses, but leaves you wanting more. A fascinating place to visit, but a relief to leave, and after a long day Ada, Amy and I were relieved to finally get into bed.

We wanted to visit the Grand Palace again and the following morning we attempted to make our way to this iconic landmark…on previous visits it had been easy to park and there were no queues. However, it was utter chaos in and around the palace…King Bhumibol Adulyadej (Rama IX) had passed away on 13 October 2016, it was now April 2017 and he had been lying in state at the Grand Palace since the end of October 2016. The nation was in mourning and we were caught up in the crowds of mourners, dressed in black and wanting to pay their respects to their beloved king, crowds of tourists trying to get in to the Grand Palace and people going about their everyday business. King Bhumibol was on the throne for almost 68 years, therefore, he was the only monarch that most of Thailand's population had ever known, and a king that had done so many positive things for his country, particularly in rural areas…I had watched a documentary on this wonderful monarch and I remember the narrator saying that "when he ascended to the throne the country loved him because he was the king, but before he died they loved the king because it was him"…you can't get a bigger compliment that that. We eventually made it through the security blanket around the palace, through the tens of thousands of mourners, and were in a short queue to enter this amazing, beautiful palace complex. The area that housed 'The Temple of the Emerald Buddha' was bustling with tourists, all attempting to comprehend the beauty of the buildings, statues, murals and gardens that surrounded them. Much of the palace was understandably closed off, as King Bhumibol was lying in state in 'Dusit Maha Prasat Throne Hall', within the grounds of the Grand Palace…you could sense the Thai nation's loss at losing a much respected and much loved king. Once our tour had finished we made our way out of the palace, following other tourists on a designated route away from the palace and past the area, shrouded in secrecy, where soldiers and construction workers were building structures for the king's elaborate funeral celebrations that were due to begin in October 2017…when we were outside the security perimeter we flagged down a taxi and headed back to the Royal Princess hotel.

Our holiday was over, another unbelievable trip had come to an end, and apart from visiting Nang and her husband we left Bangkok and headed for the Orchid Resort, Lat Krabang (near Suvanabhumi Airport). We spent our last night in this quaint little hotel, and after breakfast drove the couple of kilometres to the airport…Nang, her husband, Pechar and Toy came to see us off, and after hugs and wais all round, we took the escalator up to immigration, as our farewell party waved frantically and smiled at us, and a sadness again enveloped us all as we waved back one final time before disappearing from view behind the frosted glass and joined the queue through immigration.

Chapter 10 – Miscellaneous

The 'Thomas' Children

As you have read your way through this slightly different type of autobiography it wouldn't have escaped your attention that I have six children. They were introduced to you when I described their births, and in 'K's case, his amazing adoption (his biological father's unforgiving desertion which opened the door for me to happily become his legal father, something I grabbed with open arms and an open heart), and the children have also cropped up in other parts of the book. I am fiercely proud of my children, and as you've also seen, I am very protective and have invariably been involved in various battles with their mother; British legal system; school teachers; doctors and even the Welsh F.A. (Football Association), but only when I strongly believe they are or have been victims of some injustices of life. There have been shared experiences both good, bad and indifferent and where possible we have faced things together...as a family. Like any good parent, I love my children and their joy is my joy, but equally their pain is my pain and whilst there has been great joy with holidays; Christmases; day trips; parties etc, there has also been the pain of illnesses; injuries; and separation. I appreciate life is life and I know our shared experiences could be considered better or worse than the experiences of others, but through the laughter and tears we are still here today and still close, regardless of the trials or joyous events that life has thrown at us. I would like to share some additional experiences with you all, some of which were shared collectively, some individual classics and some you wouldn't want to see repeated in this or future generations or experienced by others. I have tried to be fair, loving, impartial, supportive and sometimes brutally honest, but I am human and therefore, imperfect and have and will make mistakes, but I have tried my best and I guess, as parents, that's all we can do.

As with most families with young children, the early years were very difficult financially. Firstly, for the first ten or so years my wages as a soldier, and in the civilian life that followed, were considerably lower than the average living wage at the time (I didn't pay tax in one job as the wages were so low). My ex-wife and I went through a period of 'robbing Peter to pay Paul' and the financial insecurity meant we went through some extremely lean periods…one particular time I remember was when she was pregnant with 'G' and the only food we had in the house (it was the day before pay day) were two tins of Kwik Save 'No Frills' vegetable soup and three slices of bread. 'K' and 'R' shared one tin and one slice of bread and my wife and I shared the other tin and had a slice of bread each. Whilst the soup was being warmed, next door's cat strolled in and started licking the butter off my wife's slice of bread - the cat was shooed away and I can confirm that the bread wasn't wasted! Despite the tough times we always made sure that every year the children had a good Christmas, which normally resulted in us paying off a loan or catalogues in those early years of marriage, finishing in November before going through the same process all over again. As a result, my wife and I didn't buy each other presents for the first few years, and this was a sacrifice, like other families, we were happy to make so our children would have a good Christmas. We must have made the right choices as we'd hear the kids say 'this is the best Christmas EVER!' year after year. Despite the financial difficulties we also managed to enjoy a few holidays…nothing exciting like Disneyworld, Spain, Greece or Turkey, but nevertheless a week in a caravan or holiday chalet in Dawlish, Ilfracombe or Filey was still a holiday…the holiday in Ilfracomble was spent with my wife's parents.These holidays still provided the children with some great and happy memories that they could look back on with fondness.

Eventually the financial strain became too much, we separated and then divorced. The difficulties, already documented, were experienced by everyone, but it also heralded the beginning of a new chapter when I bought (with a mortgage) a terraced house on High Street, Abertridwr…around 400m from the family home in Bryngelli Terrace. I made a conscious decision to try and become a better father, as toward the end of the marriage I didn't believe my skills as a father were the best, due to the worry of the financial strain we were continually under and the realization that I had never loved their mother. As a result, this had quite a negative effect on all the relationships in the family unit, therefore, the separation/divorce was probably best for all concerned. I wanted to use this fresh start to become a real 'hands-on' father not a father that turned up once every 2-3 weeks, took the children to McDonalds and then took them home again. I wanted to develop and maintain strong and emotional relationships with all my children, I wanted to give them the support, stability and a loving home that I had never experienced with my own parents. Therefore, I fought for decent access resulting in them spending every weekend (Friday to midday Sunday) and two hours on a Tuesday and two hours on a Thursday, in fact they were free to knock anytime they were passing, and during the summer evenings I would find myself playing football on 'the green' opposite the YMCA or playing tennis down Abertridwr Park with the older children. Additionally, I would have the children for 2 weeks in the summer holidays plus one of the half-terms and also alternate Christmas Eve's (one year they would come over Christmas Eve, stay overnight and return to their mother Christmas Day lunchtime, and the following year they would come to me Christmas Day afternoon and stay Christmas night) and New Years Eve's. I also made sure I attended every parents evening, sports day or Christmas Nativity plays. I made sure I provided a normal routine for them all, which involved home-cooked meals and Saturday evenings were normally spent watching Casualty and Match of the Day or we'd hire a film and get some 'goodies' in or we'd play board games (mainly 'Monopoly', trying to make sure 'G' didn't cheat). They had their own beds, wardrobes (filled with clothes), toys etc…I believe that I provided the stability, support, beans and corned beef pasties on a Friday, love they needed, somewhere they could call 'home' and somewhere they could bring their friends, and it is where I still live today and a home that has provided a sackful of memories.

Everything was pretty good but then 'Middlesbrough' happened and the equilibrium of this stable and good life was well and truly turned on its head. The family was ripped in two, with 'A' and 'Rh' moving to Middlesbrough with their mother, and the older three staying in Wales ('G' lived with me and my then second wife and her two children, whilst I ashamedly forced 'R' to live in Caerphilly and 'K' in Taffs Well, which are not episodes I am proud of. But as part of the fall-out when my second marriage ended, 'R' and 'K' eventually came to live with me and 'G'. This tumultuous event occurred when 'K' was 20 years old, 'R' was 18 years old, 'G' was 16 years old and 'A' and 'Rh' were 9 years old, and this situation put a hefty strain on a lot of relationships and was probably the main reason my second marriage ended. I had fought to keep the twins in Wales…and failed and fought to save my second marriage…and failed. Unfortunately, I was left a broken man with low self esteem and a shattered confidence resulting in me having to climb out of another hole, partially created by my ex-wife, it was a very difficult time that set me back emotionally and financially…I needed counselling to help me move forward and was forced to take a second job whilst I paid off two hefty solicitors bills that totalled between £8-9k. But we all came through it and after three years, and about a month after Amy was born (I had met Ada in Jan 2009 and in April 2010 we welcomed Amy into the world), 'A' and 'Rh' returned to Wales, and the re-building began. It was wonderful to watch the siblings re-connect and again become close (if not closer), as they were before.

That was almost ten years ago and I have watched 'K' endure some personal difficulties but he's had family support and at the time of writing seems to be in a much better emotional place. I have watched 'R' and her long-term partner, Gareth, become proud parents to two beautiful daughters (Alexa and Louisa), and buy a house about 50m from where I live. I have watched 'G' start and complete an apprenticeship as a Plumber and Pipefitter with Lorne Stewart and also qualify as an air conditioning engineer. He is now travelling and after visiting India, Malaysia, Thailand, Vietnam and Singapore he's in Australia. I have watched 'A' be very successful academically gaining a string of high grades in her GSCE's and A Levels and who is now in her final year of a Business and Finance degree at Cardiff University and on the verge of moving in with her long-term boyfriend, Matthew. I have watched 'Rh' find his niche and has become, after a few years, a successful support worker for disabled and people suffering from mental health issues and he's genuinely lucky that he has found a job he loves, and a girl he loves, Ellie. Finally, Amy is approaching her final year in junior school and she is a loving, caring and very confident young lady (like her mother) who I'm sure will have a bright future in front of her.

Looking back there are some special memories we have created and here are a few for you to hopefully enjoy…

585

The Green Metro

A few months after buying 67 High Street, I was still without a car, but that was about to change and I was soon the proud owner of a metallic light green Metro. I was over the moon and couldn't wait to show the children…their reaction wasn't what I expected!

It was Friday and after driving home from work I parked the car, the eleven year old green metro, around the corner from the house in Brookfield Street, I got out of the car took one last loving look, and feeling very pleased with myself walked to the house to wait for the children's imminent arrival. I didn't have to wait long, as a few minutes later I heard the stampede of footsteps outside the front door before the door opened and they all poured in, 'K' first, followed by 'R' ushering in the twins, 'A' and 'Rh' and 'G' brought up the rear, all out of breath from running down the hill. There was a fragmented "Hiya dad" from them all before 'K' headed to the fridge for his customary chocolate. I tried to calm the usual bedlam that was unfolding before me and just managed to stop 'Rh' and 'A' disappear upstairs in their usual game of 'chase'. I succeeded in calming them down by shouting "I'VE GOT A SURPRISE FOR YOU ALL", the intrigue got the better of them and then the whispered nagging started,
"What is it?"
"I bet it's a DVD"
"Is it a dog…are we having a dog?
"Are we going on holiday?"
"Holiday…where to?"
"I bet it's a caravan somewhere…it won't be Spain, Dad can't afford it!"
Laughing at the chaos in front of me I waved my arms and said "No, no, no…it's not a dog or a holiday…follow me"
I could hear them whispering behind me as we walked down the street and just before we turned into Brookfield Street I stopped them and asked them all to close their eyes. When I was satisfied all their eyes were closed I ushered them around the corner to where the green Metro was parked and told them to open their eyes. They all opened their eyes and the twins were jumping up and down shouting "A CAR, A CAR, A CAR…" before turning and hugging a leg each, looking up and shouting in unison, "THANK YOU DADDY". I looked at

'K', 'R' and 'G' who were all staring at the green
Metro…they were speechless.
"Well…what do you think?"
'K' broke the silence with "It's a Metro", quickly followed by
'R' with "So embarrassing!" and she tutted, turned and walked
back to the house, followed by 'K' and 'G'. Not the reaction I
was hoping for, "perhaps they'll warm to it…" I thought,
"…but at least the twins liked it…so difficult to impress a
thirteen year old, eleven year old and a nine year old" and
laughed to myself as I headed back to the house with the 'A'
and 'Rh', who were still hanging on to a leg each.

I'd like to say the older children warmed to the green metro,
but I'd be lying, they remained embarrassed by the 'green box
on wheels', as they called it' and would lie down in the car as
we drove through the village, so their friends hopefully
wouldn't see them, and if they were asked "did I see you in a
green car yesterday?", they would all deny it. The
embarrassment intensified if we went out for the day and
travelled on the M4…the old Metro would shake violently at
65mph, so I would sit in the inside lane at a steady 60mph
with the world speeding past. I can honestly say that all the
times we drove on the M4 we never overtook a single vehicle,
but we'd always get to our destination, places such as Barry
Island; Porthcawl; Ogmore-by-Sea; the Gower; Bristol Zoo
etc…even if it did take quite a bit longer. The real test for the
old Metro was always the trip back up the hill to their
mother's house on Sunday mornings, only a trip of around
400m, "what could be so difficult?" I hear you say. For those
who don't know the Aber valley, my house is located two
thirds the way up High Street, on a steady incline from Aber
square, before flattening out where the road headed to
Senghenydd at the end of our terrace block, where an Indian
takeaway was (and still is) located. However, to get to their
mother's house, there was a right turn up a hill, opposite the
Indian takeaway, possibly the steepest hill in the valley,
Bryngelli Terrace…and their mother lived three-quarters the
way up. We'd leave my house, squeeze everyone into the car
and try to build-up as much speed as we could before we got
to the Indian takeaway, praying that no-one was crossing the
pelican crossing and that no-one was driving down from
Senghenydd, so we could get as far up Bryngelli as we
possibly could. The car would lose power as we battled

587

against the steep incline and provided we'd had a clear run we'd make it to the turning to 'Top Rock', just past their mother's house, but other time's we'd fall about ten yards short…we'd all be in the car shouting "COME ON, COME ON, COME ON…" in encouragement at the 'green box', but she'd typically not listen, but when we were successful there was always a collective cheer….happy days.

We had the 'old green Metro' about twelve to fourteen months before I bought a much better (and cooler) Ford Orion, but that little old Metro served the family well for the short time we had it and even got me to Leeds and back for a wedding and to Barnsley and back for football, and it will always have a soft spot for me as it enabled me to take the children places, not just on the weekend, but also in the week…unfortunately for 'K', 'R' and 'G' it will always be a source of embarrassment and hilarity…"Kids eh!"

The Welsh F.A.

When 'G' was thirteen he played football for Caerphilly Cavaliers and one week he was sent off, not on the field during the game, but in the changing rooms, after the game had ended, by a referee on an unbelieveable power trip. I'm not saying that 'G' was innocent, but there should have been a modicum of common sense displayed by the referee before he brandished a red card. This is the story leading up to that incident, immediately after the incident and in the months that followed…when a joke resulted in me not just fighting for justice for 'G' but for all under 16s involved in football under the umbrella of the South Wales Football Association.

The referee blew the final whistle and 'G's' team, Caerphilly Cavaliers, had lost 1-0 to a gritty and determined Llantrisant side who had probably deserved the win…they were the first to every ball and wanted the win more. However, there was a glimpse of a chance for Caerphilly Cavaliers just before the end of the game that came in the guise of a thunderous shot from outside the area that hit the underside of the bar and bounced straight down (reminiscent of the Hurst goal for England in the World Cup final of 1966), and the decision could have gone either way, but with no official linesmen in junior football to support the referee, it was left to the 'man in the middle' who was stood in the centre circle facing the goal, and he decided that it wasn't a goal and waved play on, which was probably the fairest decision given the way that Llantrisant had played. As I walked back to the car with 'Rh' and 'A' the referee was striding across the park with a face like thunder, I jovially shouted across "YOU COULD HAVE DONE WITH AN OFFICIAL LINESMAN WHEN THAT SHOT HIT THE BAR AND BOUNCED DOWN REF...IT WOULD HAVE MADE YOUR LIFE EASIER" and I smiled. The referee didn't break stride and just glared at me and shouted back "IN YOUR OPINION". Despite witnessing a refereeing display by someone who made the entire game all about him...there was no leniency to boys still learning how to play and as a result he didn't give either team a chance, blowing up at every minor indiscretion which frankly spoilt the game. He had refereed the game as if it was being played by seasoned professionals, but still, I could believe what I had just heard and stood there gobsmacked for a second, thinking "who the hell does he think he is?" before continuing to the car with 'A' and 'Rh'. Around ten minutes later a couple of 'G's' team mates walked past the car and shouted "'G' HAS JUST BEEN SENT OFF IN THE CHANGING ROOMS" "WHAT?" not believing what I had just heard, and they repeated what they said. I shot out of the car, and with Rh and A marched back to the changing rooms where 'G' was stood and I asked him, "Is it true? Have you just been sent off?" 'G', nodded sheepishly confirming it was true. "What the hell for?" and he showed me what he'd done, putting his hand in the air in a nazi salute and his other hand over his top lip in the typical comic gesture...that everyone was aware was a joke, obviously everyone except this referee. I looked at the referee and laughed saying "Are you for real? He's thirteen, he doesn't even know the proper meaning of what he's just done...unbelieveable, you're having a laugh". At this point, 'G's' coach, Stuart, pulled me away as he could see how angry I was and said "Don't worry, we'll appeal"...and appeal we did, against this ridiculous decision, especially as the referee shouldn't have even entered the changing rooms without another adult being present.

The day had arrived for 'G's' disciplinary hearing in Cardiff with the South Wales F.A. and we met Stuart in the car park outside a non-descript building at a sports ground not too far away from the Heath Hospital. As we approached the building, Stuart assured me it would all be fairly relaxed…"they will call us in, ask a few questions and then we'll leave the room and the referee will then be called in and asked a few question, then, after a short deliberation by the disciplinary committee, both parties will be called in together to hear the decision…" Stuart continued "As it's a junior matter, there'll only be three or four committee members present and it'll all be carried out within an informal environment…don't worry, it'll be fine" and he winked. I felt better knowing it would be dealt with in a sympathetic manner, given 'G's' age, and smiled at Stuart as we sat down outside the committee room waiting to be called.

Around ten minutes later, the door opened and an old lady popped her around it smiling and asked "'G' Thomas?", Stuart stood up and said "Yes", looked at me and 'G' and motioned for us to follow him. We stood up and 'G' followed Stuart, with me bringing up the rear. I was totally unprepared for what was waiting for us on the other side of that previously closed door!

I was the last to enter the room and couldn't believe that the whole South Wales F.A. Disiplinary Committee (thirteen members) were facing us, and to complete this nightmare scenario, to our right, was sat the referee who had booked 'G' and was the reason why we were all here. To make matters worse he looked at me and 'G' as if we were something he'd just scraped off his shoe and I stared back thinking to myself "you are something else…you need to realise that you are nothing special…stop acting the big I am". The nightmare escalated when the panel started questioning the referee and we had to listen to lie after lie pouring out of his mouth, it was unbelieveable listening to him accuse me of being racist, and therefore, the reason why 'G' had directed a 'Sieg Heil' salute at him, he tried to justify his poor and egotistical on-field performance by blaming the behaviour of both teams, the coaches and both sets of parents in an attempt to deflect the blame and he also tried to justify walking in to the boys changing room without any other adult being present. I was struggling to keep it together listening to the verbal diarrhea spurting out of the referee's mouth, but knew I had to stay calm for 'G's' sake. Just when I thought things couldn't get any worse, members of the panel started questioning 'G' in what can only be described as a bullying manner...I was on the verge of blowing, and when an elderly gentleman and probably one of the most senior members of the committee held up the FA Wales Rules & Regulations book stating "every football player, regardless of age or ability, should know every rule in this book", and 'G', who was totally overwhelmed, started crying...I couldn't hold my tongue anymore and looked directly at this ancient bully and said "Satisfied...let me tell you, that is a load of rubbish...there are professional players that wouldn't know every rule in that book, let alone a thirteen year old who is still learning the rudiments of the game..." I looked around the room and especially at the referee, who couldn't look me in the face, and as I shook my head in disbelief I continued "...you should be ashamed of yourselves, speaking to children like this". We were excused and we made our way outside to comfort 'G', and the same lady who had called us in and who I now knew represented Rhondda Cynon Taff, came out to check that 'G' was ok. She appeared to be genuinely concerned, but it didn't stop me from telling her that I couldn't believe that this was how they dealt with junior disciplinary matters. After ''G had composed himself and a few minutes later we were called back in to hear the decision, which predictably, that the referee's original decision had been upheld and 'G' had to serve a one match ban.

Over the next few days I thought about the shocking way the South Wales F.A. had dealt with 'G's' red card. The more I thought about it the angrier I became. I decided I was going to take this further...I couldn't bear to think of other young players being put through what 'G' had been put through regardless of whether they were guilty or not, and thought "I've got to try and do something about this". I appealed the decision to the FA Wales and paid the associated fee of £90. The appeal took place in one of the large conference rooms at the Holiday Inn in the centre of Cardiff and was chaired by three senior members of FA Wales. Thankfully, 'G' didn't have to attend and the referee's exaggerated lies were beginning to unravel through a mix of inconsistencies and witnesses that contradicted these lies. The final decision meant that 'G' still had to serve a one match ban, but that was now irrelevent, this was now about child welfare and the flaws in the way the South Wales F.A. dealth with disciplinary issues. The appeal rewarded our perseverance and agreed that the South Wales F.A. were in the wrong and they were officially directed to urgently review and alter the way they dealt with junior disciplinary matters. The real bonus came when the referee announced that he would never officiate junior football match again…an equilibrium had been reached and commonsense had at last prevailed and I felt that the £90 I paid for the appeal was the best £90 I'd ever spent. I also felt that I had only reacted in a way that any other parent would have reacted to protect their child or any other child faced with similar situation.

Post Note

I have deliberately not given the referee's name in this incident as it was fourteen years ago and it would serve no purpose dragging his name through the mud, despite his lying. I would like to believe he eventually realised he was in the wrong, hence his decision not to referee junior football matches again…the best decision for him and junior football in South Wales, I'm sure he was a very good referee for senior football, but definitely not for junior football, where boys and girls are still perfecting timing tackles correctly and often play football with an innocent naivety.

Magaluf 2007

Prior to the 'flare-up' that led to the 'Middlesbrough' situation, I had booked a holiday for me and the children to Magaluf. Thankfully, despite 'Rh' and 'A' now living in Middlesbrough, the planned holiday went ahead, and in early October 2007 we all headed off to Cardiff Airport for our flight to Palma Airport in Mallorca…this would be a pivotal moment in the 'Thomas family' as it was the last time we all spent a holiday together, therefore, I consider this to be a very special memory.

I've always believed a holiday starts the minute you leave the house and this one was no different. By the time we arrived at Cardiff Airport, the excitement was building, especially in 'A' and 'Rh' who were already charging around the departure lounge with, what seemed like, limitless energy levels, no doubt, aided by sugar from the sweets and coca-cola they had enjoyed in the car…it was great to see them so happy after the turmoil of the previous five months. We didn't have to wait long before boarding the plane and after a flight of a little over two hours, we arrived at Palma Airport in Mallorca. Making sure we were all together, we collected our luggage, exited the airport and boarded the bus that would take us to our hotel…around an hour later we were being shown to our rooms at our hotel for the week, BCM Hotel, a large hotel that consisted of two large accommodation buildings separated by a large outdoor pool and sun lounger area in the centre of the complex. Magaluf may seem like a strange destination for a family holiday, but as it was the end of the season and I'd been assured that the resort would be quiet and ideal for a families, and as we explored on that first afternoon we could see that there were quite a few hotels, bars and restaurants already closed up…the normal mania, chaos, drunkenness and lewd behaviour were not something we expected to see during our stay…hopefully.

The first few evenings we were there we made our way to the Robin Hood Bar, a ten minute walk from the hotel, and luckily we had the bar to ourselves, which was great for the kids…and for me. There was small dance floor toward the back of the bar which included a karaoke, but more of that later. 'K' and 'G' were initially drawn to the 'arcade punch ball machine' in a typical teenage show of bravado…one attempting to outdo the other, with the odd attempt by the rest of us, purely to boost the boasts and testosterone levels of the two older boys. Having the place to ourselves was a big draw as it meant I could easily keep a close eye on the children, and relax and enjoy myself at the same time without worrying that they (mainly 'A' and 'Rh') maybe annoying other customers. Thankfully, the children were enjoying the sense of freedom in the Robin Hood Bar and the highlight of our time in those first few days was the karaoke, as 'R' enjoyed singing and 'A' and 'Rh' could have a go without worrying that their antics would annoy anyone and the resident DJ was great. But the real stars of the karaoke were 'K' and 'G's' with their duet of the haunting (when I say 'haunting' in this sense I mean that they frightened everyone to death) rendition of 'Hello' by Lionel Ritchie, not the sort of song you'd expect two lads to sing…when I say sing I use the term in its loosest sense. It was a one off, never forgotten performance that I will remember for as long as I live, two out of tune lads attempting to give 110% and leaving the rest of us howling with laughter as they gamely murdered this famous heart-warming tune. It is a performance that is still talked about today by all those that witnessed it, namely me, 'R', 'A' and 'Rh', but I've no doubt that the barmaid that night still tells people about the night two lads ruined an absolute classic eighties tune.

During our stay we visited the impressive upside down 'House of Katmandu', a house filled with illusions, interactive experiences, mazes and games – an amazing experience and one we all thoroughly enjoyed. We also paid a visit to Golf Fantasia, a mini golf course set in stunning grounds filled with water features and various plants, flowers and trees. As I'm the typical 'competitive dad' there was no quarter given and I probably enjoyed it more than the children did as I played…TO WIN, and win I did. Another great focal point of the holiday was the outdoor swimming pool at the hotel and as I'd bought swimming costumes for 'A' and 'Rh' that were similar to wet suits they spent hours in the pool whilst I relaxed on a sun lounger, however, there was no chance of a sun tan as it was either overcast all week or raining, and as a result the temperature was a little cooler than expected. On the last but one day the kids had been nagging for me to jump in the pool for around thirty minutes trying to convince me that "it's ok dad…it's a bit cold at first, but you'll soon warm up". Mr Gullible here, who stupidly trusted his kids, took a short run-up and jumped in the pool…"FUCK…IT'S FREEZING" I thought, as my nuts retreated to the warmth of my neck, and I could hear all the children laughing hysterically at me as I swam to the side of the pool, got out and pointed knowingly at each of the kids before dashing to my sun lounger and the sanctuary of my towel. I immediately started rubbing my neck so my nuts would return to their correct position…with the kids still laughing I gathered up my stuff and headed back to the room to get dressed and get warm.

Myself, 'A' and 'Rh' spent the majority of the last night in the hotel bar, where there was children's entertainment which included a parrot show…I managed to get a great photo, and permanent reminder of the holiday, of 'A' and 'Rh' with a Macaw parrot each which is still on display today in the house.

594

'K', 'R' and 'G' had made friends on holiday, as children always do, and spemt their last night with them. The week was finally over and we packed, headed to Palma Airport and caught the plane home. As I sat on the plane that day, I was thankful that we'd had a great holiday, but little did I know the significance of what we'd all just experienced…it was the last time we would spend an entire week together, as they have all got older we now only manage snatched moments all together at Christmases or at the occasional party. Therefore, in that respect, I consider that week in Magaluf as being a pretty special time for many reasons.

Lost on the Mountain

As with any family, we have had our fair share of funny stories whether they involve someone saying something funny, pranks, a comical episode or even events that have led to a visit to A&E. But a story that we still laugh about today started with an innocuous phone call to 'G', on his mobile, from my son, 'K'. At the time, 'K' worked at the ASDA store in Coryton (close to junction 32 of the M4 on the outskirts of Cardiff), which was around seven miles from our house in Abertridwr. Who would have thought that when 'K' rang 'G' late that night that it would lead to a humorous incident that was one of the reasons that led to 'K' and 'G' becoming affectionately known as 'The Chuckle Brothers' and resulting in me buying them, for Christmas, specially printed t-shirts with a big 'K' on the front of one and 'Chuckle Brother 1' on the back and the other with a big 'G' on the front and 'Chuckle Brother 2' on the back, respectively.

I was stood in the kitchen patiently waiting for the kettle to boil, I took a deep draw on my cigarette as 'G' answered his phone. I heard the click of the kettle…"finally…" I thought "…that took its time!" and heard 'G' say "I'll ask him now…"
"DAD?"
"Yes 'G'"
"'K' wants to know if you'll pick him up"
"WHERE IS HE?" I shouted, as I stirred my coffee.
'G' was still in the front room, sitting at the table.
"Where are you 'K'?"
I walked into the living room, sat down and I could hear 'G'
"Uh huh…hmm…alright 'K'…hang on…" He pulled the

phone away from his mouth, looked at me and said "He doesn't know Dad"

"How the hell can I pick him up if he doesn't know where he is" and I laughed, looked at 'R', who was now giggling, and I shrugged my shoulders. 'G' was now asking 'K' questions "What can you see?...what do you mean, you can see the lights of Cardiff...are you on Caerphilly mountain?...what do you mean you don't know?..."

There was a long pause and then 'G' must have had a brainwave as I heard him say

"Have you passed any signs?" and he looked at me and smiled, as if he was seeking my approval at his great question. I sarcastically nodded and gave him a 'thumbs up' and said to 'R' "they are like a double act...like the Chuckle Brothers" and 'R' again giggled and said "you're right dad".

It was then I heard 'G' say "Right 'K'...run back down the lane to where you saw the sign...it'll tell you where you are...OK 'K'...I'll hang on"

There was a long pause before I heard 'G' say "Right, what does it say 'K'" Another pause, "For fuck sake 'K'...that's no good". I got up and walked into the front room, looked at 'G', "What's the matter 'G'?...what does the sign say?"

I wasn't prepared for what 'G' told me and nearly spat my coffee out.

'G' looked at me, sighed, and said "No motorbikes on common land"

"You what!"

"No motorbikes on common land" he repeated sheepishly.

"How the hell does that help?...he could be anywhere...tell him to keep walking down the lane until he comes to a village or somewhere he recognizes...tell him to call you back"

"Unbelieveable" I muttered as I walked back to the settee.

Ten to fifteen minutes later 'K' rang 'G' back and told him he was in Groeswen, a small village on the mountain between Caerphilly and Treforest Industrial Estate...we worked out that the lights 'K' had seen were those of the industrial estate, and of Pontypridd. 'G' asked me again if I could pick up 'K'. "Tell him to stay where he is and we'll pick him up".

Within a couple of minutes 'G' and I were heading out of Abertridwr and five minutes later we found 'K' standing at the 'Groeswen' sign on the far side of the village. We pulled over and 'K' got in the back. I tutted loudly and asked 'K' "OK

'K'…what are doing walking home via the mountain if you don't know where you are going and you have no sense of direction…"

"Yeah 'K'" mocked 'G'.

"It…it…was…was a nice night…I…"

"It's fucking dark 'K'…why?...why?...why? said 'G' and his head rocked with laughter.

"He's got a point 'K'" I said and started laughing "…anyway, he's here now, leave it 'G'".

When we got back to the house 'G' told 'K' that when he originally asked him if he'd seen a sign, he meant a village sign that would tell us where he was…not any old sign. 'G' turned to me and 'R' and said "I could hear him running down the lane and panting…when he stopped and said he was in front of the sign, it was then he told me the sign read no motorbikes on common land…NO MOTORBIKES ON COMMON LAND…" he then looked at 'K' and said "fucking header".

We all burst out laughing, even 'K'...priceless, absolutely priceless!

Return of 'A' and 'Rh'

As previously stated, 'A' and 'Rh' returned from Middlesbrough in May or June 2010…as a result of their mother missing 'K', 'R' and 'G' (a huge case of "I told you so!"). It was great to have them back where they belong and for everyone to have the chance to repair the damage of the many affected relationships father/child; mother/child; sister/brother; brother/brother; grandparent/child etc, relationships that had taken years to build were damaged virtually overnight and here we were, a little under three years later, being given the chance to start afresh. I have never been happier than when the twins made that final trip back to Wales in the middle of 2010…great to have them back in Wales.

It was early May 2010 and Ada and I had just celebrated the arrival of our little girl, Amy Hannah Thomas. Little did I know at the time, but a week or so later I was to receive more good news, news that I never thought would happen…'A' and 'Rh' were coming back home to Wales. When the news sank in, the initial euphoria was nudged aside by a modicum of anger when I reflected on the emotional and financial damage that had occurred over the previous three years. But the relief and joy quickly returned as 'K', 'R', 'G' and myself, and the wider family, prepared for their almost imminent return, and the chance to re-build relationships that had been so deeply affected by their move to Middlesbrough with their mother. There was now no need for us to keep asking 'why had the move to Middlesbrough been allowed by the authorities/British legal system?', we could again look forward to a brighter future, a future where hopefully everyone could move forward…there would be new challenges ahead, but challenges that would now be easier to manage.

When 'Rh' and 'A' returned to Wales, it wasn't to Caerphilly, they moved to Newport which was much closer than Middlesbrough, being about 10 miles away. Whilst they were happy to be back in Wales and close to their family again, there was understandably a degree of resentment simmering below the surface as they had both left good friends and had been enjoying Middlesbrough. This was especially the case with 'A', who had been initially sad to leave Wales when she was nine, but who had come to accept the move and enjoy her new life in Middlesbrough. She was sad to leave her school and friends and this resentment sometimes surfaced in her attitude towards her mother. As soon as they returned I again started seeing them every weekend…I would pick them up and bring them back to Abertridwr and it was great to have all the children under the same roof again, a little manic at times, but it was great to be surrounded by the sound of their laughter (initially, with exception of Amy as she was still only a couple of months old at the time). Selfishly, I was ecstatic that they had returned, and an inner happiness and contentment swept over me at the emotional re-connection that had been made with 'A' and 'Rh'. But on a wider scale, it was great to see them re-connecting with their siblings and their paternal grand-parents, who had also felt the pain of the separation and it was great to see everyone's relationships developing and eventually becoming stronger. Having been an only child, I had tried to encourage the children to always try to remain close and to be there for each other and if there is one achievement in my life that I would be proud of more than anything else, it would be that my children remain close to each other and help each other through any difficulties they may face. Thankfully, I have already seen that this is the case and that makes me immensely proud, and I hope that as I fought for them, they will always fight to maintain their strong relationships with each other.

As a father, I have been blessed with great children, and when 'A 'and 'Rh' returned to Wales I hoped I'd be able to provide them with support with their education and hobbies and I can't tell you how good it was to see 'A' excel at school and 'Rh' to play football again, especially as he chose to play in the same team he'd played in before, Aber Valley YMCA, and I again became involved in running the team at the beginning of the 2010/11 season. I remain involved until the team finished playing in the U'16 league at the 2012/13 season, and as you saw in Chapter 7, seeing him score that first goal, since returning to Wales, when the team beat Cilfynydd, was very emotional...I didn't think I'd see him play football again, let alone score a goal.

Over the past 10 years, 'K', 'R', 'G', 'A' and 'Rh' have all stepped into adulthood, and I have watched them develop as individuals and as a group. Yes, there have been difficulties, as every family experience albeit sometimes differing ones, that are part of everyday life when growing up, but it is heart-warming to know that I have been able to guide them through some difficult periods such as bereavement; problems with their mother; relationships, gambling; debt; depression; and mental health etc. But I haven't done it on my own, whenever an individual has faced a difficult problem, we have faced them together, without criticism or condemnation, but with love, support and good old 'Welsh banter'. However, it hasn't always been easy and sometimes mistakes have been made, but it has always been done with good intentions. Amy, however, is still too young to understand or appreciate the trials that life throws at us, as she is still, to a certain degree, protected from them, having never had to face bereavement; divorce; illness etc, but as she has been blessed with siblings that love her, and who she has forged strong relationships with. I've no doubt that in future she will also benefit from their support and them from her support. Amy has already formed extremely close relationships with her nieces, Alexa and Louisa, due to their similar ages and hopefully, they'll provide the same level of support to each other as they go through life.

I love all my children and am equally proud of their achievements whether they are academic, sporting, work or personal. Additionally, I am proud of their characters, which, I might add, are all different, but most of all, I am proud of the way they support one another. They have had to deal with some extremely difficult situations throughout their respective lives, and hopefully some of the negative issues they have dealt with will equip them with the necessary tools to deal with problems/situations their own children may face. I strongly believe that trials we face in life are for a reason, and difficulties I have faced in my own life have changed me from the selfish person I was in my twenties to the understanding, loving and supportive person I am today, and my children are a huge part of that transformation…they are the best thing that ever happened to me. Having children has helped me develop as a person and as a father, and I owe them all a huge debt of gratitude. I believe, to develop as a person, having children is the single most important part of life, and I sympathise with those who can't or don't want to have children, as it could be argued their personal development could be hampered by the void of being childless. My children are my world and I have no favourites…they are loved equally and without question. 'K', 'R', 'G', 'A', 'Rh' and Amy, my only advice to you all is 'to live life without regrets', as I have tried to do.

Top Ten Music Singles

My musical tastes are quite broad, which is hardly surprising as I have been listening to music for over fifty years. I've always has a soft spot for love songs, but equally I appreciate the lyrics of songs. I have lived through the disco and glam rock of the early seventies, punk, two-tone, synth pop of the mid to late seventies and eighties, Brit pop of the nineties and so on. Additionally, I like swing (especially Dean Martin), country music, rap and have recently discovered the joy of Thai music and my 'Top Ten' reflects all these genres. If I was honest, my 'Top Ten' could have easily consisted of songs by The Jam, easily my favourite band of all time. Sadly, there are songs missing from some huge artists such as The Beatles; Elvis Presley; The Rolling Stones; Elton John; Sham 69; The

Buzzcocks; Dolly Parton; Dixie Chicks; Blondie; Dire, Straits, Oasis; Ed Sheeran etc and that is not to say I don't like these artists, as they produced many great songs which could have made my 'Top Ten'. However, I have tried to pick songs that have a deep meaning to me, but I also appreciate that the 'Top Ten' could change if I made a list tomorrow, next week, next month or even next year, such is the power of music. So here goes, if there are any you don't recognise, have a listen on You Tube...enjoy.

Name of song	**Artist**
White man in Hammersmith Palais	The Clash

This is a song that doesn't appear on any albums and is far removed from the songs on the first two Clash albums that were distinctly punk in sound and style. This song could be considered as being nearer to 'reggae' than punk, but it is a lyrical masterpiece. One line in particular shows the madness of the societies we live in, never a truer word has been sang than "If Adolf Hitler flew in today, they'd send a limousine anyway". It is a political statement that highlights everything that is wrong with the world we lived in yesterday, live in today and will live in tomorrow. It is a song that is a total opposite to those early punk hits such as *White Riot, Clash City Rockers, Janie Jones, Cheat* and *Garageland*...all great tunes in their own right, but typically raw and naive, that hightlighted the great rock voice of Joe Strummer. But *White Man in Hammersmith Palais* showed Joe's versatility as a performer...great tune.

■■

Hard to say I'm sorry	Chicago

A song that was in the charts in the autumn of 1982, and a song that I bought for Linda Hutchinson...my first love. It was an attempt to apologise for 'forbidden love', and when I hear the haunting voice of Chicago's Peter Cetera belting out this song, I smile and think of Linda, and the love we shared in that Autumn of 1982. It's not one of those well-known love songs such as The Righteous Brothers '*Unchained Melody*', The Eagles '*Hotel California*' or Dolly Parton's '*I Will Always*

Love You' (made famous by the Whitney Houston in the film *'The Bodyguard'*), but its lyrics turned out to be ironic and sadly I did end up being *'swept away...far away'* from Linda and I never had the chance to *'make it up'* to her, hence I believe I already knew we were doomed before it began and I said as much to one of my mates on the flight from Brize Norton to Ascension Island. But whilst I am not sorry I fell for Linda, I am sorry that our love caused so much hurt to others. It's funny you'd think this would be a song I wouldn't want to listen to...far from it, it reminds me of a happy time many, many years ago.

■■

Down in the Tube Station   The Jam

This song for me is lyrically the most powerful song of my generation...it typified the anger felt by many during the late seventies. It was a powerful song when I was a teenager, but it is a song that is timeless and I still get the same feelings listening to it today as I did when I was fifteen years old. The Jam re-invented themselves a few times whilst a lot of punk/mod groups from that era were one hit wonders. The Jam had a string of hit singles and best-selling albums. I believe that Paul Weller will eventually be recognised as one of the best, if not the best, songwriter this country has ever produced, and *'Down in the Tube Station'* for me will always be the pinnacle of his song writing talent...the song about a man being mugged and beaten up in the London Underground when he's on his way home. Its lyrics are captivating, and as you listen to the powerful lyrics you can picture the story unfolding...such a powerful skill to be able to write such an incredible song. A timeless classic that could still be relevant today and still be relevant tomorrow...Classic song, and one of many songs by The Jam that I could have included in this 'Top Ten'.

■■

Fix You   Coldplay

There were a few songs I could have chosen from Coldplay such as *'Yellow'*, *'The Scientist'* or *'Viva la Vida'*, but for me it has to be *'Fix You'*. It was a huge song around the same time I was experiencing a difficult period in my life as I fought for custody of 'A' and 'Rh' as part of the attempt to keep my children together. Unfortunately, the weight of British Law sides heavily with the mother and the emotional and financial fall-out was huge, resulting on the destruction of my second marriage…my second wife was unable to deal with the malicious actions of my first wife and to protect her own two children we ultimately divorced. I felt completely helpless as I watched my family being ripped apart, but I was able to take solace from the lyrics of '*Fix You*' and used them to re-build my own emotional well-being. These lyrics were very powerful and gave me the strength to carry on…they were a huge 'pick me up', a sort of self-help, and I saw the words of the song as an instruction from me to me (as if I was talking to myself). From the first line where there is a sense of failure to the last line where you tell yourself that you will try and help to repair your emotional state, the words helped me through…this song more than any other will always have a very special place in my heart. It's a song that saved me in more ways than one…it gave me strength to carry on, to become a better person, a better father and to achieve success both personally and professionally. Thank you Coldplay, for writing and releasing '*Fix You*' with almost perfect timing.

■■■■■■■■■■■■■■■■■■■■■■■■■■■■■■■■■■■■■■■

Why does it always rain on me   Travis

This is the first song I heard from Travis and this catchy tune resulted in me getting the album '*The Man Who*' on my thirty-sixth Birthday. This song was the beginning of my musical love affair with Travis, and I was lucky enough to see them live in the CIA Cardiff (now the Motorpoint Arena) in 2004 with Keane as the support act. The concert was brilliant and Fran even sang one song on his own with just the guitar…as if he was again busking on the streets, brilliant. Travis are still together and over the years they have released some classic songs such as '*Driftwood*', '*Flowers in the Window*', '*Sing*' and many more. But it is '*Why Does It Always Rain On Me?*' that just edges the others as my favourite Travis record, and whilst I've always loved strong lyrics, I am not sure what the inspiration is for the song or what it's about…for me, it is just a class song and the catchy words and tune are the reason I still love it, and Travis, twenty years after it was first released.

■■■■■■■■■■■■■■■■■■■■■■■■■■■■■■■■■■■■■■■

Just like a pill   Pink

What can I say about Pink? I believe she is such a talented
individual, not just the singing, but the dancing, the acrobatics
and more importantly…as a songwriter. She has written some
classic songs, not just individually, but also in collaborations
with other artists such as Nate Ruess from Fun for their *'Just
Give Me A Reason'*. This year I had the honour of obtaining
tickets for the Cardiff leg of the Beautiful Trauma tour at the
Principality Stadium…Wow, what a concert, easily the best
artist I've ever seen live. It was an unbelievable show, but
unlike many stars who can't sing live, Pink showed her true
class with an excellent live singing performance…she even
played my favourite Pink track *'Just Like A Pill'*. Similar to
Travis, I was hooked to this social rebel from hearing *'Just
Like a Pill'* the first time and have enjoyed her music ever
since. As an ex-soldier, I have got a soft spot for the song her
father wrote, *'My Vietnam'* which they sing together on the
album *'Missunderztood'*, the same album that includes *'Just
like a Pill'*. This song has a rawness that is obviously about the
misuse of drugs and still remains a favourite Pink song despite
the endless number of hits she has released.

■■■

The Soldier   Harvey Andrews

Just thinking about the lyrics of this song makes the hairs
stand-up on the back of my neck. A simple story of an
ordinary man who doesn't join the army out of any sense of
loyalty to his Queen or country, he joins purely to get a
job…and this kind of recruit defines the majority of the
military generation I served with, such was the political
climate in the mid to late-seventies. I joined the army in 1979
and the 'Troubles' in Northern Ireland were very much still a
major issue. I was lucky that I didn't serve on the streets in
Northern Ireland, but I did witness the fear and instability of
Northern Ireland whilst staying at Massereene Barracks in
Antrim for ten days with 24 Field Squadron rugby team in
1982. This song by Harvey Andrews is an absolute lyrical
masterpiece as it provides the humble beginnings of a simple
soldier, details, in simple terms, the essence of Northern

604

Ireland and builds to a crescendo of emotion, and the music quickens as the suspense builds, as the soldier sacrifices his own life to save others…others who call him murderer as opposed to referring to him as a friend. In this single song you get a sense of the tragedy that is Northern Ireland. It really is a powerful song which typifies the total waste of life of ordinary people (on all sides)…all in the name of religion.

■■■

Kau Jai Tur Lak Bur Toh   Ying Lee
(Your heart for my number)

With my Thai connections it was inevitable that I would listen to Thai music and this song will always have a place in my top ten. It is a catchy tune and allegedly the second most downloaded song in Asia behind '*Gangnam Style'*. It's a song that has led the way in me starting to enjoy various Thai artists such as Labanoon, Takkatan Chonlada, Tai Orathai, Gam and many others. I enjoy watching Thai music videos as they tell a story, therefore, I don't have to understand the words, but I have managed to learn the choruses of some songs. Whilst this Ying Lee song is my favourite Thai song, my favourite Thai artist is Tai Orathai…this Thai country singer has had a multitude of hits over nearly two decades, and she is not just a much loved artist, she is also a much loved person…a polite, warm and giving person who does a lot for the people of her home city Ubon Ratchathani. But it is Ying Lee's huge hit that remains my favourite song and the video on 'You Tube' of the song with its unique dance choreography is brilliant. Thai music is very different to the music produced in Britain, but its different styles and sounds are what makes it so captivating…have a look on 'You Tube', I guarantee you'll find something you like.

■■■

L'il Ole Wine Drinker Me   Dean Martin

This is undoubtedly my favourite song by the legendary Dean Martin, a man who I consider to be the greatest singer of all time…it wasn't the strong voice of a powerful rock singer, or the unique voice of someone like Bob Dylan or Johnny Rotten, no, it was because his singing was so smooth and so effortless…a natural gift and so easy to listen to. It is a song that takes me back to those nights in the NAAFI (Navy, Army and Royal Air Force Institute) at Chattenden Barracks in Kent…it was on the juke box that stood adjacent to the bar and I can still hear the groans from others if it, or the 'B' side, 'Bumming Around', was ever played…others in the NAAFI would immediately look at Mick Stupple, Jake Maiden or me and instantly blame us for putting it on…and they were right, it was always us. We loved that song and never got sick of it. It also reminds me of the late, great Alan Jenkins and the time, after a few drinks, that we sang this Dean Martin classic all the way from Caerphilly to Senghenydd and back to Abertridwr. Yes, I like many of his other songs such as '*Volare*', '*Sway*', '*Gentle on my Mind*' etc, but '*Li'l ole Wine Drinker Me*' will always be my favourite.

■■■

Anarchy in the UK   Sex Pistols

The Sex Pistols were a breath of fresh air from the dreary drivel of bland music that littered the early to mid-1970s. When bands like The Sex Pistols, The Clash, The Stranglers, Sham 69 etc came to prominence in the late 1970s, the music reflected the political anger and turmoil of the time. Their first single in 1976, '*Anarchy in the UK*' provided teenage boys, like me, with a focus that mirrored the anger and rage sweeping across the country. This 'punk' music part of a new order that swept across the country as one crisis stumbled into another, with strikes by various bodies (miners, steelworkers, bin men, firemen etc), three day weeks and general discontent everywhere. This was reflected in the punk music and the anger, hate, violence and sexual liberation of a new generation, was pouring forth from powerful 'punk' lyrics about a harsh reality. '*Anarchy in the UK*' was typical of these kinds of songs and to an impressionable thirteen year old, they were brilliant, and hearing this song reminds me of my teenage years when worries were few and life was simple and uncomplicated…whilst all around us was political chaos. Great times for teenagers…shit for adults.

■■■

Top Ten Music Albums

As with my 'Top Ten Singles' I have picked albums that mean something to me, but again there are albums missing from stars/bands such as The Rolling Stones; Squeeze; The Stranglers; Sham 69; Faith Hill; Adele; Hot Chocolate; Abba etc who all produced albums that mean a great deal to me, but I've had to choose ten and they are revealed below. Music is very subjective as we all have our own personalities and are touched by different experiences and this will reflect and influence our individual musical taste. I am happy that I enjoy many different genres of music, as sticking with one particular type of genre could result in us missing out on so much joy. Music we love can also depend on our mood at a given time, and that is a beautiful aspect to the pleasure it creates…a world without music would be a very sad and boring phenomenon, therefore, music in any form is a fantastic reflection and appreciation of life. Everyone's 'Top Ten' would be unique and also subject to change, as is the flexibility of our freedom of choice…like or dislike my choices, that is up to you, but have a go of creating your own 'Top Ten' and I bet you'll see how difficult it is. I guarantee you will forget an album or artist you love…enjoy and good luck.

Name of Album	Artist
All Mod Cons	The Jam

The Jam will always be my number one band, and their '*All Mod Cons*' album still remains my favourite. I was fifteen when it was released and my cousin, Stuart, and I were lucky to see The Jam live on the '*All Mod Cons*' tour at Bristol's Colston Hall…they were absolutely brilliant. Every song on the album is a classic and they were a huge influence on me with their songs, written as stories, that reflected life in the late-seventies, songs such as '*Mr Clean*', '*David Watts*' and '*Down in the Tube Station at Midnight*', the poignancy of '*English Rose*' the aggression of '*Billy Hunt*' and the violence of '*A Bomb in Wardour Street*'…a song that was excellent live, when there was a mock explosion at the end of the song. Whenever fans of The Jam are asked about their favourite album, opinion is split between 'All Mod Cons' and 'Setting Sons'. In truth, there is little to choose between them, but lyrically, the songs of both albums are on different levels, highlighting the song writing talent of Paul Weller better than any other album they produced. Whilst Bruce Foxton contributed to the song writing for The Jam, it was mainly Paul Weller that wrote most of the songs, and his song writing prowess continued into his solo career, but perhaps not with the same fervor as his career with The Jam. When I joined the army as a sixteen year old, The Jam were still a huge part of my life and as a result one of the lads in the troop, Simon Hunt, became 'Billy' after the 'Billy Hunt' song…a name he's still known as today by the lads of 4 troop, 66 Squadron, JLRRE. And a few years later *'English Rose'* took on a new meaning, along with *'Bitterest Pill (I ever had to swallow)'* became a reminder of a certain Yorkshire Lass. However, 'All Mod Cons' is truly an album amongst albums and easily my all-time favourite album of any artist.

■■■

Never Mind the Bollocks   Sex Pistols

Considered to be one of the most influential albums ever, and one of the songs on this album was the first single I bought…*'Holidays in the Sun'*…I'd play it again and again and again. Everything about The Sex Pistols was controversial…the clothes they wore, their bad language, the music, and at one point, they were barred from everywhere. Unfortunately, I never got to see the Pistols live, as I was only thirteen when they started, and only fifteen when Johnny Rotten was sacked during a tour of the USA. This was the only album that the original line-up recorded (there were other albums released much later…live albums etc). The punk music of the mid to late seventies reflected the anger at the time, hence the controversial nature of its music and lyrics. Our parent's and grand-parent's generations felt threatened by the music and sneering, aggressive singers and musicians of this new kind of music…whether they liked it or not, The Sex Pistols were at the forefront of this musical revolution and they, and their music, influenced so many bands that came after. Johnny Rotten in his book 'No Irish, No Blacks, No Dogs' states they were taken too serious, but given the state of Britain in the mid to late-seventies it could be argued that they had to be taken seriously as they were reflecting the anger of my generation. As a result, the songs on *'Never Mind the*

Bollocks' had to be controversial, songs such '*God Save the Queen'*, *'Bodies'*, *'Anarchy in the UK'* and *'Holidays in the Sun'*, but whatever anyone thinks of The Sex Pistols, they were a flagship for our generation, a generation that were violently dragged into the 1980s. I was an impressionable fourteen year old at the time of its release and I thought they were a breath of fresh air from the 'shit' music of the early-seventies…they were brilliant, and to this day I still find Johnny Rotten to be a complex, but fascinating, character and I definitely believe he was, and still is, misunderstood.

■■■

Desire   Bob Dylan

Bob Dylan wasn't someone I had listened to, I wasn't a fan of 'folk music' and he was considered to be a terrible singer. But when I was based at Southwood Camp, Cove, nr Farnborough in 1981 one of the lads in the room was always playing the Bob Dylan album '*Desire*' and the lyrics of a few of these songs blew me away. '*Hurricane*' told the true story of Rubin 'Hurricane' Carter, a middleweight boxer who was on the verge of challenging for the world title, but who was then wrongly convicted of a triple murder. Very moving song and Bob Dylan was involved in the campaign to free Rubin, but he still spent twenty years in jail. Another moving song is '*Joey*', a biographical song about the life and death of mobster Joey Gallo. '*Sara*' is another beautiful song and one that Bob Dylan had written for his first wife Sara Lownds,…it is easy to appreciate the love Bob Dylan had for Sara when you listen to the lyrics of this song. All in all there isn't a bad song on '*Desire*', every song is a lyrical masterpiece and it is the only Bob Dylan album I possess. I've never felt the urge to listen to other albums or songs by Bob Dylan…possibly due to the fact that I don't believe any of his other music would equal the quality of the songs on this album. It is a wonderful lyrical masterpiece.

■■■

Curtain Call (The Hits)   Eminem

Love him or hate him, Eminem is an incredible artist and this collection of his greatest hits is a fantastic legacy. The songs are a mixture of being catchy, serious, sometimes humorous

609

and emotional…not words you would normally associate with a 'rap' artist, but then Eminem is no ordinary rapper. Much of what he writes about are reflections of his own life and, it appears to me, there is a great deal of anger in some of his songs that reveal the harsh issues he has experienced in his own life. The lyrics are extremely powerful and Eminem deserves his place in the 'story of rap'…it shows how anger can be used in a positive way, but it is heart-breaking to look through a 'lyrical' window into his painful experiences. There isn't a bad song on this album as each song has it own merit…as would be expected of a greatest hits album. Each song is a story and my favourite songs are '*Stan*', '*Mocking Bird*', '*Cleanin' out my closet*' and '*When I'm Gone*'. The first time I heard '*Stan*' the escalation from someone being a huge fan to killing himself and his pregnant girlfriend was shocking, but the more you listen to it, you begin to understand the anger and frustrations of someone struggling with mental illness…very powerful lyrics. '*Mockingbird*' is an outstanding song as Eminem sings a song to his daughter, Hayley, a heartfelt plea that he's there for her despite the tragic realities of life that have torn the family apart. '*Cleaning' out my Closet*' is another classic lyrical song directed at his mother and father and the mistakes they made in the way they treated him when he was growing up, you can feel his pain and shame, at the continual moves, his mother's drug addiction and his father's abandonment. '*When I'm Gone*' is another great self-depreciating song as Eminem struggles with the balance of fame and family life. Most of Eminem's songs are hard to listen to because of the raw emotion that is evident in his lyrics…he wears his heart on his sleeve and it seems that he has used the powerful lyrics to counsel himself to deal with the difficulties he has faced. They are not songs you would listen to if you wanted to cheer yourself up…apart from '*Fack*' which is very funny. Eminem is like marmite…you either love him or hate him.

■■

Word Gets Around   Stereophonics

This isn't just an album to the Welsh, the songs are 'anthems', and sung by the unique gritty voice of Kelly Jones. Even now, after over twenty years since its release, songs from this album are still sung in the pubs in Cardiff on rugby international days…I can remember being in Jumping Jacks in Cardiff for a Wales v England game years ago and we were treated to a set of songs from this album by the Monophonics, a Stereophonics tribute band…fantastic afternoon, made better by Wales winning. They are an iconic band that are still popular today, and we are proud that these 'valley boys' are ours. This album is hit after hit… *'A Thousand Trees'*, *'Local Boy in the Photograph'*, *'Billy Davey's Daughter'*, and the anthem of all anthems…*'More Life in a Tramp's Vest'*, a great song and a great analogy. They have had a string of hits over the years, but nothing as rich and raw as the hits on this album…deservedly one of my top ten albums, an absolute classic.

■■■

Coldplay Live 2012   Coldplay

I'm not normally a fan of 'live' albums, but this is a fantastic album. It's not just the selection of great songs such as *'Yellow'*, *'Princess of China'* (with Rhianna), *'Viva La Vida'*, *'Paradise'* and my all-time Coldplay favourite *'Fix You'*, it's the interaction with the crowd throughout the whole performance. Recorded at Stade de Frances, Paris on their Mylo Xyloto tour in 2012, it is a fantastic blend of their big hits and easily their best album. I missed the opportunity of seeing them live when they played at Cardiff in 2018…a lot of friends who did go said it was easily the best concert they had been too. Listening to the 2012 concert from Paris on this CD made me understand why my friends thought the Cardiff concert was so fantastic…gutted to have missed it. The album deserves its place in my top ten, it is a truly great collection of Coldplay's hits and highlights exactly why they are considered such a good band to see live.

■■■

The Man Who   Travis

The unique easy listening style of Travis captured me from the first time I heard this brilliant album. I found Travis relaxing to listen to and this new band, who had won the 2000 Brits Awards for 'Best Album' for the '*The Man Who*' and also won 'Best British Group'…highlighting their unique and fresh music and being a wonderful addition to the history

611

of British Music with their awards. Normally, when you listen to any album by any artist for the first time there are songs that you may not like, however, with this album I instantly liked every song on 'The Man Who' which included a string of great hits such as *'Waiting to Reach You'*, *'Driftwood'*, *'Turn'* and of course, *'Why Does it Always Rain On Me'*. They went on to release some fantastic singles and albums, all of which are a joy to listen to, but nothing beats 'The Man Who'…absolute classic.

■■

Truth About Love   Pink

It is difficult to pick my favourite Pink album, but it came down to *'Missunderztood'* and *'Truth About Love'*. 'Missunderztood' is a great album and was the first Pink album I bought, and it had some great songs…such as *'Don't Let Me Get Me'*, *'Get The Party Started'*, *'Family Portrait'*, *'My Vietnam'* and of course *'Just Like A Pill'*. But I have chosen 'Truth About Love' as there are four absolute classic Pink songs that highlight her versatility as an artist. There is the catchy anthem *'Are We All We Are'*, an amazing and memorable tune which was a highlight of the concert I watched on the Beautiful Trauma tour. *'Blow Me (One Last Kiss)'*, a lyrical masterpiece about a relationship 'breaking-up', *'Try'*, another anthem that provides a lyrical self-help about carrying-on when a love has gone bad, and the excellent *'Just Give Me A Reason'*, a beautiful collaboration with Nate Reuss from Fun, an alternative love song as a couple (Pink and Nate) fight to save their love, in the guise of a lyrical conversation between them…an emotionally beautiful song. These four powerful songs highlight Pink's maturity, and that maturity is one reason why this album just edges *'Missunderztood'*, an album that was written much earlier in Pink's career. Another reason is when you look at other songs on 'Truth About Love', you appreciate the collective quality of the album, songs such as 'True Love', 'The Truth About Love', 'How Come You're Not Here', 'Walk Of Shame', 'Here Comes The Weekend', 'Where Did The Beat Go', the emotional 'The Great Escape' and the unbelievable 'Slut Like You', an extremely clever song that challenges the male dominated society in which we live…a brilliant song screaming 'equality' which, it could be argued, tips the balance in favour of women. A fantastic album by an amazing person and artist.

■■■

Abbey Road   The Beatles

I'm not a big fan of The Beatles as I think they are hugely overrated, and I have to say I am a much bigger fan of The Rolling Stones. Therefore, how could I pick an album by The Beatles in my top ten but not one by The Rolling Stones? Simple. The Rolling Stones may have produced albums that included two or three good songs, but 'Abbey Road' has a string of unusual but classic songs on it. It is an album that has fascinated me since I was a young teenager growing up in Bridgend. It has two of the most lyrically strange songs I think there has ever been written by anybody, let alone The Beatles, '*Maxwell's Silver Hammer*' and '*Octopus's Garden*'…to write songs this weird must mean there is a very unusual mind behind it, or was there another reason that they were able to produce such strange lyrics! There are also classic songs such as '*Come Together*' and '*Here Comes The Sun*'. But it's the love song '*Something*' that is my favourite song from this album. Everyone has a favourite 'love' song, some of us even enjoy more than one for various reasons, but '*Something*' is one of the most simplistic, yet, most meaningful love songs ever written. It is certainly an excellent, but bizarre album and the only album by The Beatles that I believe deserves any artistic credit. Apologies to all fans of The Beatles, but apart from this album, I generally don't enjoy the majority of the music produced by The Beatles.

■■■

The Clash LP   The Clash

This is probably my favourite punk album of all time, the energy of this album is outstanding, as the gritty and edgy voice of Joe Strummer guides us through a catalogue of great punk rock songs. I was fourteen when this was released in 1977 and when I bought the album, I played it, and played it, and played some more. I was enthralled by the raw lyrics of songs such as '*Janie Jones*', '*White Riot*', '*London's Burning*', '*Cheat*', and '*Garageland*'. '*Career Opportunities*' hinted at

613

the employment issues of the time and in an album of so many contrasts there was an almost 'reggae' feeling about '*Police and Thieves*'…perhaps an early sign of the reggae influence that was more evident in later albums. Of '*Give Em Enough Rope*' they were far removed from the raw material on this album. Sadly, Joe Strummer is no longer with us as he passed away in 2002, but the music he wrote with Mick Jones is a part of 'British Music' history, and this album is an outstanding legacy left behind by Joe Strummer and the other members of The Clash, Mick Jones, Paul Simonen and Topper Headon…True Heroes from my youth.

■■

Top Ten Films

Another difficult one, my 'Top Ten' films are a reflection of my age and maturity and I know had I created a list in my teenage years, twenties, thirties or even my forties, they would have been different to the 'Top Ten' I have created below. My current list includes six films that are based on true events, events that are extremely emotional for one reason or another, but you'll see that I have not chosen any comedy films.
It isn't that I don't like them because I have enjoyed some great ones over the years such as the 'Carry on' films; Norman Wisdom; Laurel and Hardy; Abbot & Costello and Dean Martin/Jerry Lewis classics and also later comedy greats such as Porky's; National Lampoon's Animal House and Airplane have also been favourites over the years. As are modern classics such as Step Brothers; Bridesmaids; Borat; Ted etc…it would be easier to create 'Top Tens' by genre. Another genre that's missing is 'Westerns' and it can be argued there have been great ones over the years that have included John Wayne, Alan Ladd and of course Cline Eastwood's 'spaghetti westerns'. Another omission is 'musicals' again, some great films such as The King and I; The Sound of Music; Grease; Les Miserables; Sunshine on Leith and many more, some of which could have easily made it in to my 'Top Ten'. Additionally, I absolutely love 'Disney' films, but despite some classics such as Lion King; Tangled; Aladdin; Snow White there are none in my 'Top Ten', however, there is every chance a Disney film would have been included in a 'Top Ten' list from the past. However, two

genres that would not be in any 'Top Ten' would be 'horror' and 'sci-fi' with exception of the Alien series of films which is a mixture of horror and sci-fi. I find horror boring and I just don't get sci-fi, it's just not a genre I enjoy...I have never seen a Star Wars film from beginning to end. As with music, a 'Top Ten' films is also subjective and unique to an individual, but it is likely that someone else's 'Top Ten' list would include a film I also chose. I know my army friends will be upset that 'Zulu' isn't included in my 'Top Ten'...sorry boys, although an absolute classic, it just missed out.

Top Ten Films (Spoiler Alert)

Film Title

The Impossible

Ewan McGregor, Naomi Watts, Tom Holland, Samuel Joslin, Oaklee Pendergast, Ploy Jindachot and many others

This film is based on a true story which tells of the Belon family's remarkable survival story when the 2004 Tsunami hit the hotel they were staying at in Khao Lak, Thailand. Every time I've watched this film I struggle to understand how anybody survived the devastation caused by the tsunami of 2004, a tsunami that killed more than 230,000 people, highlighting the destructive power of nature that should never be under-estimated. For anyone to survive was a miracle, but for a family of five people (mother, father and three sons aged 10, 8 and 5) to survive, was nothing short of remarkable. This amazing story unfolds as we see the family arrive in Thailand, head to the beautiful resort in Khao Lak, where they enjoy a paradise of stunning beaches and coconut groves...then their world is turned upside down as, without warning, they experience the unbelievable force of the tsunami as it hits their hotel complex. Scenes that are beyond comprehension for the viewer as one minute the family are around the pool, then the next their story of survival begins...and what a story it is. The film captured brilliantly the emotions of the various character: the family, other survivors, Thai villagers and even the hospital staff, as the destruction and loss of life becomes apparent as the tidal waters of the tsunami recede. The viewer is taken on a roller coaster of a ride as we initially follow Maria Belon being dragged along by the surge water and the injuries she sustains from foreign objects in the water. During this frightening scene she is reunited with her eldest son, Lucas. Eventually, we see them being rescued by Thai villagers before being taken to hospital, where the full sense of horror is realised. The film then cuts back to Quique Belon (father) and the other sons who have miraculously survived as well. There is a harrowing scene in the hospital when Lucas loses his mother after she gets moved when he is running around the hospital trying to reunite families…the hospital is filled with victims and the chaotic scenes are heart-breaking as unknown characters face the realization that they have lost loved ones. Then we experience the joyous moment when all members of the family are re-united at the hospital. I have been to the coastline where the tsunami hit in 2004, when we stayed in Kata, Phuket in 2013, and there is now little evidence of the devastation caused by the tsunami…the only thing I remember seeing are signs that show the direction people should head if a tsunami hits, too little, too late for the victims of the 2004 tsunami, but a reminder of the devastation and loss of life it caused. But as I witnessed in Kata, life goes on. Nevertheless, it's an astonishing story, laid out in a film that definitely highlights the strength and togetherness of the human spirit when faced with such devastating danger. A very humbling film.

■■

Empire of the Sun

Christian Bale, John Malkovich, Ben Stiller, Miranda Richardson, Nigel Havers, Leslie Phillips, Takataro Kataoka and many more

A classic Steven Spielberg movie that is set during World War II. A young Christian Bale provides an exceptional performance as the young Jim Graham, who lives with his parents in Shanghai, just prior to the Second World War breaking out. They are here when Japan invades China, and in the chaos that follows Jim is separated from his parents as people try to flee Shanghai and the horror of war. Eventually, Jim is captured by the Japanese and placed in an internment camp where he forms an unlikely friendship with Basie, an

American merchant navy man, played by John Malkovic. With their other internment camp prisoners they attempt to survive their ordeal of violence, disease and slowly being starved. Bale's performance of a boy struggling to hold onto his childhood and who becomes confused as to where his loyalties lie…with Japan or with the Allies. It is a complex part played by Bale and is considered, by some people, to be the best juvenile performance in film history. Bale is the constant throughout a mesmerizing film, a story of survival against the backdrop of war. When the Japanese eventually leave prior to surrendering and his fellow prisoners also leave, including Basie, Jim is the only person left in the camp. American soldiers eventually arrive at the camp to find Jim cycling around on a bicycle he has found, oblivious that the war in China is over. The final scene is extremely emotional as children and parents are re-united in an old greenhouse, somewhere in China. At first the two sets of people (the children on one side and parents on the other) stare silently at each other, children attempt to recognise parents and vice versa. When one mother and daughter eventually recognise each other and embrace, the stand-off is broken and parents and children start to intermingle to find their loved ones. Jim's parents are there, as is Jim, and as they attempt to find their son, Jim's mother notices a boy (Jim) looking at her husband as he walks past the boy. She shouts "Jim" and then stands in front of the boy and says again "Jim". The boy (Jim) turns to look at his mother and there is a flicker of recognition, but he's not sure, and then (after glancing at his father), gently lifts his mother's hand, looks at it before reaching for her mouth and rubbing his finger across her lip to look at the lipstick, takes his mother's hat off, touches her hair, breaks into a half-smile before embracing his mother. It is a sensitive scene played brilliantly by Bale and this sensitive and emotional end to a dramatic, and sometimes touching film shows the various sides of war including its barbarity. It is a wonderful film made even better by Bale's excellent performance.

■■

Saving Private Ryan

Tom hanks, Matt Damon, Tom Sizemore, Ted Danson, Edward Burns, Vin Diesel, Barry Pepper, Giovanni Ribisi and many more

The opening twenty minutes of this film are considered to be the most realistic scenes of war ever made. Set during the time the American troops were landing at Omaha Beach on D-Day in 1944, the opening twenty minutes are graphic and true to actual events. The reason we know this is that its first screening was in front of 'Vets' who were actually involved in those D-Day landings, and confirmed the film's accurate portrayal of the horror on the beach as landing crafts hit the beach and soldiers poured out and straight into a killing field of indiscriminate firing from German machine gun posts in the sand dunes and bunkers facing the beach. I had joined the army after years of always wanting to be a soldier after watching the 1950s Hollywood films that glorified war, making it seem heroic and gallant, but '*Saving Private Ryan*' shows the true horror of war in all its gory detail…it is not heroic, it's pointless and a total waste of human life. This film tells the story of a squad of American soldiers, led by Captain Miller (Tom Hanks), who are sent on a 'suicide' mission to find a Private Ryan (Matt Damon), to send him home to his mother, as it has been discovered that his brothers have all died, casualties of war. The mission is fraught with danger, as we see with the deaths of Private Carparzo (Vin Diesel), killed by a sniper and of T-4 Medic Wade (Giovanni Ribisi) who is shot, but can't be saved, and who dies calling for his mother in a very touching scene. Eventually, Captain Miller and his small band of men find Private Ryan, who is serving with a detachment of 101st Airborne who are defending the fictional town of Ramelle, and in particular, a bridge over the Merderet River. The tension builds as the Germans approach and in a crescendo of savagery there is probably the most disturbing scene I have ever seen in any film, even horror films. Private Mellish (Adam Goldberg) is involved in a hand-to-hand fight for survival with a German soldier. Mellish pulls his bayonet out and attempts to stab the German, but the German gets the upper hand, resulting in Mellish being on his back and the German soldier slowly pushing the knife into Mellish's chest hushing the pleading of Mellish not to kill him…extremely disturbing and haunting image that shows the barbarity of war. In the battle for Ramelle the tide eventually turns in the favour of the Americans, but not before Private Jackson (Barry Pepper), Sgt Horvath (Tom Sizemore) and even Captain Miller are killed…before Miller dies he whispers to Private Ryan "James…earn this" followed by "earn it", in reference to the sacrifice Miller and his men have made to save him. As Ryan stands there over Miller, the image changes to an old Ryan standing in front of Captain Miller's headstone in the present day Normandy war cemetery, he salutes and asks his wife if he's been a good man. It's a poignant end to an unbelievable film that accurately shows the full horror of war for the first time on film, with its harrowing portrayal of the horrors of D-Day and the battles/skirmishes that followed. It also spawned the critically acclaimed 'Band Of Brothers' which followed the fortunes, and misfortunes, of Easy Company, 101st Airborne which continued to provide the viewer with the gritty, graphic and true horrors of war.

■■

Angels with Dirty Faces

James Cagney, Pat O'Brien, Humphrey Bogart, George Bancroft, Ann Sheridan and the 'Dead End Kids'

I've got a soft spot for some old black and white movies, and the gangster films of James Cagney are a particular favourite…'Angels With Dirty Faces' was probably the first James Cagney film I watched and it just edges Cagney's performance in another classic, 'White Heat'. In 'Angels With Dirty Faces' Cagney plays Rocky Sullivan, a hoodlum who is a hero to a gang of boys that Rocky's childhood friend, Father Connolly (Pat O'Brien), who is trying to keep the gang on the straight and narrow. Throughout the film the hero worship of Rocky, by the gang, intensifies and continues to grow, especially when Rocky is sentenced to death after killing lawyer James Frazier (Humphrey Bogart). Father Connolly goes to visit Rocky on death row to plead with him to go to the electric chair kicking and screaming, as Father Connolly pleads it is the best chance he has of saving the gang of boys from a life of crime. But Rocky says he can't do that and even punches a guard as he's taken to the electric chair. However, Rocky changes his mind and pretends he's scared, crying and

619

screaming that de doesn't want to die. In the final scene of the film, Father Connolly finds the gang and tells them that Rocky died a coward, crying and screaming as he struggled to accept his fate. A powerful message sent out by the film to juvenile boys that crime doesn't pay, a message re-visited in many of Cagney's gangster films as dying was a familiar ending. The cowardice shown by Cagney when it is relayed back to the gang results in them losing all respect for Rocky, much to Father Connolly's happiness…happy that he has a chance to save the boys despite the fact he couldn't save his childhood friend. Great film and an absolute classic, but don't expect James Cagney to say "You Dirty Rat" because he never said it any of his films..

■■■

Goodbye Mr Chips

Robert Donat, Greer Garson, John Mills, Terry Killburn, Paul Herveld, Lyn Harding and many more

This is one of my all-time favourite films, a heart-warming story of a young schoolmaster, Arthur Chips (Robert Donat) who arrives at the famous public school, Brookfield, and his dedication to educate the generations of schoolboys that walk through its gates. From his early timid days as a young schoolmaster, his friendship with a fellow German teacher, Staefel (Paul Herveld), the meeting and marriage to Katherine (Greer Garson) and the sad, untimely death of her and their child during childbirth, his progression through the ranks, and his ultimate achievement when he was brought out of retirement to become Head of Brookfield during the First World War. It is a life journey with a wonderful blend of characters that deals fantastically well with the sensitive aspects that came out of the Great War (from both sides, as his friend, Staefel, is one of those 'killed in action', but for the enemy), and the same sense of loss felt in every corner of Britain and nowhere moreso than at Brookfield. It is beautifully told and this poignant story of heartbreak, friendship and respect reaches its climax as Mr Chips nears the end of his rich and rewarding life (despite the loss of his wife and unborn child), and when he hears someone say,
"He never had children you know"

But without opening his eyes, he whispers "I had hundreds of children…all boys".

Robert Donat deservedly won an Oscar for his portrayal of this enigmatic character from this 1939 film…there have been a couple of remakes with Peter O'Toole in 1969 and a TV film with Martin Clunes in 2002, both very good, but not as good as the warm and tender original, the story of Robert Donat's Mr Chips…a hero of the classroom in more ways than one.

▪▪▪

Schindler's List

Liam Neeson, Ralph Fiennes, Ben Kingsley, Embeth Davidtz, Caroline Goodall, Jonathan Sagall and many more

Another Steve Spielberg film (the third on my list) and another classic, telling the story of Oskar Schindler, a member of the Nazi Party, a flagrant womanizer and a man essentially making money out of other people's misery (a profiteer), but who goes on to save the lives of many Jews that would have ultimately perished in one way or another…a remarkable story of an unlikely hero. When Schindler acquired an enamelware factory in Krakow, Poland, he employed many Jews from the ghetto in the city, resulting in him eventually saving around 1200 Jews. It is a truly remarkable story and Spielberg's film perfectly captures the essence of the man and this astonishing story of survival. 'Schindler's List' is filmed in black and white which is a stroke of genius as it gives the film a sense of realism which creates a haunting sense of authenticity that makes it stand out against other excellent holocaust films such as 'Escape for Sobibor', 'The Boy In The Striped Pyjamas' and 'The Pianist'…all brilliant films in their own right but they are filmed in colour, and they just don't create that same level of authenticity as Schindler's List'. However, there is a sad, but poignant, episode in Schindler's List when there is an appropriate touch of colour – when the Germans come to empty the Krakow ghetto and they are rounding up people in the streets, we see a little girl wearing a red coat whereas everything else in the scene is black and white. Schindler, who has been out riding on his horse, is watching this chaotic scene and is transfixed by the little girl in the red coat (as he allegedly did in real life). When the scene cuts to mountains of dead bodies, a cart is pushed past Schindler and on the cart is the dead body of the little girl still wearing the red coat. This scene is extremely emotional and signifies the horror of the holocaust perfectly, it is also allegedly the catalyst that changed Schindler's views which resulted in him saving so many Jews. Many of the Jews that Schindler saved were held in the Krakow-Plazow concentration camp, where the camp commandant was Haupturmfurer Goeth (Ralph Fiennes), a violent and murderous character that mirrored the hard-line attitude of the Nazis and their horrendous treatment of the Jews. It is a brilliant film which finishes with the survivors (saved by Schindler) and their families honouring the man who is buried in Mount Zion Roman Catholic Franciscan Cemetery in Jerusalem.

The subject matter of the film, and others like it, is always seen as controversial, whether it's in the form of a film or a documentary, but it's important that films/documentaries are made about this subject. The world should never forget these shameful and dark events that resulted in the slaughter of around 6,000,000 Jews and countless of other minority groups such as Slavs, Gypsies, Disabled, homosexuals etc. The images seen and the stories told are still as shocking to me today as they were when I first witnessed them as a young boy watching the TV series 'The World at War', and it also gives me a new found respect and understanding of people such as Mrs Heimm, the sweet old lady at Heinrich Stahl House in East Finchley, who took me to Hampstead Fair when I was only ten years old, a sweet old lady who was also a survivor of the holocaust, who bore the tattooed number of a former concentration camp prisoner.

■■

Hamburger Hill

Dylan McDermott, Don Cheadle, Courtney B.Vance, Steven Weber, Kieu Chinh, Tim Quill and many others

There are many good films about the Vietnam War such as Platoon, We Were Soldiers, Full Metal Jacket, Casualties of War, Good Morning Vietnam, The Deer Hunter, Apocolypse Now and many, many more. But it is Hamburger Hill that is my favourite, as it tackles other issues other than the war itself. The film highlights the racial unfairness due to the way black soldiers were treated…mainly used in front line roles as opposed to cushy rear echelon roles in Saigon or safer areas. It also covers the political tensions of the time and how the American public felt about the war (there was a growing anti-war movement and soldiers returning from Vietnam were becoming vilified). The film is based on a true story about American forces attempting to take a heavily fortified hill (Hill 937) in the A Sau Valley in 1969. We are shown the total disregard for human life and the inept decicions made by higher command…ordering young American soldiers to attack well constructed NVA (North Vietnamese Army) positions in full frontal assaults…again and again and again! During the many battle scenes we see characters, we have come to know, cut down in their prime in an array of grissly ways which highlights the horrors of the Vietnam War. It is believed that the US lost 72 men with over 400 being injured and 7 MIAs (missing in action) and the Vietnamese many, many more. The loss of life in taking the hill caused controversy as it had little strategic value, and as we see at the end of the film, the Americans abandoned it shortly after taking it, which caused controversy with the American military and the public back home in the US. For me it epitomizes the Vietnam War and pointlessness and ineffectiveness of American military tactics. The characters of the infantry squad are led mainly by Sgt Frantz (Dylan McDermott), but it is Doc (the squad's medic) who steals the limelight and provides the realistic image of not just the film, but the war itself. The barbarity, horror and unmistakeable errors made by the US are highlighted in spectacular ways in this hard-hitting film…probably the first war film of the modern era that shows war for what it actually is, horrific. It drove home the reality of war and the scars it creates…on soldiers who served in Vietnam, their families and especially on a nation that despite its power, had no way of winning in Vietnam…it was lost politically, on the ground and the 'hearts and minds' tactics were totally bereft of any common sense i.e. the re-location of civilians who had lived in villages for generations turned the rural Vietnamese population against the US. It is a war that probably affected most families in the US and it probably was, still is and always will be the darkest era in American history. A timeless film, that is, by far, the best portrayal of the Vietnam War with a cast of almost unknown actors when it was released in 1987.

Absolutely amazing, but sad film that highlights that there were no real winners in the Vietnam War, as with any war.

■■

Killing Fields

Haing S.Ngor, Sam Waterston, John Malkovich, Spalding Gray, Craig T.Nelson, Julian Sands, and many others

This is another true story and is set during the 1970s in Cambodia, when the Khmer Rouge took control of their country in a bloody revolution. This revolution and its aftermath resulted in the death, via starvation, torture, murder etc of almost a quarter of Cambodia's population. Under the rule of the despot, Pol Pot, the Khmer Rouge emptied the cities, killed educated people and returned the country to 'Year Zero' and an agricultural society. The horrors of this revolution are seen in this film that is centred around the story of a friendship between Sydney Schanberg, a New York Times journalist and his local representative, Dith Pran. There are many survival stories told of people caught up in the Khmer Rouge coup such as 'First They Killed My Father' (also made into a film by Angeline Jolene) and 'Stay Alive My Son', but it is 'The Killing Fields' that was the first major film that highlighted the horror of events in Cambodia in the 1970s and the barbaric treatment of its people due to the lunacy of the Khmer Rouge as Cambodia decends into chaos. Sydney attempts to get Dith and his family to safety, but Dith changes his mind at the last minute, and whilst his family are flown to the USA and safety, he decides to stay with Sydney.

The eurphoria of the revolution soon turns to fear for the population of Phnom Penh
and Cambodia, which included Sydney and Dith, as the brutal reality of the Khmer Rouge revealed itself. Sydney and Dith were soon detained, with other foreigeners, in a large house in Phnom Penh…the nightmare begins. A remarkable story of survival unfolds as Sydney and other foreign nationals are forced to leave Cambodia whilst Dith finds himself in one of the labour/re-education camps, where he is subjected to forced labour, starvation and torture, and witness's people being murdered. He manages to escape and stumbles upon the true horror of the Khmer Rouge regime when he falls into a pit of

dead bodies and finds himself in the middle of an area where there are many similar pits collectively teeming with thousands of his dead compatriots...hence their ironic name of 'killing fields'. During this period Sydney, in New York, is desperately trying to find out what has happened to Dith. There are more twists in the story before the emotional finale when Sydney receives the news that Dith is alive, and the two are re-united in a refugee camp in Thailand in 1980. It is a truly amazing story that, whilst revealing the depth of Sydney and Dith's friendship, also highlights the horror associated with the Khmer Rouge and the non-sensical treatment of their own people.

■■■

Mississippi Burning
Gene Hackman, Willem Dafoe, Frances McDormand, Brad Dourif, R.Lee Ermey, Michael Rooker, Darius McCrary, Badja Djola, Frankie Faison and many others

This is another brutal film based loosely on a true story and is set in 1964 surrounding the the murder investigation of three civil rights activists, Chaney, Goodman and Schwerner, in Mississippi. Early in the film we are introduced to two FBI agents, who are sent to Mississippi to investigate, Agent Rupert Anderson (Gene Hackman) and Agent Alan Ward (William Dafoe)...two very different characters. As the story unfolds it reveals a hot bed of Klu Klux Klan members overflowing with racial hatred and contempt for blacks. It is shocking to see how the treatment of the blacks was portrayed in the film and the cruel arrogance of the white characters of the town that is central to the story and a true reflection of how blacks were treated in 1960s Mississippi. It is shocking to realise that these events portrayed in the film were occurring all over the 'South' during this period. It is not a surprise that given the subject matter that this is a violent film, but the performance of Gene Hackman is enthralling, and when the bodies of the three murdered men are found, Gene Hackman's character comes more to the fore. As the FBI's tactics change, mainly Anderson's doing, the perpetrators of the murders start to turn on each other and eventually the FBI have their men.

It is an outstanding film and easily one of my favourites and it is complimented by a great soundtrack, and it has to be a

625

contender as one of my favourite films of all time. I found myself 'rooting' for the underdogs in the film…the black community and the terror they had to live with every day. When you see the white supremesists arrested, tried and given lengthy prison sentences, there is a sense of justice, not just for the three murdered activists, but for the entire black community, all over the 'Deep South'. I love this film, a film that provides a great story of good prevailing over evil, violent times that deserve no credible place in history, but unfortunately, their (KKK) place in history, as a dangerous, racist and powerful organization, has been cemented and unfortunately there are still people around today that mirror the beliefs of those that murdered the three men…thankfully there are also men like Anderson who will fight those injustices.

■■■

The Notebook

Ryan Gosling Jr, Rachel McAdams, James Garner, Gena Rowlands, James Marsden, Joan Allen, Kevin Connolly, Sam Shepherd and many others

I am a bit of a softie at heart and I can't resist a good love story and there are many I have enjoyed over the years such as *An Officer and a Gentleman*; *P.S. I Love You*; *Notting Hill*; *Titanic*; *Ghost* etc, but for me, the best has to *The Notebook*. I consider this to be the ultimate love story between two people, a story that spans many decades, and there are events in the film that each and every one of us could relate to, regardless of age. It is a love that spans across the entire length of adulthood, and at first seemingly told as a story to an old lady in a nursing home by a fellow resident, and both in the latter stages of life…it is soon realised that the old couple are actually married and the man is telling the story to his wife, who has Altzheimer's, in a bid to try and get her to remember their life together. The elderly man's efforts appear futile, but it is the viewer that is taken back and forth between the past and the present on an emotional roller-coaster that starts with a chance but poignant meeting at a fairground in the 1930s.

The man, Noah, is reading to his wife, Allie, and is trying his damndest to get Allie to remember, despite the doctor telling

626

him he's wasting his time, but he wants his wife back, such is the depth of his love for her. Noah Jr doesn't just take Allie back to a time when he and Allie fell in love, he is taking us all back, and we watch a passionate love grow and develop between two young people. However, they came from different backgrounds, with Noah Jr working in a local sawmill whilst Allie's family are very wealthy and as a result they eventually successfully break them up...and we experience the painful separation of two people who's only crime is to love each other with unbridled passion. It is a beautiful, well-made and well-acted film by both the young (Ryan Gosling and Rachel McAdams) and older (James Garner and Gena Rowlands) versions of Noah Jr and Allie.

There is one point in the film that Allie appears to remember Noah Jr just for a split second, but almost immediately she sadly reverts back to not knowing Noah Jr is her husband leaving him visibly upset and heartbroken...it is a truly upsetting scene. As the story moves along we see a seven year forced separation between the young lovers before they re-kindle their love with some very emotional scenes...it is love in its basist sense, but also extremely pure. We see the coming together of two people and their fiery but passionate relationship; we see the heartache of the forced separation, a rekindling of their love and the ultimate sacrifice of Noah Jr's love for Allie in his attempts to keep their love alive in the nursing home.

As I've already stated, everyone can relate to scenes in this film, and its ability to use the raw emotion associated with love is what make it such a wonderful film. Many people experience this level of love in relationships/marriages that have lasted fifty or sixty years, and some, like me, have enjoyed fleeting moments, but like the senior Noah, I have someone in my life that I want to cherish every moment with and I totally understand Noah's actions...The Notebook may never receive its full recognition, but I hope it does, and goes on to become recognised as the classic love story.

■■

Top Ten TV Programmes

The Chase is the only programme I have included from the present, but that is not a reflection of today's TV, as there are some excellent programmes to watch such as Poldark; World on Fire; The Voice etc and there are many great investigatitive documentaries and I have enjoyed some of the Stacey Dooley programmes that have looked into some controversial subjects such as drugs; child abuse; domestic workers in tourist hotspots around the world etc. I have taken a nostalgic look at the past, hence there are a mix of programmes from the seventies, eighties, nineties and noughties. But I have left out 'soaps' as despite being a fan of Coronation Street, Eastenders and Emmerdale over the years, I barely watch them these days. Additionally, I have omitted cartoons or other programmes from my youth such as Wacky Races; Scooby Doo; Hong Kong Fuey; Top Cat; Blue Peter; Grange Hill etc, which I thoroughly enjoyed back in the day and now, but I feel that is a completely different 'Top Ten', which would also include the original Adam West, Batman and Robin TV series; Star Trek; Land of the Giants; Adams Family and many, many more. Comedy has been included in my 'Top Ten' as I believe comedy works better on TV than it does on film and I have avoided some controversial programmes such as Love Thy Neighbour and Alf Garnett for obvious reasons, I have also omitted nature programmes as I feel these deserve their own 'Top Ten' but would probably be dominated by David Attenborough. Enjoy my list and see for yourself, but you younger ones may not appreciate some of my choices as they would seem dated to you, but those of a similar generation as me will probably wear a smile as they remember these or other programmes from the same eras such as Rising Damp; Mind Your Language; The Sweeney; Absolutely Fabulous, Vicar of Dibley; Knight Rider, Tomorrow's World and so many more.

Programme

<u>Dads Army</u>

As a youngster growing up in Bridgend, Saturday night TV was always something to look forward to, and more often than not, I wasn't disappointed. Those Saturday evening programmes such *Dr Who*; *Bruce Forsythe's Generation Game*; *The Two Ronnies*; *Ironside*; *Kojak; Starsky and Hutch and Match of the Day* etc provided great entertainment and 'Saturday Night telly' was always the highlight of the week. However, there was one programme that I really looked forward to and still enjoy watching today…*Dad's Army*. It is still as funny today, if not moreso, as it was in those halcyon days of the Seventies. *Dad's Army* is a timeless comedy and centred around a Home Guard detachment in the fictitious Walmington-on-Sea, and their hilarious attempts of defending the town against the threat of a German invasion during World War II. The blend of characters was genius and was the brainchild of writers David Croft and Jimmy Perry, who also went on to write other classics such as *It Ain't Half Hot Mum, Hi-De-Hi* and *You Rang, M'Lord*? The characters of Dad's Army are probably more well known than any other comedy show, Captain Mainwaring (Arthur Lowe); Lance Corporal Jones (Clive Dunn); Sgt Wilson (John Le Mesurier); Private Pike (Ian Lavender); Private Godfrey (Arnold Ridley); Pte Walker (James Beck); Pte Frazer (John Laurie), Chief Warden (Bill Pertwee), Reverand Timothy (Frank Williams) and the verger (Edward Sinclair) provided us with week after week of hilarious comedy and inept soldiering under the command of of the bumbling Captain Mainwaring.

It is classic British comedy at its absolute best and explains why they are still televising re-runs of this well-written and well-acted show that originally ran from 1968 to 1977. A comedy that provided us with catchy phrases that I and many other people still use today such as 'You stupid boy'; 'we're doomed'; 'They don't like it uppem' and of course 'Don't panic…don't panic…' such is the legacy of this wonderful programme. Whilst the show highlights the 'Bulldog spirit' of Britain in the face of adversity, if Captain Mainwaring's squad was typical of the Home Guard (which I'm sure it wasn't), Britain would now be speaking German…absolute comic gold.

▪▪▪

Vietnam

A brilliant TV five-part mini-series that was set during the Vietnam War, highlighting Australian involvement in a controversial war, the political turmoil of the time and the rise of an anti-war movement that developed as the public's attitude toward the fighting in Vietnam changed. The Vietnam War has fascinated me for over thirty years and I have read many books, watched many films and documentaries. The horror, inept leadership and soldiering of the American troops and the conflicting ingenious and resourcefulness of the NVA (North Vietnamese Army) and Vietkong, provides a melting pot of intrigue and indecision in a war considered to be the first 'televised war'. Therefore, it is easy to see why TV coverage of the injured soldiers and body bags of dead American and Australian troops being returned their respective countries, turned public opinion against this barbaric and horrific war, as events played out their grizzly scenes in the news of homes across the world.

In this brilliant mini-series we follow the fortunes of a 'happy-go-lucky' student and budding photographer, Phil Goddard (Nicholas Eadie), son of Evelyn (Veronica Lang) and his public servant father, Douglas, (Barry Otto) and brother to a rebellious fifteen year old Megan (Nicole Kidman), as the Australian involvement in Vietnam deepened and Phil takes his chance with 'DoB lottery' for the army draft. The story escalates as Phil's gamble has a negative affect on the Goddard family as he is drafted into the army and then sent to Vietnam to fight. We follow Phil as he heads to Vietnam, survives his tour and comes back to his family, but is visibly scarred by the war. However, he decides to return to Vietnam as he misses the Vietnamese girl he had met during his first tour, and he ends up in a 'special forces' unit. He becomes dehumanized at the things he witnesses, including the killing of his Vietnamese girlfriend, who he discovers is part of the Vietkong, and eventually he is discharged and returns to Australia. However, he does not return to his family and isolates himself as he struggles with some sort of PTSD from his experiences in Vietnam. Meanwhile Megan, his sister, and his mother are actively involved with the anti-war movement. Eventually, we see Phil being re-united with his family. It is a clever, emotional, hard-hitting mini-series that covers many issues associated with the Vietnam War. Unfortunately, it's a little known mini-series, but well worth a watch.

■■

The Two Ronnies

Ronnie Corbett and Ronnie Barker , *The Two Ronnies*, complemented each other perfectly and their show was great Saturday night TV…they had it all comedy, great sketches, song and dance, innuendo and like *Dad's Army* they became an icon of Saturday night entertainment on BBC1. This was another highlight of Saturday night telly, their brand of humour suited everyone, probably the last great comedy double act of the pre-modern era that had it all, both extremely clever and funny in their own right. When I was younger the bit I didn't like was Ronnie Corbett in his chair telling a joke…but when I became older, I loved this part of the show as Ronnie Corbett continually went off at tangents before returning time and time again to finish telling the joke…very clever. Whilst there was innuendo in their 'song' routines they were so cleverly done that the suggestive element was so subtle it didn't cause offence. Ronnie Barker was way ahead of his time as a comic writer and this was clearly evident during the long run of *The Two Ronnies*. Their most famous sketch, 'Fork Handles', was a comedy masterclass, and is still funny today as the night it was first aired…absolute class. And their openings and closings to the show, as newsreaders, was also funny, as they provided hilarious comic news, and the end of the show was always Ronnie Corbett saying "And it's goodnight from me" and Ronnie Barker saying "And it's goodnight from him"…so, so funny.

■■■■■■■■■■■■■■■■■■■■■■■■■■■■■■■■■■■■■■■

Match of the Day

I have been watching *Match of the Day* for almost fifty years and even today, it is still my favourite football programme. Back in the Seventies ITV attempted to upstage *Match of the Day*, but *The Big Match* was always a poor relation to the far superior BBC programme. It's coverage of every game in the top division has always been a winner…an hour and a half of top football, all the goals, all the controversial incidents, sendings-off etc, followed by excellent analysis. The wonderful goals, players and dramas I've seen over the years is almost limitless and it's been chaired by some great hosts such as David Coleman, Jimmy Hill, Des Lyneham and Gary Lineker, and also great pundits, my favourites being Alan

Hansen and Alan Shearer, so knowledgeable. Finally, they have had some fantastic commentators over the years such as John Motson, Barry Davies and Tony Gubba.

My favourite *Match of the Day* moment has to be the Liverpool v Barnsley F.A.Cup 5th Round game in 2008 when Barnsley won 2-1 at Anfield after Brian Howard's brilliant winning goal…the stuff of dreams. The worst match has to be another Barnsley v Liverpool game, this time at Oakwell during Barnsley's only season in the Premiership in 1997/98 season. A game Barnsley controversially lost 3-2 and finished the game with eight men after having three men sent off…sadly, it was the turning point in a tough season that saw them being relegated back to the Championship. Yes, Match of the Day has been a huge part of my life and is one of the reasons I love football, long may it continue to entertain people…it was certainly the programme I wanted to watch more than any other when I was a teenager in the Seventies…great memories and an iconic class of British television.

■■

Benny Hill Show

My Gran Henson hated this programme but she still let me watch it…I can still see her sitting in her favourite chair, knitting and tutting in disgust at the slap-stick, but smutty, comedy of Benny Hill. I thought it was hilarious, especially the speeded up clips where everyone would be chasing Benny Hill to an ever familiar tune, that even people today know…even if they don't know who Benny Hill was. The 'tongue in cheek' humour was acceptable in the seventies, but it is difficult to understand the level of 'PC' that is evident in today's world, and as a result, it would probably be seen as exploiting women and they wouldn't get away with making a show like it today. Realistically, it was clean, harmless fun and that's how it should be remembered, despite the naughty and seemingly lecherous behaviour of Benny Hill. The cast of the show Henry McGhee, Sue Upton, Bob Todd, to name but a few, were as iconic as Benny Hill himself, and offered the straight element to Benny Hill's naughty behaviour, but it was his side-kick, Jackie Wright, the diminuative bald man that Benny continually slapped on the top of the head. As a teenage boy you couldn't help but laugh at the saucy sketches, and my favourite character was Fred Scuttle, an idiotic character with round-rimmed glasses, blinking eyes, pronounced lisp who continually saluted everyone and who always came up with half-brained ideas...absolutely priceless and extremely funny.

The seventies were much simpler times in the context of humour and the colourful character of *The Benny Hill Show* epitomized the halcyon days of this 'suggestive' type of humour.

■■■

The Chase

Everyone loves a quiz show and I am no different and have enjoyed many over the years such as *Sale of the Century; Mastermind; Blockbusters; Who wants to be a Millionaire?; Eggheads* and many more. It has been said that everyone likes the 'thrill of the chase' and *The Chase* has this in abundance, its this 'chase' that sets this quiz show apart from others over the years – the thrill (and fear) of the contestant is to ensure they don't get caught by 'the chaser' during the individual rounds and the 'final chase'. It's real edge of the seat stuff and the more contestants in the final chase gives the team a broader chance of winning with increased knowledge. I love the fact there is a show where the contestants are the general public, but also a celebrity show for charity. The chasers, as you would expect, are excellent and they tempt the contestants with high prize cash figures to build the cash pot, but the downside is that chaser starts just one place behind them...the gamble sometimes pays off, but sometimes it doesn't. The final chase is won by whoever scores the highest...the contestant go first and then the chaser, if the chaser gets a question wrong then the contestants get the chance to push the chaser back in the excellent game of cat and mouse, and some chases have gone down to the last second with victory going either way. Additionally, what adds to this brilliant spectacle is the host, Bradley Walsh, he is absolutely brilliant and so funny, it's as if the show was made for him. His banter with both the contestants and the chasers is hilarious and it's a toss up as to whether I watch the show for the format or because of Bradley Walsh, which is a compliment to both. Very well put

together and toughest quiz show which is enjoyed by most
people I know…long may it continue.

■■

Blackadder goes Forth

Everyone loves the rogue that is 'Blackadder' as we take a
journey through history from Medieval England through
Elizabethan and Georgian times before arriving at the First
World War and *Blackadder Goes Forth*. Each series is
excellent in its own right, but *Blackadder Goes Forth* steals it
for me…it is absolute comedy genius. Richard Curtis and Ben
Elton have taken one of the darkest times in history and
sprinkled a mix of dark humour and nostalgic comedy. It has
been said that every city, town or village suffered loss during
the First World War or 'Great War' as it is known, and to
create such iconic comedy about such a horrific and negative
war is a feat in itself. There are many scenes in the series that
are extremely funny, but on the flip side, they show the total
disregard for human life and the blend of characters in the
show provide, what could possibly be considered as one of the
best in British comedy along with the cast of Dad's
Army…both highlight the ability of the British to laugh in the
face of adversity. The stories each provide are a 'toungue in
cheek' poke at the 'establishment' and the way the
government and officers treated their soldiers. All comedy is
clever, but *Blackadder Goes Forth* takes comedy to another
level…to write a successful comedy about such a negative and
horrendous event was a stroke of genius, they would have
been vilified by society had they got it wrong. What they
achieved was a comedy that, whilst funny, also asks important
questions of how the war was perceived and highlights its
pointlessness in scenes such as Captain Blackadder (Rowan
Atkinson) ringing General Haig (Geoffrey Palmer) for a
favour (whilst on the phone Haig can be seen sweeping up
soldiers from a mock battlefield in front of him) or Captain
Darling (Tim Mcinnery) telling Brigadier Melchett (Stephen
Fry) that the scale of the land taken that day, which is about
the size of a snooker table, is 1:1 or the court martial over a
pidgeon or the misconception that the '20 minutes' was the
time pilots spent in the air, not realizing it was their life
expectancy. It appears that Captain Blackadder is the only
sane person in the whole series, such was the madness all

634

around him and that's what makes it so ironic, as he is the only one that understands that the war is pointless and he tries his best to escape the trenches via various means. However, it is the poignant end to the series that is so powerful as it dawns on the characters that they are unable to escape the command to go 'over the top', there is a moment when Captain Darling thinks the war is over as the artillery falls silent and shouts that "It's over...we've survived the Great War, 1914-1917", but Blackadder brings him down to earth with a bump telling him that they have stopped firing as it's time to go 'over the top'...the repeated slow motion action as they go over the top leaves us in no doubt that they all probably perished as the series ends...very powerful how that final scene transforms into a picture of a poppy covered field of today, as the curtain is brought down on a wonderful series.

■■■

Only Fools and Horses

This programme and its characters are still talked about in homes, pubs and workplaces, and it has to be considered as one of the most entertaining, humorous and successful programmes that Britain has ever produced. It ran from 1981 until 2003 and included sixteen 'Christmas Specials'. Everyone has their favourite episode...cleaning the chandaliers, the flourescant paint in the Chinese takeway and the cemetery, the singer who can't pronounce his Rs, the blow-up sex dolls, trip to Margate, Del Boy falling through the bar, winning the holiday (from a painting done by Rodney, when he was fourteen), Del Boy and Rodney dressed as Batman and Robin, Trigger's broom, Uncle Albert's insurance claim when he falls into a pub cellar and many, many more. The characters were undeniably brilliant and pure genius, characters such as Del Boy (David Jason); his younger brother Rodney (Nicholas Lyndhurst); Grandad (Lennard Pearce); Uncle Albert (Buster Merryfield); Trigger (Roger Lloyd Pack); Boycie (John Challis); Racquel (Tessa Peake-Jones); Cassandra (Gwyneth Strong); Marlene (Sue Holderness) and many, many more. This fantastic show brought us a feast of entertainment as Del Boy continually promises Rodney that 'this time next year we'll be millionaires' and the episodes were always centred around his money making schemes from their HQ...their flat in the fictitious tower block of Nelson

635

Mandela House in Peckham. Like Dad's Army the show provided us with some great quotes such as 'cushty', 'Rodney, you plonker'; 'Lovely jubbly'; 'During the War'; 'Dave…'; 'Mange tout, mange tout'; 'Marlene…' to name but a few. It wouldn't be an exaggeration that it is the finest light entertainment show ever to hit British TV screens as people can identify with the characters as they became an institution of British society…everyone knows a Del Boy or a Rodney or a Trigger. My own work colleagues often call me Uncle Albert and liken my stories of my army life to his 'During the war…', a comparison I'm proud of and find totally amusing.

Eventually, they did become millionaires when they sold an old clock at auction they'd found during a garage clearance, and the scene of Del Boy and Rodney in their beaten-up old yellow robin reliant with Trotters Independent Traders emblazoned on the side, screaming and shouting…and as the camera pans out to the image of the van, packed up outside Sotherby's, violently shaking die to their excitement epitomizes everything that was great and funny about the iconic '*Only Fools and Horses*'.

■■■

Becker

With exception of the iconic *Mash* and *Happy Days*, I'm not a huge fan of American comedy shows, I find their over the top and are far removed from actual reality. I never liked *Friends, Seinfeld* or other similar shows, but *Becker* was different, and although politically incorrect on so many levels, the blend of characters complimented each other perfectly, and Ted Danson's acting in the role of *Becker* was a stroke of genius…a doctor who is experiencing the bitterness of reality and hates his own life and the 'stupid' people he meets who make that life a misery on a daily basis. It doesn't sound like the foundations for great comedy, but the blend of main characters that experience the daily grind of Becker's life along with their own problems provides unexpected moments of humour as they and everyone else are repeatedly victims of Becker's acid tongue and bitterness. The characters were Dr John Becker (Ted Danson); the dizzy receptionist, Linda (Shawnee Smith); the practice manager, Margaret (Hattie

Winston); café owner and former model, Reggie (Terry Farrell), the blind newspaper vendor, Jake (Alan Desent); loser Bob (Saverio Guerra); the 2nd café owner, Christine (Nancy Travis) and others. Despite Becker's negatives, he is an excellent and dedicated doctor, but the amount of bad luck he endures and his tetchy behaviour provides some priceless humerous scenes, mixed with some equally touching moments. As un 'pc' as it sounds, Becker's derision of Bob, Jake, Reggie and Linda are hilarious and writers probably wouldn't get away with it in today's television. It has been fifteen years since the show finished, but it is well worth a watch if you get the chance…Ted Danson at his bitter, sarcastic and scathing best and by far the best modern American comedy.

■■

Top of the Pops

This was something that, as teenagers, we all loved watching and it was essential viewing, as the conversation in school on a Friday morning would always be about who was on *Top of the Pops* the previous evening and who was No1 in the charts. This was an iconic programme that was 'must see' television throughout the sixties; seventies; eighties; nineties and early noughties right up to when it ended in 2006 for all teenagers and adults alike who would settle themselves down to its usual 7.30pm Thursday evening slot (it did move to a Friday on a few occasions, but it was the Thursday night time that sticks out in my mind, as being its usual slot). Despite the majority of songs not being sung live, some songs being played via a video or accompanied by the famous Top of the Pops dance troupes of Pans People and Legs and Co, it was still a great programme, hosted by the famous DJs of the day. We all watched our favourite singers or groups, probably had our first musical crushes (mine was Suzi Quatro, when I was about ten), watched hundreds of one hit wonders, and always enjoyed the Christmas Day Top of the Pops to see who would be the Christmas No 1…the ultimate honour in the musical calendar before the Brit Awards came along. They show compilation highlight shows from different years and I always enjoy it when they show the late 1970s and early to mid 1980s, reminiscing about the good old days when worries were few and life was a lot less complicated…and that's the

637

· joy of music, it can take you back to a certain time in the past, even to a single event and even remind you of a long lost love. Yes, Top of the Pops, the music show of my and other generations and will always hold a special place in my mind and heart.

■■■

Top Ten Books/Novels

I have always loved reading, it sparks the imagination as you attempt to visualize the subject matter you are reading, whether it be a historical novel, a story of war or an auto-biography etc. The only times I have struggled to read a book is when that spark is not ignited and the visual element cannot be imagined, but that has rarely happened. The joy of reading is that there will always be a category that will grab the attention of anyone, even a person who does not like reading...it is just a case of finding that subject that draws you in and makes for a compelling read. This top ten is not something that you may enjoy reading yourself, you may be intrigued by some or reviled by others, but there may be one that you think 'I might give that one a try'. My 'top ten' will reveal my love for history or true stories...there are no crime or romance books and there are some notable omissions such as books by James Herbert (The Fog, The Rats etc), Nelson Mandela's autobiography, Second World War books or the Enid Blyton books I read as a youngster (Castle of Adventure, Valley of Adventure etc) or the many auto-biographies of great Welsh rugby players I have read highlighting my love of rugby (there is one rugby auto-biography that I have included that may surprise a few). Lastly, I could have included some of the children's books I studied during my last module at the OU, Children's Literature, such as Little Women, Swallows and Amazons, Tom's Midnight Garden, Junk, Treasure Island, Coram Boy, Roll of Thunder, Hear my Cry and Where the World Ends, all outstanding books and I have to admit I nearly included Junk, a gritty, hard-hitting story (based on actual events) of the horrors of heroin addiction. But I also haven't included comic books such as the annuals of Dandy and Beano, as good as they are, they were books I really enjoyed when I was younger and were responsible for starting on my reading journey...I wanted this top ten to be about stories with meanings. Additionally, this top ten is going to be

638

slightly different to the other top tens in that I am only going to reveal an overview of what the book is about and there will be no big reveal as to the outcomes of each book, just in case any of you decide to pick one of them up and to read them yourselves. My first choice is three books as they form a trilogy, by my favourite author of all time, Alecander Cordell...so here goes:

Names of Books	**Authors**
Rape of the Fair Country/ Hosts of Rebecca/ Song of the Earth	Alexander Cordell.

These three books are a trilogy of historical fiction that are centred around true events that occurred in South Wales during the Industrial Revolution. The stories involve a fictional family, the Mortymer's, and their trials, loves and struggles during a dark period in Welsh history. They are novels that are riddled with joy, sadness, love, hardship (disease, starvation, poverty, injustices and fights with the iron and mine owners (and the establishment) for safer working conditions and a better standard of living). The books highlight the lives of a working class family and the dangers of living in this period, when the lives of the working class were considered cheap and meaningless. The books are a roller-coaster of emotions and should you read them I know you will laugh, cry, empathise and even experience anger and sadness at events in each book. Additionally, I believe anyone who reads these books will think of their own ancestors and the struggles they may have endured...I know I did. These books are not only important to me as a reference to our own past, they have also led me to name three of my children after characters from these attritional novels. My eldest daughter, 'R', is named after a character in *Song of the Earth* and 'Rh's second name comes from the main character (Iestyn, prounounced 'yes tin') in *Rape of the Fair Country*. 'A' is named after a character in another Alexander Cordell book *Land of my Fathers*. As a proud Welshman, I have read each book many times and I treasure them and everything they reveal.

■■

To Kill a Mockingbird   Harper Lee

This is an absolute classic and was a book I first read when I
was in comprehensive school and again when I was an
adult…I enjoyed it both times, but reading it as an adult I was
better placed to understand the racial issues presented in the
book. It is a disturbing story with an intriguing set of
characters led by the main character, Scout, the young
daughter of Atticus Finich, a lawyer in a small Alabama town.
It identifies the racial inequality in 1930s America,
particularly in the 'Deep South' and centres around the trial of
a black man accused of an alleged rape by one of the town's
white residents…excellent read and an eye opener into the
racial tensions of small town America, particularly in places
like Alabama and Mississippi.

■■

Stay Alive, My Son   Pin Yathay

This is the story of one family's survival in Cambodia
following the rise to power of the Khmer Rouge in 1975. A
family that was forced to leave Phnom Penh and found
themselves being moved from one labour camp to another as
they worked as peasants in the fields under horrifying
conditions. It is one of the thousands of stories that have
emerged from Cambodia in recent times about a period where
almost a third of the country's population perished. They are
comparable with the more famous atrocities associated with
the 'Holocaust' and yet, in some respects, more
incomprehensible. If you decide to read this it will open your
eyes to the horrors the Khmer Rouge meted out to the majority
of their compatriots…another compelling read about what one
man is capable of enduring at the hands of another.

■■

Nam   Mark Baker

This is similar to the 'voices' series of books that provided the
memories of civilians, servicemen and women covering
various events during World War II. The 'voices' books were
written from taped recordings of thousands upon thousands of
people who were interviewed about their individual

640

experiences in World War II. Similarly, Nam is a book that re-tells the experiences of many American servicemen and women who served in the Vietnam campaign. It is a true reflection of what they experienced or witnessed and in parts can be very graphic and could be considered by some as upsetting. The author travelled around America interviewing many people who served and tell their individual experiences of their time in training, their operational tours in Vietnam, War Stories and how they coped when they returned to the USA. It is a book without a beginning and in many senses a book without an end, as many veterans struggle to deal with a war that left many with mental and physical scars. I have many books about Vietnam such as *13th Valley, Chickenhawks, If I Die in a Combat Zone, The Tunnels of Cu Chi, Dispatches, Tiger Force, Vietnam: The Ten Thousand Day War* and many more, which are all excellent books in their own right. But there is something about this book that is gritty and brutally honest with sometimes a 'matter of fact' attitude from the former soldiers, airmen, marines, doctors and nurses who are being interviewed. If you want an honest reflection of what Vietnam was like without sugar-coating anything, then this is the book you must read if you are going to read a book about the American involvement in Vietnam.

■■

A People's History of Britain   Rebecca Fraser

This is a comprehensive book about British history that begins in 55B.C. and finishes in 2002 and it covers every major event in-between. If you like history I would recommend this book as it is an excellent read. It is not an academic, high-brow read it is written in a way that makes it an enjoyable read...I say that as when I was studying for my degree one or two of the history books I had to read were mind numbingly boring and were as painful as head-butting broken glass. This is special for another reason, it was a gift from a man who was the inspiration for my love of history and a major influence in my life, but who is sadly no longer with us, Bernard Stokes. A much loved man and the husband of my mother's cousin Beth and father to my cousins Nick (who also sadly passed away a few years ago) and Maggie. I have many memories of Bernard that involve history, but still haven't been able to confirm whether Monmouthshire is still at war with Germany, as he

641

once told me (Bernard claimed that when war was declared there were disputes over whether Monmouthshire was in England or Wales and therefore, when the declaration was signed it was signed by England, Scotland, Wales, Northern Ireland and Monmouthshire. When World War II ended the dispute had been resolved and the Declaration of Peace was only signed by the four home countries, meaning Monmouthshire was still at war with Germany). This was probably another case of Bernard teasing me, but it's something I have never forgotten. Bernard was a legend and is still sorely missed by all who knew him and this book acts as permanent reminder of the esteem I still hold for this great man and as a result the most precious book I have in my collection. It is a book that I know will help my daughter, Amy, with history when she starts comprehensive school in around eighteen months. Highly recommended.

■■■

Thailand: A Short History   David K.Wyatt

My connections with Thailand are well documented and during one trip I visited Asia Books in the Central Plaza in Khon Kaen, a shop that has a good selection of books in various lanuages including English. This book caught my eye because of my love of history and I saw it as an opportunity to not only enjoy reading about Thai history, but I thought it would help me understand the Thai people and perhaps reveal the reasoning behind Thai customs, especially their obsession with 'saving face'. It really is an excellent read and similar to *A People's History of Britain* it is written in a non-condescending way, that many history books are written, and is extremely informative, interesting and revealing. The history of Thailand (formerly Siam) and its inter-woven histories with Laos, Cambodia, Burma (Myanmar), Malaysia, Vietnam and the colonial powers of Britain and France is absolutely fascinating, as is its reverence of the Thai people toward the Thai Royal family. If you are visiting Thailand or have a connection with the country and you want to learn about Thailand's past then this is the book to read. Brilliant from beginning to end.

■■■

Rotten: No Irish - No Blacks – No Dogs   John Lydon

There are those who don't like John Lydon (otherwise know
as Johnny Rotten), and I think that is purely that they just
don't understand him and still see him as the obnoxious and
sometimes arrogant person who fronted the Sex Pistols…a
punk band of the late-Seventies who stuck two fingers up to
the British establishment. But this is an intriguing read and a
book I thoroughly enjoyed…yes, John Lydon is a complex
character but there is evidence of his humanity in this book
and that there is a lot more to him than the reviled figure many
believe is the real John Lydon. There is no doubt that he was a
high profile figure during my early to late teens, but there is a
warmth evident in this book that transposes the controversial
figure that was influential to many of my generation. After
reading this book I have a new found respect for this
outspoken legend. I defy any of you not to change your
attitude about John Lydon after reading this excellent, honest
and enthralling book.

■■■

Martin Johnson: The Autobiography   Martin Johnson

There are many of my fellow Welshman throwing their arms
in the air shouting 'How could you?' but as a lifelong rugby
fan, you have to admit that Martin Johnson is a much
respected figure in and out of rugby circles…he would
probably be in many people's all time Greatest ever World
XV. Remember, this is the only British rugby player that has
captained a World Cup winning team when England beat
Australia 20-17 in 2003. He was capped 82 times for England.
He captained the British Lions to a series win over South
Africa in 1997 and was part of a successful Leicester side and
captained them to two European Cups in 2001 & 2002 aswell
as four domestic championships. He was an incredible player
with a fanstatic career. I remember the Martin Johnson before
he achieved all these wonderful accolades, when he first came
back from New Zealand in 1991 and came to work with me
for two weeks…he was delivering stationery to our customers
in Leicestershire, and he was a humble, quietly spoken young
man and was an absolute gentleman. He went on to become
one of the best second rows ever in world rugby and was an

643

outstanding leader. If you only read one autobiography of a rugby player, make sure it's this one…share the highs and lows of this incredible player's journey and a man who will always remain an absolute legend.

■■■■■■■■■■■■■■■■■■■■■■■■■■■■■■■■■■■■■■■

The Story of English   Robert McCrum

As the name suggests this is the story of English from its early beginnings right up to the English we know today. It's a book that tells of us the origins of many of the words we use today and take for granted that they are of English origin. It tells how English has been adapted into local dialects in some parts of the world creating new mixed languages. It also reveals how English is now recognised as the number one international language. It is a fascinating book that reveals many unknowns and confirms other things that we believe are correct. This was another gift, a thank you from a wonderful woman, June Davies, who I used to help at Ystrad Mynach College in teaching English to foreign learners…a voluntary position I have now enjoyed for over five years. This book is well worth a read, with its strong hint of history it is another book I thoroughly enjoyed.

■■■■■■■■■■■■■■■■■■■■■■■■■■■■■■■■■■■■■■■

The Book Thief   Markus Zusak

This is an incredible book with a very unusual narration technique seeing the lives of the characters from an angle that I don't think has ever been used before. It is an extraordinarily clever book and you cannot help but become emotionally attached to its many different characters, especially its main characters Leisel, her adoptive parents, Rosa and Hans Hubermann, her friend Rudy, and the young Jewish man, Max. It is set in a small German town during World War II and it is the first time I've seen World War II portrayed through the eyes of ordinary Germans. I don't want to say any more about this book other than it has been adapted into a film, which is as excellent as the book. Therefore, if you don't like reading, there's always the film. However, to those who do like reading and haven't read this book, I would strongly recommend making this the next book you read...you will not be disappointed. It's difficult to pigeon hole this book, it was written for adults but has been labelled as a book for young adults (teenagers), I don't think it matters as it is just an amazing read. If I was you, I'd be putting my coat on and heading for the nearest bookstore or ordering it on-line...whichever, make sure you read it as I know you will love it as much as I did.

Epilogue

I've done it, I've achieved my lifelong dream of writing a book. Am I happy with the finished article? Could I have written things differently? Could the layout have been different? Should I have been more graphic or descriptive in my writing? etc...the answer to all these questions and more is 'Yes', but this is how it's ended up...pages of humour, love, adventure, sadness, triumph, anger, respect, pride and sadly...death, but most of all it's been a work of 'reflection' and the whole book has been a joy to write, even remembering events that had a detrimental effect on my life and well-being. Remembering people, events, places and life in general is not going to be all sweetness and light, as that does not reflect real life...good things happen and bad things happen. Have I been surprised by how my understanding of some people and events has changed? Again, 'Yes', there have been many instances where my outlook on someone or something that happened, has totally changed and emotionally, that has been difficult to deal with at times. But it has also been wonderful (and sad) remembering people such as my grandparents, my mother and other family members or friends who are no longer with us, remembering happy times from the distant and more recent past. Remembering my achievements in life, academically, personally or on the sporting front, aswell as my failings in those same areas, it has all been extremely uplifting. But remembering the people I shared those moments with, has been nothing short of fantastic, as I have known many characters in my life from within the family, from school, from the Royal Engineers, from sport, friends and most recently from my time spent at Nuaire and in the Caerphilly area, mainly Abertridwr. Each shared moment is a moment cherished, as it has made me the man I am today, and I thank you all for your company on this journey however big or small part you played.

Some people are probably asking "Why set the book out as a series of short stories?". The answer is fairly simple. I started writing a book around ten to twelve years ago, a conventional auto-biography that would have run from 'Birth to present day' and had written around 120 pages. Unfortunately, I lost it all when my laptop was taken in for repair. However, when I started this book I had started studying for my degree with the Open University and one of the modules I studied included a section on 'short stories' and it spawned the idea to again start writing a book, but this time as a series of short stories. Additionally, the essay writing I had started for my OU assignments had taught me the importance of writing an outline plan for each essay, therefore, this was also incorporated in the idea. The base plan of writing an auto-biography as a series of short stories was born and was quickly followed by the idea to write not only an introduction to the book, but an introduction to each chapter and also to each story…this meant that anyone reading the book can flick through the pages to any point and just read any story of their choice, giving the reader much more freedom to read what they want. The next stage was to create the chapter titles to determine how my life story would be told. Lastly, the individual stories allowed me to be more selective in what I wrote about…I wanted it to be a celebration of my life (good and bad), it was never my intention to write a book that involved me slating people who crossed my path (apart from the odd one), I just wanted to write an honest book that reflected my own understanding of people I met along the way and the events that occurred during my life. Another reason, and the main one, is that I wanted to write a book that my children could read and simply say "that's my dad", something to remember me by as they continue on their own journeys in life. With that in mind, my proudest achievement is that there is nothing in the book that my older children don't know about, there are no revelations that will horrify them…they know everything about me, I have no dark secrets I have kept from them. How many of you can say that to your children? I accept that those of you who are included in the stories in this book, may remember things slightly differently to how I've told them, we do not have identical memories and we will perceive events differently, our memories of them will understandably differ, but that doesn't mean they are wrong. They are just how I remember them. I'd like to think that there maybe some of you that have forgotten some of the events in the book and I hope these stories serve as a prompt for you to remember things you may have forgotten, and in turn, I hope these now remembered memories bring you joy. At the same time, I also hope that something I may have written about, may help some of you deal with difficulties in your own life or understand things that may have happened to you. And remember, never turn away a helping hand…we all need someone to help us through tough times when we are faced with bereavement, divorce, job losses, illness, injury etc…and as I found out during dark periods in my life, YOU ARE NOT ALONE, people will be there for you.

Writing this book has been a breath of fresh air and I think it's fair to say that I haven't led a sheltered, reclusive life…it's been a hundred miles an hour from the beginning and I can't believe I've crammed so much in. I have to pinch myself sometimes when I realise that I have only lived one life. If someone had said to me when I was a child living in Bridgend, I'd meet the people I've met, I'd see the many places I've lived in and visited, experience the things I have (especially the scrapes I've got myself into), or end up being married to a beautiful Thai lady, then I'd think that person was obviously smoking something that they shouldn't. Growing up in Bridgend, I thought it would be a place I would always live, that I'd get married to a childhood sweetheart, buy a house, have children, grow old, have grand-children and then, like my maternal grand-parents, die and be cremated or buried in Bridgend…and for some people that's probably what has or will happen. However, that's not always the reality, and for me that's exactly how it didn't turn out…my life has turned into a roller-coaster of emotional and memorable events that have shaped the person I am today…gone is that small, innocent Welsh boy who used to run around the playground in Laleston Primary School, all those years ago, when life was simple with no real worries. I'm now a man covered in the battle scars of life who has enjoyed every damn minute and would do it all again in a heartbeat, especially if it meant I could share it again with so many wonderful people…and yes, I know it means that I'd also have to share it again with some right twats, but that's life.

My life certainly isn't extraordinary and hasn't been perfect, but who wants perfection when you can have chaos and fun. I've lived life to the full, and as I touched upon in the beginning of the last chapter, I believe my experiences have enabled me to become a better father, they have provided me with the tools to help my own children deal with difficulties they have faced or may face in the future, and hopefully they will remember this and pass on that wisdom when counselling/advising their own children (my grand-children) with any future difficulties they may face. One thing that I definitely wasn't looking for in writing this book is 'sympathy', I wanted to 'reflect' on events in my life to gain a better understanding of why people acted the way they did? Why the decisions of others had such an impact on my life? Or what were the reasons behind certain life events? Whilst bad things have happened in my life, they have happened for a reason and are a mix of my bad life choices and them being just 'one of those things'. Therefore, we can beat ourselves up about them, feel sorry for ourselves or, as we used to say in the army, "pick ourselves up, dust ourselves down and crack on". Yes, it's easier said than done and I, like others, have struggled at times to dig myself out of a hole, regardless of whether it was of my own making or the fault of someone else. Sometimes you can pick yourself up immediately, but as I've discovered, other times it can take a little longer, depending on the situation. But eventually, you push the demons aside, get your life back together and come out the other side a stronger person...I could so easily have been a statistic and not been here to write this book, but I AM still here and thankful to those people (you know who you are) who helped me during those dark periods.

In the first paragraph I have intimated that via 'reflection' my understanding of some people and situations has changed and this is evident in how I perceived the relationship between my maternal grandmother and grandfather as being 'cold', since writing this book, my opinion has changed and I now realise that they loved each other very much and that I had witnessed that love when I was a teenager, especially in the way my grandmother cared for my grandfather following a series of strokes he suffered in 1976. Another perception that has been blown out of the water was how idyllic my life was as a child...I think it's extremely sad that I only have one real memory of doing something together with my mother and father and I guess that was an important place to start the book. However, that aside, I can now see that my childhood wasn't idyllic, as my early life was surrounded by half-truths, lies and abandonment...it's no wonder that I joined the army at sixteen and became distant from my family in the eighties and early nineties. Another realization that revealed itself was that I had never been 'in love' with my first wife, as she had always believed. This came about as I finally understood that I hadn't got over my love for Linda Hutchinson until the early 2000s (twenty plus years after the relationship had physically ended). The loss of Linda resulted in a monumentus and pivitol time in my life when I had to change my whole thinking. The plan of leaving the army in 1984 and settling down in Barnsley with Linda was sadly destroyed for one reason or another, and this was something I emotionally struggled to deal with for many, many years…despite signing-on again in the army for an amended 9 year stretch, thinking I was enjoying life and having new relationships, I can now see this was not the case. Writing the book has left me in no doubt that this huge emotional change in my life had turned me into a very selfish person, who purposely destroyed relationships and remained unhappy until my first wife and I divorced in 2000. Thankfully, seeing Linda in 2001 at her brothers wedding, as a happy mother and wife had replaced the image of a seventeen year old Linda running off crying in 1982, enabling me to finally begin my own emotional healing.

One of the worse things I have had to reflect upon and try to understand in writing this book, is the damage caused by child abuse…this is a very difficult subject to comprehend. The destructive elements associated with child abuse have been evident in a previous relationship I discussed in Chapter 8. …the figures of people who have suffered indirectly because of child abuse must be in their millions. Hindsight and reflection are wonderful things and it has resulted in an unhealthy acceptance that it is not something I can change on my own…we have to deal with it the best we can and that, sadly, is the way it will probably always be. Whilst I am an indirect victim of child abuse, I have to remember that I was not the abused and our pain is miniscule in comparison to that suffered by my former partner and others. The damage caused by one person's selfish actions many years ago left my ex-partner with major trust issues and suffering from mental illness. Sadly, she will continue to suffer and carry those horrific memories with her until she passes away at some point in the future. In some respects, using reflection, has allowed me to understand the rash decisions she has made that have caused a lot of pain, and that she would have probably been a different person today had the abuse not taken place.

Reflection has allowed me to be diligent and to be very aware of child abuse and it has allowed me to protect my own children from the devastating damage child abuse can cause. It is an evil that has no place in any society across the globe and has to be considered as one of the most destructive evils of mankind.

As I reflect on my time in the army, I know I wasn't the best soldier the world has ever seen, but despite the fact that I was never sent to a 'theatre of war', I am still proud to have served my country for ten and a half years and even prouder that it was as a Sapper. Yes, I served in the Falklands for six months and I was involved in exercises in the UK, Germany and Denmark, but it was the rugby or football pitches where my time was predominantly spent and I can now reflect on that time more obejectively. In my late teens and early twenties it was great to skip work details, win trophies and share the triumphs with some great people, who have remained lifelong friends. But, in hindsight, I can now appreciate that sport, particularly rugby, ruined my career as a soldier and ultimately led me to refusing my full Corporal when I was twenty-five and leaving the army after 9 years adult service twenty-one months later. The original plan was to serve my country for 22 years or longer, but that wasn't to be and perhaps with what happened after I left in 1990 (First Gulf War, the horrific events in the Balkans in the Nineties, the second Gulf War between 2001 and 2003 and Afghanistan), it was probably a blessing I left when I did. Nevertheless, I'm still proud to have put my hand up and volunteered to serve my Queen and Country for ten and a half years from the age of sixteen and a half...the memories made during that period will never, ever leave me and they are something I cherish (very difficult for civilians who have never served to know what that feels like and it is not something that is easily explained). As a result, I am proud of my 'Uncle Albert' nickname given to me by friends/colleagues at Nuaire.

Even writing and looking back on my sporting career, I understand that I wasn't a fantastic rugby or football player, I was probably an average player at best...I was blessed that I played with many great players in many great teams over the years and hence I enjoyed a fairly successful career. It was probably more down to luck than skill, I guess I was just in the right place at the right time, but I do admit that I could kick and I did have a pretty good sidestep (borne purely out of fear), Michael Stupple continually tells people "Huw could side-step you from a mile out". Unfortunately, my downfall was my size…I was only small (10st soaking wet and 5ft 8in). Therefore, Michael Stupple, Gerry Hoolachan and Jake Maiden will tell you I would never have made it as a prop…I had to settle to play as one of God's chosen own - outside half (No 10) or at full-back (No 15). But sport has provided me with great memories and lifelong friends and I am proud of the successes we collectively achieved, especially on the rugby field. But my funniest sporting memory has to be that night in the boxing ring at Maidstone back in 1985, when I got knocked out in 1 minute and 48 seconds…possibly the shortest boxing career on record. As a young child and young teen my dream, like many others, was to be a famous professional sportsman. But as I look back on a life that has been dominated by sport, in one capacity or another, I have come to realise that if I had been successful in just one sport then it is highly unlikely I would have been able to enjoy the many other sports I played over the years. Additionally, becoming a professional sportsman may have provided financial security, but the negative aspects of fame wouldn't have been something I believe I would have been able to cope with as a person. I have enjoyed playing rugby, football, tennis, badminton, squash, cricket, hockey, cross country running, athletics, volleyball, ice skating, table tennis, boxing and many more with varying degrees of success. I was always competitive when I played sport and played to win, but I always tried to play with a smile on my face and accepted defeat graciously if beaten by a better player or a better team. Additionally, sport played in the right spirit crosses social boundaries and creates unlikely friendships that you wouldn't necessarily experience in other aspects of life…and I believe that the memories they provide is probably the reason why we all enjoy playing some kind of sport.

My understanding of love, life and death has changed dramatically in writing this book as my experiences in these extremely complex areas have been both joyous and painful. It his made me understand 'Huw Thomas' better and understand why others in my life made the decisions they did, decisions that greatly affected me as both a child and as an adult. I now know that due to the fact I didn't see my father for three years as a small child, my mother moving into a flat (leaving me with my grandparents) when I was around eight and the failed relationship with Linda, are why I have seriously struggled with rejection. This was clearly evident when relationships ended, as I found it extremely difficult to deal with and this led to some very serious situations or bad decisions such as attempted suicide or purposely ending relationships, some of which, have been covered in this book. I also have a better understanding of some of the other decisions I made and the reasoning behind them, decisions that were sometimes justified such as joining the army, returning to Wales from Long Eaton or fighting for my children in a bitter custody battle. None of us have practice runs in life to see the impact of a decision, we have to make the best judgement call we can at the time with the information we have…sometimes we get it right and sometimes we don't. Like Jean said many years ago 'life's ard' and she was absolutely spot on…everyone experiences some sort of 'trial' in their life and how we deal with them will, in most cases, be different, highlighting how complex we all are as individuals. I have tried to be honest in this book with my feelings and my abilities, not just on the sports field, but more importantly as a father. I was 'ok' as a father when married to my ex-wife, but I believe I became a much better father following the divorce. Yes, I have made mistakes, but I have tried to be loving, supportive and understanding and although I haven't always got it right, I have always tried to do my best and I think my children appreciate that. I've come to greatly appreciate some of the major influences and role models in my life such as my maternal and paternal grandparents; my father and Shirley, my mother and Den; my Uncle Ivor, Bernard and Beth Stokes (Beth is the first cousin of my mother); Mr Owens and Mr Phillips (maths and history teachers respectively at Brytntirion Comprehensive School), Sgts Scholey, Kerr & Osborne (training instructors at J.L.R.R.E.); Gareth Davies (Army & Combined Services Senior Rugby Coach); Tiny Bott (24 Field Squadron RE Sergeant Major); Derek Deacon (Long Eaton Rugby); Alan Jenkins (my work colleague at Nuaire, neighbour and great friend); Alun Morton (another former Nuaire great); my wife Ada, my own children, so many of my peers and even ex-girlfriends. Thanks to you all for many different reasons, you have all played an important role at

653

some point in my life in creating the more rounded, content and happy Huw Thomas you see today who is at peace with the world and all its faults. Similarly, I must also thank all the negative people that have entered my life, who tried their utmost to destroy me, but who ultimately failed. Whether we like it or not, our characters are made up from positive and negative influences throughtout our lives, its how we choose to use those influences that is the key. I believe it's a strength and not a weakness to admit we are flawed or imperfect, as our imperfections highlight our humanity and define our humility. I know I'm not perfect, I know I've made mistakes and that I've hurt people…I so wish I hadn't, but I also know that I am no different to anyone else, I'm not a better person or a worse person than any of you, I am just different, we are all different and that's what makes us unique and special and that is something worth remembering. Through my own reflection, self-analysis and analysis of the characters and events in my life, I've enjoyed the whole experience of writing this multi faceted book. Similarly, I hope you've enjoyed reading this book as much as I enjoyed writing it and I hope you've enbraced the roller-coaster of emotion that is evident throughout, the informative parts of the 'travel journal' type chapter of my Thai trips and the 'top tens' towards the end…I have tried to include a variety of subjects in the book that hopefully appeal to the personal choice of many and I hope there was something that made you laugh, cry or gasp in astonishment/horror, or even helped in some way. If I can offer any advice it would be '*try not to take things too seriously, learn to laugh at yourselves and have fun…lots of fun. We are here once so make the most of it and remember to treat others the way you'd expect to be treated yourselves…no matter how bad people may treat you*'. It's easy for me to say that and I know it's advice that, at times, I didn't follow myself, hence the reason I'm saying it now as I saw the hurt I sometimes caused to others. Additionally, try not to have any regrets…I only admit to one, I could have had many more, but I prefer to call other possible regrets 'alternative life opportunities' that normally set you on a different path…no one knows how their life will pan out, every day when we step out of bed in the morning, we are stepping into the unknown, so try and embrace whatever that brings.

I've achieved a personal goal in more ways than one and you maybe wondering what's next for Huw Thomas or you may simply not care. Anyway, I am going to try and continue to live life to the full for as long as my health lets me or before the 'big sleep'. I am going to continue working at Nuaire, hopefully for many, many years and qualify as a teacher next year which will enable me to get a part-time job in a local college teaching English to foreign learners (this is more of a hobby as it is something I enjoy, and I have been an unpaid teaching assistant for five years, helping out in a two hour class once a week). There is still so much I'd like to see and do, and we are currently looking at re-visiting Thailand at the end of the next year (should have been this year, but postponed due to COVID-19) with a few days in Cambodia, but we'll see what happens. I'd like to visit Euro-Disney at some point in the next couple of years and who knows where else we might go. On the literary front, if this book is the only book I write then it's something I'm proud of, but I have got ideas bubbling away about some childrens books (a series of books for younger children with a central character…I can't say anymore or I might give the game away. And I have an idea for a possible 'trilogy' of historical fiction books for older children in their early teens), so watch this space. But mainly, I am going to enjoy spending time with family and creating more memories.

Good luck and good health to all, especially as we are in the grip of the COVID-19 pandemic. This is a scary time the likes of which none of us have ever seen and hopefully will ever see again and I hope everyone stays safe during this unprecendented and fearful period.

Cheers and love to all

Huw Thomas, November 2020

GLOSSARY

Numerical

4 tonner

This was the affectionate name for the Bedford MK, our main form of transport in the army. It took us on exercise, to the ranges, dropped us off on night's out etc and it was bloody cold and uncomfortable, but we all wanted to be 'Tail Gate Romeo's' so we could catch the eyes of local girls.

24 hour ration pack

A ration pack that provided a soldier enough calories to sustain a him/her in the field for one day. They came in four menus: A, B, C or D. Each pack contained a breakfast, tinned main meal and snacks (rolo's, a chocolate bar and dextrose sweets for energy) and ingredients to make a warm drink. There was also a tin opener, toilet roll, matches, hexamine blocks and mini collapsible cooker.

2ic

This is the 'second in command' of a squadron or regiment and normally holds the rank of Captain.

252 Charge Sheet

This was a form that was completed if a soldier committed any type of offence. The report would include the soldier's personal information and include the details of the offence.

In typical military tradition the soldier would be marched in to the office of the commanding officer, who would read the charge to the soldier. The soldier would be found guilty or not guilty. If guilty, he or she she would be asked if they'd accept the award and then be punished accordingly.

30m Rifle Range

Most camps had a 30m rifle range which was used for firing small arms such as the SMG (sub machine gun) and Browning 9mm pistol.

37 Pattern Webbing

This is the army issue ammunition sandy coloured pouches, small pack, large pack, belt, straps, water bottle and holder that a soldier would use in the field to carry his equipment such as rifle cleaning kit, spare clothes, mess tins, 24 hour ration pack, groundsheet and bivouac (see 'bivouac'). This was used in World War II and we still used this when I joined the

Junior Leaders (see 'J.L.R.R.E.') at sixteen.

3Ss

The three Ss are 'shit, shower and shave.'

58 Pattern Webbing

Similar to the 37 pattern webbing for use to carry a soldiers equipment (as detailed above) in the field. This more modern version was green coloured and consisted of a large pack, yoke, right and left ammo pouches, kidney pouch, water bottle and pouch, poncho roll and belt.

A

Ablutions

Army slang for a room or block that contains wash basins, showers, baths and toilets.

APC

Armoured personnel carrier.

Armoury

A building on a military site where weapons are stored.

ASEAN

The Assoctiation of SouthEast Asian Nations. A regional intergovernmental organization made up ten countries, Brunei, Cambodia, Indonesia, Laos, Malaysia, Myanmar,

Phillipines, Singapore,
Thailand and Vietnam.

Assault course

A course of permanent or
semi-permanent obstacles
(i.e. six ft wall, rope
walklways, 12ft wall,
water filled ditches,
horizontal or vertical
cargo nets to climb under
or over etc) that are used
for train soldiers.

AWOL

Absent WithOut Leave. A
term used for a military
person who has not
returned from leave or has
absconded from military
camp/base and failed to
attend a parade. This term
is only used in peacetime.
If the country was at war
this would be elevated to
'desertion' which carries a
more serious punishment

B

Bailey Bridge

A type of portable, pre-
fabricated, truss bridge. It
was a British development
in 1940-41 for use in
World War II. It was used
extensively by British,
Canadian and American
combat engineers,
especially after the war
ended and the
infrastructure of large
parts of Europe was re-
built. An iconic military
invention praised by
General Eisenhower.

Bamboozled	Cheated or tricked.
Basher	A bivouac that used to make a personal shelter for an individual soldier when in the field.
Beasting	The description of the process of instilling discipline into new recruits in the armed forces.
Best Clobber	Best clothes or outfit.
BFT	Battle Fitness Test. A fitness test that involved running three miles. The first mile and a half was run collectively as a troop (or squad), which had to be completed in eleven and a half minutes. The second half of the test also had to be completed in eleven and a half minutes (under 30s) but was run as individuals. The time may seem excessive to some, but a squad of men had soldiers of mixed fitness levels and the time was deemed a fair time for all.
Billet	A building where soldiers are lodged temporarily.
Blind side (rugby)	The opposite of open side. The 'narrow' side between

Brigadier A rank in the British Army, below Major General but above Colonel.

Burgermeister Chairman of the executive council in a German town or city. Similar to a Mayor in the UK, but with more power.

Butt A slang word in Wales for mate, pal or friend etc.

C

CAFCASS Children And Family Court Advisory and Support Service. A non-departmental public body in England set-up to promote the welfare of children and families involved in family court.

Camaradarie A mutual trust or friendship that develops between people who spend a lot of time together.

Cam cream Camouglage cream. A cream soldiers use to conceal the shine and contours of the face to help conceal soldiers.

Capt Captain. A military rank below major but above lieutenant.

CCF	Combined Cadet Force. Similar to Army Cadets sponsored by Ministry of Defence. Normally found in private schools.
CFT	Combat Fitness Test. During the 1980s this involved a forced march of around 8 miles in full kit (58 pattern webbing and rifle), carrying a fellow soldier a 100m and a task specific to army and the soldiers' Corps.
Chaplain (Army)	A religious representative of the army that assists soldiers and their families.
Chong kraben	A lower-body wraparound cloth (Thai)
Chedi	Alternative name for a Buddhist stupa (see 'stupa').
CND	Campaign for Nuclear Disarmament. An organization that fights for nuclear disarmament in Britain and globally.
Combat engineer	Is a solider that performs a variety of construction and demolition tasks that will assist friendly forces or hamper the enemy respectively. Roles include bridge-building, mine clearance, bridge demolition, minelaying, booby traps etc. Otherwise

known as a 'Sapper' or 'Oggy'

Coarctation

A congenital narrowing of a short section of the aorta.

Coastel

A floating hotel that was sent to the Falkland Islands in 1983 to accommodate soldiers.

CO

Commanding Officer. This was normally a Lieutenant Colonel (rank below Colonel but above Major). And would be in command of a regiment (normally between 800-1000 soldiers).

Copse

A small group of trees.

Condominium

A building or complex of buildings of individually owned apartments (Thailand).

Corps

A branch of the army assigned to a particular kind of work (i.e. Corps of Royal Engineers, Royal Army Ordinance Corps, Royal Army Medical Corps etc).

Cpl

Corporal. A rank below Sergeant but above Lance Corporal.

Crap Hat

A degoratory term used by members of the Parachute Regiment when describing

soliders from other parts
of the army.

CS Gas

A powerful form of tear
gas used to control riots.

D

Decontamination pads

A small specialised pad
issued to soldiers to use to
decontaminise themselves
and their equipment after a
chemical attack.

Dias

A raised, sometimes
covered, platform where
troops are viewed and
salutes are taken.

DMS Boots

Directly **M**oulded **S**ole
boots formerly worn by
soldiers before they were
replaced by 'combat high
boots' in the early 1980s.

DoB

Date of Birth.

Drill

Military practice and
rehearsal of prescribed
movements (i.e. marching,
familiarization of weapons
etc).

DUKW

A six-wheel-drive
amphibious vehicle used
by US military. (Britain
acquired 2,000 through
lend-lease. They were
used during World War II
and during the Malayan
Campaign between 1948-
60).

E

Eisteddford

A competitive festival of music and poetry in Wales.

EMT

Early Morning Training at Junir Leaders Regiment, Dover or 'going for a run' as we liked to call it…in three ranks dressed in red PT vest, green denim works trousers, puttees and DMS boots.

Escort

When a serviceman or woman accompanies an accused soldier on 'OCs orders' (see 'OCs orders') as a possible form of restraint should the said soldier attempt to attack the OC (see 'OC').

Exercise

A military exercise or war game is the employment of military resources in training for military operations. Testing strategies should soldiers face actual combat situations.

F

Fascine

A bundle of plastic pipes bound together and tied to the front of armoured vehicles and used to fill in small trenches or laid on marshy ground to allow military vehicles to cross difficult areas.

FEBA

Forward Edge of the Battle Area. Line of troops and weapon coverage closest to the enemy.

FIBS

Falkland Islands Broadcasting Station. The local Falkland Islands radio station run from a house in Port Stanley and comically unprofessional, but still a source of great comfort and hilarity to us soldiers who served there in the early eighties, following the conflict.

Fieldcraft

The techniques we were taught to enable us to live, move and observe in the field whilst remaining undetected.

Fire at Will

A command that allows soldiers to fire weapons at their own discretion and at their own chosen targets.

Forced March

A fast march by soldiers with full kit c/w weapons over a long distance.

Forceps

An instrument shaped like a pair of large spoons or salad tongs that is used is a type of assisted vaginal delivery. The tongs are placed around the head of

666

the baby to help guide the baby out of the birth canal.

G

Glad rags

Best party clothes for a night out on the town.

Gunfire

A mixture of tea and a splash of rum traditionally given to soldiers on Christmas Day if they are serving away from home. It is believed to have originated in the 1890s as a form of a morale boost before a morning battle.

Gunners

Nickname of the Royal Artillery...arch rivals of the more superior Royal Engineers.

Guard of honour

A group of soldiers detailed to ceremonially welcome an important dignitary. Additionally, often used at military weddings to honour the happy couple as they leave the church.

Guardroom

A room in a military camp used to accommodate a guard detail and part of the guardhouse that also includes cells to detain prisoners.

H

Harbour Area	A defined area that is deemed as a temporary base for a group of soldiers when in the field.
Haulamtic	Large dump truck.

I

I.R.A.	Irish Republican Army. Depending which side of the fence you are on would depend on how these are described. The British Government, the majority of the general public on Mainland UK and Protestants would describe them as terrorist organization in Northern Ireland during 'The Troubles'. However, Catholics in Northern Ireland and I.R.A. sympthisers, in the UK or globally, would see them as a legitimate army fighting for a united Ireland.
Illtyd Williams Cup	The cup that U'11s Junior School rugby teams would play for in the Bridgend area of South Wales.
Isaan	Pronounced 'eesan'. This is the area of NE Thailand, otherwise known as the 'Korat Plateau. It is bordered to the North and East by the Mekong River and the rural areas of Isaan are considered to be some

of the poorest areas of Thailand.

J

J.L.R.R.E.

Junior Leaders Regiment Royal Engineers. A training regiment at Old Park Barracks, Dover for young 'Junior Sappers' (Between 16-17 years old). After 12 months of training soldiers will be transferred to 1 & 3 Training Regiments RE to continue their Combat Engineering training, before being posted to the first regiment or squadron.

Jock

Affectionate nickname for someone born in Scotland.

Junior Ranks

Normally Corporals and below.

J/Spr

Junior Sapper. Rank held by Junior Leader's serving at J.L.R.R.E. Through training others may have been promoted to J/LCpl, J/Cpl, J/Sgt etc purely for the duration of their time at Dover. Everyone would revert to Sapper when posted to 1&3 Traing Regiments RE for the B3 Combat Engineer training.

K

Kata Noi	Kata is a town/beach on the west coast of Phuket, Thailand. Kata Noi is the smaller beach/town just to the south (separated from Kata by a small headland). 'Noi' means 'small' in Thai, hence Kata Noi…Small Kata.
Koh	This is the Thai word for island (i.e. Koh Samui, Koh Tao, Koh Chang etc).
L	
LCpl	Lance Coporal. Rank in British Army that is above Sapper (Private) but below Corporal.
Lt	Lieutenant. Rank in British Army that is above Second Lietenant but below Captain.
Lug Oiles	This is how they say 'ears' in the dialect spoken in and around Barnsley, South Yorkshire.
M	
MACC	Military Aid to the Civil Community. This is a building project that is carried out by a Royal Engineers unit that benefits a civilian community.
Maggot	Green army sleeping bag.

Main Square	Main parade square in an army camp where military parades are conducted (i.e. Squadron Parade, Remembrance Day Parade etc).
Maj	Major. Rank in British Army that is above Captain but below Lieutenant Colonel.
MAMC	Military Aid to the Military Community. This is a building project that is carried out by a Royal Engineers unit that benefits a military camp.
Manky	Dirty and unpleasant.
Mark time	When a soldier or soldiers march on the spot without moving forward.
Mess Tins	A set of of two rectangular metal dishes with fold in handles that are an integral part of a soldier's mess kit. One is slightly smaller than the other so that it can fit inside the large mess tin as a space saver when packing kit in 37 or 58 pattern webbing.
Mexeflote	This is a landing raft used by the British Royal Logistic Corps to move equipment from ship to shore.

MGB	Medium Girder Bridge. A lightweight, man portable bridge that can be assembled without heavy lifting equipment. It can carry loads up to the weight of a main battle tank (approximately 60 tons).
Miners Fortnight	In Wales, this was the last week of July and first week of August and a time when historically miners used to take the two weeks summer holiday.
Mint Crisp	A sort of Millionaire's shortcake, but in place of the caramel was a mint cream.
Mor lam	A traditional Lao form of song in Laos and Isaan. Mor lam means 'expert song' or 'expert singer'. It is a common event in Isaan to attend a Mor lam in a village. Travelling shows will set-up huge stages and provide a free show to the village. They are a visual and musical treat for everyone who attends.

N

N.A.A.F.I.	Navy, Army and Air Force Institute. A company created by the British government in 1920 to run recreational

facilities needed by the British Armed Forces. They would run the bars on a military camp and usually had snooker tables and provided discos for Junior Ranks. Additionally, they would also run shops on military camps and in the adjoining married quarters selling goods to servicemen and women and their families.

Navy Shore Patrol

The Royal Navy equivalent of the Royal Military Police and to be avoided at all costs in places like Portsmouth, Plymouth and Weymouth due to their fierce, no-nonsense reputation.

NBC

Nuclear, Biological and Chemical. An integral part of servicemen and womens training involved learning about the effects of these horrific types of warfare and how best to deal with them. Particularly important during the Cold War.

Nehru-style Jacket

Traditional white jacket with straight collar and five buttons.

No2 Dress Uniform

A khaki service dress uniform that included an open collared jacket worn over a collared shirt and tie, trousers of the same material as jacket, peaked cap, highly polished (bulled) boots, belt and lanyard (specific to Corps).

O

Oath of Allegiance

As soldiers we swore an 'Oath of Allegiance' to our monarch Queen Elizabeth II. This was normally carried out in the Army Careers Office just prior to joining the British Army.

OC

Office Commanding. An OC was normally a Major and was in charge of a squadron with a strength of around two hundred men.

OC's Orders

To be placed on OC's Orders meant a soldier had committed an offence. This could be something as minor as being late for parade or more serious charges such as theft, or assault. More serious charges were dealt with by the CO of a regiment which could lead to dishonourable discharges or sentences to be carried out in the military prison at Colchester.

Officers Mess

A building that would house officers of the rank

of Second Lieutenant and above and would include accommodation, a bar, mess hall and a day lounge etc.

On stag
Slang for being on sentry or guard duty in a military camp or in the field.

Orderly Corporal
Slang 'Orderly Dog'. A Corporal or Lance Corporal who would report directly to the Squadron Sergeant Major, sharing the same office and being responsible for producing 'Daily Orders' etc.

P

Pad's wife
A slang term for a soldier's wife.

Parade(s)
A formation of soldiers, normally in three ranks for ceremonial purposes, inspections, PT or to ensure all soldiers are present and correct and that there are no absentees…welfare of each soldier is paramount and daily works parades are important.

Para flare
A pyrotechnic that produces a bright light (without an explosion) and used to illuminate an area for defensive

	countermeasures in military operations. Can also be used as a distress signal.
Parkin	A gingerbread cake traditionally made with oatmeal and black treacle. Often associated with Yorkshire.
Passing-Out Parade	Passing out is the completion of a military course (i.e. many soldiers take part in a passing out parade when they complete their basic training).
PT	Physical Training (military). This took many forms such as troop runs, circuit training in the gymnasium, swimming, assault courses, sport and forced marches etc.
Pha Nung	A cloth (normally silk) worn around the lower part of the body that resembles a long skirt.
Posted/posting	This comes from the military word 'post' (military installation). It is the act of a soldier being transferred from one camp to another camp.
Prasat	A Khmer and Thai term meaning 'castle', 'palace' or 'temple' (from Sanskrit 'prasada').

PVR Pre Voluntary Release. The act of a soldier being released early from the army. During training there would be a set period where a soldier would be able to request to leave and there would be no cost (provided they were over 18. If under 18, they would need their parent's permission). Once a soldier has been posted to his adult unit they would have to serve a minimum of 3 years, after that a soldier could apply for a PVR, which would have to be approved by the army, but there would be a cost involved. This was how it worked during the 1980s, this might have changed at the time of writing.

Q

QM Quartermaster. Normally an 'ex ranker' (commissioned from the ranks) with rank of Captain and in charge of supplies. N.B. During my time at 24 Field Squadron RE we had two wonderful QMs…Captain Bobby Lampard (footballer Frank Lampard's uncle) and Captain Jim Benson (the Jester on the roof in an earlier story).

Quadrangle	Normally a rectangular space or courtyard enclosed on four sides (we called the area where we used to parade 'the quadrangle' despite it only being enclosed on three sides). This was where Jock Martin and I were famously tied to chairs in our pants and hosed down by the rest of the Squadron.
Quick change parade	A series of parades one after the other where soldiers, normally as a punishment, would have to continually change their uniforms, parade again and get inspected and so on…it would normally go on for 2-3 hours.

R

Ramayana	This is an ancient Sanskrit epic story which follows Prince Rama's quest to rescue his beloved wife Sita from the clutches of Ravana with the help of an army of monkeys. It is traditionally attributed to the sage Vlmiki circa 500 BCE to 100 BCE.
RE	Royal Engineers. The finest and largest Corps in the British Army with a wonderful, outstanding and colourful history.

RE 200	This was the celebrations in 1987 when the Royal Engineers celebrated their 200th Anniversary of receiving the 'Royal' prefix changing from the Corps of Engineers to the Corps of Royal Engineers.
Rebro	Re-broadcast. A method where radio operators act as an intermediary between two army units that are located too far apart for normal radio traffic (messages would be passed through the 'rebro' and forwarded on).
Regiment	A military unit with a strength of 1000 to 1200 soldiers.
Regimental Bath	This was a bath that was reserved for 'Grots' (soldiers with hygiene issues). The offending soldier would be forcibly stripped and thrown into a cold bath that included a few additional (not so nice) surprises and bleach. The soldier would then be scrubbed with bass brooms. This was harsh but a means of changing the ways of a soldier that was letting the troop down.
REMF	Rear Echelon MotherFucker. An affectionate but derogatory

word for clerks, storemen and radio users in the British Army. Adapted from the US frontline soldiers who served in Vietnam and used the word to describe those soldiers who had cushy posts as clerks or storeman etc either back in the main camps or in Saigon.

REMRO

Royal Engineer Manning & Records Office. The office that looks after the personal records of all serving and ex-serving members of the Royal Engineers. When I was a serving solider this was based in Brighton but has since moved to Glasgow.

Respirator

Often called a 'gas mask', it protected soldiers from fumes or gases during wars or riots.

Reveille

A signal historically sounded by a bugle or drum to wake personnel in the armed forces. Only experienced once staying in the Light Infantry barracks in Shrewsbury where we were staying for an Army U21 rugby fixture against Shropshire…it didn't end well for the bugler as he was pelted with rugby boots. The word 'reveille' was still used as a term for getting up in the morning (but no bugler on Royal Engineer camps).

RFA
Royal Fleet Auxillary. Primary role to supply Royal Navy with fuel, supplies and ammunition. The 'Round Table class landing ship logistics' LSLs such as RFA Sir Galahad and RFA Sir Tristram were used in the Falklands Conflict...the former being bombed and set ablaze with the loss of many members of the Welsh Guards and the latter damaged. When we returned from the Falkland Islands in April 1983 we sailed to Ascension Island on the RFA Sir Geraint.

RHQ
Regimental HeadQuarters. The main building in a regiment that houses the CO and RMS and the main orderly office, post room etc.

Route denial
Demolition of bridges, roads, railways, canals, laying of minefields and setting of booby traps etc to slow the advance of enemy soldiers.

R&R
Rest and Recuperation. It was a short period where servicemen and women would spend away from their role whilst on a tour

of duty (i.e. our R&R in the Falkland Islands was 24 hours spent on a huge water tanker in the outer harbour at Port Stanley getting pissed).

RSM

Regimental **S**ergeant **M**ajor. This would be a Warrant Officer Class 1, the highest non-commissioned rank in the British Army and responsible for camp discipline…this man was a 'God' in military terms and to be avoided at all costs (as seen when I was told "the RSM wants to see you") when I was a young 17 year old Sapper at Dover – see Chapter 2).

RSME

Royal **S**chool of **M**ilitary **E**ngineering. When I was a serving soldier in 24 Field Squadron RE at Chattenden we shared the barracks with 12 RSME Regiment RE where Section Commanders, Field Sergeants, Young Officers, Plant Operatives and Search (for soldiers being sent to Northern Ireland) courses etc were held. It was a busy camp back in the eighties.

S

Sabai costumes

A shawl like garment or breast cloth. The sabai is

worn by both men and women on Thailand, about a foot wide and is draped diagonally around the chest, covering one shoulder while its end drops behind the back.

Salute

A gesture of respect or polite recognition, typically made by non-commissioned servicemen and women when meeting an officer (and leaving).

Sapper

A soldier with the rank of Private in the Royal Engineers is a 'Sapper'. It is also used as a general term to describe any member of the Royal Engineers, and one that serving and ex-serving members of the Corps are proud to be called.

Scrote

A worthless, obnoxious person.

Sentry

A soldier stationed at a pre-determined point to stand guard and prevent passage to any authorised personnel.

Sergeants Mess

A building that included accommodation, a bar, a mess room for Sergeants, Staff Seargeants and Warrant Officers Class 1 and 2.

Sgt	Sergeant. A rank in the British Army above a Corporal but below Staff Sergeant.
Shenanigans	Stupid or high-spirited behaviour or mischief
...she wasn't a full ticket	Not of sound mind, crazy.
SLR	Self Loading Rifle. The standard issue weapon of most soldiers during the 1970s and 1980s before that change to the SA80.
SNCOs	Senior Non-Commissioned Officers. Sgts, SSgts, WO1s & WO2s.
Songkran	A festival celebrating the traditional Thai New Year, held in April and marked by the throwing and sprinkling of water. A huge event in the Thai Calendar and a time for 'family' and paying respects to parents.
Squaddie	An informal/slang name for a soldier.
Squaddie Basher	Civilian who is part of a group of like-minded people who set out to beat-up soliders. Cowardly acts, as a large group would often ambush and attack a soldier on his own (see Chapter 2).

Squadron	An army unit of normally around 200-220 soldiers.
SSgt	Staff Sergeant. A British Army rank above a Sergeant but below a Warrant Officer Class 2.
SSM	Squadron Sergeant Major. Similar to an RSM, but in charge of discipline in a Squadron and held the rank of Warrant Officer Class 2 which is above the rank of Staff Sergeant but lower than a Warrant Officer Class 1.
Starch	A spray used when ironing to stiffen fabric or clothing.
Stupa	A dome-shaped building erected as a Buddhist shrine.
T	
Taff	A nickname given to people born and bred in Wales. Proud to have been called Taff during my time as a soldier, and still proud to be called Taff today by the same friends.
Three month warning order	Military equivalent of a 'final written warning' in a civilian job.
Tin helmet/tin hat	Steel helmet worn by soldiers and military

personnel during combat or in war zones.

Tracer rounds

Bullets or cannon-calibre rounds that are built with a small pyrotechnic charge in their base. Used as a marking tool for other soldiers to fire at a particular target.

Transit Camp (military)

A camp that provides temporary accommodation for soldiers (i.e. camps used for training exercises or camps set-up for soldiers in a foreign theatre).

U

-

V

Ventouse

A vacuum device used in the assistance of delivering a baby.

W

Wai greeting

This is a Thai greeting that has various levels of respect. The hands are pressed together in a prayer-like fashion but depending on who is being given the wai (i.e. monk, teacher, parents, someone of equal status, someone younger etc) will depend on the position of the hand and the extent of the bow.

Wat

This is the Thai word for temple.

Water bowser

Mobile water tank used in emergencies or as a means of clean warter for soliders when they are on exercise in the field (i.e. Salisbury Plain etc).

WRAC

Women's Royal Army Corps. The female branch of the army during my time in the 1980s (ended in 1992).

WRVS

Women's Royal Voluntary Service. A voluntary organization concerned with helping people in need throughout the UK. When I was stationed at Dover we had WRVS representative based on the camp. Her name was Fanny Morgan and she helped many a junior solder through a crisis...amazing woman.

<u>X</u>

-

<u>Y</u>

Yomp   A squad of soldiers march
                                  with heavy equipment
                                  over difficult terrain.

Z

Zulu time   Grenwich Mean Time.
                                  Zule time was used used
                                  in the forces (i.e. 2100 hrs
                                  zulu, 0830 hrs zulu etc)

Printed in Great Britain
by Amazon

83809190R10393